Goochland County Virginia

Court Order Books

1728-1731

Ann K. Blomquist

HERITAGE BOOKS
2007

HERITAGE BOOKS
AN IMPRINT OF HERITAGE BOOKS, INC.

Books, CDs, and more—Worldwide

For our listing of thousands of titles see our website at
www.HeritageBooks.com

Published 2007 by
HERITAGE BOOKS, INC.
Publishing Division
65 East Main Street
Westminster, Maryland 21157-5026

Copyright © 2007 Ann K. Blomquist

Other books by the author:

Goochland County, Virginia Court Order Book 3, 1731-1735

Goochland County, Virginia Court Order Book 5, 1741-1745

*Southam Parish Land Processioning, 1747-1784
Goochland, Cumberland, and Powhatan Counties, Virginia*

The Vestry Book of Southam Parish, Cumberland County, Virginia, 1745-1792

The Vestry Book of South Farnham Parish, Essex County, Virginia, 1739-1779

All rights reserved. No part of this book may be reproduced or transmitted in any form or by any means, electronic or mechanical, including photocopying, recording or by any information storage and retrieval system without written permission from the author, except for the inclusion of brief quotations in a review.

International Standard Book Number: 978-0-7884-3746-5

Contents

Introduction — i

Map — ix

Sample Pages — x

The Court Orders
  Order Book 1   1728-1730 — 1
  Order Book 2   1730-1731 — 240

Appendices — 415
  Court Officials — 416
  Glossary and Abbreviations — 417

Bibliography — 420

Index — 421

INTRODUCTION

The Goochland County Court Order Books 1 and 2, 1728-1731 contains the varied and interesting proceedings of a colonial county court. Local residents brought suit against each other and answered for their crimes while the court laid the county levy and kept order in the community.

The Court Orders

Goochland County was formed in 1728 from Henrico County. The Act passed by the General Assembly gave the boundaries as "the division be made by a Line on the North side of James River beginning at the mouth of Tuckahoe Creek thence up the said Creek to Chumley's Branch thence along a line of marked Trees North Twenty degrees East to Hanover County And on the south side James River beginning at the lower Manachin Creek from thence along a line of marked Trees in a direct course to the south of Skinquarter Creek on Appomattox River And that part of the County lying below the said line shall for ever hereafter be called and known by the name of Henrico county And that part of the County lying above the said line shall be called and known by the name of Goochland County."[1] The upper reaches of the county were not defined until the formation of Albemarle County in 1744. This original Goochland County comprises the modern counties of Goochland, Albemarle, Cumberland, and Powhatan.

The effective date of the new county was May 1, 1728. The first Court met within three weeks, on May 21, 1728, and set about creating new governmental bodies. The Gentlemen Justices immediately appointed justices of the peace, justices of the chancery, the clerk of the court, the sheriff, and a surveyor.

These records include a wide variety of transactions for the public good and between individuals. For the public welfare, roads were ordered to be cleared, surveyors were assigned, and bridges were built. Prices for liquor and meals were established, and ordinaries were licensed.

Beginning immediately, a courthouse for the county was planned and then ordered in August 1730. (p 4, 7, 172, 257) A levy of 10,000 pounds of tobacco was allotted to James Skelton for building a 36 foot by 20 foot building with an expected completion date of November 1731. (p 261)

The county would also need a prison. Both the courthouse and the prison were to be located on the north side of the James River near the Atkinson Ferry. (p 7) At the May 1730 Court, Sheriff Tarlton Fleming complained that the jail was insufficient and that he would not be responsible for any prisoners who escaped. (p 217) Edward Scot was assigned the task of viewing the prison for its strength and report back to the next Court. (p 230) In December 1730, Edward Scot was permitted to undertake building a prison "to be built near the Court house of the County at his own cost & charge of the following dimentions and after the manner hereafter expressed. the Prison to be twenty four foot long twelve foot wide in the clear the timbers in the sides ends floor and ceiling to be framed close to each other and to be eight inches thick, the lower floor to be laid with inch planks a partition to be made with a door in it and a lock thereto, two inside Chimneys, one outside door to be well secured with a good lock bar and other iron-work, the roof sides and ends to be covered with clap boards sap'd, the upper floor to be laid with clap boards, for which Prison the Court agree to pay the said Scot at the laying the next County levy ten thousand pounds of tobacco with Cask and Conveniency." Thomas Prosser promised to provide a lock on the outside door and another for the partition door of the prison. (p 292-293)

Scot built the prison and at the August 1731 Court, three of the Gentlemen Justices were appointed to view the prison. They reported that the prison had been built according to the contract, so the Court accepted the prison. (p 396). Curiously, without providing any specific reason, Sheriff Fleming again objected that the building was insufficient. (p 396)

The Court helped maintain order in the community by administering justice. Some of the crimes mentioned were assault, beatings, drunkenness, stealing, swearing, and murder. Sentences included fines, whipping, and incarceration.

Whipping was a public punishment. In November 1728, a pillory, whipping post, and pair of stocks were ordered to be built. (p 44) John Williams was paid 540 pounds for erecting them. (p 144) They were soon put to use: in July 1729, John Innis was given 20 lashes for stealing; in January 1730, Negro Cuffy was sentenced to 39 lashes for stealing; in June 1730, William Hardcastle received 5 lashes for accidentally shooting a horse; and in September 1731, Elizabeth Poe had 5 lashes for stealing a hoe. (p 126, 178, 234, 410)

Several criminal cases appear in the entries. In November 1728, Frances Green was accused of killing her illegitimate infant and sent to Williamsburg for her trail. Costs for her case amounted to 3083 pounds of tobacco. (p 45, 46, 143, 144) Negro Cuffy was acquitted of poisoning Negro Kate, but he was sentenced to 39 lashes for having stolen goods in his possession. (p 177, 178)

Proper conduct was demanded by the Court. Thomas Prosser presented a very unusual case for the Court. Prosser was a leading citizen and served as an attorney before the Court. At the June 1728 Court, he presented his commission from Lt. Governor William Gooch and took the oath as a deputy attorney for the Court. (p 5, 59) In October 1729, he was granted a salary of 1000 pounds of tobacco per year for representing the King in the Goochland Court. (p 145) In August 1730, Prosser ran afoul of the Court when he defied their order to refrain from questioning witnesses outside of the Court. (p 258-259) Prosser's response that he would "ask what questions he pleased on behalf of his client" brought an order to be taken into custody. When Prosser refused to post a £50 bond for good behavior, he was jailed. To proceed with the case of Luke Wiles, plaintiff, against Stephen Hughes, defendant, the Court demanded a paper concerning the case from Prosser in jail, who refused to produce it. He was returned to Court and even there, he "would not trouble himself to look for it." (p 259)

Back in jail, when the sheriff attempted to look for the paper, Prosser defended himself "with his naked sword" and refused to return to Court. In retaliation, the Court decided to "keep him in gaol without victuals or drink until he shall deliver up his sword and such other offensive weapons as shall be found on him, and also his papers that search may be make for the said declaration, and if the declaration if not found that the Sherif keep him in irons until the next Court." (p 259-260)

By September 1730, the conflict between Prosser and Court had somewhat cooled, perhaps because he had remained in jail, and Prosser posted a bond for good behavior. (p 263) His appeal to revoke his fine was denied and he was barred from any further appearances as an attorney before the Court. (p 263) The September 1730 Levy Court paid him 1530 pounds of tobacco for seventeen months of his services as the county attorney (p 281) In November 1730, he petitioned the Court for reinstatement to the bar and was readmitted by the Court. (p 283) Ironically, in November 1730, Prosser pledged to give a lock for the outside door of the prison. (p 293) Having exhibited good behavior for a year, in September 1731, Prosser was released from his bond. (p 413)

The ages of Negro slaves were established by the Court. Wills, inventories of estates, and assignment of administrations are included in these records. The Court extended its protection to women, orphans, and servants. In January 1729, indentured servant Daniel Fauquinou petitioned the court for his release from his master Peter David. (p 57-58) In November 1729, John Huston was granted his "freedom dues" from his master Fredorick Cox. (p 163) Both masters were ordered to provide their freed servants with the customary payment with 10 bushels of corn, a musket worth 20 shillings, and 30 shillings of money or goods.

The Court "permitted" Sarah Atkinson to operate the county ferry, setting the ferry fees at three pence for a man and three pence for a horse. (p 74) For a woman to be paid out of county monies is rather surprising. The usual ferryman's stipend of 800 pounds of tobacco per year was included by the October 1729 Levy Court. (p 87) Mrs. Atkinson received 301 pounds of tobacco. Mrs. Atkinson was paid 301 pounds of tobacco, indicating that she had kept the ferry about four and a half months during 1729. (p 143-144) Mrs. Atkinson died before May 1730 because Stephen Hughes was granted the operation of the ferry. (p 220) As the administrator of her estate, the September 1730 Levy Court paid Hughes 499 pounds of tobacco for her operation of the ferry from October first until the May Court. The Court then transferred operation of the ferry to Hughes and increased the stipend to 1500 pounds of tobacco. (p 281) At the November 1730 Court, the fee was raised to 1600 pounds per annum. (p 285)

Many of the entries between individuals in this order book involve the actions of Trespass and Debt. Unfortunately, the suits do not include specific details. In the modern sense, we think of trespass as an uninvited incursion onto someone's property. But in the colonial era, trespass also included using someone else's land. Since property boundaries were sometimes ambiguous, landowners had to carefully protect their lines against encroachment by neighbors. Suits of debt probably include monies, goods, and services owed by persons. Since few of the suits enumerate stolen livestock, the suits of debt probably also included this type of petty offense. Other routine entries include deeds of sale.

In an era when most people had only two names (a Christian first name and their surname), five people appear here with three names: John

Peter Bondurant, James Theophilus Dillon, John Sutton Farrar, John James Flournoy, and Jane Magdalene L'Grand.

Since these order books are early court records for Goochland County, they have suffered some damage over the years. There are numerous torn pages, especially at the beginning of Book 2. The reader of this transcription will find many bracketed words and sentences. Sometimes the missing words could be inferred based on routine entries, but other times, the missing sections are unknown.

Henry Wood was the Clerk of the Court, so the records are written in his hand. Throughout this volume, the handwriting of the Court Clerk is beautiful and legible. The formation of some letters was slightly different than modern handwriting, but in context, nearly all of the writing is readable. Spelling was not standardized yet so some noticeable differences in spelling appear in these records: "beleive" for believe and "goal" for gaol (jail). Names were often written phonetically and changed from one entry to the next.

This court order book covers the time period when the method of recording dates was different from modern notation. During this era, the first day of the year was considered to be March 25 with the months of January and February as the last months of the year. So dates labeled as "January 1731" should be considered as January 1732 by the modern reader. Modern dates have been noted in brackets.

The County Levy

To pay for the variety of public business for the county, the county court levied a tax called a titheable. Levy courts were conducted in September 1728, October 1729, and September 1730.

Since the county government was just beginning, their first levies are rather variable. The Court levied a low of 22,640 pounds of tobacco in 1728 and a high of 40,288 pounds in 1730. A major expense each year was the payment of 200 pounds of tobacco for each wolf head returned to the Court. The expense of the wolves' heads ranged from 22% to 28% of the Court's budget. To a modern citizen, this seems like a disproportionate expenditure for the county at a time when roads and other county improvements were needed.

During this period, the number of titheables in the county increased, while the tax per poll also increased from 20 to 32 pounds of tobacco.

The table below includes the major and interesting expenses paid by the county in pounds of tobacco.

	1728	1729	1730
Wolf heads	6 400	8 600	9 000
Clerk	1 080	1 080	1 080
Sheriff	1 080	1 080	1 080
Burgesses	6 800		
Counting tobacco plants	4 624	3 824	
Run county line	630	7 450	
Ferry		801	1 124
Trials		3 083	400
Courthouse			10 000
Bridge			6 000
Total Levy	22 640	33 785	40 288
# of Titheables	1132	1165	1259
& Tax per poll	@ 20	@ 29	@ 32
Wolf Heads %	28.3%	25.5%	22.3%

Parishes in the County

Parishes were separate entities from county civil government. However, the parish vestry acted in a semi-governmental capacity in the community including caring for the poor and for orphans. For example, the parish church wardens "bound out" orphans to responsible persons to be raised and taught a trade.

The two parishes of Goochland County during this era were St. James Parish and King William Parish. St. James Parish had been formed in 1720 as part of Henrico County.[2] For the most part, when Goochland County was formed in 1728, St. James Parish coincided with the civil boundaries of the county.[3] However, there is an exception to this general statement.

Even before the formation of St. James Parish, King William Parish existed. Protestant Huguenot refugees from Catholic France fled Europe and, in July 1700, some of them settled in Virginia at Manakintown in Henrico County. In December 1700, King William Parish was officially created to provide a separate parish for the French Protestant refugees.[4] King William Parish in Goochland County was south of the James River along the River but the King William Parish boundaries were not clearly delineated in the legislation.[5] Any person in this record who is identified as living in King William Parish should be researched as a possible French Huguenot.

Editorial Methods and Notes

These records were previously transcribed by Dennis R. Hudgins and a limited number of copies were printed by Goochland County Historical Society in 1997. Mr. Hudgins provided his transcription to this editor for this new publication. The Order Books have been proofread, re-formated, and newly indexed with supplementary materials added. The introduction, analysis, formatting, indexing, and preparation were done by Ann Blomquist.

This transcription is based on microfilm of the original book provided by the Library of Virginia. The microfilm is available from the Library of Virginia as Goochland County Court Records, Reel 21.

Some style decisions were made for this publication. The overall philosophy has been to modernize the text as little as possible. Some punctuation has been updated, but where modern writers would have included some commas, they are lacking in the original. The reader will need to supply some punctuation for improved understanding of each record. Due to the size of this volume and the difficulty in reading small type, superscripts were not used by the transcriber. So, abbreviations like " ordy " for " ord^y " look strange but should be decipherable to the modern reader as the word "ordinary."

The editor wishes to make grateful acknowledgment to Dennis Hudgins; to the Library of Virginia; and to my husband John Blomquist for his computer wizardry, support, and encouragement.

July 2007
Orlando, Florida

Ann Kicker Blomquist

Notes

1. Cocke, *Parish Lines, Diocese of Virginia*, p 48; 4 Hening 240, by title only; Morgan P. Robinson, *Virginia Counties: Those Resulting from Virginia Legislation*, Bulletin of the Virginia State Library, Vol IX, 1916.
2. Cocke, *Parish Lines, Diocese of Southern Virginia*, p 132.
3. Cocke, *Parish Lines, Diocese of Southern Virginia*, p 133.
4. Cocke, *Parish Lines, Diocese of Virginia*, p 55-56; 3 Hening 201.
5. See map from on page ix.

Map by permission of Eric Grundset
Historical Boundary Atlas of Central Virginia

At a Court held for the County of Goochland the third ~~Tuesday in September~~ being the seventeenth day of ~~September~~ Anno Domini 1728.

Present. Thomas Randolph, John Woodson, Carlton Hix, Allen Howard Gent. Justices.

In the action of Detinue between Joseph Bradley plaintiff and Hirith Cox Defendant the following jury are sworn to wit. George Payne, William Womack, James Howlin, Henry Harper, Robert Hughes, John McBride, Nathaniel Basset, John Lanis, James Taylor, William Saunders, Bartholomew Stovall, James Spe— s who having received their charge withdraw and after some ti— return with their Verdict which on the plts motion is ordered to be recorded and is as followeth "We find for the plt twenty shillings Currant money. Whereupon it is considered by the Co— that the plaintiff do recover against the Defendant the said s— of twenty shillings Currant money by the jurors in their Ve—— aforesaid assessed with costs and an Attorneys ffee.

In the action of Debt between Richard Ward plaintiff and William Watkins Deft the parties submit themselves to the Court for tryal— upon the witnesses being heard it is considered by the Court that the p— do recover against the Deft the sum of five hundred pounds of to— with Costs and an Attorneys ffee.

In the action of Debt between James Taylor plaintiff and Mary— Deft the Defendant comes into Court and confesses her self indebted unto the plt in the sum of nine pounds two shillings Currant mo— whereupon it is considered by the Court that the plaintiff do recover against the Deft the said sum of nine pounds two shillings Currant money with Costs and an Attorneys ffee.

Portion of page 23 from Court Order Book 1

At a Court held for Goochland County the third Tuesday in July being the twentieth day of the Month Anno Dom. MDCCXXXI.

Present William Mayo, Daniel Stoner, George Pain, Anthony Hoggatt, Gent. Justices.

Chastains deed to Horses
Stephen Chastain acknowledges a deed from himself to Mary Horse to be his Act and deed and it is thereupon admitted to record.

Present William Cabbell Gent.

Horses Inventory
Anne Epperson presents an Inventory of the Estate of Francis Horse deceased which is ordered to be recorded.

Bollings Inventory
Stephen Hughes presents an Inventory of the Estate of James Bolling deceased which is ordered to be recorded.

Cannon vs Stephens
In the Action of Debt between William Cannon Plt. and Edward Scot Administrator of John Stephens decd. Deft. an Imparlance granted the Defendant.

Cannon vs Strange
In the Action of Trespass on the case between William Cannon Plt. and Alexander Strange Deft. the Sherif having made return that the Deft. is not to be found and he failing to appear on the Plts. motion an Alias Capias is awarded against the Defend. returnable to the next Court.

Portion of page 150 from Court Order Book 2

Goochland County
Order Book 1
1728 - 1730
May 21 1728 - June 16 1730

[1]   May Court 1728
At a Court held for the County of Goochland the third Tuesday in May being the twenty first day of the month Annoq. Domini 1728.

[A Comm]ission from the Honble. William Gooch Esqr. his Majesties Lieut. Governor & Commander in Chief of this Dominion to Thomas Randolph, John Fleming, William Mayo, John Woodson, Daniel Stoner, Rene Laforce, Tarlton Fleming, Allin Howard, and Edward Scot, Gent. to be Justices of the Peace for this County is read as also the Dedimus for administring oaths, then Tarlton Fleming & Allin Howard Gent. Administer the Oaths appointed by act of Parliament to be taken instead of the Oaths of Allegiance & Supremacy the oath appointed to be taken by an act of Parliament made in the Sixth Year of the reign of her late Majesty Queen Anne Entituled an act for the Security of her Majesties person and Government and of the Succession of the Crown of Great Brittain in the protestant line unto Thomas Randolph and William Mayo Gent. who also Subscribed the Test take the oath of a Justice of the peace and of a Justice in Chancery and then administer the Said oaths unto John Woodson, Tarlton Fleming, and Allin Howard Gent. who also Subscribed the Test.

Wood Sworn Clerk   Henry Wood produces a Commission from the Honble. John Carter Esqr. Secretary of this Colony to be Clerk of this County Court which being [re]ad the Said Henry Wood takes the oaths appointed to be taken by act of Parliament instead of the oaths of allegiance and Supremacy the oath appointed to be taken by an act of Parliament made the 6th year of the reign of her late Majesty Queen Ann [Entituled an Act] for the Security of her [Majesties person and Government and of the Succession of the Crown of Great Brittain in the protestant line unto ...] [torn] [and take the Oath]

[2]   May Court 1728
of a County Court Clerk, and is admitted to the [torn] Office. On the motion of the Said Henry [Wood it] is ordered to be recorded.

Stoner Sworn Sherif   Daniel Stoner Gent. produces a Commission f[rom the Honble.] William Gooch Esqr. his Majesties Lieut. Governor [and Com]mander in Chief of this Dominion to be Sheriff of this County being read the Said Daniel Stoner, William Mayo, and Allin Howard, Gent. enter into bond according to Law and acknowledging the Same to be their act and Deed it is ordered to be recorded then Daniel Stoner and Thomas Walker take the oaths appointed by act of Parliament to be taken instead of the oaths of allegiance and Surpremacy the oath appointed to be taken by an Act of Parliament made in the sixth Year of the reign of her late Majesty Queen Ann Entituled an act for the Security of her Majesties person and Government and of the Succession to the Crown of Great Brittain in the protestant line, and Subscribe the Test, Daniel Stoner also takes the oath of A Sherif and Thomas Walker the Oath of an under Sherif.

Present Thomas Randolph, John Woodson, Tarlton Fleming and Allin Howard, Gent. Justices.

Mayo Sworn Surveyor   William Mayo Gent. produces a Commission from the Honble. Peter Beverly Esqr. Surveyor Generall of this Colony to be Surveyor of this County which being read the Said William Mayo takes the oaths appointed by Act of Parliament to be taken instead of the Oaths of Allegiance and Supremacy the oath appointed to be taken by An Act of Parliament made in the Sixth Year of the reign of her late Majesty Queen Ann [etc. - torn] person and [torn] of Great Brittain

[3]   May Court 1728
in the protestant line, Subscribed the Test, and takes the oath of A Surveyor.

Present William Mayo Gent.

Cox's will proved   The Last will and Testament of George Cox Deceased is presented to the Court by Martha Cox his Executrix who makes Oath thereto and the Same being proved by the oaths of the witnesses thereto it is admitted to record and on the motion of the Said Executrix and her performance what is usual in Such Cases Certificate is

Granted her for obtaining a probate thereof in due form Daniel Stoner & Robert Hughes Securitys Ordered that John Saunders, Joel Chandler, Robert Hughes and Bartholomew Stoveall or any 3 of them being first Sworn by Some Justice of the peace do appraise the Estate of George Cox Deceased and that Martha Cox the Executrix do return an Inventory thereof to the next Court.

Crooms deed to Michaux Daniel Croom acknowledges a deed with the Levery of Seizin endorsed from himself to Jacob Michaux to be his act & Deed and it is thereupon admitted to record, then Elizabeth his wife of the Said Daniel (She being first privately examined) relinquishes her right of Dower in the Land by the Said deed conveyed which is also admitted to record.

Michaux deed to Croom Jacob Michaux and John Michaux acknowledge a deed with the Livery of Seizin endorsed from themselves to Daniel Croom to be their act and Deed and it is thereupon admitted to record, then Sarah wife of the Said John (She being first privately examined) relinquishes her right of Dower in the Land by the Said deed conveyed which is also ordered to be recorded.

Vigne's will proved The Last will and Testament of Adam Vigne Deceased is presented in Court by Stephen Monford and the Same being proved by the oath of Bartholomew Dupuy (who also makes oath that he Saw the other [Witnesses] who are Since dead Subscribe their Names thereto) it

[4]   May Court 1728
is admitted to record. Stephen Monford also presents a paper containing a Translation of the Said will which being Sworn to by Daniel Guerrant Junr. is also ordered to be recorded.

Bibe levy Free On the petition of Thomas Bibe he is Exempt from paying of Levys.

Clerks Fees to be paid by attornys On the motion of Henry Wood it is entered as a rule that every Attorny be answerable to the Clerk of this Court for all Fees that shall accrue upon any action by him Commenced and presented in the Name and on the behalf of any person or persons resideing in this County.

Moor levy Free On the petition of Thomas Moor he is exempt from paying of Levys.

County line to be runn   William Mayo Gent. Surveyor, and John Woodson and Tarlton Fleming Gent. Justices, are appointed to meet the Surveyor and Justices of Henrico County to runn the dividing line between the Countys of Henrico and Goochland at Such time as they Shall agree on between this and the 10th day of June next.

Lists of the titheables to be taken   The Following persons are appointed to take the Lists of tithables, to wit, John Woodson Gent. below Beaverdam Creek, and Allin Howard Gent. above the Said Creek, William Mayo Gent. in that part of St. James's parish on the South Side James River and Tarlton Fleming in King William parish.

Constables Sworn   John Macbride, Joseph Bingley, and Bartholomew Stovall appointed and Sworn Constables.

Stoner protests agt. the County   On the motion of Daniel Stoner Gent. Sherif his protest against the County for all damages that Shall happen unto him [for] a prison is entered.

[5]   June Court 1728
Prison & Court house to be built   Thomas Randolph and Allin Howard Gent. are appointed to treat with workmen about building a prison and Court house and to make report of their proceedings therein to the next Court.

Then the Court adjourned to the 3rd Tuesday in next Month.
                                                            Test. Henry Wood ClCurt.

****

At the Court held for Goochland County the third Tuesday in June being the 18th day of the Month Annoq. Domi. 1728.

Justices Sworn   Thomas Randolph and William Mayo Gent. administer the oaths appointed by act of parliament to be taken instead of the oaths of Allegiance & Supremacy the oath appointed to be taken by an act of parliament made in the Sixth Year of the reign of her late Majesty Queen Anne Entituled an act for the Security of her Majestys person and Government and of the Succession to the Crown of Great Brittain in the protestant line unto John Fleming Gent. who Subscribed the Test and takes the oath of a Justice of the peace and of a Justice in Chancery.

Present. Thomas Randolph, John Fleming, William Mayo, Allin

Howard, Gent. Justices.

Prosser Sworn Depy. attorny   Thomas Prosser Gent. produces a commission from the Honble. William Gooch Esqr. his Majestys Lieut. Governour & Commander in chief of this Dominion to be Deputy attorny of this Court which being read the Said Thomas Prosser takes the oaths appointed to be taken by act of parliament instead of the oaths of Allegiance and Supremacy the oath appointed to be taken by an act of parliament made in the Sixth Year of the reign of her late Majesty Queen Anne Entituled an act for the Security of her Majestys person and Government and of the Succession [to the]

[6]   June Court 1728
Crown of Great Brittain in the protestant line and Subscribes the test.

Agees deed to Bruise   Mathew Agee acknowledges a deed with the Livery of Seiz'n endorsed from himself to Peter Bruise to be his act and deed and it is thereupon admitted to record, then Anne wife of the Said Mathew (She being first privately examined) relinquish her right of Dower in the Land by the Said deed conveyed wch. is also admitted to record.

Agee deed to Smith   Mathew Agee acknowledges a deed with the livery of Seizin endorsed from himself to John Smith to be his act and Deed and it is thereupon admitted to record, then Anne wife of the Said Mathew (She being first privately examined) relinquished her right of Dower in the Land by the said Deed conveyed which is also admitted to record.

Snugs an Orphan to be bound   Ordered that the Churchwardens of King William parish bind William Snugs an Orphan according to the Direction of the Act of Assembly.

Champaigne vs Pruit   In the action of Trespass between Peter Champaigne Plt. and Thomas Pruit Deft. the Deft. pleads not guilty and for tryal puts himself upon the Country and the Plt. likewise.

Alvis vs Sorrell   In the action of Case between George Alvis Plt. and John Sorrell Deft. the Sherif haveing returned the Deft. not to be found and he failing to appear on the Plts. attorney's motion is ordered that an alias Capias do issue against the Deft. returnable to the next Court.

[7]   [June Court 1728]
The action of Case between Stephen Hughes Plt. and William Cressy Deft. is dismist neither party appearing.

Moor vs Walker   In the action of Debt between Thomas Moor Plt. and John Walker Deft. the Deft. pleads he oweth nothing and for tryall puts himself upon the Country and the Plt. Likewise.

Vanderhood vs Taber   In the action of Trespass on the Case between Henry Vanderhood Plt. and John Tabor Deft. the Deft. pleads non assumpsit and for tryal puts himself upon the Country and the Plt. likewise.

Vanderhood vs Quin   In the action of trespass on the Case between Henry Vanderhood Plt. and John Quin Deft. William Cabbell enters himself Special Bail for the Deft. and an imparlance is Granted him.

Rocket vs Quin   In the action of Case between Baldwin Rocket Plt. and John Quin Deft. William Cabbell enters himself Special Bail for the Deft. an imparlance is Granted him.

May vs Hudson   In the action of Debt Between William May Plt. and John Hudson Deft. for Seven Hundred and fifty pounds of tobacco Sweet Scented and Cask the Deft. appears and confesses the Same to be due whereupon it is considered by the Court that the Plt. do recover against the Deft. Seven Hundred and fifty pound of Sweet Scented Tobacco and Cask with Costs als. Exo.

Carner vs Rapene   In the action of Trespass on the Case between Susanna Carner Plt. and Anthony Rapene Deft. the Deft. pleads he oweth nothing and for tryall puts himself upon the Country and the Plt. Likewise.

Syme vs Hoggat   In the action of Case between John Syme Plt. and Anthony Hoggat Deft. the Deft. not appearing Judgment is Granted to the Plt. [torn] Thomas Walker his Common Bail for what Damages the [Plt.]

[8]   June [Court 1728]
Shall recover in this Suit unless the Said Deft. Shall appear at next Court and answer the Said action.

May vs Morris   In the action of Trespass on the Case between William May Plt. and John Morris Deft. the Deft. not appearing Judgment Granted to the Plt. against him and Andrew Pruit his Common Bail what Damages the Plt. Shall recover in this Suit to be Discharged upon the Defts. appearing at next Court.

GOOCHLAND COUNTY ORDER BOOK 1 1728-1730

Adams vs Richards   In the action of Trespass on the Case between Ebenezer Adams Plts. and John Richards Deft. the Deft. being in Custody of the Sherif pleads he oweth nothing and for tryal puts himself upon the Country and the Plt. likewise.

Bradley vs Cox   In the action of Detinue between Joseph Bradley Plt. and Fredorick Cox Deft. an imparlance is Granted the Deft.

Carner vs Quin   In the action of Case between Susanna Carner Assee. of John Brown Plt. and John Quin Deft. an imparlance is Granted the Deft.

The action of Case between Jacob Winfree Plt. and John Martin Deft. is Dismist neither party appearing.

Chastains Negroes   Those Negroes belonging to Stephen Chastain are Judged of the following ages. Jack eleven, Jenny eleven Years of age.

    Present Tarlton Fleming Gent.

Micheaux deed to Croom   Judith the wife of Jacob Micheaux (She being first privately examined) relinquished her right of Dower in the Land conveyed at the last Court by Jacob & John Micheaux to Daniel Croom which is ordered to be Certified on the Said Deed and recorded.

[9]   June Court 1728
Ferry to be kept   William Mayo and Allen Howard Gent. are appointed to agree with Sarah Atkinson for keeping Ferry one Year of a Court day to Set over foot people only to Court.

Cox's Invy   Martha Cox presents upon oath an Inventory of the Estate of George Cox Deceased which is ordered to be recorded.

Rapene deed to Harriss   Anthony Rapene acknowledges a deed with the Livery of Seizin endorsed from himself to John Harris to be his act and Deed and it is thereupon admitted to record then Margaret wife of the Said Anthony (She being first privately examined) relinquished her right of Dower in the Land by the Said Deed conveyed which is also admitted to record.

Court house placed   Upon consideration thereof had it is the Opinion of this Court that the Court house and prison be built on the North side James River at the most convenient place near to Atkinsons Ferry.

Surveyors of the road The Following Surveyors of the roads are appointed Vizt. William Womack from Tuckahoe Creek to Stony Creek, George Paine from Stoney Creek to Beverdam Creek, John Webb from Beverdam Creek to Treasurers runn, Leonard Ballow from thence to the Bird, Joseph Thomas from the Bird to Patricks Ford, James Nowlin from the river road up the Back road to the Bridge over Beverdam Creek below Major Bollings Mill, John Mackbride from that Bridge up the said Back road untill it meets the river road, Tarlton Fleming Gent. from the County line to fine Creek, John Quin from fine Creek to Solomons Creek, John Saunders from Solomons Creek to Deep Creek, George Stoveall from Deep Creek to Muddy Creek, Mathew Cox from Muddy Creek to Willis's Creek, and it is ordered that George Stoveall and Mathew Cox with the Several Titheables in each of their precincts do meet at Muddy Creek to repair the bridge over the Same as often as there shall be occasion. Nathaniel Basset of the road from John Fords towards Appamatox ridge, Stephen Chastain of the River road from

[10] July Court 1728
the County line on the South side James River to the Coal pit.

News will to be proved On the motion of William New it is ordered that Mary New be Summoned to appear at the next Court to prove Edmund News will.

Then the Court Adjourned to the third Tuesday in Next Month.
Test. Henry Wood ClCurt.

****

At the Court held for the Goochland County the third Tuesday in July being the Sixteenth day of the Month Annoq. Domini 1728.
Present. John Fleming, William Mayo, John Woodson, Tarlton Fleming, Allin Howard, Gent. Justices.

Stoners deeds to Mayo Daniel Stoner acknowledges two Several Deeds from himself to William Mayo to be his acts & Deeds, John Cox proves one of the Said Deeds & Thomas Turpin the other to be the acts & Deeds of Mary Stoner and they are thereupon admitted to record.

Mayo's deed to Stoner William Mayo acknowledged a deed from himself to Daniel Stoner to be his act & Deed & it was thereupon admitted to record.

Tindals deed to Diggs   Thomas Tindal acknowledges a deed with the Livery of Seizin endorsed and the receipt of the consideration money from himself to Dudley Diggs to be his act and Deed and it is thereupon admitted to record.

Randolphs negroes judged   These negroes belonging to Richard Randolph are Judged of the Following ages, Nero twelve, Charles Eleven.

Lyles negro judged   Toby a negro belonging to David Lyles is judged to be ten Years old.

[11]   July Court 1728
L'villan's negroes judged   These negroes belonging to John L'villan are Judged of the following ages, Robin twelve, Hannah eleven.

Champaigne vs Pruit   The tryal of the issue in the action of Tresspass Between Peter Champaigne Plt. and Thomas Pruit Deft. is referred to the next Court.

Alvis vs Sorrell   In the action of Case between George Alvis Plt. and John Sorrell Deft. the Deft. failing to appear Judgment is Granted the Plt. against the Deft. and Edward Scot his Common Bail for what Damages shall be recovered in this Suit to be Discharged upon the Defts. appearance at the next Court.

Moore vs Walker   In the action of Debt between Thomas Moore Plt. and John Walker Deft. for four pounds Sixteen Shillings & eight pence Currant money due by bill dated the eighteen day of February in the Year of our Lord one thousand Seven Hundred and twenty four   George Paine, Wm. Womack, James Cocke, William Cabbell, Nowel Burton, John Webb, Jacob Micheaux, Leonard Ballow, Peter Baize, Richard Oglesby, Thomas Ballow, Thomas Edwards, the Jury are Sworn to try the issue joyned who haveing agreed on their Verdict on the Plts. motion it is recorded in these words "Wee find for the Plaintif nine Shillings Currt. money Geo: Paine foreman." whereupon it is considered by the Court that the Plaintif do recover against the Deft the Said Sum of nine Shillings Currant money by the Jurors aforesaid in their Verdict aforesaid assessed and the Costs of this Suit with the attornys Fee.

Vanderhood vs Tabor   The action of Trespass on the Case between Henry Vanderhoode Plt. and John Taber Deft. is dismist the Plt. not prosecuting the Same.

Vanderhood vs Quin   In the action of Trespass on the Case between Henry Vanderhood Plt. and John Quin Deft. the Deft. failing to plead on the Plts. motion Judgment by nihil dicit is Granted him for what

[12]   July Court 1728
Damages Shall be recovered against the Deft. to be Discharged if he Shall plead at the next Court.

Rocket vs Quin   In the action of Case between Baldwin Rocket Plt. and John Quin Deft. by consent of the parties the Declaration is amended the Deft. acknowledging himself indebted unto the Plt. in the Sum of nine pounds eight Shillings & Six pence it is considered by the Court that the Plt. do recover against the Deft. nine pounds eight Shillings and Six pence Currant money with Costs and an Attornys Fee.

Carner vs Rapene   In the action of Trespass on the Case between Susanna Carner Plt. and Anthony Rapene Deft. the parties Submit the tryal of the issue to the Court whereupon the witnesses being heard it is considered that the Plt. do recover against the Deft. three pounds Currant money with costs and an Attornys Fee.

Syme vs Hogat   In the action of Case between John Syme Plt. and Anthony Hoggat Deft. Judgment by nihil dicit is Granted the Plt. against the Deft. to be discharged if the Deft. Shall plead at the next Court.

May vs Morriss   In the action of Trespass between William May Plt. and John Morris Deft. the conditional Judgment entered at the Last Court is confirmed and a writ of inquiry of damages is ordered to be executed at the next Court the Deft. having ten days notice thereof Given him by the Sherif.

Adams vs Richards   In the action of Trespass on the Case between Ebenezer Adams Plt. and John Richards Deft. the Deft. acknow'ging himself indebted unto the Plt. in the Sum of five pounds Seventeen Shillings and four pence it is considered by the Court that the Plt. do recover against the Deft. five pounds Seventeen Shillings and four pence Currant money with costs and an Attornys Fee.

[13]
Prides deed to Watkins   John Pride acknowledges a deed with the Livery of Seizin endorsed from himself to Thomas Watkins to be his act and Deed and is thereupon admitted to record.

Bradley vs Cox   In the action of Detinue between Joseph Bradley Plt. and Frederick Cox Deft. Judgment by nihil dicit is Granted the Plt. against the Deft. to be discharged if the Deft. Shall plead at the next Court.

Carner vs Quin   In the action of Case between Susanna Carner Assignee of John Brown Plt. and John Quin Deft. Judgment by nihil Dicit it is Granted the Plt. against the Deft. to be discharged if the Deft. Shall plead at the next Court.

New vs New   The order entered last Court on the motion of William New against Mary New is discontinued.

May vs Field   In the action of Case between William May Plt. and John Field Deft. an Alias Capias is awarded against the Deft. returnable to the next Court.

The action of Case between Luke Wilds Plt. and Thomas Pruit Deft. is dismist no prosecution.

Dickinson vs Hughes   In the action of Case between John Dickinson Plt. and Stephen Hughes Deft. the Plt. failed to file his declaration [on] time on the Defts. motion he is Nonsuited and it is thereupon considered that the Deft. do recover against the Plt. five Shillings Currant money with Costs and an Attornys Fees.

Burton vs Watkins   In the action of Debt between Nowel Burton Plt. and William Watkins Deft. an imparlance is Granted the Deft.

Ward vs Watkins   In the action of Debt between Richard Ward Plt. and William Watkins Deft. John Maxey & William Barnes become Special Bail for the Deft. who pleads he oweth nothing and for tryal puts himself upon the Country and Plt. Likewise.

[14]   July Court 1728
Moor vs Taylor   In the action of Debt between Edward Moore Plt. and John Taylor Deft. an imparlance is Granted the Deft.

The action of Debt. between Anthony Rapene Plt. and Joseph Woodson Deft. is dismist the Plt. not prosecuting the Same.

Moore vs Stubblefield   In the action of Trespass on the Case between Edward Moore Plt. and John Stubblefield Deft. an imparlance is Granted the Deft.

The action of Debt between Adam Buttery Plt. and John Lawson Deft. is dismist neither party appearing.

The action of Debt between John Bolling Plt. and John Quin Deft. is dismist the Plt. not presenting the Same.

Thornton vs Salmon   In the action of Trespass on the Case between John Thornton Plt. and Thomas Salmon Deft. the Deft. failing to appear Judgment is Granted the Plt. against the Deft. and Thomas Edwards his Bail for what damages the Plt. Shall recover in this Suit to be Discharged if the Deft. Shall appear at the next Court.

Ward vs Bryan   In the action of Trespass on the Case between Richard Ward Plt. and Thomas Bryan Deft. the Deft. being in Custody of the Sherif acknowledges himself indebted unto the Plt. in the sum of Six pounds Seven Shillings whereupon it is Considered that the Plt. do recover against the Deft. Six pounds Seven Shillings Currant money with Costs and an attornys Fee.

The action of Case between Nowel Burton Plt. and John Burgamy Deft. is Dismist neither party appearing.

The action of Debt between Tabitha Evans Plt. and Thomas Walton Junr. Deft. is Dismist neither party appearing.

[15]   [July Court 1728]
Williams vs Hogat   In the action of Trespass on the Case Between Edward Williams Plt. and Phillip Hoggat Deft. the Deft. failing to appear Judgment is Granted the Plt. against the Deft. and Welcome Wi[llia]m[s] Bail for what Damages the Plt. shall recover in [this su]it to be Discharged if the Deft. Shall appear at the Next C[ourt.]

Paine vs Carner   John Paine having attended this day as a witness for [Susanna Carner] vs. Anthony Rapene it is ordered that the Said Susan[na Carner do] pay [him] for the Same thirty pounds of tobacco with Costs.

Guerrant vs Carner   Daniel Guerrant Junr. haveing attended this day as [witness] for [Susa]nna Carner vs. Anthony Rapene it is ordered that the [said Susanna] do pay him for the same thirty pounds of Tobacco w[ith costs].

Hodges deed to Hodges   Robert Hodges acknowledges a deed with Liv[ery of Seizen endor]sed from himself to William Hodges to be his a[ct and deed and is] thereupon admitted to record.

Wotars deed to Hodges   William Wotars acknowledges a deed with Live[ry of Seiz'n endors]ed from himself to Robert Hodges to be his act an[d deed and is] thereupon admitted to record.

Hodges deed to Hodges   Robert Hodges acknowledges a deed with Livery [of Seiz'n endorsed] from himself to John Hodges to be his act and De[ed and is there]upon admitted to record.

Hodges deed to Wotars   Robert Hodges acknowledges a deed with Live[ry of Seiz'n endorsed] from himself to William Wotars to be his act a[nd deed and is] thereupon admitted to record.

Woodsons Ordiny. lycense   On the motion of Joseph Woodson leave is Grante[d him to keep an] Ordinary Joseph Parsons and Daniel Croom Secur[ities] [torn] of John Bolling, Thomas Prosser [torn].

[16]   [July Court 1728]
[Constables Sworn]   [torn] is Sworn constable.

[Rates of Liquors Settled] [torn] of Liquors &c. are Settled as Follows Vizt. Rum at ten Shillings [Pr. Gallon], French Brandy at twenty Shillings Pr. Gallon, Madera Wine Pr. [torn] Shillings and Six pence Pr. quart, European Strong Beer at [torn] quart, American Strong Beer at twelve pence Pr. quart, [Rum Punch of] Double refined Sugar at fifteen pence Pr. quart, of Brown [Sugar at] twelve pence, French Brandy punch at two Shillings Pr. quart, [torn] at twelve pence, diet for a Servant Six pence, one Lodging [torn], Corn at four pence Pr. Gallon, Stableage & fodder or pas[turage] for one night for a Horse Six pence.

Then the Court Adjourned to the third Tuesday next Month.
                                         Test. Henry Wood ClCur.

****

At the Court held for the County of Goochland the third Tuesday in August being the twentieth day of the Month Annoq. Domini 1728 Present. Thomas Randolph, John Fleming, William Mayo, Tarlton Fleming, Allin Howard, Gent. Justices.

[Moreman to Burks]   [??] Moreman Acknowledges a deed with the Livery of Seizin [endorsed] from himself to Samuel Burks to be his act and Deed. [torn] thereupon admitted to record. then Susan wife of the said [torn] she being first privately examined) relinquishes her right [torn] the Land by the Said Deed conveyed which is also [admitted to record.]

[torn]   [torn] acknowledges a deed with ye. Livery of Seiz'n and [torn] consideration money and [torn]

[17]   August Court 1728
Burks deed to Howard   John Burk acknowledges a deed with the Livery of Seizin endorsed from himself to James Howard to be his act and Deed and it is thereupon admitted to record, then Catherine wife of the Said John (She being first privately examined) relinquishes her right of Dower in the land by this deed conveyed which is also admitted to record.

Champaigne vs Pruit   In the action of Trespass between Peter Champaigne Plt. and Thomas Pruit Deft. the Deft. files a new plea, to which the Plt. Demurrs Generally and the Defendant joyns in Demurrer.

Alvis vs Sorrell   In the action of Case between George Alvis Plt. and John Sorrell Deft. the Defendant failing to plead Judgment by Nihil Dicit is Granted the Plt. for what Damages Shall be recovered in this Suit to be discharged if the Deft. Shall plead at the next Court.

Vanderhood vs Quin   In the action of Trespass on the Case between Henry Vanderhoode Plt. and John Quin Deft. the Defendant pleads he oweth nothing and the Suit is thereupon referred.

Syme vs Hoggat   In the action of Case between John Syme Plt. and Anthony Hoggat Defendant the Defendant pleads he oweth nothing and for Tryall puts himself upon the Country and the Plt. Likewise.

May vs Morris   In the action of Trespass on the Case between William May Plt. and John Morris Defendant the Pla[i]ntif waives the executing the writ of inquiry and the Defendant acknowledging himself indebted to the Plt. in the Sum of three pounds it is considered by the Court that the Plantif Do recover against the Deft. three pounds Currant money with Costs and attorny Fee.

Bradley vs Cox   In the action of Detinue between Joseph Bradley Plt. and Frederick Cox Defendant the Defendant pleads non detinet and for tryall puts himself upon the Country and the Plt. Likewise.

Carner vs Quin   In the action of Case between Susanna Carner Plt. and

John Quin Deft. the Defendant pleads non assumpsit [and for Tryal puts himself upon] the Country and the Plaintif Likew[ise.]

[May vs Field] The action of Case between William [May] [torn] Defendant is Dismist the Plt. not pr[osecuting] [torn]

[18] August Court 1728
Burton vs Watkins In the action of Debt between Nowel Burton Plaintif and William Watkins Defendt. the Defendt. failing to plead Judgment by in Dicit is Granted the Plt. for what Damages Shall be recovered this Suit to be discharged if ye. Defendant Shall plead at the next Court.

Ward vs Watkins The action of Debt Between Richard Ward Plaintif and William Watkins Defendant is referred at the Plaintif's Cost.

Moore vs Taylor In the action of Debt between Edward Moore Plaintif and John Taylor Defendant Judgment by nihil dicit is Granted the Plt. for what Damages Shall be recovered in this Suit to be Discharged if the Defendant shall plead at the next Court.

Present. John Woodson Gent.

Moore vs Stubblefd In the action of Tresspass on the Case between Edward Moore Plaintif and John Stubblefield Defendant Judgment by nihil Dicit is Granted the Plt. for what Damages Shall be recovered in this Suit to be Discharged if the Deft. Shall plea the next Court.

Thornton vs Salmon The action of Trespass on the Case between John Thornton Plaintif and Thomas Salmon Defendant is referred [torn] the Plt. Costs.

Williams vs Hoggat In the action of Trespass on the Case between Edward Williams Plaintif and Phillip Hoggat Defendant the Deft. confess[es] himself indebted unto the Plaintif the Sum of twenty five Shillin[g]s it is considered by the Court the Plaintif do recover agt. the Defendt. twenty five Shillings Currant money with costs and an Attornys Fee.

[Cox deed to Randolph] [torn] [acknowle]dges a deed with Livery of Seizin endor[torn] Thomas Randolph to be his act and Deed [torn] admitted to record.

[19]   August Court 1728
Hodges deed to Parsons   Robert Hodges acknowledges a deed with the Livery of Seizin endorsed from himself to Joseph Parsons to be his act and Deed and it is thereupon admitted to record.

Quin deed to Nolun   John Quin and Susanna his wife (She being first privately examined) Acknowledges a deed with the Livery of Seizin endorsed from themselves to Thomas Nolun to be their act and Deed and it is thereupon admitted to record.

Bingley Sworn Sub Sherif   Joseph Bingley takes the oaths appointed to be taken by act of Parliament instead of the oaths of allegiance & Supremacy the oaths appointed to be taken by an act of parliament made in the Sixth year of the reign of her late Majesty Queen Anne Entituled an act for the Security of her Majestys person and Government and of the Succession of the Crown of Great Brittain in the protestant line, Subscribes the Test and takes the oath of an Undersherif and is thereupon admitted to the execution of that Office.

Rogers vs Strange   In the action of Debt between Robert Roge[r]s Plt. and Alexander Strange Defendant the Deft. acknowledging himself indebted to the Plt. ten Shillings it is considered by the Court the Plt. do recover against the Defendt. ten Shillings Currant money with costs and an attornys Fee.

Jackson vs Utley   In the action of Debt between John Jackson Plaintif and John Utley Defendant on the Defendants motion an imparlance is Granted him.

Macon vs Wharton   In the action of Case between John Macon Plaintif and Thomas W[h]arton Defendant the Deft. being in Custody of the Sherif pleads he oweth nothing and for tryall puts himself upon the Country and the Plt. Likewise.

The action of Case between Robert Napier Plt. and John Dickinson Defendant is Dismist neither party appearing.

The action of Case between Stephen Hughes Plt. and Stephen Crump Defendant is Dismist neither party appearing.

The action of Trespass on the Case Between Joseph Woodson Plt. and Joseph Ashlin Deft. is Dismist neither party appearing.

The action of case between Thomas Pavement Plaintif and Jacob Brooks Defendant is Dismist neither party appearing.

[20] August Court 1728

Taylor vs Griffith   In the action of Debt between James Taylor Plaintif and Mary Griffith Defendant an Alias Capias is awarded against the Deft. returnable to the next Court.

Ware vs Kent   In the action of Case between Susanna Ware Plt. and William Kent Defendant the Deft. appear and Acknowledging himself indebt[ed] unto the Plt. in the Sum of one pound eighteen Shilling[s] and three pence three farthings it is considered by the Court that the Plt. Do recover against the Defendant the Sum of one pound eighteen Shillings and three pence three Farthings Currant money with Costs and an Attornys Fee.

Right vs Wilson   In the action of Case between John Right Plaintif and Richard Wilson Defendant Thomas Nolun becomes Special Bail for the Deft. who Acknowledging himself indebted unto the Plt. in the Sum of one pound Six Shillings and Eleven pence it is considered by the Court that the Plt. do recover against the Deft. the Sum of one pound Six Shillings and Eleven pence Currant money with Costs and an Attorneys Fee.

Stoveall vs Taylor   In the action of Trespass between George Stoveall Plaintif and John Taylor and Avis his wife Defendants the Defendants plead not Guilty and for Tryall put themselves upon the Country and the Plt. Likewise.

Saunders vs Franklin   In the action of Trespass between John Saunders Plaintif and John Franklin Defendant the Deft. pleads not Guilty and for tryall puts himself upon the Country and the Plaintif Likewise.

Saunders vs Taylor   In the action of Case between John Saunders Plt. and John Taylor Defendant the Defendant pleads he oweth nothing and for tryal puts himself upon the Country and the Plaintif Likewise.

Saunders vs Tayler   In the action of Trespass between John Saunders Plaintiff and John Tayler Defendant the Defendant pleads not Guilty and for Tryall puts himself upon the Country and the Plantif Likewise.

The action of Trespass between Peter Dept Plaintif and Benjamin Simon Defendant is Dismist No Prosecution.

[21] August Court 1728

Rogers vs Marchbanks   In the action of Trespass on the Case between Robert Rogers Plt. and George Marchbanks Defendant for one pound nine Shillings and Seven pence Currant money, Thomas Randolph Gent. on behalf of the Defendant brings into Court the Sum Sued for and Consents to pay the Costs whereupon it is Considered by the Court that the Plaintif do recover against the Deft. the Costs of this Suit & an Attornys Fee.

The action of Case between James Hook Plaintiff and John Smith Deft. is Dismist Neither party appearing.

Atkinson vs Raynolds   In the action of Debt between Elizabeth Atkinson assignee of Henry Atkinson Plaintif and William Raynolds Deft. the Deft. Confesses himself indebted unto the Plt. in the Sum of one pound one shilling and Six pence Currant money whereupon it is considered by the Court that the Plt. do recover against the Defendt. the Sum of one pound one Shilling and Six pence Currant money with Costs.

In the action of Case between James Tayler Plt. and John Quin Deft. the Suit is Dismist the Plt. not prosecuting the Same.

Utley vs Napier   In the action of Debt between John Utley Plt. and Bouth Napier Deft. on the Defts. motion a Special imparlance is Granted him.

Scot vs Paine   In the action of Debt Between Waltor Scott Plt. and John Paine Deft. the Deft. acknowledging himself indebted unto the Plt. in the Sum of twenty Shillings Credit in Captn. Richard Randolphs Store it is considered by the Court that the Plt. do recover against the Deft. the Sum of twenty Shillings Credit in Captn. Richard Randolphs Store with Costs and an Attornys Fee.

Hook vs Quin   In the action of Case between James Hook Plt. and John Quin Deft. on the Defendants Motion an imparlance is Granted him

The action of Case between David Mims Plaintif and Thomas Moor Deft. is Dismist neither party appearing.

Uttley vs Napier   In the action of Case between John Utley Plt. and Bouth Napier Deft. on the Defendants motion an imparlance is Granted him.

[22]   August Court 1728
Utley vs Napier   In the action of Debt Between John Utley Plt. and Bouth Napier Deft. on the Defts. motion Oyer of the Bond is Granted him.

May vs Richards   In the action of Debt between William May Plt. and John Richards Deft. Judgment is Granted the Plt. against the Deft. and Bouth Napier his common Bail for what Damages Shall be recovered this Suit to be Discharged if the Deft. Shall appear at the next Court.

Bryan vs Scot   In the action of Trespass between Thomas Bryan Plt. and Edward Scot Deft. Judgment is Granted the Plt. against the Deft. and John Mcbride his Common Bail for what Damages Shall be recovered this Suit to be Discharged if the Deft. Shall appear at the next Court.

The action of Debt between William New Plt. and Mary New Defendt. is Dismist Neither party appearing.

McDaniel vs Brooks   The attachment obtained by Henry Mcdaniel against Jacob Brooks is continued to the Next Court.

Scot refuses to Swear unto the Comisn. of Peace   Edward Scott Gent. comes into Court and being requested thereto he refuseth to Swear into the Commission of the Peace.

Bingleys deed to Guerrant   Joseph Bingley acknowledges a deed with the Leivery of Seizin endorsed from himself to Daniel Guerrant Junr. to be his act and Deed and it is thereupon admitted to record then Judy wife of the Said Joseph (She being first privately examined) relinquishes her right of Dower in the Land by the Said Deed conveyed which is also admitted to record.

Surveyor of the road   Anthony Hoggat is appointed Surveyor of the back road over Tuckahoe Creek from the County line upwards.

Then the Court adjourned to the third Tuesday in Next month.
                                            Test. Henry Wood ClCur.

****

[23]   September Court 1728
At the Court held for the County of Goochland the third Tuesday in September being the Seventeenth day of the Month Annoq. Domini

1728. Present. Thomas Randolph, John Woodson, John Fleming, Tarlton Fleming, Allin Howard Gent. Justices.

Bradley vs Cox   In the action of Detinue between Joseph Bradley Plaintif and Frederick Cox Defendant the following Jury are sworn to wit. George Paine, William Womack, James Nowlin, Henry Harper, Robert Hughes, John Macbrid, Nathaniel Basset, John Laine, James Taylor, William Saunders, Bartholomew Stoveall, James Spears, who having received their charge withdraw and after some time return with their Verdict which on the Plts. motion is ordered to be recorded and is as followeth "Wee find for the Plt. twenty shillings Currant money." Whereupon it is considered by the Court that the Plaintif do recover against the Defendant the said Sum of twenty Shillings Currant money by the Jurors in their Verdict aforesaid assessed with costs and an Attornys Fee.

Ward vs Watkins   In the action of Debt between Richard Ward Plaintif and William Watkins Deft. the parties Submit themselves to the Court for tryal wh[ere]upon the witnesses being heard it is considered by the Court that the Plt. do recover against the Deft. the Sum of five hundred pounds of tobo. with Costs and an Attornys Fee.

Taylor vs Griffith   In the action of Debt between James Taylor Plaintif and Mary Griffith Deft. the Defendant comes into Court and confesses her self indebted unto the Plt. in the sum of nine pounds two shillings Currant money whereupon it is considered by the Court that the Plaintif do recover against the Deft. the said Sum of nine pound two shillings Currant money with Costs and an Attornys Fee.

[24]   September Court 1728
Carnar vs Quin   In the action of Case between Susanna Carner Plt. and John Quin Deft. the parties Submit themselves to the Court for tryal whereupon they being heard it is considered by the Court that the Plaintif do recover against the Deft. the Sum of thirty shillings Currant money with Costs and an Attorneys Fee.

Mcdanl. vs Brooks   Jacob Brooks having privately departed from his usual place of abode in this County indebted unto Henry Mcdaniel in the sum of Seven pounds ten shillings Currant money he obtained an Attachment ag[st.] the Estate of the said Jacob which attchmt. is returned executed in these words "12th of July 1728. Attached in the hands of William Womack
19th. attached in the hands of Thos. Whiteman one hand saw two

Chissells
19th. attached in the hands of Edward Hatcher one saddle two peices of leather.
19th. attached in the hands of Henry Mcdaniel one horse wch. I have in Custody." The said Henry makes oath to the Justness of his debt and it is thereupon considered that he do recover against the said Jacob Brooks the sum of Seven pounds ten shillings Currant money with Costs and an attornys Fee. William Womack appears [and] confesses himself indebted unto the said Jacob in the sume of Seven hundred pounds of tobacco which being valued at ten shillings Pr. Centum is ordered to be paid by the said William Womack unto the said Henry Macdaniel towards Satisfaction of the Judgment aforesaid.

Syme vs Hoggat   In the action of Case between John Syme Plaintif and Anthony Hoggat Defendant the following Jury are sworn George Paine, William W[omack], James Nowlin, Henry Harper, Robert Hughes, John Mcbrid, Nathaniel Basset, John Laine, James Taylor, William Saunders, Bartholomew Stoveall, James Spears, who having received their charge withdrew and after some time return with their Verdict which on the Plaintifs motion is ordered to be recorded and is as followeth "Wee find for the Plaintif fifty two shillings Currant money." Whereupon it is considered by the Court that the Plaintif do recover against the Defendant the said

[25]   September Court 1728
said Sum of fifty two shillings by the Jurors in their Verdict aforesd. assessed with Costs and a Lawyers Fee.

Laforce's will provd   The last will & testament of Rene Laforce deceased is presented in Court by William Kennon & Richard Randolph two of his Executors who make oath thereto and the same being proved by the oaths of Thomas and Catherine Farrar two of the witnesses thereto it is admitted to record and on the motion of the said Executors and their performing what is usual in such cases Certificate is granted them for obtaining a probate thereof in due form John Woodson & Tarlton Fleming Securities.

Surveyor of the road   Nicholas Cox is appointed Surveyor of the road from Richard Parkers on let alone Creek the best way down to the Manakin Town road and it is ordered that the Inhabitants near the said road be exempt from clearing any other road.

Justice sworn   Edward Scot Gent. takes the Oaths appointed to be taken by act of parliament instead of the Oaths of Allegiance & Supremacy the Oath appointed to be taken by an Act of Parliament made in the Sixth year of the reign of her late Majesty Queen Anne Entitled an Act for the Security of her Majestys person and Government and of the succession to the Crown of Great Brittain in the Protestant line, and Subscribes the Test.

Surveyor of the road   William Womack is appointed Surveyor of the road from Tuckahoe Bridge to Woodsons Mill Creek.

Champaigne vs Pruit   In the Action of Trespass between Peter Champaigne Plaintif and Thomas Pruit Defendant the Court having heard the Arguments on the Demurrer are of Opinion the same is not good in Law, then the Plaintif take issue on the Defendants plea the tryal whereof is referred.

Alvis vs Sorrell   In the Action of Case between George Alvis Plaintif and John Sorrell Defendant the Defendant pleads nonassumpsit and for tryal puts himself upon the Country and the Plaintif likewise.

[26]   September Court 1728
Vanderhd. vs Quin   In the action of Trespass on the Case between Henry Vanderhood Plaintif and John Quin Deft. the Defendant pleads he oweth nothing and for tryall puts himself upon the Country and the Plaintif likewise.

Burton vs Watkins   In the action of Debt between Nowel Burton Plaintif and William Watkins Defendant the Defendant pleads he oweth nothing and for tryal puts himself upon the Country and the Plaintif likewise.

Moor vs Taylor   In the action of Debt between Edward Moor Plaintif and John Taylor Deft. the Defendant acknowledges himself indebted unto the Plaintif in the sume of five hundred and Sixty pounds of tobacco whereupon it is considered by the Court that the Plaintif do recover against the Deft. five hundred and Sixty pounds of tobacco with costs and an Attornys Fee.

Moor vs Stubblefd   In the action of Trespass on the Case between Edward Moor Plaintif and John Stubblefield Defendant the Defendant failing to appear and the Plaintif having at last Court obtained Judgment by nihil dicit, the said Judgment is confirmed for what damages shall be found upon executing a writ of inquiry at the next Court of which the

Sherif is ordered to give the Defendant notice by serving him with a copy of this order.

Thornton vs Salmon   The action of Trespass on the Case between John Thornton Plaintif and Thomas Salmon Deft. is referred at the Plaintifs cost.

Jackson vs Utley   In the action of Debt between John Jackson Plaintif and John Utley Defendant the Defendant failing to plead Judgment is granted the Plaintif against the Deft. for what damages shall be recovered in this Suit to be discharged never the less if the Defendant pleads at the next Court.

Macon vs Wharton   The Action of Case between John Macon Plaintif and Thomas Wharton Defendant is referred to the next Court for tryall.

[27]   September Court 1728
Utley vs Napier   In the action of Debt between John Utley Plt. and Bouth Napier Deft. the last Courts order is continued.

In the action of Case between John Utley Plaintif and Bouth Napier Deft. the last Courts order is continued.

In the Action of Debt between John Utley Plaintif and Bouth Napier Deft. the last Courts order is continued.

Hook vs Quin   In the action of Case between James Hook Plaintif and John Quin Defendt. the Deft. failing to plead Judgment is granted the Plaintif against the Deft. for what damages shall be recovered in this Suit to be discharged never the less if the Defendt. pleads at the next Court.

May vs Richards   In the action of Debt between William May Plaintif and John Richards Defendant at last Court the Plaintif obtained a conditional Judgment for What damages should be recovered in this Suit against the Defendant and Bouth Napier his Common Bail the Deft. now fails to appear and the Plaintif makes oath to the Justness of his Debt whereupon the said Judgment is confirmed and it is considered by the Court that the Plaintif do recover against the Defendant and Bouth Napier the Sum of two pounds two shillings and two pence Currant money with Costs.

Bryan vs Scot   In the action of Trespass between Thomas Bryan Plaintif and Edward Scot Defendant the Deft. failing to plead judgment is granted the Plaintif against the Defendant for what damages shall be recovered in this Suit to be discharged never the less if the Deft. pleads at the next Court.

Chiswell vs Hoggat   In the action of Case between Charles Chiswell Plaintif and Anthony Hoggat Defendt. an imparlance is granted the Defendant.

[Chiswell] vs Napier   In the action of Case between Charles Chiswell Plaintif and Bouth Napier Deft. an Imparlance is granted the Defendant.

[28]   September Court 1728
Stoveall vs Taylor   In the action of Trespass between George Stoveall Plaintif and John Taylor and Avis his wife Defendants the following Jury are sworn to Wit, George Paine, William Womack, James Nowlin, Henry Harper, Robert Hughes, John Macbrid, Nathll. Basset, John Laine, James Taylor, William Saunders, and James Spears, who having received their charge withdraw and after some time return with their Verdict which on the Defendants motion is ordered to be recorded and is as followeth "Wee find for the Defendant. George Paine Foreman." whereupon it is considered by the Court that the suit be dismist with costs and that the Defendants go hence without day.

Saunders vs Taylor   In the action of Trespass between John Saunders Plaintif and John Taylor Defendant the following Jury are sworn, to wit, George Paine, William Womack, James Nowlin, Henry Harper, Robert Hughes, John Macbrid, Nathaniel Basset, John Laine, James Taylor, William Saunders, and James Spears, who having received their charge with draw and after sometime return with their Verdict which at the Defendts. motion is ordered to be recorded and is as followeth "Wee find for the Defendant. George Paine Foreman." whereupon it is considered by the Court that the Deft. go hence without day and that he recover against the Plaintif his Costs in this behalf expended.

Chiswell vs Stubblefield   In the action of Case between Charles Chiswell Plaintif and John Stubblefield Defendant the Defendt. failing to appear Judgment is granted the Plaintif against the Deft. and Joseph Woodson his Bail for what damages shall be recovered in this Suit to be discharged never the less if the Defendant appears at the next Court.

Bottom vs Taylor   In the action of Trespass the Case between William Bottom Plaintif and James Taylor Defendant an imparlance is granted the Defendant.

In the action of Case between William Bottom Plaintif and James Taylor Defendant an imparlance is granted the Defendant.

[29]   September Court 1728
Napier vs Scot   In the action of Debt between Bouth Napier Plaintif and Edward Scot Administration of the Goods and Chattles of Paul Green Deceased Defendant the Deft. failing to appear judgment is granted the Plaintif against the Deft. for what damages shall be recovered in this Suit to be discharged nevertheless upon the appearance of the Defendant at the next Court.

The action of Case between James Turner Plaintif and John Robertson Deft. is dismist no prosecution.

Gill vs Spears   In the action of Trespass on the Case between John Gill Plaintif and Robert Spears Deft. an imparlance is granted the Defendant.

The action of case between William Merewether Plaintif and John Stubblefield Defendant is dismist no prosecution.

The action of Debt between Joseph Woodson Plaintif and John Micheaux Defendant is dismist no appearance.

Chamberln. vs Marchbanks   In the action of Debt between William Chamberlaine Plaintif and George Marchbanks Deft. an imparlance is granted the Defendant.

In the action of Debt between William Chamberlaine Plaintif and George Marchbanks Deft. an imparlance is granted the Defendant.

Saunders vs Franklin   In the action of Trespass between John Saunders Plaintif and John Franklin Deft. the suit is referred at the Plaintifs cost.

[Saunders] vs Taylor   The action of Case between John Saunders Plaintif and John Taylor Defendant is referred at the Defendants cost.

Quin vs Bradly   John Quin having attended this day as a witness for Joseph Bradley vs Frederick Cox it is ordered that the said Joseph do pay him thirty pounds of tobacco with Costs.

Chandler vs Bradley   Joel Chandler having attended this day as a witness for Joseph Bradley vs Frederick Cox it is ordered that the said Joseph do pay him thirty pounds of tobacco with Costs.

[30]
Hix vs Bradley   Marmaduke Hix having attended this day as a witness for Joseph Bradley against Frederick Cox it is ordered that the said Joseph do pay him thirty pounds of tobacco with Costs.

Mann vs Bradley   John Man having attended this day as a witness for Joseph Bradley against Frederick Cox it is ordered that the said Joseph do pay him thirty pounds of tobacco with Costs.

Dawson vs Bradley   Thomas Dawson having attended this day as a witness for Joseph Bradley against Frederick Cox it is ordered that the said Joseph pay him thirty pounds of tobacco with Costs.

Bradley vs Cox   Ordered that no more than three witness be allowed Joseph Bradley in his bill of Costs vs Frederick Cox.

Powel vs Taylor   Roger Powel having attended this day as a witness for John Taylor ads John Saunders it is ordered that the said John Taylor do pay him thirty pounds of tobacco with Costs.

Stoveall vs Saunders   Bartholomew Stoveall having attended this day as a witness for John Saunders vs John Taylor it is ordered that the said John Saunders do pay him thirty pounds of tobacco with Costs.

Hix vs Taylor   Marmaduke Hix having attended this day as a witness for John Taylor ads John Saunders it is ordered that the said John Taylor do pay him thirty pounds of tobacco with Costs.

Low vs Taylor   Amey Low having attended this day a witness for John Taylor ads John Saunders it is ordered that the said John Taylor do pay her thirty pounds of tobacco with costs.

Scruggs vs Saunders   John Scrugs having attended this day as a witness for John Saunders vs John Taylor it is ordered that the said John Saunders do pay him thirty pounds of tobacco with Costs.

Saunders vs Stoveall   John Saunders Junr. having attended this day as a witness for George Stoveall vs John Taylor & Uxorem it is ordered that the said George do pay him thirty pounds of tobacco with Costs.

[31]   September Court 1728
Then the Court adjourned 'till to morrow morning nine aClock
                              Test. Henry Wood ClCur.

****

At the Court continued and held for Goochland County the eighteenth day of September 1728. Present. Thomas Randolph, John Woodson, John Fleming, Tarlton Fleming, Allin Howard, Gent. Justices.

Marshalls negros to be listd   On the petition of Alexander Marshall it is ordered that five negros belonging to him be added to the List of titheables.

Surveyor of the road   Ordered that a road be cleared from the Widow Johnsons by the race paths on the South side of William Knights from thence between Peter Harrisses and John Guns to Thomas Murrells, and Constantine Perkins is appointed Surveyor thereof.

Surveyor of the road   Ordered that a convenient road be cleared from the Ferry landing through the lowground of Jacob Micheaux for the upper and lower Inhabitants on the South side James River and John Quin is appointed Surveyor thereof.

Sampson levy Free   On the petition of Stephen Sampson he is exempt from payment of Levys for four years.

The action of Debt between Henry Harper Plaintif and Edward Scot Admr. of Paul Green deceased Defendt. is dismist neither party appearing.

The action of Debt between John Laine Plaintif and Edward Scot Admr. of Paul Green deceased Defendant is dismist neither party appearing.

Alvis vs Mims   In the action of Case between George Alvis Plaintif and Lyonel Mims Defendant the Sherif having returned the Defendant not to be found and he failing to appear an Alias Capias is ordered to issue against him returnable to the next Court. On the Plaintifs motion leave is granted him to mend the declaration.

[32]   September Court 1728
Alvis vs Utley   In the Action of Case between George Alvis Plaintif and John Utley Deft. the Deft. failing to appear Judgment is granted the Plaintif against the Defendt. and Robert Willis his common Bail for what damages shall be recovered in this Suit to be discharged never the less if the Defendant appears at the next Court. On the motion of the Plaintif leave is granted him to mend the declaration.

Nolun vs Waders   In the action of Case between Thomas Nolun Plaintif and William Waders Deft. an Imparlance is granted the Defendt.

Scot vs Napier   In the action of Case between Edward Scot Plaintif and Bouth Napier Defendt. an imparlance is granted the Defendant.

Pruit vs Maxey   In the action of Trespass between Thomas Pruit Plaintif and Nathaniel Maxey Defendt. the Plaintif having failed to file his declaration on the Defendants motion he is Nonsuited and it is thereupon considered by the Court that the Defendant do recover against the Plaintif five shillings Currant money with Costs and an Attornys Fee.

Cabbell vs Ashlin   In the action of Debt between William Cabbell Assignee of Roger Powell Plaintif and Joseph Ashlin Defendt. the Sherif returned that the Defendant is not to be found and he failing to appear it is ordered that an Alias Capias do issue against him returnable to the next Court.

Buttery vs Lawson   In the action of Case between Adam Buttery Plaintif and John Lawson Deft. the Sherif having returned that the Defendt. is not to be found and he failing to appear it is ordered that an Alias Capias do issue against him returnable to the next Court.

[33]   September Court 1728
Winfrey vs Martin   In the action of Case between Jacob Winfrey Plaintif and John Martin Defendant the Sherif having returned that the Defendant is not to be found and he failing to appear it is ordered that an Alias Capias do issue against him returnable to the next Court.

Towns vs Hoggat   In the action of Debt between William Towns Plaintif and Anthony Hoggat Defendant on the Defendants motion an imparlance is granted him.

Taylor vs Ashlin   In the action of Case Between Elizabeth Taylor Executrix of James Taylor deceased Plaintif and Joseph Ashlin Deft. the Defendant failing to appear Judgment is granted the Plaintif for what damages shall be recovered in this Suit against the Defendant and William Lewis his Common Bail to be discharged never the less if the Defendant appears at the next Court.

The action of Debt between Robert Napier Plaintif and John Dickinson Defendt. is dismist neither party appearing.

GOOCHLAND COUNTY ORDER BOOK 1 1728-1730   29

The action of Case between Thomas Pavement Plaintif and Jacob Brooks Defendant is dismist the Plaintif not prosecuting the same.

Waders vs Nolun & Quin   In the action of Debt between William Waders Plaintif and Thomas Nolun and John Quin Defendant an Imparlance is granted the Defendants.

Burton vs Woodson   In the action of Case between Robert Burton Plaintif and William Woodson Executor of Benjamin Woodson deceased Defendant a Special imparlance is granted the Defendant.

Then the Court Adjourned to the third Tuesday in next Month.
                              Test. Henry Wood ClCur.

****

[34]   County Levy Court 1728
At the Court held for the County of Goochland the 18th day of September 1728. for laying the County levy. Present. Thomas Randolph, John Woodson, Tarlton Fleming, Allin Howard, Gent. Justices.

		tobacco	cask
Goochland County	Dr.		
To Henry Wood Clerk		1000	80
To Daniel Stoner Sheriff		1000	80
To Richard Randolph Gent. Burgess		3400	
To John Bolling Junr. Gent. Burgess		3400	
To Josiah Paine & John McBrid for counting 1795286 Tobo. plants		1496	
To Wm. Cabbell & Nowel Burton for counting 1850906 Tobo. plants		1542	
To Joseph Bingley & David Leseur for counting 449800 Tobo. plants.		375	
To Jacob Micheaux & Joell Chandler for counting 1104663 Do.		920	
To Joseph Ashlin & James Nevill for counting 349156 Do.		291	
To Charles Raley for one Wolfe head Certified by Thos. Randolph.		200	
To Wm. Cannon for 7 Do. Certified by Tarlton Fleming		1400	
To Marmaduke Hix for one Do. Certified by Thos. Randolph		200	

To Stephen Mallett for one Do.		
Certified by Thos. Randolph	200	
To John Scrugs for 3 do.		
Certified by Wm. Mayo	600	
To. Marmaduke Hix for one Do.		
Certified by Tarlton Fleming	200	
To Henry Webb for one Do.		
Certified by Allen Howard.	200	
To Abraham Micheaux for 7 Do.		
Certified by John Woodson	1400	
To John Cressy for one Do.		
Certified by Allen Howard	200	
To Wm. Cressy for one Do. Certified by Do.	200	
To James Holman for 3 Do.		
Certified by Thos. Randolph	600	
To Andrew Spradley for 2 Do. Certified by Do.	400	
To Do. for 3 Certified by John Woodson	600	
To Henry Baily 3 days attendance in		
running the County line	90	
To Isaac Sallee 6 days Do.	180	
To John Legrand 6 days Do.	180	

[35]   County Levy Court 1728.]

Brought Forward	20274	160
To Ashford Hughes 3 days Attendance		
in running the County line	90	
To Wm. Sallee 3 days Do.	90	
	20454	160
Salary	2045	
Cask	160	
	22659	160

Do. Cr.		
By 1132 Titheables at 20 lbs. Tobo. pr. poll	22640	
Due to the Sheriff	19	
	22659	

Ordered that Daniel Stoner Gent. Sherif do Collect of every titheable person in the County the Sum of 20 lbs. of tobacco pr. poll and that in Case of refusal or non payment thereof he levy by distress, and that he also make payment of the severall Sums of tobacco to the respective Creditors for whom the same is leveyed. the said Danl. Stoner enters into bond Allin Howard becomes his Security.

Test. Henry Wood ClCur.

****

At the Court held for Goochland County the Nineteenth day of November 1728. Present. Thomas Randolph, John Fleming, John Woodson, Tarlton Fleming, Allen Howard, Gent. Justices.

Burtons deed to Randolph   Nowel Burton acknowledges a deed from himself to Thomas Randolph to be his act and Deed and it is thereupon admitted to record.

Champaigne vs Pruit   In the Action of Trespass between Peter Champaigne Plaintif and Thomas Pruit Defendant at last Court the Demurrer taken by the Plaintif to the Defendants Plea was overuled, and issue on the said Plea was taken by the Plaintif, the

[36]   November Court 1728
Defendants Attorny now moves that the tryall of the said issue may be waived which being granted, and the premises being seen and by the Court of Our Lord the King here fully understood it seems to the Justices here that the Plea of the said Thomas above in barr Pleaded and the matter in the same contained is good and Sufficient in Law to Quash the Bill aforesaid of the aforesaid Peter therefore it is considered that the said Peter take noting by his writt aforesaid and that the said Thomas go hence without day, and that he recover against the Plaintif his costs by him in this behalf expended and a Lawyers Fee.

Lafeats will   The last will and testament of Tobias Lafeat deceased is presented in Court by Esther Jouany one of his Executors who makes oath thereto and the same being proved by the oath of Anthony Benning and affirmation of Anthony Morgan a Quaker it is admitted to record and on the motion of the said Esther and her performing what is usual in such cases Certificate is granted her for Obtaining a Probate thereof in due form. Anthony Rapene & Anthony Benning Securities.

Ordered that Stephen Chastain, John L'villan, John Chastain, and Peter Ford, or any 3 of them being first Sworn by some Justice of the Peace do Appraise the Estate of Tobias Lafeat deceased.

Grand Jury Presentments   Pursuant to An Act of Assembly of this Colony the Following Grand Jury are Sworn. George Paine, Robert Adams, Nowel Burton, John Mcbride, Robert Burton, Thomas Wadley,

Stephen Cox, James Nowlin, William Kent, Constant Perkins, Peter Baise, Martin Duncan, Daniell Guerrant Junr., Stephen Chastain, John Harris, William Lansdon, James Taylor, Stephen Woodson, William Woodson, William Cabbell, who having received their charge withdraw and after sometime return with their Presentments which are as follow Vizt. "William Cabbell and George Skeeman present Francis Ellidge for Adultery. Wm. Cabbell Geo. Skeeman 1 ejus sigill. ??? The Jury present Martha Watkins for bringing a base born child. Wm. Cabbell and John Mackbride present Mary Stephens for bringing a base born child. Wm. Cabbell. Jno. Mcbrid. Geo. Payne Foreman."

[37]   November Court 1728
Ordered that the severall persons presented be Summon'd to appear at the next Court and answer the same.

Alvis vs Sorrell   In the action of case between George Alvis Plt. and John Sorrell Defendt, Anthony Hoggat, Thomas Christian, Leonard Ballow, Ashford Hughes, William Sallee, John Gunn, Robert Hughes, Benjamin Woodson, Anthony Benning, Peter Ford, John Pryer, John Micheaux, the Jury are Sworn to try the issue joyned who bringing in their Verdict in these words "Wee find for the Plaintif Six Pounds and eight pence half penny Currant money Antho. Hoggat Foreman." the said Verdict at the Plts. motion is recorded and it is considered by the Court that the Plt. recover against the said Deft. the said Sum of Six pounds and eight pence half penny Currant money damages by the Jurors aforesaid in their said Verdict Assessed with the Costs of this Suit and a Lawyers Fee.

Vanderhood vs Quin   In the action of Trespass on the Case between Henry Vanderhood Plt. and John Quin Deft. the tryall of the issue being Submitted to the Court it is by the same considered that the Plaintif recover against the Deft. the Sum of Six pounds Seven shillings and eight pence Currant money with the costs of this Suit and a Lawyers Fee.

Burton vs Watkins   In the Action of Debt between Nowel Burton Plaintif and William Watkins Deft. the Plt. failing to prosecute his Suit the Defts. motion is Nonsuited and it is considered by the Court that the Deft. recover against the Plt. five shillings Currant money with his Costs by him in this behalf expended and a Lawyers Fee.

Moor vs Stubblefield   The action of Trespass on the Case between Edward Moor Plt. and John Stubblefield Deft. is continued to the next Court.

[The handwriting is different for the next 3 items]

Thornton vs Salmon   In the Action of Trespass on the Case between John Thornton Plt. and Thomas Salmon Defendant the Parties Submit themselves to the Court for tryall whereupon it is considered by the Court that the Plaintif do recover against the Defendt. three pounds Currant money with Costs of this Suit and a Lawyers Fee.

Hudspith's deed to Fauqua   Ralph Hudspith acknowledges a deed with the Livery of Seizin endorsed from himself to Joseph Fauqua to be his Act and deed and it is thereupon admitted to record.

[38]   November Court 1728
Jackson vs Utley   In the Action of debt between John Jackson Plaintif and John Utley Deft. the Parties Submit themselves to the Court for tryall whereupon it is considered that the Plaintif do recover against the Deft. the Sum of five pounds seventeen shillings Currant money with the Costs of this Suit and a Lawyers Fee.

[The original handwriting style resumes.]

Macon vs Wharton   The action of Case between John Macon Plt. and Thomas Wharton Deft. is continued to the next Court at the Plts. cost.

Holland vs Becket   In the action of Case between Michaell Holland Plaintif and John Becket Deft. the parties Submit themselves to the Court for tryall where upon it is considered that the Plt. do recover against the Deft. the Sum of one pound Six shillings Currant money with the Costs of this Suit and a Lawyers Fee.

Utley vs Napier   The two actions of Debt and the Action of Case between John Utley Plaintif and Bouth Napier Deft. are continued to the next Court.

Hook vs Quin   In the Action of Case between James Hook Plt. and John Quin Defendt. the Defendant Pleads non Assumpsit and for tryal puts himself upon the Country and the Plaintif likewise.

Taylors deed to Dickins   James Taylor acknowledges a deed with the Livery of Seizin endorsed from himself to Thomas Dickins to be his Act and deed and it is thereupon admitted to record.

Gathwrites acct. agt. Saunders   Michaell Gathwrite exhibits an Acct.

against Thomas Saunders and makes oath that the Sum thereof is justly due to him which is ordered to be Certified thereon.

Dickins accts. vs Meaux and Merrewether   Thomas Dickins exhibits an Acct. agt. the Estate of John Meaux dec'd and one against David Merrewether and makes oath that the several Sums thereof are justly due to him which is ordered to be Certified on the same accounts.

Hoggat & Scots deed to Randolph   Anthony Hoggat and Edward Scot acknowledge a deed with the Livery of Seizin endorsed from themselves to Thomas Randolph to be their act and deed and it is thereupon admitted to record.

[39]   November Court 1728
East vs Champaigne   William East having attended two days as a witness for Peter Champaigne against Thomas Pruit it is ordered that the said Peter do pay him Sixty pounds of tobacco with Costs.

Bryan vs Scott   The action of Trespass between Thomas Bryan Plt. and Edward Scot Defendant is dismist no appearance.

Chiswell vs Hogg[at]t   In the Action of Case between Charles Chiswell Plt. and Anthony Hoggat Defendt. the Parties Submit themselves to the Court for tryall where upon it is considered that the Plt. do recover against the Deft. the Sum of eleven pounds Currant money with the Costs of this Suit and a Lawyers Fee.

Chiswell vs Stubblefield   In the Action of Case between Charles Chiswell Plt. and John Stubblefield Deft. the Deft. failing to appear on the Plts. motion the conditional Judgment granted at September Court against the Deft. and Joseph Woodson is confirmed for so much damages as shall be found upon executing a writ of enquiry at the next Court of which the Sherif is ordered to give the Defendant notice.

Chiswell vs Napier   In the Action of Case between Charles Chiswell Plt. and Bouth Napier Deft. Judgment by nihil dicit is granted the Plt. for what damages shall be recovered against the Defendt. to be discharged nevertheless of the Deft. pleads at the next Court.

Bottom vs Taylor   In the action of Trespass on the Case between William Bottom Plt. and James Taylor Defendant the Defendant Pleads non assumpsit and for tryal puts himself upon the Country and the Plt. likewise.

Bottom vs Taylor   In the Action of Case between William Bottom Plt. and James Taylor Deft. the Parties Submit themselves to the Court for tryall whereupon it is considered that the Plt. do recover against the Defendt. ten busshells of wheat with the costs of this Suit & a Lawyers Fee.

Napier vs Scot   In the action of Debt between Bouth Napier Plt. and Edward Scot Admr. of the goods chattles rights & credits of Paul Green deceased Deft. the Suit is continued at the Plts. cost.

[40]   November Court 1728
Gill vs Spears   In the Action of Trespass on the Case between John Gill Plt. and Robert Spears Deft. pleads not guilty and for tryall puts himself upon the Country and the Plt. likewise.

Chamberlaine vs Marchbanks   In the Action of Debt between William Chamberlaine Plt. and George Marchbanks Deft. the Plt. not being resident within this Colony and his Attorny having failed at his first appearance to give Security for the payment of all such damages costs and charges as should be awarded to the Deft. the Deft. now moves that the suit may be dismist, whereupon Thos. Prosser as Attorny of the Plt. offers to become Security as aforesaid which being refused by the Court as not being in time, it is thereupon considered that the Deft. go hence without day and that he recover against the Plt. his Costs by him in this behalf expended and a Lawyers Fee.
   From which Judgmt. Thomas Prosser as Attorny of William Chamberlaine Appeals to the 6th day of the next General Court and enters himself Security.

Chamberlaine vs Marchbanks   In the Action of Debt between William Chamberlaine Plt. and George Marchbanks Deft. the Plt. not being resident within this Colony and his Attorny having failed at his first appearance to give Security for the payment of all such damages Costs and charges as should be awarded to the Deft. the Deft. now moves that the Suit may be dismist, whereupon Thos. Prosser as Attorny of the Plt. offers to become Security as aforesaid which being refused by the Court as not being in time, it is thereupon considered that the Deft. go hence without day and that he recover against the Plt. costs by him in this behalf expended and a Lawyers Fee.
   From which Judgment Thomas Prosser as Attorny of William Chamberlaine Appeals to the 6th day of the next General Court and enters himself Security.

Adams deed to Sorrell   Robert Adams acknowledges a deed with the Livery of Seizin endorsed from himself to John Sorrell to be his Act and deed and it is thereupon admitted to record Mourning wife of the said Robert being first privately examined relinquishes her Dower in the land by the said Deed

[41]   November Court 1728
conveyed which is also ordered to be recorded.

Adams deed to Johnson   Robert Adams and Mourning his wife She being first privately examined acknowledge a deed from themselves to Charles Johnson to be their act and deed and the same with the Livery of Seizin endorsed which they also acknowledge is admitted to record.

Saunders vs Franklin   In the Action of Trespass between John Saunders Plt. and John Franklin Deft. Anthony Hoggat, Thos. Christian, Leonard Ballew, John Guin, John Pryer, John Micheaux, William Sallee, Anthony Benning, As[h]ford Hughes, Peter Ford, Robert Hughes, Benjamin Woodson, the Jury are sworn to try the issue joyned, who bringing in their Verdict in these words "Wee find for the Plt. twenty shillings Currant Antho. Hoggat Foreman." the said Verdict at the Plts. motion is recorded and it is considered by the Court that the Plt. do recover against the Deft. the said Sum of twenty shillings Currant damages by the Jurors aforesaid in the said Verdict assessed with Costs to the value of twenty shillings Currant only.

Saunders vs Taylor   In the action of Case between John Saunders Plt. and John Taylor Defendt. the tryal of the issue joyned being Submitted to the Court it is thereupon considered that the Plt. recover against the Defendant the Sum of four pounds eleven shillings and seven pence Currant money with the Costs of this Suit and a Lawyers Fee.

Alvis vs Mims   In the Action of Case between George Alvis Plt. and Lionel Mims Deft. the Parties Submit themselves to the Court for tryall whereupon it is considered that the Plt. do recover against the Deft. the Sum of Seven pounds eleven shillings and two pence Currant money with the Costs of this Suit and a Lawyers Fee.

Alvis vs Utley   In the Action of Case between George Alvis Plt. and John Utley Deft. the Deft. failing to Plead Judgment by nihil dicit is granted the Plt. for what damages shall be recovered against the Deft to be discharged nevertheless if the Deft. pleads at the next Court.

Alvis vs Woodson   In the action of Case between George Alvis Plt. and Benjamin Woodson Deft. the Deft. failing to appear on the Plts. motion the conditional Judgment granted at September Court against the Deft. and Bouth Napier is confirmed for

[42]   November Court 1728
for what damages shall be recovered upon executing a writ if inquiry at the next Court of which the Sherif is ordered to give the Deft. notice.

Nolun vs Waders   In the action of Case between Thos. Nolun Plaintif and William Waders Deft. time is granted the Plt. to mend his declaration.

Scot vs Napier   In the action of Case between Edward Scot Plt. and Bouth Napier Deft. the Deft. failing to plead on the Plts. motion Judgment by nihil dicit is granted him for what damages shall be recovered against the Deft. to be discharged nevertheless if the Deft. pleads at the next Court.

Cabbell vs Ashlin   In the Action of Debt between William Cabbell Assee. of Roger Powell Plt. and Joseph Ashlin Deft. the Deft. failing to appear judgment is granted the Plt. for what damages shall be recovered against the Deft. and Jas. Nevils to be discharged nevertheless if the Deft. appears at the next Court.

Buttery vs Lawson   In the action of Case between Adam Buttery Plt. and John Lawson Deft. the Sherif having returned the Deft. not to be found on the Plts. motion a Pluries Capias is awarded against him.

Winfrey vs Martin   In the Action of Case between Jacob Winfrey Plt. and John Martin Deft. the Sherif having returned the Deft. not to be found on the Plts. motion a Pluries Capias is awarded against him.

Towns vs Hoggat   In the action of Debt between William Towns Plt. and Anthony Hoggat Deft. the Deft. failing to plead on the Plts. motion Judgment by nihil dicit is granted him for what damages shall be recovered against the Deft. to be discharged neverthe[le]ss if the Deft. pleads at the next Court.

Taylor vs Ashlin   In the Action of Case between Elizabeth Taylor Executrix of James Taylor Plt. and Joseph Ashlin Deft. the Defts. failure to appear on the Plts. motion the conditional Judgment granted at September Court against the Deft. and William Lewis is confirmed for what damages shall be recovered upon executing a writ of inquiry at the next Court of which the Sherif is ordered to give the Defts. notice.

Waders vs Nolun & Quin   In the action of Debt between William Waders Plt. and Thomas Nolun and John Quin Defts. the Defts. failure to plead on the Plts. motion Judgment by nihil dicit is granted him for what damages shall be recovered against

[43]   November Court 1728
against the Defts. to be discharged if the Defts. plead at the next Court.

Burton vs Woodson   In the action of Case between Robert Burton Plt. and William Woodson Executr. of the last will & testament of Benjamin Woodson deceased Deft. time is granted the Plt. to mend the declaration.

The action of Case between Allin Howard Plt. and Francis Hamilton Deft. is dismist the Plt. not prosecuting the same.

Pruit vs Maxey   In the action of Trespass between Thomas Pruit Plt. and Nathaniel Maxey Deft. an Imparlance is granted the Deft.

Clopton vs Alexander   In the Action of Debt between William Clopton Junr. Plt. and John Alexander Deft. the Deft. is in Custody of the Sherif for lack of Special Bail, and failing to plead Judgment by nihil dicit is granted the Plt. for what damages shall be recovered in this Suit against the Deft. to be discharged upon the Defts. pleading at the next Court.

Holland vs Utley   In the Action of Case between Michaell Holland Plt. and John Utley Defendt. the Parties Submit themselves to the Court for tryall whereupon it is considered by the Court that the Plt. do recover against the Deft. the Sum of Seventeen pounds three shillings and nine pence Currant money with the costs of this Suit & a Lawyers Fee.

The Action of Case Between Michael Holland Plt. and Charles Cannon Deft. is dismist the Plt. not prosecuting the same.

Then the Court Adjourned 'till to morrow morning ten a Clock
                                                Test. Henry Wood ClCur.

****

At the Court continued and held for Goochland County the twentieth day of Novem. 1728. Present. Thomas Randolph, John Fleming, John Woodson, Tarlton Fleming, Allin Howard, Gent. Justices.

Hughes vs Crump   In the Action of Case between Stephen Hughes Plt. and Stephen Crump Deft. the Deft. failing to appear Judgment is granted the Plt. against the Deft. and John Bostick for what damages shall be recovered in this Suit to be discharged if the Deft. appears at the next Court.

[44]   November Court 1728
Littlepage vs Crump   In the Action of Debt between Frances Littlepage Plt. and Stephen Crump Deft. the Deft. failing to appear on the Plts. motion Judgment is granted her against the Deft. and Nowel Burton & Bouth Napier the Defts. Bail for what Damages shall be recovered in this Suit to be discharged if the Defendant shall appear at the next Court.

Chastains will   The last will & testament of Peter Chastain deceased is presented in Court by John and Peter Chastain his Executors who make oath thereto and the same being proved by the oaths of Thomas Randolph and Daniel Guerrant Junr. two of the witnesses thereto it is admitted to record, and on the motion of the said Executors and their performing what is usuall in such cases Certificate is granted them for obtaining a probate thereof in due form William Sallee and Thomas Jevodan Securities.
   Ordered that Stephen Chastain, Anthony Rapene, John L'villan, and Abraham Sallee, or any 3 of them being first sworn by some Justice of the Peace do Appraise the Estate of Peter Chastain deceased.

Holland vs Hoggat   In the Action of Case between Michael Holland Plt. and Anthony Hoggat Deft. an imparlance is granted the Deft.

Rapene vs Bingley   In the action of Trespass on the Case between Anthony Rapene Plt. and Joseph Bingley Deft. time is granted the Plt. to mend his declaration.

The action of Case between John Woodson Plt. and Michael Canady Deft. is dismist the Plt. not prosecuting the same.

The action of Case between Thomas Wharton Plt. and Robert Napier Deft. is dismist the Plt. not prosecuting the same.

The action of Debt between Samuel Allin Plt. and Michael Canady Deft. is dismist neither party appearing.

Holland vs Saunders   In the Action of Case Between Michael Holland Plt. and Thomas Saunders Defendt. An Alias Capias is awarded against the Defendt. returnable to the next Court.

Bryan vs Quin   In the action of Case between Thoms. Bryan Plt. and John Quin Deft. an imparlance is granted the Deft.

[45]   November Court 1728
Burton vs Watkins   In the action of Debt between Nowell Burton Assee of Allin Frazur Assee. of Michael Canady Plt. and William Watkins Deft. the Defendant failing to appear on the Plts. motion Judgment is granted him against the Deft. and Daniel Stoner Gent. Sherif for what damages shall be recovered in this Suit to be discharged if the Deft. shall appear at the next Court.

Tyre vs Utley   In the action of Trover between James Tyre &c. Plt. and John Utley Deft. the Deft. failing to appear Judgment is granted the Plt. against the Deft. and Daniel Stoner Gent. Sherif for what damages shall be recovered in this Suit to be discharged if the Deft. shall appear at the next Court.

Maxey vs Pruit   In the action of Debt between Nathaniel Maxey Plt. and Thomas Pruit Deft. the Deft. failing to plead Judgment for nihil dicit is granted the Plt. against the Deft. for what damages shall be recovered in this Suit to be discharged if the Deft. shall plead at the next Court.

The action of Case between Michael Holland Plt. and Arnold Thomason Deft. is dismist the Plt. not prosecuting the same.

Holland vs Richard   In the Action of Case between Michael Holland Plt. and John Richard Deft. an Alias Capias is awarded against the Deft. returnable to the next Court.

Waddil vs Edwards   In the Action of Case between William Waddill Junr. Plt. and Thomas Edwards Deft. an imparlance is granted the Deft.

The action of Debt between Thomas Dickins Plt. and John Farguson Deft. is dismist the Plt. not prosecuting the same.

The Action of Debt between Samuel Chamberlaine Plt. and John Kerby Deft. is dismist the Plt. not prosecuting the same.

Ware vs Saunders   In the action of Case between Susanna Ware Plt. and Thomas Saunders Deft. an Alias Capias is awarded against the Defendant returnable to the next Court.

Holland vs Logan   In the action of Case between Michael Holland Plt. and Alexander Logan Deft. the Deft. failing to appear Judgment is granted the Plt. against the Deft. and Thomas Edwards for what damages shall be recovered in this suit to be discharged if the Deft. appears at the next Court.

[46]   November Court 1728
Carnar vs Atkinson   In the action of Case between Susanna Carnar Plt. and Henry Atkinson Deft. an Alias Capias is awarded against the Deft. returnable to the next Court.

The action of Case between Henry Macdaniel Plt. and Michael Canady Deft. is dismist. the Plt. being dead.

Mcdaniels Admn. grant'd   Thomas Randolph comes into Court and makes oath that Henry Macdaniel died without any will as far as he knows or beleives and upon his giving Security for his just and faithfull Administration of the said Deceadents estate Certificate is granted him for obtaining Letters of Administration in due form. John Fleming and John Woodson Securities. Ordered that Robert Adams, George Paine, Robert Burton, and Robert Woodson or any three of them being first Sworn by some Justice of the Peace do appraise the Estate of Henry Macdaniel Deceased.

Bingley vs Wiers   In the action of Case between Joseph Bingley Plt. and John Wiers Defendt. the Deft. failing to appear conditional Judgment is granted the Plt. against the Deft. and Edward Williams to be discharged if the Defendt. shall appear at the next Court.

Spencer vs Gallemore   In the Action of Case between Samuel Spencer Plt. and William Gallemore Deft. an Alias Capias is awarded against the Deft. returnable to the next Court.

Pattison vs King   In the action of Trespass between David Pattison Plt. and Martin King Deft. an imparlance is granted the Defendant.

Webber vs Baker   In the action of Case between Philip Webber Plt. and Francis Baker Deft. time is granted the Plt. to mend his declaration.

Hughes vs Lax   In the action of Case between Ashford Hughes Plt. and William Lax Deft. an Alias Capias is awarded against the Deft. returnable to the next Court.

Hughes vs Haws   In the action of Case between Robert Hughes Plt. and Henry Haws Deft. Stephen Hughes becomes Special Bail for the Defendt. who pleads he oweth nothing and for tryal puts himself upon the Country and the Plt. likewise.

Dickason vs Hughes   In the action of Case between John Dickason Plt. and Stephen Hughes Deft. an imparlance is granted the Defendant.

[47]   November Court 1728
Gee vs Thomas   In the action of Trespass on the Case between Gilbert Gee Plt. and Rowland Thomas Defendant the Defendant failing to appear Judgment is granted the Plt. against the Defendant and Daniel Stoner Gent. Sherif for what damages shall be recovered in this Suit to be discharged of the Deft. appears at the next Court.

Woodson vs Allen   In the action of Case between Josiah & Stephen Woodson Executors of Jacob Woodson deceased Plts. and Samuel Allen Deft. an Alias Capias is awarded against the Defendt. returnable to the next Court.

The Action of Trespass between Andrew Pruit Plt. and Charles Johnson Deft. is dismist the Plt. not prosecuting the same.

Bolling vs Tapley   In the Action of Trespass on the Case between John Bolling Plt. and John Tapley Deft. an Alias Capias is awarded against the Deft. returnable to the next Court.

Walker vs Curd   In the action of Trespass on the Case between William Walker Plt. and Edward Curd Deft. an Alias Caps. is awarded against the Deft. returnable to the next Court.

The action of Case between Edward Williams Plt. and Peter Ware Deft. is dismist the Plt. not prosecuting the same.

White vs Webber   In the action of Case between Samuel White Plt. and Philip Webber Deft. an imparlance is granted the Deft.

The action of Debt between Joseph Woodson Plt. and John Micheaux Deft. is dismist neither party appearing.

Turner vs Powel   In the action of Detinue between James Turner Plt. and Richard Powell Deft. the Deft. pleads non detinet and for tryall puts himself upon the Country and the Plt. likewise.

New vs Morriss   In the action of Debt between William New Plt. and Hugh Morris and Sarah his wife Executrix of Edmund New deceased time is granted the Plt. to mend his declaration.

[48]   November Court 1728
King vs Pattison   In the action of Trespass on the Case between Martin King Plt. and David Pattison Junr. Deft. an imparlance is granted the Deft.

Laine vs Christian   In the action of Case between John Laine Plt. and John Christian Deft. an Alias Capias is awarded against the Defendt. returnable to the next Court.

Davis vs Sallee   In the action of Trespass on the Case between John Davis Plt. and William Sallee Deft. a Special imparlance is granted the Defendant.

Vaughn vs Williams   In the Action of Trover between George Vaughn Plt. and John Williams Deft. time is granted the Plt. to mend his declaration.

Raley vs Quin   In the action of Debt between Charles Raley Plt. and John Quin Defendant an imparlance is granted the Defendt.

Williams vs Quin   In the action of Debt between John Williams Plt. and John Quin Defendt. an imparlance is granted the Defendant.

Chamberlaine vs Marchbanks   In the action of Debt between William Chamberlaine Plt. and George Marchbanks Deft. the Plt. not being resident in the Colony Thomas Prosser enters himself Security for the payment of all such costs & damages as shall be awarded to the Deft. and time is granted the Plt. to mend his declaration.

Stidum vs Bingley   In the Action of Case between Benjamin Stidum Plt. and Joseph Bingley Deft. time is granted the Plt. to mend his declaration.

Barnes vs Pruit   In the Action of Debt between William Barnes Plt. and Thomas Pruit Deft. Roger Pratt enters himself Special Bail for the Deft. and an imparlance is granted the Defendt.

Lansdon vs Wiers   In the Action of Case between William Lansdon Plt. and John Wiers Deft. the Deft. failing to appear Judgment is granted the Plt. against the Deft. and William East for what damages shall be recovered in this Suit to be discharged if the Defendt. shall appear at the next Court.

Harriss vs Pratt In the Action of Case between John Harriss Plt. and Roger Pratt and Peter Ford Defts. failing to appear Judgment is granted the Plt. against the Defts. and Daniel Stoner Gent. Sherif for what damages shall be

[49] November Court 1728
recovered in this Suit to be discharged if the Defts. appear at the next Court.

New vs Calvit In the action of Case between William New Deft. and Peter Calvit Deft. Joseph Bingley enters himself Special Bail for the Deft. and an imparlance is granted the Defendant.

Baise vs Moor In the action pf Case between Edward Baize Plt. and William Moor Deft. time is granted the Plt. to mend his declaration.

Harper vs Scot In the Action of Trespass on the Case between Henry Harper Plt. and Edward Scot &c. Administrator of Paul Green Deft. an imparlance is granted the Deft.

Laine vs Scot In the action of Trespass on the Case between John Laine Plt. and Edward Scot Administrator &c. of Paul Green deceased Deft. an imparlance is granted the Deft.

Boccards Admn Peter Boccard comes into Court and makes Oath that Stephen Boccard deceas'd died without any will as far as he knows or beleives and on his giving Security for his just & faithfull and Administration of the said Deceadents Estate Certificate is granted him for obtaining Letters of Administration in due form. William Lansdon & Peter Dep Securities.
Ordered that Peter Ford, Stephen Chastain, Anthony Rapene, Nicholas Souille, or any three of them being first Sworn by some Justice of the Peace do appraise the Estate of Stephen Boccard deceased.

Stocks &c. to be built Ordered that Allin Howard Gent. do agree with some person for the Erecting a pillory, whipping post and a pair of Stocks for the use of the County.

Surveyor appointed Allin Howard Gent. is appointed Surveyor of the road from the Court house into the back road above Major Bollings mill.

Henry Wood is appointed Surveyor of the road from Tuckahoe Creek mill to Manakin Town Ferry.

Stephen Hughes is appointed Surveyor of the road from the Court house Ferry down the South side of James River the most convenient way for the lower Inhabitants to come to Court, and it is ordered that the Inhabitants between the main road and the River clear the said road.

[50] November Court 1728

Turner vs Saunders   Joanna Turner having attended this day as a witness for John Saunders vs. John Taylor it is ordered that the said John Saunders do pay her thirty pounds of tobacco with Costs.

Then the Court adjourned to the third Tuesday in next Month
Test. Henry Wood ClCur.

****

At a Court called and held for Goochland County the twentieth day of November 1728. for the tryall of Frances Green. Present. Thomas Randolph, John Fleming, John Woodson, Tarlton Fleming, Allin Howard Gent. Justices.

Frances Green being brought to the Bar and accused with the Murther of her Bastard Child, upon hearing the Prisoner and consideration of the Depositions of the witnesses, it is the Opinion of the Court that the said Frances Green ought to be tryed for the crime aforesaid before the Court of Oyer and Terminer to be held at Williamsburgh on the Second Tuesday in December next.

Thomas Murrel comes into Court and acknowledges himself indebted unto Our Sovereign Lord the King his Heirs &c. in the Sum of one hundred pounds Sterling to be leveyed of the goods chattles &c. of the said Thomas Murrell On condition nevertheless that if Elizabeth wife of the said Thomas do appear before the Court of Oyer and Terminer to be held at Williamsburgh on the Second Tuesday in December next to give Evidence between Our Sovereign Lord the King and Frances Green then the said Recognizance to be void.

Benjamin Bradshaw comes into Court and acknowledges himself indebted unto Our Sovereign Lord the King in the Sum of one hundred pounds Sterling to be levyed of the Goods Chattles &c. of the said Benjamin

Bradshaw. On Condition nevertheless that if the said Benjamin and

[51] December Court 1728
Anne his wife do Appear before the Court of Oyer & Terminer to be held at Williamsburg on the Second Tuesday in December next to give Evidence between Our Sovereign Lord the King and Frances Green then the said Recognizance to be void.

> Test. Henry Wood ClCur.

****

At the Court held for Goochland County the 3rd Tuesday in December being the 17th day of the Month Anno Domini 1728. Present. Thomas Randolph, William Mayo, John Woodson, Tarlton Fleming, Allen Howard, Gent. Justices.

Moor vs Stubblefield   The action of Trespass on the Case between Edward Moor Plt. and John Stubblefield Deft. is continued to the next Court.

Macon vs Wharton   The action of Case between John Macon Plt. and Thomas Wharton Deft. is continued to the next Court.

Utley vs Napier   In the two Actions of Debt and Action of Case between John Utley Plt. and Bouth Napier Deft. John Woodson, Tarlton Fleming, and Henry Wood by consent of the parties are appointed to Examine state & settle the several differences and accounts in dispute between them and to make report of their proceedings therein to the next Court. Thursday the nineteenth of this month is appointed for Auditing the same.

Hook vs Quin   In the Action of Case between James Hook Plt. and John Quin Deft. the parties Submit themselves to the Court for tryal whereupon it is considered that the Plt. do recover of the Deft. four pounds Credit in a Store with the costs of this Suit and a Lawyers Fee.

Littlepage vs Crump   In the Action of Debt between Frances Littlepage Plt. and Stephen Crump Deft. at last Court the Plt. obtained a condl. Judgment against the Defendt. and Nowel Burton and Bouth Napier who were returned his Bail the Deft. now failing to appear on the Plts. motion the said Judgment is confirmed

[52] December Court 1728

confirmed and it is thereupon considered by the Court that the Plt. do recover against the Deft. and Nowel Burton & Bouth Napier the Sum of four pounds six Shillings Currant money and eighty seven pounds of tobo. with the costs of this Suit and a Lawyers Fee.

Turner vs Powell   In the Action of Detinue between James Turner Plt. and Richard Powell Deft. the Plt. failing to Prosecute his Suit on the Defendants motion he is Nonsuited and it is thereupon considered by the Court that the Deft. do recover agt. the Plt. five shillings Currant money with costs and a Lawyers Fee.

Chiswell vs Stubblefield   In the Action of Case between Charles Chiswell Plt. and John Stubblefield Deft. Anthony Hoggat, Robert Burton, John Harriss, Nathll. Basset, William Moor, John Macbrid, Amos Lad, Henry Harper, James Spears, John Webb, Ashford Hughes, Peter Ware, the Jury are Sworn to enquire of the damages who after some time return their Verdict in these words "Wee find for the Plt. six pounds and a penny Currant money Antho. Hoggat Foreman" wch. Verdict on the Plts. motion is ordered to be recorded And it is thereupon considered by the Court that the Plt. do recover against the Deft. and Joseph Woodson his Bail the said Sum of six pounds one penny Currant money by the Jurors aforesaid in their Verdict Assessed with the costs of this Suit and a Lawyers Fee.

Woodson vs Horseley   In the Action of Case between John Woodson Plt. and Robert Horseley Deft. the parties Submit themselves to the Court for tryal whereupon it is considered by the Court that the Plt. do recover against the Deft. five hundred pounds of tobo. with the Costs of this Suit and a Lawyers Fee.

Fauquinoe vs David   Upon the Complaint of Danl. Fauquinoe against his Master Peter David it is ordered that the said Daniel do remain with the Sherif until next Court and that the said Peter be Summoned to appear and answer the Complaint aforesd.

Hughes vs Crump   In the Action of Case between Stephen Hughes Plt. and Stephen Crump Deft. the Deft. failing to appear the Plts. motion the conditional Judgment formerly granted in this Suit against the Deft. and John Bostick is confirmed for so much damages as shall be found upon executing a writ of enquiry at the next Court

[53]   December Court 1728
of which the Sherif is ordered to give the Deft. notice by serving him with a copy of this Order.

Holland vs Logan   In the Action of Case between Michael Holland Plt. and Alexander Logan Defendant the Defendant failing to appear on the Plts. motion the conditional Judgment formerly granted in this Suit against the Deft. and Thomas Edwards is confirmed for so much damages as shall be found upon executing a writ of inquiry at the next Court of which the Sherif is ordered to give the Defendant notice by Serving him with a Copy of this order.

Bingley vs Wiers   In the Action of Case between Joseph Bingley Plt. and John Wiers Deft. the Deft. failing to appear on the Plts. motion the conditional Judgment formerly granted in this Suit against the Defendant and Edward Williams is confirmed for so much damages as shall be found upon executing a writ of inquiry at the next Court of which the Sherif is ordered to give the Deft. notice by Serving him with a Copy of this Order.

Gee vs Thos   In the Action of Trespass on the Case between Gilbert Gee Plt. and Rowland Thomas Deft. the Deft. failing to appear on the Plts. motion the conditional Judgment formerly granted in this Suit against the Deft. and Daniel Stoner Gent. Sherif is confirmed for so much damages as shall be found upon executing a writ of inquiry at the next Court of which the Sherif is ordered to give the Deft. notice by Serving him with a Copy of this order.

Pleasants deed to Rand[olp]h   John Pleasants acknowledges a deed with the Livery of Seizin endorsed from himself to Thomas Randolph to be his act and deed and it is thereupon admitted to record.

Chiswell vs Napier   The action of Case between Charles Chiswell Plt. and Booth Napier Deft. is continued at the Defts. cost.

Alvis vs Utley   The action of Case between George Alvis Plt. and John Utley Deft. is continued at the Defts. costs.

[54]   December Court 1728
Napier vs Scot   In the Action of Debt between Bouth Napier Plt. and Edward Scot Admr. of Paul Green deceased Deft. the Deft. failing to plead on the Plts. motion Judgment by nihil dicit is granted him against the Defendant for what damages shall be recovered in this Suit to be discharged if the Deft. shall plead at the next Court.

Alvis vs Woodson   The action of case between George Alvis Plt. and Joseph Woodson Deft. is continued.

Nolun vs Wotars   In the action of Case between Thos. Nolun Plt. and William Wotars Deft. the Deft. failing to plead Judgment by nihil dicit is granted against the Deft. for what damages shall be recovered in this Suit to be discharged if the Deft. pleads at the next Court.

Scot vs Napier   In the Action of Case between Edward Scot Plt. and Bouth Napier Deft. the Deft. pleads he oweth nothing and for tryall puts himself upon the Country and the Plt. likewise.

Cabbell vs Ashlin   In the Action of Debt between William Cabbell Plt. and Joseph Ashlin Deft. John Webb enters himself Special Bail for the Deft. who failing to plead Judgment by nihil dicit is granted against him for what damages shall be recovered in this Suit to be discharged if the Deft. pleads at the next Court.

Buttery vs Lawson   The action of Case between Adam Buttery Plt. and John Lawson Deft. is dismist the Plt. not prosecuting the same.

Winfrey vs Martin   In the Action of Case between Jacob Winfrey Plt. and John Martin Deft. a pluries Caps. is awarded against the Deft. returnable to the next Court.

Gill vs Spears   The action of Trespass on the Case between John Gill Plt. and Robert Spears Deft. is continued at the Plts. costs.

[55]   December Court 1728
Bottom vs Taylor   In the Action of Trespass on the Case between William Bottom Plt. and James Taylor Deft. Anthony Hoggat, Robert Burton, John Harriss, Nathaniel Basset, William Moor, John Macbrid, Amos Lad, Henry Harper, James Spears, John Webb, Ashford Hughes, Peter Ware, the Jury are Sworn, who after some time bring in their Verdict in these words "Wee find for the Deft. Anthony Hoggat Foreman." which Verdict at the Defts. motion is recorded, and it is thereupon considered by the Court that the Defendant go hence without day and that he recover against the Plt. his costs in this behalf expended and a Lawyers Fee.

Towns vs Hoggat   The action of Debt between William Towns Plt. and Anthony Hoggat Defendant is continued at the Defendants Costs.

Taylor vs Ashlin   In the Action of Case between Elizabeth Taylor Executrix of James Taylor deceased Plt. and Joseph Ashlin Deft. the parties Submit themselves to the Court for tryall, whereupon it is considered that the Plt. do recover against the Deft. one hundred eighty one and a quarter pound[s] of tobacco with costs.

Wotars vs Nolun and Quin   In the Action of Debt between William Wotars Plt. and Thomas Nolun and John Quin Defts. the Defts. file a plea to which the Plt. Demurrs generally and the Defts. joyn in Demurrer.

Burton vs Woodson   In the Action of Case between Robert Burton Plt. and William Woodson Executor &c. of Benjamin Woodson deceased Deft. the Plt. amends his declaration and the Deft. failing to plead Judgment by nihil dicit is granted against him for what damages shall be recovered in this Suit to be discharged if the Deft. appears at the next Court and Pleads.

Pruit vs Maxey   In the Action of Trespass between Thomas Pruit Plt. and Nathll. Maxey Deft. the Deft. pleads not guilty and for tryal puts himself upon the Country and the Plt. likewise.

[56]   December Court 1728
Landsdon vs Wiers   In the Action on the Case Between William Landsdon Plt. & John Wiers Deft. at last Court the Plt. Obtained a Conditional Judgmt. agt. the Deft. & William East, the Deft. now failing to appear Joseph Bingley on the behalf of the Deft. Submitts the Tryall to the Court Whereupon it is Considered that the Plt. recover agt. the Deft. & William East Two hundred pounds of Tobacco with Cost and a Lawyers Fee. [The handwriting is different for this entry.]

Clopton vs Alexander   In the Action of Debt between William Clopton Junr. and John Alexander Deft. on the Plts. motion leave is granted him and thereupon he mends his declaration the Deft. being in Custody of the Sherif for lack of Special Bail pleads he oweth nothing and for tryall Submits himself to the Court and the Plt. likewise whereupon it is considered that the Plt. do recover against the Deft. three pounds twelve shillings and six pence Currant money and eight hundred and forty eight pounds of tobacco with Costs and a Lawyers Fee.

Holland vs Hoggat   In the action of Case between Michael Holland Plt. and Anthony Hoggat Deft. on the motion of the Sherif leave is granted him to mend his return of the writ the Deft. failing to plead Judgment by nihil dicit is granted against him for what damages shall be recovered in this Suit to be discharged never the less if the Deft. pleads at the next Court.

Rapene vs Bingley   The action of Trespass on the Case between Anthony Rapene Plt. and Joseph Bingley Deft. is continued at the Plts. cost.

Holland vs Saunders   In the Action of Case between Michaell Holland Plt. and Thomas Saunders Deft. an Alias Caps. is awarded against the Deft. and returnable to the next Court.

Burton vs Watkins   In the action of Debt between Nowell Burton Assignee of Michael Canady Assignee of Allin Frazer Plt. and William Watkins Deft. the Deft. failing to plead Judgment by nihil dicit is granted against him for what damages shall be recovered in this Suit to be discharged if the Deft. shall plead at the next Court.

Bryan vs Quin   In the action of Case between Thomas Bryan Plt. and John Quin Deft. the Deft. failing to Plead on the Plts. motion Judgment by nihil dicit is granted against

[57]   December Court 1728

against him for what damages shall be recovered in this Suit to be discharged if the Deft. shall plead at the next Court.

Tyre vs Utley   In the action of Trover between James Tyre Plt. and John Utley Deft. the Deft. failing to plead Judgment by nihil dicit is granted him for what damages shall be recovered in this Suit to be discharged if the Deft. shall plead at the next Court.

Howls Administr. granted   Mary Relict of William Howl deced relinquishing John Pleasants comes into Court and (being a Quaker) makes his Solemn affirmation that William Howl deceased died without making any will so far as he knows or beleives and on his motion and giving Security for his just and faithfull administration of the said Deceadents Estate Certificate is granted him for obtaining Letters of Administration in due form. John Woodson, Henry Wood Securities.

Ordered that Edward Maxey, Francis James, Robert Hughes and John Harriss or any three of them being first Sworn by some Justice of the Peace do Appraise the Estate of William Howl deceased.

Present John Fleming Gent.

Maxey vs Pruit   The action of case between Nathll. Maxey Plt. and Thomas Pruit Deft. is continued.

Griffith discharged of Exa   Mary Griffith comes into Court and makes Oath that a certain Schedule by her Subscribed containeth a true full and perfect account of her Estate according to the form prescribed in One Act of Assembly of this Colony for the Releif of Insolvent Debtors, and on her motion it is ordered that She be discharged the Custody of the Sherif at the Suit of James Taylor.

Morgans bill vs Howl   Edward Morgan exhibits a bill and makes oath that he never received any Satisfaction for the same from William Howl deceased which is ordered to be Certified thereon.

Woodson's deed to Randolph   John Woodson acknowledges a deed with the Livery of Seizin endorsed from himself to Thomas Randolph to be his act and deed Edward Scot, Joseph Scot, and Thomas Dickins prove the same deed to be the Act and deed of Robert Woodson Junr. and it is thereupon admitted to record.

[58]   December Court 1728
Leseur vs Taylor   David Leseur having attended this day a witness for James Taylor ads William Bottom it is ordered that the said James do pay him for the same thirty pounds of tobacco with Costs.

Benning vs Taylor   Anthony Benning having attended this day as a witness for James Taylor ads William Bottom it is ordered that the said James do pay him for the same thirty pounds of tobacco with Costs.

Chastain vs Bottom   Peter Chastain having attended this day as a witness for William Bottom vs James Taylor it is ordered that the said William do pay him for the same thirty pounds of tobacco with Costs.

Hook vs Bottom   On the motion of James Hook a witness for William Bottom vs James Taylor it is ordered that the said William do pay him for one days attendance thirty pounds of tobacco with Costs.

Holland vs Richard   In the action of Case between Michaell Holland Plt. and John Richard Deft. the Deft. being in Custody of the Sherif for lack of Special Bail pleads he oweth nothing and for tryall Submits himself to the Court and the Plt. likewise whereupon it is considered that the Plt. do recover against the Deft. Six hundred pounds of Sweet Scented tobacco with Costs and a Lawyers Fee.

Waddill vs Edwards   In the action of Case between William Waddill Plt. and Thomas Edwards Deft. the Deft. failing to plead Judgment by nihil dicit is granted him agt. the Deft. for what damages shall be recovered in this Suit to be discharged if the Deft. shall plead at the next Court.

Ware vs Saunders   In the action of Case between Susanna Ware Plt. and Thomas Saunders Deft. an Alias Capias is awarded the Deft. returnable to the next Court.

Carnar vs Atkinson   The action of Case between Susanna Carnar Plt. and Henry Atkinson Deft. is dismist the Plt. not prosecuting the same.

[59]   December Court 1728
Spencer vs Gallemore   In the Action of Case between Samuel Spencer Plt. and William Gallemore Deft. an Als. Caps. is awarded against the Deft. returnable to the next Court.

Dick's. acct. vs Farrall   Thomas Dickins exhibits an Account due to him from Daniel Farral and makes oath he never received any Satisfaction for the same which is ordered to be Certified thereon.

Pattison vs King   In the action of Trespass between David Pattison Plt. and Martin King Deft. the Deft. failing to plead Judgment is granted against him by nihil dicit for what damages shall be recovered in this Suit to be discharged if the Deft. pleads at the next Court.

Webber vs Baker   In the action of Case between Philip Webber Plt. and Francis Baker Deft. the Deft. pleads he oweth nothing and for tryal puts himself upon the Country and the Plt. likewise.

Hughes vs Lax   In the action of Case between Ashford Hughes Plt. and William Lax Deft. on the Plts. motion leave is granted him to mend his declaration.

Hughes vs Haws   The action of Case between Robert Hughes Plt. and Henry Haws Deft. is dismist the Plt. not prosecuting the same.

Dickinson vs Hughes   In the Action of Case between John Dickinson Plt. and Stephen Hughes Deft. the Deft. failing to plead Judgment by nihil dicit is granted against him for what damages shall be recovered in this Suit to be discharged if the Deft. pleads at the next Court.

Woodson vs Allin   In the action of Case between Josiah & Stephen

Woodson Executors of Jacob Woodson deceased Plts. and Samuel Allin Deft. an Alias Caps. is awarded against the Deft. returnable to the next Court.

Bolling vs Tapley   In the action of Trespass on the Case between John Bolling Plt. and John Tapley Deft. a Pluries Caps. is awarded against the Deft. returnable to the next Court.

[60]   December Court 1728
Walker vs Curd   In the Action of Trespass on the Case between William Walker Plt. and Edward Curd Deft. a Pluries Caps. is awarded against the Deft. returnable to the next Court.

White vs Webber   The action of Case between Samuel White Plt. and Philip Webber Deft. is continued.

New vs Morriss   In the Action of Debt between William New Plt. and Hugh Morriss and Sarah his wife Executrix &c. of Edmund New deceased Defts. on the Defts. motion Oyer is granted them.

King vs Pattison   In the Action of Trespass on the Case between Martin King Plt. and David Pattison Deft. the Deft. pleads not guilty and for tryal puts himself upon the Country and the Plt. likewise.

Laine vs Christian   In the Action of Case between John Laine Plt. and John Christian Deft. on the Plts. motion time is granted him to mend his declaration.

Davis vs Sallee   In the Action of Trespass on the Case between John Davis Plt. and William Sallee Deft. the Deft. failing to plead Judgment by nihil dicit is granted against him for what damages shall be recovered in this Suit to be discharged if the Deft. shall plead at the next Court.

Vaughn vs Williams   In the Action of Trover between George Vaughn Plt. and John Williams Deft. the Plt. files a new declaration and an imparlance is granted the Deft.

Raley vs Quin   In the Action of Debt between Charles Raley Plt. and John Quin Deft. the Deft. failing to plead Judgment by nihil dicit is granted against him for what damages shall be recovered in this Suit to be discharged if the Deft. pleads at the next Court.

Williams vs Quin   In the Action of Debt between John Williams Plt.

and John Quin Deft. the Deft. failing to plead judgment by nihil dicit is granted against him for what damages shall be recovered in this Suit to be discharged if the Deft. pleads at the next Court.

[61]   December Court 1728
Chamberln. vs Marchbks   In the Action of Debt between William Chamberlaine Plt. and George Marchbanks Deft. the Plt. files a new declaration & the Deft. failing to Plead Judgment by nihil dicit is granted against him for what damages shall be recovered in this Suit to be discharged if the Deft. pleads at the next Court.

Stidum vs Bingley   The action of Case between Benjamin Stidum Plt. and Joseph Bingley Deft. is continued at the Plts. costs.

Barnes vs Pruit   In the Action of Debt between William Barnes Plt. and Thomas Pruit Deft. the Deft. failing to plead Judgment by nihil dicit is granted him for what damages shall be recovered in this Suit to be discharged if the Deft. pleads at the next Court.

Harris vs Prat   In the Action of Case between John Harris Plt. and Roger Pratt and Peter Ford Defts. the Defts. failing to plead Judgment by nihil dicit is granted against them for what damages shall be recovered in this Suit to be discharged if the Defts. plead at the next Court.

New vs Calvit   In the action of Case between William New Plt. and Peter Calvit Deft. the Deft. failing to plead Judgment by nihil dicit is granted against him for what damages shall be recovered in this Suit to be discharged if the Deft. pleads at the next Court.

Baise vs Moor   In the Action of Case between Edward Baise Plt. and Willm. Moor Deft. the Deft. failing to Plead Judgment by nihil dicit is granted against him for what damages shall be recovered in this Suit be discharged if the Deft. pleads at the next Court. The Plt. files a new declaration.

Harper vs Scot   In the Action of Trespass on the Case between Henry Harper Plt. and Edward Scot Admr. of Paul Green deceased Deft. the Parties submit themselves to the Court for tryall whereupon it is considered that the Plt. do recover against the Deft. Admr. as aforesaid the Sum of one pound ten shillings Currant money and four hundred and Sixteen pounds of tobacco with Costs.

[62]   December Court 1728

Laine vs Scot   In the Action of Trespass on the Case between John Laine Plt. and Edwd. Scot Admr. &c. of Paul Green deceased Deft. the Parties Submit themselves to the Court for tryal whereupon it is considered that the Plt. do recover against the Deft. Admr. as aforesaid Seven hundred and fifty pounds of tobacco with Cask and the Costs of this Suit.

Scot vs Wiers   On the Attachment obtained by Edward Scot against the Estate of John Wiers it is ordered that Subpœnas do issue against Peter Ford and Roger Prat to declare what is in their hands or possession belonging to the said John Wiers, and the Attachment is continued.

The attachment obtained by William Kent against Thos. Pruit is dismist the said William not prosecuting the same.

The action of Case between John Woodson Plt. and Bartholomew Cox Deft. is dismist the Plt. not prosecuting the same.

The action of Case between Ashford Hughes Plt. and William Lax Deft. is dismist the Plt. not prosecuting the same.

The Action of Trespass between John Franklin Plt. and William Daviss Deft. is dismist the Plt. not prosecuting the same.

The Action of Trespass between John Quin Plt. and Robert Allin Junr. Deft. is dismist the Plt. not prosecuting the same.

Rogers vs Alexander   In the Action of Debt between Robert Rogers Plt. and John Alexander Deft. the Deft. being in Custody of the Sherif for lack of Special Bail confesses Judgment for two pounds fourteen shillings and eleven pence Currant money which he is ordered to pay unto the Plt. with Costs and a Lawyers Fee.

The action of Case between William Cabbell Plt. and John Burks Deft. is dismist the Plt. not Prosecuting the same.

The Action of Debt between Charles Johnson Plt. and Abraham Sutlet Deft. is dismist the Plt. not prosecuting the same.

[63]   December Court 1728

Randolph vs Canady   In the Action of Case between Thomas Randolph Admr. &c. of Henry Macdaniel deceased Plt. and Michael Canady Deft.

the Deft. failing to appear Judgment is granted against him and James Nowlin his Bail for what damages shall be recovered in this Suit to be discharged if the Deft. shall appear at the next Court.

Prosser vs Dendy   In the Action of Case between Thomas Prosser and Elizabeth his Wife Admx. &c. of John Skelton deceased and William Dendy Deft. an Alias Caps. is awarded against the Deft. returnable to the next Court.

Dean vs Canady   In the Action of Case between Richard Dean Plt. and Michael Canady Deft. the Deft. failing to appear Judgment is granted against him and John Chambers his Bail for what damages shall be recovered in this Suit to be discharged if the Deft. shall appear at the next Court.

The action of Debt between Richard Dean Plt. and Jacob Capoon Deft. is dismist the Plt. not prosecuting the same.

Taylor vs Saunders   In the Action of Trespass on the Case between John Taylor Plt. and John Saunders Deft. time is granted the Plt. to mend his declaration.

Nowlin vs Burton   In the Action of Case between James Nowlin Plt. and Nowel Burton Deft. the Plt. having failed to file his declaration on the Defendants motion he is Nonsuited and it is considered that the Deft. recover against the Plt. five shillings Currant Money and his costs by him in this behalf expended.

Then the Court adjourned to the third Tuesday in the next Month.
Test. Henry Wood ClCur.

****

[64]   January Court 1728 [1729]
At a Court held for the County of Goochland the third Tuesday in January being the twenty first day of the Month Annoq Domini 1728. Present. Thomas Randolph, William Mayo, John Woodson, Allen Howard, Gent. Justices.

Fauquinou vs David   On the Petition of David [Daniel] Fauquinou vs Peter David praying the Petitioner may be adjudged Free &c. The Parties being heard it is the Opinion of the Court that the Petitioner is Free, and it is ordered that the said Peter David do pay and deliver unto him ten bushells of Indian Corn a Musquett or Fuzee of the value of twenty shillings and thirty shillings or the value thereof in goods with Costs.

Alexander discharged of Exo   John Alexander comes into Court and makes oath that a certain Schedule by him Subscribed containeth a true full & perfect account of all his Estate according to the form prescribed by one Act of Assembly of this Colony for releif of Insolvent Debtors, and on his motion it is ordered that he be discharged the Custody of the Sherif at the Suit of William Clopton Junr.

Surveyor of road   Ordered that the titheables of James Moss, David Clarkson, Thomas Golsby, George Thompson, Samuel Butler, Andrew Pruit do assist in clearing the road from Tuckahoe Mill to Ferry over James River at the Manackin Town.

Surveyor of road   Ordered that the road from John Fords towards Appamatox Ridge be continued over the branches of Fine Creek, Nathaniel Basset is appointed Surveyor thereof.

Then the Court Adjourned to the third Tuesday in next Month.
                                Test. Henry Wood ClCur.

****

[65]   February Court 1728 [1729]
At a Court held for the County of Goochland the third Tuesday in February being the eighteenth day of the month Annoq Domi 1728. Present. William Mayo, John Woodson, Tarlton Fleming, Allin Howard, Gent. Justices.

Alvis vs Woodson   In the Action of Case between George Alvis Plt. and Benjamin Woodson Deft. at November Court Judgment was confirmed against the Deft. and Bouth Napier his Common Bail for what damages the Plt. should recover upon executing a writ of inquiry of damages the following Jury are now Sworn to wit, William Cabbell, Robert Hughes, Joell Chandler, John Webb, Thomas Murrell, Thomas Wadloe, Ashford Hughes, William Lansdon, Samuell Allin, Stephen Cox, Thomas Edwards, William Woodson, who after some time bring in their Verdict in these words "Wee find for the Plt. the Sum of four pounds ten shillings and five pence Current money William Cabbell Foreman." the said Verdict on the Plts. motion is recorded and it is considered that the Plt. do recover against the Deft. and Bouth Napier the Said Sum of four pounds ten shillings and five pence Current money damages by the Jurors aforesaid in their said Verdict assessed with Costs and a Lawyers Fee.

Pruit vs Maxey   In the action of Trespass between Thomas Pruit Plt. and Nathaniell Maxey Deft. William Cabbell, Joell Chandler, John Webb, Thomas Murrell, Thomas Wadloe, Ashford Hughes, William Lansdon, Samuell Allin, Stephen Cox, Thomas Edwards, William Woodson, Robert Hughes, the Jury are Sworn who after some time bring in their Verdict in these words "Wee find for the Plt. twenty Shillings Currant money William Cabbell Foreman." The sd Verdict on the Plts. motion is recorded and the Court being of Opinion that the Battery is fully proved it is considered that the Plt. do recover agst. the Deft. twenty shillings Currant money damages by the Jurors aforesd. in their said Verdict assessed with Costs and a Lawyers Fee.

[66]   February Court 1728 [1729]
Prosser's Comn. recd   On the motion of Thomas Prosser his Commission to be Deputy Attorny at this Court is ordered to be recorded.

Macon vs Wharton   In the Action of Case between John Macon Plt. and Thomas Wharton Deft. William Cabbell, Bouth Napier, Joell Chandler, John Webb, Thos. Murrell, Thomas Wadloe, Ashford Hughes, William Lansdon, Saml. Allin, Stephen Cox, Thos. Edwards, William Woodson, the Jury are Sworn who after some time return their Verdict which on the Plts. motion is ordered to be recorded and is as followeth "Wee find for the Plt. the Sum of three pounds eighteen shillings and six pence Currant money William Cabbell Foreman." the Deft. files his reasons for arresting the Judgment on the Verdict aforesaid, the arguing whereof is referred to the next Court.

Marshall vs Moseley &c   On the Petition of Alexander Marshall ordered that Arthur Moseley and Samuell Hancocke be Sumoned to appear at the next Court and make their Objections thereto.

Jordan Eliza. chooses her Guardian   On the motion of Elizabeth Jordan She is permitted to choose Thomas Randolph Gent. her Guardian who accepts the charge John Woodson Gent. and Henry Wood Securities.

Moor vs Stubblefd   In the [Action] of Trespass on the Case between Edward Moor Plt. and John Stubblefield Deft. the Executing the writ of inquiry is waved and Wm. Cabbell enters himself Common Bail for the Deft. and confesses Judgmt. for one pound Six Shillings and Seven pence half penny Currant money whereupon it is considered by the Court that the Plt. do recover against the Deft. and William Cabbell the said Sum of one pound Six shillings and Seven pence half penny Currant money with Costs and a Lawyers Fee.

[67] February Court 1728 [1729]
Utley vs Napier   The two Actions of Debt and Action of Case between John Utley Plt. and Bouth Napier Deft. are continued to the next Court.

Chiswell vs Napier   In the Action of Case between Charles Chiswell Plt. and Bouth Napier Deft. the Deft. pleads non assumpsit and for tryall puts himself upon the Country and the Plt. likewise.

Napier vs Scot   In the Action of Debt between Bouth Napier Plt. and Edward Scot Admr. &c. of Paul Green deceased Deft. the Deft. pleads not guilty and for tryal puts himself upon the Country and the Plt. likewise.

Alvis vs Utley   In the Action of Case between George Alvis Plt. and John Utley Deft. the Deft. pleads he oweth nothing and for tryal puts himself upon the Country and the Plt. likewise.

Nolun vs Wotars   In the Action of Case between Thomas Nolun Plt. and William Wotars Deft. the Plt. files a new Declaration and an imparlance is granted the Deft.

Scot vs Napier   In the Action of Case between Edward Scot Plt. and Booth Napier Defend. the Parties Submit themselves to the Court for tryal whereupon it is considered by the Court that the Plt. do recover against the Deft. two pounds thirteen shillings and three pence Currant money and Sixty eight and three quarters pounds of tobacco with the Costs of this Suit and A Lawyers Fee.

Cabbell vs Ashlin   In the Action of Debt between William Cabbell Assignee of Roger Powell Plt. and Joseph Ashlin Deft. the Deft. pleads he oweth nothing and for tryal Submits himself to the Court and the Plt. likewise whereupon it is considered by the Court that the Plt. recover against the Deft. one pound nine shillings and eight pence Current money with the Costs of this Suit and an Attornys Fee.

Burton vs Woodson   The Action of Case between Robert Burton Plt. and William Woodson Executr. &c. of Benjamin Woodson deceased Det. is continued.

[68]   February Court 1728 [1729]
Winfrey vs Martin   In the Action of Case between Jacob Winfree Plt. and John Martin Deft. the Deft. by James Martin appears and pleads he oweth nothing and for tryal Submits himself to the Country and the Plt. likewise.

Towns vs Hoggat   In the Action of Debt between William Towns Plt. and Anthony Hoggat Deft. the Defendt. pleads he oweth nothing and the Suit is thereupon continued.

Wotars vs Nolun & Quin   In the Action of Debt between William Wotars Plt. and Thomas Nolun and John Quin Defts. came as well the said William Wotars by Thomas Prosser his Attorney as the said Tho. Nolun and John Quin by John Quin Attorney upon which the premises being seen and by the Court of Our Lord the King here fully understood it seems to the Justices here that the Plea of the said Thomas Nolun and John Quin above in barr pleaded and the matter in the same contained is not good and Sufficient in Law to Quash the Bill aforesaid of the aforesaid William Wotars therefor it is ordered that a writ of enquiry of damages be recorded at the next Court of which the Sherif is to give the Defts. notice by service them with a Copy of this order.

Hughes vs Crump   The action of Case between Stephen Hughes Plt. and Stephen Crump Deft. is continued.

Holland vs Hoggat   In the action of Case between Michael Holland Plt. and Anthony Hoggat Deft. the Deft. demurrs generally and pleads he oweth nothing and the Plt. takes issue thereon.

Rapene vs Bingley   In the action of Trespass on the Case between Anthony Rapene Plt. and Joseph Bingley Deft. the Plt. files a new declaration and an imparlance is granted the Deft.

Hughes vs Lax   On the motion of Ashford Hughes John Woodson and Tarlton Fleming Gent. are appointed to take the Deposition of William Bryan in the Suit between the said Ashford Hughes and William Lax.

[69]   February Court 1728 [1729]
Gill vs Spears   In the action of Trespass on the Case between John Gill Plaintiff and Robert Spears Deft. the following Jury are Sworn, William Cabbell, Robert Hughes, Joell Chandler, John Webb, Thomas Murrell, Thomas Wadloe, Ashford Hughes, William Lansdon, Samuel Allin, Stephen Cox, Thomas Edwards, William Woodson, who after some time

return their Verdict which on the Plts. motion is ordered to be recorded and is as followeth "Wee find for the Plt. one shilling Current money William Cabell Foreman." whereon it is considered by the Court that the Plt. do recover against the Defendant one shilling Current money with costs to the value thereof.

Holland vs Saunders   In the action of Case between Michaell Holland Plt. and Thomas Saunders Defendant the Deft. failing to appear Judgment is granted the Plt. against the Deft. and Daniel Stoner Gent. for what damages shall be recover'd in this Suit to be discharged if the Deft. appears at the next Court.

Burton vs Watkins   In the action of Debt between Nowel Burton Plt. and William Watkins Deft. the Deft. pleads not guilty and the Suit is thereupon continued.

Bryan vs Quin   In the Action of Case between Thomas Bryan Plt. and John Quin Deft. the Deft. pleads he oweth nothing and for tryal puts himself upon the Country and the Plt. likewise.

Tyre vs Utley   The action of Trover between James Tyre Plt. and John Utley Defendant is continued.

Maxey vs Pruit   In the action of Debt between Nathaniel Maxey Plt. and Thomas Pruit Deft. the Deft. pleads not guilty and for tryall puts himself upon the Country and the Plt. likewise.

Waddill vs Edwards   In the Action of Case between William Waddill Plt. and Thomas Edwards Deft. the Defendant pleads non assumpsit and for tryall puts himself upon the Country and the Plt. likewise.

[70]   February Court 1728 [1729]
Ware vs Saunders   In the Action of Case between Susanna Ware Plt. and Thomas Saunders Deft. the Deft. failing to appear Judgment is granted the Plt. against the Deft. and Daniel Stoner Gent. Sherif for what damages shall be recover'd in this Suit to be discharged if the Deft. appears at the next Court.

Holland vs Logan   The action of Case between Michael Holland Plt. and Alexander Logan Deft. is continued.

Bingley vs Wiers   The Action of Case between Joseph Bingley Plt. and John Wiers Deft. is dismist the Plt. not prosecuting the same.

Spencer vs Gallemore   In the Action of Case between Samuel Spencer Plt. and William Gallemore Deft. a Pluries Capias is awarded against the Deft. returnable to the next Court.

Pattison vs King   In the Action of Trespass between David Pattison Plt. and Martin King Deft. the Deft. pleads not guilty and for tryall puts himself upon the Country and the Plt. likewise.

Webber vs Baker   In the action of Case between Philip Webber Plt. and Francis Baker Deft. is continued at the Plts. cost.

Hughes vs Lax   The action of Case between Ashford Hughes Plt. and William Lax Deft. is continued.

Dickinson vs Hughes   In the Action of Case between John Dickinson Plt. and Stephen Hughes Deft. the Deft. pleads he oweth nothing and for tryal puts himself upon the Country and the Plt. likewise.

Gee vs Thomas   The action of Trespass on the Case between Gilbert Gee Plt. and Rowland Thomas Deft. is continued.

Bolling vs Tapley   The Action of Trespass on the Case between John Bolling Plt. and John Tapley Deft. is dismist the Plt. not prosecuting the same.

[71]   February Court 1728 [1729]
Woodson vs Allin   In the Action of Case between Josiah Woodson and Stephen Woodson Executors &c. of Jacob Woodson deceased Plts. and Samuell Allin Deft. the Deft. failing to appear Judgment is granted the Plts. against the Deft. and Daniel Stoner Gent. Sherif for what damages shall be recovered in this Suit to be discharged if the Deft. appears at the next Court.

Walker vs Curd   In the Action of Trespass on the Case between William Walker Plt. and Edward Curd Deft. the Pluries Capias is continued returnable to the next Court.

White vs Webber   In the Action of Case between Samuell White Plt. and Philip Webber Deft. the Deft. failing to Plead Judgment by nihil dicit is granted the Plt. against the Deft. for what damages shall be recovered in this Suit to be discharged if the Deft. pleads at the next Court.

New vs Morriss   In the Action of Debt between William New Plt. and

Hugh Morriss & Sarah his wife Executrix &c. of Edmund New deceased Defts. on the motion of the Defts. leave is granted them to plead severall matters and thereupon they file pleas and time is granted the Plt. to reply.

King vs Pattison   The action of Trespass on the Case between Martin King Plt. and David Pattison Deft. is continued.

Laine vs Christian   The action of Case between John Laine Plt. and John Christian Deft. is continued.

Basset vs Gill   Nathaniel Bassett having attended three days as a witness for John Gill vs Robert Spears it is ordered that the said John Gill do pay him for the same ninety pounds of tobacco with Costs.

Barnes vs Spears   William Barnes having attended two days as a witness for Robert Spears ads John Gill it is ordered that the said Robert Spears do pay him for the same sixty pounds of tobacco with Costs.

[72]   February Court 1728 [1729]
Davis vs Sallee   In the Action of Trespass on the Case between John Davis Plt. and William Sallee Deft. the Deft. pleads non assumpsit and for tryall puts himself upon the Country and the Plt. likewise.

Vaughn vs Williams   In the Action of Trover between George Vaughn Plt. and John Williams Deft. the Deft. failing to Plead Judgment by nihil dicit is granted the Plt. against the Deft. for what damages shall be recovered in this Suit to be discharged if the Deft. pleads at the next Court.

Raley vs Quin   In the Action of Debt between Charles Raley Plt. and John Quin Deft. the Deft. pleads non assumpsit and for tryal puts himself upon the Country and the Plt. likewise.

Williams vs Quin   In the Action of Debt between John Williams Plt. and John Quin Deft. the Deft. pleads non assumpsit and for tryall puts himself upon the Country and the Plt. likewise.

Chamberlain vs Marchbanks   In the Action of Debt between William Chamberlaine Plt. and George Marchbanks Deft. the Deft. pleads nil debet and for tryall puts himself upon the Country and the Plt. likewise.

Stidum vs Bingley   In the Action of Case between Benjamin Stidum Plt. and Joseph Bingley Deft. the Deft. demurrs generally and the Suit is continued.

Barnes vs Pruit   In the Action of Debt between William Barnes Plt. and Thomas Pruit Deft. the Deft. pleads not guilty and the Suit is deferred.

Wood to send for Statutes   The Court being of Opinion the Statutes at large are necessary for the County's use, Henry Wood is impowered and desired to send to England for them.

Constable Sworn   Mathew Bingley is sworn Constable in the stead of Joseph Bingley.

Pruit vs Pruit   Hugh Prewit having attending this day as a witness for Thomas Pruit vs Nathaniell Maxey it is ordered that the said Thomas do pay him thirty pounds of tobacco with Costs.

[73]   March Court 1728 [1729]
Surveyor of road   Jacob Micheaux is appointed Surveyor of the road from fine Creek to Solomons Creek, and from the Ferry to the main road upwards.

Then the Court adjourned to the third Tuesday in next Month
                                    Test. Henry Wood Cl Cur.

****

At a Court held for Goochland County the third Tuesday in March being the eighteenth day of the month Annoque Domini 1728 [1729]. Present, William Mayo, John Woodson, Tarlton Fleming, Allin Howard, Gent. Justices

Harris vs Pratt   In the Action of Case between John Harris Plt. and Roger Pratt and Peter Ford Defts. the Defts. plead non assumpserunt and for tryall put themselves upon the Country and the Plt. likewise.

Jones deed to Lansdon   Hester Jones acknowledges a deed from herself to William Lansdon to be her Act and Deed and it is thereupon admitted to record.

Lansdon's deed to Jones   William Lansdon acknowledges a deed from himself to Hester Jones to be his Act and deed and it is thereupon admitted to record.

Lafeats Invy   Hester Jones presents upon oath an Inventory of the Estate of Tobias Lafeat deceased which is ordered to be recorded.

Burtons deed to Farrar   Nowel Burton acknowledges a deed with the Livery of Seizin endorsed from himself to John Sutton Farrar to be his Act and Deed and it is thereupon admitted to record.

New vs Calvit   In the Action of Case between William New Plt. and Peter Calvit Deft. the Deft. pleads non assumpsit and for tryal puts himself upon the Country and the Plaintif likewise.

[74]   March Court 1728 [1729]
Fords deed to Ford   Peter Ford acknowledges a deed from himself to John Ford to be his Act and Deed and it is thereupon admitted to record, then Judith wife of said Peter Ford (She being first privately examined) relinquishes her right of Dower in the land of by the said Deed conveyed which is also admitted to recorded.

Webbs deed to Moseby   Henry Webb acknowledges a deed with the Livery of Seizin endorsed from himself to Richard Moseby to be his Act and Deed and it is thereupon admitted to record, then Agnes wife of the said Henry (She being first privately examined) relinquishes her right of dower in the land by this deed conveyed which is also admitted to record.

Baise vs Moore   In the Action of Case between Edward Baise Plt. & William Moor Deft. leave is granted the Dft. to plead several matters and thereupon he files pleas and tenders in Court three shillings Currant money which the Plt. refuses to accept.

Randolph vs Canady   The Action of Case between Thomas Randolph Plt. and Michael Canady Deft. is dismist the Plt. not prosecuting the same.

Scot vs Wiers   On the Attachment obtained by Edward Scot against the Estate of John Wiers the Sherif hath made the following return "Atached all the tobacco of John Wyers in the hand of Peter Fourd and Roger Pratt Pr. me Joseph Bingley S Sherif November the 1 day 1728." the Plt. makes oath to his account and it is thereupon considered that he do recover against the Deft. two hundred pounds of tobacco with Costs and a Lawyers Fee. the said Peter Fourd and Roger Pratt having declared what is in their hands or possession belonging to John Wiers it is ordered that his Judgment be levyed on the same.

Prosser vs Dendy   In the Action of Case between Thomas Prosser and

Elizabeth his wife Administratrix of John Shelton deceased Plts. and William Dendy Deft. a Pluries Capias is awarded against the Deft. returnable to the next Court.

[75] March Court 1728 [1729]
Dean vs Canady The Action of Case between Richard Dean Plt. and Michael Canady Deft. is dismist the Plt. not prosecuting the same.

Taylor vs Saunders In the Action of Trespass on the Case between John Taylor Plt. and John Saunders Deft. the Plt. files a new declaration, the Deft. Pleads not guilty and for tryal puts himself upon the Country and the Plt. likewise.

Grandjurys Presentmts Ordered that the Subp'as. against the Severall persons presented by the Grand jury be continued returnable to the next Court.

Towns vs Hoggat In the Action of Trespass between William Towns Plt. and Anthony Hogat Deft. the Plt. files a new declaration and the Deft. failing to appear Judgmt. is granted the Plt. against the Deft. and Thomas Randolph for what damages shall be recovered in this Suit to be discharged if the Deft. appears at the next Court.

Williams vs Ware In the Action of Case between Edward Williams Plt. and Peter Ware Deft. the Plt. files a new declaration and an imparlance is granted the Deft.

The Action of Case between Baldwin Rocket Plt. and Thomas Saunders Deft. is dismist the Plt. not prosecuting the same.

Mullin vs Phelps In the Action of Trespass between Mary Mullin Plt. and John Phelps Deft. the Plt. failing to prosecute his Suit the Defts. motion is Nonsuited and it is ther?upon considered that the Deft. do recover of the Plt. five shillings Current money with Costs and a Lawyers Fee.

Moss vs Taylor In the Action of Trespass on the Case between Thomas Moss Plt. and James Taylor Deft. the Plt. files a new Declaration and an imparlance is granted the Deft.

The Action of Case between William Merrewether Plt. and Andrew Spradlin Deft. is dismist the Plt. not prosecuting the same.

[76]   March Court 1728 [1729]

Clark vs Cannon   In the Action of Case between Christopher Clark Plt. and William Cannon Deft. an imparlance is granted the Deft.

Clark vs Bolling   In the Action of Case between Christopher Clark Plt. and James Bolling Deft. the Deft. being in Custody of the Sherif confesses himself indebted unto the Plt. in the Sum of Seven hundred and six pounds of tobacco which he is ordered to pay unto the Plt. with Costs and a Lawyers Fee.

Clark vs Gallemore   In the Action of Case between Christopher Clerk Plt. and William Gallemore Deft. the Deft. failing to Plead on the Plts. motion Judgment is granted him against the Deft. and Daniel Stoner Gent. Sherif for what damages shall be recovered in this Suit to be discharged nevertheless if the Deft. shall appear and plead at the next Court.

Atkinson vs Benning   In the Action of Trespass between Sarah Atkinson Plt. and Anthony Benning Deft. a Special imparlance is granted the Deft.

Atkinson vs Leseur   In the Action of Case between Sarah Atkinson Plt. and David Leseur Deft. a Special imparlance is granted the Deft.

Atkinson vs Taylor   In the Action of Case between Sarah Atkinson Plt. and James Taylor Deft. a Special imparlance is granted the Deft.

Hughes vs Cone   In the Action of Case between Robert Hughes Plt. and John Cone Deft. an imparlance is granted the Deft.

Doran vs Marchbanks   In the Action of Case between John Doran Administrator &c. of Julius King deceased Plt. and George Marchbanks Deft. the Deft. pleads he oweth nothing and for tryall puts himself upon the Country and the Plt. likewise.

Jeffs vs Martin   In the Action of Case between John Jeffs Plt. and John Martin Deft. an Alias Capias is awarded against the Deft. returnable to the next Court.

[77]   March Court 1728 [1729]

Taylor vs Lowe   In the Action of Trespass on the Case between John Taylor Plt. and Thomas Lowe and Amey his wife Defts. a special imparlance is granted the Defts.

Gathwrite vs Saunders   In the Action of Case between Michaell Gathwrite Plt. and Thomas Saunders Deft. the Deft. confesses himself indebted unto the Plt. in the sum of one pound one shillings and Six pence Currant money which he is ordered to pay unto the Plt. with costs and a Lawyers Fee.

The Action of Case between Allin Howard Plt. and Henry Reynolds Deft. is dismist the Plt. not prosecuting the same.

Paine vs Huckaby   In the Action of Debt between John Paine Plt. and John Huckaby Deft. a Special imparlance is granted the Defendant.

Morgan vs Pleasants   In the Action of Case between Edward Morgan Plt. and John Pleasants Administrator &c. of William Howl deceased Deft. the Plts. account being proved and the Deft. making no objection thereto it is considered by the Court that the Plt. do recover against the Deft. Admr. as aforesaid the Sum of three pounds thirteen shillings and three pence Currant money and one hundred and ninety eight pounds of Sweet Scented tobacco with the Costs of this Suit.

Present. Thomas Randolph, John Fleming, Gent.

Vanderhood vs Worley   In the Acton of Case between Henry Vanderhood Plt. and John Worley Deft. for three pounds nine shillings and four pence Current money the Deft. being returned not to be found by the Sherif and failing to appear an Attachment is awarded against the Estate returnable to the next Court.

Rocket vs Baldrige   On the Attachment obtained by Baldwin Rocket against the Estate of Thomas Baldridge the Sherif hath made the following return "February the 13th. day 1728 Attached in the hands of Sarah Woodson, Warham Easly, Nowel Burton, Stephen Woodson, Joseph Parsons, Jacob Winfrey Pr. Joseph Bingley Sub Sherif." which severall persons aforesaid are ordered to be sumoned to appear at the next Court to discover the said Thomas Baldridges effects in their hands.

[78]   March Court 1728 [1729]
Dean vs Napier   In the Action of Case between Richard Dean Plt. and Robert Napier Junr. Deft. the Sherif having made return that the Deft. is not to be found and he failing to appear an Attachment is awarded against the Estate for the Sum of five pounds thirteen shillings and eight pence Current money returnable to the next Court.

Mayo vs Quin &c   In the Action of Debt between William Mayo Plt. and John Quin and John Micheaux Defts. John Micheaux enters himself Special Bail for John Quin and Oyer is granted the Defts.

Hughes &c. deed to Cox   Robert Hughes and Sarah Atkinson acknowledge a deed with the Livery of Seizin endorsed from themselves to Mathew Cox to be their Act and deed and it is thereupon admitted to record.

Holland vs Burton   In the Action of Case between Michaell Holland Plt. and Nowel Burton Deft. the Deft. confesses himself indebted unto the Plt. in the Sum of three pounds six shillings and two pence Currant money which he is ordered to pay him with Costs and a Lawyers Fee.

Holland vs Jeffs   In the Action of Case between Michaell Holland Plt. and John Jeffs Deft. the Deft. failing to appear Judgment is granted the Plt. against the Deft. and Charles Johnson for what damages shall be recovered in this Suit to be discharged nevertheless if the Deft. Shall appear at the next Court.

Carol vs Burton   In the Action of Case between Elizabeth Carol Executrix of Roger Carol deceased Plt. and Nowell Burton Deft. the Deft. pleads he oweth nothing and for tryall puts himself upon the Country and the Plt. likewise.

Hix vs Salley   The Action of Trespass between Marmaduke Hix Plt. and William Sallee Deft. is continued at the Plaintifs cost.

Ware vs Wms   In the Motion of Trespass between Peter Ware Plt. and Edward Williams Deft. the Deft pleads not guilty and for tryall puts himself upon the Country and the Plt. likewise.

Hughes vs Dean   In the Action of Case between Robert Hughes Plt. and Richard Dean Deft. an imparlance is granted the Deft.

[79]   March Court 1728 [1729]
Ware vs Wms   In the Action of Case between Peter Ware Plt. and Edward Williams Deft. James Holman enters himself Speciall Bail for the Deft. who Pleads he oweth nothing and for tryall puts himself upon the Country and the Plt. likewise.

Cannon vs Burgess   In the Action of Trespass on the Case between William Cannon Plt. and Daniel Burgess Deft. the Court being of

Opinion that Bail returned by the Sherif is insufficient on the Plts. motion Judgment is granted him against the Deft. and Daniel Stoner Gent. Sherif for what damages shall be recovered in this Suit to be discharged nevertheless if the Deft. shall appear at the next Court.

Spencer vs Quin   In the Action of Trespass on the Case between Peter Spencer Plt. and John Quin Deft. William Cabbell enters himself Special Bail for the Deft. to whom an imparlance is granted.

Turner vs Powell   In the Action of Detinue between James Turner Plt. and Richard Powel Deft. time is granted the Plt. to mend his declaration.

Dale vs Gunn   In the Action of Case between Christopher Dale Plt. and John Gunn Deft. the Deft. failing to appear Judgment is granted the Plt. against the Deft. and Daniel Stoner Gent. Sherif for what damages shall be recovered in this Suit to be discharged nevertheless if the Deft. shall appear at the next Court.

Alexander vs Chandler   In the Action of Case between John Alexander Plt. and Joell Chandler Deft. the Deft. failing to appear Judgment is granted the Plt. against the Deft. and Daniel Stoner Gent. for what damages shall be recovered in this Suit to be discharged nevertheless if the Deft. shall appear at the next Court.

The action of Trespass on the Case between Baldwin Rocket Plt. and Benjamin Woodson Deft. is dismist the Plt. not prosecuting the same.

The Action of Case between Michaell Holland Plt. and Stephen Woodson Deft. is dismist the Plt. not Prosecuting the same.

[80]   March Court 1728 [1729]
Clark vs Martin   In the Action of Case between Christopher Clark Plt. and Francis Martin Deft. the Deft. confesses himself indebted unto the Plt. in the Sum of one pound and seven pence half penny Currant money which he is ordered to pay unto the Plt. with Costs and a Lawyers Fee.

The Action of Case between Stephen Hughes Plt. and Thomas Moor Deft. is dismist the Plt. not prosecuting the same.

Randolph vs Wotars   The Action of Debt between Thomas Randolph Plt. and William Wotars Deft. is continued.

The Action of Case between Thomas Randolph Plt. and Thomas Moor

Deft. is dismist the Plt. not prosecuting the same.

The Action of Case between John Quin Plt. and Robert Downing Deft. is dismist the Plt. not prosecuting the same.

Allin vs Dickins   In the Action of Case between Samuell Allin Plt. and Thomas Dickins Deft. time is granted the Plt. to mend his declaration.

Cabbell vs Nolun   In the Action of Case between William Cabbell Assignee of John Quin Plt. and Thomas Nolun Deft. a Special imparlance is grant the Deft.

Burton vs Quin   In the Action of Case between Nowell Burton and John Quin Deft. William Cabbell becomes Special Bail for the Deft. and an imparlance is grant him.

Quin vs May   In the Action of Case between John Quin Plt. and William May Deft. a Special imparlance is granted the Deft.

The Action of Debt. between Richard Dean Plt. and John Scrugs Deft. is dismist the Plt. not prosecuting the same.

May vs Ashlin   The Action of Case between William May Plt. and Joseph Ashlin Deft. is continued.

[81]   March Court 1728 [1729]
Bolling vs Bullington   In the Action of Debt between John Bolling Plt. and John Bullington Deft. the Deft. confesses himself indebted unto the Plt. in the sum of two thousand four hundred pounds of tobacco which he is ordered to pay unto the Plt. and the Costs and a Lawyers Fee.

Ballews Admn   Thomas Randolph comes into Court and makes oath that Giles Ballew departed this life without making any will so far as he knows or beleives and on his motion and giving Security for his just and faithfull Administration of the sd Deceadents Estate is granted him for obtaining Letters of Administration in due form. John Fleming Security.

Ordered that John Chastain, Abraham Sallee, Thos. Jevodan, and Isaac Sallee, or any three of them being first Sworn by some Justice of the Peace do Appraise the Estate of Giles Ballew deced.

The Action of Debt between Stephen Hughes Plt. and George Eastham Deft. is dismist the Plt. not prosecuting the same.

Cannon vs Matlock   In the Action of Case between William Cannon Plt. and William Matlock Deft. the Deft. failing to appear Judgment is granted the Plt. against the Deft. and Stephen Hughes and George Eastham for what damages shall be recovered in this Suit to be discharged nevertheless if the Deft. shall appear at the next Court.

Hinson vs Nash   In the Action of Case between John Hinson Plt. and Samuel Nash Deft. the Deft. failing to appear Judgment is granted the Plt. against the Deft. and David Pattison for what damages shall be recovered in this Suit to be discharged nevertheless if the Deft. shall appear at the next Court.

The Action of Case between Giles Allegre Plt. and Thomas Conner Deft. is dismist the Plt. not prosecuting the same.

Holland vs Allin   In the Action of Case between Michael Holland Plt. and Samuel Allin Deft. the Deft. confesses himself indebted uno the Plt. in the Sum of two pounds eighteen shillings and a penny Current money which he is ordered to pay unto the Plt. with Costs and a Lawyers Fee.

[82]   March Court 1728 [1729]
Capoon vs Sublet   In the Action of Case between Jacob Capoon Plt. and Peter Lewis Sublet Deft. the Deft. failing to appear Judgment is granted the Plt. against the Deft. and Daniel Stoner Gent. Sherif for what damages shall be recovered in this Suit to be discharged nevertheless if the Deft. shall appear at the next Court.

The Action of Case between Thomas Wharton Plt. and Robert Napier Junr. Deft. is dismist the Plt. not prosecuting the same.

Westbrook vs Clark   In the Action of Case between James Westbrook and Frances his wife Executrix &c. of Edward Bass deceased Plts. and John Clark Deft. an Alias Capias is awarded against the Deft. returnable to the next Court.

The action of Case between Tarlton Fleming Plt. and James Raley Deft. is dismist neither party appearing.

The Action of Case between Daniel Burgess Plt. and Joshua Stephens Deft. is dismist neither party appearing.

Then the Court adjourned till tomorrow morning 10 aClock.
                                      Test. Henry Wood ClCur.

****

At a Court continued and held for Goochland County the nineteenth day of March 1728 [1729]. Present. Thomas Randolph, John Fleming, William Mayo, Tarlton Fleming, Allin Howard, Gent. Justices.

Justices recomended   The Court considering that there are not a Sufficient number of Justices

[83]   March Court 1728 [1729]
in the Commission of Peace, and that hereby the business of the Court is sometimes delayed, George Paine, William Cabbell, and James Holman are therefore recommended to the Honble. William Gooch Esqr. his Majesties Lieut. Governor as persons proper to be added to the said Commission.

Adams deed to Chamberlaine   Daniel Stoner, Thomas Prosser and Thomas Dickins prove a deed with the Livery of Seizin endorsed from Ebenezer Adams to William Chamberlaine to be the Act and deed of the said Ebenezer Adams, and it is thereupon admitted to record.

Ferry appoint'd   Sarah Atkinson is permitted to keep Ferry and the rate of Ferriage for a man is Settled at three pence and for a Horse at three pence.
    William Mayo and Daniel Stoner Gent. are desired to agree with her for keeping a County Ferry.

Surveyor of the road   David Walker is appointed Surveyor of the road from Courthouse into the back road above Major Bollings mill.

Macon vs Wharton   In the Action of Case between John Macon Plt. and Thomas Wharton Deft. the Deft. waives the Errors filed in Arrest of Judgment and files a bill of Injunction in Chancery and time is granted the Plt. to answer it.

Utley vs Napier   In the two Actions of Debt and Action of Case between John Utley Plt. and Bouth Napier Deft. Tarlton Fleming Gent. and Henry Wood are appointed to Examine State and Settle the matters in dispute between them and to report their proceedings therein to the next Court.

Chiswell vs Napier   In the Action of Case between Charles Chiswell Plt. and Booth Napier Deft. George Paine, William Lansdon, Peter Ware,

Thomas Murrell, William Sallee, John Webb, William Woodson, John Laine, Ashford Hughes, Thomas Edwards, David Pattison, Thomas Jevodan, the Jury are Sworn, who after some time return with their Verdict which on the Plts. motion is ordered to be recorded and is as followeth "Wee find the Plt. Six pounds Seventeen shillings and eight pence Currant money Geo. Paine Foreman." the Deft. files his reasons for arresting the Judgmt.

[84] March Court 1728 [1729]
on the said Verdict the arguing thereof is referred to the next Court.

Napier vs Scot   In the Action of Debt between Bouth Napier Plt. and Edward Scot Admr. &c. of Paul Green deceased the Plt. Demurrs generally to the Defts. plea and the Deft. joyns in Demurrer the arguing whereof is referred to the next Court.

Alvis vs Utley   In the Action of Case between George Alvis Plt. and John Utley Deft. the Parties Submit the tryal of the issue joyned to the Court and it is thereupon considered that the Plt. do recover against the Deft. the Sum of three pounds nineteen shillings Currant money with the Costs of this Suit and a Lawyers Fee.

Nolun vs Wotars   In the Action of Case between Thomas Nolun Plt. and William Wotars Deft. the Deft. pleads non assumpsit and for tryall puts himself upon the Country and the Plt. likewise.

Winfrey vs Martin   In the Action of Case between Jacob Winfrey Plt. and John Martin Deft. George Paine, William Lansdon, Peter Ware, Thos. Murrell, William Sallee, John Webb, William Woodson, John Laine, Ashford Hughes, Thomas Edwards, David Pattison, Thomas Jevodan, the Jury are Sworn, who after some time return with their Verdict which on the Plts. motion is ordered to be recorded and is as followeth "Wee find for the Plt. two pounds ten shillings Current money Geo. Paine Foreman" Whereupon it is considered by the Court that the Plt. do recover against the Deft. the Sum of two pounds ten shillings Current Money by the Jurors aforesaid in their said Verdict assessed with the Costs of this Suit and a Lawyers Fee.

Towns vs Hoggat   In the Action of Debt between William Towns Plt. and Anthony Hoggat Deft. the Plt. Demurrs generally to the Defts. plea and the Deft. joyns in Demurrer the arguing whereof is referred.

Wotars vs Nolun &c   The Action of Debt between William Wotars Plt.

and Thomas Nolun and John Quin Deft. is dismist the Plt. not prosecuting the same.

Burton vs Woodson   In the Action of Case between Robert Burton Plt. and William Woodson Executor of Benja. Woodson deceased Deft. the Deft. pleads he oweth nothing.

[85]   March Court 1728 [1729]
Hughes vs Crump   In the Action of Case between Stephen Hughes Plt. and Stephen Crump Deft. George Paine, John Barnit, William Lansdon, Peter Ware, Thomas Murrell, William Sallee, John Webb, William Woodson, John Laine, Thomas Edwards, David Pattison, Thomas Jevodan, the Jury are Sworn to enquire of the damages who after some time return with their Verdict which on the Plts. motion is ordered to be recorded and is as followeth "Wee find for the Plt. eleven shillings and Six pence Current money Geo. Paine Foreman" And it is thereupon considered by the Court that the Plt. do recover against the Deft. And John Bostick the sum of eleven shillings and Six pence Current money by the Jurors aforesaid in their said Verdict and the Costs of this Suit with a Lawyers Fee.

Holland vs Hoggat   In the Action of Case between Michael Holland Plt. and Anthony Hoggat Deft. the Deft. confesses himself indebted unto the Plt. in the Sum of eight hundred and thirty pounds of tobacco Sweet Scented, whereupon it is ordered that he do pay the same unto the Plt. with costs and a Lawyers Fee.

Rapene vs Bingley   In the Action of Trespass on the Case between Anthony Rapene Plt. and Joseph Bingley Deft. the Deft. pleads not guilty and for tryall puts himself upon the Country and the Plt. likewise.
    John Woodson and Tarlton Fleming Gent. are appointed to take the deposition of Isaac Parents in the Suit between Anthony Rapene and Joseph Bingley.

Holland vs Saunders   In the Action of Case between Michael Holland Plt. and Thomas Saunders Deft. the Deft. failing to appear the conditional Judgment entered in this Suit agst. the Deft. and Daniel Stoner Gent. Sherif is confirmed for so much as a Jury shall find upon executing a writ of enquiry of damages at the next Court of which the Sherif is ordered to give the Deft. notice by serving him with a copy of this order. Plaintif proves his Account Ordered to be Certified thereon.

Burton vs Watkins   In the Action of Debt between Nowel Burton Plt.

and William Watkins Deft. the Plt. demurrs generally to the Defts. plea and the Deft. joyns in Demurrer.

[86]   March Court 1728 [1729]
Woodson vs Allin   In the Action of Case between Josiah Woodson and Stephen Woodson Executors &c. of Jacob Woodson deceased Plts. and Samuel Allin Deft. the Deft. failing to appear the conditional Judgment formerly entered in this Suit agst. the Deft. and Daniel Stoner Gent. Sherif is confirmed for so much as a Jury shall find upon executing a writ of enquiry of damages at the next Court of which the Sherif is ordered to give the Deft. notice by Serving him with a Copy of this order.

Randolph vs Moor   On the Attachment obtained by Thomas Randolph against the Estate of Thomas Moor the Sherif hath made the following return, "Executed the 15 day of March 1728. Pr. me Danl. Stoner Sherif." the Deft. not appearing the Plt. makes oath to his account and it is thereupon considered by the Court that he do recover against the Deft. the sum of three pounds Current money with the Costs of this Suit and a Lawyers Fee.

Hughes vs Moor   On the Attachment obtained by Stephen Hughes against the Estate of Thomas Moor the Sherif hath made the following return "March the 10th day Attach of Thomas Moors Estate tow [two] hand pack hoddes [hogsheads] of tobbo a quantity of Corn in the Ears 1 Chest 1 pail 1 bedsted 1 table 1 tubb 1 bread tray 1 basket Pr. Thos. Walker Sub Sherif." the Deft. failing to appear the Plt. (being a Quaker) makes his Solemn affirmation to his account and it is thereupon considered by the Court that he do recover against the Deft. the sum of three pounds five shillings Current money with the Costs of this Suit and a Lawyers Fee.

Dickins vs Dickinson   On the Attachment obtained by Thos. Dickins against the Estate of John Dickinson the Sherif hath made the following return "Feby. 10: 1728. Attached in the hands of Richard Powell and Robert Carter Pr. Thos. Walker Sub Sherif." the Deft. failing to appear the Plt. makes oath to his Account and it is thereupon considered by the Court that the Plt. do recover against the Deft. the Sum of thirty Shillings Current money with

[87]   March Court 1728 [1729]
the Costs of this Suit and a Lawyers Fee.
    Richard Powell appears and acknowledges upon oath that three barrells of Indian Corn and Six shillings and three pence is due from him

to John Dickinson; And Robert Carter that there are in his possession belonging to the said John Dickinson One Barrow, One old rug, a par of old blankets, an old Drawing knife, a Coopers old Croes, whereupon it is ordered that the said Judgment be leveyed thereon.

Bryan vs Quin   In the Action of Case between Thomas Bryan Plt. and John Quin Deft. Anthony Hoggat, John Barnit, William Lansdon, Peter Ware, Thomas Murrell, William Sallee, John Webb, William Woodson, John Laine, Thomas Edwards, David Pattison, Thomas Jevodan, the Jury are Sworn, who after some time return with their Verdict which on the Defts. motion is ordered to be recorded and is as followeth "Wee find for the Deft. Anthony Hoggat Foreman." Whereupon it is considered by the Court that the Deft. go hence without day and that he recover against the Plt. his costs by him in this behalf expended and a Lawyers Fee.

Tyre vs Utley   In the Action of Trover between James Tyre Plt. and John Utley Deft the writ being in an Action of Trover and the Plts. attorny avering that he directed the Sherif to fill it up in an Action of the Case by consent of the Plts. attorny and at his motion the Sherif makes oath that the writ is according to the directions of the Plts. attorny. the Defendt. Demurrs generally and the Plt. joyns in Demurrer.

Ware vs Saunders   In the Action of Case between Susanna Ware Plt. and Thomas Saunders Deft. the Suit is continued.

Spencer vs Gallemore   In the Action of Case between Samuel Spencer Plt. and William Gallemore Deft. the Deft. failing to appear at the return of the Pluries Capias on the Plts. motion a Pluries Capias de novo is awarded against him returnable to the next Court.

Walker vs Curd   The action of Trespass on the Case between William Walker Plt. and Edward Curd Deft. is dismist the Plt. not prosecuting the same.

[88]   March Court 1728 [1729]
Hughes vs Lax   In the Action of Case between Ashford Hughes Plt. and William Lax Deft. the Deft. pleads he oweth nothing non detinet and for tryal puts himself upon the Country and the Plt. likewise.

White vs Webber   In the Action of Case between Samuel White Plt. and Philip Webber Deft. the Deft. pleads he oweth nothing and for tryal puts himself upon the Country and the Plt. likewise.

New vs Morriss   In the Action of Debt between William New Plt. and Hugh Morriss and Sarah his wife Executrix &c. of Edmund New Deceased Defts. the Plt. takes issue on the Defts. Pleas and joyns in Demurrer.

Laine vs Christian   In the Action of Case between John Laine Plt. and John Christian Deft. an imparlance is granted the Deft.

Dickinson vs Hughes   In the Action of Case between John Dickinson Plt. and Stephen Hughes Deft. William Cabbell, Thomas Edwards, William Lansdon, John Laine, David Pattison, John Webb, Peter Ware, Thomas Jevodan, William Salle, Fredorick Cox, John Prier, Mathew Cox, the Jury are Sworn, who after some time return with their Verdict which on the Plts. motion is admitted to record and is as followeth "Wee find for the Plt. the sum of two pounds ten shillings Currant money Pr. William Cabbell Foreman." Whereupon it is considered by the Court that the Plt. do recover against the Deft. the said Sum of two pounds ten shillings Current money by the Jurors in their Verdict aforesaid with the Costs of this Suit and a Lawyers Fee.

Vaughan vs Williams   In the Action of Trover between George Vaughan Plt. and John Williams Deft. the Deft. pleads not guilty and for tryal puts himself upon the Country and the Plt. likewise.

Stidum vs Bingley   In the Action of Case between Benjamin Stidum Plt. and Joseph Bingley Deft. the Plt. joyns in Demurrer with the Deft. the arguing whereof is referred to the next Court.

[89]   March Court 1728 [1729]
Barnes vs Pruit   In the Action of Debt between William Barnes Plt. and Thomas Pruit Deft. the Plt. Demurrs Generally to the Defts. Plea and the Deft. joyns in Demurrer the arguing whereof is referred to the next Court.

Thomas vs Jeffs   In the Action of Case between Michael Thomas Plt. and John Jeffs Deft. the Deft. failing to appear Judgment is granted the Plt. against the Deft. and Daniel Stoner Gent. Sherif for what damages shall be recovered in this Suit to be discharged nevertheless if the Deft. shall appear at the next court.

The Action of Trespass on the Case between Edward Scot Plt. and Francis Farcee Deft. is dismist the Plt. not prosecuting the Same.

Pruit vs Baldwin   In the Action of Trespass between Andrew Pruit Plt.

and Henry Baldwin Deft. time is granted the Plt. to mend his declaration.

Maxey vs Pruit   The Action of Debt between Nathaniel Maxey Plt. and Thomas Pruit Deft. is dismist the Plt. not prosecuting the Same.

Waddill vs Edwards   In the Action of Case between William Waddill Plt. and Thomas Edwards Deft. Anthony Hoggat, John Barnit, William Lansdon, Peter Ware, Thos. Murrell, William Sallee, John Webb, William Woodson, John Laine, Fredorick Cox, David Pattison, Thomas Jevodan, the Jury are Sworn, the Deft. files a Demurrer to the Evidence whereupon the Jury are discharged and time is granted the Plt. to consider the same.

Holland vs Logan   In the Action of Case between Michael Holland Plt. and Alexander Logan Deft. the Deft. appears and acknowledges himself indebted unto the Plt. the sum of one pound nineteen shillings and a penny Currant money which he is ordered to pay unto the Plt. and a Lawyers Fee.

Pattison vs King   The Action of Trespass between David Pattison Plt. and Martin King Deft. is continued at the Plts. Cost.

[90]   March Court 1728 [1729]
Webber vs Baker   In the Action of Case between Philip Webber Plt. and Francis Baker Deft. Peter Ware, Thomas Edwards, William Lansdon, Mathew Cox, William Sallee, John Webb, William Woodson, John Laine, Fredorick Cox, David Pattison, Thomas Jevodan, John Prier, the Jury are Sworn who after some time return with their Verdict which on the Defts. motion is ordered to be recorded and is as followeth "Wee find for the Deft. Peter Ware Foreman." Whereupon it is considered by the Court that the Deft. go hence without day and that he recover against the Plt. his costs by him in this behalf expended and a Lawyers Fee.

The Action of Trespass on the Case between Joseph Good Plt. and John Martin Junr. Deft. is dismist neither party appearing.

Martin vs Quin   In the Action of Trespass between Francis Martin Plt. and John Quin Deft. time is granted the Plt. to mend his declaration.

Randolph vs Quin   In the Action of Trespass on the Case between Thos. Randolph Plt. and John Quin Deft. William Cabbell enters himself Special bail for the Deft. and an imparlance is granted him.

Woodson vs Woodson   In the Action of Trespass on the Case between

Robert Woodson and James Holman Plts. and William Woodson Deft. an imparlance is granted the Defendt.

The Action of Debt between Ambrose Bradford Plt. and Thomas Dickins is dismist neither party appearing.

Thomas vs Gee   In the Action of Case between Rowland Thomas Plt. and Gilbert Gee Deft. time is granted the Plt. to mend his declaration.

[91]   March Court 1728 [1729]
Martin vs Rapene   In the Action of Case between John Martin Junr. Plt. and Anthony Rapene Deft. an imparlance is granted the Deft.

Bingley vs Rapene   In the Action of Trespass between Joseph Bingley Plt. and Anthony Rapene Deft. a Special imparlance is granted the Deft.

Cabbell vs Wade   In the Action of Trespass on the Case between William Cabbell Plt. and Robert Wade Deft. a Special imparlance is granted the Deft.

The Action of Trespass between John Jeffs Plt. and Henry Baldwin Deft. is dismist the Plt. not prosecuting the same.

Ditoway vs Pleasants   In the Action of Case between Barbary Ditoway Plt. and John Pleasants Administrator &c. of William Howl deceased Deft. the Deft. failing to appear Judgment is granted the Plt. against the Deft. and Daniel Stoner Gent. Sherif for what damages shall be recovered in this Suit to be discharged nevertheless if the Deft. appears at the next Court.

Chastain vs Pleasants   In the Action of Case between Stephen Chastain Plt. and John Pleasants Administrator &c. of William Howl deceased Deft. the Deft. failing to appear Judgment is granted the Plt. against the Deft. and Daniel Stoner Gent. Sherif for what damages shall be recovered in this Suit to be discharged nevertheless if the Deft. appears at the next Court.

Atkinson vs Lax   In the Action of Case between Henry Atkinson Plt. and William Lax Deft. an imparlance is granted the Deft.

Barnit vs Webber   John Barnit having attended three days as a witness for Philip Webber vs Francis Baker it is ordered that the said Philip do pay him the same ninety pounds of tobacco with Costs.

Utley vs Webber   John Utley having attended three days as a witness for Philip Webber vs Francis Baker it is ordered that the said Philip do pay him for the same ninety pounds of tobacco with Costs.

[92]   March Court 1728 [1729]
Dickins vs Macon   In the Action of Trespass on the Case between Thomas Dickins Plt. and John Macon Deft. an imparlance is granted the Deft.

Hughes vs Macon   In the Action of Case between Stephen Hughes Plt. and John Macon Deft. the Deft. failing to appear Judgment is granted the Plt. against the Deft. and Daniel Stoner Gent. Sherif for what damages shall be recovered in this Suit to be discharged nevertheless if the Deft. shall appear at the next Court.

Macon vs Hughes   In the Action of Debt between John Macon Plt. and Stephen Hughes Deft. Ashford Hughes enters himself Special Bail for the Deft. for whom an imparlance is granted.

Macon vs Fleming   In the Action of Debt between John Macon Plt. and Tarlton Fleming Deft. the Deft. pleads he oweth nothing and for tryal puts himself upon the Country and the Plt. likewise.

The Action of Debt between Thomas Randolph Plt. and Edward Williams Deft. is dismist the Plt. not prosecuting the same.

Gee vs Thos   The Action of Trespass on the Case between Gilbert Gee Plt. and Rowland Thomas Deft. is dismist the Plt. not prosecuting the same.

King vs Pattison   The Action of Trespass on the Case between Martin King Plt. and David Pattison Junr. Deft. is continued at the Defts. cost.

Raley vs Quin   The Action of Debt between Charles Raley Plt. and John Quin Deft. is continued at the Defts. cost.

Chamberlaine vs Marchbanks   The Action of Debt between William Chamberlaine Plt. and George Marchbanks Deft. is continued at the Defts. cost.

The Attachment obtained by George Alvis against the Estate of Thomas Moor is dismist the said George not prosecuting the same.

[93]   March Court 1728 [1729]
Williams vs Quin   In the Action of Debt between John Williams Plt. and John Quin Deft. the parties Submit themselves to the Court for tryal whereupon it is considered that the Plt. do recover against the Deft. the sum of two pounds thirteen shillings and three pence Currant money with the costs of this Suit and a Lawyers Fee.

Davis vs Sallee   In the Action of Trespass on the Case between John Davis Plt. and William Sallee Deft. William Cabbell, Mathew Cox, John Pryer, Thomas Edwards, Jacob Winfrey, Jacob Micheaux, John Mcbride, William Lansdon, John Laine, David Pattison, John Webb, William Woodson, the Jury are Sworn, who after some time return their Verdict which on the Defts. motion is ordered to be recorded and is a followeth "Wee find for the Deft. Pr. Wm. Cabbell Foreman." whereupon it is considered by the Court that the Deft. go hence without day and that he recover against the Plt. his costs by him in this behalf expended and a Lawyers Fee.

The attachment obtained by Ashford Hughes against the Estate of John Dickinson is dismist the said Ashford not prosecuting the same.

The Attachment obtained by Stephen Hughes against the Estate of James Bolling is dismist the said Stephen not prosecuting the same.

Marshall vs Moseley   The Petition of Alexander Marshall against Arthur Moseley and Samuel Handcocke is dismist the Petitioner not prosecuting the same.

Sherifs recommend'd   Pursuant to the Directions of an Act of Assembly of this Colony intitled An Act Prescribing the method of appointing Sherifs &c. Daniel Stoner Tarlton Fleming, and Allin Howard Gent. are recommended to the Honble William Gooch Esqr. his Majestys Lieut. Governour of whom one may be appointed to Execute the Office of Sheriff of this County for the ensuing year.

[94]   March Court 1728 [1729]
Cox acct. vs Harriss   John Cox presents an Account against David Harriss and makes oath that the ballance thereof (being twenty shillings) is justly due to him which is ordered to be certified thereon.

Then the Court adjourned to the third Tuesday in next Month.
                                                    Test. Henry Wood Clcur.

****

At a Court held for Goochland County the third Tuesday in May being the twentieth day of the month Annoq Domini 1729.

Justices Sworn   A Commission from the Honble. William Gooch Esqr. his Majesties Lieut. Governor and Commander in chief of this Dominion to Thomas Randolph, John Fleming, William Mayo, John Woodson, Daniel Stoner, Rene Laforce, Tarlton Fleming, Allin Howard, Edward Scot, George Paine, William Cabbell, James Holman, Gent. to be Justices of the Peace for this County is read as also the Dedimus for Administring the Oaths and Test therein mentioned then Allin Howard and George Pain Gent. administer the Oaths appointed by Act of Parliament to be taken instead of the Oaths of Allegiance and Supremacy the Oath appointed to be taken by an Act of Parliament made in the 1st year of the reign of his late Majesty King George the First Entituled An Act for the further Security of his Majestys person and Government and the Succession of the Crown in the Heirs of the late Princess Sophia being protestants and for extinguishing the hopes of the pretended Prince of Wales and his open and secret abettors unto Thomas Randolph and John Fleming Gent. who Subscribe the Test take the Oath of a Justice of the Peace and of a Justice in Chancery and then

[95]   May Court 1729
Administer the said Oaths and Tests unto William Mayo, John Woodson, Tarlton Fleming, Allin Howard, George Paine, William Cabbell, and James Holman Gent.

Stoner sworn Sherif   Daniel Stoner Gent. produces a Commission from the Honble. William Gooch Esqr. his Majesties Lieut. Governor & Commander in chief of this Dominion to be Sherif of this County which being read the said Daniel Stoner together with William Mayo and Thomas Prosser Gent. enter into bond according to Law and acknowledging the same to be their Act and deed it is ordered to be recorded then Daniel Stoner, John Bowie, Thomas Walker and Joseph Bingley take the Oaths appointed to be taken by Act of Parliament instead of the Oaths of Allegiance and Supremacy the Oath appointed to be taken by an Act of Parliament made in the 1st year of his reign of his late Majesty King George the First Entituled an Act for the further Security of his Majestys person and Government and the Succession of the Crown in the Heirs of the late Princess Sophia being protestants and for extinguishing the hopes of the pretended Prince of Wales and his open and secret abettors and Subscribe the Test. Daniel Stoner also takes the

GOOCHLAND COUNTY ORDER BOOK 1 1728-1730   85

Oath of a Sherif and John Bowie, Thomas Walker and Joseph Bingley take the Oath of an Undersherif.

Present. Thomas Randolph, John Fleming, William Mayo, John Woodson, Tarlton Fleming, Allin Howard, George Paine, William Cabbell, James Holman Gent.

Tulys deed to Scot   John Tuly acknowledges a deed with the Livery of Seizin endorsed from himself to Edward Scot to be his Act and Deed and it is thereupon admitted to record then Sarah wife of the said John (She being first privately examined) relinquishes her right of Dower in the land by the said Deed conveyed which is also admitted to record.

Fleming deed to Hughes   John Fleming Gent. acknowledges a deed with the Livery of Seizin endorsed from himself to Stephen Hughes to be his Act and deed and it is thereupon admitted to record.

[96]   May Court 1729
Lansdon deed to Benning   William Lansdon and Esther his wife (she being first privately examined) acknowledge a deed with the Livery of Seizin endorsed from themselves to Anthony Benning and Elizabeth his wife to be their Act and Deed and it is thereupon admitted to record.

Benning deed to Lansdon   Anthony Benning and Elizabeth his wife (She being first privately examined) acknowledge a deed with the Livery of Seizin endorsed from themselves to William Lansdon and Esther his wife to be their Act and Deed and it is thereupon admitted to record.

Ford deed to Bingley   John Ford acknowledges a deed with the Livery of Seizin endorsed from himself to Joseph Bingley to be his Act and deed and it is thereupon admitted to record then Anne his wife (she being first privately examined) relinquishes her right of Dower in the land by the said Deed conveyed which is also admitted to record.

William Lansdons deed to Ford   William Lansdon and Hesther his wife (She being first privately examined) acknowledge a deed with the Livery of Seizin endorsed from themselves to John Ford to be their Act and Deed and it is thereupon admitted to record.

Holman deed to St. James's Parish   James Holman acknowledges a deed with the Livery of Seizin endorsed from himself to the Vestrymen of St. James's parish to be his Act and Deed and it is thereupon admitted to record then Sarah his wife (She being first privately examined) relinquishes her right fo Dower in the land by the deed conveyed which is also admitted to record.

Carnar's deed to Chamboon   Susanna Karnar acknowledges a deed with the Livery of Seizin endorsed from herself to Gideon Chamboon to be her Act and deed and it is thereupon admitted to record.

Birks deed to Howard   John Birks acknowledges a deed with the Livery of Seizin endorsed from himself to James Howard to be his Act and Deed and it is thereupon admitted to record, then Katherine his wife (She being first privately examined) relinquishes her right of Dower in the land by the said Deed conveyed which is also admitted to record.

[97]   May Court 1729
Dumas deed to Prosser   Jeremiah Dumas acknowledges Deeds of Lease and Release and a Bond from himself to Thomas Prosser to be his Act and Deed and they are thereupon admitted to record, then Unity wife of the said Jeremiah (She being first privately examined) relinquishes her right of Dower in the land by the said Deeds conveyed which is also admitted to record. Esther Jones also comes into Court and relinquishes her right of the Dower in the land by the said Deeds conveyed which is also admitted to record.

Randolph deed to Digges   Thomas Randolph acknowledges a deed with the Livery of Seizin endorsed from himself to Dudley Digges to be his Act and Deed and it is thereupon admitted to record.

Holmans negro judged   Cain a negro belonging to James Holman is judged to be 12 years old.

Hix's negro judged   Fanny a negro belonging to Daniel Hix is judged to be 12 years old.

Surveyors of the road   Constant Perkins is appointed Surveyor of the road from Thomas Murrel's to the back road. Anthony Hoggat from Tuckahoe Creek mill towards Hanover County as far as the County line.

Lists of titheable to be taken   The following persons are appointed to take the lists of Titheables, John Woodson Gent. below Beverdam Creek, Allin Howard Gent. above the said Creek, William Mayo Gent. in that part of St. James's Parish lying on the South side of James River, and Tarlton Fleming Gent. in King William Parish.

Bullington Levy Free   On the Petition of John Bullington he is exempt from payment of Levys.

Ferry appd   Stephen Hughes on behalf of Sarah Atkinson agrees to keep Ferry at the Courthouse for eight hundred pounds of tobacco Pr. Annum and to set over all persons living in the County on Court days and all other publick days and the Sherif and his Officers at all times.

Prosser vs Dendy   The Action of Case between Thomas Prosser and Elizabeth his wife Admx. &c. of John Shelton deceased Plts. and William Dendy Deft. is dismist the Plts. not prosecuting the same.

[98]   May Court 1729
Harriss vs Pratt   In the Action of Case between John Harriss Plt. and Roger Pratt and Peter Ford Defts. the parties Submit themselves to the Court for tryal whereupon it is considered that the Plt. do recover against the Defendants eight hundred pounds of tobacco with Cask and conveniency and the Costs of this Suit and a Lawyers Fee.

Wadley vs Harriss   On the motion of Thomas Wadloe an Evidence for John Harriss vs Roger Pratt & Peter Ford it is ordered that the said John do pay him for one days attendance and thirty pounds of tobacco with Costs.

Maxey vs Harriss   On the Motion of John Maxey a witness for John Harriss vs Roger Pratt and Peter Ford it is ordered that the said John Harriss do pay him for one days attendance thirty pounds of tobacco with costs.

Radford vs Harriss   On the Motion of John Radford a witness for John Harriss to Roger Pratt and Peter Ford it is ordered that the said John Harriss do pay him for one days attendance thirty pounds of tobacco with Costs.

Lyles vs Harriss   On the Motion of David Lyles a witness for John Harriss vs Roger Pratt and Peter Ford it is ordered that the said John Harriss do pay him for one days attendance thirty pounds of tobacco with Costs.

Paine vs Harriss   John Paine having attended one day a witness for John Harriss vs Roger Pratt and Peter Ford it is ordered that the said John Harriss do pay him for one days attendance thirty pounds of tobacco with Costs.

New vs Calvit   In the Action of Case between William New Plt. and Peter Calvit Deft. the Deft. acknowledges himself indebted unto the Plt. in the sum of three pounds Current money and four hundred pounds of tobacco whereupon it is ordered that he do pay the same unto the Plt. with Costs and a Lawyers Fee.

Baise vs Moor   In the Action of Case between Edward Baize Plt. and William Moor Deft. the Plt. Demurrs generally to the Defts. Pleas and the Deft. joyns in Demurrer.

Taylor vs Saunders   The Action of Trespass on the Case between John Taylor Plt. and John Saunders Deft. is continued at the Plts. cost.

[99]   May Court 1729
Towns vs Hoggat   In the Action of Trespass between William Towns Plt. and Anthony Hoggat Deft. Oyer of the Plaintifs account is granted the Defendant.

Williams vs Ware   In the Action of Case between Edward Williams Plt. and Peter Ware Deft. the Deft. pleads non assumpsit and for tryal puts himself upon the Country and the Plt. likewise.

Moss vs Taylor   In the Action of Trespass on the Case between Thomas Moss Plt. and James Taylor Deft. the Plt. files a new declaration and an imparlance is granted the Deft.

Surveyor of the road   Warham Easly is appointed Surveyor of the road from Richard Parkers on Letalone Creek the best way down to the Manakin Town road and it is ordered that the Inhabitants near the said road be exempt from clearing any other road.

New vs Morriss   In the Action of Debt between William New Plt. and Hugh Morriss and Sarah his wife Executrix &c. of Edmund New deceased Defts. the Defts. attorny agrees to file us Errors in Arrest of Judgment if the Verdict of the Jury be for the Plt. the following Jury are sworn. Anthony Hoggat, Robert Burton, Nowel Burton, John Harriss, Ashford Hughes, Robert Hughes, Leonard Ballew, Thomas Wadloe, Thomas Edwards, William Lansdon, Peter Ware, William Woodson, upon the return of the Jury with their Verdict the Plt. being called three several times fails to appear whereupon on the motion of the Defts. attorny the Verdict is recorded in these words "Wee of the Jury find that Mary wife of Hugh Morriss was Executrix &c. of the will of Edmund New deceased. Secondly Wee find by the Evidence of David Pattison that the said

Edmund New acknowledged his hand and Seal to the bond Specified &c. but without delivery. thirdly Wee find no consideration. Wherefore if the Law is for the Plt. Wee find fifty pounds Currant otherwise for the Deft. A. Hoggat Foreman." The Court being of Opinion the Law is for the Defts. it is considered that the Defts. go hence without day and that they recover against the Plt. their Costs by them in this behalf expended and a Lawyers Fee.

Christian vs New   On the motion of Thomas Christian a witness for William New vs Hugh Morriss & Sarah his wife it is ordered that the said William do pay him for one days attendance thirty pounds of tobacco with costs.

[100]   May Court 1729
Clark vs Cannon   In the Action of Case between Christopher Clark Plt. and William Cannon Deft. the Deft. pleads he oweth nothing and for tryal puts himself upon the Country and the Plt. likewise.

Clark vs Gallemore   In the Action of Case between Christopher Clark Plt. and William Gallemore Deft. the Deft. failing to appear the Conditional Judgment granted last Court against the Deft. and Daniel Stoner Gent. Sherif is confirmed for so much damages as shall be found upon executing a writ of enquiry at next Court of which the Sherif is ordered to give the Deft. notice by Serving him with a copy of this order.

Atkinson vs Benning   In the Action of Trespass between Sarah Atkinsson Plt. and Anthony Benning Deft. the Deft. pleads not guilty and for tryal puts himself upon the Country and the Plt. likewise.

Atkinson vs Leseur   In the Action of Trespass between Sarah Atkinson Plt. and David Leseur Deft. the Deft. pleads not guilty and for tryal puts himself upon the Country and the Plt. likewise.

Atkinson vs Taylor   In the Action of Trespass between Sarah Atkinson Plt. and James Taylor Deft. the Deft. pleads not guilty and for tryall puts himself upon the Country and the Plt. likewise.

Hughes vs Cone   In the Action of Case between Robert Hughes Plt. and John Cone Deft. the Deft. failing to plead Judgment by nihil dicit is granted against him for what damages shall be recovered in this Suit to be discharged if the Deft. pleads at the next Court.

Doran vs Marchbank   The Action of Case between John Doran Admr.

&c. of Julius King deceased Plt. and George Marchbanks Deft. is continued at the Plts. cost.

Jeffs vs Martin   In the Action of Case between John Jeffs Plt. and John Martin Deft. a Pluries Capias is awarded against the Deft. returnable to the next Court.

Taylor vs Lowe   In the Action of Trespass on the Case between John Taylor Plt. and Thomas Lowe and Amy his wife Defts. the Defts. failing to plead Judgment by nihil dicit is granted against them for what damages shall be recovered in this Suit to be discharged if the Defts. plead at the next Court.

[101]   May Court 1729
Paine vs Huckaby   The Action of Debt between John Paine Plt. and John Huckaby Deft. is dismist the Plt. not prosecuting the same.

Mayo vs Quin   In the Action of Debt between William Mayo Plt. and John Quin & John Micheaux Defts. the Deft. Quin appears and acknowledging that there is due unto the Plt. the Sum of four pounds sixteen shillings and five pence Currant money upon ballance of a Bond it is considered that the Plt. do recover against the Defts. the said Sum with Interest after the rate of Pr. Centum Pr. Annum from the tenth day of November 1725 untill the same shall be paid with costs and a Lawyers Fee.

Vanderhood vs Worley   The Attachment issued in the Action of Case between Henry Vanderhoode Plt. and John Worley Deft. is continued returnable to the next Court.

Holland vs Jeffs   In the Action of Case between Michael Holland Plt. and John Jeffs Deft. the Deft. failing to appear the Conditional Judgment granted at last Court against the Deft. and Charles Johnson his Bail is confirmed for so much damages as shall be found upon executing a writ of enquiry at next Court of which the Sherif is ordered to give the Deft. notice by Serving him with a copy of this order.

Dale vs Gunn   In the Action of Case between Christopher Dale Plt. and John Gunn Deft. the Deft. failing to appear the Conditional Judgment granted at last Court against the Deft. and Daniel Stoner Gent. Sheriff is confirmed for somuch damages as shall be found upon executing a writ of enquiry at the next Court of which the Sherif is ordered to give the Deft. notice by Serving him with a Copy of this order.

Capoon vs Sublet   In the Action of Case between Jacob Capoon Plt. and Peter Lewis Sublet Deft. the Deft. failing to appear the Conditional Judgment granted at last Court against the Deft. and Daniel Stoner Gent. Sherif is confirmed for so much damages as shall be found upon executing a writ of enquiry at the next Court of which the Sherif is ordered to give the Deft. notice by serving him with a Copy of this order.

[102]   May Court 1729
Carol vs Burton   The Action of Trespass on the Case between Elizabeth Carol Executrix &c. of Roger Carol deceased Plt. and Nowel Burton Deft. is dismist the Plt. not prosecuting the same.

Hix vs Salley   The Action of Trespass between Marmaduke Hix Plt. and William Sallee Deft. is dismist the Plt. not prosecuting the same.

Hughes vs Dean   In the Action of Case between Robert Hughes Plt. and Richard Dean Deft. the Deft. pleads he oweth nothing and for tryal puts himself upon the Country and the Plt. likewise.

Cannon vs Burgess   In the Action of Trespass on the Case between William Cannon Plt. and Daniel Burgess Deft. the Conditional Judgment granted at the last Court against the Deft. and Daniel Stoner Gent. Sherif is confirmed the Deft. failing to appear and it is thereupon considered by the Court that the Plt. do recover against the Deft. and Daniel Stoner Gent. Sherif four hundred pounds of tobacco with Costs and a Lawyers Fee.

Spencer vs Quin   In the Action of Trespass on the Case between Peter Spencer Plt. and John Quin Deft. the Deft. failing to Plead Judgment by nihil dicit is granted against him for what damages shall be recovered in this Suit to be discharged if the Deft. shall plead at the next Court.

Turner vs Powell   In the Action of Detinue between James Turner Plt. and Richard Powell Deft. the Deft. pleads non Detinet and for tryall puts himself upon the Country and the Plt. likewise.

Alexander vs Chandler   The Action of Case between John Alexander Plt. and Joell Chandler Deft. is continued.

Roc[ke]t vs Baldrige   On the Attachment obtained by Baldwin Rocket against the Estate of Thomas Baldrige the Sherif hath made the following return "February the 13th. day 1728. Attached in the hands of Sarah Woodson, Warham Easly, Nowel Burton, Stephen Woodson, Joseph

Parsons, Jacob Winfree, Pr. Joseph Bingley Sub Sher." the Plt. makes oath to this Debt and it is thereupon considered that he do recover against the Deft. six pounds Currant money with Costs and an Attornys Fee. Warham Easly acknowledges that there is in his Possession a horse belonging to the said Thomas Baldrige.

[103]   May Court 1729
Allin vs Dickins   In the Action of Case between Samuell Allin Plt. and Thomas Dickins Deft. the Plt. files a new declaration and an imparlance is granted the Defendant.

Cabbell vs Nolun   In the Action of Debt between William Cabbell Deft. and Thomas Nolun Deft. the Deft. failing to plead Judgment by nihil dicit is granted against him for what damages shall be recovered in this Suit to be discharged if the Deft. shall plead at the next Court.

Burton vs Quin   In the Action of Case between Nowel Burton Plt. and John Quin Deft. the Deft. failing to plead Judgment by nihil dicit is granted against him for what damages shall be recovered in this Suit to be discharged if the Deft. shall plead at the next Court.

Quin vs May   In the Action of Case between John Quin Plt. and William May Deft. the Deft. pleads he oweth nothing and for tryal puts himself upon the Country and the Plt. likewise.

May vs Ashlin   In the Action of Case between William May Plt. and Joseph Ashlin Deft. the Deft. appears and acknowledges himself indebted unto the Plt. in the sum of two hundred and twenty seven pounds of tobacco whereupon it is considered that the Plt. do recover against the Deft. the said Sum of tobacco with Costs.

Cannon vs Matlock   In the Action of Case between William Cannon Plt. and William Matlock Deft. the Deft. failing to appear the Judgment granted at the last Court against the Deft. and Stephen Hughes and George Eastham his Bail is confirmed and it is thereupon considered by the Court that the Plt. do recover against the Deft. and Stephen Hughes and George Eastham the Sum of three pounds twelve shillings and three pence Currant money with Costs and an Attornys Fee.

Hinson vs Nash   In the Action of case between John Hinson Plt. and Samuell Nash Deft. the Deft. being in Custody of the Sherif for lack of Special Bail acknowledges himself indebted unto the Plt. in the Sum of one pounds eight shillings and six pence Currant money whereupon it is considered by the Court that the Plt. do recovered against the Deft. the said sum with Costs and a Lawyers Fee.

Constable sworn   Joseph Ashlin is sworn a Constable in the room of Bartholomew Stoveall.

[104]   May Court 1729
Dean vs Napier   In the Action of Case between Richard Dean Plt. and Robert Napier Junr. Deft. the same is continued.

Westbrook vs Clark   In the Action of Case between James Westbrook and Frances his wife Executrix &c. of Edward Bass deceased Plts. and John Clark Deft. a Pluries Capias is awarded against the Deft. returnable to the next Court.

Randolph vs Wotars   The Action of Debt between Thomas Randolph Plt. and William Wotars Deft. is continued.

Then the Court adjourned 'till to morrow morning nine of the Clock.
                                                            Henry Wood ClCur.

****

At a Court continued and held for Goochland County the 21st day of May Annoq Domini 1729. Present. Thomas Randolph, John Fleming, John Woodson, Tarlton Fleming, George Paine, William Cabbell, Gent. Justices.

Hoggats Ordiny. Lycense   On the motion of Anthony Hoggat Lycense is granted him to keep an Ordinary at his House, Stephen Hughes and Henry Wood Securities.

Ware vs Williams   In the Action of Trespass between Peter Ware Plt. and Edward Williams Deft. Richard Dean, William Lansdon, William Woodson, John Macbride, Joell Chandler, Robert Hughes, Ashford Hughes, Richard Oglesby, John Webb, John Laine, John Paine, Jacob Micheaux, the Jury are sworn who after some time return their Verdict which on the Defts. motion is ordered to be recorded and is as followeth "Wee find for the Deft. Richard Dean Foreman" whereupon it is considered by the Court that the Deft. go hence without day and that he recover against the Plt. his costs by him in this behalf expended and a Lawyers Fee.

[105]   May Court 1729
Ware vs Williams   In the Action of Case between Peter Ware Plt. and Edward Williams Deft. the parties Submit themselves for tryal to the Court whereupon it is considered that the Plt. do recover against the Deft. the sum of nineteen shillings and ten pence Currant money with Costs and a Lawyers Fee.

Macon vs Wharton   The Action of Case between John Macon Plt. and Thomas Wharton Deft. is continued.

Utley vs Napier   In the two actions of Debt and Action of Case between John Utley Plt. and Bouth Napier Deft. George Paine & William Cabbell Gent. are appointed to examine state & settle the severall accounts and matters in dispute between them and to report their proceedings therein to the next Court.

    Present. William Mayo Gent.

Burton vs Watkins   In the Action of Debt between Nowel Burton Assignee of Allin Frazer Assee. of Michael Canady Plt. and William Watkins Deft. came as well the said Nowel Burton by John Quin his attorny as the said William Watkins by Thos. Prosser his attorny upon which the premises being seen and by the Court of Our Lord the King here fully understood it seems to the Justices here that the Plea of the said William Watkins above in bar pleaded and the matter therein contained is not good and Sufficient in Law to Quash the bill aforesaid of the said Nowel Burton therefore it is ordered that a writ of enquiry of damages be executed at the next Court of which the Sherif is to give the Deft. notice by serving him with a Copy of this order.

Thomas vs Jeffs   In the Action of Case between Michael Thomas Plt. and John Jeffs Deft. the Deft. failing to appear the Conditional Judgment granted at last Court against the Deft. and Daniel Stoner Gent. Sherif is confirmed for what damages shall be recovered in this Suit upon executing a writ of enquiry at the next Court of which the Sherif is ordered to give the Deft. notice by serving him with a Copy of this order.

Dittoway vs Pleasants   In the Action of Case between Barbary Ditoway Plt. and John Pleasants Admr. &c. of William Howl deceased Deft. the Deft. failing to appear the Conditional Judgment

[106]   May Court 1729
Judgment granted at last Court against the Deft. and Daniel Stoner Gent.

Sherif is confirmed for so much damages as shall be found upon executing a writ of enquiry at the next Court of which the Sherif is ordered to give the Deft. notice by serving him with a Copy of this order.

Chastain vs Pleasants   In the Action of Case between Stephen Chastain Plt. and John Pleasants Admr. &c. of William Howl deceased Deft. the Deft. failing to appear the conditional Judgment granted at last Court against the Deft. and Daniel Stoner Gent. Sherif is confirmed for what damages shall be recovered upon executing a writ of enquiry of damages at the next Court of which the Sherif is ordered to give the Deft. notice by Serving him with a Copy of this order.

Chiswell vs Napier   In the Action of Case between Charles Chiswell vs Bouth Napier the Court having heard the Arguments on the reasons filed by the Deft. to stay the Judgment it is the opinion of the Court that the same are not good in Law to stay the Judgment aforesaid whereupon it is considered that the Plt. do recover against the Deft. the Sum of six pounds seventeen shillings and eight pence Currant money by the Jurors in their verdict assessed with the costs of this Suit & a Lawyers Fee.

Napier vs Scot   In the Action of Debt between Bouth Napier Plt. and Edward Scot Admr. &c. of the goods and chattles of Paul Green Deft. came as well as the said Bouth by his attorny Thomas Dickins as the said Edward by his Attorny Thomas Prosser upon which the Premises being seen and by the Court of our Lord the King here fully understood it seems to the Justices here that the Plea of the said Edward above in Bar Pleaded and the matter in the same contained is good and Sufficient in Law to Quash the bill aforesaid of the aforesaid Bouth, whereupon the Plt. takes issue on the Plea aforesaid the tryall whereof is referred.

Towns vs Hoggat   In the Action of Debt between William Towns Plt. and Anthony Hoggat Deft. came as well the said William by Thomas Prosser his atty as the said Anthony by Thomas Dickins his attorny upon which the Premises being seen and by the Court of Our Lord the King here fully understood it seems to the Justices

[107]   May Court 1729
here that the Plea of the said Anthony above in barr pleaded and the matter in the same is good and Sufficient in Law to Quash the bill aforesd. of the aforesaid William whereupon the Plt. takes issue on the Plea aforesaid the tryall whereof is referred.

Nolun vs Wotars   In the Action of Case between Thomas Nolun Plt.

and William Wotars Deft. the following Jury are sworn, Richard Dean, William Lansdon, John Mcbrid, Joell Chandler, Ashford Hughes, John Webb, Richard Oglesby, John Paine, Jacob Micheaux, Nowell Burton, Samuell Allin, John Laine, who after some time return with their Verdict which is ordered to be recorded and is as followeth "Wee find by first Evidence that the Deft. was to finish the house without any consideration. Wee find by the second Evidence that the Deft. had a Jobb of work to do in Hanover and that he told him so, if the Law be for the Plt. then Wee find for the Plt. seven shillings and Six pence Currant money otherwise for the Deft. the arguing of which Verdicts is referred."

Burton vs Woodson   In the Action of Case between Robert Burton Plt. and William Woodson Executor &c. of Benjamin Woodson Deft. the Plt. takes issue on the Defts. plea the tryall whereof is referred.

Tyre vs Utley   In the Action of Trover between James Tyre Plt. and John Utley Deft. came as well the said James by Thomas Prosser his attorny and the said John by Thos. Dickins his attorny upon which the premises being seen and by the Court of our Lord the King here fully understood it seems to the Justices here that the Writ of the aforesaid James is not good and Sufficient in Law to maintain the Action aforesaid of the aforesaid James whereupon it is considered by the Court that the Deft. go hence without day and the he recover against the Plt. his costs by him in this behalf expended. and a Lawyers Fee.

Rapene vs Bingley   The action of Trespass on the Case between Anthony Rapene Plt. and Joseph Bingley Deft. is continued.

Holland vs Saunders   The action of Case between Michaell Holland Plt. and Thos. Saunders Deft. is continued.

[108]   May Court 1729
Mayo Sworn Survr   William Mayo Gent. produces a Commission from the Honble. John Robinson Esqr. Surveyor General of this Colony to be Surveyor of this County which being read the said William Mayo takes the Oaths appointed to be taken by Act of Parliament instead of the Oaths of Allegiance and Supremacy the Oath appointed to be taken by an Act of Parliament made in the 1st year of the reign of his late Majesty King George the First intituled An Act for the further Security of his Majestys Person and Government and the Succession of the Crown in the Heirs of the late Princess Sophia being Protestants and for extinguishing the hopes of the Pretended Prince of Wales and his open and Secret abettors, and Subscribes the Test, and takes the Oath of a Surveyor.

Ware vs Saunders   In the Action of Case between Susanna Ware Plt. and Thomas Saunders Deft. Edward Scot becomes Special Bail for the Deft. who thereupon Pleads he oweth nothing.

Bellamy ordd. to be Sumd   Ordered that Mary Bellamy be Sumoned to appear at the next Court to accept or refuse the administration of the Estate of John Bellamy deceased.

Spencer vs Gallemore   In the Action of Case between Samuel Spencer Plt. and William Gallemore Deft. the Deft. failing to appear a Pluries Capias is awarded against him returnable to the next Court.

Hughes vs Lax   In the Action of Case between Ashford Hughes Plt. and William Lax Deft. the same is continued.

Woodson vs Allin   In the Action of Case between Josiah Woodson &c. Executors &c. of Jacob Woodson Deceased Plts. and Samuel Allin Deft. the same is continued.

Laine vs Christian   In the Action of Case between John Laine Plt. and John Christian Deft. the Deft. failing to appear & plead Judgment by nihil dicit is granted against him for what damages shall be recovered in this Suit to be discharges nevertheless if the Deft. shall plead at the next Court.

[109]   May Court 1729
Stidum vs Bingley   In the Action of Case between Benjamin Stidum Plt. and Joseph Bingley Deft. came as well the said Benjamin by Thos. Prosser his attorny at the said Joseph by Thomas Dickins his Attorny upon which the premises being Seen and by the Court of Our Lord King here fully understood it seems to the Justices here that the Declaration of the aforesaid Benjamin is not good and Sufficient in Law to maintain the Action aforesaid of the aforesd. Benjamin therefore it is considered that the said Benjamin take nothing by his writ, and that the said Joseph go hence without day and that he recover against the said Benjamin his costs by him in this behalf expended and a Lawyers Fee.

Barnes vs Pruit   In the Action of Debt between William Barnes Plt. and Thomas Pruit Deft. the Plt. failing to Prosecute his Suit on the Defts. motion he is nonsuited and it is thereupon considered that the Deft. do recover against the Plt. shillings Currant money with Costs and an Attorneys Fee.

Pruit vs Baldwin   The action of Trespass between Andrew Pruit Plt. and Henry Baldwin Deft. is dismist the Plt. not prosecuting the same.

Waddill vs Edwards   In the Action of Case between William Waddill Plt. and Thomas Edwards Deft. came as well the said William by Thomas Dickins as the said Thomas Edwards by Thomas Prosser his attorny upon which the premises being seen and by the Court of our Lord the King here fully understood it seems to the Justices here that the Demurrer taken by the Deft. to the Plts. Evidence is not good and Sufficient in Law whereupon time is granted the Defendant to file a Bill of Injunction in Chancery.

Martin vs Gunn   In the action of Trespass between Francis Martin Plt. and John Gunn Deft. the Deft. failing to plead Judgment by nihil dicit is granted against him for what damages shall be recovered in this Suit to be discharged if the Deft. shall plead at the next Court.

Randolph vs Quin   In the Action of Trespass on the Case between Thomas Randolph Plt. and John Quin Deft. the Deft. acknowledges himself indebted unto the Plt. in the Sum of six pounds and eleven pence Currant money whereupon it is considered that the Plt. do recover against the Deft. the said Sum wth. costs and an Attornys Fee.

[110]   May Court 1729
Woodson &c. vs Woodson   In the Action of Trespass on the Case between Robert Woodson and James Holman Plts. and William Woodson Deft. the Deft. failing to plead Judgmt. by nihil dicit is granted against him for what damages shall be recovered in this Suit to be discharged if the Deft. pleads at the next Court.

Thomas vs Gee   In the Action of Case between Rowland Thomas Plt. and Gilbert Gee Deft. the Plt. mends his declaration and the Deft. failing to plead Judgment by nihil dicit is granted against him for what damages shall be recovered in this Suit to be discharged if the Deft. pleads at the next Court.

In the Action of Case between John Martin Plt. and Anthony Rapene Deft. the Deft. failing to Plead Judgment by nihil dicit is granted against him for what damages shall be recovered in this Suit to be discharged if the Deft. pleads at the next Court.

Bingley vs Rapene   In the Action of Trespass between Joseph Bingley Plt. and Anthony Rapene Deft. the Deft. failing to plead Judgment by nihil dicit is granted against him for what damages shall be recovered in this Suit to be discharged if the Deft. pleads at the next Court.

Cabbell vs Wade   In the action of Trespass on the Case between William Cabbell Plt. and Robert Wade Deft. the Deft. failing to Plead Judgment by nihil dicit is granted against him for what damages shall be recovered in this Suit to be discharg'd if the Deft. pleads at the next Court.

Atkinson vs Lax   In the Action of Case between Henry Atkinson Plt. and William Lax Deft. Stephen Hughes becomes special Bail for the Deft. who failing to plead Judgment by nihil dicit is granted against him for what damages shall be recovered in this Suit to be discharged if the Deft. shall plead at the next Court.

Dickins vs Macon   In the Action of Trespass on the Case between Thomas Dickins Plt. and John Macon Deft. William Cabbell Gent. is appointed to examine state and settle the several accounts in dispute between them.

Denton vs Nolun   On the motion of Thomas Denton of Hanover County a witness for Thomas Nolun agst. William Wotars it is considered that the Thomas Nolun do pay him for two days attendance & for coming and returning thirty five miles once according to Law with Costs.

[111]   May Court 1729
Paine vs Ware   On the motion of George Paine Junr. a witnes. for Peter Ware vs Edward Williams it is ordered that the said Peter do pay him for two days attendance according to Law with Costs.

Cox vs Ware   On the motion of John Cox a witness for Peter Ware vs Edward Williams it is ordered that the said Peter do pay him for two days attendance according to Law with Costs.

Vaughan vs Williams   In the Action of Trover between George Vaughan Plt. and John Williams Deft. the following Jury are Sworn Richard Dean, William Lansdon, John Mcbrid, Joell Chandler, Ashford Hughes, John Webb, Richard Oglesby, John Paine, Jacob Micheaux, Nowel Burton, Saml. Allin, John Laine, who after some time return their Verdict in these words "Wee find for the Plt. Six pounds Currant money or his said Horse and twenty shillings Currant money damage Richard Dean Foreman." which Verdict at the Plts. motion is recorded   And it is considered that the Plt. do recover against the Deft. the Horse aforesaid or Six pounds Currt. money and twenty shillings Currant money damage by the Jurors aforesaid in their said Verdict assessed with the Costs of this Suit and a Lawyers Fee.

Tuley vs Morriss   On the motion of John Tuly a witness for Hugh Morriss and Sarah his wife ads William New it is ordered that the said Hugh do pay him for four days attendance with Costs according to Law.

  Present. Allin Howard Gent.

Hughes vs Macon   In the Action of Case between Stephen Hughes Plt. and John Macon Deft. Samuell Allin & John Webb become Special bail for the Deft. who failing to plead Judgment by nihil dicit is granted him for what damages shall be recovered in this Suit to be discharged if the Deft. pleads at the next Court.

Macon vs Hughes   In the Action of Debt between John Macon Plt. and Stephen Hughes Deft. the Deft. failing to plead Judgment by nihil dicit is granted against him for what damages shall be recovered in this Suit to be discharged if the Deft. pleads at the next Court.

  Absent. Thos. Randolph, John Fleming, John Woodson Gent.

Macon vs Fleming   In the action of Debt between John Macon Plt. and Tarlton Fleming Deft. the parties Submit themselves to the Court for tryal whereupon it is considered that the Plt. do recover against the Deft. eight hundred and fifteen pounds of tobacco with the Costs of this Suit and a Lawyers Fee.

[112]   May Court 1729
  Present. Thomas Randolph, John Fleming Gent.

Raley vs Quin   In the action of Debt between Charles Raley Plt. and John Quin Deft. the parties Submit themselves to the Court for tryall whereupon it is considered that the Plt. do recover against the Deft. the Sum of three pounds Seven shillings and Six pence Currant money with the Costs of this Suit and a Lawyers Fee.

Chamberlaine vs Marchbanks   The Action of Case between William Chamberlaine Plt. and George Marchbanks Deft. is continued.

Alsup vs Vaughan   On the motion of Benjamin Alsup of Hanover County a witness for George Vaughn against John Williams it is ordered that the said George do pay him for two days attendance for coming and returning thirty miles once according to Law.

Pate vs Vaughan   On the motion of Benjamin Pate of Hanover County a witness for George Vaughan against John Williams it is ordered that the said George do pay him for two days attendance and for coming and returning thirty miles once according to Law.

Micheaux vs Raley   In the Action of Debt between Jacob Micheaux Plt. and Charles Raley Deft. an imparlance is granted the Defendant.

Wade vs Daviss   In the Action of Trespass on the Case between Robert Wade Plt. and William Daviss Deft. an imparlance is granted the Deft.

Lad vs Coleman   In the Action of Case between Constantine Lad Plt. and Samuel Coleman Deft. the Defendt. acknowledges himself indebted unto the Plt. in the sum of twenty shillings Currant money which he is ordered to pay him with Costs.

Fleming vs Pleasants   In the Action of Debt between John Fleming Plt. and John Pleasants Admr. &c. of William Howl deceased Deft. the Deft. failing to appear Judgment is granted against him and Daniel Stoner Gent. Sherif for what damages shall be recovered in this Suit to be discharged if the Deft. appears at the next Court.

The Action of Case between Dudley Digges and John Franklin Deft. is dismist the Plt. not prosecuting the same.

[113]   May Court 1729
Carnar vs Atkinson   In the Action of Trespass on the Case between Susanna Carnar Plt. and Henry Atkinson Deft. Tarlton Fleming Gent. is appointed to examine state and settle the several Accounts in dispute between them and to make report of his proceeding therein to the next Court.

The action of Case between Nowell Burton Plt. and Robert Carter Deft. is dismist neither party appearing.

Amos vs Raley   On the motion of John Amos a witness for Charles Raley vs Quin, it is ordered that the said Charles do pay him for four days attendance according to Law with Costs.

Hughes vs Raley   On the motion of Stephen Hughes a witness for

Charles Raley vs John Quin it is ordered that the said Charles do pay him for four days attendance according to Law with Costs.

Anderson vs Hoggat. In the Action of Case between Mary Anderson Plt. and Philip Hoggat Deft. the Deft. failing to appear Judgment is granted against the Deft. and Danl. Stoner Gent. Sherif for what damages shall be recovered in this Suit to be discharged if the Deft. shall appear at the next Court.

The Action of Trespass on the Case between John Woodson Plt. and Thomas Ballew Deft. is dismist the Plt. not prosecuting the same.

Woodson vs Taylor   In the Action of Case between John Woodson Plt. and John Taylor Deft. the Deft. failing to appear Judgment is granted the Plt. against the Defendt. and Daniel Stoner Gent. Sherif for what damages shall be recovered in this Suit to be discharged if the Deft. appears at the next Court.

Pavement vs Coleman   In the Action of Case between Thomas Pavement Plt. and Saml. Coleman Deft. the Deft. pleads he oweth nothing and for tryal puts himself upon the Country and the Plt. likewise.

Randolph vs Bullington   In the Action of Case between Thomas Randolph Plt. and John Bullington Deft. the Deft. failing to appear Judgment is granted the Plt. and the Deft. and Robert Carter his Bail for what damages shall be recovered in this Suit to be discharged if the Deft. appears at the next Court.

The Attachment obtained by Thomas Randolph against the Estate of John Dickinson is dismist the said Thomas not prosecuting the same.

[114]   May Court 1729
The Action of Case between James Holman Plt. and John Pritchett Deft. is dismist neither party appearing.

Taylor vs Swett   In the Action of Trespass between James Taylor Plt. and Robert Swett Deft. an imparlance is granted the Deft.

The Action of Case between Dudley Digges Plt. and William Gates Deft. is dismist neither party appearing.

The Action of Case between Dudley Digges Plt. and John Scrugs Defendant is dismist neither party appearing.

The Action of Debt between Richard Dean Plt. and Marmaduke Hix Deft. is dismist neither party appearing.

Dean vs Huson   In the Action of Debt between Richard Dean Plt. and John Huson Deft. the Deft. being in Custody of the Sherif pleads he oweth nothing and for tryal puts himself upon the Country and the Plt. likewise.

The Action of Case between John McCulloch Plt. and Jacob Brooks Deft. is dismist neither party appearing

The Action of Case between Thomas Randolph Plt. and John Stone Deft. is dismist neither party appearing.

Then the Court adjourned to the third Tuesday in next Month.
Test. Henry Wood ClCur.

****

At a Court held for Goochland County the third Tuesday in June being the Seventeenth day of the month Annoq Domi. 1729. Present. William Mayo, John Woodson, Tarlton Fleming, George Paine, William Cabbell, Gent. Justices.

[115]   June Court 1729
Court to meet at certain hours   Ordered to be entered as a rule that the Court meet at ten of the Clock in the months of March, Aprill, May, June, July, and August, and at eleven of the Clock in the other Six months.

Capoon's deed to Chastain   Jacob Capoon and Elizabeth his wife (She being first privately examined) acknowledge a deed with the Livery of Seizin endorsed from themselves to Stephen Chastain to be their Act and Deed and it is thereupon admitted to Record.

Present. Allin Howard Gent.

Jeffs vs Martin   In the Action of Case between John Jeffs. Plt. and John Martin Deft. the Deft. failing to appear a Pluries Capias is awarded against him returnable to the next Court.

V'rhoode vs Worley   The Action of Case between Henry Vanderhoode Plt. and John Worley Defendant is dismist the Plt. not prosecuting the same.

Alexander vs Chandler   In the Action on the Case between John
Alexander Plt. and Joell Chandler Deft. the Deft. failing to appear the
Conditional Judgment granted at last Court against the Deft. and Daniel
Stoner Gent. Sherif is confirmed for what damages shall be recovered
upon executing a writ of inquiry at next Court of which the Sherif is
ordered to give the Deft. notice by serving him with a Copy of this order.

Dean vs Napier   In the action on the Case between Richard Dean Plt.
and Robert Napier Junr. Deft. Stephen Hughes becomes Special Bail for
the Deft. who pleads he oweth nothing and for tryall puts himself upon
the Country and the Plt. likewise.

Westbrook vs Clark   In the Action on the Case between James
Westbrook Plt. and John Clark Deft. the Deft. failing to appear a Pluries
Capias is awarded against him returnable to the next Court.

Spencer vs Gallemore   In the action on the Case between Samuel
Spencer Plt. and William Gallemore Deft. the Deft. failing to appear a
Pluries Capias is awarded against him returnable to the next Court.

    Present. James Holman Gent.

Hughes vs Cone   In the Action on the Case between Robert Hughes
Plt. and John Cone Deft. the Deft. Pleads he oweth nothing and for tryal
puts himself upon the Country and the Plt. likewise.

[116]   June Court 1729
Thomas vs Jeffs   In the Action on the Case between Michael Thomas
Plt. and John Jeffs Deft. Anthony Hoggat, Peter Ware, Nowel Burton,
George Marchbanks, Leonard Ballew, William Womack, Robert Burton,
John Harriss, Nathll. Bassett, William Woodson, Richard Oglesby, David
Pattison, the Jury are Sworn to enquire of the damages, who after some
time return with their Verdict which on the Plts. motion is admitted to
record and is as followeth "Wee find for the Plt. twenty nine pounds of
tobacco Anthony Hoggat Foreman." whereupon it is considered by the
Court that the Plt. do recover against the Deft. and Daniel Stoner Gent.
Sherif twenty nine pounds of tobacco damages by the Jurors aforesaid in
their said Verdict assessed with the Costs of this Suit and a Lawyers Fee.

Hughes vs Dean   In the Action on the Case between Robert Hughes
Plt. and Richard Dean Defendant, Peter Ware, Nowel Burton, George
Marchbanks, Leonard Ballew, William Womack, Robert Burton, Anthony
Hoggat, John Harriss, Nathl. Bassett, William Woodson, Richard Oglesby,

David Pattison, the Jury are sworn and afterwards by consent of Parties dismist without hearing their Evidence, wherefore George Paine & William Cabbell Gent. are appointed to Examine State and Settle the Several accounts in dispute and to report their proceedings therein to the next Court.

Woodson & Holmn. vs Woodson   In the Action of Trespass on the Case between Robert Woodson and James Holman Plts. and William Woodson Deft. the Deft. pleads he oweth nothing and for tryall puts himself upon the Country and the Plts. likewise.

Hughes vs Macon   In the Action on the Case between Stephen Hughes Plt. and John Macon Deft. the Deft. pleads he oweth nothing and for tryall puts himself upon the Country and the Plt. likewise.

Macon vs Hughes   In the Action of Debt between John Macon Plt. and Stephen Hughes Deft. the Deft. files a Plea and the Plt. takes issue thereon.

Scot's deed to Hughes   Edward Scot and John Scot Junr. acknowledge a deed with the Livery of Seizin endorsed from themselves to Stephen Hughes to be their Act and deed and it is thereupon admitted to record, then Anne wife of the said Edward (she being first privately examined) relinquishes her right of Dower in the land by this deed conveyed which is also admitted to record.

[117]   June Court 1729
Scot & Hughes deed to Scot   Edward Scot & Stephen Hughes acknowledge a deed with the Livery of Seizin endorsed from themselves to John Scot Junr. to be their Act and Deed and it is thereupon admitted to record then Anne wife of the said Edward and Elizabeth wife of the said Stephen (they being first privately examined) relinquish their right of Dower in the land by this deed conveyed which is also admitted to record.

Scot & Hughes deed to Cox   Edward Scot, John Scot Junr. & Stephen Hughes acknowledge with the Livery of Seizin endorsed from themselves to Nicholas Cox to be their Act and Deed and it is thereupon admitted to record, then Anne wife of the said Edward and Elizabeth wife of the said Stephen (they being first privately examined) acknowledge their right of Dower in the land by this deed conveyed to be relinquished unto the said Nicholas Cox which is also admitted to record.

Parish's deed to Joplin   John Parish acknowledges a deed with the

Livery of Seizin endorsed from himself to Thomas Joplin to be his Act and deed and it is thereupon admitt'd to record.

Parish's deed to Watkins   John Parish acknowledges a deed with the Livery of Seizin endorsed from himself to Joseph Watkins to be his Act and Deed and it is thereupon admitted to record.

        Present. Thomas Randolph Gent.

White vs Webber   The Action of Case between Samuel White Plt. and Philip Webber Deft. is continued at the Defts. cost.

Baise vs Moor   The Action of Case between Edward Baize Plt. and William Moor Deft. is continued at the Defts. cost.

Towns vs Hoggat   The Action of Trespass between Wm. Towns Plt. and Anthony Hoggat Deft. is continued at the Plts. cost.

Woodson deed to Randolph   John Dandrige, Job Moor, and William Womack prove a deed with the Livery of Seizin endorsed from Robert Woodson to Thomas Randolph to be the Act and deed of Robert Woodson and it is thereupon admitted to record, then Sarah widow and Relict of the said Robert Woodson relinquishes her right of Dower in the land by the said Deed conveyed which is admitted to record.

Williams vs Ware   The Action of Case between Edward Williams Plt. and Peter Ware Deft. is continued at the Plts. cost.

[118]   June Court 1729
Utley vs Napier   The Action of Debt between John Utley Plt. and Bouth Napier Deft. is continued at the Defts. cost.

Utley vs Napier   In the Action of Case between John Utley Plt. and Booth Napier Deft. the Auditors make report of their proceedings which on the Plts. motion is admitted to record and is as followeth "Pursuant to an order of Goochland County Court wee have proceeded to examine state & settle the Severall accounts in dispute between John Utley Plt. and Bouth Napier Deft. in the Action on the Case and find the ballance due to the said John Utley to be two pounds seventeen shillings and Six pence Currant money Given under our hands the twelfth day of June 1729. Geo. Payne, Willm. Cabbell." Whereupon it is considered by the Court that the Plt. do recover against the Deft. the sum of two pounds seventeen shillings and Six pence Currant money and the cots of this Suit with a

Lawyers Fee.

Utley vs Napier. In the Action of Debt between John Utley Plt. and Bouth Napier Deft. time is granted the Plt. to mend his declaration.

Woodsons will   The last will & Testament of Robert Woodson Deceased is presented in Court by Thomas Randolph, William Womack, and Sarah Woodson, his Executors & Executrix who make oath thereto and the same being proved by the Oaths of John Dandrige and Job Moor it is admitted to record and on the motion of the said Exrs. & Executrix and their performing what is usual in such Cases Certificate is granted them for obtaining a probate thereof in due form John Woodson and Allin Howard entring themselves Securities for the same.

Pattison vs King   In the Action of Trespass between David Pattison Plt. and Martin King Deft. the following Jury are Sworn. Anthony Hoggat, Peter Ware, Nowel Burton, George Marchbanks, Leonard Ballew, William Womack, Robert Burton, John Harriss, Nathll. Bassett, Richard Oglesby, Fredorick Cox, who after some time return with their Verdict which on the Plts. motion is ordered to be recorded and is as followeth "Wee find for the Plt. ten shillings Currant money Anthony Hoggat Foreman." whereupon it is considered that the Plt. do recover against the Defendant ten shillings Currant money with costs to the value of ten shillings Currant money.

Quin vs May   The action of Case between John Quin Plt. and William May Deft. is continued at the Defts. cost.

[119]   June Court 1729
Moss vs Taylor   The Action of Trespass on the Case between James Moss Plt. and James Taylor Deft. is continued at the Plts. cost.

Clark vs Cannon   The action of Case between Christopher Clark Plt. and William Cannon Deft. is continued at the Plts. cost.

Clark vs Gallemore   The action of Case between Christopher Clark and William Gallemore Deft. is continued at the Plts. cost.

Atkinson vs Benning   The Action of Case between Sarah Atkinson Plt. and Anthony Benning Deft. is continued at the Defts. cost.

Atkinson vs Leseur   The Action of Case between Sarah Atkinson Plt. and David Leseur Deft. is continued at the Defts. cost.

Atkinson vs Taylor   The Action of Case between Sarah Atkinson Plt. and James Taylor Deft. is continued at the Defts. cost.

Doran vs Marchbanks   The Action on the Case between John Doran Admr. &c. of Julius King deceased Plt. and George Marchbanks Deft. is continued at the Plts. cost.

Taylor vs Lowe &c   The Action of Trespass on the Case between John Taylor Plt. and Thomas Lowe and Amey his wife Defts. is continued at the Defts. cost.

Spencer vs Quin   In the Action of Trespass between Peter Spencer Plt. and John Quin Deft. the Deft. pleads he oweth nothing and for tryal puts himself upon the Country and the Plt. likewise.

Allin vs Dickins   In the Action of Case between Samuell Allin Plt. and Thomas Dickins Deft. the Deft. failing to plead Judgment by nihil dicit is granted against him for what damages shall be recovered in this Suit to be discharged nevertheless if the Deft. shall plead at the next Court.

Cabbell vs Nolun   The Action of Debt between William Cabbell Assee. of John Quin Plt. and Thomas Nolun Deft. is continued at the Defts. cost.

Burton vs Quin   In the Action of Case between Nowell Burton Plt. and John Quin Deft. the Deft. pleads he oweth nothing and for tryal puts himself upon the Country and the Plt. likewise.

[120]   June Court 1729
Randolph vs Wotars   The Action of Debt between Thomas Randolph Plt. and William Wotars Deft. is continued at the Defts. cost.

Macon vs Wharton   The Action of Case between John Macon Plt. and Thomas Wharton Deft. is continued at the Defts. cost.

King vs Pattison   In the Action of Trespass on the Case between Martin King Plt. and David Pattison Junr. Deft. the following Jury are Sworn, Anthony Hoggat, Peter Ware, Nowel Burton, George Marchbanks, Leonard Ballew, William Womack, Robert Burton, John Harriss, Nathaniel Basset, William Woodson, Richard Oglesby, Fredorick Cox, who after some time return their Verdict in these words "Wee find for the Deft. Anthony Hoggat Foreman." which Verdict on the Defts. motion is ordered to be recorded and it is thereupon considered by the Court that the Deft. go hence without day and that he recover against the Plt. his costs by him in this behalf expended and a Lawyers Fee.

Christian vs Pattison   On the motion of John Christian a witness for David Pattison Junr. vs Martin King it is ordered that the said David do pay him for three days attendance according to Law with Costs.

Webb vs Pattison   On the motion of Henry Webb a witness for David Pattison Junr. vs Martin King it is ordered that the said David do pay him for five days attendance according to Law with Costs.

Napier vs Scot   The Action of Debt between Bouth Napier Plt. and Edward Scot Admr. &c. of Paul Green deceased Deft. is continued at the Defts. cost.

Towns vs Hoggat   The Action of Debt between William Towns Plt. and Anthony Hoggat Deft. is continued at the Plts. cost.

Nolun vs Wotars   The Action of Case between Thomas Nolun Plt. and William Wotars Deft. is continued at the Defts. cost.

Burton vs Woodson   The Action of Case between Robert Burton Plt. and William Woodson Executor &c. of Benjamin Woodson deceased Deft. is continued at the Defts. cost.

Rapene vs Bingley   The Action of Trespass on the Case between Anthony Rapene Plt. and Joseph Bingley Deft. is continued at the Plts. cost.

[121]   June Court 1729
Holland vs Saunders   The Action of Case between Michael Holland Plt. and Thomas Saunders Deft. is continued at the Plts. cost.

Hughes vs Lax   The Action of Case between Ashford Hughes Plt. and William Lax Deft. is dismist the Plt. not prosecuting the same.

Dickinson vs King   Frances Dickinson a witness for Martin King ads David Pattison Junr. having attended Seven days it is ordered that the said Martin do pay her for the same according to Law with Costs.

Turner vs Powell   In the Action of Detinue between James Turner Plt. and Richard Powell Deft. the following Jury are Sworn, Anthony Hoggat, Peter Ware, Nowel Burton, George Marchbanks, Leonard Ballew, William

Womack, Robert Burton, John Harriss, Nathll. Bassett, William Woodson, Richard Oglesby, Fredorick Cox, who after some time return with their Verdict which on the Defts. motion is ordered to be recorded and is as followeth "Wee find for the Deft. Anthony Hoggat Foreman." wherefore it is considered by the Court that the Deft. go hence without day and that he recover against the Plt. his costs by him in this behalf expended and a Lawyers Fee.

Laine vs Christian   The Action of Case between John Laine Plt. and John Christian Deft. is continued at the Plts. cost.

Waddill vs Edwards   The action of Case between William Waddil Plt. and Thomas Edwards Deft. is continued at the Defts. cost.

Martin vs Gunn   The Action of Trespass between Francis Martin Plt. and John Gunn Deft. is continued at the Plts. cost.

Thomas vs Gee   The Action of Case between Rowland Thomas Plt. and Gilbert Gee Deft. is continued at the Plts. cost.

Martin vs Rapene   The Action of Case between John Martin Plt. and Anthony Rapene Deft. is continued at the Defts. cost.

Bingley vs Rapene   The Action of Trespass between Joseph Bingley Plt. and Anthony Rapene Deft. is continued at the Defts. cost.

Cabbell vs Wade   The Action of Trespass on the Case between William Cabbell Plt. and Robert Wade Deft. is continued at the Defts. cost.

Dittoway vs Pleasants   The Action of Case between Barbary Dittoway Plt. and John Pleasants Deft. is dismist the Plt. not prosecuting the same.

[122]   June Court 1729
Chastain vs Pleasants   The Action of Case between Stephen Chastain Plt. and John Pleasants admr. &c. of William Howl deceased Deft. is dismist the Plt. not prosecuting the same.

Atkinson vs Lax   The action of Case between Henry Atkinson Plt. and William Lax Deft. is continued at the Plts. cost.

Dickins vs Macon   In the Action of Trespass on the Case between Thomas Dickins Plt. and John Macon Deft. the Defendt. pleads he oweth nothing and for tryall puts himself upon the Country and the Plt. likewise.

Chamberlaine vs Marchbanks   The Action of Debt between William Chamberlaine Plt. and George Marchbanks Deft. is dismist the Deft. consenting to pay the Costs.

Micheaux vs Raley   The Action of Debt between Jacob Micheaux Plt. and Charles Raley Deft. is dismist the Plt. not prosecuting the same.

Wade vs Davis   The action of Trespass on the Case between Robert Wade Plt. and William Davis Deft. is dismist the Plt. not prosecuting the same.

Fleming vs Pleasants   The action of Debt between John Fleming Plt. and John Pleasants Admr. &c. of William Howl deceased Defendant is continued.

Howls Invy. recorded   John Pleasants a Quaker Presents the Inventory and Appraisment of the Estate of William Howl deceased and makes his Solemn affirmacon thereto whereupon it is admitted to record.

Carnar vs Atkinson   The Action of Trespass on the Case between Susanna Carnar Plt. and Henry Atkinson Defendt. is continued.

Anderson vs Hoggat   In the Action on the Case between Mary Anderson Plt. and Philip Hoggat Deft. the Deft. failing to appear the Conditional Judgment granted at last Court against the Deft. and Daniel Stoner Gent. is confirmed for one pound fifteen shillings and it is thereupon considered that the Plt. do recover against the Deft. and Daniel Stoner Gent. Sherif the Sum of One pound fifteen shillings Currant money with Costs of this Suit & a Lawyers Fee.

Woodson vs Taylor   In the Action on the Case between John Woodson Plt. and John Taylor Deft. the Deft. appears and acknowledges himself indebted unto the Plt. in the sum of five hundred pounds of tobacco with Cask and conveniency whereupon it is ordered that the Deft. do pay the same unto the Plt. with Costs and a Lawyers Fee.

[123]   June Court 1729

Pavement vs Coleman   The Action of Case between Thomas Pavement Plt. and Samuell Coleman Deft. is continued at the Defts. cost.

Randolph vs Bullington   The action of Case between Thomas Randolph Plt. and John Bullington Deft. is continued to the next Court.

Taylor vs Swett   The Action of Trespass between James Taylor Plt. and Robert Swett Deft. is dismist the Plt. not prosecuting the same.

Dean vs Huson   The action of Debt between Richard Dean Plt. and John Huson Deft. is continued at the Defts. cost.

Briggs vs Swett   In the Action on the Case between Charles Brigs Plt. and Robert Swett Deft. Wm. Lansdon the Defts. common Bail comes into Court and consents that Judgment be entered against him for eight pounds three shillings and nine pence half penny Currant money wherefore it is considered by the Court that the Plt. do recover against the said William Lansdon the sum aforesaid with the Costs of this Suit & a Lawyers Fee.

Temple vs Burton   The Action of Trespass on the Case between Joseph Temple Plt. and Nowel Burton Deft. is continued at the Plts. cost.

Kenny &c. vs Dean   The Action of Debt between William Kenny & William Morriss Plts. and Richard Dean Deft. is continued at the Plts. cost.

Nolun vs Quin   In the Action of Trespass between Thomas Nolun Plt. and John Quin Deft. a Special imparlance is granted the Deft.

Nolun vs Quin   In the action of Debt between Thomas Nolun Plt. and John Quin Deft. Oyer is granted the Defendant.

Read vs Downie   The Action of Case between Clem Read Plt. and Robert Downie Deft. is continued at the Plts. Cost.

Grundy vs Utley   The action of Debt between Joseph Grundy Plt. and John Utley Deft. is continued at the Plts. Cost.

Wood vs Utley   The action of Case between Henry Wood Plt. and John Utley Deft. is continued.

Moseby vs Taylor   The action of Debt between Richard Moseby Plt. and John Taylor Deft. is continued at the Plts. cost.

[124]   June Court 1729
The action of Debt between William Chamberlaine Plt. and John Alexander Defendant is dismist the Plt. not prosecuting the same.

Jones vs Locket   In the Action on the Case between Rees Jones Plt. and Thomas Locket Deft. the Deft. failing to appear Judgment is granted against him & Daniel Stoner Gent. Sherif for what damages shall be recovered in this Suit to be discharged nevertheless if the Defendant shall appear at the next Court.

Tryce vs Utley   The Action of Trespass on the Case between James Tryce Plt. and John Utley Deft. is continued at the Plts. cost.

Alvis vs Sorrell   The Action of Debt between George Alvis Plt. and John Sorrell Deft. is continued at the Plts. cost.

Levins vs Farrar   In the Action on the Case between Richard Levins Plt. and William Farrar Deft. the Deft. failing to appear an Alias Capias is awarded against the Deft. returnable to the next Court.

Pruit vs Johnson   In the Action on the Case between Andrew Pruit Plt. and Charles Johnson Deft. an imparlance is granted the Defendant.

Bottom vs Fauquinou   In the Action on the Case between William Bottom Plt. and Daniel Fauquinou Defendt. John Bowie enters himself Special Bail for the Defendt. and on behalf of the Deft. acknowledges that there is due unto the Plt. thirty shillings Currant money, whereupon it is considered by the Court that the Plt. do recover against the Deft. thirty shillings Currant money with the Costs of this Suit and a Lawyers Fee.

The Action of Trespass on the Case between William Cabbell Plt. and John Moor Deft. is dismist the Plt. not prosecuting the same.

The Action of Trespass on the Case between Jacob Capoon Plt. and Francis Force Deft. is dismist neither party appearing.

Woodson vs Baize   In the Action of Trespass on the Case between John Woodson Plt. and Edward Baize Deft. the Deft. failing to appear Judgment is granted the Plt. against the Defendant and Thomas Murrell his Bail for what damages shall be recovered in this Suit to be discharged nevertheless if the Deft. shall appear at the next Court.

Ligon vs Watkins   The action of Case between Mathew Ligon Plt. and William Watkins Deft. is continued at the Plts. cost.

[125]   June Court 1729
May vs Jackson   In the Action on the Case between William May Plt.

and Joseph Jackson Deft. the Plt. having failed to file his declaration on the Defendants motion he is nonsuited and it is thereupon considered that the Deft. do recover against the Plt. five shillings Currant money and his costs by him in this behalf expended and a Lawyers Fee.

McCulloch vs Brooks   In the Action of Case between John McCulloch Plt. and Jacob Brookes Deft. the Deft. failing to appear an Alias Capias is awarded against him returnable to the next Court.

Smith vs Taylor   In the Action of Trespass on the Case between James Smith Plt. and John Taylor Deft. the Deft. appears and acknowledges himself indebted unto the Plt. forty shillings Currant money whereupon it is considered that the Plt. do recover against the Deft. forty shillings Currant money with the Costs of this Suit & a Lawyers Fee.

Taylor vs Lansdon   In the Action of Trespass between James Taylor Plt. and William Lansdon Deft. on the Defts. motion an imparlance is granted him.

The Action of Salt and Battery between Peter David Plt. and Anthony Sharrone Deft. is dismist neither party appearing.

Woodson vs Allin   In the Action of Case between Josiah & Stephen Woodson Executors &c. of Jacob Woodson Deceased Plts. and Samuell Allin Deft. the Defendant appears and acknowledges himself indebted unto the Plts. thirty shillings and seven pence Currant money whereupon it is considered that the Plaintifs do recover against the Defts. the said Sum with the Costs of this Suit and a Lawyers Fee.

Bellamys will   The last will & testament of John Bellamy deceased is presented in Court by Mary Bellamy and proved by the oaths of William Woodson & Elizabeth Cabbell, and on the motion of the said Mary and her performing what is usual in such Cases Certificate is granted her for obtaining Letters of Administration with the will annexed on the goods chattles rights and Credits of the said John Bellamy deceased in due form Amos Lad and Roger Powell Securities.

Ordered that Robert Adams, Nowell Burton, William Woodson, and Samuel Allin or any three of them being first Sworn by some Justice of the Peace do appraise the Estate of John Bellamy deceased.

Bellamy chooses her Guardian   Judith Bellamy comes into Court and chooses William Cabbell her Guardian who accepts the charge George Paine becoming his Security.

Hughes vs Turner   On the motion of Elizabeth Hughes a witness for James Turner vs Richard Powell it is ordered that the said James do pay her for two days attendance according to Law with Costs.

[126]   June Court 1729
Lyles vs Powell   On the motion of David Lyles a witness for Richard Powell ads James Turner it is ordered that the said Richard do pay him for three days attendance according to Law with Costs. One day only to be taxed in the bill of Costs.

Then the Court adjourned to the third Tuesday in next month.
Test. Henry Wood ClCur.

****

At a Court held for Goochland County the third Tuesday in July being the fifteenth day of the month Annoq Domi. 1729. Present. William Mayo, Allin Howard, George Paine, William Cabbell Gent. Justices.

Taylor vs Saunders   The Action of Trespass on the Case between John Taylor Plt. and John Saunders Deft. is continued at the Defts. cost.

Dale vs Gunn   The action of Case between Christopher Dale Plt. and John Gunn Deft. is continued at the Plts. cost.

Capoon vs Sublet   The Action of Case between Jacob Capoon Plt. and Peter Lewis Sublet Deft. is continued at the Plts. cost.

Burton vs Watkins   The Action of Debt between Nowel Burton Assee. of Allin Frazer Assee. of Michael Canady Plt. and William Watkins Deft. is continued at the Plts. cost.

Ware vs Saunders   The Action of Case between Susanna Ware Plt. and Thomas Saunders Deft. is continued at the Plts. cost.

Jeffs vs Martin   The Action of Case between John Jeffs Plt. and John Martin Deft. is continued at the Plts. cost.

Alexander vs Chandler   The Action of Case between John Alexander Plt. and Joell Chandler Deft. is continued at the Plts. cost.

Dean vs Napier   The Action of Case between Richard Dean Plt. and

Robert Napier Junr. Deft. is continued at the Plts. cost.

[127] July Court 1729
Westbrook vs Clark   The Action of Case between James Westbrook and Frances his wife Executrix &c. of Edward Bass Deceased Plts. and John Clark Deft. is dismist the Plts. not prosecuting the same.

Spencer vs Gallemore   The Action of Case between Samuell Spencer Plt. and William Gallemore Deft. is continued at the Plts. cost.

Hughes vs Cone   The Action of Case between Robert Hughes Plt. and John Cone Deft. is continued.

Hughes vs Dean   The Action of Case between Robert Hughes Plt. and Richard Dean Deft. is continued at the Defts. cost.

Present. James Holman Gent.

Woodson &c. vs Woodson   The Action of Trespass on the Case between Robert Woodson & James Holman Plts. and William Woodson Deft. is continued.

Hughes vs Macon   The Action of Case between Stephen Hughes Plt. and John Macon Deft. is continued at the Plts. cost.

Macon vs Hughes   The Action of Debt between John Macon Plt. and Stephen Hughes Deft. is continued at the Defts. cost.

White vs Webber   The Action of Case between Samuel White Plt. and Philip Webber Deft. is continued at the Plts. cost.

Baize vs Moor   The Action of Case between Edward Baize Plt. and William Moor Deft. is continued at the Plts. cost.

Moss vs Taylor   The Action of Trespass on the Case between Thomas Moss Plt. and James Taylor Deft. is continued at the Defts. cost.

Clark vs Cannon   The Action of Case between Christopher Clark Plt. and William Cannon Deft. is continued at the Defts. cost.

Clark vs Gallemore   The Action of Case between Christopher Clark Plt. and William Gallemore Deft. is dismist the Plt. not prosecuting the same.

Atkinson vs Benning The Action of Trespass between Sarah Atkinson Plt. and Anthony Benning Deft. is continued at the Plts cost.

Atkinson vs Leseur The Action of Trespass between Sarah Atkinson Plt. and David Lesseur Deft. is continued at the Plts. cost.

Atkinson vs Taylor The Action of Trespass between Sarah Atkinson Plt. and James Taylor Deft. is continued at the Plts. cost.

[128] July Court 1729
Doran vs Marchbks The Action of Case between John Doran Admr. &c. of Julius King deceased Plt. and George Marchbanks Deft. is continued at the Defts. cost.

Taylor vs Lowe The Action of Trespass on the Case between John Taylor Plt. and Thomas Lowe and Amey his wife Defendants is continued at the Plts. cost.

Spencer vs Quin The Action of Trespass on the Case between Peter Spencer Plt. and John Quin Deft. is continued.

Allin vs Dickins The Action of Case between Samuell Allin Plt. and Thomas Dickins Deft. is continued at the Defts. cost.

Cabbell &c. vs Nolun The Action of Debt between William Cabbell Assee. of John Quin Plt. and Thomas Nolun Deft. the Deft. Pleads he oweth nothing and for tryal puts himself upon the Country and the Plt. likewise.

Burton vs Quin The Action of Case between Nowel Burton Plt. and John Quin Deft. is continued.

Quin vs May The Action of Case between John Quin Plt. and William May Deft. is continued at the Plts. cost.

Randolph vs Wotars The Action of Debt between Thomas Randolph Plt. and Thomas Wharton Deft. is continued at the Plts. cost.

Macon vs Wharton The Action of Case between John Macon Plt. and Thomas Wharton Deft. is continued at the Plts. cost.

Utley vs Napier In the Action of Debt between John Utley Plt. and Bouth Napier Deft. Oyer is granted the Deft.

Utley vs Napier   In the Action of Debt between John Utley Plt. and Bouth Napier Deft. Oyer is granted the Defendt.

Harding's deed to Thomas   Thomas Harding acknowledges a deed with the Livery of Seizin endorsed from himself to Edward Thomas to be his Act and Deed and it is thereupon admitted to record then Mary wife of the said Thomas Harding (she being first privately examined) relinquishes her right of Dower in the land by the said Deed conveyed which is also admitted to record.

Napier vs Scot   The Action of Debt between Bouth Napier Plt. and Edward Scot Admr. &c. of Paul Green Deft. is continued at the Plts. cost.

Burton vs Woodson   The Action of Case between Robert Burton Plt. and William Woodson Executor &c. of Benjamin Woodson deceased Deft. is continued at the Plts. cost.

[129]   July Court 1729
Towns vs Hoggatt   In the Action of Debt between William Towns Plt. and Anthony Hoggat Deft. the following Jury are Sworn Richard Dean, Robert Burton, William Woodson, John Utley, Thomas Christian, John Mcbride, William Lansdon, Nowell Burton, Ashford Hughes, James Taylor, Peter Baze, who after some time return with their Verdict which on the Defts. motion is admitted to record and is as followeth "Wee find for the Deft. Richard Dean Foreman." wherefore it is considered by the Court that the Deft. go hence without day and that he recover against the Plt. his Costs by him in this behalf expended and a Lawyers Fee.

Nolun vs Wotars   In the Action on the Case between Thomas Nolun Plt. and William Wotars Deft. the Arguments on the Speciall Verdict being heard and by the Court of Our Lord the King here fully understood it seems to the Justices here that the Law arising thereon is with the Deft. wherefore it is considered that the Defendt. go hence without day and that he recover against the Plt. his Costs by him in this behalf expended and a Lawyers Fee.

Rapene vs Bingley   The Action of Trespass on the Case between Anthony Rapene Plt. and Joseph Bingley Deft. is continued at the Defendants cost.

Holland vs Saunders   In the Action on the Case between Michael Holland Plt. and Thomas Saunders Deft. the Plt. having formerly obtained a Conditional Judgment against the Deft. and Daniel Stoner

Gent. Sheriff, the following Jury are now sworn to enquire of the damages Richard Dean, Robert Adams, Robert Burton, William Woodson, John Utley, Thomas Christian, John Mcbride, William Lansdon, Nowell Burton, Ashford Hughes, James Taylor, Peter Baize, who after some time return with their Verdt. which on the Plts. motion is admitted to record and is as followeth "Wee find for the Plt. twenty seven Shillings and ten pence Damages. Richard Dean Foreman." Wherefore it is Considered by the Court that the Plt. do recover against the Deft. and Daniel Stoner Gent. Sherif the Sum of twenty seven shillings and ten

[130]   July Court 1729
ten pence Damages by the Jurors aforesaid in their said Verdict assessed with the Costs of this Suit and a Lawyers Fee.

Laine vs Christian   In the Action on the Case between John Laine Plt. and John Christian Deft. the Plt. files a new declaration, the Deft. files Plea and the Plt. takes issue thereon.

Waddill vs Edwards   The Action of Case between William Waddill Plt. and Thomas Edwards is continued at the Plts. Cost

Towns vs Hoggat   In the Action of Trespass on the Case between William Towns Plt. and Anthony Hoggatt Deft. Thomas Randolph, William Mayo, and George Paine Gent. or any two of them are appointed to examine State & settle the Severall accts. in dispute on Friday the eighth day of August next at the House of Thomas Randolph aforesaid and it is ordered (if either party fail to appear) that upon the other partys producing his papers and Evidences, the Auditors do account ex parte, and that their report be recorded and Judgment entered thereon.
   Ordered that the Clerk issue Supœnas for the witnesses to attend at the Audit.

Hoggat vs Towns   In the action on the Case between Anthony Hoggat Plt. and William Townes Deft. Thomas Randolph, William Mayo, and George Paine Gent. or any two of them are appointed to examined State and settle the severall accounts in dispute on Friday the eighth day of August next at the House of Thomas Randolph aforesaid and it is ordered (if either party fail to appear) that upon the other partys producing his papers and Evidences, the Auditors do account ex parte, and that their Report be Recorded and Judgmt. entered thereon.
   Ordered that the Court issue Supœnas for the witnesses to attend at the Audit.

[131]   July Court 1729
Martin vs Gunn   The Action of Trespass between Francis Martin Plt. and John Gunn Deft. is continued at the Defts. cost.

Thomas vs Gee   In the Action on the Case between Rowland Thomas Plt. and Gilbert Gee Deft. time is granted the Plt. to mend his declaration.

Martin vs Rapene   The Action of Case between John Martin Plt. and Anthony Rapene Deft. is continued at the Plts. Cost.

Bingley vs Rapene   The Action of Trespass between Joseph Bingley Plt. and Anthony Repene Deft. is continued at the Plts. Cost.

Cabbell vs Wade   In the Action of Trespass on the Case between William Cabbell Plt. and Robert Wade Deft. the Deft. demurs generally and time is granted the Plt. to mend his declaration.

Atkinson vs Lax   In the Action of Case between Henry Atkinson Plt. and William Lax Deft. the parties submit themselves to the Court for tryall whereupon it is Considered that the Plt. do recover against the Defendt. two pounds Current money with Costs and a Lawyers Fee.

Williams vs Ware   In the Action on the Case between Edward Williams Plt. and Peter Ware Deft. the following Jury are Sworn   Richard Dean, Robert Adams, Robert Burton, William Woodson, John Utley, Thomas Christian, John Mcbride, William Lansdon, Nowell Burton, Ashford Hughes, James Taylor, Peter Baize, who after some time return their Verdict which on the Plts. motion is admitted to Record and is as followeth "Wee find for the Plt. ten pounds Currant money   Richard Dean Foreman." wherefore it is considered by the Court that the Plt. do recover against the Deft. the Sum of ten pounds Currant money damages by the Jurors aforesaid in their said Verdict assessed with the Costs of this Suit and a Lawyers Fee.

Dickins vs Macon   The Action of Trespass on the Case between Thomas Dickins Plt. and John Macon Deft. is continued at the Plts. Cost.

Fleming vs Pleasants   The Action of Debt between John Fleming Plt. and John Pleasants Administrator &c. of William Howl deceased Deft. is continued at the Plts. cost.

[132]   July Court 1729
Carnar vs Atkinson   The Action of Trespass on the Case between

Susanna Carnar Plaintif and Henry Atkinson Defendt. is Continued at the Plts. Cost.

Pavement vs Coleman   The Action of Case between Thomas Pavement Plt. and Samuell Coleman Defendt. is Continued at the Plts. Cost.

Randolph vs Bullington   The Action of Case between Thomas Randolph Plt. and John Bullington Deft. is continued at the Plts. Cost.

Dean vs Huson   The Action of Debt between Richard Dean Plt. and John Huson Defendt. is continued at the Plaintifs Cost.

Temple vs Burton   In the Action of Trespass on the Case between Joseph Temple Plt. and Nowell Burton Deft. an Imparlance is granted the Defendant.

Kenny &c. vs Dean   In the Action of Debt between William Kenny and William Morris Plts. and Richard Dean Defendt. the Deft. acknowledges himself indebted unto the Plts. in the Sum of eight hundred and ninety two pounds of sweet scented Tobacco whereupon it is considered by the Court that the Plaintifs do recover against the Defendant. the said Sum of eight hundred and ninety two pounds of Sweet scented Tobacco with Cask and Conveniency with Costs and an Attornys Fee.

Nolun vs Quin   In the Action of Trespass between Thomas Nolun Plt. and John Quin Deft. time is granted the Plt. to mend his declaration.

Nolun vs Quin   In the Action of Debt between Thomas Nolun Plt. and John Quin Defendt. the Deft. failing to plead Judgment by nihil dicit is granted against him for what damages shall be recovered in this Suit to be discharged if the Defendant Pleads at the next Court.

Read vs Downie   In the Action of Case between Clem Read Plt. and Robert Downie Deft. William Cabbell enters himself Special Bail for the Deft. and an imparlance is granted him.

Grundy vs Utley   In the Action of Debt between Joseph Grundy Plt. and John Utley Defendt. the Deft. acknowledges himself indebted unto the Plt. in the Sum of two Pounds ten shillings Currant money and

[133]   July Court 1729
one hundred and fifty one pounds of Tobacco whereupon it is considered by the Court that the Plt. do recover against the Deft. the said Sum of two

pounds ten shillings Currant money and one hundred and fifty one pounds of Tobacco with costs and ten Shillings for a Lawyers Fee.

Wood vs Utley   The Action of Case between Henry Wood Plt. and John Utley Defendant is continued.

Moseby vs Taylor   In the Action of Debt between Richard Moseby Plaintif and John Taylor Defendt. time is granted the Plt. to mend his Declaration.

Jones vs Locket   In the Action on the Case between Rice Jones Plaintif and Thomas Locket Deft. the Deft. failing to appear the Conditional Judgment granted at last Court against the Defendant and Daniel Stoner Gent. Sheriff is confirmed for so much Damages as shall be found upon executing a writ of Inquiry at the next Court of which the Sheriff is ordered to give the Defendt. notice by serving him with a Copy of this Order.

Tryce vs Utley   In the Action of Trespass on the Case between James Tryce Plaintif and John Utley Defendt. the Defendant acknowledges himself indebted unto the Plt. in the Sum of five pounds Currant money whereupon it is considered by the Court that the Plt. do recover against the Deft. the said Sum of five pounds Currant money with Costs and an Attornys Fee.

Alvis vs Sorrell   In the Action of Debt between George Alvis Plt. and John Sorrell Defendt. the Deft. not appearing and the Sheriff having failed to return Bail Judgment is granted the Plt. against the Deft. and Daniel Stoner Gent. Sheriff for what damages shall be recovered in this Suit to be discharged nevertheless if the Deft. appears at the next Court.

Levins vs Farrar   The Action of Case between Richard Levins Plaintif and William Farrar Deft. is dismist the Plt. not prosecuting the same.

Pruit vs Johnson   The Action of Case between Andrew Pruit Plaintif and Charles Johnson Defendt. is continued at the Defendants Cost.

[134]   July Court 1729
Woodson vs Baize   The Action of Trespass on the Case between John Woodson Plaintif and Edward Baize Defendt. is continued at the Plts. Cost.

Ligon vs Watkins   The Action of Case between Mathew Ligon Plaintif and William Watkins Defendt. is dismist the Plt. not prosecuting the same.

McCulloch vs Brooks   In the Action of Case between John McCulloch Plt. and Jacob Brooks Deft. the Defendant failing to appear at the return of the Alias Capias a Pluries Capias is awarded against him returnable to the next Court.

Taylor vs Lansdon   The Action of Trespass between James Taylor Plaintif and William Lansdon Defendant is continued at the Plts. Cost.

Holland vs Jeffs   In the Action of the Case between Michaell Holland Plaintif and John Jeffs Defendt. Edward Scott comes into Court and on behalf of the Defendant consents to pay two pounds twelve shillings in Tobacco at ten shillings Pr. Cent. with which the Plt. being satisfied it is therefore considered by the Court that the Plt. do recover against the said Edward Scot five hundred and twenty pounds of Tobacco with the Costs of this Suit and a Lawyers Fee.

~~Collins vs Perrin~~   The Action of Trespass between Mathew Collins Plt. and George Perrin Defendt. is dismist neither party appearing.

Dickins vs Fauquinou   The Action of Case between Thomas Dickins Plaintif and Daniel Fauquinou Deft. is continued at the Plts. Cost.

Martin vs Woodson   The Action of Case between John Martin Plaintif and Joseph Woodson Executor &c. of John Woodson deceased Defendt. is continued at the Plts. Cost.

Martin vs Woodson   The Action of Case between John Martin Plt. and Joseph Woodson Defendt. is continued at the Plts. Cost.

Lad vs Cannon   In the Action of Case between Amos Lad Plt. and William Cannon Defendt. the Sherif having made return that the Defendt. is not to be found and he failing to appear an Alias Capias is awarded against

[135]   July Court 1729
him returnable to the next Court.

Dean vs Cragwarr   In the Action of Trespass on the Case between Richard Dean Plaintif and William Cragwarr Defendt. the Plt. failed to file his declaration on the Defts. motion he is Nonsuited and it is thereupon considered by the Court that the Deft. recover against the Plt. five shillings Currant money damages with the Costs of this Suit and a Lawyers Fee.

Cox vs Dean   In the Action of Trespass between Fredorick Cox Plaintif and Richard Dean Deft. an Imparlance is granted the Defendt.

The Petition of Elizabeth Webster against John Burgess is dismist the Petitioner not prosecuting the same.

Huson vs Bingley   In the Action of Trespass between John Huson Plt. and Mathew Bingley Deft. the Sheriff having made return that the Defendant is not to be found and he failing to appear an Alias Capias is awarded against him returnable to the next Court.

Johnson vs Quin   The Action of Case between Daniel Johnson Plaintif and John Quin Defendt. is continued at the Plts. Cost.

Taylor vs Quin   The Action of Debt between James Taylor Plaintif and John Quin Defendt. is continued at the Plts. Cost.

Woodson vs Moreman   The Action of Case between John Woodson Plaintif and Andrew Moreman Defendt. is continued at the Plts. Cost.

Bumpuss vs Moreman   In the Action of Trespass on the Case between Samuell Bumpuss Assignee of Robert Bumpuss Plt. and Andrew Moreman Defendant William Cabbell enters himself Special Bail for the Defendt. and an imparlance is granted him.

Napier vs Cox   In the Action of Case between Robert Napier Junr. Plaintif and Bartholomew Cox Defendant time is granted the Plt. to mend his declaration.

[136]   July Court 1729
Hook vs Maxey   The Action of Case between James Hook Plaintif and John Maxey Defendt. is continued at the Plts. Cost.

Wiles vs Atkinson   The Action of Debt between Luke Wiles Plt. and Sarah Atkinson and Stephen Hughes Executor and Executrix &c. of Thomas Atkinson Deceased Deft. is continued at the Defendants Cost.

Pennington vs Baily   The Action of Trespass between Paul Pennington Plt. and Henry Baily Deft. is continued at the Plts. Cost.

Randolph vs Lax   In the Action of Trespass between Thomas Randolph Plt. and William Lax Defendt. the Deft. pleads not Guilty and for tryall puts himself upon the Country and the Plt. likewise.

Marchbanks vs Croom   In the Action of Case between George Marchbanks Plaintif and Daniel Croom Defendt. an imparlance is granted the Defendt.

Woodson vs Williams   On the motion of Joseph Woodson a Witness for Edward Williams vs Peter Ware it is ordered that the said Edward do pay him for one days attendance thirty pounds of Tobacco with Costs.

Woodson vs Williams   On the motion of Sarah Woodson a witness for Edward Williams vs Peter Ware it is ordered that the said Edward do pay her for two days attendance sixty pounds of Tobacco with Costs.

Sorrell vs Williams   On the motion of John Sorrell a witness for Edward Williams vs Peter Ware it is ordered that the said Edward do pay him for one days attendance thirty pounds of Tobacco with Costs.

Lewis vs Williams   On the motion of John Lewis a witness for Edward Williams vs Peter Ware it is ordered that the said Edward do pay him for two days attendance sixty pounds of Tobacco with Costs.

Saunders vs Ware   On the motion of William Saunders a witness for Peter Ware ads Edward Williams it is ordered that the said Peter do pay him for three days attendance ninety pounds of Tobacco with Costs.

[137]   July Court 1729
Cox vs Ware   On the motion of Nicholas Cox a witness for Peter Ware ads Edward Williams it is ordered that the said Peter do pay him for two days attendance sixty pounds of Tobacco with Costs.

Bellamy chooses her Guardian   On the motion of Mary Bellamy she is permitted to choose William Cabbell her Guardian who accepts the Charge George Paine enters himself Security.

The Action of Case between Edward Baize Plaintif and John Woodson Deft. is dismist the Plt. not prosecuting the same.

Wiles vs Hughes   The Action of Trespass on the Case between Luke Wiles Plt. and Stephen Hughes Deft. is continued at the Defendts. Cost.

The Action of Case between John Martin Plt. and Joseph Woodson Executor &c. of John Woodson deceased Deft. is dismist neither party appearing.

The Action of Debt between Edward Scot Plt. and Thomas Applebury Defendt. is dismist the Plt. not prosecuting the same.

Salmon vs Edwards   The Action of Case between Thomas Salmon Plaintif and Thomas Edwards Deft. is continued at the Plts. Cost.

Hughes's Ordinary Lycence   On the motion of Stephen Hughes Lycence is granted him to keep Ordinary in this County. William Cabbell and Henry Wood entring themselves Securities.

Then the Court adjourned to the third Tuesday in next month.

****

At a Court called for Goochland County the thirty first day of July 1729 for the Tryall of John Innis.

[138]   [July/August Court 1729]
Present. Thomas Randolph, William Mayo, George Paine, William Cabbell Gent. Justices.

John Innis being brought to the Barr and accused with Stealing a side of tanned Leather of the Value of nine pence from John Sorrell upon hearing the Witnesses and the said John Innis, the Court are of Opinion he is guilty of the Fact, and it is thereupon ordered that he receive on his bare back twenty lashes at the Common whipping post well laid on and that he be thereafter discharged, paying Fees.

****

At a Court held for Goochland County the third Tuesday in August being the nineteenth day of the month Annoq Domini 1729. Present William Mayo, Allin Howard, George Paine, William Cabbell Gent. Justices.

Thomas's negro judged   Roger a negro boy belonging to Phillip Thomas is judged to be eleven years old.

Present John Woodson Gent.

Lansdon sworn Constable   William Lansdon is sworn Constable in the stead of Mathew Bingley.

Absent John Woodson Gent.

Woodson sworn Surveyor   John Woodson Gent. produces a Comission from the Honble. John Robinson Esqr. Surveyor General of this Colony to be an Assisting Surveyor to William Mayo Gent. Principal Surveyor of this County which being read William Mayo and Allin Howard Gent. Administer the Oaths appointed to be taken by Act of Parliament instead of the Oaths of Allegiance and Supremacy, the Oath appointed to be taken by an Act of Parliament made in the first year of the Reign of His late

[139]   August Court 1729
late Majesty King George the First intituled an Act for the further Security of his Majesty's Person and Government and the Succession of the Crown in the Heirs of the late Princess Sophia being Protestants and for extinguishing the hopes of the Pretended Prince of Wales and his open and Secret abettors, unto John Woodson Gent. who Subscribes the Test and takes the Oath of a Surveyor.

Present John Woodson Gent.

Phenix vs Towns   On the motion of Abraham Phenix of Hanover County a witness for William Townes vs Anthony Hoggatt it is ordered that the said William do pay him for one days attendance and for coming and returning Thirty three miles once one hundred and fifty nine pounds of Tobacco with Costs.

Lewis's deed to Cocke   William Lewis acknowledges a deed with the Livery of Seizin endorsed from himself to James Cocke to be his Act and Deed and it is thereupon admitted to record, then Mary wife of the said William (she being first privately examined) relinquishes her right of Dower in the Land by this deed conveyed which is also admitted to Record.

Ogee's deed to Woodson   Mathew Ogee acknowledges a deed with the Livery of Seizin endorsed from himself to Samuel Woodson to be his Act and Deed and it is thereupon admitted to record then Anne wife of the said Mathew (She being first privately examined) relinquishes her right of Dower in the Land by the said Deed conveyed which is also admitted to record.

Sanders deed to Dickins   John Sanders acknowledges a Deed with the Livery of Seizin endorsed from himself to Thomas Dickins to be his Act and Deed and it is thereupon admitted to record.

Taylor vs Sanders   In the Action of Trespass on the Case between John Taylor Plt. and John Saunders Defendt. the following Jury are Sworn. Nowell Burton, David Pattison, William Lansdon, Thomas Christian, John Webb, Thomas Murrell, Ashford Hughes, Frodorick Cox, John Prier, Joell Chandler, James Taylor, William Woodson who after some time bring in their Verdict which on the Plts. motion is admitted to record and is as followeth "Wee find for the Plt.

[140]   August Court 1729
Plt. twenty Shillings Currant money. Nowell Burton Foreman." whereupon it is considered by the Court that the Plt. do recover against the Defendant twenty shillings Currant money damages by the Jurors aforesaid in their said Verdict assessed and two hundred and forty pounds of Tobacco for Costs.

   Present Thomas Randolph Gent.

Lewis vs Saunders   On the motion of William Lewis a witness for John Saunders ads John Taylor it is ordered that the said John Saunders do pay him for three days attendance ninety pounds of Tobacco with Costs.

Scrug's vs Saunders   On the motion of John Scruggs a witness for John Saunders ads John Taylor it is ordered that the said John Saunders do pay him for three days attendance ninety pounds of Tobacco with Costs.

Reed vs Taylor   On the motion of Thomas Reed a witness for John Taylor vs John Saunders it is ordered that the said John Taylor do pay him for two days attendance Sixty pounds of Tobacco with Costs.

Hathaway vs Taylor   On the motion of David Hathaway a witness for John Taylor vs John Saunders it is ordered that the said John Taylor do pay him for three days attendance ninety pounds of Tobacco with Costs.

Stoveall vs Taylor   On the motion of Thomas Stoveall a witness for John Taylor vs John Saunders it is ordered that the said John Taylor do pay him for three days attendance ninety pounds of Tobacco with Costs.

Jeffs vs Martin   In the Action of Case between John Jeffs Plt. and John Martin Defendant the Sheriff having returned on the Pluries Capias that the Defendant is not to be found and he failing to appear a Pluries Capias is awarded against him returnable to the next Court.

Spencer vs Gallemore   The Action of Case between Samuell Spencer Plt. and William Gallemore Defendant is dismist the Plt. not prosecuting the same.

[141]   August Court 1729
Hughes vs Dean   In the Action of Case between Robert Hughes Plt. and Richard Dean Defendt. the Auditors make the following report which on the Plts. motion is admitted to record.

Dr. Richard Dean	
To 1 hhd Tobo. & Cask Nt.	749
To Ashford Hughes note	120
To pd. by William Cragwarr more to Cragwarr further	85
	42½
	996½
Cr.	
By his bill 69/3 @ 2d	415½
By 2 Levys	115
By Secretary's Fees	80
By Clerks Fees	59
By Sheriffs Fees	20
By a note for Costs on Askew exo.	51
By Quit rents 170 Acres	41
By Costs on Stoners Warrt.	10
	791½
By ballance due to R Hughes	205
	996½

"Pursuant to an order of Goochland County Court Wee have Settled the above account and find the ballance due to Robert Hughes to be two hundred and five pounds of Tobacco the value of which wee refer to be settled by the Court. Witness our hands the 26th. day of June 1729. Geo. Payne. Willm. Cabbell." the Court are of Opinion the Tobacco shall be valued at two pence Pr. pound and it is thereupon Considered that the Plt. do recover against the Defendant thirty four shillings and two pence Currant Money with the Costs of this Suit and a Lawyers Fee.

Powell vs Hughes   On the motion of Roger Powell a Witness for Robert Hughes vs Richard Dean it is ordered that the said Robert do pay him for three days attendance 90 lbs. of Tobacco with Costs.

Cragwarr vs Hughes   On the motion of William Cragwarr a Witness for Robert Hughes vs Richard Dean it is ordered that the said Robert do pay him for three days attendance ninety pounds of Tobacco with Costs.

Hughes vs Hughes   On the motion of Ashford Hughes a Witness for Robert Hughes vs Richard Dean it is ordered that the said Robert do pay him for three days attendance ninety pounds of Tobacco with Costs.

[142]   August Court 1729
Easly's deed to Kilpatrick   Warham Easly acknowledges a deed with the Livery of Seizin endorsed from himself to Alexander Kilpatrick to be his Act and deed and it is thereupon admitted to record, then Sarah wife of the said Warham (She being first privately examined) relinquishes her right of Dower in the Land by the said Deed conveyed which is also admitted to Record.

Easly's deed to Cardwell   Warham Easly acknowledges a deed with the Livery of Seizin endorsed from himself to Thomas Cardwell to be his Act and deed and it is thereupon admitted to record, then Sarah wife of the said Warham (she being first privately examined) relinquishes here right of Dower in the Land by the said Deed conveyed which is also admitted to Record.

Napier's deed to Randolph   Bouth Napier acknowledges his Deeds with the Livery of Seizin endorsed on each Deed from himself to Thomas Randolph to be his Acts and Deeds and they are thereupon admitted to record, then Sarah wife of the said Bouth (She being first privately examined) relinquishes her right of Dower in the land conveyed by each Deed which is also admitted to Record.

Napier's deed to Webber   Bouth Napier acknowledges Deeds of Lease and Release and a bond from himself to Phillip Webber to be his severall Acts and Deeds and they are thereupon admitted to record, then Sarah wife of the said Bouth (She being first privately examined) relinquishes her right of Dower in the land by the said Deeds conveyed which is also admitted to Record.

Moreman's deed to Wade   Andrew Moreman acknowledges a Deed with the Liver of Seizin endorsed from himself to Robert Wade to be his Act and Deed and it is thereupon admitted to record then Susanna Wife of the said Andrew (She being first privately examined) relinquishes her right of Dower in the Land by the said Deed conveyed which is also admitted to Record.

[143]   August Court 1729
Dale vs Gunn   The Action of Case between Christopher Dale Plt. and John Gunn Defendant is continued at the Plts. Cost.

Capoon vs Sublett   In the Action on the Case between Jacob Capoon Plt. and Peter Lewis Sublett Defendant at May Court last Judgment was Confirmed against the Defendant and Daniel Stoner Gent. Sheriff for what damages the Plt. should recover upon executing a writ of inquiry of Damages and thereupon the following Jury are now Sworn. Nowel Burton, John Prior, Joell Chandler, William Woodson, Thomas Christian, Ashford Hughes, John Harriss, William Lansdon, James Taylor, Fredorick Cox, John Webb, David Pattison, who after some time bring in their Verdict which on the Plts. motion is ordered to be recorded and is as followeth "Wee find for the Plt. one pounds thirteen shillings and Six pence Currant money Nowell Burton Foreman." wherefore it is Considered by the Court that the Plt. do recover against the Defendant and Daniel Stoner Gent. Sheriff the said Sum of one pound thirteen shillings and Six pence Currant money damages by the Jurors aforesaid in their said Verdict assessed and the Costs of this Suit with a Lawyers Fee.

Surveyor of the road   David Walker is appointed Surveyor of the Road from the Court house unto the back road above Major Bollings mill and it is ordered that the severall male labouring titheables of Joseph Woodson, Henry Adkins, William May, Richard Cocke, William Moor, Edward Curd, Abraham Perkins, and John Moor do assist in Clearing the said road.

Ware vs Saunders   The Action of Case between Susanna Ware Plt. and Thomas Saunders Defendant is continued.

Dean vs Napier   The Action of Case between Richard Dean Plt. and Robert Napier Junr. Defendant is continued at the Plts. Cost.

Hughes vs Cone   In the Action on the Case between Robert Hughes Plt. and John Cone Defendant George Paine and William Cabbell Gent. are appointed to examine state and settle the severall accounts in dispute between them

[144]   August Court 1729
them and to report their proceedings therein to the next Court.

Woodson &c vs Woodson   The Action of Trespass on the Case between Robert Woodson and James Holman Plt. and William Woodson Defendant is continued at the Plts. Cost.

Hughes vs Macon   In the Action on the Case between Stephen Hughes Plt. and John Macon Defendant the following Jury are Sworn   Thomas Christian, John Webb, Fredorick Cox, John Prier, Joell Chandler, William Woodson, David Pattison, James Taylor, John Harriss, George Marchbanks, Andrew Moreman, William Lansdon, who after some time bring in their Verdict, the Defendt. files his reasons why the said Verdict ought not to be recorded, the arguments whereon are referred to be heard at the next court.

Macon vs Hughes   In the Action of Debt between John Macon Plt. and Stephen Hughes Defendant the following Jury are Sworn   Thomas Christian, John Webb, Fredorick Cox, John Prier, Joell Chandler, William Woodson, David Pattison, James Taylor, John Harriss, George Marchbanks, Andrew Moreman, William Lansdon, At the arising of the Court the Jury not agreed it is ordered that the Sheriff do keep them together untill they have agreed upon their Verdict, that they Seal up the same and deliver it to the Sheriff and that they appear at next Court to present the same.

White vs Webber   In the Action on the Case between Samll. White Plt. and Phillip Webber Defendant the Parties Submitt themselves to the Court for tryall whereupon it is considered that the Plt. do recover against the Deft. ten bushells of Indian Corn, thirty shillings or the value thereof in Goods a well fixt Musquet or Fuzee of the value of twenty shillings, and eight shillings and nine pence Currant money with Costs and an Attorneys Fee.

Moss vs Taylor   In the Action of Trespass on the Case between Thomas Moss Plt. and James Taylor Deft. the Defendant failing to plead on the Plts. motion Judgment by nihil dicit is granted against him for what damages

[145]   August Court 1729
damages shall be recovered in this Suit to be discharged nevertheless if the Defendant Pleads at the next Court.

Clerk vs Cannon   The Action of Case between Christopher Clerk Plt. and William Cannon Defendant is continued.

Taylor vs Lowe &c   In the Action of Trespass on the Case between John Taylor Plt. and Thomas Lowe & Amey his wife Defts. on the Defts. motion leave is granted them to plead severall matters, and thereupon they file Pleas, and time is granted the Plaintif to reply.

Spencer vs Quin   In the Action of Trespass on the Case between Peter Spencer Plt. and John Quin defendant the Parties Submitt themselves to the Court for tryall whereupon it is considered that the Plt. do recover against the Deft. three hundred five & a half pounds of Tobacco with Costs and an Attornys Fee.

Allin vs Dickins   The Action of Case between Samuell Allin Plt. and Thomas Dickins Defendant is dismist the Plt. not prosecuting the same.

Then the Court adjourned to the third Tuesday in next month.

****

At a Court held for Goochland County the third Tuesday in September being the Sixteenth day of the month Annoq Domini 1729. Present. John Woodson, Allin Howard, William Cabbell, James Holman Gent. Justices.

Robinson to be listed   On the Petition of Isaac Robinson it is ordered that he be added to the lists of titheables.

Scots Negro's judged   These Negroes belong to Edward Scott are judged to be of the following ages, Jupiter seven, and Betty nine years of age.

[146]   September Court 1729
Tuly's Negro judged   Hannah a Negro girl belonging to John Tuly is Judged to be eight years of age.

Bradleys deed to Randolph   Joseph Bradley acknowledges a deed from himself to Isham Randolph to be his act and deed and it is thereupon admitted to Record.

Surveyor of the Road   Stephen Chastain is appointed Surveyor of the Road from Fine Creek to the County line below the lower Manakin Creek.

Randolph vs Wotars   The Action of Debt between Thomas Randolph Plt. and William Wotars Defendt. is continued.

Burton vs Watkins   In the Action of Debt between Nowell Burton Assee. of Allin Frazer Assee. of Michaell Canady Plt. and William Watkins Defendant at May Court a writ if inquiry of damages was awarded and therefore the following Jury are now Sworn. Anthony Hoggat, John Mcbride, Thomas Nolun, Stephen Woodson, Robert Burton, John Christian, Peter Ware, Ashford Hughes, Bouth Napier, John Laine, Bartholomew Stoveall, Benjamin Woodson, who after some time bring in their Verdict which on the Plts. motion is admitted to Record and is as followeth "Wee find for the Plt. Six hundred and thirty pounds of Tobo. according to Bill Anthony Hoggatt Foreman." wherefore it is considered by the Court that the Plt. do recover against the Defendt. the said Sum of Six hundred and thirty pounds of Tobo. by the Jurors aforesaid in their Verdict Assessed and the Costs of this Suit with a Lawyers Fee.

Alexander vs Chandler   In the Action of Case between John Alexander Plt. and Joell Chandler Defendt. the Plt. having at a former Court obtained a Judgt. against the Defendt. and Daniel Stoner Gent. Sheriff for so much damages as should be found upon executing a writ of inquiry of damages the following Jury are now Sworn. Anthony Hogat, John Mcbride, Thomas Nolun, Stephen Woodson, Robert Burton, John Christian, Peter Ware, Ashford Hughes, Bouth Napier, John Laine, Bartholomew Stoveall, Benjamin Woodson, who after some time return with their Verdict which on the Plts. motion is admitted to Record and is as followeth "Wee find for the Plt. twenty seven shillings & six pence Currant Anthony Hoggat Foreman" Wherefore it is considered by the Court that the Plt. do recover against the Deft. and Daniel

[147]   September Court 1729
Stoner Gent. Sheriff the said Sum of twenty seven shillings and Six pence Currant money by the Jurors aforesaid in their said Verdict assessed with the Costs of this Suit and a Lawyers Fee.

    Present Tarlton Fleming Gent.

Macon vs Wharton   In the Action on the Case between John Macon Plt. and Thomas Wharton Defendt. the Plt. being respondent in Chancery files his Answer to the Defendants Bill of Injunction, and Tarlton Fleming, George Paine and William Cabbell, Gent. are appointed to Examine State and Settle the Accounts in dispute between them and to make report of their Proceedings therein to the next Court.

Easly's deed to Mayo   George Carrington proves upon oath a deed from Robert Easly to Joseph Mayo and also the Livery of Seizin thereon endorsed to be the Act and deed of the said Robert Easly, he also makes oath that he saw George Mayo, and Sarah Mayo Subscribe their names as witnesses to the said Deed and to the Livery of Seizin endorsed thereon, and the same was thereupon admitted to record.

Huson Fined   John Huson being committed to Prison by Thomas Randolph Gent. for a breach of the Peace committed last Court day after the rising of the Court, appears now according to the Condition of his Recognizance and his offence being considered by the Court it is ordered that he be fined to Our Sovereign Lord the King in the Sum of ten shillings Currant money, and that the Sheriff take the said John Huson into his Custody and him safely keep untill he pay the fine aforesaid, and untill he enter into Bond in the Sum of ten pounds Currt. money with one good and sufficient Security with Condition for his good behaviour for one year, and that the said John Huson pay Costs.

Davis Willm. fined   William Davis being committed to Prison by Thomas Randolph Gent. for a breach of the Peace committed last Court day after the rising of the Court, appears now according to the Condition of his Recognizance and his offence being considered by the Court it is ordered that he be fined to Our Sovereign Lord the King in the Sum of fifty shillings Currant money and that the Sheriff take the said William Davis into his Custody and him safely keep untill he pay the fine aforesaid and untill he enter into bond in the

[148]   September Court 1729
the Sum of ten pounds Currant money with one good and sufficient Security with Condition for his good behaviour for one year and that the said William Davis pay Costs.

Davis George fined   George Davis being committed to Prison by Thomas Randolph Gent. for a breach of the Peace committed last Court day after the rising of the Court appears now according to the Condition of his Recognizance and his Offence being considered by the Court it is ordered that he be fined to Our Sovereign Lord the King in the Sum of fifty shillings Currant money, and that the Sheriff take the said George Davis into his Custody and him safely keep untill he pay the fine aforesaid and untill he enter into Bond in the Sum of ten pounds Currt. money with one good and sufficient Security with Condition for his good behaviour for one year and that the said George Davis pay Costs.

Laine vs Christian   In the Action on the Case between John Laine Plt. and John Christian Defendt. came as well the said John Laine by Thomas

Prosser his Attorney as the said John Christian by Thomas Dickins and Griffith Bowen his Attorneys upon which the Premises being seen and by the Court of Our Lord the King here fully understood it seems to the Justices here that the Plea of the said John Christian above in Abatement Pleaded and the matter in the same contained is good and sufficient in Law to Quash the Bill aforesaid of the said John Laine therefore it is considered that the said John Laine take nothing by his writt aforesaid and that the said John Christian go hence without day and that he recover against the said John Laine his costs by him in this behalf expended and a Lawyers Fee.

Surveyor of the road   Henry Wood is appointed Surveyor of the Road from Tuckahoe Creek mill to the main River road, and it is ordered that the severall male labouring Titheables of Thomas Wadloe, Joseph Watkins, Thomas Joplin, James Moss, David Clarkson, Thomas Golsby, George Thompson, Samuell Butler, Andrew Pruit, John Sorrell, Mathew Collins, George Perrin, Robert Burton, and Henry Wood do assist in clearing the same.

[149]   September Court 1729
Doran vs Marchbanks   In the Action on the Case between John Doran Admr. &c. of Julius King deceased Plt. and George Marchbanks Defendant the Parties Submit themselves to the Court for tryall whereupon the accounts being examined it is considered that the Defendant go hence without day and that he recover against the Plt. his Costs by him in this behalf expended.

Macon vs Hughes   In the Action of Debt between John Macon Plt. and Stephen Hughes Defendt. the Jury sworn at the last Court not having agreed their Verdict, it is ordered that the Sheriff keep them together untill they are agreed, that the Jury Seal up their Verdict and deliver it to the Sherif, and that they appear and Present it to the next Court.

Present George Paine Gent.

Cabbell vs Nolun   In the Action on the Case between William Cabbell Assignee of John Quin Plt. and Thomas Nolun Defendant the following Jury are sworn Anthony Hoggat, John Mcbrid, Stephen Woodson, Robert Burton, Peter Ware, Bouth Napier, Bartholomew Stoveall, John Laine, Benjamin Woodson, Samuell Allin, Thomas Wadloe, Richard Oglesby, At the rising of the Court the Jury not being agreed it is ordered that the Sheriff do keep them together untill they have agreed on their Verdict, that they Seal up the same and deliver it to the Sheriff, and that they appear at next Court to present the same.

Gathwrite deed to Cannon   Ephraim Gathwrite acknowledges a deed with the Livery of Seizin endorsed from himself to William Cannon to be his Act and Deed and it is thereupon admitted to record.

Waddill vs Edwards   In the Action on the Case between William Waddill Junr. Plt. and Thomas Edwards Defendt. the Defendt. files a Bill of injunction in Chancery to stay proceedings at Common Law.

Martin vs Gunn   In the Action of Trespass between Francis Martin Plt. and John Gunn Deft. the Defendant files a Plea.

[150]   September Court 1729
Thomas vs Gee   In the Action on the Case between Rowland Thomas Plt. and Gilbert Gee Deft. the Plt. files a new declaration and an Imparlance is granted the Defendant.

Martin Rapene   In the Action of Case between John Martin Junr. Plt. and Anthony Rapene Defendt. on the Defendants motion leave is granted him to plead severall matters and thereupon he files Pleas.

Bingley vs Rapene   In the Action of Trespass between Joseph Bingley Plt. and Anthony Rapene Deft. on the Defendants motion leave is granted him to plead severall matters and thereupon he files Pleas.

Cabbell vs Wade   In the Action of Trespass on the Case between William Cabbell Plt. and Robert Wade Defendt. on the Defts. motion leave is granted him to plead severall matters and thereupon he files Pleas.

Dickins vs Macon   The Action of Trespass on the Case between Thomas Dickins Plt. and John Macon Defendant is dismist the Plt. not prosecuting the same.

Fleming vs Pleasants   In the Action of Debt between John Fleming Plt. and John Pleasants Admr. &c. of William Howl deceased Defendt. the Defendant failing to appear Judgment is granted the Plt. against the Defendant and Daniel Stoner Gent. Sherif for what damages shall be recovered in this Suit to be discharged nevertheless if the Defendant appears at the next Court.

Carnar vs Atkinson   In the Action of Trespass on the Case between Susanna Carnar Plt. and Henry Atkinson Defendt. the Defendt. failing to appear Judgment is granted the Plt. against the Defendant and Daniel Stoner Gent. Sherif for what damages shall be recovered in this Suit to be discharged nevertheless if the Defendant appears at the next Court.

[151]   September Court 1729
Randolph vs Bullington   The Action of Case between Thomas Randolph Plt. and John Bullington Defendt. is continued.

Temple vs Burton   In the Action of Trespass on the Case between Joseph Temple Plt. and Nowell Burton Defendant time is granted the Plt. to mend his declaration.

Bibe vs Morriss   On the motion of Elizabeth Bibe a witness for Hugh Morriss & Sarah his wife Executrix &c. of Edmund New decd. ads William New it is ordered that the said Hugh do pay her for one days attendance thirty pounds of Tobacco with Costs.

Weldy vs Morriss   On the motion of William Weldy a witness for Hugh Morriss & Sarah his Wife Executrix &c. of Edmund New deceased ads William New it is ordered that the said Hugh do pay him for one days attendance thirty pounds of Tobacco with Costs.

Lad & Powel vs Thompson   On the Petition of Amos Lad & Roger Powell against Samuell Thompson & Mary his Wife Admx. &c. of John Bellamy deced. it is ordered that the said Samuell & Mary be Sumoned to appear at the next Court to answer the same.

Nolun vs Quin   In the Action of Trespass between Thomas Nolun Plt. and John Quin Defendant on the Defendts. motion an imparlance is granted him.

Nolun vs Quin   In the Action of Debt between Thomas Nolun Plt. and John Quin Defendt. the Defendant Demurrs generally.

Read vs Downie   In the Action of Case between Clem Read Plt. and Robert Downie Defendt. the Plt. files a new declaration and a special imparlance is granted the Defendant.

Wood vs Utley   The Action of Case between Henry Wood Plt. and John Utley Deft. is dismist the Plt. not prosecuting the same.

Moseby vs Taylor   In the Action of Debt between Richard Moseby Plt. and John Taylor Deft. the Plt. files a new declaration and a special imparlance is granted the Defendant.

[152] September Court 1729
Alvis vs Sorrell   In the Action of Debt between George Alvis Plt. and John Sorrell Defendt. the Plt. files a new declaration and a special imparlance is granted the Defendant.

Pruit vs Johnson   In the Action of Case between Andrew Pruit Plt. and Charles Johnson Defendt. the Plt. files a new declaration and a special imparlance is granted the Defendant.

Woodson vs Baize   In the Action of Trespass on the Case between John Woodson Plt. and Edward Baize Defendt. the Defendt. failing to appear Judgment is granted the Plt. against the Defendt. and Daniel Stoner Gent. Sherif for what damages shall be recovered in this Suit to be discharged nevertheless if the Defendant appears at the next Court.

McCulloch vs Brooks   The Action of Case between John McCulloch Plt. and Jacob Brooks Defendt. the Sherif having returned the Deft. not to be found and he failing to appear on the Pluries Capias the same is continued against him returnable to the next Court.

Taylor vs Lansdon   In the Action of Trespass between James Taylor Plt. and Wm. Lansdon Defendt. the Defendant pleads not guilty and the Suit is continued.

Dickins vs Fauquinou   In the Action of Case between Thomas Dickins Plt. and Daniel Fauquinou Defendt. the Defendant failing to appear Judgment is granted the Plt. against the Deft. and Joseph Watkins his Common Bail for what damages shall be recovered in this Suit to be discharged nevertheless if the Defendt. appears at the next Court.

Arrington's deed to Micheaux   Samuell Arrington acknowledges a deed with the Livery of Seizin endorsed from himself to John Micheaux to be his act and deed and it is thereupon admitted to Record then Jane wife of the said Samuell (She being first privately examined) relinquishes her right of Dower in the land by this Deed conveyed which is also admitted to Record.

[153] September Court 1729
Webbs Petn. to turn Road   On the Petition of Henry Webb leave is granted him to turn the road now going through his Plantation above licking hole [Creek] provided he make a new road as good as the old one.

Martin vs Woodson   In the Action of Case between John Martin Plt. and Joseph Woodson Executor &c. of John Woodson deceased Defendant an imparlance is granted the Defendant.

Martin vs Woodson   In the Action of Case between John Martin Plt. and Joseph Woodson Defendt. an Imparlance is granted the Defendant.

Lad vs Cannon   In the Action of Case between Amos Lad Plt. and William Cannon Defendt. an Imparlance is granted the Defendant.

Cox vs Dean   In the Action of Trespass between Fredorick Cox Plt. and Richard Dean Defendt. the Defendant Pleads not guilty and the Suit is continued.

Huson vs Bingley   The Action of Trespass between John Huson Plt. and Mathew Bingley Defendt. is dismist the Plt. not prosecuting the same.

Johnson vs Quin   In the Action on the Case between Daniel Johnson Plt. and John Quin Defendt. an Imparlance is granted the Defendant.

Taylor vs Quin   In the Action of Debt between James Taylor Plt. and John Quin Defendt. William Cabbell becomes special Bail for the Defendt. and time is granted the Plt. to mend his declaration.

Woodson vs Moreman   The Action of Case between John Woodson Plt. and Andrew Moreman Defendt. is dismist the Plt. not prosecuting the same.

Bumpuss vs Moreman   In the Action of Trespass on the Case between Samuell Bumpuss Plt. and Andrew Moreman Defendt. the Plt. files a new declaration and a special Imparlance is granted the Defendant.

Napier vs Cox   In the Action of Case between Robert Napier Junr. Plt. and Bartholomew Cox Defendt. the Plt. files a new declaration and a special Imparlance is granted the Defendant.

[154]   September Court 1729
Hook vs Maxey   The Action of Case between James Hook Plt. and John Maxey Defendt. is dismist the Plt. not prosecuting the same.

Wiles vs Hughes &c   In the Action of Debt between Luke Wiles Plt. and Stephen Hughes and Sarah Atkinson Executor & Executrix &c. of Thomas Atkinson deceased Defendts. the Defendants file a Plea and the

Suit is continued.

Pennington vs Baily   In the Action of Trespass between Paul Pennington Plt. and Henry Bailey Defendt. the Defendant Pleads not guilty and the Suit is continued.

Randolph vs Lax   The Action of Trespass between Thomas Randolph Plt. and William Lax Deft. is dismist the Plt. not prosecuting the same.

Wiles vs Hughes   In the Action of Trespass on the Case between Luke Wiles Plt. and Stephen Hughes Defendt. the Defendant files a Plea and the Suit is continued.

Marchbanks vs Croom   In the Action of Case between George Marchbanks Plt. and Daniell Croom Defendt. the Defendant appearing and failing to Plead Judgment by nihil dicit is granted against him for what damages shall be recovered in this Suit to be discharged nevertheless if the Defendant Pleads at the next Court.

Salmon vs Edwards   In the Action of Case between Thomas Salmon Plt. and Thomas Edwards Defendt. time is granted the Plt. to mend his declaration.

May vs Jackson   In the Action of Case between William May Plt. and Joseph Jackson Defendt. the Plt. files a new declaration and an Imparlance is granted the Defendant.

New vs Morris   In the Action of Debt between William New Plt. and Hugh Morris and Mary his Wife Executrix &c. of Edmund New deceased Defendants. Oyer of the Bond is granted them.

[155]
New vs Morris   In the Action of Case between William New Plt. and Hugh Morris and Mary his wife Executrix &c. of Edmund New deceased Defendts. the Plaintif having failed to file any declaration on the Defendts. motion he is nonsuited and it is thereupon considered that the Defendants do recover against the Plt. five shillings Currant money together with their Costs by them in this behalf expended and a Lawyers Fee.

The Action of Case between John Utley Plt. and Thomas Randolph Defendant is dismist neither party appearing.

The Action of Trespass on the Case between Edward Scot Plt. and John Martin Junr. Defendt. is dismist the Plt. not prosecuting the same.

Holland vs Woodson   In the Action on the Case between Michaell Holland Plt. and Benjamin Woodson Defendt. the Plt. files a new declaration.

Holland vs Woodson   In the Action of Debt between Michaell Holland Plt. and Benjamin Woodson Defendt. the Plt. files a new declaration.

Holland vs Napier   In the Action of Case between Michaell Holland Plt. and Bouth Napier Defendt. the Plt. files a new declaration and an imparlance is granted the Defendant.

Ward vs Dean   In the Action of Trespass on the Case between Seth Ward Plt. and Richard Dean Defendt. the Plt. files a new declaration and an imparlance is granted the Defendant.

Ward vs Dean   In the Action of Trespass on the Case between Seth Ward Plt. and Richard Dean Defendt. the Plt. files a new declaration and an imparlance is granted the Defendant.

Taylor vs Lowe   In the Action of Trespass on the Case between John Taylor Plt. and Thomas Lowe Defendant the Defendant failing to appear Judgment is granted the Plt. against the Defendt. and Daniel Stoner Gent. Sherif for what damages shall be recovered in this Suit to be discharged nevertheless if the Defendant appears at the next Court.

[156]   September Court 1729
Stidum vs Bingley   In the Action of Debt between Benjamin Stidum Plt. and Joseph Bingley and William Lansdon Deft. an imparlance is granted the Defendants.

Dickins vs New   In the Action on the Case between Thomas Dickins Plt. and William New Defendt. time is granted the Plt. to mend his declaration.

Holmes vs Dickins   In the Action of Trespass on the Case between Charles Holmes Plt. and Thomas Dickins Defendt. the Defendant acknowledges himself Indebted unto the Plt. thirty four shillings and a half penny Currant money whereupon it is considered by the Court that the Plt. do recover against the Defendant the said Sum with Costs and a Lawyers Fee.

Then the Court adjourned to the third Tuesday in next Month.

****

At a Court held for Goochland County the first day of October 1729 for laying the County Levy. Present William Mayo, John Woodson, Allin Howard, George Paine, William Cabbell, Gent. Justices.

	Tobacco	Cask
Goochland County Dr.		
To Henry Wood Clerk.	1000	80
To Do. for attending the tryall of Frances Green	200	
To Do. for the Virginia Laws and a Record Book	1600	
To Daniel Stoner Sheriff	1000	80
To Wm. Cabbell & Nowell Burton for counting 1695982 plants.	1411	

[157]   County Levy Court 1729

To David Lesseur & Peter David for ct. 425585 plants.	351
To Jno. Mcbrid & Josias Paine for 1762708.	1466
To Jos. Ashlin & Jos. Hooper for 716991.	596
To Sarah Atkinson for keeping Ferry from May Court after the rate of 800 lb Tobacco Pr. Annum.	301
To Edd. Williams for three Wolves heads Certified Pr. Jas. Holman.	600
To Wm. Holliday for three Do. Certified by Do.	600
To James Barrett for two Do. Certified by Do.	400
To Wm. Kent Constable for sumoning a Jury on Frances Greens child	50
To Henr. Raynold for two Wolves heads Certified by Wm. Cabbell	400
To Thos. Ballew for one Do. Certified by John Fleming	200
To Thos. Ballew for one Do. Certified by Geo. Paine	200
To Andw. Spradlin for three do. Certd. by Tarlton Fleming	600
To Andw. Spradlin for one Do. Certd. by Allin Howard	200
To Henr. Reynolds for one Do. Certd. by Allin Howard	200
To Geo. Stoveall for three Do. Certd. by John Woodson	600
To Luke Wiles for two Do. Certd. by Wm. Cabbell	400
To John Felps for four Do. Certd. by Tarlton Fleming	800
To John Laine for one Do. Certd. by Tarlton Fleming	200
To Henr. Baily for one Do. Certd. by Allin Howard	200
To Henr. Baily for one Do. Certd. by Wm. Cabbell	200
To Danl. Stoner Sherif for Insolvents @ 20 Pr. Poll	520
To Do. for Sundry's as Pr. his Account	1360

To David Lawson for one Wolfes head Certd. by Allin Howard	200	
To Robt. Willis for one Do. Certd. by George Paine	200	
To Henr. Reynolds for one Do. Certd. by Allin Howard	200	
To Jno. Dawson for one Do. Certd. by Allin Howard	200	
To Abram. Micheaux for eight Do. Certd. by Allin Howard	1600	
To Thos. Murrell & Benja. Bradshaw for guarding Frances Green 29 days each 725	1450	
To Peter Baize, John Wilkinson, David Pattison for Guarding Frances Green to Williamsburgh each 300 lbs. Tobacco	900	
To Thos. Christian for Guarding Fras. Green 3 days at Wmsburgh	150	
To Willm. Cabbell for an Inquest & Sumoning a Jury on the Body of James Pritchet	283	
To Allin Howard for on Inquest on Willm. Laine	133	

[158]   County Levy Court 1729
        Brought forward

To Allin Howard for an Inquest on Fras. Greens Child	133	
To Jno. Mcbrid for sumoning a Jury on Wm. Laine	50	
To Richd. Perkins for the loss of his Horse a month in carrying Frances Green to Williamsburgh	200	
To Wm. Mayo Surveyor for his Acct. for running the County lines	3450	
To Jno. Woodson & Tarlton Fleming Gent. for attending at running the County lines each 2000	4000	
To John Williams for Pillory &c.	500	40

Present Tarlton Fleming Gent.

To Jos. Woodson for keeping Ferry from July 1728 untill May 1729	500	
To Thos. Edwards for one Wolfs head Certd. Pr. Tarln. Fleming	200	
	30604	200
Sallary	3060	
Cask	200	
	33264	
Due to the County	521	
	33785	

Do.	Cr.
By 1165 Titheables @ 29 Pr. Poll	33785

Ordered that Daniel Stoner Sherif do Collect of every Titheable Person in this County twenty nine pounds of Tobacco and in Case of refusal or nonpayment that he levey the same by Distress. Daniel Stoner enters into bond Tarlton Fleming Security.

Ordered that Robert Saunders be added to the List taken by William Mayo Gent.

****

[159]   October Court 1729
At a Court held for Goochland County the third Tuesday in October being the twenty first day of the month Annoq Domi. 1729. Present William Mayo, John Woodson, Tarlton Fleming, Allin Howard, George Paine, William Cabbell, Gent. Justices.

James's deed to Lansdon & Uxor   Francis James acknowledges a deed with the Livery of Seizin endorsed from himself to William Lansdon & Esther his wife to be his Act and deed and it is thereupon admitted to Record.

Christian's Negro Judg'd   Jack a Negro belonging to Thomas Christian is judged to be ten Years old.

Christians Negro Judg'd   Kate a Negro belonging to James Christian is judged to be ten Years old.

Cox's deed to Chamberlaine   John Quin, Thomas Edwards, and Thomas Dickins, come into Court and upon their Corporal Oaths prove deeds of Lease & Release from Fredorick Cox to William Chamberlaine to be the Acts and Deeds of the said Fredorick Cox and they are thereupon admitted to Record.

Calvet an Orphan to bound out   Ordered that the Churchwardens of St. James's Parish do bind out William Calvet an Orphan according to Law.

Prosser to be allowed a Sallary   On the motion of Thomas Prosser who hath obtained a Commission from the Honble. William Gooch Esqr. his Majesty's Lieut. Governour to appear at this Court on behalf of the King it is the Opinion of the Court that a thousand pounds of Tobacco & Cask be annually allowed the said Thomas Prosser to Commence from the first day of May last past in full Recompence and reward for all Services he shall perform on his Majestys behalf.

Atkinson vs Benning   The Action of Trespass between Sarah Atkins Plt. and Anthony Benning Defendant is continued at the Plts. cost.

[160]   October Court 1729
Atkinson vs Leseur   The Action of Trespass between Sarah Atkinson Plt. and David Lesseur Defendt. is continued at the Plts. Cost.

Atkinson vs Taylor   The Action of Trespass between Sarah Atkinson Plt. and James Taylor Defendt. is continued at the Plts. Cost.

Burton vs Quin   In the Action on the Case between Nowell Burton Plt. and John Quin Deft. the Parties submit themselves to the Court for tryall whereupon it is considered that the Plt. do recover against the Defendt. Seventy six pounds of tobacco and five shillings Currt. money with the Costs of this Suit and a Lawyers Fee.

Present   James Holman Gent.

Fleming vs Pleasants   In the Action of Debt between John Fleming Plt. and John Pleasants Admr. &c. of William Howl deceased Defendt. the Defendt. failing to appear the Conditional Judgment formerly granted in this Suit against the Defendt. and Daniel Stoner Gent. Sherif is confirmed for so much damages as shall be found upon executing a Writ of Inquiry at the next court of which the Sherif is ordered to give the Deft. notice by serving him with a Copy of this Order.

Carnar vs Atkinson   In the Action of Trespass on the Case between Susanna Carnar Plt. and Henry Atkinson Defendt. the Defendt. failing to appear the Conditional Judgment formerly granted in this Suit against the Defendt. and Daniel Stoner Gent. Sherif is confirmed for so much damages as shall be found upon executing a Writ of Inquiry at the next Court of which the Sherif is ordered to give the Deft. notice by serving him with a copy of this Order.

Woodson vs Baize   In the Action of Trespass on the Case between John Woodson Plt. and Edward Baize Defendant the Defendt. failing to appear the Conditional Judgment formerly granted in this Suit against the Deft. and Daniel Stoner Gent. Sheriff is confirmed for so much damages as shall be found upon executing a Writ

[161]   October Court 1729
of Inquiry at the next Court of which the Sherif is ordered to give the Defendt. notice by serving him with a Copy of this Order.

Dickins vs Fauquinou   In the Action of Case between Thomas Dickins Plt. and Daniel Fauquinou Deft. the Defendt. failing to appear the Conditional Judgment formerly granted in this Suit against the Deft. and Joseph Watkins his Common Bail is confirmed for so much damages as shall be found upon executing a Writ of Inquiry at the next court of which the Sherif is ordered to give the Deft. and the said Joseph Watkins notice by serving them with a Copy of this Order.

Utley vs Napier   In the Action of Debt between John Utley Plt. and Bouth Napier Deft. leave is granted the Deft. to plead severall matters and thereupon he files pleas and the Suit is continued.

Utley vs Napier   In the Action of Debt between John Utley Plt. and Bouth Napier Defendt. the Deft. failing to plead Judgment by nihil dicit is granted against him for what damages shall be recovered in this Suit to be discharged nevertheless if the Defendant pleads at the next Court.

Lansdon's deed to James   William Lansdon and Esther his wife (she being first privately examined) acknowledges a deed with the Livery of Seizin endorsed from themselves to Francis James to be their act and deed and it is thereupon admitted to Record.

Napier vs Scot   The Action of Debt between Bouth Napier Plt. and Edward Scot Admr. &c. of Paul Green Deceased Deft. is continued at the Plts. Cost.

Burton vs Woodson   In the Action of Case between Robert Burton Plt. and William Woodson Executor &c. of the last will and testament of Benjamin Woodson Deceased Defendt. the Parties being at issue on a plea of nil debet the following Jury are sworn to try the same   Anthony Hoggat, James Taylor, Nathaniel Basset, Thomas Christian, William Lansdon, Joell Chandler, John Mcbrid,

[162]   October Court 1729
Peter Ware, Joseph Lewis, Thomas Wadloe, Thomas Edwards, George Marchbanks, who after some time return their Verdict which on the Plts. motion is ordered to be recorded and is as followeth "Wee find for the Plt. one thousand four hundred eighty eight pounds of Tobo. Antho. Hoggat Foreman." The Defts. Attorny offers reasons to stay the

Judgments being entered up which reasons being disallowed by the Court as tending only to delay the Judgment it is thereupon Considered that the Plt. do recover against the Defendant the said Sum of one thousand four hundred eighty eight pounds of Tobacco by the Jurors aforesaid in their said Verdict assessed and also the Costs of this Suit of the Goods and Chattles which were of the aforesaid Benjamin's at the time of his death in the hands of the said William to be administered if so much in his hands there be, and if not so much then the Costs aforesaid of the proper Goods and Chattles of the aforesaid William to be levyed. From which Judgment the said William Woodson Appeals to the Sixth day of the next Generall Court William Cabbell entring himself Security.

Jeffs vs Martin   In the Action of Case between John Jeffs Plt. and John Martin Defendt. the Sherif having made return on the Alias Capias that the Defendant is not to be found and he failing to appear another Alias Capias is awarded against him returnable to the next Court.

Hughes vs Cone   In the Action on the Case between Robert Hughes Plt. and John Cone Defendt. the Auditors formerly appointed in this Suit now offer their report which is ordered to be recorded in these words Vizt. "Pursuant to an order of Goochland Court Wee have proceeded to examine state and settle the Account between Robert Hughes Plt. and John Cone Defendant and Wee find that there is due to Robert Hughes three pounds sixteen shillings and ten pence Currt. money and three barrells three bushells Indian Corn to be paid in kind by January next to the said Hughes by the said Cone Pr. us Geo. Payne, Wm. Cabbell.

[163]   October Court 1729
Cabbell. August the 20th. 1729." and it is thereupon considered by the Court that the Plt. do recover against the Deft. the said sum of three pounds sixteen shillings and ten pence Currt. money and three Barrells three bushells of Indian Corn which the Costs of this Suit and a Lawyers Fee.

Coroners appointed   The Court taking into Consideration that there are no Coroners in the County do thereupon recommend Tarlton Fleming and William Cabbell Gentlemen proper to execute that Office.

Moss vs Taylor   In the Action of Trespass on the Case between Thomas Moss Plt. and James Taylor Defendt. the Defendant pleads he oweth nothing and for tryall puts himself upon the Country and the Plt. likewise.

Taylor vs Lowe & Uxor   In the Action of Trespass on the Case between John Taylor Plt. and Thomas Lowe and Amey his wife Defendts. the Plt. takes Issue on the Defts. Plea.

The Action of Case between William Bottom Plt. and John Burgess Defendt. is dismist the Plt. not prosecuting the same.

The Action of Case between Edward Baize Plt. and Edward Maxey Defendt. is dismist the Plt. not prosecuting the same.

Martin vs Bondurant   In the Action of Case between John Martin Junr. Plt. and John Peter Bondurant Defendt. the Defendt. acknowledges himself indebted unto the Plt. twenty shillings Currant money whereupon it is considered by the Court that the Plt. do recover against the Defendant twenty shillings Currant money with Costs and an Attornys Fee.

Lankford vs Lankford   In the Action of Trespass between John Lankford Plt. and West Lankford Defendt. the Plt. having failed to file his declaration on the Defendants motion he is nonsuited and it is thereupon considered by the Court that the Defendt. do recover against the Plt. five shillings Currant money together with his Costs by him in this behalf expended and a Lawyers Fee.

[164]   October Court 1729
Harrison vs Mckenny   In the Action of Debt between Benjamin Harrison Plt. and Daniel Mckenny Defendant the Sherif having made return that the Defendt. is not to be found and he failing to appear an Alias Capias is awarded against the Deft. returnable to the next Court.

Davis vs Stoveall   The Action of Debt between George Davis Plt. and Bartholomew Stoveall Defendt. is continued.

Skeyman vs Burk   In the Action of Trespass between George Skeyman Plt. and Theodorick Burk Defendt. the Defendt. failing to appear Judgment is granted against him and Samuel Burk his Common Bail for what damages shall be recovered in this Suit to be discharged nevertheless if the Defendant appears at the next Court.

Randolph vs Wotars   The Action of Debt between Thomas Randolph Plt. and William Wotars Defendt is dismist the Plt. being dead.

Macon vs Wharton   In the Action on the Case between John Macon Plt.

and Thomas Wharton Defendt. the Plt. in the Action who is respondent in Chancery is fined twelve pence Currant money for want of a sufficient answer to the Complainants Bill, and time is granted the Respondent to mend his answer.

Macon vs Hughes   The Action of Debt between John Macon Deft. and Stephen Hughes Defendt. is continued.

Cabbell vs Nolun   The Action of Debt between William Cabbell Assee. of John Quin Plt. and Thomas Nolun Defendt. is continued.

Waddill vs Edwards   The Action on the Case between William Waddill Junr. Plt. and Thomas Edwards Defendt. is continued.

Martin vs Gunn   In the Action of Trespass between Francis Martin Plt. and

[165]   October Court 1729
John Gunn Defendant the Plt. files his Replication and time is granted the Defendant to Rejoyn.

Thomas vs Gee   In the Action on the Case between Rowland Thomas Plt. and Gilbert Gee Defendt. the Defendant appears but failing to Plead Judgment by nihil dicit is granted against him for what damages shall be recovered in this Suit to be discharged nevertheless if the Defendant shall plead at the next Court.

Nolun vs Quin   In the Action of Trespass between Thomas Nolun Plt and John Quin Defendt. the Defendant appears but failing to Plead Judgment by nihil dicit is granted against him for what damages shall be recovered in this Suit to be discharged nevertheless if the Defendant shall plead at the next Court.

Read vs Downie   In the Action on the Case between Clem Read Plt. and Robert Downie Defendt. the Defendant appears but failing to Plead Judgment by nihil dicit is granted against him for what damages shall be recovered in this Suit to be discharged nevertheless if the Defendt. shall plead at the next Court.

Moseby vs Taylor   In the Action of Debt between Richard Moseby Plt. and John Taylor Defendt. the Defendant appears but failing to Plead Judgment by nihil dicit is granted against him for what damages shall be recovered in this Suit to be discharged nevertheless if the Defendant shall plead at the next Court.

Alvis vs Sorrell   In the Action of Debt between George Alvis Plt. and John Sorrell Defendt. the Defendant appears but failing to Plead Judgment by nihil dicit is granted against him for what damages shall be recovered in this Suit to be discharged nevertheless if the Defendant shall plead at the next Court.

Pruit vs Johnson   In the Action on the Case between Andrew Pruit Plt. and Charles Johnson Defendant the Defendt. appears but failing to Plead Judgment by nihil dicit is granted against him for what damages

[166]   October Court 1729
shall be recovered in this Suit to be discharged nevertheless if the Defendant shall Plead at the next Court.

Martin vs Woodson   In the Action on the Case between John Martin Plt. and Joseph Woodson Executor &c. of John Woodson deceased Deft. the Defendant appears but failing to Plead Judgment by nihil dicit is granted against him for what damages shall be recovered in this Suit to be discharged nevertheless if the Deft. shall Plead at the next Court.

Martin vs Woodson   In the Action on the Case between John Martin Plt. and Joseph Woodson Defendt. the Defendant appears but failing to Plead Judgment by nihil dicit is granted against him for what damages shall be recovered in this Suit to be discharged nevertheless if the Defendant shall Plead at the next Court.

Taylor vs Quin   In the Action of Debt between James Taylor Plt. and John Quin Defendt. the Defendant appears but failing to Plead judgment by nihil dicit is granted against him for what damages shall be recovered in this Suit to be discharged nevertheless if the Defendant shall Plead at the next Court.

Bumpuss vs Moreman   In the Action of Trespass on the Case between Samuell Bumpuss Plt. and Andrew Moreman Defendt. the Defendt. appears but failing to Plead Judgment by nihil dicit is granted against him for what damages shall be recovered in this Suit to be discharged nevertheless if the Defendant shall Plead at the next Court.

Napier vs Cox   In the Action on the Case between Robert Napier Junr. Plt. and Bartholomew Cox Defendt. the Defendant appears but failing to Plead Judgment by nihil dicit is granted against him for what damages shall be recovered in this Suit to be discharged nevertheless if the Defendant shall Plead at the next Court.

May vs Jackson   In the Action on the Case between William May Plt. and Joseph Jackson Defendt. the Defendant appears but failing

[167]   October Court 1729

to Plead Judgment by nihil dicit is granted against him for what damages shall be recovered in this Suit to be discharged nevertheless if the Defendant shall Plead at the next Court.

Holland vs Woodson   In the Action on the Case between Michaell Holland Plt. and Benjamin Woodson Defendt. the Defendant appears but failing to Plead Judgment by nihil digit is granted against him for what damages shall be recovered in this Suit to be discharged nevertheless if the Defendant shall Plead at the next Court.

Holland vs Woodson   In the Action of Debt between Michaell Holland Plt. and Benjamin Woodson Defendt. the Defendant appears but failing to Plead Judgment by nihil dicit is granted against him for what damages shall be recovered in this Suit to be discharged nevertheless of the Defendant shall Plead at the next Court.

Holland vs Napier   In the Action on the Case between Michaell Holland Plt. and Bouth Napier Defendt. the Defendant appears but failing to Plead Judgment by nihil dicit is granted against him for what damages shall be recovered in this Suit to be discharged nevertheless if the Defendant shall Plead at the next Court.

Ward vs Dean   In the Action of Trespass on the Case between Seth Ward Plt. and Richard Dean Defendt. the Defendant appears but failing to Plead Judgment by nihil dicit is granted against him for what damages shall be recovered in this Suit to be discharged nevertheless if the Defendant shall Plead at the next Court.

Ward vs Dean   In the Action of Trespass on the Case between Seth Ward Plt. and Richard Dean Defendt. the Defendant appears but failing to Plead Judgment by nihil dicit is granted against him for what damages shall be recovered in this Suit to be discharged nevertheless if the Defendant shall Plead at the next Court.

Stidum vs Bingley   In the Action of Debt between Benjamin Stidum Plt. and Joseph Bingley and William Lansdon Defendts. the Defendants appear but failing to Plead Judgment by nihil dicit is granted against

[168] October Court 1729
them for what damages shall be recovered in this Suit to be discharged nevertheless if the Defendants shall Plead at the next Court.

Dickins vs New   In the Action on the Case between Thomas Dickins Plt. and William New Defendt. the Plt. files a new declaration and the Defendant appearing but failing to Plead Judgment by nihil dicit is granted against him for what damages shall be recovered in this Suit to be discharged nevertheless if the Defendant shall Plead at the next Court.

Martin vs Rapene   In the Action on the Case between John Martin Junr. Plt. and Anthony Rapene Defendt. the Plt. takes issue on the Defendants Pleas and the Suit is continued.

Bingley vs Rapene   In the Action of Trespass between Joseph Bingley Plt. and Anthony Rapene Defendt. the Plt. takes issue on the Defendts. Pleas and the Suit is continued.

Cabbell vs Wade   The Action of Trespass on the Case between William Cabbell Plt. and Robert Wade Defendt. is continued at the Plts. Cost.

Randolph vs Bullington   The Action on the Case between Thomas Randolph Plt. and John Bullington Defendt. is dismist the Plt. being dead.

Temple vs Burton   In the Action of Trespass on the Case between Joseph Temple Plt. and Nowell Burton Defendt. time is granted the Plt. to mend his declaration.

Nolun vs Quin   In the Action of Debt between Thomas Nolun Plt. and John Quin Defendt. the Plt. joyns the Demurrer with the Defendant and the Suit is continued.

McCulloch vs Brookes   The Action on the Case between John McCulloch Plt. and Jacob Brookes Defendant is dismist neither party appearing.

[169] October Court 1729
Taylor vs Lansdon   In the Action of Trespass between James Taylor Plt. and William Lansdon Defendt. the Plt. takes issue on the Defendts Plea and the Suit is continued.

Lad vs Cannon   In the Action on the Case between Amos Lad Plt. and William Cannon Defendt. the Plt. failing to Prosecute his Suit on the Defendants motion he is nonsuited and it is thereupon considered by the Court that the Defendant go hence without day and that he recover against the Plt. five shillings Currt. money with his Costs by him in this behalf expended and a Lawyers Fee.

Cox vs Dean   In the Action of Trespass between Fredorick Cox Plt. and Richard Dean Defendt. the Plt. failing to Prosecute his Suit on the Defendts. motion he is nonsuited and it is thereupon considered by the Court that the Defendant go hence without day and that he recover against the Plt. five shillings Currant money with his Costs by him in this behalf expended and a Lawyers Fee.

Wiles vs Hughes & Atkinson   In the Action of Debt between Luke Wiles Plt. and Stephen Hughes and Sarah Atkinson Executor and Executrix &c. of Thomas Atkinson deceased Defendants the Plt. failing to Prosecute his Suit on the Defendants motion he is nonsuited and it is therefore considered by the Court that the Defendants go hence without day and that they recover against the Plt. five shillings Currant money with their Costs by them in this behalf expended and a Lawyers Fee.

Wiles vs Hughes   In the Action of Trespass on the Case between Luke Wiles Plt. and Stephen Hughes Defendant the Plt. failing to Prosecute his Suit on the Defendants motion he is nonsuited and it is thereupon considered by the Court that the Defendant go hence without day and that he recover against the Plt. five shillings Currant money with his Costs by him in this behalf expended and a Lawyers Fee.

Johnson vs Quin   The Action of Case between Daniell Johnson Plt. and John Quin Defendant is dismist the Plt. not prosecuting the same.

[170]   October Court 1729
Pennington vs Baily   In the Action of Trespass between Paul Pennington Plt. and Henry Baily Defendt. the Plt. takes issue on the Defendts. Plea and the Suit is continued.

Marchbanks vs Croom   In the Action on the Case between George Marchbanks Plt. and Daniell Croom Defendt. leave is granted the Deft. to Plead severall matters and thereupon he files Pleas and the Suit is continued.

Salmon vs Edwards   In the Action on the Case between Thomas

Salmon Plt. and Thomas Edwards Defendt. time is granted the Plt. to mend his declaration.

New vs Morriss   In the Action of Debt between William New Plt. and Hugh Morriss and Mary his wife Executrix &c. of Edmund New deceased Defendts. the Defendants Demurr generally to the Declaration and the Suit is continued.

Taylor vs Lowe   The Action of Trespass on the Case between John Taylor Plt. and Thomas Lowe Defendt. is continued at the Plts. cost.

Lad & Powell vs Thompson   The Petition of Amos Lad and Roger Powell against Samuell Thompson and Mary his Wife Administratrix &c. of John Bellamy deceased is continued.

Scot vs Moseley   In the Action on the Case between Edward Scot Plt. and William Moseley Defendt. the Defendant acknowledges himself indebted unto the Plt. in the Sum of two pounds nineteen shillings and a penny Currant money whereupon it is considered by the Court that the Plt. do recover against the Defendant the said Sum with Costs of this Suit and a Lawyers Fee.

Huson vs Cox   On the Petition of John Huson vs Fredorick Cox ordered that a Subpœna do issue against the said Cox returnable to the next Court.

Wharton proves Accts   Thomas Wharton exhibits an Account against Elizabeth Harriss

[171]   October Court 1729
for one hundred and forty pounds of Tobacco and against Edward Harriss for Seven shillings Currant money and makes Oath that the same is justly due to him which is ordered to be Certified thereon.

Then the Court adjourned 'till to Morrow morning eleven of the Clock.

****

At a Court continued and held for Goochland County the twenty second day of October Annoq Domi. 1729. Present. William Mayo, Tarlton Fleming, George Paine, James Holman, Gent. Justices.

Quin vs May   In the Action on the Case between John Quin Plt. and

William May Defendt. the following Jury are sworn, John Mcbrid, Peter Ware, James Taylor, Joell Chandler, William Woodson, Joseph Lewis, William Lansdon, Thomas Christian, John Prier, John Laine, Thomas Murrell, Robert Carter, who after some time bring in their Verdict which on the Plts. motion is ordered to be recorded and is as followeth "Wee find for the Plaintive three pounds Currant money Jno. Mcbrid." the Defendt. files reasons in arrest of Judgment the arguing whereof is referred to the next Court.

Micheaux vs Turner   In the Action on the Case between Jacob Micheaux Plt. and James Turner Defendt. the Sherif having made return that the Defendant is not to be found and he failing to appear on the Plts. motion an Attachment is awarded him against the Defendants Estate returnable to the next Court.

Tindall vs Woodson   In the Action on the Case between Thomas Tindall Plt. and John Woodson Defendt. the Plt. having failed to file his declaration on the Defendants motion he is nonsuited and it is thereupon considered by the Court that the Defendant go hence without day and that he recover against the Plt. five shillings Currant money

[172]   October Court 1729
with his Costs by him in this behalf expended and a Lawyers Fee.

Towns vs Hoggat   The Action of Trespass between William Townes Plt. and Anthony Hoggat Defendt. is continued.

Hoggat vs Townes   The Action on the Case between Anthony Hoggatt Plt. and William Townes Defendt. is continued.

Cannon vs Felps   In the Action on the Case between William Cannon Plt. and John Felps Defendt. the Defendant appears but failing to plead Judgment by nihil dicit is granted against him for what damages shall be recovered in this Suit to be discharged nevertheless if the Defendant shall Plead at the next Court.

Pigg vs Allin   In the Action on the Case between John Pigg Junr. Plt. and Samuell Allin Defendt. an imparlance is granted the Defendant.

Pigg vs Woodson   In the Action on the Case between John Pigg Junr. Plt. and William Woodson Defendt. a Special imparlance is granted the Defendant.

Boston vs Cox   The Action on the Case between Hugh Boston Plt. and Nicholas Cox Defendt. is continued at the Defendants cost.

Micheaux vs Woodson   In the Action on the Case between Jacob Micheaux Plt. and Joseph Woodson Defendt. a Special imparlance is granted the Defendant.

Jones vs Quin   In the Action on the Case between Esther Jones Executrix &c. of Tobias Lafeit deceased Plt. and John Quin Defendt. an imparlance is granted the Defendant.

Scot vs Phelps   In the Action on the Case between Edward Scot Plt. and John Phelps Defendt. the Defendant acknowledges himself indebted unto the Plt. in the Sum of five pounds six shillings and

[173]   October Court 1729
eleven pence Currant money whereupon it is considered by the Court that the Plt. do recover against the Defendt. the said Sum with the Costs of this Suit and a Lawyers Fee.

Present John Woodson Gent.

Scot vs Pritchet   In the Action on the Case between Edward Scot Plt. and John Pritchet Defendt. the Sherif having made return that the Defendant is not to be found and he failing to appear an Alias Capias is awarded against the Defendant returnable to the next Court.

Scot vs Swift   In the Action on the Case between Edward Scot Plt. and William Swift Defendt. an imparlance is granted the Defendt.

Henson vs Saunders   In the Action of Trespass on the Case between Benjamin Henson Plt. and Thomas Saunders Defendt. the Defendant failing to appear Judgment is granted against him and Daniel Stoner Gent. Sherif for what damages shall be recovered in this Suit to be discharged nevertheless if the Defendant appears at the next Court.

Cabbell vs Kent   In the Action on the Case between William Cabbell Plt. and William Kent Defendt. the Defendant failing to appear Judgment is granted against him and Daniel Stoner Gent. Sherif for what damages shall be recovered in this Suit to be discharged nevertheless if the Defendant appears at the next Court.

Prosser vs Wotars   In the Action on the Case between Thomas Prosser

Plt. and William Wotars Defendt. the Defendant failing to appear Judgment is granted against him and Daniel Stoner Gent. Sherif for what damages shall be recovered in this Suit to be discharged nevertheless if the Defendant appears at the next Court.

Womack vs Burton   In the Action of Debt between William Womack Plt. and Nowell Burton Defendt. the Defendant failing to appear Judgment is granted against him and Thomas Dickins his Common Bail for what damages shall be recovered in this Suit to be discharged nevertheless

[174]
if the Defendant appears at the next Court.

Cannon vs Swift   In the Action on the Case between John Cannon Plt. and William Swift Defendt. an Imparlance is granted the Deft.

Prier vs White   In the Action on the Case between Rebecca Prier by Samuel Prier her next friend Plt. and Edward White Defendant time is granted the Plt. to mend her declaration.

Cabbell vs Allin   In the Action of Debt between William Cabbell Plt. and Samuel Allin Defendt. the Defendant acknowledges himself indebted unto the Plt. in the Sum of four pounds ten Shillings and seven pence Currant money and one hundred and five and a half pounds of Tobacco whereupon it is considered by the Court that the Plt. do recover against the Defendant the said money and Tobacco with the Costs of this Suit and a Lawyers Fee.

Womack vs Pritchet   In the Action of Debt between William Womack Plt. and John Pritchet Defendant the Sherif having made return that the Defendt. is not to be found and he failing to appear an Alias Capias is awarded against the Defendant returnable to the next Court.

Bowie vs Fauquinou   In the Action of Trespass on the Case between John Bowie Plt. and Daniel Fauquinou Defendt. the Defendant acknowledges himself indebted unto the Plt. in the sum of thirty shillings Currant money and two hundred and thirteen pounds of Tobacco whereupon it is considered by the Court that the Plt. do recover against the Defendant the said money and tobacco with the Costs of this Suit and a Lawyers Fee.

Ashlin vs Mcbrid   In the Action of Trespass between Joseph Ashlin Plt.

and John Mcbrid Defendt the Defendant Pleads not guilty and for tryall puts himself upon the Country and the Plt. likewise and the Suit is continued.

[175]   October Court 1729
Hopkins vs Martin   In the Action of Trespass between Evan Hopkins Plt. and Francis Martin Defendant a Special imparlance is granted the Defendant.

Rapene vs Bingley   In the Action of Trespass on the Case between Anthony Rapene Plt. and Joseph Bingley Defendant the following Jury are sworn John Mcbrid, Thomas Christian, Samuell Allin, Stephen Woodson, James Taylor, Joseph Lewis, John Laine, John Prier, Joell Chandler, John Taylor, John Felps, Thomas Wadloe, who after some time bring in their Verdict which Verdict Thomas Prosser Attorny for the Plt. moves may not be received because he Saith that the Jury have found against their Evidence, upon consideration whereof it is the Opinion of the Court that the Jury's Verdict is not contrary to their Evidence, and on the Defendants motion the same is admitted to record and is as followeth "Wee find for the Defendant John Mcbrid." whereupon it is considered by the Court that the Defendant go hence without day and that he recover against the Plt. his Costs by him in this behalf expended and a Lawyers Fee.

Grand Jury to be Summoned   Pursuant to an Act of Assembly of this Colony intituled an Act concerning Jurys it is ordered that the Sheriff do Summon twenty four Freeholders of his County to appear at the next Court and serve as Grand jury men.

Tuckahoe bridge to be built   John Woodson and Allin Howard are appointed to meet Richard Randolph and Joseph Mayo Gent. on Saturday the eighth day of November next at Tuckahoe Bridge to treat with workmen about rebuilding the same.

Surveyor of the road   Phillip Thomas is appointed Surveyor of the road from Richard Parkers on let alone Creek the best way down to the Manakin Town road, and it is ordered that the titheables dwelling on the South side the said road do clear the same.

Woodson vs Woodson   In the Action of Trespass on the Case between Robert Woodson

[176]   October Court 1729
and James Holman Plts. and William Woodson Defendant Tarlton Fleming Gent. is appointed to examine State and settle the severall Accounts in dispute between them and to report his proceedings therein to the next Court.

Bingley vs Rapene   On the motion of Judith Bingley a witness for Anthony Rapene vs Joseph Bingley it is ordered that the said Anthony do pay her for eight days attendance two hundred and forty pounds of tobacco with Costs.

Mallet vs Rapene   On the motion of Stephen Mallet a witness for Anthony Rapene vs Joseph Bingley it is ordered that the said Anthony do pay him for seven days attendance two hundred and ten pounds of tobacco with Costs.

Parentan vs Rapene   On the motion of Isaac Parentan a witness for Anthony Rapene vs Joseph Bingley it is ordered that the said Anthony do pay him for eight days attendance two hundred and forty pounds of tobacco with Costs.

Pratt vs Bingley   On the motion of Roger Pratt a witness for Joseph Bingley ads Anthony Rapene it is ordered that the said Joseph do pay him for eight days attendance two hundred and forty pounds of tobacco with Costs.

Perro vs Bingley   On the motion of Daniel Perro a witness for Joseph Bingley ads Anthony Rapene it is ordered that the said Joseph do pay him for three days attendance ninety pounds of tobacco with Costs.

Bingley vs Quin   On the motion of Joseph Bingley a witness for John Quin vs Willm. May it is ordered that the said John do pay him for one days attendance thirty pounds of tobacco with Costs.

****

[177]   November Court 1729
At a Court held for Goochland County the third Tuesday in November being the Eighteenth day of the Month Annoq Domi. 1729. Present. William Mayo, Tarlton Fleming, Allin Howard, George Payne, William Cabbell Gent. Justices.

Grand Jury Sworn   Pursuant to an Act of Assembly of this Collony, the following Persons are Sworn Grand Jury Men of this County John Mcbrid, Bouth Napier, Amos Lad, John Gunn, Henry Harper, John Pryer, Robert Carter, John Webb, Andrew Moreman, Thomas Christian Junr, James Nowlin, William May, Benjamin Woodson, Constant Perkins, Thomas Wadloe, James Taylor, Samuell Thompson, who after some time Return with their Presentments which are Ordered to be Recorded and are as follow "Amos Lad and Henry Harper Present Judith Ballew for having one Bastard Child. Robert Carter and Constant Perkins Present John Burks for a Common Swearer. Wee Present the Surveyor of Tuckahoe Bridge for not keeping the Bridge in Repair. Amos Lad, Robert Carter, and Samuell Thompson, Present John Woodson Gent. Surveyor of Bever dam Bridge and Road for that the said Bridge and Road is not in Repair Jno. McBrid."

Ordered that the Clerk of this Court do Issue Subpœna's against the several Persons who are Presented by the Grand Jury.

Carters deed to Hulsey Robert Carter acknowledges a Deed with the Livery of Seizin endorsed from himself to Susannah Hulsey to be his Act and Deed and it is thereupon admitted to Record then Mary wife of the said Robert (She being first privately Examined) relinquishes her Right of Dower in the Land by the said Deed Conveyed which is also Admitted to Record.

Hulseys deed to Hulsey Susannah Hulsey acknowledges a Deed with the Livery of Seizin endorsed from herself to Charles Hulsey to be her Act and Deed and it is thereupon admitted to Record.

[178] November Court 1729
Epes deed to Ligon Francis Epes acknowledges a Deed with the Livery of Seizin endorsed from himself to Matthew Ligon to be his Act and Deed and it is thereupon Admitted to Record.

Christians deed to Christian Thomas Christian acknowledges a Deed from himself to James Christian to be his Act and Deed and it is thereupon Admitted to Record.

Macon vs Hughes In the Action of Debt between John Macon Plt. and Stephen Hughes Defendt. by Consent of the Parties the Jury formerly Sworn are discharged and Griffith Bowen, Thomas Prosser, and Thomas Dickins are Appointed to Examine State and Settle the Several matters in Dispute and to Report their Proceedings therein to the next Court.

Hughes vs Macon In the Action on the Case between Stephen Hughes

Plt. and John Macon Defendt. by Consent of the Parties the Arguments on the Reasons filed in stay of Judgment are waived and Griffith Bowen, Thomas Prosser, and Thomas Dickins are Appointed to Examine State and Settle the Severall matters in Dispute and to Report their Proceedings therein to the next Court.

Wood vs Taylor   In the Action of Trespass on the Case between Henry Wood Plt. and John Taylor Defendt. the Deft. appears and acknowledges himself Indebted unto the Plt. in the Sum of Twenty three Shillings and Six pence Currt. Money and four hundred and twenty eight pounds of Tobacco whereupon it is Considered by the Court that the Plt. do Recover against the Deft. the said Money and Tobacco with Costs.

Sims vs Phelps   In the Action of Trespass on the Case between Mathew Sims Plt. and John Phelps Defendt. on the Defts. motion a Special Imparlance is granted him.

LaVillain vs Woodson   In the Action on the Case between John LaVillain and Joseph Woodson Defendt. on the Defts. motion a Special Imparlance is granted him.

[179]   November Court 1729
Woodson vs Napier   In the Action on the Case between William Woodson Plt. and Bouth Napier Defendt. on the Defts. motion a Special Imparlance is granted him.

Rapine vs Bingley   In the Action of Trespass on the Case between Anthony Rapine Plt. and Joseph Bingley Defendt. on the Defts. motion a Special Imparlance is granted him.

Innis vs Mcbrid   In the Action of Trespass between John Innis Plt. and John Mcbrid Defendt. on the Defts. motion a Special Imparlance is granted him.

Collins vs Morriss   In the Action of Trespass between Mathew Collins Plt. and John Morriss Defendt. the Sheriff having made Return that the Deft. is not to be found and he failing to Appear an Alias Capias is Awarded against him returnable to the next Court.

Scott vs Pritchet   In the Action on the Case between Edward Scot Plt. and John Pritchet Defendt. the Sheriff having made Return on the Alias Capias that the Defendt. is not to be found and he failing to Appear a Pluries Capias is Awarded against him Returnable to the next Court.

Scoyles vs Bondurant   In the Action on the Case between William Scoyles Plt. and John Peter Bondurant Defendt. the Deft. Pleads that he Oweth nothing and time is granted the Plt. to Reply.

Chastain vs Easly   In the Action on the Case between John and Peter Chastain Exrs. &c. of Peter Chastain Deceasd. Plts. and William Easley Deft. the Deft. failing to Appear on the motion of the Plts. Judgment is granted him against the Deft. and Daniel Stoner Gent. Sheriff for what damages shall be Recovered in this Suit to be discharged nevertheless by the Appearance of the Defendt. at the next Court.

David vs Coutain   The Action on the Case between Peter David Plt. and John Coutain Deft. is dismiss'd the Plt. not Prosecuting the same.

[180]   November Court 1729
Cabbell vs Kent   The Action on the Case between William Cabbell Plt. and William Kent Defendt. is Dismiss'd the Plt. not Prosecuting the same.

Micheaux vs Woodson   The Action on the Case between Jacob Micheaux Plt. and Joseph Woodson Defendt. is Dismiss'd the Plt. not Prosecuting the same.

Huson vs Cox   On the Petition of John Huson against Fredorick Cox Praying an Order for his Freedom Dues it is Considered by the Court that the Petitioner do recover against the said Fredorick ten bushells of Indian Corn, thirty Shillings in Money or the Value thereof in Goods and a well fix'd Musquet or Fuzee of the Value of twenty Shillings at least with the Costs of this Petition.

Woodson vs Woodson   The Action of Trespass on the Case between Robert Woodson and James Holman Plts. and William Woodson Deft. is continued.

Womack vs Pritchet   The Action of Debt between William Womack Plt. and John Pritchet Defendt. is continued.

Cannon vs Phelps   The Action on the Case between William Cannon Plt. and John Phelps Defendt. is continued.

Hopkins vs Martin   In the Action of Trespass between Evan Hopkins Plt. and Francis Martin Defendt. the Deft. appears but failing to Plead On the Plts motion Judgment by nihil dicit is granted against the Deft. for what Damages shall be Recovered in this Suit to be Discharged nevertheless if the Deft. shall Plead at the next Court.

Cannon vs Swift   In the Action on the Case between John Cannon Plt. and William Swift Deft. the Deft. appears but failing to Plead On the Plts. motion Judgment by nihil dicit is granted against the Deft. for what Damages shall be recovered in this Suit to be discharged nevertheless if the Defendant shall Plead at the next Court.

[181]   November Court 1729
Henson vs Sanders   In the Action of Trespass on the Case between Benjamin Henson Plt. and Thomas Saunders Defendt. the Deft. appears but failing to Plead On the Plts. motion Judgment by nihil dicit is granted against the Deft. for what Damages shall be Recovered in this Suit to be Discharged nevertheless if the Deft. shall Plead at the next Court.

Scott vs Swift   In the Action on the Case between Edward Scott Plt. and William Swift Defendt. the Deft. appears but failing to Plead on the Plts. motion Judgment by nihil dicit is granted against the Deft. for what Damages shall be Recovered in this Suit to be Discharged nevertheless if the Deft. shall Plead at the next Court.

Jones &c. vs Quin   In the Action on the Case between Esther Jones Exx. &c. of Tobias Lafait Plt. and John Quin Defendt. the Deft. appears but failing to Plead on the Plts. motion Judgment by nihil dicit is granted against the Deft. for what Damages shall be Recovered in this Suit to be Discharged nevertheless if the Deft. shall Plead at the next Court.

Pigg vs Woodson   In the Action on the Case between John Pigg Junr. Plt. and William Woodson Deft. the Defendt. appears but failing to Plead On the Plts. motion Judgment by nihil dicit is granted against the Deft. for what Damages shall be Recovered in this Suit to be Discharged nevertheless if the Deft. shall Plead at the next Court.

Pigg vs Allin   In the Action on the Case between John Pigg Junr. Plt. and Samuel Allin Deft. the Defendt. appears but failing to Plead on the Plts. motion Judgment by nihil dicit is granted against the Deft. for what Damages shall be Recovered in this Suit to be Discharged nevertheless if the Defendant shall Plead at the next Court.

Womack vs Burton   In the Action of Debt between William Womack Plt. and Nowell Burton Defendt. the Deft. failing to Appear on the Plts. motion the Conditionall Judgment formerly Granted against the Deft. and Thomas Dickins his Common Bail is Confirmed for so much Damages as shall be found upon Executing a Writ of Inquiry at the next Court of which the Sheriff is ordered to give the Deft. and the said Thomas Dickins

[182]   November Court 1729
notice by serving them with a Copy of this Order.

Prosser vs Wotars   In the Action on the Case between Thomas Prosser Plt. and William Wotars Defendt. the Deft. failing to appear on the Plts. motion the Conditionall Judgment formerly granted against the Deft. and Daniel Stoner Gent. Sheriff is Confirmed for so much damages as shall be found upon Executing a Writ of Inquiry at the next Court of which the Sheriff is ordered to give the Deft. notice by serving him with a Copy of this Order.

Prier vs White   In the Action on the Case between Rebecca Prier by Edward Pryer her Father and next Friend Plt. and Edward White Deft. the Plt. failing to prosecute her Suit on the Defts. motion She is nonsuited and it is thereupon considered by the Court that the Deft. do Recover against the Plt. for five shillings Currt. money together with the Costs by him in this behalf expended and a Lawyers Fee.

Micheaux vs Turner   In the Action on the Case between Jacob Micheaux Plt. and James Turner Deft. Joseph Woodson enters himself Special Bail for the Deft. who Pleads he oweth nothing and for tryall thereof puts himself upon the Country and the Plt. likewise.

Boston vs Cox   In the Action on the Case between Hugh Boston Plt. and Nicholas Cox Defendt. on the Plts. motion time is granted him to mend his Declaration.

Quin vs May   In the Action on the Case between John Quin Plt. and William May Defendt. the Deft. appears and acknowledges himself Indebted unto the Plt. in the sum of forty five shillings Currt. money whereupon it is considered by the Court that the Plt. do recover against the Deft. the said money with the Costs of this Suit and a Lawyers Fee.

Townes vs Hoggat   In the Action of Trespass between William Townes Plt. and

[183]   November Court 1729
Anthony Hoggat Defendt. the Report of the Auditors formerly appointed in this Suit being now presented on the Plts. motion it is admitted to

Record and is as followeth "Goochland County ss In Obedience to an Order made last July Court by the Worshipfull the Justices of Goochland County in Court sitting in order that a final end of all Differences between William Townes of the one part and Anthony Hoggat of the other part might be made fully compleated and perfected the said Court by the assent consent and approbation of the Parties abovementioned did constitute nominate and appoint Us Thomas Randolph, William Mayo, George Pain Gent. Arbitrators indifferently chosen and approved by the said William Townes and Anthony Hoggat that we the said Thomas Randolph, William Mayo, George Pain Gent. should award, Arbitrate, determine, and Judge of and concerning all and all manner of Accou[nt]s, suits, Judgment, Executions, Accompts, Reckonings, Trespasses, Controversies, and demands whatsoever had, made, move, stirred, between the said William Townes and Anthony Hoggat from the beginning of the World untill the day of the date of these presents and whereas it was ordered by the Worshipfull the said Court that we should return such award of, and concerning the Premises betwixt the Parties abovesaid made, compleated, and perfected to the next Court in Course, which should be the third Tuesday in August of this present Year 1729. Now be it known that we the said Thomas Randolph, William Mayo, George Pain Gent. Arbitrators as aforesaid taking upon us the Charge of the said award, and Arbitrament and having heard and understood the sayings and Allegations of both the said Parties concerning the Premises do thereupon make and put in writing this our Award, Arbitration, and Judgment under our hands & seals between the said Parties for and concerning the Premises in manner and form following, First we do award, Arbitrate, and determine by these Presents That the said Anthony Hoggat pay unto the said William Towns the Sum of Five pounds Five shillings & two pence Current money which we Judge to be to be the Ballance due besides Costs Given under our Hands the 15th September 1729. Thoms. Randolph, Wm. Mayo." Whereupon it is considered by the Court that the Plt. do recover against the Deft. five pounds five shillings and two pence Currt. money with Costs of this Suit and a Lawyers Fee.

From which Judgment the Defendt. Appeals to the Sixth day of

[184] November Court 1729
of the next General Court Stephen Hughes entring himself Security for the same.

Phenix vs Townes   On the motion of Abraham Phenix of Hanover County a Witness of William Townes vs Anthony Hoggat it is Ordered that the said William do pay him for one days attendance and for coming and returning thirty five miles once one hundred and sixty five pounds of

Tobacco with Costs.

Hoggat vs Townes   In the Action on the Case between Anthony Hogat Plt. and William Townes Defendt. the Deft. moves that the Plts. Suit may be dismiss'd and the Plt. thereupon moves that it may proceed whereupon the Court being of opinion that the Plts. cause of action in this Suit was examined settled and allowed by the Auditors in the Suit between William Townes Plt. and Anthony Hoggat Deft. it is Considered that the Deft. go hence without Day and that he recover against the Plt. his Costs by him in this behalf expended and a Lawyers Fee.

[blank] from which Judgment the Plt. Appeals to this sixth day of the next General Court Stephen Hughes entring himself Security for the same.

Marchbanks acct. vs Birch   George Marchbanks exhibits an Acct. against Edward Birch and makes Oath that the Ballance thereof being six pounds seventeen shillings and three pence half penny is justly due to him and that he never received any Satisfaction for the same which is ordered to be Certified thereon.

Marchbanks deeds to Chamberlayne   Ebenezer Adams comes into Court and proves upon Oath Deeds of Lease and Release from George Marchbanks to William Chamberlayne to be the Acts and Deeds of the said George Marchbanks and they are thereupon admitted to Record.

Then the Court adjourned to the third Tuesday in next month.

****

[185]   December Court 1729
At a Court called for Goochland County the second day of December 1729 for the Tryall of John Huetson. Present. John Woodson, Tarlton Fleming, Allin Howard, George Payne, Gent. Justices.

Thomas Dickins is admitted Council for the Prisoner.

John Huetson being brought to the Barr and accused with the felonious taking from the body of George Alves five pounds seven shillings and eleven pence upon Examination of the Witnesses it is the Opinion of the Court that the said John Huetson is not guilty and he is thereupon Acquitted.

****

At a Court held for Goochland County the third Tuesday in December being the sixteenth day of the Month Annoq Domi 1729. Present. William Mayo, John Woodson, Tarlton Fleming, Allin Howard, William Cabbell, James Holman Gent. Justices.

Fleming sworn Coroner Tarlton Fleming Gent. produces a Commission from the Honble. William Gooch Esqr. his Majesty's Leiut. Governor and Commander in Chief of this Dominion to be one of the Coroners of this County which being read the said Tarlton Fleming takes the Oaths appointed by Act of Parliament to be taken instead of the Oaths of Allegiance and Supremacy, the Oath appointed to be taken by an Act of Parliament made in the sixth year of the Reign of her late Majesty Queen Anne Entituled an Act for the Security of her Majesty's person and Government and of the Succession to the Crown of Great Brittain in the

[186]   December Court 1729
the Protestant line, Subscribed the Test and takes the Oath of a Coroner.

Cabbell sworn Coroner   William Cabbell Gent. Produces a Commission from the Honble. William Gooch Esqr. his Majesty's Lieut. Governor and Commander in chief of this Dominion to be one of the Coroners of this County which being Read the said William Cabbell takes the Oaths appointed by Act of Parliament to be taken instead of the Oaths of Allegiance and Supremacy the Oath appointed to be taken by an Act of Parliament made in the sixth year of the Reign of her late Majesty Queen Anne Entituled an Act for the security of her Majesty's person and Government and of the Succession to the Crown of Great Brittain in the Protestant line Subscribed the Test and takes the Oath of a Coroner.

Farrars deed to Barnet   John Farrar acknowledges a Deed from himself to John Barnit to be his Act and Deed and it is thereupon Admitted to Record.

Stovealls' deed to Quin   Bartholomew Stoveall acknowledges a deed with the Livery of Seizin endorsed from himself to John Quin to be his Act and Deed and it is thereupon admitted to Record.

Sorrells' deed to Pumfree   John Sorrell acknowledges a deed from himself to Sylvanus Pumfree, Margaret Pumfree and Sylvanus Pumfree Junr. to be his Act and Deed and it is thereupon Admitted to Record.

Carr's Administration   William Cabbell comes into Court and makes Oath that Joell Carr Deceased, died without any will as far as he knows or believes and on his motion and giving security for his Just and faithfull administration of the said Decedents Estate Certificate is granted him for obtaining Letters of Administration in due form   Thomas Prosser and Thomas Dickins entring themselves Securities for the same.

Ordered that Amos Lad, Thomas Murrell, James Nowlin

[187]   December Court 1729
and John Gunn, or any three of them being first sworn by some Justices of the peace do Appraise the Estate of Joell Carr deceased and that William Cabbell the Administrator do return an Inventory thereof to the next Court.

Surveyor of the Road   On the motion of Henry Cary Gent. leave is granted him to Clear a Road from Buckingham downwards the most convenient way and Edward Wood is appointed Surveyor thereof.

Atkinson vs Benning   In the Action of Trespass between Sarah Atkinson Plt. and Anthony Benning Defendt. the following Jury are sworn Richard Dean, John Prier, Mathew Cox, Robert Adams, John Mcbrid, Peter Jefferson, Henry Harper, Samuell Allin, Nowell Burton, Thomas Christian, Thomas Christian Junr. Thomas Wadloe, who after some time return with their Verdict which on the Plts. motion is admitted to Record and is as followeth "Wee find for the Plt. six pence Sterling Richard Dean Foreman." the Deft. moves that the Judgment may be entered for no more Costs them the Jury have found Damages whereupon the Court being of opinion that full Costs ought to be tax'd it is considered that the Plt. do recover against the Deft. six pence Sterling by the Jurors aforesaid in their said Verdict assessed with the Costs of this Suit and a Lawyers Fee.

From which Judgment the Deft. Appeals to the sixth day of the next Generall Court David Lesseur entring himself Security for the same.

Macon vs Hughes   The Action of Debt between John Macon Plt. and Stephen Hughes Defendt. is continued.

Hughes vs Macon   The Action on the Case between Stephen Hughes Plt. and John Macon Defendt. is continued.

Lankford vs Macon   On the motion of West Lankford of New Kent County a Witness for John Macon ads Stephen Hughes it is ordered that the said John Macon do pay him for four days attendance and for coming and returning forty five miles four times seven hundred and eighty pounds of Tobacco with Costs.

Syms vs Phelps   In the Action of Trespass on the Case between Mathew Syms Plt. and

[188]   December Court 1729
John Phelps Defendt. the Deft. appears but failing to plead on the Plts. motion Judgment by nihil dicit is granted against the Deft. for what damages shall be recovered in this Suit to be discharged nevertheless if the Deft. shall plead at the next Court.

La Villain vs Woodson   In the Action on the Case between John LaVillain Plt. and Joseph Woodson Defendt. the Deft. appears but failing to plead on the Plts. motion Judgment by nihil dicit is granted against the Deft. for what damages shall be recovered in this Suit to be discharged nevertheless if the Deft. shall plead at the next Court.

Woodson vs Napier   In the Action on the Case between William Woodson Plt. and Bouth Napier Defendt. the Deft. appears but failing to plead on the Plts. motion Judgment by nihil dicit is granted against the Deft. for what damages shall be recovered in this Suit to be discharged nevertheless if the Deft. shall plead at the next Court.

Innis vs Mcbrid   In the Action of Trespass between John Innis Plt. and John Mcbrid Defendt. the Deft. appears but failing to plead on the Plts. motion Judgment by nihil dicit is granted against the Deft. for what damages shall be recovered in this Suit to be discharged nevertheless if the Deft. shall plead at the next Court.

Innis vs Mcbrid   In the Action on the Case between John Innis Plt. and John Mcbrid Defendt. the Deft. appears but failing to plead on the Plts. motion Judgment by nihil dicit is granted against the Deft. for what damages shall be recovered in this Suit to be discharged nevertheless if the Deft. shall plead at the next Court.

Collins vs Morriss   In the Action of Trespass between Mathew Collins Plt. and John Morriss Defendt. the Sheriff having made Return on the Alias Capias that the Deft. is not to be found and he failing to appear a Pluries Capias is Awarded against him returnable to the next Court.

Rapine vs Bungley   In the Action of Trespass between Anthony Rapine Plt.

[189] December Court 1729
and Joseph Bingley Defendt. the Deft. pleads he is not Guilty and for tryall thereof puts himself upon the Country and the Plt. likewise.

Scoyles vs Bondurant   In the Action on the Case between William Scoyles Plt. and John Peter Bondurant Defendt. the Parties submit themselves to the Court for tryall whereupon it is considered that the Plt. do recover against the Defendt. twenty nine shillings and six pence Currt. money with the Costs of this Suit and a Lawyers Fee.

Taylor vs Scoyles   On the motion of James Taylor a Witness for William Taylor vs John Peter Bondurant it is ordered that the said William Scoyles do pay him for two days attendance sixty pounds of tobacco with Costs.
Ordered that only one days attendance be taxed in the bill of Costs.

Ditoway vs Scoyles   On the motion of Barbary Dittoway a Witness for William Scoyles vs John Peter Bondurant it is ordered that the said William Scoyles do pay her for one days attendance thirty pounds of tobacco with Costs.

Chastain vs Easly   In the Action on the Case between John and Peter Chastain Exrs. &c. of Peter Chastain decd. Plts. and William Easly Defendt. the Plts. file a new declaration the Deft. appears and pleads that he oweth nothing and for tryall submits himself to the Court and the Plts. likewise whereupon it is considered that the Plt. do recover against the Deft. forty shillings and three pence Currt. money with Costs of this Suit and a Lawyers Fee.

Woodson &c. vs Woodson   In the Action of Trespass on the Case between Robert Woodson and James Holman Plts. and William Woodson Defendt. the report of the Auditors formerly appointed in this Suit being now presented on the Plts. motion it is admitted to Record and is as followeth "Persuant to an order of Goochland County Court to me directed, bearing date the 21th. day of October 1729. to Examined state & Settle accounts between Robert Woodson and James Holman Plaintiff's and William Woodson Defendant. Having perused the accounts do find the Ballance due to the Pla[i]ntiffs, one pound fifteen shillings and three farthings Current money. Witness my hand this 27th of October 1729. Tarlton Fleming" Whereupon it is considered by the Court that the Plts

[190] December Court 1729
do recover against the Deft. one pound fifteen shillings and three farthings Currt. money with the Costs of this Suit and a Lawyers Fee.

Court house to be build   Ordered that the Sheriff do give publick notice in this County that at the next Court the building of the Court house will be lett to Workmen.

Then the Court adjourned 'till to morrow morning ten of the Clock.

****

At a Court continued and held for Goochland County the seventeenth day of December Annoq Domi 1729. Present. William Mayo, John Woodson, Allin Howard, William Cabbell Gent. Justices.

Atkinson vs Lesseur   In the Action of Trespass between Sarah Atkinson Plt. and David Lesseur Defendt. the following Jury are Sworn Richard Dean, William Lansdon, David Pattison, Henry Harper, John Prier, John Laine, Joseph Farrar, Bouth Napier, John Mcbrid, Mathew Cox, John Taylor, Robert Carter, who after some time return with their Verdict which on the Defts. motion is admitted to Record and is as followeth "Wee find for the Defendant Richard Dean Foreman." Whereupon it is considered by the Court that the Deft. go hence without day and that he recover against the Plt. his Costs by him in this behalf expended and a Lawyers Fee.

Franklin vs Atkinson   On the motion of John Franklin a Witness for Sarah Atkinson vs Davis Lesseur it is ordered that the said Sarah do pay him for eight days attendance two hundred and forty pounds of tobacco with Costs.

[191]   December Court 1729
Lax vs Atkinson   On the motion of William Lax a Witness for Sarah Atkinson vs David Lesseur it is ordered that the said Sarah do pay him for eight days attendance two hundred and forty pounds of tobacco with Costs.

Hook vs Lesseur   On the motion of James Hook a Witness for David Lesseur ads Sarah Atkinson it is ordered that the said David do pay him for six days attendance one hundred and eighty pounds of tobacco with Costs.

Atkinson vs Taylor   In the Action of Trespass between Sarah Atkinson Plt. and James Taylor Defendt. the following Jury are now Sworn Richard Dean, Jacob Micheaux, David Pattison, Henry Harper, John Prier, John Laine, Joseph Farrar, Bouth Napier, John Mcbrid, Mathew Cox, John

Taylor, Robert Carter, the Jury not being returned at the rising of the Court it is ordered that the Sheriff do keep them together untill they have agreed on their Verdict that then they seal up the same and deliver it to the Sheriff and that they appear to present it at the next Court.

Ferry appointed   On the motion of Dudley Digges Gent. leave is granted him to keep a Ferry from the point of the Fork of James River to both sides of the River and from each side to the point of Fork the rate of Ferriage two pence for a man and two pence for a horse.

Hopkins vs Martin   In the Action of Trespass between Evan Hopkins Plt. and Francis Martin Defendt. on the Defts. motion leave is granted him to plead several matters whereupon he files pleas and time is granted the Plt. to reply.

Surveyor of the Road   Ordered that a Road be cleared from the Ferry landing on the South side of James River opposite to the point of Fork in such manner as to pass by a Gravelly fall of Willis's Creek about three quarters of a mile below a plantation belonging to William Mayo Gent. and from thence the best way the ground will admit to the main Road, and from the Ferry landing on the North side of James River opposite to the point of Fork the best way the ground will admit to

[192]   December Court 1729
the River road   James Nevill is appointed Surveyor of both the said Roads.
   Ordered that the titheables inhabiting on the South side of James River above Willis's Creek do clear that part of the road lying between the said Creek and the Ferry landing and that the titheables of Benjamin Harrison Gent. do clear the other part of the Road lying below the said Creek.

Womack vs Burton   In the Action of Debt between William Womack Plt. and Nowell Burton Deft. John Quin appears on behalf of the Deft. and confesses a Judgment to the Plt. for five pounds Currant money whereupon it is considered by the Court that the Plt. do recover against the Deft. the said sum with the Costs of this Suit and a Lawyers Fee.

Womack vs Pritchet   The Action of Debt between William Womack Plt. and John Pritchet Defendt. is dismist the Plt. not prosecuting the same.

Cannon vs Swift   In the Action on the Case between John Cannon Plt. and William Swift Defendt. the Deft. pleads he oweth nothing and time is granted the Plt. to reply.

Henson vs Sanders   In the Action of Trespass on the Case between Benjamin Henson Plt. and Thomas Saunders Defendt. the Deft. pleads he oweth nothing and for tryall thereof puts himself upon the Country and the Plt. likewise.

Scott vs Swift   In the Action on the Case between Edward Scot Plt. and William Swift Defendt. the Deft. pleads he oweth nothing and for tryall thereof puts himself upon the Country and the Plt. likewise.

Scott vs Pritchet   In the Action on the Case between Edward Scott Plt. and John Pritchet Defendt. the Sheriff having made Return on the Pluries Capias that the Deft. is not to be found and he failing to appear on the Plts. motion a Pluries Capias de novo is awarded against the Deft. returnable to the next Court.

Jones &c. vs Quin   In the Action on the Case between Esther Jones Exx. &c. of Tobias Lafait Plt. and John Quin Defendt. the Deft. pleads

[193]   December Court 1729
he oweth nothing and for tryall thereof submits himself to the Court and the Plt. likewise whereupon it is considered that the Plt. do recover against the Deft. one pound & eighteen Shillings Credit in a Store with the Costs of this Suit and a Lawyers Fee.

Michaux vs Turner   In the Action on the Case between Jacob Michaux Plt. and James Turner Defendt. Stephen Hughes and Joseph Woodson are appointed to Examine, state and Settle the severall matters in dispute and to report their proceedings therein to the next Court.

Boston vs Cox   The Action of Case between Hugh Boston Plt. and Nicholas Cox Deft. is Continued.

Pigg vs Woodson   In the Action on the Case between John Pigg Junr. Plt. and William Woodson Defendt. on the Plts. motion time is granted him to mend his Declaration.

Pigg vs Allin   In the Action on the Case between John Pigg Junr. Plt. and Samuell Allin Defendt. on the Plts. motion time is granted him to mend his Declaration.

Cannon vs Phelps   The Action on the Case between William Cannon

Plt. and John Phelps Defendt. is dismist the Plt. not prosecuting the same.

Grand Jury vs Turner   Upon the Presentment of the Grand Jury against Hannah Turner the said Hannah failing to appear it is ordered that a Capias do Issue against her returnable to the next Court.

Grand Jury vs Birks   On the Presentment of the Grand Jury against John Burks for Swearing the said John comes into Court and acknowledges himself guilty whereupon it is ordered that he pay unto the Churchwardens of St. James's Parish five shillings Currt. money with Costs.

Grand Jury vs Ballew   The Present of the Grand Jury against Judith Ballew is continued to the next Court.

[194]   December Court 1729
Dickins vs Wharton   In the Action of Trespass on the Case between Thomas Dickins Plt. and Thomas Wharton Defendt. the Deft. failing to appear and the Sheriff having taken insufficient Bail on the motion of the Plt. Judgment is granted him against the Deft. and Daniell Stoner Gent. Sheriff for what damages shall be recovered in this Suit to be discharged nevertheless by the appearance of the Deft. at the next Court.

Vanderhood vs Ashlin   The Action of Trespass on the Case between Henry Vanderhood Plt. and Joseph Ashlin Deft. is dismist neither party appearing.

Woodson vs Micheaux   In the Action of Trespass on the Case between Joseph Woodson Plt. and Jacob Micheaux Defendt. the Plt. having failed to file his declaration on the Defts. motion he is nonsuited and it is thereupon considered by the Court that the Deft. do Recover against the Plt. five shillings Currt. money together with his Costs by him in this behalf expended and a Lawyers Fee.

Alvis vs Huetson   In the Action of Detinue between George Alvis Plt. and John Huetson Defendt. the Deft. pleads non detinet and for tryall thereof puts himself upon the Country and the Plt. likewise.

Murrell vs Wotars   The Action of Trespass on the Case between Thomas Murrell Plt. and William Wotars Defendt. is dismissed neither party appearing.

Wood vs New   In the Action of Trespass on the Case between Henry

Wood Plt. and William New Defendt. the Deft. failing to appear and the Sheriff having not returned any Bail on the motion of the Plt. Judgment is granted him against the Deft. and Daniell Stoner Gent. Sheriff for what damages shall be recovered in this Suit to be discharged nevertheless by the Appearance of the Deft. at the next Court.

Johnson vs Fenton   In the Action of Trespass on the Case between William Johnson

[195]   December Court 1729
Plt. and Thomas Fenton Defendt. the Sheriff having made Return that the Deft. is not to be found and he failing to appear an Alias Capias is awarded against him returnable to the next Court.

Wood vs Thompson   In the Action of Trespass on the Case between Henry Wood Plt. and Samuell Thompson Defendt. the Deft. failing to appear Judgment is granted against him and George Payne, Nowell Burton and Samuell Allin his Common Bail for what damages shall be recovered in this Suit to be discharged nevertheless by the appearance of the Deft. at the next Court.

Dennet vs Burnet   The Action on the Case between John Dennet Plt. and John Burnet Defendt. is dismist neither party appearing.

Wiles vs Hughes   In the Action of Trespass on the Case between Luke Wiles Plt. and Stephen Hughes Defendt. on the Defts. motion an Imparlance is granted him.

Wiles vs Hughs & Atkinson   In the Action of Debt between Luke Wiles Plt. and Stephen Hughes and Sarah Atkinson Executor & Exx. &c. of Thomas Atkinson deced. Defts. on the motion of the Defendts. an Imparlance is granted them.

Ware vs Saunders   In the Action of Trespass on the Case between Susanna Ware Plt. and William Sanders Defendt. the Deft. failing to appear and the Sheriff having not returned any Bail on the motion of the Plt. Judgment is granted her against the Deft. and Daniel Stoner Gent. Sheriff for what damages shall be recovered in this Suit to be discharged nevertheless by the appearance of the Defendt. at the next Court.

Davis vs Scruggs   In the Action of Trespass on the Case between George Davis Plt. and John Scruggs Defendt. the Sheriff having made Return that the Defendt. is not to be found and he failing to appear an

Alias Capias is awarded against him returnable to the next Court.

Lad & Powell vs Thompson   On the Petition of Amos Lad and Roger
Powell against

[196]   December Court 1729
Samuell Thompson and Mary his Wife the Sheriff having returned the said Samuell Summoned and he failing to appear on the motion of the Petitioners a Capias is awarded against him returnable to the next Court.

Then the Court adjourned to the third Tuesday in next Month.

****

At a Court called for Goochland County the nineteenth day of January 1729 [1730] for the tryall of Cuffey a negro man slave belonging to Anthony Benning.

A Commission from the Honble. William Gooch Esqr. his Majesty's Lieut. Governour and Commander in chief of this Dominion to John Fleming, William Mayo, John Woodson, Tarlton Fleming, Allen Howard, Edward Scot, George Paine, William Cabbell, and James Holman, Gent. to be Justices of Oyer and Terminer for the tryall of Cuffey a negro man slave belonging to Anthony Benning being read as also the Dedimus for administring the oaths and Test therein mentioned, John Woodson and George Paine Gent. administer the oaths appointed by Act of Parliament to be taken instead of the oaths of Allegiance and Supremacy, the Oath appointed to be taken by an Act of Parliament made in the first year of the Reign of his late Majesty King George the first Entituled an Act for the further Security of his Majestys persons and Government and the Succession of the Crown in the Heirs of the late Princess Sophia being Protestants and for extinguishing the Hopes of the pretended Prince of Wales and his open and secret abettors

[197]   [January 1730]
unto John Fleming and William Mayo Gent. who Subscribe the Test, take the Oath for duly executing the Office of a Commissioner of Oyer and Terminer, and then administer the said Oaths and Test unto John Woodson and George Paine Gent.

The Prisoner being brought to the Barr an Indictment against him for feloniously administring Poison to Kate a negro woman belonging to Anthony Rapine being read the Prisoner pleads not guilty the Witnesses and the Prisoners Defence being heard it is the Opinion of the Court that he is not guilty and he is thereupon acquitted.

The said Negro Cuffy being again brought to the Barr an Indictment against him for feloniously breaking and entring into the dwelling house of Peter Ware in this County and stealing thereout divers Goods the Property of the said Peter Ware being read the Prisoner pleads he is not guilty the Witnesses and the Prisoners defence being heard it is the Opinion of the Court that he is not guilty of the felony but upon consideration of the goods being found in the Possession of the Prisoner and his not discovering the same it is ordered that the Prisoner do receive on his bare back thirty nine lashes well laid on at the Common Whipping post and that he be then discharged.

****

At a Court held for Goochland County the twenty ninth day of January 1729 [1730] for the Proof of Publick Claims. Present. John Fleming, William Mayo, John Woodson, Allin Howard Gent. Justices.

The Act concerning Publick Claims is read.

[198] [January 1730]
Stephen Hughes a Quaker Exr. &c. of Thomas Atkinson deceased makes his Solemn Affirmation that he never received any satisfaction for taking up Edward Cable a Servant man belonging to Thomas Martin, and that he beleives his Testator Thomas Atkinson to whom the Certificate is granted never received any satisfaction for the same, which is ordered to be Certified to the Generall Assembly for allowance.

A Petition for a Town of Warwick is Presented to William Mayo Gent. and ordered to be Certified to the Generall Assembly.

A Proposition for a Town at or near the Falls of James River on the North side of James River is Presented by the Subscribers thereto and ordered to be Certified to the Generall Assembly.

A Proposition for the improvement of Trade and encouragement of Navigation, by regulating the manner of exporting Tobacco, paying the Publick Levies, and setling a bounty on linnen Cloth, is Presented by the Subscribers thereto and ordered to be Certified to the Generall Assembly.
                                                    Test. Henry Wood ClCur.

****

At a Court held for Goochland County the third Tuesday in February being the seventeenth day of the Month Annoq Domi. 1729 [1730]. Present. John Fleming, Tarlton Fleming, Allin Howard, George Paine, William Cabbell, James Holman, Gent. Justices.

Pavement vs Coleman   In the Action on the Case between Thomas Pavement Plt.

[199]   February Court 1729 [1730] and Samuell Coleman Defendt. the following Jury are Sworn Richard Dean, Robert Adams, Nicholas Cox, Jacob Micheaux, Mathew Cox, Stephen Woodson, Ashford Hughes, John Mcbrid, Nowell Burton, William Lansdon, James Taylor, John Prier, who after some time return with their Verdict which on the Plts. motion is admitted to Record and is as followeth "Wee find for the Plt. fourteen shillings Currant money and three pounds fourteen shillings and seven pence half penny Credit in a Store, Richard Dean Foreman." wherefore it is considered by the Court that the Plt. do recover against the Deft. the said Sums of fourteen shillings Currant money and three pounds fourteen shillings and seven pence half penny Credit in a Store by the Jurors aforesaid in their said Verdict assessed with the Costs of this Suit and a Lawyers Fee.

Bibe's will proved   The last will and testament of Thomas Bibe is presented in Court by Elizabeth Bibe his Executrix who makes Oath thereto and the same being proved by the oaths of the Witnesses thereto it is admitted to Record and on the motion of the said Executrix and her performing what is usuall in such cases Certificate is granted her for obtaining a Probate thereof in due form Francis Martin and John Webb Securities.

Stewart's deeds to Poveall   John Stewart acknowledges Deeds of Lease and Release from himself to John Poveall to be his several Acts and Deeds and they are thereupon admitted to Record.

Hollands deeds to Chiles   Michaell Holland acknowledges a Deed with the Livery of Seizin endorsed and a Bond from himself to Henry Chiles to be his severall Acts and Deeds and they are thereupon admitted to Record.
    Edward Moor, Thomas Prosser, and Joseph Fox prove upon oath a Power of Attorney from Judith wife of the said Michaell to Henry Wood to be the Act and Deed of the said Judith which is admitted to Record,

then Henry Wood by virtue of the said power of Attorny relinquishes the said Judith's right of Dower in the land by the said deed conveyed which is also ordered to be Recorded.

[200]   February Court 1729 [1730]
Pratt's Administration   Mary Pratt comes into Court and makes Oath that Roger Pratt deceased died without any will as far as she knows or believes and on her motion and giving security for her Just and faithfull Administration of the said Deceadents Estate Certificate is granted her for obtaining Letters of Administration in due form Peter Ford and Joseph Bingley entring themselves Securities for the same.
    Ordered that Anthony Rapene, Stephen Chastain, Nicholas Suillie, and John Paine or any three of them being first sworn by some Justice of the Peace do Appraise the Estate of Roger Pratt deceased and that Mary Pratt the Administratrix do return an Inventory thereof to the next Court.

Baizes will proved   The last will and testament of Peter Baize is Presented in Court by Sarah Baize his Executrix who makes Oath thereto and the same being proved by the Oaths of Elisabeth Bibe and Edward White two of the Witnesses thereto it is admitted to Record and on the motion of the said Executrix and her performing what is usuall in such cases Certificate is granted her for obtaining a Probate thereof in due form Robert Adams and John Webb Securities.

Adams's deed to Chiles   Robert Adams acknowledges a Deed with the Livery of Seizin endorsed and a Bond from himself to Henry Chiles to be his severall Acts and Deeds and they are thereupon admitted to Record.

        Present William Mayo Gent.

Dean vs Huson   In the Action of Debt between Richard Dean Plt. and John Huson Defendt. the following Jury are Sworn John Mcbrid, Robert Adams, Nicholas Cox, Jacob Micheaux, Mathew Cox, Stephen Woodson, Ashford Hughes, Nowell Burton, William Lansdon, James Taylor, John Prier, Joseph Farrar, who after some time return with their Verdict which on the Defendts. motion is admitted to Record and is as followeth "Wee find for

[201]   February Court 1729 [1730]
the Defendant John Mcbrid Foreman." Whereupon it is considered by the Court that the Deft. go hence without day and that he recover against the Plt. his Costs by him in this behalf expended and a Lawyers Fee.

GOOCHLAND COUNTY ORDER BOOK 1 1728-1730   181

Jones vs Locket   The Action on the Case between Rice Jones Plt. and Thomas Locket Defendt. is dismist the Plt. not Prosecuting the same.

Nolun's Administration   Agnes Nolun comes into Court and makes Oath that Thomas Nolun deceased died without any will as far as she knows or believes and on her motion and giving security for her Just and faithfull Administration of the said Deceadents Estate Certificate is granted her for obtaining Letters of Administration in due form, John Woodall and Nicholas Wilkinson entring themselves Securities for the same.
   Ordered that Jacob Micheaux, Robert Hughes, Fredorick Cox, and Thomas Walker or any three of them being first sworn by some Justice of the Peace do Appraise the Estate of Thomas Nolun deceased and that Agnes Nolun the Administratrix do return an Inventory thereof to the next Court.

Jordan Eliza. chooses her Guardian   On the motion of Elizabeth Jordan she is permitted to choose John Harriss Gent. her Guardian who accepts the charge Thomas Dickins and John Quin Securities.

Bates Flemg. chooses his Guardian   On the motion of Fleming Bates he is permitted to choose John Woodson Gent. his Guardian who accepts the charge Thomas Dickins and John Quin Securities.

Dale vs Gunn   The Action on the Case between Christopher Dale Plt. and John Gunn Defendt. is continued at the Plts. Cost.

Ware vs Saunders   The Action on the Case between Susanna Ware Plt. and Thomas Saunders Defendt. is continued at the Plts. Cost.

Dean vs Napier   In the Action on the Case between Richard Dean Plt. and Robert Napier Junr. Defendant the following Jury are Sworn Robert Adams,

[202]   February Court 1729 [1730]
Nicholas Cox, Mathew Cox, Stephen Woodson, John Mcbrid, Nowell Burton, William Lansdon, James Taylor, John Prier, Joseph Farrar, David Walker, Fredorick Cox, At the rising of the Court the Jury not being agreed it is ordered that the Sheriff do keep them together untill they have agreed on their Verdict and that they appear to morrow and Present the same to the Court.

Clark vs Cannon   The Action of Case between Christopher Clark Plt.

and William Cannon Defendt. is dismist the Plt. not Prosecuting the same.

Utley vs Napier   In the Action of Debt between John Utley Plt. and Bouth Napier Defendt. the Plt. takes issue on the Defts. Pleas and the Suit is continued.

Utley vs Napier   In the Action of Debt between John Utley Plt. and Bouth Napier Defendt. the Deft. Pleads he oweth nothing and for tryall thereof puts himself upon the Country and the Plt. likewise.

Napier vs Scot &c   In the Action of Debt between Bouth Napier Plt. and Edward Scot Administrator &c. of Paul Green deceased Defendt. the following Jury are Sworn   John Harriss, John Laine, William Walker, Samuell Allin, John Phelps, Thomas Edwards, Bartholomew Stoveall, Jacob Micheaux, Thomas Baily, George Stoveall, Leonard Ballew, John Taylor, who after some time return with their Verdict which on the Defts. motion is admitted to Record and is as followeth "Wee find for the Defendant John Harriss Foreman." Whereupon it is considered by the Court that the Defendt. go hence without day and that he recover against the Plt. his Costs by him in this behalf expended and a Lawyers Fee.

[203]   February Court 1729 [1730]
Jeffs vs Martin   In the Action on the Case between John Jeffs Plt. and John Martin Defendt. the Sheriff having returned on the Pluries Capias that the Defendant is not to be found and he failing to appear a Pluries Capias de novo is awarded against him returnable to the next Court.

Harrison vs Mckenny   The Action of Debt between Benjamin Harrison Plt. and Daniell Mckenny is dismist the Plt. not prosecuting the same.

Morgan vs Huson   On the motion of Anthony Morgan a Witness for John Huson ads Richard Dean it is ordered that the said John do pay him for four days attendance one hundred and twenty pounds of tobacco with Costs.

Daviss vs Stoveall   The Action of Debt between George Daviss Plt. and Bartholomew Stoveall Deft. is dismist the Plt. not prosecuting the same.

Skeyman vs Burk   In the Action of Trespass between George Skeyman Plt. and Theodorick Burk Defendt. the Deft. appears but failing to Plead Judgment by nihil dicit is granted against him for what damages shall be recovered in this Suit to be discharged nevertheless if the Defendant shall

Plead at the next Court.

Taylor vs Lowe   In the Action of Trespass on the Case between John Taylor Plt. and Thomas Lowe Defendt. the Deft. appears but failing to Plead Judgment by nihil dicit is granted against him for what damages shall be recovered in this Suit to be discharged nevertheless if the Defendt. shall Plead at the next Court.

Macon vs Wharton   The Action on the Case between John Macon Plt. and Thomas Wharton Deft. is continued at the Plts. Cost.

Cabbell vs Nolun   The Action of Debt between William Cabbell Assignee of John Quin Plt. and Thomas Nolun Defendt. is dismist the Defendt. being dead.

[204]   February Court 1729 [1730]
Waddill vs Edwards   In the Action on the Case between William Waddill Junr. Plt. and Thomas Edwards Defendt. Thomas Prosser Thomas Dickins and Tarlton Fleming or any two of them are appointed to Examine, State and Settle the matters in dispute between them and to report their Proceedings therein to the next Court.

Moss vs Taylor   In the Action of Trespass on the Case between Thomas Moss Plt. and James Taylor Defendt. the following Jury are Sworn John Harriss, John Laine, William Walker, Samuell Allin, John Phelps, Thomas Edwards, Bartholomew Stoveall, John Taylor, Jacob Micheaux, Thomas Bailey, George Stoveall, William Woodson, who after some time return with their Verdict which on the Defts. motion is admitted to Record and is as followeth "Wee find for the Defendant John Harriss Foreman." Whereupon it is considered by the Court that the Defendt. go hence without day and that he recover against the Plt. his Costs by him in this behalf expended and a Lawyers Fee.

Fauquinou vs Moss   On the motion of Mary Fauquinou a Witness for Thomas Moss vs James Taylor it is ordered that the said Thomas do pay her for two days attendance sixty pounds of tobacco with Costs.

Moss vs Moss   On the motion of William Moss of New Kent a Witness for Thomas Moss vs James Taylor it is ordered that the said Thomas do pay him for four days attendance and for coming and returning forty eight miles three times six hundred and seventy two pounds of tobacco with Costs.

Thomas vs Gee   In the Action on the Case between Rowland Thomas Plt. and Gilbert Gee Defendt. on the Defts. motion leave is granted him to Plead severall matters whereupon he files Pleas and time is granted the Plt. to report and to

[205]   February Court 1729 [1730]
mend his declaration.

Griffith's Administration   Thomas Moss comes into Court and makes Oath that John Griffith deceased died without any will as far as he knows or believes and on his motion and giving security for his Just and faithfull administration of the said Deceadents Estate Certificate is granted him for obtaining Letters of Administration in due form   Thomas Prosser entring himself Security for the same.

Martin vs Gunn   In the Action of Trespass between Francis Martin Plt. and John Gunn Defendt. the following Jury are Sworn   John Harris, John Laine, William Walker, Samuell Allin, James Nowlin, Thomas Edwards, Bartholomew Stoveall, John Taylor, Jacob Micheaux, Thomas Bailey, George Stoveall, William Woodson, who after some time return with their Verdict which on the Plts. motion is admitted to Record and is as followeth "Wee find for the Plt. thirty two shillings Sterling Damage John Harriss Foreman."   the Court being of opinion that the Battery is fully proved it is thereupon considered that the Plt. do recover against the Defendt. the said sum of thirty two shillings Sterling Damages by the Jurors aforesaid in their said Verdict assessed with full Costs and a Lawyers Fee.

Cabbell vs Wade   The Action of Trespass on the Case between William Cabbell Plt. and Robert Wade Defendt. is dismist the Plt. not prosecuting the same.

Fleming vs Pleasants   In the Action of Debt between John Fleming Plt. and John Pleasants Administrator &c. of William Howl deceased Deft. the Deft. failing to appear on the Plts. motion and his making Oath to the Justness of his Debt Judgment is granted him against the Defendts. Administrator as aforesaid for six pounds fourteen shillings and two pence Currant money and two hundred and forty five pounds of tobacco with Costs.

[206]   February Court 1729 [1730]
Temple vs Burton   In the Action of Trespass on the Case between Joseph Temple Plt. and Nowell Burton Defendt. the Plt. files a new

declaration the Defendt. pleads he oweth nothing and for tryall thereof puts himself upon the Country and the Plt. likewise.

Nolun vs Quin   The Action of Trespass between Thomas Nolun Plt. and John Quin Defendt. is dismist the Plt. being dead.

Nolun vs Quin   The Action of Debt between Thomas Nolun Plt. and John Quin Defendt. is dismist the Plt. being dead.

Read vs Downie   In the Action on the Case between Clem Read Plt. and Robert Downie Defendt. the Deft. failing to appear on the Plts. motion the Conditionall Judgment formerly Granted against the Deft. is confirmed for so much Damages as shall be found upon Executing a Writ of Inquiry at the next Court of which the Sheriff is ordered to give the Deft. notice by serving him with a copy of this order.

Moseby vs Taylor   The Action of Debt between Richard Moseby Plt. and John Taylor Defendt. is continued.

Alves vs Sorrell   In the Action of Debt between George Alves Plt. and John Sorrell Defendt. the Deft. failing to appear on the Plts. motion the Conditionall Judgment formerly Granted against the Defendt. is confirmed for so much Damages as shall be found upon Executing a Writ of Inquiry at the next Court of which the Sheriff is ordered to give the Defendt. notice by serving him with a copy of this order.

Dickins vs Fauquinou   The Action on the Case between Thomas Dickins Plt. and Daniell Fauquinou Deft. is dismist the Plt. not prosecuting the same.

Pruit vs Johnson   In the Action on the Case between Andrew Pruit Plt. and

[207]   February Court 1729 [1730]
Charles Johnson Defendt. time is granted the Plt. to mend his declaration.

Martin vs Woodson &c   In the Action on the Case between John Martin Plt. and Joseph Woodson Execr. &c. of John Woodson deceased Defendt. the Deft. failing to appear on the Plts. motion and his making Oath to the Justness of his Debt Judgment is granted him against the Deft. Executr. as aforsaid for two pounds five shillings Currt. money with Costs.

Martin vs Woodson   In the Action on the Case between John Martin Plt. and Joseph Woodson Defendt. the Defendt. failing to appear on the Plts. motion and his making Oath to the Justness of his Debt Judgment is granted him against the Deft. for one pound seven shillings Currt. money with Costs and a Lawyers Fee.

Taylor vs Quin   In the Action of Debt between James Taylor Plt. and John Quin Defendt. time is granted the Plt. to mend his declaration.

Bumpuss vs Moreman   The Action of Trespass on the Case between Samuell Bumpuss Plt. and Andrew Moreman Defendt. is continued at the Defts. cost.

Napier vs Cox   In the Action on the Case between Robert Napier Junr. Plt. and Bartholomew Cox Defendt. the Deft. pleads non detinet and for tryall thereof puts himself upon the Country and the Plt. likewise.

Marchbanks vs Croom   In the Action on the Case between George Marchbanks Plt. and Daniell Croom Deft. time is granted the Plt. to mend his declaration.

Salmon vs Edwards   In the Action on the Case between Thomas Salmon Plt. and Thomas Edwards Defendt. the Deft. Demurrs generally without writing and time is granted the Plt. to consider.

May vs Jackson   In the Action on the Case between William May Plt. and Joseph Jackson Defendt. the Deft. pleads he oweth nothing and for tryall thereof puts himself upon the Country and the Plt. likewise.

[208]   February Court 1729 [1730]
New vs Morriss &c   In the Action of Debt between William New Plt. and Hugh Morriss and Mary his wife Executrix &c. of Edmund New deceased Defendts. the Defendts. waive the Demurrer and the Suit is continued at the defendts. cost.

Holland vs Woodson   The Action on the Case between Michaell Holland Plt. and Benjamin Woodson Defendt. is dismist the Plt. not prosecuting the same.

Holland vs Woodson   The Action of Debt between Michaell Holland Plt. and Benjamin Woodson Defendt. is dismist the Plt. not prosecuting the same.

Holland vs Napier   In the Action on the Case between Michaell Holland Plt. and Bouth Napier Defendt. the Deft. Pleads he oweth nothing and for tryall thereof puts himself upon the Country and the Plt. likewise.

Ward vs Dean   In the Action of Trespass on the Case between Seth Ward Plt. and Richard Dean Defendt. the Deft. pleads he oweth nothing and for tryall thereof puts himself upon the Country and the Plt. likewise.

Ward vs Dean   In the Action of Trespass on the Case between Seth Ward Plt. and Richard Dean Defendt. the Deft. Pleads he oweth nothing and for tryall thereof puts himself upon the Country and the Plt. likewise.

Stidum vs Bingley &c   In the Action of Debt between Benjamin Stidum Plt. and Joseph Bingley and William Lansdon Defts. the Defendts. Plead they oweth nothing and for tryall thereof put themselves upon the Country and the Plt. likewise.

Dickins vs New   In the Action on the Case between Thomas Dickins Plt. and William New Defendt. the Deft. failing to appear on the Plts. motion the conditionall Judgment formerly granted against

[209]   February Court 1729 [1730]
the Deft. is confirmed for so much Damages as shall be found upon executing a Writ of Inquiry at the next Court of which the Sheriff is ordered to give the Deft. notice by serving him with a copy of this order.

Wood vs Napier   In the Action of Trespass on the Case between Henry Wood Plt. and Bouth Napier Defendt. the Deft. pleads he oweth nothing and for tryall thereof puts himself upon the Country and the Plt. likewise.

Sims vs Phelps   In the Action of Trespass on the Case between Mathew Sims Plt. and John Phelps Defendt. the Deft. pleads he is not guilty and for tryall thereof puts himself upon the Country and the Plt. likewise.

Collins vs Morriss   In the Action of Trespass between Mathew Collins Plt. and John Morriss Defendt. the Sheriff having returned on the Pluries Capias that the Defendt. is not to be found and he failing to appear a Pluries Capias de novo is awarded against him returnable to the next Court.

L'Villain vs Woodson   The Action on the Case between John L'Villain Plt. and Joseph Woodson Defendt. is continued.

Woodson vs Napier   In the Action on the Case between William Woodson Plt. and Bouth Napier Defendt the Deft. pleads he oweth nothing and for tryall thereof puts himself upon the Country and the Plt. likewise.

Mcbrid vs Martin   On the motion of John Mcbrid a Witness for Francis Martin vs John Gunn it is ordered that the said Francis do pay him for five dayes attendance one hundred and fifty pounds of tobacco with Costs.

Westbrook vs Martin   On the motion of James Westbrook a Witness for Francis Martin vs John Gunn it is ordered that the said Francis do pay him for five days attendance 150 lbs. of tobacco with Costs.

Paine vs Martin   On the motion of George Paine Junr. a Witness for Francis Martin vs John Gunn it is ordered that the said Francis do pay him for four days attendance one hundred and twenty pounds of tobacco with Costs.

[210]   February Court 1729 [1730]
Parish vs Gunn   On the motion of John Parish of Hanover County a Witness for John Gunn ads Francis Martin it is ordered that the said John do pay him for two days attendance and for coming and returning eight miles once one hundred and forty four pounds of tobacco with Costs.

Serjeant vs Gunn   On the motion of Mary Serjeant a Witness for John Gunn ads Francis Martin it is ordered that the said John do pay her for two days allowance sixty pounds of tobacco with Costs.

Then the Court adjourned till to morrow morning ten of the Clock.

****

At a Court continued and held for Goochland County the eighteenth day of February Annoq Domi 1729 [1730]. Present. John Fleming, William Mayo, Tarlton Fleming, Allin Howard, William Cabbell, Gent. Justices.

Rapene vs Bingley   The Action of Trespass on the Case between Anthony Rapene Plt. and Joseph Bingley Defendt. is continued at the Plts. Cost.

Innis vs Mcbrid   In the Action of Trespass between John Innis Plt. and

John Mcbrid Defendt. on the motion of the Plt. leave is granted him to fill up the blanks in his declaration. the Deft. pleads he is not guilty and for tryall thereof puts himself upon the Country and the Plt. likewise.

Innis vs Mcbrid   In the Action on the Case between John Innis Plt. and John Mcbrid Defendt. the Deft. pleads he oweth nothing and for tryall thereof puts himself upon the Country and the Plt. likewise.

Atkinson vs Taylor   The Action of Trespass between Sarah Atkinson Plt. and James Taylor Defendt. is continued.

[211]   February Court 1729 [1730]
Cabbell vs Pattison   On the Complaint of William Cabbell Gent. against John Lewis, David Pattison Junr. and Thomas Pattison, for a breach of their good behaviour and contempt of his Authority as a Justice of the Peace it is ordered that the Sheriff do take into his Custody the said John Lewis, David Pattison Junr. and Thomas Pattison, and them safely keep in the Goal of his County untill they severally enter into bond each in the Sum of one hundred pounds Sterling with good and sufficient Security for their appearance at the next Court to be held for this County and for their good behaviour towards all his Majestys Subjects till then.

Prosser vs Nowlin &c   On the Complaint of Thomas Prosser Gent. against James Nowlin and Robert Napier Junr. for a breach of the Peace it is ordered that the Sheriff do take into his Custody the said James Nowlin and Robert Napier Junr. and them safely keep in the Goal of his County untill they severally enter into bond each in the Sum of ten pounds Sterling with good and sufficient Security for their appearance at the next Court to be held for this County and for their good behaviour towards all his Majestys Subjects till then.

Hopkins vs Martin   In the Action of Trespass between Evan Hopkins Plt. and Francis Martin Defendt. the Plt. takes issue on the Defts. Pleas and the Suit is continued.

Cannon vs Swift   The Action on the Case between John Cannon Plt. and William Swift Defendt. is dismist the Plt. not prosecuting the same.

Henson vs Saunders   The Action of Trespass on the Case between Benjamin Henson Plt. and Thomas Saunders Defendt. is continued.

Micheaux vs Turner   In the Action on the Case between Jacob Micheaux Plt. and James Turner Defendt. Stephen Hughes and Joseph

Woodson being formerly appointed Auditors. William Cabbell Gent. is now added to them and the Suit is continued.

Bingley vs Rapene   In the Action of Trespass between Joseph Bingley Plt. and Anthony Rapene Defendt. the following Jury are Sworn Nowell Burton, Mathew Cox, Bouth Napier, David Walker, John Mcbrid,

[212]   February Court 1729 [1730]
Francis Martin, Henry Webb, Jacob Micheaux, Robert Carter, William Lansdon, Joseph Farrar, John Prier, who after some time return with their Verdict which on the Plts. motion is admitted to Record and is as followeth "Wee find for the Plt. forty five shillings Sterling money Nowell Burton Foreman." Whereupon it is considered by the Court that the Plt. do recover against the Deft. the said Sum of forty five shillings Sterling money by the Jurors aforesaid in their said Verdict assessed with the Coss of this Suit and a Lawyers Fee.

Boston vs Cox   In the Action on the Case between Hugh Boston Plt. and Nicholas Cox Defendt. the Deft. appears but failing to Plead Judgment by nihil dicit is granted against him for what damages shall be recovered in this Suit to be discharged nevertheless if the Deft. shall plead at the next Court.

Wiles vs Hughes   In the Action of Trespass on the Case between Luke Wiles Plt. and Stephen Hughes Defendt. the Deft. appears but failing to Plead Judgment by nihil dicit is granted against him for what damages shall be recovered in this Suit to be discharged nevertheless if the Deft. shall Plead at the next Court.

Wiles vs Hughes & Atkinson   In the Action of Debt between Luke Wiles Plt. and Stephen Hughes & Sarah Atkinson Exr. & Exx. of Thomas Atkinson decd Defendts. the Defts. appear but failing to Plead Judgment by nihil dicit is granted against them for what damages shall be recovered in this Suit to be discharged nevertheless if the Defts. shall Plead at the next Court.

Pigg vs Woodson   In the Action on the Case between John Pigg Junr. Plt. and William Woodson Deft. the Plt. files a new Declaration.

Pigg vs Allin   In the Action on the Case between John Pigg Junr. Plt. and Samuell Allin Deft. the Plt. files a new Declaration.

[213]   February Court 1729 [1730]
Dickins vs Wharton   In the Action of Trespass on the Case between Thomas Dickins Plt. and Thomas Wharton Defendt. John Quin appears on behalf of the Deft. and confesses a Judgment to the Plt. for one pound ten shillings Currant money whereupon it is considered by the Court that the Plt. do recover against the Deft. the said Sum with the Costs of this Suit and a Lawyers Fee.

Wood vs New   The Action of Trespass on the Case between Henry Wood Plt. and William New Defendt. is continued.

Surveyor of the road   John Prier is appointed Surveyor of the Road from lower Bever dam Bridge to little licking hole Creek.

Johnson vs Fenton   In the Action of Trespass on the Case between William Johnson Plt. and Thomas Fenton Defendt. the Sheriff having returned on the Pluries Capias that the Defendt. is not to be found and he failing to appear a Pluries Capias de novo is awarded against him returnable to the next Court.

Ware vs Saunders   In the Action of Trespass on the Case between Susanna Ware Plt. and William Saunders Deft. time is granted the Plt. to mend her Declaration.

Davis vs Scruggs   In the Action of Trespass on the Case between George Daviss Plt. and John Scruggs Defendt. the Deft. failing to appear and the Sheriff on the Alias Capias having not returned any Bail on the motion of the Plt. Judgment is granted him against the Deft. and Daniell Stoner Gent. Sheriff for what damages shall be recovered in this Suit to be discharged nevertheless by the appearance of the Deft. at the next Court.

Wood vs Thompson   In the Action of Trespass on the Case between Henry Wood Plt. and Samuell Thompson Defendt. the Deft. failing to appear on the Plts. motion the Conditionall Judgment formerly granted against the Deft. & George Paine, Nowell Burton, & Samuell Allin his common bail is confirmed for so much damages as shall be found upon Executing a Writ of Inquiry at the next Court of which the Sheriff is ordered to give the Deft. and the said George Paine

[214]   February Court 1729 [1730]
Nowell Burton & Samuell Allin notice by serving them with a Copy of this Order.

Grand Jury vs Hannah Turner   Upon the Presentment of the Grand Jury against Hannah Turner the Sheriff having made return on the Capias that the said Hannah is not to be found and she failing to appear an Alias Capias is awarded against her returnable to the next Court.

Grand Jury vs Judith Ballew   Upon the Presentment of the Grand Jury against Judith Ballew the said Judith being returned Summoned and she failing to appear it is ordered that a Capias do Issue against her returnable to the next Court.

Lad & Powell vs Thompson   The Petition of Amos Lad and Roger Powell against Samuell Thompson is dismist neither party appearing.

Cox vs Wotars   In the Action of Trespass on the Case between Mathew Cox Plt. and William Wotars Defendt. the Deft. failing to appear and the Sheriff having not returned any Bail on the motion of the Plt. Judgment is granted him against the Deft. and Daniell Stoner Gent. Sheriff for what damages shall be recovered in this Suit to be discharged nevertheless by the Appearance of the Deft. at the next Court.

Taylor vs Lowe & Uxor   In the Action of Trespass on the Case between John Taylor Plt. and Thomas Lowe and Amey his wife Defts. Tarlton Fleming & William Cabbell Gent. or either of them are appointed to Examine state and settle the severall matters in dispute and to report their proceedings therein to the next Court.

Martin vs Rapene   The Action on the Case between John Martin Junr. Plt. and Anthony Rapene Deft. is continued at the Plts. cost.

Woodson vs Baize   The Action of Trespass on the Case between John Woodson Plt. and Edward Baize Defendt. is continued.

[215]   February Court 1729 [1730]
Cox vs Dean   In the Action of Trespass between Fredorick Cox Plt. and Richard Dean Defendt. the Deft. pleads he is not guilty and for tryall thereof puts himself upon the Country and the Plt. likewise.

Taylor vs Hopkins   In the Action of Trespass between James Taylor Plt. and Evan Hopkins Deft. a special Imparlance is granted the Defendant.

Bolling vs Wotars   The Action of Trespass on the Case between John Bolling Plt. and William Wotars Deft. is dismist neither Party appearing.

Bingley vs Boccor   The Action on the Case between Joseph Bingley Plt. and Peter Boccor Defendt. is dismist neither Party appearing.

Napier vs Bingley   On the motion of Mary Napier a Witness for Joseph Bingley vs Anthony Rapene it is ordered that the said Joseph do pay her for ten days attendance three hundred pounds of tobacco with Costs.

Woodson vs Bingley   On the motion of Benjamin Woodson a Witness for Joseph Bingley vs Anthony Rapene it is ordered that the said Joseph do pay him for ten days attendance three hundred pounds of tobacco with Costs.

Cocke vs Rapene   On the motion of William Cocke of Henrico a Witness for Anthony Rapene ads Joseph Bingley it is ordered that the said Anthony do pay him for five days attendance and for coming and returning thirty six miles three times six hundred and twenty four pounds of tobacco with Costs.

Pennington vs Bailey   In the Action of Trespass between Paul Pennington Plt. and Henry Bailey Defendt. the following Jury are Sworn Nowell Burton, Mathew Cox, Bouth Napier, David Walker, John Mcbrid, Francis Martin, Henry Webb, Jacob Micheaux, Robert Carter, William Lansdon, Joseph Farrar, John Prier, who after some time return with their Verdict which on the Plts. motion is admitted to Record and is as followeth "Wee find for the Plt. two shillings Sterling money Nowell Burton Foreman." the Court being of opinion that the Battery is fully proved it is thereupon considered that the Plt. do recover against the Deft. the said Sum of two shillings Sterling money

[216]   February Court 1729 [1730]
money by the Jurors aforesaid in their said Verdict assessed with full Costs and a Lawyers Fee.

Smith vs Pennington   On the motion of James Smith a Witness for Paul Pennington vs Henry Bailey it is ordered that the said Paul do pay him for six days attendance one hundred and eighty pounds of tobacco with Costs.

Burton vs Pennington   On the motion of Nowell Burton a Witness for Paul Pennington vs Henry Bailey it is ordered that the said Paul do pay him for one days attendance thirty pounds of tobacco with Costs.

Logan vs Wotars   In the Action on the Case between Alexander Logan

Plt. and William Wotars Defendt. the Deft. failing to appear and the Sheriff having not returned any Bail on the motion of the Plt. Judgment is granted him against the Deft. and Daniel Stoner Gent. Sheriff for what damages shall be recovered in this Suit to be discharged nevertheless by the Appearance of the Defendt. at the next Court.

Rocket vs Thompson   In the Action of Trespass on the Case between Baldwin Rocket Plt. and Samuell Thompson Defendt. the Deft. failing to appear on the motion of the Plt. Judgment is granted him against the Deft. and John Birks his common Bail for what damages shall be recovered in this Suit to be discharged nevertheless by the Appearance of the Deft. at the next Court.

Scot vs Utley   In the Action on the Case between Edward Scot Plt. and John Utley Defendt. the Deft. failing to appear on the motion of the Plt. Judgment is granted him against the Deft. and Anthony Hoggat his common Bail for what damages shall be recovered in this Suit to be discharged nevertheless by the Appearance of the Defendt. at the next Court.

Lad vs Cannon   In the Action on the Case between Amos Lad Plt. and William Cannon Defendant an Imparlance is granted the Defendt.

[217]   February Court 1729 [1730]
Mullin vs Wotars   The Action of Trespass on the Case between Patrick Mullin Plt. and William Wotars Deft. is dismist neither party appearing.

Armstrong vs Southerland   The Action on the Case between Robert Armstrong Plt. and George Southerland Defendt. is dismist neither party appearing.

Harbour vs Jeffs   The Action on the Case between Thomas Harbour Plt. and John Jeffs Defendt. is dismist the Plt. not Prosecuting the same.

Bryant vs Carnar   The Action of Trespass between James Bryant Plt. and Susanna Carnar Deft. is dismist neither party appearing.

Pruit vs Boccor   In the Action of Trespass on the Case between Hugh Pruit Plt. and Peter Boccor Defendt. the Plt. having failed to file his declaration on the Defts. motion he is nonsuited and it is thereupon considered by the Court that the Deft. go hence without day and that he recover against the Plt. five shillings Currant money together with his Costs by him in this behalf expended and a Lawyers Fee.

Dickins vs Lansdon   The Action on the Case between Thomas Dickins Plt. and William Lansdon Defendt. is dismist the Plt. not Prosecuting the same.

Redford vs Lankford   In the Action of Trespass on the Case between John Redford Plt. and West Lankford Defendt. the Plt. having failed to file his declaration on the Defts. motion he is nonsuited and it is thereupon considered by the Court that the Deft. go hence without day and that he recover against the Plt. five shillings Currant money together with his Costs by him in this behalf expended and a Lawyers Fee.

Agee vs Sutleth   In the Action of Trespass on the Case between Mathew Agee Plt. and Abraham Sutleth Deft. an Imparlance is granted the Deft.

Croom vs Hardwick   The Action of Trespass on the Case between Daniell Croom Plt. and Robert Hardwick Deft. is dismist the Plt. not prosecuting the same.

May vs Taylor   In the Action of Trespass between William May Plt. and John Taylor Defendt. the Deft. pleads he is not guilty and for tryall thereof

[218]   February Court 1729 [1730]
puts himself upon the Country and the Plt. likewise.

Dickins vs Cone   In the Action on the Case between Thomas Dickins Plt. and John Cone Defendt. John Quin Attorny for the Defendt. appears and confesses a Judgment to the Plt. for forty shillings Currant money Whereupon it is considered by the Court that the Plt. do recover against the Deft. the said Sum with Costs.

Woodson &c. vs Lester   In the Action on the Case between Tarlton Woodson Assee. of Jeremiah Lester Plt. and Henry Lester Defendt. the Deft. failing to appear and the Sheriff not having returned sufficient Bail on the Plts. motion Judgment is granted him against the Deft. and Daniell Stoner Gent. Sheriff for what damages shall be recovered in this Suit to be discharged nevertheless if the Deft. shall appear at the next Court.

Allegre vs Stidum   In the Action on the Case between Giles Allegre Plt. and Benjamin Stidum Defendt. the Deft. failing to appear and the Sheriff not having returned any Bail on the Plts. motion Judgment is granted him against the Defendt. and Daniell Stoner Gent. Sheriff for what damages shall be recovered in this Suit to be discharged nevertheless if the Deft. shall appear at the next Court.

Macon vs Hughes   The Action of Debt between John Macon Plt. and Stephen Hughes Defendt. is dismist the Plt. not prosecuting the same.

Hughes vs Macon   The Action on the Case between Stephen Hughes Plt. and John Macon Defendt. is dismist the Plt. not prosecuting the same.

Award inter Hughes & Macon   Thomas Prosser, Griffith Bowen, & Thomas Dickins present a Report of an Award between Stephen Hughes and John Macon which on their motion is ordered to be Recorded.

Scot vs Pritchet   In the Action on the Case between Edward Scot Plt. and John Pritchet Defendt. the Sheriff having made return on the Pluries Capias that the Deft. is not to be found and

[219]   February Court 1729 [1730]
he failing to appear on the Plts. motion a Pluries Capias de novo is awarded against him returnable to the next Court.

Alves vs Huetson   In the Action of Detinue between George Alves Plt. and John Huetson Defendt. leave is granted the Plt. to mend his declaration and the Suit is continued.

Scot vs Swift   The Action on the Case between Edward Scot Plt. and William Swift Defendt. is continued.

Ashlin vs Mcbrid   The Action of Trespass between Joseph Ashlin Plt. and John Mcbrid Deft. is dismist the Plt. not Prosecuting the same.

Daviss vs Pattison complaint   On the Complaint of William Daviss against David Pattison Junr. for assaulting and beating him it is ordered that the Sheriff do take into his Custody the said David Pattison Junr. and him safely keep in the Goal of his County untill he enter into bond in the Sum of Fifty pounds Sterling with good and sufficient Security for his Appearance at the next Court to be held for this County and for his good behaviour towards all his Majesty's Subjects untill then.

Taylor vs Lansdon   In the Action of Trespass between James Taylor Plt. and William Lansdon Defendt. the Plt. failing to Prosecute his Suit on the Defts. motion he is nonsuited and it is thereupon considered by the Court that the Deft. go hence without day and that he recover against the Plt. five shillings Currant money together with his Costs by him in this behalf expended and a Lawyers Fee.

Bingley vs Lansdon   On the motion of Joseph Bingley a Witness for William Lansdon ads James Taylor it is ordered that the said William do pay him for five days attendance one hundred and fifty pounds of tobacco with Costs.

Carnar vs Atkinson   In the Action of Trespass on the Case between Susanna Carnar Plt. and Henry Atkinson Defendt. Thomas Prosser Attorny for the Deft. appears and confesses a Judgment to the Plt. for two hundred

[220]   February Court 1729 [1730]
and sixty seven pounds of tobacco Whereupon it is considered by the Court that the Plt. do recover against the Deft. the said sum with the costs of this Suit and a Lawyers Fee.

Daviss vs Pattison recogn   William Daviss and John Quin come into Court and acknowledge themselves unto our Sovereign Lord the King his Heirs &c. each in the Sum of ten pounds Sterling to be levyed of the Goods Chattles &c. of the said William Daviss & John Quin, On Condition nevertheless that if the said William Daviss & John Quin do appear at the next Court to give Evidence on behalf of our Sovereign Lord the King against David Pattison Junr. then the said Recognizance to be Void.

Prosser vs Wotars   In the Action on the Case between Thomas Prosser Plt. and William Wotars Defendt. the following Jury are Sworn John Mcbrid, Mathew Cox, Bouth Napier, Nowell Burton, David Walker, Francis Martin, Henry Webb, Jacob Micheaux, Robert Carter, William Lansdon, Joseph Farrar, John Prier, who after some time return with their Verdict which on the Plts. motion is admitted to Record and is as followeth "Wee find for the Plt. forty shillings Currant money John Mcbrid Foreman." Whereupon it is considered by the Court that the Plt. do recover against the Deft. and Daniell Stoner Gent. Sheriff the said Sum of forty shillings Currant money by the Jurors aforesaid in their said Verdict assessed with the Costs of this Suit and a Lawyers Fee.

Bever dam Bridge   Ordered that the Bridge over Bever dam Creek below Bollings Mill be kept in repair by the titheables who clear the Road below the said Bridge.

Then the Court adjourned to the third Tuesday in next Month.

****

[221]   March Court 1729 [1730]
At a Court held for Goochland County the third Tuesday in March being the seventeenth day of the month Annoq Domi 1729 [1730].
Present. William Mayo, Allin Howard, George Paine, James Holman Gent. Justices.

Surveyor of the Roads   On the motion of Ebenezer Adams on behalf of himself and others it is ordered that a road be cleared from Bever dam Bridge near John Priers to pass by John Rights Plantation cross wild Boar swamp near Elk lick by William Owens Plantation cross the North branch of the Bird to Elk ford on the Bird to end at Martin Kings. John Prier is appointed Surveyor of the said road from Bever dam Bridge to John Rights; John Laine from John Rights to Great Licking hole, Martin Dunkin from Great Licking hole to the South branch of the Bird, John Bostick from the South branch of the Bird to Elk ford, Martin King from Elk ford to the River.

Dale vs Gunn   The Action on the Case between Christopher Dale Plt. and John Gunn Defendt. is continued at the Plts. cost.

   Present William Cabbell Gent.

Ware vs Saunders   In the Action on the Case between Susanna Ware Plt. and Thomas Saunders Defendt. the Parties submit themselves to the Court for tryall whereupon the Plts. oath and the Defts. allegation being considered it is ordered that the Deft. pay unto the Plt. the Sum of four pounds five shillings and one penny Currant money together with the Costs of this Suit and a Lawyers Fee.

Reynolds's deed to Wade   Henry Reynolds acknowledges a Deed with the Livery of Seizin endorsed from himself to Robert Wade to be his Act and Deed and it is thereupon admitted to Record.

Moreman's deed to Stone   Andrew Moreman acknowledges a Deed with the Livery of Seizin endorsed from him self to Thomas Stone to be his Act and Deed and it is thereupon admitted to Record.

[222]   March Court 1729 [1730]
Reynolds's deed to Barringer   Henry Reynolds acknowledges a Deed

with the Livery of Seizin endorsed from himself to Joseph Barringer to be is Act and deed and it is thereupon admitted to Record.

Dean vs Napier   The Action on the Case between Richard Dean Plt. and Robert Napier Defendt. is continued.

Pattison's deed to Michell   David Pattison Junr. Thomas Pattison and Silvester Prophet prove a deed with the Livery of Seizin endorsed from David Pattison to Thomas Michell and Archelaus Michell to be the Act and deed of the said David Pattison and it is thereupon admitted to Record.

Utley vs Napier   The Action of Debt between John Utley Plt. and Bouth Napier Defendt. is continued.

Utley vs Napier   The Action of Debt between John Utley Plt. and Bouth Napier Defendt. is dismist the Plt. not prosecuting the same.

Jeffs vs Martin   In the Action on the Case between John Jeffs Plt. and John Martin Defendt. the Sheriff having returned on the Pluries Capias that the Deft. is not to be found and he failing to appear a Pluries Capias de novo is awarded against him returnable to the next Court.

Skeyman vs Burk   The Action of Trespass between George Skeyman Plt. and Theodorick Burk Defendt. is continued.

Macon vs Wharton   The Action on the Case between John Macon Plt. and Thomas Wharton Defendt. is continued.

Waddill vs Edwards   The Action on the Case between William Waddill Junr. Plt. and Thomas Edwards Defendt. is continued.

Thomas vs Gee   In the Action on the Case between Rowland Thomas Plt. and Gilbert Gee Defendt. the Plt. files his Replication and time is granted the Deft. to Rejoyn.

[223]   March Court 1729 [1730]
Temple vs Burton   The Action of Trespass on the Case between Joseph Temple Plt. and Nowell Burton Defendt. is continued at the Defts. cost.

Read vs Downie   The Action on the Case between Clem Read Plt. and Robert Downie Defendt. is continued at the Plts. cost.

Moseby vs Taylor   In the Action of Debt between Richard Moseby Plt. and John Taylor Defendt. the Deft. pleads he is not guilty and for tryall thereof puts himself upon the Country and the Plt. likewise.

Alves vs Sorrell   In the Action of Debt between George Alves Plt. and John Sorrell Deft. the following Jury are Sworn to enquire of the damages John Mcbrid, John Pryer, Thomas Christian, Richard Dean, William Lansdon, Robert Carter, William Walker, John Laine, Thomas Wadloe, Constant Perkins, David Walker, Fredorick Cox, who after some time return with their Verdict which on the Plts. motion is admitted to Record and is as followeth "Wee find for the Plt. four pounds seven shillings and four pence John Mcbrid Foreman." Wherefore it is considered by the Court that the Plt. do recover against the Deft. the said Sum of four pounds seven shillings and four pence by the Jurors aforesaid in their said Verdict assessed with the costs of this Suit and a Lawyers Fee.

Pruit vs Johnson   In the Action on the Case between Andrew Pruit Plt. and Charles Johnson Defendt. an imparlance is granted the Defendant.

Taylor vs Quin   The Action of Debt between James Taylor Plt. and John Quin Defendt. is continued at the Plts. cost.

Bumpuss vs Moreman   In the Action of Trespass on the Case between Samuell Bumpuss Plt. and Andrew Moreman Defendt. on the Defts. motion leave is granted him to plead severall matters whereupon he files pleas and the Plt. takes Issue thereon.

Marchbanks vs Croom   The Action on the Case between George Marchbanks Plt. and Daniell Croom Defendt. is continued at the Plts. cost.

[224]   March Court 1729 [1730]
Salmon vs Edwards   In the Action on the Case between Thomas Salmon Plt. and Thomas Edwards Defendt. the Deft. waives his Demurrer and the Suit is continued.

   Present John Woodson Gent.

New vs Morriss &c   In the Action of Debt between William New Plt. and Hugh Morriss and Mary his wife Executx. &c. of Edmund New deced Defts. on the motion of the Defts. leave is granted them to plead several matters whereupon they file Pleas and time is granted the Plt. to reply.

Taylor vs Lowe   In the Action of Trespass on the Case between John Taylor Plt. and Thomas Lowe Defendt. the Deft. pleads he is not guilty and for tryall thereof puts himself upon the Country and the Plt. likewise.

Mcloughland vs Alves   On the motion of James Mcloughland of Hanover County a Witness for George Alves vs John Sorrell it is ordered that the said George do pay him for one days attendance and for coming and returning twenty one miles one hundred and twenty three pounds of tobacco with costs.

Dean vs Ware   On the motion of Richard Dean a Witness for Susanna Ware vs Thomas Saunders it is ordered that the said Susanna do pay him for one days attendance thirty pounds of tobacco with costs.

Napier vs Cox   In the Action on the Case between Robert Napier Junr. Plt. and Bartholomew Cox Defendt. the following Jury are Sworn John Mcbrid, John Prier, Thomas Christian, William Lansdon, Robert Carter, John Laine, Thomas Wadloe, Constant Perkins, Thomas Christian Junr, David Walker, Joseph Farrar, William Walker, who after some time return with their Verdict which on the Defts. motion is admitted to Record and is as followeth "Wee find for the Defendt. John Mcbrid Foreman." Whereupon it is considered by the Court that the Deft. go hence without day

[225]   March Court 1729 [1730]
and that he recover against the Plt. his costs by him in this behalf expended and a Lawyers Fee.

Collins vs Morriss   In the Action of Trespass between Mathew Collins Plt. and John Morriss Defendt. the Sheriff having returned on the Pluries Capias that the Deft. is not to be found and he failing to appear a Pluries Capias de novo is awarded against him returnable to the next Court.

L'Villain vs Woodson   In the Action on the Case between John L'Villain Plt. and Joseph Woodson Defendt. the Deft. pleads he oweth nothing and for tryall thereof puts himself upon the Country and the Plt. likewise.

   Present John Fleming Gent.

Cox vs Cox   On the motion of Fredorick Cox a Witness for Bartholomew Cox ads Robert Napier Junr. it is ordered that the said Bartholomew do pay him for one days attendance thirty pounds of tobacco with costs.

Cox vs Cox   On the motion of John Cox a Witness for Bartholomew Cox ads Robert Napier Junr. it is ordered that the said Bartholomew do pay him for one days attendance thirty pounds of tobacco with Costs.

Chandler vs Cox   On the motion of Joell Chandler a Witness for Bartholomew Cox ads Robert Napier Junr. it is ordered that the said Bartholomew do pay him for one days attendance thirty pounds of tobacco with costs.

Present Tarlton Fleming Gent.

Pattison Thos. fined   Thomas Pattison having been taken into the Custody of the Sheriff pursuant to an order of the last Court for a Breach of the Peace by him committed and for his rescuing a Prisoner from the Sheriff now appears according to the Condition of his Recognizance and his Offence being considered by the Court it is ordered that he be fined to

[226]   March Court 1729 [1730]
Our Sovereign Lord the King in the Sum of fifty shillings Sterling and that the Sheriff take into his Custody the said Thomas Pattison and him safely keep untill he pay the fine aforesaid and untill he enter into bond in the Sum of twenty pounds Sterling with one good and sufficient Security conditioned for his good behaviour for one year and a day and that the said Thomas Pattison pay Costs.

Lewis fined   John Lewis having been taken into the Custody of the Sheriff pursuant to an order of the last Court for a Breach of the Peace by him committed and for Striking William Cabbell Gent. now appears according to the Condition of his Recognizance and his Offence being considered by the Court it is ordered that he be fined to Our Sovereign Lord the King in the Sum of five pounds Sterling and that the Sheriff take into his Custody the said John Lewis and him safely keep untill he pay the fine aforesaid, and untill he enter into bond with one good and sufficient Security in the Sum of twenty pounds Sterling conditioned for his good behaviour for one year and a day and that the said John Lewis pay Costs.

Pattison David Junr. fined   David Pattison Junr. having been taken into the Custody of the Sheriff pursuant to an order of the last Court for a Breach of the Peace by him committed and for endeavouring by words to deter the Sheriff from carrying a Prisoner to Goal now appears according to the Condition of his Recognizance and his Offence being considered by the Court it is ordered that he be fined to our Sovereign Lord the King in the Sum of twenty shillings Sterling and that the Sheriff take into his Custody the said David Pattison Junr. and him safely keep untill he pay the fine aforesaid and untill he enter into bond in the Sum of twenty pounds Sterling with one good and sufficient Security conditioned for his good behaviour for one year and a day and that the said David Pattison Junr. pay Costs.

Pattison David Junr. fined   David Pattison Junr. having been taken into the Custody of the Sheriff pursuant to an order of the last Court for a Breach

[227]   March Court 1729 [1730]
of the Peace by him committed and for assaulting and beating George Davis and William Davis now appears according to the Condition of his Recognizance and his Offence being considered by the Court it is ordered that he be fined to Our Sovereign Lord the King in the Sum of four pounds Sterling and that the Sheriff take into his Custody the said David Pattison Junr. and him safely keep untill he pay the fine aforesaid and untill he enter into bond in the Sum of twenty pounds Sterling with one good and sufficient Security conditioned for his good behaviour for one year and a day and that the said David Pattison Junr. pay Costs.

Napier bound to good behaviour   Robert Napier Junr. having been taken into the Custody of the Sheriff Pursuant to an order of the last Court for a Breach of the Peace by him committed now appears according to the Condition of his Recognizance and his Offence being considered by the Court, it is ordered that the Sheriff take into his Custody the said Robert Napier Junr. and him safely keep untill he enter into bond in the Sum of ten pounds Sterling with one good and sufficient Security conditioned for his good behaviour for one year and a day and that the said Robert Napier Junr. pay Costs.

May vs Jackson. The Action on the Case between William May Plt. and Joseph Jackson defendt. is continued at the Plts. Cost.

Holland vs Napier   The Action on the Case between Michaell Holland Plt. an Bouth Napier Defendt. is continued at the Defts. Cost.

Ward vs Dean   In the Action of Trespass on the Case between Seth Ward Plt. and Richard Dean Defendt. the Deft. appears and confesses a Judgment to the Plt. for four hundred and seventy pounds of tobacco and eight pounds thirteen shillings Currant money whereupon it is considered by the Court that the Plt. do recover against the Deft. the said Sums with the Costs of this Suit and a Lawyers Fee.

Ward vs Dean   In the Action of Trespass on the Case between Seth Ward Plt. and Richard Dean Defendt. the Deft. appears and confesses a Judgment to the Plt. for three hundred and forty pounds of tobacco whereupon it

[228]   March Court 1729 [1730]
is considered by the Court that the Plt. do recover against the Deft. the said sum with the Costs of this Suit and a Lawyers Fee.

Rapene vs Bingley   In the Action of Trespass on the Case between Anthony Rapene Plt. and Joseph Bingley Deft. the following Jury are Sworn Bouth Napier, Thomas Christian, Mathew Cox, Andrew Moreman, James Taylor, Samuell Allin, Peter Jefferson, Thomas Christian Junr, Thomas Turpin, Thomas Wadloe, John Laine, William Walker, who upon hearing their Evidence withdraw.
    Then the Court adjourned for half an hour:.

    Present. John Fleming, William Mayo, Tarlton Fleming, Allin Howard, George Paine, William Cabbell, Gent.

The Jury after some time return with their Verdict which being read the Defts. Attorny moves that the same may not be Recorded but that a new tryall may be granted which being considered it is the Opinion of the Court that there be a new tryall and the Deft. being Under Sheriff it is ordered that the Coroner do Impannel the Jury.

Parentan vs Rapene   On the motion of Isaac Parentan a Witness for Anthony Rapene vs Joseph Bingley it is ordered that the said Anthony do pay him for one days attendance thirty pounds of tobacco with Costs.

Then the Court adjourned till to morrow morning ten of the Clock.

    ****

At a Court continued and held for Goochland County the eighteenth day of March Annoq Domi 1729 [1730]. Present. John Fleming, William Mayo, Tarlton Fleming, Allin Howard, George Paine, William Cabbell, Gent. Justices.

[229]   March Court 1729 [1730]
Micheaux vs Turner   In the Action on the Case between Jacob

Micheaux Plt. and James Turner Defendt. the Report of the Auditors appointed in this Suit is now presented in Court which on the Defts. motion is ordered to be Recorded and is as followeth "Persuant to an order of the Worshipfull Justices of the Court Goochland dated February 18th. 1729. We the Subscribers have proceeded to Examine State and Settle the several Accounts and maters in dispute Between Jacob Micheaux Plaintiff and James Turner Defendant and we finde the said Plaintiff to be Indebted to the said Defendant the Sum of Eight shillings and three pence Current money As Witness our hands William Cabbell, Sten. Hughes, Jos: Woodson." Whereupon it is considered by the Court that the Deft. go hence without day and that he recover against the Plt. his Costs by him in this behalf expended.

Boston vs Cox   In the Action on the Case between Hugh Boston Plt. and Nicholas Cox Defendt. by consent of the Parties Allin Howard and George Paine Gent. are appointed Arbitrators in this Suit and it is agreed that the Defts. testimony be taken before them and that the Judgment be entered according to their Report.

Pigg vs Woodson   In the Action on the Case between John Pigg Junr. Plt. and William Woodson Defendt. the Deft. pleads non assumpsit and for tryall thereof puts himself upon the Country and the Plt. likewise.

Pigg vs Allin   In the Action on the Case between John Pigg Junr. Plt. and Samuell Allin Defendt. the Deft. appears but failing to Plead Judgment by nihil dicit is granted against him for what damages shall be recovered in this Suit to be discharged nevertheless if the Deft. shall Plead at the next Court.

Lad vs Cannon   In the Action on the Case between Amos Lad Plt. and William Cannon Defendt. the Deft. appears but failing to Plead Judgment by nihil dicit is granted against him for what damages shall be recovered in this Suit to be discharged nevertheless if the Deft. shall plead at the next Court.

Wood vs New   The Action of Trespass on the Case between Henry Wood Plt. and William New Deft. is continued.

[230]   March Court 1729 [1730]
Johnson vs Fenton   In the Action of Trespass on the Case between William Johnson Plt. and Thomas Fenton Defendt. the Sheriff having returned on the Pluries Capias that the Deft. is not to be found and he failing to appear a Pluries Capias de novo is awarded against him

returnable to the next Court.

Dickins vs New   In the Action on the Case between Thomas Dickins Plt. and William New Defendt. Griffith Bowen appears on behalf of the Deft. and confesses a Judgment to the Plt. for thirty five shillings Currant money Whereupon it is considered by the Court that the Plt. do recover against the Deft. the said Sum with the Costs of this Suit and a Lawyers Fee.

Wood vs Napier   In the Action of Trespass on the Case between Henry Wood Plt. and Bouth Napier Defendt. Thomas Dickins appears on behalf of the Deft. and confesses a Judgment to the Plt. for twenty four shillings and a penny Currant money Whereupon it is considered by the Court that the Plt. do recover against the Deft. the said Sum with Costs.

Stidum vs Bingley   The Action of Debt between Benjamin Stidum Plt. and Joseph Bingley and William Lansdon Defts. is continued

Sims vs Phelps   The Action of Trespass on the Case between Mathew Sims Plt. and John Phelps Defendt. is continued at the Plts. Cost.

Innis vs Mcbrid   In the Action of Trespass between John Innis Plt. and John Mcbrid Defendt. the following Jury are Sworn   Richard Oglesby, Thomas Murrell, Fredorick Cox, John Laine, William Cannon, Bouth Napier, William Lansdon, Thomas Saunders, James Taylor, John Prier, Hugh Morriss, Richard Moseby who after some time return with their Verdict which being read the Plts. Attorny moves that the same may not be Recorded but that a new tryall may be granted which being considered it is the Opinion of the Court that there be a new tryall.

Hoggat vs Innis   On the motion of Anthony Hoggat a Witness for John Innis

[231]   March Court 1729 [1730]
vs John Mcbrid it is ordered that the said John Innis do pay him for two days attendance sixty pounds of tobacco with Costs.

Hoggat vs Innis   On the motion of Eleanor Hoggat a Witness for John Innis vs John Mcbrid it is ordered that the said John Innis do pay her for one days attendance thirty pounds of tobacco with Costs.

Walker vs Innis   On the motion of John Walker a Witness for John Innis vs John Mcbrid it is ordered that the said John Innis do pay him for two days attendance sixty pounds of tobacco with Costs.

Cabbell vs Mcbrid   On the motion of William Cabbell a Witness for John Mcbrid ads John Innis it is ordered that the said John Mcbrid do pay him for one days attendance thirty pounds of tobacco with Costs.

Innis vs Mcbrid   In the Action on the Case between John Innis Plt. and John Mcbrid Defendt. the parties submit themselves to the Court for tryall and upon hearing of the parties and examining of the Witnesses it is considered that the Deft. go hence without day and that he recover against the Plt. his Costs by him in this behalf expended and a Lawyers Fee.

Hughes vs Mcbrid   On the motion of Stephen Hughes a Witness for John Mcbrid ads John Innis it is ordered that the said John Mcbrid do pay him for one days attendance thirty pounds of tobacco with Costs.

Hughes vs Mcbrid   On the motion of Robert Hughes a Witness for John Mcbrid ads John Innis it is ordered that the said John Mcbrid do pay him for one days attendance thirty pounds of tobacco with Costs.

Hoggat vs Innis   On the motion of Anthony Hoggat a Witness for John Innis vs John Mcbrid it is ordered that the said John Innis do pay him for two days attendance sixty pounds of tobacco with Costs.

Hoggat vs Innis   On the motion of Eleanor Hoggat a Witness for John Innis vs John Mcbrid it is ordered that the said John Innis do pay her for one days attendance thirty pounds of tobacco with Costs.

[232]   March Court 1729 [1730]
Atkinson vs Taylor   In the Action of Trespass between Sarah Atkinson Plt. and James Taylor Defendt. it is ordered that the Jurors sworn in this cause failing to appear at the next Court be fined each in the Sum of four hundred pounds of tobacco and the Suit is continued.

Woodson vs Napier   In the Action on the Case between William Woodson Plt. and Bouth Napier Defendt. the Parties submit themselves to the Court for tryall and upon hearing of the Parties and Examining of the Witnesses it is considered that the Deft. go hence without day and that he recover against the Plt. his Costs by him in this behalf expended and a Lawyers Fee.

Hopkins vs Martin   In the Action of Trespass between Evan Hopkins

Plt. and Francis Martin Defendt. the following Jury are Sworn Bouth Napier, Richard Oglesby, Thomas Murrell, Fredorick Cox, John Laine, William Cannon, William Lansdon, Thomas Saunders, James Taylor, John Prier, Hugh Morriss, Richard Moseby, who after some time return with their Verdict which on the Defts. motion is admitted to Record and is as followeth "Wee find for the Defendt. Bouth Napier Foreman." Whereupon it is considered by the Court that the Deft. go hence without day and that he recover against the Plt. his costs by him in this behalf expended and a Lawyers Fee.

Mcbrid vs Martin   On the motion of John Mcbrid a Witness for Francis Martin ads Evan Hopkins it is ordered that the said Francis do pay him for one days attendance thirty pounds of tobacco with Costs.

Wiles vs Hughes   In the Action of Trespass on the Case between Luke Wiles Plt. and Stephen Hughes Deft. the Deft. pleads non assumpsit and for tryall thereof puts himself upon the Country and the Plt. likewise.

Wiles vs Hughes &c   In the Action of Trespass on the Case between Luke Wiles Plt. and Stephen Hughes & Sarah Atkinson Exr. & Execx. of Thomas Atkinson deced Defts. the Defts. plead non assumpsit and for tryall thereof

[233]   March Court 1729 [1730]
put themselves upon the Country and the Plt. likewise.

Ware vs Saunders   In the Action of Trespass on the Case between Susanna Ware Plt. and William Saunders Deft. time is granted the Plt. to mend her Declaration.

Davis vs Scruggs   The Action of Trespass on the Case between George Davis Plt. and John Scruggs Defendt. is dismist the Plt. not Prosecuting the same.

Cox vs Wotars   In the Action of Trespass on the Case between Mathew Cox Plt. and William Wotars Defendt. the Deft. failing to appear on the Conditionall Judgment formerly Granted against the Deft. and Daniell Stoner Gent. Sheriff is confirmed for so much Damages as shall be found upon Executing a Writ of Inquiry at the next Court of which the Sheriff is ordered to give the Deft. notice by serving him with a Copy of this Order.

Taylor vs Lowe & Uxor   The Action of Trespass on the Case between

John Taylor Plt. and Thomas Lowe and Amey his Wife Defendts. is continued.

Taylor vs Hopkins   In the Action of Trespass between James Taylor Plt. and Evan Hopkins Deft. the Deft. files a Plea and time is granted the Plt. to reply.

Logan vs Wotars   In the Action on the Case between Alexander Logan Plt. and William Wotars Defendt. the Deft. failing to appear the Conditionall Judgment formerly Granted against the Deft. and Daniell Stoner Gent. Sheriff is confirmed for so much Damages as shall be found upon Executing a Writ of Inquiry at the next Court of which the Sheriff is ordered to give the Deft. notice by serving him with a Copy of this Order.

Rocket vs Thompson   In the Action of Trespass on the Case between Baldwin Rocket Plt. and Samuell Thompson Defendt. the Deft. failing to appear the Conditional Judgment formerly Granted against the Deft. and John Birks his Common Bail is confirmed for so much Damages as shall be found upon executing a Writ of Inquiry at the next Court of which the Sheriff is ordered to give the Deft. and the said John Birks notice by serving them with a Copy of this Order.

Scot vs Utley   In the Action on the Case between Edward Scot Plt. and John Utley Deft.

[234]   March Court 1729 [1730]
the Deft. failing to appear the Conditionall Judgment formerly Granted against the Deft. and Anthony Hoggat his Common Bail is confirmed for so much Damages as shall be found upon Executing a Writ of Inquiry at the next Court of which the Sheriff is ordered to give the Deft. and the said Anthony Hoggat notice by serving them with a Copy of this Order.

Agee vs Sutlief   The Action of Trespass on the Case between Mathew Agee Plt. and Abraham Sutlief Defendt. is continued.

May vs Taylor   The Action of Trespass between William May Plt. and John Taylor Defendt. is continued.

Woodson &c. vs Lester   In the Action on the Case between Tarlton Woodson Assee. of Jeremiah Lester Plt. and Henry Lester Defendt. Richard Moseby enters himself Special Bail for the Deft. who pleads he oweth nothing and the Suit is continued.

Allegre vs Stidum   In the Action on the Case between Giles Allegree Plt. and Benjamin Stidum Defendt. the Deft. being in Custody of the Sherif for lack of Special Bail pleads he oweth nothing and for tryall thereof puts himself upon the Country and the Plt. likewise. Thomas Prosser appears as Attorny for the Sheriff in this Suit.

Scot vs Pritchet   In the Action on the Case between Edward Scot Plt. and John Pritchet Defendt. the Sherif having made return on the Pluries Capias that the Deft. is not to be found and he failing to appear a Pluries Capias de novo is awarded against him returnable to the next Court.

Scot vs Swift   In the Action on the Case between Edward Scot Plt. and William Swift Defendt. the Parties Submit themselves to the Court for tryall whereupon the Plts. oath being considered it is ordered that the Deft. pay unto the Plt. the Sum of eleven pounds seventeen shillings and two pence Currant money together with the costs of this Suit and a Layers Fee.

[235]   March Court 1729 [1730]
Henson vs Saunders   In the Action of Trespass on the Case between Benjamin Henson Plt. and Thomas Saunders Defendt. the following Jury are Sworn Richard Moseby, Richard Oglesby, Thomas Murrell, Fredorick Cox, John Laine, William Cannon, Bouth Napier, William Lansdon, James Taylor, John Prier, Hugh Morriss, William Woodson, who after some time return their Verdict which on the Plts. motion is admitted to Record and is as followeth "Wee find for the Plt. forty five shillings Currt. money Richard Moseby Foreman." the Defts. Attorny files Reasons in arrest of Judgment the arguing of which is referred to the next Court.

Wetherford vs Henson   On the motion of William Wetherford of Hanover County a Witness for Benjamin Henson vs Thomas Saunders it is ordered that the said Benjamin do pay him for three days attendance one of the days at thirty pounds of tobacco, and the other two at sixty pounds of tobacco each for coming and returning sixteen miles once one hundred and ninety eight pounds of tobacco with Costs.

Cabbell vs Woodson   On the motion of William Cabbell a Witness for William Woodson vs Bouth Napier it is ordered that the said William do pay him for two days attendance sixty pounds of tobacco with Costs.

Grand Jury vs Hannah Turner   Upon the Presentment of the Grand Jury against Hannah Turner the Sheriff having made return on the Alias Capias that the said Hannah is not to be found and she failing to appear a Pluries Capias is awarded against her returnable to the next Court.

Grand Jury vs Judith Ballew   Upon the Presentment of the Grand Jury against Judith Ballew the said Judith by her Attorny Griffith Bowen, pleads She is not Guilty and for tryall puts her self upon the Country and the Kings Attorny in like manner.

Dickins vs Pride   On the Petition of Thomas Dickins for an Acre of John Prides land it is Ordered that a Summons do Issue against the said Pride returnable to the next Court.

Lewis vs Woodson   On the motion of William Lewis of Henrico a Witness for William

[236]   March Court 1729 [1730]
Woodson Exr. &c. of Benjamin Woodson deced ads Robert Burton it is ordered that the said William do pay him for six days attendance and for coming and returning thirty two miles four times seven hundred and forty four pounds of tobacco with Costs.

Sherifs recommended   Pursuant to an Act of Assembly of this Colony intitled an Act Prescribing the method of appointing Sheriffs &c. Tarlton Fleming, Allin Howard, and George Paine, Gent. are recommended to the Honble William Gooch Esqr. His Majesty's Lieut. Governour of whom one may be appointed to Execute the Office of Sheriff of this County for the ensuing year.

Murrell vs Mcbrid   The Action on the Case between Thomas Murrell Plt. and John Mcbrid Deft. is dismist the Plt. not prosecuting the same.

Murrell vs Ashlin   The Action on the Case between Thomas Murrell Plt. and Joseph Ashlin Deft. is dismist the Plt. not prosecuting the same.

Woodson vs Atkinson   The Action on the Case between John Woodson Plt. and Henry Atkinson Deft. is dismist the Deft. being dead.

Swift vs Howard   In the Action of Trespass on the Case between William Swift Plt. and Allin Howard Deft. an Imparlance is granted the Deft.

Moreman vs Mullin   The Action on the Case between Andrew Moreman Plt. and Patrick Mullin Deft. is dismist the Plt. not prosecuting the same.

Wood vs Thompson   In the Action of Trespass on the Case between Henry Wood Plt. and Samuell Thompson Deft. the following Jury are sworn to enquire of the Damages   Richard Moseby, Richard Oglesby, Thomas Murrell, Fredorick Cox, John Laine, William Cannon, Bouth Napier, William Lansdon, James Taylor, John Prier, Hugh Morriss, William Woodson, who after some time return with their Verdict which upon the Plts. motion is admitted to Record and is as followeth "Wee find for the Plt. three pounds eight shillings Current money and two hundred and sixty eight

[237]   March Court 1729 [1730]
pounds of tobacco Richard Moseby Foreman." Wherefore it is considered by the Court that the Plt. do recover against the Deft. and George Paine, Nowell Burton, and Samuell Allin, his Bail the said Sums of three pounds eight shillings Current money, and two hundred and sixty eight pounds of tobacco by the Jurors aforesaid in their said Verdict assessed with Costs.

Martin vs Rapene   In the Action on the Case between John Martin Junr. Plt. and Anthony Rapene Defendt. the following Jury are Sworn   Bouth Napier, Richard Oglesby, Thomas Murrell, Fredorick Cox, John Laine, William Lansdon, William Cannon, David Pattison Junr, John Prier, Hugh Morris, Richard Moseby, William Woodson, who after some time return with their Verdict which on the Defts. motion is admitted to Record and is as followeth "Wee find for the Defendt. Bouth Napier Foreman." Whereupon it is considered by the Court that the Defendt. go hence without day and that he recover against the Plt. his Costs by him in this behalf expended and a Lawyers Fee.

Johnson vs Pruit   In the Action of Trespass on the Case between Charles Johnson and Elizabeth his Wife Plt. and Andrew Pruit Deft. an Imparlance is granted the Deft.

Saunders vs Saunders   On the motion of John Saunders of Hanover County a Witness for Thomas Saunders ads Benjamin Henson it is ordered that the said Thomas do pay him for five days attendance and for coming and returning sixteen miles five times five hundred and forty pounds of tobacco with Costs.

Taylor vs Martin   On the motion of James Taylor a Witness for John Martin Junr. vs Anthony Rapene it is ordered that the said John do pay him for seven days attendance two hundred and ten pounds of tobacco with Costs.

Quantain vs Martin   On the motion of John Quantain a Witness for John Martin Junr. vs Anthony Rapene it is ordered that the said John do pay him for six days attendance one hundred and eighty pounds of tobacco with Costs.

Boccar vs Rapene   On the motion of Peter Boccar a Witness for Anthony Rapene ads John

[238]   March Court 1729 [1730]
Martin Junr. it is orderd that the said Anthony do pay him for two days attendance sixty pounds of tobacco with Costs.

May vs Morriss   In the Action of Trespass between William May Plt. and John Morris Defendt. the Sheriff having made return that the Deft. is not to be found and he failing to appear an Alias Capias is awarded against him returnable to the next Court.

Quin vs Nolun   In the Action of Debt between John Quin Plt. and Agnes Nolun Administx. &c. of Thomas Nolun deced Defendt. time is granted the Plt. to mend his declaration.

New vs Morriss   In the Action of Trespass between William New Plt. and Hugh Morriss Defendt. a Special Imparlance is granted the Deft.

Then the Court adjourned to the third Tuesday in next Month.

****

At a Court held for Goochland County the third Tuesday in May being the nineteenth day of the Month Annoq Domi 1730. Present. William Mayo, Allin Howard, George Payne, William Cabbell, James Holman, Gent. Justices.

Fleming sworn Sherif   Tarlton Fleming Gent. produces a Commission from the Honble. William Gooch Esqr. his Majesty's Lieut. Governour and Commander in chief of this Dominion to be Sherif of this County which being read the said Tarlton Fleming together with William Mayo, and Allin Howard, Gent. enter into bond according to Law and acknowledging the same to be their Act and deed it is ordered to be recorded then Tarlton Fleming and Joseph Dabbs take the Oaths appointed to be taken by Act of Parliament instead of the Oaths of Allegiance and Supremacy the Oath appointed to be taken by an Act of Parliament made in the First year of

[239] May Court 1730
the Reign of his late Majesty King George the First Entituled an Act for the further Security of his Majesty's Person and Government and the Succession of the Crown in the Heirs of the late Princess Sophia being Protestants and for extinguishing the hopes of the Pretended Prince of Wales and his open and secret abettors and Subscribe the Test. Tarlton Fleming also takes the Oath of a Sherif and Joseph Dabbs takes the Oath of an Under Sherif.

Mays deeds to Chamberlayne   William May acknowledges Deeds of Lease and Release and a Receipt thereon endorsed from himself to William Chamberlayne to be his Act and deed and they are thereupon admitted to Record then Anne wife of the said William (she being first privately examined) relinquishes her right of Dower in the land by the said Deeds conveyed which is also admitted to Record.

Mayo & other Officers take oaths   Major William Mayo, and Captain Allin Howard come into Court and take the Oaths appointed to be taken by Act of Parliament instead of the Oaths of Allegiance and Supremacy, the Oath appointed to be taken by an Act of Parliament made in the first year of the Reign of his late Majesty King George the First Entituled an Act for the further Security of his Majesty's Person and Government and the Succession of the Crown in the Heirs of the late Princess Sophia being Protestants and for extinguishing the hopes of the Pretended Prince of Wales and his open and secret abettors and Subscribe the Test.

Gregory's deed to Knight   Samuell Gregory acknowledges a deed with the Livery of Seizin endorsed from himself to William Knight to be his Act and deed and it is thereupon admitted to Record.

Curds deed to Walker   Edward Curd acknowledges a deed with the Livery of Seizin endorsed from himself to William Walker to be his Act and deed and it is thereupon admitted to Record.

Scot vs Bowie   In the Action on the Case between Edward Scot Plt. and John Bowie Defendt. Griffith Bowen Attorney for the Deft. appears and confesses a Judgment to the Plt. for seven pounds eleven shillings and eleven pence Currt. money Whereupon it is considered by the Court that the Plt.

[240] May Court 1730
do recover against the Deft. the said Sum with Costs. by consent of the Plt. Execution is to stay eleven months if the Deft. so long live.

Smith levy free   On the Petition of John Smith he is exempt from payment of Levys during the continuance of his present indisposition.

Howl an Orphan to be bound out   On the Petition of Mary Howl it is ordered that Daniel Stoner Gent. one of the Church wardens of St. James's Parish do bind unto John Peter Bondurant Susanna Howl an Orphan according to Law.

Hughes's will proved   The last will and testament of Sarah Hughes is presented in Court by Robert Hughes her Executor who makes Oath thereto and the same being proved by the oath of William Creesey one of the Witnesses thereto it is admitted to Record and on the motion of the said Executor and his performing what is usuall in such cases Certificate is granted him for obtaining a Probate thereof in due form Stephen Hughes and Mathew Cox Securities.
    Ordered that Jacob Micheaux, John Webb, Thomas Walker, Fredorick Cox, or any three of them being first sworn by some Justice of the Peace do Appraise the Estate of Sarah Hughes deceased and that Robert Hughes her Executor do return an Inventory thereof to the next Court.

Calvit an Orphan to be bound out   Ordered that William Calvit an Orphan be bound by William Mayo Gent. one of the Church wardens of St. James's Parish to Joseph Bingley according to Law.

Pratts Inventory   Mary Pratt Presents the Inventory and Appraisment of the Estate of Roger Pratt deceased which is admitted to Record.

Cones Administration   Mary Cone comes into Court and makes Oath that John Cone deceased died without any will as far ash she knows or believes and on her motion and giving security for her just and faithfull Administration of the said Deceadents Estate Certificate is granted her for obtaining Letters of Administration in due form. Mathew Cox and Robert Hughes entring themselves Securities

[241]   May Court 1730
for the same.
    Ordered that Fredorick Cox, John Cox, Thomas Walker, Ashford Hughes, or any three of them being first sworn by some Justice of the Peace do Appraise the Estate of John Cone deceased and that Mary Cone the Administratrix do return an Inventory thereof to the next Court.

Chastain vs Cones   Stephen Chastain presents an Account of the funeral

Expences of John Cone deceased and makes Oath thereto whereupon it is ordered that Mary Cone Administratrix of the said John Cone do pay unto the said Stephen Chastain out of the said Deceadents Estate one pound ten shillings and six pence with Costs.

Baize's Administration   Thomas Murrell comes into Court and makes Oath that Edward Baize deceased died without any will as far as he knows or believes and on his motion and giving Security for his just and faithfull Administration of the said Deceadents Estate Certificate is granted him for obtaining Letters of Administration in due form, John Quin and John Mcbrid entring themselves Securities for the same.
  Ordered that John Gunn, Constant Perkins, Amos Lad, James Nowlin, or any three of them being first sworn by some Justice of the Peace do Appraise the Estate of Edward Baize deceased and that Thomas Murrell the Administrator do return an Inventory thereof to the next Court.

Stoveall's deed to Saunders   George Stoveall acknowledges a deed with the Livery of Seizin endorsed from himself to John Saunders to be his Act and deed and it is thereupon admitted to Record then Elizabeth wife of the said George (she being first privately examined) relinquishes her right of Dower in the land by the said Deed conveyed which is also admitted to Record.

Stoveall's deed to Saunders   George Stoveall acknowledges a deed with the Livery of Seizin endorsed from himself to John Saunders to be his Act and deed and it is thereupon admitted to Record then Elizabeth wife of the said George (she being first privately examined) relinquishes her right of Dower in the land by the said Deed conveyed which is also admitted to Record.

Chamberlayne Acct. vs Thompson   John Saunders exhibits an Acct. against John Thomason and makes Oath

[242]   May Court 1730
that the Ballance thereof being ten pounds twelve shillings and nine pence half penny is justly due to William Chamberlayne and that he never received any satisfaction for the same which is ordered to be Certified thereon.

Chamberlayne Acct. vs Dockrey   John Saunders exhibits an Account against James Dockrey and makes Oath that the Ballance thereof being forty nine pounds of tobacco and three pounds eighteen shillings and two pence half penny is justly due to William Chamberlayne and that he never received any satisfaction for the same which is ordered to be Certified thereon.

Chamberlayne Acct. vs Allin   John Saunders exhibits an Account against David Allin and makes Oath that the Ballance thereof being three hundred and five pounds of tobacco and five pounds eighteen shillings is justly due to William Chamberlayne and that he never received any satisfaction for the same which is ordered to be Certified thereon.

Atkinson's Administration   Stephen Hughes comes into Court and makes his solemn Affirmation that Sarah Atkinson deced died without any will as far as he knows or believes and on his motion and giving Security for his just and faithfull Administration of the said Deceadents Estate Certificate is granted him for obtaining Letters of Administration in due from John Quin and Robert Hughes entring themselves Securities for the same.

Wright Eliza. to appear & prove John Wrights will   On the motion of Stephen Hughes it is ordered that Elizabeth widow of John Wright deceased be Summoned to appear at the next Court to prove the last will and testament of the said John Wright or refuse the Execution thereof.

Fleming protests agt. the prison   Tarlton Fleming Gent. Sherif Protests against the Justices of this County for all damages, Costs, and sums of money or tobacco that shall or may be recovered against him by reason of the escape of any Prisoner

[243]   May Court 1730
or Prisoners who shall escape out of the Goal of this County the said Goal not being sufficient as he thinks.

Allegres Acct. vs Stidum   Giles Allegre exhibits an Account against Benjamin Stidum and makes Oath that the Ballance thereof being seven pounds eleven shillings and seven pence is justly due to him and that he never received any satisfaction for the same which is ordered to be Certified thereon.

Dean vs Napier   In the Action on the Case between Richard Dean Plt. and Robert Napier Junr. Defendt. the Jury sworn in February not appearing it is ordered that in this and every cause wherein a Jury shall be hereafter sworn if any of the Jurors shall fail to appear at another day than that on which they are sworn they shall be fined each in the Sum of four hundred pounds of tobacco and the Suit is continued.

Rapine vs Bingley   The Action of Trespass on the Case between Anthony Rapine Plt. and Joseph Bingley Defendt. is continued at the Defts. Cost.
  John Woodson and George Payne Gent. are appointed to take Isaac Parentan's deposition in this Cause on Monday the twenty fifth Instant.

Woodson vs Baize   The Action of Trespass on the Case between John Woodson Plt. and Edward Baize Defendt. is dismist the Deft. being dead.

Cox vs Dean   The Action of Trespass between Fredorick Cox Plt. and Richard Dean Deft. is continued at the Plts. cost.

Dale vs Gunn   The Action on the Case between Christopher Dale Plt. and John Gunn Defendt. is dismist the Plt. being dead.

Utley vs Napier   The Action of Debt between John Utley Plt. and Bouth Napier Defendt. is dismist the Plt. not prosecuting the same.

Jeffs vs Martin   The Action on the Case between John Jeffs Plt. and John Martin Defendt. is dismist the Plt. not prosecuting the same.

Skeyman vs Burk   The Action of Trespass between George Skeyman Plt. and Theodorick Burk Defendt. is dismist the Plt. not prosecuting the same.

[244]   May Court 1730
Macon vs Wharton   In the Action on the Case between John Macon Plt. and Thomas Wharton Defendt. the Plt. files a demurrer in Chancery and the Suit is continued.

Waddill vs Edwards   The Action on the Case between William Waddill Junr. Plt. and Thomas Edwards Defendt. is continued.

Thomas vs Gee   In the Action on the Case between Rowland Thomas Plt. and Gilbert Gee Defendt. the Deft. takes issue on the Plts. replication and the Suit is continued.

Temple vs Burton   In the Action of Trespass on the Case between Joseph Temple Plt. and Nowell Burton Defendt. the following Jury are Sworn, Richard Moseby, Nicholas Cox, William Woodson, William Lansdon, Ashford Hughes, John Prier, John Williams, James Barret, John

Merriman, John Mcbrid, Henry Webb, William Cannon, who after some time return with their Verdict which is recorded in these words "Wee find an Acct. from Joseph Temple charg'd to Noel Burton for six pounds seven shillings and one penny, Wee find a Record from Hanover County Court in these words Hanover ss. September 5th. 1729. Sworn to in Court by the within named John Darracote Test Arthur Clayton C.C. if the said Evidence shall be adjudged good wee find for the Plt. the said Sum of six pounds seven shillings and one penny otherwise wee find for the Deft. Richard Mosby Foreman." the Arguments on which Verdict are referred to be heard at the next Court.

Read vs Downie   The Action on the Case between Clem Read Plt. and Robert Downie Defendt. is continued at the Plts. cost.

Franklin vs Atkinson   On the motion of John Franklin a Witness for Sarah Atkinson vs Anthony Benning it is ordered that the said Sarah do pay him for eight days attendance two hundred and forty pounds of tobacco with costs.

Franklin vs Atkinson   On the motion of John Franklin a Witness for Sarah Atkinson vs James Taylor it is ordered that the said Sarah do pay him for eight days attendance two hundred and forty pounds of tobacco with costs.

[245]   May Court 1730

Hook vs Benning   On the motion of James Hook a Witness for Anthony Benning ads Sarah Atkinson it is ordered that the said Anthony do pay him for eight days attendance two hundred and forty pounds of tobacco with costs.

Hook vs Taylor   On the motion of James Hook a Witness for James Taylor ads Sarah Atkinson it is ordered that the said James Taylor do pay him for six days attendance one hundred and eighty pounds of tobacco with costs.

Dickins's Acct. vs Jeffs   Thomas Dickins exhibits an Account against John Jeffs and makes Oath that the Ballance thereof being one pound ten shillings is justly due to him and that he never received any satisfaction for the same which is ordered to be Certified thereon.

Pruit vs Johnson   In the Action on the Case between Andrew Pruit Plt. and Charles Johnson Defendt. the Deft. appears but failing to plead on the Plts. motion Judgment by nihil dicit is granted him against the Deft.

for what damages shall be recovered in this Suit to be discharged nevertheless if the Deft. shall plead at the next Court.

Salmon vs Edwards   In the Action on the Case between Thomas Salmon Plt. and Thomas Edwards Defendt. the Deft. appears but failing to plead on the Plts. motion Judgment by nihil dicit is granted him against the Deft. for what damages shall be recovered in this Suit to be discharged nevertheless if the Deft. shall plead at the next Court.

Taylor vs Quin   The Action of Debt between James Taylor Plt. and John Quin Defendt. is continued at the Plts. cost.

Ferry to be kept   Orderd that George Payne and William Cabbell Gent. treat with Stephen Hughes about keeping the Ferry at the Court house and that they report their proceedings therein to the next Court.

Marchbanks vs Croom   The Action on the Case between George Marchbanks Plt. and Daniell Croom Defendt. is continued at the Plts. cost.

New vs Morriss &c   The Action of Debt between William New Plt. and Hugh Morriss and Mary his wife Executrix &c. of Edmund New deced Defts. is dismist

[246]   May Court 1730
the Plt. not prosecuting the same.

Collins vs Morriss   In the Action of Trespass between Mathew Collins Plt. and John Morriss Defendt. the Sherif having returned on the Pluries Capias that the Deft. is not to be found and he failing to appear on the Plts. motion a Pluries Capias de novo is awarded against him returnable to the next Court.

Boston vs Cox   The Action on the Case between Hugh Boston Plt. and Nicholas Cox Defendt. is continued.

Pigg vs Woodson   The Action on the Case between John Pigg Junr. Plt. and William Woodson Defendt. is continued at the Plts. cost.

Pigg vs Allin   In the Action on the Case between John Pigg Junr. Plt. and Samuell Allin Defendt. on the Defts. motion leave is granted him to plead severall matters whereupon he files Pleas and the Suit is continued.

Wood vs New   In the Action of Trespass on the Case between Henry Wood Plt. and William New Defendt. the Deft. failing to appear on the Plts. motion the Conditionall Judgment formerly granted against the Deft. and Daniell Stoner Gent. late Sherif is confirmed for so much damages as shall be found upon Executing a Writ of Inquiry at the next Court of which the Sherif is ordered to give the Deft. and the said Daniell Stoner notice by serving them with a Copy of this Order.

Johnson vs Fenton   In the Action of Trespass on the Case between William Johnson Plt. and Thomas Fenton Defendt. the Sherif having returned on the Pluries Capias that the Deft. is not to be found and he failing to appear on the Plts. motion a Pluries Capias de novo is awarded against him returnable to the next Court.

Atkinson vs Taylor   The Action of Trespass between Sarah Atkinson Plt. and James Taylor Defendt. is dismist the Plt. being dead.

Ware vs Saunders   In the Action of Trespass on the Case between Susanna Ware Plt. and William Saunders Deft. the Plt. files a new declaration.

[247]   May Court 1730
Taylor vs Lowe & Uxor   The Action of Trespass on the Case between John Taylor Plt. and Thomas Lowe and Amey his wife Defendts. is continued.

Taylor vs Hopkins   In the Action of Trespass between James Taylor Plt. and Evan Hopkins Deft. the Plt. takes issue on the Defts. Pleas and the Suit is continued.

Henson vs Saunders   In the Action of Trespass on the Case between Benjamin Henson Plt. and Thomas Saunders Defendt. the Deft. waives his reasons in Arrest of Judgment and by consent of the Parties a new tryall is ordered at the next Court.

Moseby vs Taylor   The Action of Debt between Richard Moseby Plt. and John Taylor Defendt. is continued at the Defts. cost.

Bumpuss vs Moreman   The Action of Trespass on the Case between Samuell Bumpuss Plt. and Andrew Moreman Defendt. is continued at the Plts. cost.

Capoon levy free   On the Petition of Jacob Capoon he is exempt from payment of Levys.

Smith levy free   On the Petition of George Smith he is exempt from payment of Levys.

Goddard levy free   On the Petition of William Goddard he is exempt from payment of Levys for this year.

Noluns Inventory   Agnes Nolun presents the Inventory and Appraisment of the Estate of Thomas Nolun deceased which is admitted to Record.

Taylor vs Lowe   In the Action of Trespass on the Case between John Taylor Plt. and Thomas Lowe Defendt. the following Jury are sworn Anthony Hoggat, Nicholas Cox, William Woodson, William Lansdon, John Prier, John Mcbrid, Henry Webb, John Williams, James Barret, John Merriman, William Cannon, Francis Martin, upon the return of the Jury the Plt. being called and failing to appear on the Defts. motion he is nonsuited and it is thereupon considered by the Court that the Deft. go hence without day and that he recover against the Plt. five shillings Currant money according to the Act of Assembly in that Case made and provided, together with his Costs by him in this behalf expended and a Lawyers Fee.

L'villain vs Woodson   The Action on the Case between John Levillain Plt. and Joseph Woodson Deft.

[248]   May Court 1730
is continued at the Plts. cost.

May vs Jackson   The Action on the Case between William May Plt. and Joseph Jackson Defendt. is continued at the Defts. cost.

Holland vs Napier   In the Action on the Case between Michael Holland Plt. and Bouth Napier Defendt. the following Jury are sworn Anthony Hoggat, William Lansdon, John Mcbrid, John Prier, Henry Webb, John Williams, James Barret, William Woodson, John Merriman, Thomas Christian, Francis Martin, William Cannon, who after some time return with their Verdict which on the Plts. motion is admitted to Record and is as followeth "Wee find for the Plt. three pounds thirteen shillings and four pence half penny Antho. Hoggat Foreman." Whereupon it is considered by the Court that the Plt. do recover against the Deft. the said sum of three pounds thirteen shillings and four pence half penny by the

Jurors aforesaid in their said Verdict assessed with the Costs of this Suit and a Lawyers Fee.

Wade vs Holland   On the motion of Robert Wade a Witness for Michael Holland vs Bouth Napier it is ordered that the said Michael do pay him for five days attendance one hundred and fifty pounds of tobacco with Costs.

Jevodon vs Taylor   On the motion of Thomas Jevodon a Witness for James Taylor ads Sarah Atkinson it is ordered that the said James do pay him for six days attendance one hundred and eighty pounds of tobacco with Costs.

Then the Court adjourned till to morrow morning ten of the Clock.

****

At a Court continued and held for Goochland County the twentieth day of May Annoq Domi. 1730. Present. William Mayo, Allin Howard, George Payne, William Cabbell, Gent. Justices.

[249]   May Court 1730
Lists of tithables to be taken   The Following persons are appointed to take the lists of Titheables   George Payne Gent. below Beverdam Creek, Allin Howard Gent. above the said Creek including the Fork of the River, William Cabbell Gent. in that part of St. James's Parish lying on the South side of James River, and James Holman Gent. in King William Parish.

Wood takes oaths   Captain Henry Wood comes into Court and takes the Oaths appointed to be taken by Act of Parliament instead of the Oaths of Allegiance and Supremacy, the Oath appointed to be taken by an Act of Parliament made in the First year of the Reign of his late Majesty King George the First Entituled an Act for the further Security of his Majesty's Person and Government and the Succession of the Crown in the Heirs of the late Princess Sophia being Protestants and for extinguishing the hopes of the pretended Prince of Wales and his open and secret abettors, and Subscribes the Test.

Alves vs Huetson   In the Action of Detinue between George Alves Plt. and John Huetson Deft. the following Jury are sworn   Anthony Hoggat, William Lansdon, John Mcbrid, John Prier, John Williams, John Payne, William Woodson, John Merriman, Thomas Christian, Francis Martin, William Cannon, Nowell Burton, who after some time return with their

Verdict which on the Plts. motion is admitted to Record and is as followeth "Wee find for the Plt. five pounds nine shillings and ten pence half penny Antho. Hoggat Foreman" the Defts. attorny files reasons in Arrest of Judgment the arguments on which are referred to be heard at the next Court.

Barret to be fined   James Barret being yesterday Summoned [to appear] as a Jury man to attend the Court this day and failing to appear it is ordered that he be fined to our Sovereign Lord the King in the Sum of four hundred pounds of tobacco and that he pay Costs, on condition that if at the next Court he shew sufficient cause for his non appearance this order to be void.

Lad vs Cannon   The Action on the Case between Amos Lad Plt. and William Cannon Deft. is continued.

Agee vs Sutleith   The Action of Trespass on the Case between Mathew Agee Plt. and Abraham Sutleith Deft. is continued at the Plts. cost.

[250]   May Court 1730
Woodson &c. vs Leister   In the Action on the Case between Tarlton Woodson Assignee of Jeremiah Leister Plt. and Henry Leister Defendt. the Plt. files a new declaration the Deft. pleads he oweth nothing and for tryall thereof puts himself upon the Country and the Plt. likewise.

Scot vs Pritchet   In the Action on the Case between Edward Scot Plt. and John Pritchet Defendt. the Sherif having returned on the Pluries Capias that the Deft. is not to be found and he failing to appear on the Plts. motion a Pluries Capias de novo is awarded against him returnable to the next Court.

Johnson & Uxor vs Pruit   In the Action of Trespass on the Case between Charles Johnson and Elizabeth his wife Plts. and Andrew Pruit Defendt. the Plts. file a new declaration and an Imparlance is granted the Defendant.

May vs Morriss   In the Action of Trespass between William May Plt. and John Morriss Defendt. the Sherif having made return on the Alias Capias that the Deft. is not to be found and he failing to appear on the Plts. motion a Pluries Capias is awarded against him returnable to the next Court.

Quin vs Nolun   In the Action of Debt between John Quin Plt. and

Agnes Nolun Admx. &c. of Thomas Nolun deceased Defendt. the Plt. files a new declaration, and on the Defts. motion leave is granted her to Plead severall matters whereupon she files pleas and the Plt. takes issue thereon.

New vs Morriss   The Action of Trespass between William New Plt. and Hugh Morriss Defendt. is dismist the Plt. not prosecuting the same.

Grand Jury vs Hannah Turner   Upon the Presentment of the Grand Jury against Hannah Turner the Sherif having made return on the Pluries Capias that the said Hannah is not to be found and she failing to appear a Pluries Capias de novo is awarded against her returnable to the next Court.

Grand Jury vs Judith Ballew   The Present of the Grand Jury against Judith Ballew is continued.

[251]   May Court 1730
Dickins vs Pride   The Petition of Thomas Dickins against John Pride is continued.

Epperson vs Amos   The Action on the Case between Francis Epperson Plt. and John Amos Defendt. is dismist neither party appearing.

Quantain vs Robinson   In the Action on the Case between John Quantain Plt. and John Robinson Defendt. the Plt. having failed to file his declaration on the Defts. motion he is nonsuited and it is thereupon considered by the Court that the Deft. go hence without day and that he recover against the Plt. five shillings Currant money according to the Act of Assembly in that Case made and provided together with his Costs by him in this behalf expended and a Lawyers Fee.

Murrell vs Dale   The Action of Debt between Thomas Murrell Plt. and Christopher Dale Defendt. is dismist the Defendt. being dead.

Allin vs Gates   In the Action of Trespass on the Case between Charles Allin Plt. and William Gates Defendt. the Sherif having made return that the Deft. is not to be found and he failing to appear on the Plts. motion an Attachment is awarded against the Defts. Estate returnable to the next Court.

Rocket vs Denton   The Action of Debt between Baldwin Rocket Plt. and Thomas Denton Defendt. is dismist the Plt. not prosecuting the same.

Scot vs Williams   In the Action on the Case between Edward Scot Plt. and Edward Williams Defendt. the Deft. failing to appear and the Sherif having taken insufficient Bail on the motion of the Plt. Judgment is granted him against the Deft. and Daniell Stoner Gent. late Sherif for what damages shall be recovered in this Suit to be discharged nevertheless by the appearance of the Deft. at the next Court.

Scot vs Revis   In the Action on the Case between Edward Scot Plt. and Edward Revis Deft. the Deft. appears and confesses a Judgment to the Plt. for six pounds two shillings and eight pence Currant money Whereupon it is considered by the Court that the Plt. do recover against the Deft. the said Sum together with the costs of his Suit and a Lawyers Fee.

[252]   May Court 1730

Scot vs Womack   In the Action on the Case between Edward Scot Plt. and William Womack surviving Executor and James Barret & Sarah his wife Executrix &c. of Robert Woodson deced Defendts. the Defts. failing to appear and the Sherif not having returned any Bail on the motion of the Plt. Judgment is granted him against the Defts. and Daniell Stoner Gent. late Sherif for what damages shall be recovered in this Suit to be discharged nevertheless if the Defts. shall appear at the next Court.

Ward vs Farrar   In the Action of Debt between Seth Ward Plt. and John Farrar Deft. time is granted the Plt. to mend his declaration.

Woodson vs Arrington   In the Action on the Case between John Woodson Plt. and Samuell Arrington Defendt. George Stoveall enters himself Special Bail for the Deft. who pleads he oweth nothing and for tryall thereof puts himself upon the Country and the Plt. likewise

Pruit vs Boccar   In the Action on the Case between Hugh Pruit Plt. and Peter Boccar Defendt. an imparlance is granted the Deft.

Sallee &c. vs Bowey   In the Action of Trespass on the Case between Isaac Sallee Assee. of Thomas Gevedon Plt. and John Bowey Deft. an imparlance is granted the Deft.

Webber vs White   In the Action of Trespass on the Case between Phillip Webber Plt. and Edward White Defendt. the Sherif having made return that the Deft. is not to be found and he failing to appear on the

Plts. motion an Alias Capias is awarded against the Deft. returnable to the next Court.

Scot vs Wiers   On the Scire facias between Edward Scot Plt. and John Wiers Defendt. the Sherif having made return that the Deft. is not to be found and he failing to appear on the Plts. motion an Alias Scire facias is awarded against the Deft. returnable to the next Court.

Jackson &c. vs Southerland   In the Action of Trespass on the Case between John Jackson Assignee of Edward Birch Plt. and George Southerland Defendt. an imparlance is granted the Defendant.

[253]   May Court 1730
Armstrong vs Southerland   The Action of Trespass on the Case between Robert Armstrong Plt. and George Southerland defendt. is dismist the Plt. not prosecuting the same.

Wood vs Woodson   The Action on the Case between Henry Wood Plt. and Benjamin Woodson Deft. is dismist the Plt. not prosecuting the same.

Levins vs Farrar   In the Action on the Case between Richard Levins Plt. and John Sutton Farrar Defendt. the Sherif having made return that the Deft. is not to be found and he failing to appear on the Plts. motion an Alias Capias is awarded against the Deft. returnable to the next Court.

Digges vs Quin   In the Action on the Case between Dudley Digges Plt. and John Quin Defendt. an imparlance is granted the Deft.

Digges vs Ware   The Action on the Case between Dudley Digges Plt. and Peter Ware Defendt. is dismist the Plt. not prosecuting the same.

Digges vs Napier   In the Action on the Case between Dudley Digges Plt. and Bouth Napier Deft. an imparlance is granted the Defendt.

Scot vs Lawson   In the Action on the Case between Edward Scot Plt. and Jonas Lawson Defendt. the Deft. failing to appear and the Sherif not having returned any Bail on the Plts. motion Judgment is granted him against the Deft. and Daniell Stoner Gent. late Sherif for what damages shall be recovered in this Suit to be discharged nevertheless if the Deft. shall appear at the next Court.

Happer vs Woodson   In the Action on the Case between William Happer Plt. and Joseph Woodson Defendt. an imparlance is granted the

Deft.

Happer &c. vs Woodson   In the Action on the Case between William Happer Assignee of William Arrington Plt. and Joseph Woodson Deft. an imparlance is granted the Deft.

Happer vs Harper   In the Action on the Case between William Happer Plt. and Henry Harper Deft. the Deft. failing to appear and the Sherif not having returned any Bail on the Plts. motion Judgment is granted him against the Deft. and Daniell Stoner Gent. late Sherif for what damages shall be recovered in this Suit to be discharged nevertheless if the Deft. shall appear at the next Court.

[254]   May Court 1730
Digges vs Agee   In the Action on the Case between Dudley Digges Plt. and Mathew Agee Deft. the Deft. failing to appear and the Sherif not having returned any Bail on the Plts. motion Judgment is granted him against the Deft. and Daniell Stoner Gent. late Sherif for what damages shall be recovered in this Suit to be discharged nevertheless if the Deft. shall appear at the next Court.

Stidum vs Bingley &c   In the Action of Debt between Benjamin Stidum Plt. and Joseph Bingley and William Lansdon Defts. the following Jury are Sworn Nowel Burton, John Mcbrid, John Prier, John Williams, John Payne, John Laine, William Woodson, John Merriman, Thomas Christian, Francis Martin, William Cannon, Ashford Hughes, who after some time return with their Verdict which on the Plts. motion is admitted to Record and is as followeth "Wee find for the Plt. Nowel Burton Foreman." Whereupon it is considered by the Court that the Plt. do recover against the Deft. eight hundred pounds of tobacco and Cask with Interest thereon after the rate of six Pr. Centum Pr. Annum from the tenth day of January one thousand seven hundred and twenty eight together with the Costs of this Suit and a Lawyers Fee.
   Upon a Suggestion of the Defts. that there is Equity in this Cause it is ordered that Execution be stayed untill next Court that they may file a Bill of Injunction in Chancery.

Digges vs Dillon   In the Action on the Case between Dudley Digges Plt. and James Theophilus Dillon Defendt. the Deft. being ruled to Special Bail and failing therein and being in Custody of the Sherif confesses a Judgment to the Plt. for eight pounds one shilling and seven pence half penny Currt. money Whereupon it is considered by the Court that the Plt. recover against the Deft. the said Sum together with the Costs of this Suit and a Lawyers Fee.

Digges vs Saunders   In the Action on the Case between Dudley Digges Plt. and John Saunders Defendt. the Deft. failing to appear and the Sherif not having returned any Bail on the Plts. motion Judgment is granted him against the Deft. and Daniell Stoner Gent. late Sherif for what damages shall be recovered in this Suit to be discharged nevertheless if the Deft. shall appear at the next Court.

[255]   May Court 1730
Digges vs Rapene   In the Action on the Case between Dudley Digges Plt. and Anthony Rapene Defendt. an imparlance is granted the Deft.

Clarkson &c. vs Clarkson   In the Action of Trespass between James Clarkson and John Roberts Plts. and David Clarkson Defendt. the Plt. having failed to file his declaration on the Defts. motion he is nonsuited and it is thereupon considered by the Court that the Deft. go hence without day and that he recover against the Plt. five shillings Currant money according to the Act of Assembly in that Case made and provided together with his Costs by him in this behalf expended and a Lawyers Fee.

Wood vs Pratt   The Action on the Case between Henry Wood Plt. and Mary Pratt Administx. &c. of Roger Pratt deced Defendt. is continued.

Clopton &c. vs Marchbanks   In the Action of Debt between Joyce Clopton, William Acrill, & John Syme Executx. & Executors &c. of William Clopton deced Plts. and George Marchbanks Deft. an imparlance is granted the Deft.

Allegre vs Stidum   In the Action on the Case between Giles Allegre Plt. and Benjamin Stidum Deft. the Deft. being ruled to Special Bail and failing therein and being in Custody of the Sherif confesses a Judgment to the Plt. for seven pounds eleven shillings and seven pence Currt. money Whereupon it is considered by the Court that the Plt. do recover against the Deft. the said Sum together with the Costs of this Suit and a Lawyers Fee.

Prison bounds marked   Ordered that the bounds marked by Stephen Hughes by the direction of this Court be the bounds of the Goal of this County.

Payne vs Stidum   On the motion of John Payne a Witness for Benjamin Stidum vs Joseph Bingley & William Lansdon it is ordered that the said

Benjamin do pay him for two days attendance sixty pounds of tobacco with Costs.

Ford vs Stidum   On the motion of James Ford a Witness for Benjamin Stidum vs Joseph Bingley & William Lansdon it is ordered that the said Benjamin do pay him for two days attendance sixty pounds of tobacco with Costs.

Mallet vs Stidum   On the motion of Stephen Mallet a Witness for Benjamin Stidum vs Joseph Bingley

[256]   May Court 1730
Bingley & William Lansdon it is ordered that the said Benjamin do pay him for two days attendance sixty pounds of tobacco with Costs.

Wooldridge vs Bingley &c   On the motion of Thomas Wooldridge a Witness for Joseph Bingley & William Lansdon ads Benjamin Stidum it is ordered that the said Joseph & William do pay him for two days attendance sixty pounds of tobacco with Costs.

Roberts vs Bingley &c   On the motion of Maurice Roberts a Witness for Joseph Bingley & William Lansdon ads Benjamin Stidum it is ordered that the said Joseph & William do pay him for two days attendance sixty pounds of tobacco with Costs.

Prison to be examined   Edward Scot is appointed to view and enquire into the strength of the Prison and to report to the next Court what may be necessary to make it sufficient to hold a Prisoner.

Then the Court adjourned to the third Tuesday in the next Month.

****

At a Court held for Goochland County the third Tuesday in June being the sixteenth day of the Month Annoq Domi. 1730. Present. William Mayo, Allin Howard, William Cabbell, James Holman, Gent. Justices.

Holman takes oaths   Captain James Holman comes into Court and takes the Oaths appointed to be taken by Act of Parliament instead of the Oaths of Allegiance and Supremacy the Oath appointed to be taken by an Act of Parliament made in the First year of the Reign of

[257]   June Court 1730
his late Majesty King George the First Entituled an Act for the further Security of his Majesty's Person and Government and the Succession of the Crown in the Heirs of the late Princess Sophia being Protestants and for extinguishing the hopes of the pretended Prince of Wales and his open and secret abettors and Subscribes the Test.

Thompson Sworn Sub Sherif   Joseph Thompson comes into Court and takes the Oaths appointed to be taken by Act of Parliament instead of the Oaths of Allegiance and Supremacy, the Oath appointed to be taken by an Act of Parliament made in the First year of the Reign of his late Majesty King George the First Entituled an Act for the further Security of his Majesty's Person and Government and the Succession of the Crown in the Heirs of the late Princess Sophia being Protestants and for extinguishing the hopes of the pretended Prince of Wales and his open and secret abettors, Subscribes the Test and takes the Oath of an Undersherif and is thereupon admitted to the Execution of that Office.

Calvets deeds to Holman   Peter Calvet acknowledges Deeds of Lease and Release from himself to James Holman to be his Act and deed and they are thereupon admitted to Record.

Wrights will proved   The last will and testament of John Wright is presented in Court by Elizabeth Wright his Executrix who makes Oath thereto and the same being proved by the Oaths of Edward Scot and John Williams two of the Witnesses thereto it is admitted to record and on the motion of the said Executrix and her performing what is usuall in such Cases Certificate is granted her for obtaining a Probate thereof in due form Nowell Burton and Joseph Woodson Securities.
    Ordered that John Williams, Jacob Winfrey, John Merriman, Joseph Bingley, or any three of them being first sworn by some Justice of the Peace do Appraise the Estate of John Wright deceased and that Elizabeth Wright his Executrix do return an Inventory thereof to the next Court.

Christian's Negro Judg'd   Guy a Negro boy belonging to James Christian is judged to be eleven years of Age.

[258]   June Court 1730
Christian's Negro judg'd   Tom a Negro boy belonging to Robert Christian is judged to be ten years of Age.

Baize's Inventory   Thomas Murrell presents the Inventory and Appraisment of the Estate of Edward Baize deceased which is admitted to Record.

Hix & Moss deed to Cox Marmaduke Hix and William Moss acknowledge a deed with the Livery of Seizin endorsed from themselves to Nicholas Cox to be their Act and Deed and it is thereupon admitted to Record then Agnes wife of the said Marmaduke, and Elizabeth wife of the said William (they being first privately examined) relinquish their right of Dower in the land by the said deed conveyed which is also admitted to Record.

Hix's deed to Moss Marmaduke Hix acknowledges a deed with the Livery of Seizin endorsed from himself to William Moss to be his Act and deed and it is thereupon admitted to Record then Agnes wife of the said Marmaduke (she being first privately examined) relinquishes her right of Dower in the land by the said deed conveyed which is also admitted to Record.

Syms vs Phelps The Action of Trespass on the Case between Mathew Syms Plt. and John Phelps Defendt. is continued at the Defts. Cost.

Innis vs Mcbrid The Action of Trespass between John Innis Plt. and John Mcbrid Defendt. is continued at the Plts. Cost.

Wiles vs Hughes The Action of Trespass on the Case between Luke Wiles Plt. and Stephen Hughes Defendt. is continued at the Defts. Cost.

Wiles vs Hughes & Atkinson The Action of Trespass on the Case between Luke Wiles Plt. and Stephen Hughes & Sarah Atkinson Execr. & Execx. of Thomas Atkinson deceased Defendts. is continued at the Defts. Cost.

Cox vs Wotars In the Action of Trespass on the Case between Mathew Cox Plt. and William Wotars Defendt. the following Jury are sworn to enquire of

[259] June Court 1730
the damages Nowel Burton, William Woodson, Thomas Turpin, Richard Oglesby, George Southerland, Samuell Burks, Henry Webb, Thomas Murrell, Joseph Farrar, William Cannon, Joseph Jackson, Thomas Wadloe, who after some time return with their Verdict which on the Plts. motion is admitted to Record and is as followeth "Wee find for the Plt. three pounds fifteen shillings and six pence Currant money. Nowell Burton Foreman." Wherefore it is considered by the Court that the Plt.

do recover against the Deft. and Daniell Stoner Gent. late Sherif the said Sum of three pounds fifteen shillings and six pence Currant money by the Jurors aforesaid in their said Verdict assessed together with the Costs of this Suit and a Lawyers Fee.

Logan vs Wotars   In the Action on the Case between Alexander Logan Plt. and William Wotars Defendt. the following Jury are sworn to enquire of the damages   Nowell Burton, William Woodson, Thomas Turpin, Richard Oglesby, George Southerland, Samuell Burks, Henry Webb, Thomas Murrell, Joseph Farrar, William Cannon, Joseph Jackson, Thomas Wadloe, who after some time return with their Verdict which on the Plts. motion is admitted to Record and is as followeth "Wee find for the Plt. two pounds twelve shillings Currant money Nowell Burton Foreman." Wherefore it is considered by the Court that the Plt. do recover against the Deft. and Daniell Stoner Gent. late Sherif the said Sum of two pounds twelve shillings Currant money by the Jurors aforesaid in their said Verdict assessed together with the Costs of this Suit and a Lawyers Fee.

Rocket vs Thompson   In the Action of Trespass on the Case between Baldwin Rocket Plt. and Samuell Thompson Defendt. the Deft. appears and confesses a Judgment to the Plt. for five pounds two shillings and two pence farthing Currant money whereupon it is considered by the Court that the Plt. do recover against the Deft. the said Sum with the Costs of this Suit and a Lawyers Fee.

Scot vs Utley   The Action on the Case between Edward Scot Plt. and John Utley Defendt. is continued at the Defts. Cost.

May vs Taylor   The Action of Trespass between William May Plt. and John Taylor Defendt. is continued at the Defts. Cost.

[260]   June Court 1730
Dean vs Napier   In the Action on the Case between Richard Dean Plt. and Robert Napier Junr. Defendt. Robert Adams, Nicholas Cox, Mathew Cox, Stephen Woodson, John Mcbrid, Nowell Burton, William Lansdon, James Taylor, John Prier, Joseph Farrar, David Walker, Fredorick Cox, the Jury sworn last February Court now bring in their Verdict which on the Plts. motion is admitted to Record and is as followeth "Wee find for the Plt. five hundred and sixty eight pounds of tobacco to be paid at Benjamin Woodsons house where he now dwells. John Mcbrid Foreman." Whereupon it is considered by the Court that the Plt. do recover against the Deft. the said Sum of five hundred and sixty eight

pounds of tobacco at the dwelling house of Benjamin Woodson by the Jurors aforesaid in their said Verdict assessed together with the Costs of this Suit and a Lawyers Fee.

Runalls's will proved   The last will and testament of William Runals is presented in Court by William Runals his Executor who makes Oath thereto and the same being proved by the Oath of William Barnes one of the Witnesses thereto it is admitted to Record and on the motion of the said Executor and his performing what is usuall in such cases Certificate is granted him for obtaining a Probate thereof in due form Stephen Hughes and Ashford Hughes Securities.

Rapene vs Bingley   The Action of Trespass on the Case between Anthony Rapine Plt. and Joseph Bingley Defendt. is continued at the Defts. Cost.

Wood vs New   The Action of Trespass on the Case between Henry Wood Plt. and William New Defendt. is continued.

Runals Mary chooses her Guardian   On the motion of Mary Runals she is permitted to choose Stephen Hughes her Guardian who accepts the charge Tarlton Fleming Gent. and Ashford Hughes Securities.

   Present George Payne Gent.

[261]   June Court 1730
Rex vs Hardcastle   William Hardcastle appears upon a Recognizance taken before Allin Howard Gent. and is accused by George Payne Junr. of shooting his horse the Evidences being examined the Court are of Opinion that by shooting a Gun in the night and not knowing at what he shot the said William Hardcastle is guilty of a misbehaviour and it is thereupon ordered that he do receive on his bare back at the Common whipping Post five lashes and that he be thereafter discharged.

Carr's Inventory   William Cabbell presents the Inventory and Appraisment of the Estate of Joell Carr deceased which is admitted to Record.

Cone's Inventory   Mary Cone presents the Inventory and Appraisment of the Estate of John Cone deceased which is admitted to Record.

Swift vs Holland   In the Action of Trespass on the Case between William Swift Plt. and Allin Howard Defendt. the Deft. pleads he oweth nothing.

Kelly levy free   On the Petition of John Kelly he is exempt from payment of levys for this year.

Sadler levy free   On the Petition of William Sadler he is exempt from payment of levys for this Year.

Atkinson's Inventory   Stephen Hughes presents the Inventory and Appraisment of the Estate of Sarah Atkinson deceased which is admitted to Record.

Cox vs Dean   The Action of Trespass between Fredorick Cox Plt. and Richard Dean Defendt. is continued at the Defendants Cost.

Macon vs Wharton   The Action on the Case between John Macon Plt. and Thomas Wharton Defendt. is continued.

Waddill vs Edwards   The Action on the Case between William Waddill Junr. Plt. and Thomas Edwards

[262]   June Court 1730
Edwards Defendt. is continued.

Thomas vs Gee   The Action on the Case between Rowland Thomas Plt. and Gilbert Gee Defendt. is continued at the Defts. Cost.

Temple vs Burton   The Action of Trespass on the Case between Joseph Temple Plt. and Nowell Burton Defendt. is continued at the Defts. Cost.

Read vs Downie   The Action on the Case between Clem Read Plt. and Robert Downie Defendt. is continued at the Plts. Cost to be tryed at next Court by consent of Parties.

Hughes's Inventory   Robert Hughes presents the Inventory and Appraisment of the Estate of Sarah Hughes deceased which is admitted to Record.

Pruit vs Johnson   The Action on the Case between Andrew Pruit Plt. and Charles Johnson Defendt. is continued at the Defts. Cost.

Taylor vs Quin   In the Action of Debt between James Taylor Plt. and John Quin Defendt. the Plt. files a new declaration.

Marchbanks vs Croom   In the Action on the Case between George Marchbanks Plt. and Daniell Croom Defendt. the Plt. files a new declaration and an Imparlance is granted the Defendant.

Salmon vs Edwards   The Action on the Case between Thomas Salmon Plt. and Thomas Edwards Defendt. is continued at the Plts. Cost.

Collins vs Morriss   In the Action of Trespass between Mathew Collins Plt. and John Morriss Defendt. the Sherif having made return on the Pluries Capias that the Deft. is not to be found and he failing to appear on the Plts. motion a Pluries Capias de novo is awarded against the Deft. returnable to the next Court.

Boston vs Cox   The Action on the Case between Hugh Boston Plt. and Nicholas Cox Defendt. is continued at the Plts. Cost.

[263]   June Court 1730

Pigg vs Woodson   In the Action on the Case between John Pigg Junr. Plt. and William Woodson Defendt. the Parties submit themselves to the Court for tryall whereupon the Parties being heard and their accounts examined and that he recover against the Plt. his Costs by him in this behalf expended together with a Lawyers Fee.

Pigg vs Allin   In the Action on the Case between John Pigg Junr. Plt. and Samuell Allin Defendt. the Plt. Demurrs generally to the Defts. Plea and the Deft. joyns in Demurrer.

Alsup levy free   On the Petition of William Alsup he is exempted from payment of levys.

Johnson vs Fenton   The Action of Trespass on the Case between William Johnson Plt. and Thomas Fenton Defendt. is dismist the Plt. not prosecuting the same.

Ware vs Saunders   In the Action of Trespass on the Case between Susanna Ware Plt. and William Saunders Defendt. the Deft. appears but failing to Plead on the Plts. motion Judgment by nihil dicit is granted against the Deft. for what damages shall be recovered in this Suit to be discharged nevertheless if the Deft. shall plead at the next Court.

Taylor vs Lowe & Uxor   The Action of Trespass on the Case between John Taylor Plt. and Thomas Lowe & Amey his wife Defendts. is continued at the Plts. Cost.

Taylor vs Hopkins   The Action of Trespass between James Taylor Plt. and Evan Hopkins Defendt. is continued at the Plts. Cost.

Bumpuss vs Moreman   The Action of Trespass on the Case between Samuell Bumpuss Assignee of Robert Bumpuss Plt. and Andrew Moreman Deft. is continued.

L'villain vs Woodson   The Action on the Case between John L'Villain Plt. and Joseph Woodson Defendt. is continued at the Defts. Cost.

[264]   June Court 1730
May vs Jackson   The Action on the Case between William May Plt. and Joseph Jackson Defendt. is continued at the Defts. Cost.

Alves vs Huetson   In the Action of Detinue between George Alves Plt. and John Huetson Defendt. came as well the said George by his Attorny Thomas Prosser as the said John by his Attornys John Quin & Thomas Dickins upon which the Premises being seen and by the Court of Our Lord the King here fully understood and it seems to the Justices here that the Bill aforesaid of the aforesaid George is insufficient in Law to maintain the Action aforesaid therefore it is considered that the said George take nothing by his writt that the said John go hence without day and that he recover against the said George his costs by him in this behalf expended and a Lawyers Fee.

From which Judgment the said George Alves Appeals to the sixth day of the next General Court.

Lad vs Cannon   The Action on the Case between Amos Lad Plt. and William Cannon Defendt. is continued at the Defts. Cost.

Agee vs Sutleith   In the Action of Trespass on the Case between Mathew Agee Plt. and Abraham Sutleith Defendt. the Plt. files a new declaration and an Imparlance is granted the Deft.

Woodson &c. vs Leister   In the Action on the Case between Tarlton Woodson Assignee of Jeremiah Leister Plt. and Henry Leister Defendt. the following Jury are sworn Thomas Turpin, Thomas Wadloe, William Lansdon, James Taylor, John Prier, William Woodson, George Southerland, Joseph Watkins, Henry Webb, Thomas Murrell, William Cannon, Joseph Jackson, who after some time return with their Verdict which is recorded in these words "Wee find the Bill of Henry Lester payable to Jeremiah Lester bearing date the 11th. day of January 1728 [1729]. Wee find the said Bill to be assigned to Tarlton Woodson the 1st.

October 1729. Wee find the Certificate bearing date the 11th. day of June 1730. by the Assignor after the Assignee had brought Suit against Henry Lester who gave the Bill now if

[265]   June Court 1730
upon the whole the Law be with the Plaintiff wee find for the Plaintiff four hundred ninety eight pounds of tobacco, if the Law be with the Defendant Wee find for the Defendt. Thomas Turpin Foreman." the Arguments on which Verdict are referred to be heard at the next Court.

Rapene vs Pratt   Anthony Rapene presents an Account against the Estate of Roger Pratt deceased and makes Oath that the Ballance thereof being three pounds three shillings and six pence Currant money is Justly due to him and that he never received any satisfaction for the same, the Administratrix Mary Pratt making no objection it is ordered that the said Mary do pay him out of the said deceadents Estate the said Sum with Costs.

Stidum discharged from Exo   Benjamin Stidum comes into Court and makes Oath that a certain Schedule by him Subscribed containeth a true full and perfect account of all his Estate according to the form Prescribed in One Act of Assembly of this Colony for Relief of Insolvent Debtors, and on his motion it is ordered that he be discharged the Custody of the Sherif at the Suit of Giles Allegre.

Dillon discharged from Exo   James Theophilus Dillon comes into Court and makes Oath that a certain Schedule by him Subscribed containeth a true full and perfect account of all his Estate according to the form Prescribed in One Act of Assembly of this Colony for Relief of Insolvent Debtors, and on his motion it is ordered that he be discharged the Custody of the Sherif at the Suit of Dudley Digges.

Fleming takes oaths   Captain Tarlton Fleming comes into Court and takes the Oaths appointed to be taken by Act of Parliament instead of the Oats of Allegiance and Supremacy the Oath appointed to be taken by an Act of Parliament make in the First year of the Reign of his late Majesty King George the First Entituled an Act for the further Security of his Majestys Person and Government and the Succession of the Crown in the Heirs of the late Princess Sophia being Protestants and for extinguishing the hopes of the pretended Prince of Wales and his open and secret

[266]   June Court 1730
abettors and Subscribes the Test.

Howls Acct. Dr. & Cr   John Pleasants presents an Account Dr. and Cr. of the Estate of William Howl deceased which being examined and approved is ordered to be recorded.

Wood vs Pratt &c   In the Action on the Case between Henry Wood Plt. and Mary Pratt Administratrix &c. of Roger Pratt deced Defendt. the Plt. makes Oath to the Ballance of his Account and it is ordered that the said Mary Admx. as aforesaid do pay him out of the said deceadents Estate in her hands eighteen shillings Currant money with the costs of this Suit.

Then the Court adjourned to the third Tuesday in next Month.

[End of No. 1 Order Book]

Goochland County
Order Book 2
1730 - 1731
July 21 1730 - September 21 1731

[page 1 is mostly destroyed. Court was held July 21 1730.]

[2]   July Court 1730
Justice of the Peace do Appraise the Estate of John Scot Junr. deceased and that Samuell Scot his Executor do return an Inventory thereof to the next Court.

May vs Morriss   The Action of Trespass between William May Plt. and John Morriss Defendt. is dismist the Plt. not prosecuting the same.

Quin vs Nolun   In the Action of Debt between John Quin Plt. and Agnes Nolun Administratrix of the Goods Chattels right and credits of Thomas Nolun deceased Defendt. for eighty eight pounds Currant mony due by bond the following Jury are Sworn, Richard Dean, Thomas Edwards, Thomas Turpin, Anthony Hoggat, Nicholas Cox, Stephen Woodson, Joseph Watkins, George Southerland, John Williams, Joseph Bingley, James Nevils, Thomas Edwards, who after some time r[eturned] their Verdict which at the Plaintifs motion is ordered to be [torn] recorded and is as followeth "Wee find for the Plaintif seven[teen pounds] fourteen shillings and one penny half penny Currant money [with] Interest from the 19th day of September 1729. Richard Dean Fore[man"]. Whereupon it is considered by the Court that the Plt. do recover against the Deft. the said sum of seventeen pounds fourteen shillings and one penny half penny Currant money with Interest thereon after the rate of six Pr. Cent Pr. Annum from the nineteenth day of September 1729. by the Jurors aforesaid in their said Verdict assessed, and also the Costs of this Suit of the Goods and Chattels which were of the aforesaid Thomas Nolun's at his death in the hands of the said Agnes to be administred if so much in her hands there be, and if not so much, then the Costs aforesaid of the proper Goods and Chattels of the aforesaid Agnes to be levied.

Allin vs Gates   The Action of Trespass on the Case between Charles Allin Plt. and William Gates Defendt. is dismist the Plt. not prosecuting the same.

Surveyor of the Road   On the Petition of Marmaduke Hix it is Ordered that a Road be cleared from the upper branch of Fine Creek cross the fork of Deep Creek thence up the ridge between Deep Creek and Muddy Creek and that the several male labouring titheables living between the other two Roads do assist in clearing the same.

[3]   July Court 1730
Marmaduke Hix is appointed Surveyor thereof.

Surveyor of the Road   Nicholas Cox is appointed Surveyor of the River Road on the South side of James River from Deep Creek to Muddy Creek in the room of George Stoveall.

Scot vs Williams   In the Action on the case between Edward Scot Plt. and Edward Williams Defendt. the Deft. failing to appear on the Plts. motion the Conditionall Judgment formerly granted against the Deft. and Daniell Stoner Gent. late Sherif is confirmed for so much damages as shall be found upon executing a writ of Inquiry at the next Court of which the Sherif is ordered to give the Deft. and the said Daniell Stoner notice by serving them with a Copy of this Order.

[Scot vs Wo]mack &c   In the Action on the Case between Edward Scot Plt. and William Womack surviving Executor and James Barret & Sarah his wife Executrix &c. of Robert Woodson deced Defendts. the Plt. makes Oath to this account and thereupon the Defts. appear and confess a Judgment [to] the Plt. for eleven pounds fourteen shillings and four pence half [penny] Currant money with Interest from this day untill the said sum shall be paid Wherefore it is considered by the Court that the Plt. do recover against the Defts. the said sum with Costs and Interest thereon after the rate of 6 Pr. Centum Pr. Annum from this day untill the same shall be paid of the Goods and Chattels which were of the aforesaid Robert Woodson's at his death in the hands of the said William Womack and James Barret to be administred if so much in their hands there be, and if not so much, then the Costs aforesaid of the proper Goods and Chattels of the aforesaid William Womack and James Barret to be levied. By consent of the Plt. Execution is to stay untill the first day of May next.

Ward vs Farrar   The Action of Debt between Seth Ward Plt. and John Farrar Deft. is continued at the Plts. Cost.

Absent John Woodson Gent.

[4]   July Court 1730
Woodson vs Arrington   In the Action on the Case between John Woodson Plt. and Samuell Arrington Defendt. the parties submit themselves to the Court for tryall whereupon they being heard and their Accounts considered it is ordered that the Deft. do pay unto the Plt. one pound two shillings and three pence Currant money together with the Costs of the Suit and a Lawyers Fee.

Present John Woodson Gent.

Levins vs Farrar   In the Action on the Case between Richard Levins Plt. and John Sutton Farrar Defendt. the Deft. appears but failing to plead Judgment by nihil dicit is granted against him for what damage shall be recovered in this Suit to be discharged nevertheless if the Deft. shall plead at the next Court.

Pruit vs Boccar   In the Action on the Case between Hugh Pruit Plt. and Peter Boccar Defendt. time is granted the Plt. to mend his declaration.

Sallee vs Bowie   In the Action of Trespass on the Case between Isaac Sallee Assignee of Thomas Gevodon Plt. and John Bowie Defendant the Deft. appears but failing to Plead Judgment by nihil dicit is granted against him for what damages shall be recovered in this Suit to be discharged nevertheless if the Deft. shall plead at the next Court.

Webber vs White   In the Action of Trespass on the Case between Phillip Webber Plt. and Edward White Defendt. the Sherif having returned on the Alias Capias that the Deft. is not to be found and he failing to appear a Pluries Capias is awarded against him returnable to the next Court.

Henson vs Saunders   In the Action of Trespass on the Case between Benjamin Henson Plt. and Thomas Saunders Defendt. the following Jury are Sworn Nowell Burton, Richard Oglesby, Constant Perkins, Samuell Allin, William Cannon, William Moor, Thomas Wadloe, John Laine, Sanburn Woodson, John Phelps, William Woodson, James Barret, who after some time being in their Verdict

[5]   July Court 1730
which on the Defendts. motion is ordered to be recorded and is as followeth "Wee find for the Defendt. Nowell Burton Foreman." Whereupon it is considered by the Court that the Plt. take noting by his writ aforesaid that the Deft. go hence without day and that he recover against the Plt. his Costs by him in this behalf expended and a Lawyers Fee.

Chamberlayne vs Saunders   On the motion of William Chamberlayne of New Kent County a Witness for Thomas Saunders ads Benjamin Henson it is ordered that the said Thomas do pay him for two days attendance and for coming and returning sixty miles twice four hundred and eighty pounds of tobacco with Costs.

Howard vs Saunders   On the motion of Allin Howard a Witness for Thomas Saunders ads Benjamin Henson it is ordered that the said Thomas do pay him for one days attendance thirty pounds of tobacco with Costs.

Saunders vs Saunders   On the motion of John Saunders of Hanover County a Witness for Thomas Saunders ads Benjamin Henson it is ordered that the said Thomas do pay him for two days attendance and coming and returning sixteen miles twice two hundred and sixteen pounds of tobacco with Costs.

Scot vs Wiers   On the Scire Facias brought by Edward Scot against John Wiers to renew a Judgment of this Court dated the 18th day of March 1728 [1729] for two hundred pounds of tobacco and the costs of Suit being one hundred and sixty seven pounds of tobacco and fifteen shillings Currant money or one hundred and fifty pounds of tobacco the Sherif having made return on the Alias Scire Facias that the Defendt. is not to be found and he failing to appear on the Plts. motion the said Judgment is renewed and it is thereupon considered by the Court that the Plt. do recover against the Defendt. three hundred and sixty seven pounds of tobacco and fifteen shillings Currant money or one hundred and fifty pounds of tobacco with the Costs of this Suit.

Jackson vs Southerland   In the Action of Trespass on the Case between John Jackson Assignee

[6]   July Court 1730
of Edward Birch Plt. and George Southerland Deft. the Deft. appears but failing to plead Judgment by nihil dicit is granted against him for what

damages shall be recovered in this Suit to be discharged nevertheless if the Deft. shall plead at the next Court.

Present John Fleming Gent.

Digges vs Quin   The Action on the Case between Dudley Digges Plt. and John Quin Deft. is dismist the Plt. not prosecuting the same.

Digges vs Napier   In the Action on the Case between Dudley Digges Plt. and Bouth Napier Defendt. the Deft. appears but failing to plead Judgment by nihil dicit is granted against him for what damages shall be recovered in this Suit to be discharged nevertheless if the Deft. shall plead at the next Court.

Scot vs Lawson   In the Action on the Case between Edward Scot Plt. and Jonas Lawson Defendt. the Deft. failing to appear on the Plts. motion the conditional Judgment for [torn] against the Deft. and Daniell Stoner Gent. late [torn] firmed for so much damages as shall be found upon [obtaini]ng a writ of Inquiry at the next Court of which the [torn] [is o]rdered to give the Deft. and the said Daniell Stoner [Gent. late Sherif] by serving them with a Copy of this Order.

Happer vs Woodson   In the Action on the Case between William Happer Plt. and Joseph Woodson Deft. the deft. pleads he oweth nothing.

Happer &c. vs Woodson   In the Action on the Case between William Happer Assignee of William Arrington Plt. and Joseph Woodson Defendt. the Deft. pleads he oweth nothing.

Happer vs Harper   In the Action on the Case between William Happer Plt. and Henry Harper Defendt. the Deft. pleads he is not guilty.

Digges vs Agee   The Action on the Case between Dudley Digges Plt. and Mathew Agee Deft. is dismist the Plt. not prosecuting the same.

[7]   July Court 1730

Digges vs Saunders   In the Action on the Case between Dudley Digges Plt. and John Saunders Defendt. the Deft. failing to appear on the Plts. motion the conditionall Judgment formerly granted against the Deft. and Daniell Stoner Gent. late Sherif is confirmed for so much damages as shall be found upon executing a writ of Inquiry at the next Court of which the Sherif is ordered to give the Deft. and the said Daniel Stoner notice by serving them with a Copy of this Order.

Digges vs Rapene   In the Action on the Case between Dudley Digges Plt. and Anthony Rapene Defendt. the Deft. appears but failing to plead Judgment by nihil dicit is granted against him for what damages shall be recovered in this Suit to be discharged nevertheless if the Deft. shall plead at the next Court.

Clopton &c. vs Marchbanks   In the Action of Debt between Joyce Clopton Executrix & William Acrill & John Syme, Executors &c. of William Clopton deced Plts. and George Marchbanks Defendt. the Deft. pleads he oweth nothing.

Stidum vs Bingley &c   In the [Action of] Debt between Benjamin Stidum Plt. and Joseph Bingl[ey William] Lansdon Defts. the Defts. file a Bill of Inquiry Chancery and time is granted the Plt. to answer it.

Moseby vs Taylor   In the [Action of] Debt between Richard Moseby Plt. and John Taylor Defend[ant the follo]wing Jury are sworn Thomas Edwards, George March[banks, A]mos Lad, James Taylor, Thomas Turpin, Joseph Watkins, J[ohn] Williams, Joseph Bingley, John Prier, Joseph Gill, George Southerland, Thomas Edwards, who after some time bring in their Verdict which on the Plts. motion is admitted to record and is as followeth " Wee find the Defendt. guilty. Thos. Edwards Foreman." the Defts. Attorny files reasons in arrest of the Judgment the arguing of which is referred to the next Court.

Pennington's Administration   John Fleming Gent. Executor of the last will and Testament of Thomas Randolph deceased comes into Court and makes Oath [according to Law] that Paul Pennington deceased died without making any will as far as he knows or believes and on his motion and giving Security

[8]   July Court 1730
for his just and faithfull Administration of the said Deceadents Estate Certificate is granted him for obtaining letters of Administration in due form William Mayo Gent. entring himself Security for the same.

Ordered that William Womack, Stephen Cox, John Williams, Daniell Hix or any three of them being first sworn by some Justice of the Peace do Appraise the Estate of Paul Pennington deceased and that John Fleming Gent. Executor &c. of Thomas Randolph deceased the Administrator do return an Inventory thereof to the next Court.

Grand Jury vs Hannah Turner   Upon the Presentment of the Grand Jury against Hannah Turner the Sherif having made return on the Pluries Capias that the said Hannah is not to be found and she failing to appear a Pluries Capias de novo is awarded against her returnable to the next Court.

Grand Jury vs Judith Ballew   The tryal of the issue on the Presentment of the Grand Jury against Judith Ballew is referred to the next Court.

Dickins vs Pride   The Petition of Thomas Dickins against John Pride is continued for a new Summons to Issue.

Syms vs Pride   On the motion of George Sims of Hanover County a Witness for Benjamin Henson vs Thomas Saunders it is ordered that the said Benjamin do pay him for two days attendance and for coming and returning twenty miles twice, two hundred and forty pounds of tobacco with Costs.

Morriss vs Henson   On the motion of John Morriss of Hanover County a Witness for Benjamin Henson vs Thomas Saunders it is ordered that the said Benjamin do pay him for two days attendance and for coming and returning twenty five miles twice, two hundred seventy pounds of tobacco with Costs.

Wetherford vs Henson   On the motion of William Wetherford of Hanover County a Witness for Benjamin Henson vs Thomas Saunders it is ordered that

[9]   July Court 1730
the said Benjamin do pay him for one days attendance and for coming and returning sixteen miles once one hundred and eight pounds of tobacco with costs.

Digges vs Hughes   In the Action of Trespass on the Case between Dudley Digges Plt. and Stephen Hughes Defendt. an Imparlance is granted the Defendt.

Digges vs Dickins   The Action on the Case between Dudley Digges Plt. and Thomas Dickins Deft. is dismist the Plt. not prosecuting the same.

Digges vs Mullin   In the Action on the Case between Dudley Digges Plt. and Patrick Mullin Deft. the Sherif having made return that the Deft. is not to be found and he failing to appear an Alias Capias is awarded against him returnable to the next Court.

Digges vs Lively   The Action of Trespass on the Case between Dudley Digges Plt. and Mark Lively Deft. is dismist the Plt. not prosecuting the same.

Digges vs Arrington   The Action of Trespass on the Case between Dudley Digges Plt. and William Arrington Deft. is dismist the Plt. not prosecuting the same.

Digges vs Taylor   In the Action of Trespass on the Case between Dudley Digges Plt. and James Taylor Deft. Edward Scot enters himself Special Bail fo the Deft. on whose motion an Imparlance is granted him.

Digges vs Burks   In the Action of Trespass on the Case between Dudley Digges Plt. and Richard Burks Deft. Samuell Burks enters himself Special Bail for the Deft. on whose motion an Imparlance is granted him.

Digges vs Williams   In the Action of Trespass on the Case between Dudley Digges Plt. and John Williams Defendt. Jacob Winfrey enters himself Special Bail for the Deft. who appears and confesses a Judgment to the Plt. for five pounds eight shillings and nine pence half penny Currant money Whereupon it is considered by the Court that the Plt. do recover against the Deft. the said Sum together with the Costs of this Suit and a Lawyers Fee.

[10]   July Court 1730
Wood Vs Woodson   In the Action on the Case between Henry Wood Plt. and Joseph Woodson Defendt. the Deft. failing to appear on the Plts. motion Judgment is granted him against the Deft. and Tarlton Fleming Gent. Sherif for what damages shall be recovered in this Suit to be discharged nevertheless if the Deft. shall appear at the next Court.

Wood vs Johnson   The Action of Trespass on the Case between Henry Wood Plt. and Charles Johnson Deft. is dismist the Plt. not prosecuting the same.

Cox vs Napier   In the Action on the Case between Bartholomew Cox Plt. and Robert Napier Junr. Deft. time is granted the Plt. to mend his declaration.

Scot vs Thompson.   The Action of Debt between Edward Scot Plt. and Samuell Thompson Deft. is dismist the Plt. not prosecuting the same.

Bradley vs Saunders   The Action of Trespass on the Case between Joseph Bradley Plt. and Joseph Saunders Deft. is dismist neither party appearing.

Thomas vs May   In the Action of Trespass on the Case between William Thomas Plt. and William May Deft. the Plt. files a new declaration and an imparlance is granted the Deft.

Parish vs Watkins   In the Action of Trespass on the Case between John Parish Junr. Plt. and Joseph Watkins Deft. the Plt. files a new declaration and an imparlance is granted the Defendt.

Locket vs James   In the Action of Trespass between Thomas Locket Plt. and Francis James Deft. the Plt. files a new declaration and an imparlance is granted the Defendt.

Elliot vs Walker   In the Action of Trespass on the Case between James Elliot Executr &c. of John Chiles deced. Plt. and Thomas Walker Deft. the Plt. files a new declaration and an imparlance is granted the Defendt.

Winston vs Nolun   In the Action of Debt between Isaac Winston Plt. and Agnes Nolun.

[11]   July Court 1730
Administratrix &c. of Thomas Nolun deced Defendt. the Plt. files a new declaration and an Imparlance is granted the Defendant.

Hambleton vs Nolun   In the Action of Debt between James Hambleton Plt. and Agnes Nolun Administratrix &c. of Thomas Nolun deced Deft. the Plt. files a new declaration and an Imparlance is granted the Defendant.

Paslay vs Saunders   In the Action of Trespass on the Case between William Paslay Plt. and Thomas Saunders Defendt. the Plt. files a new declaration the Deft. pleads he oweth nothing and for tryal thereof puts himself upon the Country and the Plt. likewise.

Hoggatt vs Dickins   In the Action of Trespass on the Case between Anthony Hoggatt Plt. and Thomas Dickins Deft. an Imparlance is granted the Deft.

Dillon vs Bondurant   The Action of Trespass between James Theophilus Dillon Plt. and John Peter Bondurant Defendt. is dismist the

Plt. not prosecuting the same.

Cooker vs Nolun   In the Action on the Case between Samuel Cooker Plt. and Agnes Nolun Administratrix of the goods Chattles Rights and Credits of Thomas Nolun deced Defendt. the Deft acknowledges her self indebted unto the Plt. eight hundred pounds of tobacco convenient in Cask whereupon it is considered by the Court that the Plt. do recover against the Deft. the said sum of eight hundred pounds of tobacco convenient in Cask and also the Costs of this Suit of the goods and Chattles which were of the aforesaid Thomas Nolun's at his death in the hands of the said Agnes to be administred if so much in her hands there be and if not so much then the Costs aforesaid of the proper goods and Chattles of the aforesaid Agnes to be levied.

Scott vs Burton   The Action on the Case between Edward Scott Plt. and Robert Burton Defendt. is dismist the Plt. not prosecuting the same.

Scott vs Burton   In the Action on the Case between Edward Scott Plt. and Nowell Burton

[12]   July Court 1730
Defendt. the Deft. appears and confesses a Judgment to the Plt. for two pounds eight shillings 5 pence Currant mony whereupon it is considered by the Court that the Plt. do recover against the Deft. the said sum with Costs.

Digges vs Walker   The Action on the Case between Dudley Digges Plt. and William Walker Defendt. is dismist the Plt. not prosecuting the same.

Worley vs Locket   In the Action of Trespass on the Case between John Worley Plt. and Thomas Locket Defendt. the Plt. files a new declaration the Deft. pleads he is not guilty and for tryal thereof puts himself upon the Country and the Plt. likewise.

Worley vs Locket   In the Action of Slander between John Worley Plt. and Thomas Locket Defendt. the Plt. having failed to file his declaration on the Defts. motion he is nonsuited and it is thereupon considered by the Court that the Deft. go hence without day and that he recover against the Plt. five shillings Currant money according to the Act of Assembly in that Case made and provided together with his Costs by him in this behalf expended and a Lawyers Fee.

Hughes vs Write   The Action of Trespass on the Case between Stephen

Hughes Plt. and Elizabeth Wright Deft. is dismist neither party appearing.

Then the Court adjourned 'till to morrow morning ten of the clock.

****

At a Court continued and held for Goochland County the twenty second day of July Annoq. Dom. 1730. Present. William Mayo, John Woodson, Allin Howard, William Cabbell, Gent. Justices

[13]   July Court 1730
Hannah an Orphan to be bound out   Ordered that the Church wardens of St. James's Parish do bind unto Amos Lad, Hannah an Orphan Mulatto Girl and that the said Amos cause her to be learned to read sew and spin.

Macon vs Wharton. In the Action on the Case between John Macon Plt. and Thomas Wharton Defendt. the Deft. files a new Bill of Injunction in Chancery and time is granted the Plt. to answer.

Waddill vs Edwards   The Action on the Case between William Waddill Junr. Plt. and Thomas Edwards Defendt. is continued.

     Present George Payne Gent.
     Absent Allin Howard Gent.

Swift vs Howard   In the Action of Trespass on the Case between William Swift Plt. and Allin Howard Defendt. the Deft. pleads he oweth nothing and for tryal thereof puts himself upon the Country and the Plt. likewise.

     Present Allin Howard Gent.

Temple vs Burton   In the Action of Trespass on the Case between Joseph Temple Plt. and Nowell Burton Defendt. the Arguments on the Special Verdict being heard it is the Opinion of the Court that the law arising thereon is for the Defendt. wherefore it is considered that the said Joseph take nothing by his writt that the said Nowell go hence without day and that he recover against the said Joseph his Costs by him in this behalf expended and a Lawyers Fee.
    From which Judgment the said Joseph Appeals to the sixth day of the next Generall Court.

Syms vs Phelps   In the Action of Trespass on the Case between

Mathew Syms Plt. and John Phelps Defendt. the Plt. failing to prosecute his Suit on the Defts. motion he is nonsuited and it is thereupon considered by the Court that the Deft. go hence without day and that he recover against the Plt. five shillings Currant money according to the Act

[14] July Court 1730
of Assembly in that Case made and provided together with his Costs by him in this behalf expended and a Lawyers Fee.

Innis vs Mcbrid   In the Action of Trespass between John Innis Plt. and John Mcbrid Defendt. the following Jury are Sworn Thomas Turpin, Robert Hughes, Stephen Woodson, Richard Oglesby, Amos Lad, Hugh Morris, Joseph Watkins, William Farrar, John Harris, Thomas Wadloe, Edward Williams, Joseph Bingley, who after some time return with their Verdict which on the Plts. motion is admitted to Record and is as followeth "Wee find for the Plt. one shilling damage, Thomas Turpin Foreman." Whereupon it is considered by the Court that the Plt. do recover against the Deft. the said Sum of one shilling damage by the Jurors aforesaid assessed and one shilling costs.
From which Judgment the Plt. Appeals to the sixth day of the next General Court.

Wadloe vs Phelps   On the motion of Thomas Wadloe a Witness for John Phelps ads Matthew Syms it is ordered that the said John do pay him for seven days attendance two hundred and ten pounds of tobacco with Costs.

Pruit vs Johnson   In the Action on the Case between Andrew Pruit Plt. and Charles Johnson Defendt. the Deft. pleads he oweth nothing and time is granted the Plt. to mend his declaration.

Taylor vs Quin   In the Action of Debt between James Taylor Plt. and John Quin Defendt. an Imparlance is granted the Defendant.

Marchbanks vs Croom   In the Action on the Case between George Marchbanks Plt. and Daniell Croom Defendt. the Deft. pleads non Assumpsit and for tryal thereof puts himself upon the Country and the Plt. likewise.

Johnson vs Edwards   The Action on the Case between Thomas Salmon Plt. and Thomas Edwards Defendt. is continued at the Defts. cost.

Collins vs Morriss   In the Action of Trespass between Mathew Collins

Plt. and

[15]   July Court 1730
John Morriss Defendt. the Sherif having returned on the Pluries Capias that the Deft. is not to be found and he failing to appear a Pluries Capias de novo is awarded against him returnable to the next Court.

Boston vs Cox   In the Action on the Case between Hugh Boston Plt. and Nicholas Cox Defendt. William Cabbell Gent. is added to the Arbitrators formerly appointed and the Suit is continued.

Pigg vs Allin   In the Action on the Case between John Pigg Junr. Plt. and Samuell Allin Defendt. the Plea formerly filed in this Suit is waived by consent of Parties and repleader is ordered.

Walker vs Innis   On the Motion of John Walker a Witness for John Innis vs John Mcbrid it is ordered that the said John Innis do pay him for five days attendance one hundred and fifty pounds of tobacco with Costs.

Cabbell vs Mcbrid   On the motion of William Cabbell a Witness for John Mcbrid ads John Innis it is ordered that the said John Mcbrid do pay him for one days attendance thirty pounds of tobacco with costs.

Rapene vs Bingley   In the Action of Trespass on the Case between Anthony Rapene Plt. and Joseph Bingley Defendt. the following Jury are Sworn Anthony Hoggat, Richard Oglesby, William Farrar, John Harris, Thomas Turpin, Amos Lad, Hugh Morriss, Edward Williams, John Taylor, Stephen Woodson, Robert Hughes, Joseph Watkins, who after some time return with their Verdict which on the Plts. motion is admitted to Record and is as followeth "Wee find for the Plt. one shilling Ster. Antho. Hoggat Foreman" the Court being of Opinion that the Trespass was wilfully and maliciously committed it is thereupon considered that the Plt. do recover against the Deft. the said sum of one shilling Sterling by the Jurors aforesaid in their said Verdict assessed with Costs and a Lawyers Fee.

Ware vs Saunders   In the Action of Trespass on the Case between Susanna Ware Plt.

[16]   July Court 1730
and William Saunders Defendt. the Deft. pleads conditions performed and the Suit is continued.

Chastain's deed to Scot   Peter Chastain acknowledges a Deed from himself to Edward Scot to be his Act and deed and it is thereupon admitted to Record.

Flournoy vs Martin   In the Action of Trespass on the Case between John James Flournoy Plt. and Francis Martin Deft. a Special imparlance is granted the Deft.

Flournoy vs Martin   In the Action of Debt between John James Flournoy and Elizabeth his wife Executrix &c. of Orlando Jones deced Plts. and Francis Martin Defendt. on the Defts. motion Oyer is granted him.

Scot vs Mims   The Action on the Case between Edward Scot Plt. and Lionell Mims Deft. is dismist neither party appearing.

Thompson vs Edwards   In the Action of Trespass on the Case between Samuell Thompson and Mary his wife Plts. and Thomas Edwards of Beverdam Deft. the Sherif having made return that the Deft. is not to be found and he failing to appear an Alias Capias is awarded against him returnable to the next Court.

Bradley vs Saunders   In the Action of Trespass on the Case between Joseph Bradley Plt. and John Saunders Defendt. the Sherif having made return that the Deft. is not to be found and he failing to appear an Alias Capias is awarded against him returnable to the next Court.

Dean vs Logan   The Action of Trespass on the Case between Richard Dean Plt. and Alexander Logan Defendt. is dismist neither party appe[a]ring.

Napier vs Ashlin   In the Action on the Case between Bouth Napier Plt. and Joseph Ashlin Defendt. the Deft. failing to appear on the Plts. motion Judgment is granted him against the Deft. and Thomas Walker his common Bail for what damages shall be recovered in this Suit to be discharged nevertheless if the Deft.

[17]   July Court 1730
shall appear at the next Court.

Mayo &c. vs Dawson   In the Action of Debt between William Mayo and Daniell Stoner Gent. Church wardens of St. James's Parish Plts. and Elizabeth Dawson Defendt. the Sherif having made return that the Deft.

is not to be found and she failing to appear an Alias Capias is awarded against her returnable to the next Court.

Prosser vs Napier   In the Action of Trespass on the Case between Thomas Prosser Plt. and Bouth Napier Defendt. the Plt. files a new declaration and a Special imparlance is granted the Defendant.

Rocket vs Burton   In the Action of Trespass on the Case between Baldwin Rocket Plt. and Nowell Burton Defendt. the Deft. failing to appear on the Plts. motion Judgment is granted him against the Deft. and Robert Burton his common Bail for what damages shall be recovered in this Suit to be discharged nevertheless if the Deft. shall appear at the next Court.

Scot vs Farrar   In the Action of Trespass on the Case between Edward Scot Plt. and William Farrar Defendt. the Plt. files a new declaration and makes Oath to his Account the Deft. appears and confesses a Judgment to the Plt. for two pounds ten shilling and four pence Currant money whereupon it is considered by the Court that the Plt. do recover against the Deft. the said sum together with the Costs of this Suit and a Lawyers Fee.

Scot vs Chumley   The Action of Trespass on the Case between Edward Scot Plt. and William Chumbley Defendt. is dismist the Plt. not prosecuting the same.

Scot vs Allin   In the Action of Trespass on the Case between Edward Scot Plt.

[18]   July Court 1730
and Samuell Allin Defendt. the Deft. appears and confesses a Judgment to the Plt. for three pounds eleven shillings and nine pence Currant money whereupon it is considered by the Court that the Plt. do recover against the Deft. the said sum with Costs.

Scot vs Ware   In the Action of Debt between Edward Scot Plt. and Peter Ware Defendt. for fifty pounds Currant Money due by bond the Sherif having made return that the Deft. is not to be found and he failing to appear on the Plts. motion an Attachment is awarded against the Defts. estate returnable to the next Court.

Scot vs Ware   In the Action of Debt between Edward Scot Plt. and Peter Ware Defendt. for fifty pounds Currant money due by bond the

Sherif having made return that the Deft. is not to be found and he failing to appear on the Plts. motion an Attachment is awarded against the Defts. estate returnable to the next Court.

Scot vs Ware   In the Action of Trespass on the Case between Edward Scot Plt. and Peter Ware Defendt. for five pounds damages the Sherif having made return that the Deft. is not to be found and he failing to appear on the Plts. motion an Attachment is awarded against the Defts. estate returnable to the next Court.

Ford vs Williams   In the Action of Trover and Conversion between Peter Ford Plt. and Edward Williams Defendt. a Special imparlance is granted the Defendant.

Digges vs Payne   The Action of Trespass on the Case between Dudley Digges Plt. and Josiah Payne Defendt. is continued.

Digges vs Woodson   The Action of Trespass on the Case between Dudley Digges Plt. and Benjamin Woodson Defendt. is dismist the Plt. not prosecuting the same.

Digges vs Lad   In the Action on the Case between Dudley Digges Plt. and Amos Lad Defendt. the Deft. appear and confesses a Judgment to the Plt. for thirty shillings and ten pence half penny Currant

[19]   July Court 1730
money whereupon it is considered by the Court that the Plt. do recover against the Deft. the said Sum with Costs.

Digges vs Saunders   The Action of Trespass on the Case between Dudley Digges Plt. and Thomas Saunders Defendt. is dismist neither party appearing.

Woodson vs Napier   In the Action of Trespass on the Case between William Woodson Plt. and Bouth Napier Defendt. the Plt. files a new declaration the Sherif having made return that the Deft. is not to be found and he failing to appear an Alias Capias is awarded against him returnable to the next Court.

Ward vs Dean   In the Action of Debt between Seth Ward Plt. and Richard Dean Deft. the Deft. pleads he oweth nothing and for tryal thereof puts himself upon the Country and the Plt. likewise.

Ford vs Pruit   In the Action of Trespass on the Case between James Ford Plt. and Thomas Pruit Deft. a Special imparlance is granted the Deft.

Wood vs Woodson   The Action of Debt between Henry Wood Plt. and Benjamin Woodson Defendt. is dismist the Plt. not prosecuting the same.

Woods vs Burton   In the Action of Debt between Henry Wood Plt. and Nowell Burton Defendt. the Deft. failing to appear on the Plts. motion Judgment is granted him against the Deft. and Robert Burton his common Bail for what damages shall be recovered in this Suit to be discharged nevertheless if the Deft. shall appear at the next Court.

Turpin vs Hook &c   In the Action on the Case between Mathew Turpin Assignee of John Welsh Plt. and James Hook and John Peter Bilboe Defts. a Special imparlance is granted the Defendants.

Dickins vs Taylor   The Action of Trespass on the Case between Thomas Dickins Plt. and James Taylor Deft. is dismist the Plt. not prosecuting the same.

Scot vs Daniell   In the Action of Detinue between Edward Scot Plt. and James Daniell

[20]   July Court 1730
Defendt. the Sherif having made return that the Deft. is not to be found and he failing to appear an Alias Capias is awarded against him returnable to the next Court.

Mayo &c. vs Nunnary   In the Action of Debt between William Mayo and Daniell Stoner Gent. Church wardens of St. James's Parish Plts. and Judith Nunnary Deft. the Sherif having made return that the Deft. is not to be found and she failing to appear an Alias Capias is awarded against her returnable to the next Court.

Mayo vs Parker   The Action of Trespass between William Mayo Plt. and Richard Parker Defendt. is dismist.

Scot vs Webb   The Action of Trespass between Edward Scot and Joseph Scot Plts. and William Webb Deft. is dismist the Plts. not prosecuting the same.

Scot &c. vs Pruit   In the Action of Trespass on the Case between Edward Scot Administrator of John Stephens Plt. and Thomas Pruit

Defendt. time is granted the Plt. to mend his declaration.

Lad & Powell vs Thompson   On the Petition of Amos Lad and Roger Powell against Samuell Thompson it is ordered that the said Samuell be Summoned to appear at the next Court to answer the same.

Lyles vs Atkinson   On the motion of David Lyles of Prince George County a Witness for Sarah Atkinson vs Anthony Benning it is ordered that the said Sarah do pay him for six days attendance and for coming and returning twelve miles four times five hundred and four pounds of tobacco with Costs.

Bryan to Sue in forma Pauperis   On the Petition of William Bryan he is admitted to Sue in forma Pauperis and Thomas Prosser is appointed his Attorney.

Court house to be built   Ordered that the Sherif do give publick notice in this County that on Saturday next the Justices will meet at Dover mill to agree with workmen about the building the Court house.

[21]   July Court 1730
Taylor vs Lowe   The Action of Trespass on the Case between John Taylor Plt. and Thomas Lowe & Amey his wife Defendts. is continued.

Lad vs Cannon   In the Action on the Case between Amos Lad Plt. and William Cannon Defendt. the Deft. pleads he is not guilty and for tryal thereof puts himself upon the Country and the Plt. likewise.

Agee vs Sutleith   In the Action of Trespass on the Case between Mathew Agee Plt. and Abraham Sutleith Deft. the Deft. pleads non assumpsit and for tryal thereof puts himself upon the Country and the Plt. likewise.

Woodson vs Leister   [In the Action] on the Case between Tarlton Woodson Asignee of Jer[torn] [Lei]ster Plt. and Henry Leister Defendt. the Plt. failing to pro[torn] Suit on the Defts. motion he is nonsuited and it is ther[efore con]sidered by the Court that the Deft. go hence without day and [that he] recover against the Plt. five shillings Currant money according to the Act of Assembly in that Case made and provided together with his Costs by him in this behalf expended and a Lawyers Fee.

L'villain vs Woodson   In the Action on the Case between John L'villain Plt. and Joseph Woodson Defendt. the Deft. appears and confesses a

Judgment to the Plt. for Six pounds fourteen shillings and eight pence Currant money whereupon it is considered by the Court that the Plt. do recover against the Deft. the said Sum together with the Costs of this Suit and a Lawyers Fee.

Barret's fine revok'd James Barret's excuse for not appearing at May Court on the pannel of the Jury being allowed, the conditional fine then imposed on him is hereby revoked.

Souillie vs Rapene On the motion of Nicholas Souillie a Witness for Anthony Rapene vs Joseph Bingley it is ordered that the said Anthony do pay him for five days attendance one hundred and fifty pounds of tobacco with Costs.

[22] July Court 1730
Scot vs Rapene On the motion of Edward Scot a Witness for Anthony Rapene vs Joseph Bingley it is ordered that the said Anthony do pay him for one days attendance thirty pounds of tobacco with Costs.

Then the Court adjourned to the third Tuesday in next Month.

****

At a Court held for Goochland County the third Tuesday in August being the eighteenth day of the Month Annoq. Dom. 1730. Present. John Fleming, William Mayo, Allin Howard, George Payne, William Cabbell, Gent. Justices.

Wiles vs Hughes In the Action of Trespass on the Case between Luke Wiles Plt. and Stephen Hughes Defendt. the following Jury are Sworn Peter Ware, Amos Lad, Stephen Woodson, Martin King, George Southerland, Henry Harper, Joseph Jackson, John Taylor, Nicholas Cox, Thomas Locket, Thomas Turpin, Peter Jefferson, [after] which by consent of [the] parties Nicholas Cox a Juror is withdrawn and the Suit is continued.

       Absent Allin Howard Gent.

Prosser imprisoned Thomas Prosser [attorney] for Luke Wiles vs Stephen Hughes asking severall q[uestions] the Defendant before any witnesses were sworn in the Cau[se] and being told by the Court that he ought not to proceed in that m[anner], but that he ought to suffer the witnesses first to be sworn, and then to ask leave [if such] questions as he should prop[ose] might be asked them, and there[upon it is] said Thomas Prosser [in] saying that if could not be Su[ffer'd to] speak for his Client he should think injustice done his Client a[nd t]hat he would ask what questions he pleased [on behalf of his Client] it is the Opinion of the Court that the said Thomas Prosser enter into bond with good and Sufficient Security

[23]   August Court 1730
Security for his good behaviour which he refusing to give it is ordered that the Sherif take into his Custody the said Thomas Prosser and him safely keep in the Goal of his County untill he enter into bond with good and sufficient Security in the Sum of fifty pounds Currant money conditioned for his good behaviour for one year and a day.

Prosser fin'd   Upon Thomas Prosser's being committed to Prison pursuant to the former order, the Jury who were sworn in the Cause between Luke Wiles Plt. and Stephen Hughes Defendt. proceeding to try the same are informed by the Clerk that after he had read the declaration, at the request of Thomas Prosser aforesaid he delivered it to him, and thereupon the Sherif being sent to the Goal to demand of him the said declaration, and his answer to the Sherif being, that if he had it he would keep it, the Clerk is thereupon ordered to go to the Goal and demand of him the said declaration, and upon the return of the Clerk, he reports to the Court that the said Thomas Prosser's answer to him was that he was a Prisoner and would not unbundle his papers to look for any declaration, and thereupon the Sherif is ordered to bring the said Thomas Prosser into Court, who upon his appearance and his being asked to deliver to the Clerk the said declaration, answered, that he did not know if he had it or not, and that he would not trouble himself to look for it, but that he was a Prisoner and would answer every thing he should do as such and that he would justifie his whole behaviour so long as he was worth a penny, upon consideration of the Premises it is the opinion of the Court that he is guilty of a breach of his behaviour and it is thereupon ordered that he be fined to our Sovereign Lord the King in the Sum of five pounds Virginia money and that the Sherif keep him in the Goal of this County until he pay the said fine with Costs.

Prosser to be guarded and ironed   Thomas Prosser being together w[ith hi]s papers ordered to be brought in[to Cour]t that the declaration mentioned in the former order may [be searc]hed for the S[herif] makes return that he defends himself in [the Goal] with his naked sword and refuses to come before the Court, or to suffer his [papers] to be brought into Court, whereupon it is ordered that the Sherif do Summon a

Sufficient

[24]   August Court 1730
Guard to keep him in Goal without victuals or drink untill he deliver up his Sword and such other offensive weapons as shall be found on him, and also his papers that search may be made for the said declaration, and if the said declaration is not found that the Sherif keep him in irons untill the next Court.

Burks deeds to Holland   Samuell Burks acknowledges deeds of Lease and Release from himself to Michael Holland to be his Acts and deeds and they are thereupon admitted to Record.

Hix's deed to Holman   Daniell Hix acknowledges a deed with the Livery of Seizin endorsed from himself to James Holman to be his Act and deed and it is thereupon admitted to record, then Joan wife of the said Daniell (She being first privately examined) relinquishes her right of Dower in the land by the said deed] conveyed which is also admitted to record.

Hix's deed to Thompson   Daniell Hix acknowledges a deed with [the] Livery of Seizin endorsed from himself to George Thompson [to] be his Act and deed and it is thereupon admitted to record th[en Jo]an wife of the said Daniell (She being first privately exam[ined)] relinquishes her right of Dower in the land by the said [deed] conveyed which is also admitted to record.

Hix's deed to Golsby   Daniell Hix ackno[wledges] a deed [with the] Livery of Seizin [endorsed] from him[self to Thomas Golsby Junr. to be] his Act and deed and it is there[upon admitted to record, then] Joan wife of the said Daniell (S[he being first privately examin]ed) relinquishes her right of Dow[er in the land by the said deed] conveyed which is also admitted [to record.] [much of this entry is missing but can inferred]

David's will proved   The last will and Te[stament of] Peter David deceased is presented in Court by Anne David his Executrix who makes oath thereto and the same being proved by the Oaths of John Chastain and John Legrand two of the witnesses thereto it is admitted to record and on the motion of the said Executrix

[25]   August Court 1730
and her performing what is usual in such Cases Certificate is granted her for obtaining a Probate thereof in due form John Chastain and Anthony Benning Securities.

Ordered that Edward Scott, David Lesseur, Isaac Sallee, John Legrand, or any three of them being first sworn by some Justice of the Peace do appraise the Estate of Peter David deceased and that Anne David the Executrix do return an Inventory thereof to the next Court

Present Allin Howard Gent.

Scots titheables [assi]gn'd to be listed   On the motion of Edward Scott ordered that his titheable be added to the Lists.

Levey to be Laid   Ordered that the County levey be laid at the next Court.

Court house to be built   Upon [treat]ing with workmen about the building a Court house thirty six feet [long] and twenty feet wide from outside to outside, it is the Opinion of the Court that Mr. James Skelton may undertake the same [for] the consideration of ten thousand pounds of tobacco in Cask con[venient] to be paid him on or before the tenth day of June next, and [torn] thousand pounds of tobacco in Cask convenient to be paid him on [or] before the tenth day of June which shall be in the year of our Lord 1732 the Court house is to be finished by November [torn] 1731, a[ccor]ding to the manu[torn] Articles of Agreement which the Clerk is ord[ered] [torn] to the next Court to be approved.

Davis's Administration   John Q[uantin] [torn] makes oath that William Davis deceased died [without a will] as far as he knows or believes and on his motion [and] Security for his just and faithfull Administration of the said deceadents Estate Certificate is granted him for obtaining Letters of Administration in due form Edward Scot Security.

Ordered that James Taylor, Joseph Scot, David Lesseur, Stephen Cox, or any three of them being first sworn by some Justices of the Peace do appraise the Estate of William Davis deceased

[26]   August Court 1730
and that John Quantin the Administrator do return an Inventory thereof to the next Court.

Then the Court adjourned to the third Tuesday in next Month.

****

At a Court held for Goochland County the third Tuesday in September being the fifteenth day of the Month Annoq. Domi. 1730.

Present. John Fleming, William Mayo, Allin Howard, James Holman, Gent. Justices.

Hollands deeds to Chiles   Michaell Holland acknowledges deeds of Lease and Release from himself to Henry Chiles to be his Acts and deeds and they are thereupon admitted to Record.

Dickins's Negro judged   Rochester a Negro boy belonging to Thomas Dickins is judged to be nine years of age.

Present. William Cabbell Gent.

Hoggat's Ordinary Lycense   [On the] motion of Anthony Hoggat a Lycense is granted him to keep an [Ordi]nary at his dwelling house in Goochland County Thomas Dickins [and] Samuell Allin Securities.

Powell to be listed   On the Petition of Richard Powell he is Ordered to be added to the List of titheables.

Hopkins to be listed   On the Petition of Evan Hopkins he is Ordered to be added to the List of titheables.

Wiles vs Hughes   In the Action of Trespass on the Case between Luke Wiles Plt. and Stephen Hughes and Sarah Atkinson Executor & Executrix of Thomas Atkinson deced

[27]   September Court 1730
deceased Defendts. the following Jury are sworn Peter Ware, William Lansdon, John Prier, Amos Lad, George Stoveall, Joell Chandler, Bartholomew Stoveall, George Southerland, Henry Harper, Peter Jefferson, John Laine, Joseph Watkins, who after some time return with their Verdict which on the Plts. motion is admitted to record and is as followeth "Wee find for the Plt. two pounds eleven shillings and nine pence half penny Peter Ware Foreman." Whereupon it is considered by the Court that the Plt. do recover against the Defts. the said sum of two pounds eleven shillings and nine pence half penny by the Jurors aforesaid in their said Verdict assessed and also the Costs of this Suit of the goods and Chattles which were of the aforesaid Thomas Atkinson at his death in the hands of the said Stephen Hughes and Sarah Atkinson to be administred if so much in their hands there be and if not so much then the Costs aforesaid of the proper Goods and chattels of the aforesaid Stephen Hughes and Sarah Atkinson to be levied. the Plt. acknowledges this Judgment to be in satisfaction of a note for two pounds fourteen

shillings and four pence Currant money which note is mis[la]id.

Absent. Allin Howard Gent.

Randolph permitted to clear road   On the motion of Isham Randolph leave is granted him to clear a road from his Plantation above Treasurers Runn unto the main Road along a ridge of land passing by the Plantation of Joseph Jackson.

Prosser gives bond for behaviour   Griffith Bowen moving on behalf of Thomas [Prosser] that he may be released from his imprisonment upon his giving bond for his good behaviour it is ordered that the Sherif take a bond of the said Thomas Prosser payable to our Sovereign Lord King George the Second his Heirs and Successors with good and sufficient Security in the Sum of fifty pounds Currant money conditioned for the said Thomas Prosser's good behaviour for one year and a day to commence from this day and that after the Execution of the said bond the said Thomas Prosser be discharged from his imprisonment.

[28]   September Court 1730
Prosser denied an Appeal   Thomas Prosser moves for an Appeal from the Order made at the last Court for fining him whereupon it is the Opinion of the Court that an Appeal ought not to be granted.

Prosser turn'd from the Barr   Upon consideration of the behaviour of Thomas Prosser at the last Court it is the Opinion of the Court that he ought not to appear again as an Attorny at this Barr.

Scot vs Utley   The Action on the Case between Edward Scot Plt. and John Utley Deft. is continued.

Present. Allin Howard Gent.

Stoveall vs Wiles   On the motion of George Stoveall a Witness for Luke Wiles vs Stephen Hughes & Sarah Atkinson it is Ordered that the said Luke do pay him for six days attendance one hundred and eighty pounds of tobacco with Costs.

Easly vs Wiles   On the motion of Warham Easly of Henrico [County a] Witness for Luke Wiles vs Stephen Hughes & Sarah Atkinson [it is] Ordered that the said Luke do pay him for two days attendance ou[t] of the said days at thirty pounds of tobacco & the other at 60 [torn] for coming and returning thirty five miles once, one hundred and ninety five pounds of tobacco with Costs.

Ashlin vs Hughes &c   On the motion of Joseph Ashlin a Witness for Stephen Hughes and Sarah Atkinson ads Luke Wiles it is Ordered that the said Stephen & Sarah do pay him for two days attendance sixty pounds of tobacco with Costs.

Atkinson vs Hughes &c   On the motion of Henry Atkinson a Witness for Stephen Hughes and Sarah Atkinson ads Luke Wiles it is Ordered that the said Stephen & Sarah do pay him for two days attendance 60 lbs. of tobacco with Costs.

Atkinson vs Hughes &c   On the motion of Elizabeth Atkinson a Witness for Stephen Hughes and Sarah Atkinson ads Luke wiles it is Ordered that the said Stephen and

[29]   September Court 1730
and Sarah do pay him for two days attendance sixty pounds of tobacco with Costs.

May vs Taylor   In the Action of Trespass between William May Plt. and John Taylor Defendt. the following Jury are Sworn Peter Ware, William Lansdon, John Prier, Amos Lad, George Stoveall, Joell Chandler, Bartholomew Stoveall, George Southerland, Henry Harper, Peter Jefferson, John Laine, Joseph Watkins, who after some time return with their Verdict which on the Plts. motion is admitted to record and is as followeth " Wee find for the Plt. five shillings Currant money Peter Ware Foreman." the Court being of Opinion that the Battery is fully proved it is thereupon considered that the Plt. do recover against the Deft. the said sum of five shillings Currant money by the Jurors aforesaid in their said Verdict assessed with Costs and a Lawyers Fee.

Edwards vs May   On [the] motion of Thomas Edwards a Witness for William May vs [John] Taylor it is Ordered that the said William do pay him for five [days] attendance one hundred and fifty pounds of tobacco with Costs.

Creesey vs May   On the motion of John Creesey a Witness for William May vs John Taylor it is Ordered that the said William do pay him for two days attendance sixty pounds of tobacco with Costs.

Creesey vs Taylor   On the motion of William Creesey a Witness for John Taylor ads William May it is Ordered that the said John do pay him for four days attendance one hundred & twenty pounds of tobacco with Costs.

Wood vs New   The Action of Trespass on the Case between Henry Wood Plt. and William New Defendt. is continued.

Thomas vs Gee   The Action on the Case between Rowland Thomas Plt. and Gilbert Gee Defendt. is continued.

Read vs Downie   The Action on the Case between Clem Read Plt. and Robert Downie Defendt. is continued.

[30]   September Court 1730
Bumpuss vs Moreman   The Action of Trespass on the Case between Samuell Bumpuss Plt. and Andrew Moreman Defendt. is continued.

Scot vs Pritchet   The Action on the Case between Edward Scot Plt. and John Pritchet Deft. is dismist the Plt. not prosecuting the same.

Johnson vs Pruit   The Action of Trespass on the Case between Charles Johnson & Elizabeth his wife Plt. and Andrew Pruit Defendt. is continued.

Scot vs Williams   In the Action on the Case between Edward Scot Plt. and Edward Williams Defendt. the Deft. appears and confesses a Judgment to the Plt. for eleven shillings and four pence Currant money whereupon it is considered by the Court that the Plt. do recover against the Deft. the said sum together with the Costs of this Suit and a Lawyers Fee.

Ward vs Farrar   The Action of Debt between Seth Ward Plt. and John Farrar Defendt. is continued at the Plts. Cost.

Cox vs Dean   In the Action of Trespass between Frederick Cox Plt. and Richard Dean Defendt. the following Jury are sworn Peter Ware, William Lansdon, John Prier, Amos Lad, Joell Chandler, Bartholomew Stoveall, George Southerland, Henry Harper, John Laine, Joseph Watkins, James Taylor, Luke Wiles, who after some time bring in their Verdict which on the Defts. motion is admitted to Record and is as followeth "Wee find for the Defendant. Peter Ware Foreman." Whereupon it is considered by the Court that the Plt. take noting by his writt aforesaid that the Deft. go hence without day and that he recover against the Plt. his Costs by him in this behalf expended and a Lawyers Fee.

Taylor vs Hopkins   In the Action of Trespass between James Taylor Plt. and Evan Hopkins Defendt. the following Jury are sworn Peter Ware, William Lansdon, John Prier, Amos Lad, Joell Chandler, Bartholomew Stoveall, George Southerland, Henry Harper, John Laine, Joseph Watkins, Joseph Jackson, Luke Wiles, who after some time bring in their Verdict which on the Defts. motion is admitted to Record and is as followeth "Wee find for the Defendant Peter Ware Foreman." Whereupon it is considered by the Court that the Plt. take nothing by his writt aforesaid that the Deft. go hence without day

[31]   September Court 1730
day and that he recover against the Plt. his Costs by him in this behalf expended and a Lawyers Fee.

Hughes vs Hopkins   On the motion of Robert Hughes a Witness for Evan Hopkins ads James Taylor it is Ordered that the said Evan do pay him for five days attendance one hundred and fifty pounds of tobacco with Costs.

Bingley vs Taylor   On the motion of Joseph Bingley a Witness for James Taylor vs Evan Hopkins it is Ordered that the said James do pay him for four days attendance one hundred and twenty pounds of tobacco with Costs.

Lansdon vs Taylor. On the motion of William Lansdon a Witness for James Taylor vs Evan Hopkins it is Ordered that the said James do pay him for two days attendance sixty pounds of tobacco with Costs.

Levins vs Farrar   The Action on the Case between Richard Levins Plt. and John Sutton Farrar Defendt. is continued.

Pruit vs Boccar   The Action on the Case between Hugh Pruit Plt. and Peter Boccar Deft. is continued.

Sallee vs Bowie   The Action of Trespass on the Case between Isaac Sallee Assignee of Thomas Gevodan Plt. and John Bowie Deft. is continued.

Webber vs White   The Action of Trespass between Phillip Webber Plt. and Edward White Defendt. is continued.

Jackson vs Southerland   The Action of Trespass on the Case between John Jackson Assignee of Edward Birch Plt. and George Southerland

Defendt. is continued.

Digges vs Napier   In the Action on the Case between Dudley Digges Plt. and Bouth Napier Defendt. the Deft. pleads he oweth nothing and for tryal thereof puts himself upon the Country and the Plt. likewise.

Scot vs Lawson   The Action on the Case between Edward Scot Plt. and Jonas Lawson Deft. is dismist the Plt. not prosecuting the same.

[32]   September Court 1730
Happer vs Woodson   In the Action on the Case between William Happer Plt. and Joseph Woodson Defendt. the Deft. pleads he oweth nothing and for tryal thereof puts himself upon the Country and the Plt. likewise.

Happer &c. vs Woodson   In the Action on the Case between William Happer Assignee of William Arrington Plt. and Joseph Woodson Defendt. the Deft. pleads he oweth nothing and for tryal thereof puts himself upon the Country and the Plt. likewise.

Happer vs Harper   The Action on the Case between William Happer Plt. and Henry Harper Defendt. is continued.

Digges vs Saunders   The Action on the Case between Dudley Digges Plt. and John Saunders Defendt. is dismist the Plt. not prosecuting the same.

Digges vs Rapene   The Action on the Case between Dudley Digges Plt. and Anthony Rapene Defendt. is dismist the Plt. not prosecuting the same.

Clopton &c. vs Marchbanks   The Action of Debt between Joyce Clopton Executrix & William Acrill and John Syme Executors &c. of William Clopton deced Plts. and George Marchbanks Defendt. is continued.

May vs Jackson   In the Action on the Case between William May Plt. and Joseph Jackson Defendt. the following Jury are sworn Peter Ware, James Taylor, John Prier, Amos Lad, John Taylor, Bartholomew Stoveall, George Southerland, Henry Harper, John Laine, Joseph Watkins, Thomas Walker, Luke Wiles, who after some time return with their Verdict which on the Plts. motion is admitted to Record and is as followeth "Wee find for the Plaintif two pounds four shillings and nine pence   Peter Ware

Foreman." Whereupon it is considered by the Court that the Plt. do recover against the Deft. the said sum of two pounds for shillings and nine pence Currant money by the Jurors aforesaid in their said Verdict assessed together with the Costs of this Suit and a Lawyers Fee.

Bibe vs May   On the motion of Elizabeth Bibe a Witness for William May vs Joseph Jackson it is Ordered that the said William do pay her for seven days attendance two hundred and ten pounds of tobacco with Costs.

[33]   September Court 1730
Stidum vs Bingley &c   The Action of Debt between Benjamin Stidum Plt. and Joseph Bingley & William Lansdon Defts. is continued.

Moseby vs Taylor   The Action of Debt between Richard Moseby Plt. and John Taylor Defendt. is continued.

Grand Jury vs Hannah Turner   The Presentment of the Grant Jury against Hannah Turner is dismist.

Walker to be listed   On the motion of Thomas Walker he is Ordered to be added to the List of Titheables.

Dickins vs Pride   The Petition of Thomas Dickins against John Pride is dismist.

Digges vs Hughes   The Action of Trespass on the Case between Dudley Digges Plt. and Stephen Hughes Defendt. is continued at the Defts. cost.

Digges vs Mullin   In the Action on the Case between Dudley Digges Plt. and Patrick Mullin Defendt. the Deft. failing to appear on the Plts motion Judgment is granted him against the Deft. and Tarlton Fleming Gent. sherif for what damages shall be recovered in this Suit to be discharged nevertheless if the Deft. shall appear at the next Court.

Digges vs Taylor   The Action of Trespass on the Case between Dudley Digges Plt. and James Taylor Defendt. is continued.

Digges vs Burks   In the Action of Trespass on the Case between Dudley Digges Plt. and Richard Burks Deft. the Deft. pleads he oweth nothing and for tryal thereof puts himself upon the Country and the Plt. likewise.

Wood vs Woodson   In the Action of the Case between Henry Wood Plt. and Joseph Woodson Defendt. the Deft. failing to appear on the Plts. motion the conditional Judgment formerly granted against the Deft. and Tarlton Fleming Gent. Sherif is confirmed for so much damages as shall be found upon executing a writt of Inquiry at the next Court of which the Sherif is ordered to give the Deft. notice by serving him with a copy of this order.

[34]   September Court 1730
Fleming's acknowledgment of receit to Burton   John Fleming acknowledges an endorsement on a deed of Mortgage from Nowell Burton to Thomas Randolph to be his Act and deed which is ordered to be recorded.

Cox vs Napier   The Action on the Case between Bartholomew Cox Plt. and Robert Napier Junr. Defendt. is dismist the Plt. not prosecuting the same.

Then the Court adjourned 'till to morrow morning then of the Clock.

****

At a Court continued and held for Goochland County the sixteenth day of September Annoq. Domi. 1730. Present. John Fleming, William Mayo, Allin Howard, George Payne, William Cabbell, Gent. Justices.

Worley vs Locket   In the Action of Trespass on the Case between John Worley Plt. and Thomas Locket Defendt. the following Jury are sworn John Mcbrid, John Prier, Amos Lad, Francis Martin, Mathew Cox, Samuell Allin, Luke Wiles, George Stoveall, Edward Hatcher, Thomas Edwards, Jacob Micheaux, Benjamin Bradshaw, who after some time return with their Verdict which on the Defts. motion is admitted to record and is as followeth "Wee find for the Defendt. John Mcbrid Foreman." Whereupon it is considered by the Court that the Plt. take nothing by his writt aforesaid that the Deft. go hence without day and that he recover against the Plt. his Costs by him in this behalf expended and a Lawyers Fee.

Spears vs Locket   On the motion of Robert Spears a Witness for Thomas Locket ads John Worley it is Ordered that the said Thomas do pay him for three days attendance ninety pounds of tobacco with Costs.

[35]   September Court 1730

Spears vs Locket   On the motion of James Spears a Witness for Thomas Locket ads John Worley it is Ordered that the said Thomas do pay him for three days attendance ninety pounds of tobacco with Costs.

Akin vs Locket   On the motion of James Akin of Henrico County a Witness for Thomas Locket ads John Worley it is Ordered that the said Thomas do pay him for four days attendance one of the said days at thirty pounds of tobacco and the other three at sixty pounds of tobacco each and for coming and returning forty miles twice four hundred and fifty pounds of tobacco with Costs, and for four Ferriages.

Locket vs Locket   On the motion of Thomas Locket Junr. a Witness for Thomas Locket ads John Worley it is Ordered that the said Thomas do pay him for four days attendance one hundred and twenty pounds of tobacco with Costs.

Pennington's Inventory   John Fleming presents the Inventory and Appraisment of the Estate of Paul Pennington deceased which is Ordered to be recorded.

Thomas vs May   The Action of Trespass on the Case between William Thomas Plt. and William May Defendt. is continued.

Locket vs James   The Action of Trespass between Thomas Locket Plt. and Francis James Defendt. is continued.

Parish vs Watkins   The Action of Trespass on the Case between John Parish Junr. Plt. and Joseph Watkins Defendt. is continued.

Elliot vs Walker   The Action of Trespass on the Case between James Elliott Executor &c. of John Chiles deced Plt. and Thomas Walker Deft. is continued.

Winston vs Nolun   The action of Debt between Isaac Winston Plt. and Agnes Nolun Administratrix of Thomas Nolun deced Deft. is continued.

Hambleton vs Nolun   The Action of Debt between James Hambleton Plt. and Agnes Nolun Admx. &c. of Thomas Nolun deced Deft. is continued.

[36]   September Court 1730

Pasley vs Saunders   The Action of Trespass on the Case between

William Pasley Plt. and Thomas Saunders Defendt. is continued.

Hoggat vs Dickins   The Action of Trespass on the Case between Anthony Hoggat Plt. and Thomas Dickins Defendt. is dismist the Plt. not prosecuting the same.

March vs Wharton   The Action on the Case between John Macon Plt. and Thomas Wharton Defendt. is continued.

Waddill vs Edwards   The Action on the Case between William Waddill Junr. Plt. and Thomas Edwards Defendt. is continued.

Swift vs Howard   In the Action of Trespass on the Case between William Swift Plt. and Allin Howard Defendt. the Plt. failing to prosecute his Suit on the Defts. motion he is nonsuited and it is thereupon considered by the Court that the Deft. go hence without day and that he recover against the Plt. five shillings Currant money according to the Act of Assembly in that Case made and proceed together with his Costs by him in this behalf expended and a Lawyers Fee.

Pruit vs Johnson   The Action on the Case between Andrew Pruit Plt. and Charles Johnson Defendt. is continued.

Taylor vs Quin   The Action of Debt between James Taylor Plt. and John Quin Deft. is dismist the Plt. not prosecuting the same. the Deft. consents to pay the Costs of this Suit and a Lawyers Fee.

Marchbanks vs Croom   In the Action on the Case between George Marchbanks Plt. and Daniell Croom Defendt. by consent of Parties all matters in the difference between them are referred to the determination of George Payne Gent. and his award is to be made the Judgment of this Court.

Salmon vs Edwards   The Action on the Case between Thomas Salmon Plt. and Thomas Edwards Defendt. is continued.

[37]   September Court 1730
Collins vs Morriss   The Action of Trespass between Mathew Collins Plt. and John Morriss Defendt. is dismist the Plt. not prosecuting the same.

Boston vs Cox   The Action on the Case between Hugh Boston Plt. and Nicholas Cox Defendt. is continued.

Pigg vs Allin   In the Action on the Case between John Pigg Junr. Plt. and Samuell Allin Defendt. the Deft. pleads he oweth nothing and for tryall thereof puts himself upon the Country and the Plt. likewise.

Ware vs Saunders   In the Action of Trespass on the Case between Susanna Ware Plt. and William Saunders Defendt. the Deft. pleads conditions performed and for tryall thereof puts himself upon the Country and the Plt. likewise.

Flournoy vs Martin   The Action of Trespass on the Case between John James Flournoy Plt. and Francis Martin Defendt. is continued.

Flournoy vs Martin   The Action of Debt between John James Flournoy & Elizabeth his wife Executrix &c. of Orlando Jones deceased Plts. and Francis Martin Defendt. is continued.

Thompson vs Edwards   In the Action of Trespass on the Case between Samuell Thompson and Mary his Wife Plts. and Thomas Edwards of Bever dam Defendt. time is granted the Plts. to mend their declaration.

Bradley vs Saunders   In the Action of Trespass on the Case between Joseph Bradley Plt. and John Saunders Defendt. an imparlance is granted the Deft.

Napier vs Ashlin   In the Action on the Case between Bouth Napier Plt. and Joseph Ashlin Defendt. time is granted the Plt. to mend his declaration.

Mayo &c. vs Dawson   The Action of Debt between William Mayo & Daniell Stoner Gent. Church wardens of St. James's Parish and Elizabeth Dawson Deft. is continued.

Prosser vs Napier   In the Action of Trespass on the Case between Thomas Prosser Plt. and Bouth Napier Defendt. the Deft. appears but failing to Plead Judgment

[38]   September Court 1730
by nihil dicit is granted against him for what damages shall be recovered in this Suit to be discharged nevertheless if the Deft. shall plead at the next Court.

Rocket vs Burton   The Action of Trespass on the Case between Baldwin Rocket Plt. and Nowell Burton Defendt. is continued at the Plts.

cost.

Scot vs Ware   In the Action of Debt between Edward Scot Plt. and Peter Ware Deft. the Deft. appears and confesses a Judgment to the Plt. for twenty five pounds Currant money with Interest from the tenth day of May 1729. untill the same shall be paid whereupon it is considered by the Court that the Plt. do recover against the Deft. the said sum of twenty five pounds Currant money with Interest thereon after the rate of Sex Pr. Centum Pr. Annum from the said tenth day of May untill the said sum shall be paid with the Costs of this Suit and a Lawyers Fee.

Burton vs Worley   On the motion of John Burton of Prince George County a Witness for John Worley vs Thomas Locket it is Ordered that the said John do pay him for three days attendance and for coming and returning twenty four miles twice three hundred and twenty four pounds of tobacco with Costs and for four Ferriages.

Russell vs Worley   On the motion of John Russell of Henrico County a Witness for John Worley vs Thomas Locket it is Ordred that the said John do pay him for three days attendance and for coming and returning forty five miles twice four hundred and fifty pounds of tobacco with Costs and for four Ferriages.

Mcdermore vs Worley   On the motion of Michaell Mcdermore of Prince George County a Witness for John Worley vs Thomas Locket it is ordered that the said John do pay him for three days attendance one of the said days at thirty pounds of tobacco and the other two at sixty pounds of tobacco each and for coming and returning twenty four miles once two hundred and twenty two pounds of Tobacco with Costs and for two Ferriages.

[39]   September Court 1730
Cannon's ear mark   On the motion of William Cannon his ear mark is ordered to be recorded as followeth one swallow fork on the right ear, a Crop and under keel on the left ear.

Scot vs Ware   In the Action of Debt between Edward Scot Plt. and Peter Ware Defendt. the Deft. appears and confesses a Judgment to the Plt. for fifteen pounds fourteen shillings Currant money with Interest from the tenth day of May 1730, until the same shall be paid whereupon it is considered by the Court that the Plt. do recover against the Deft. the said sum of fifteen pounds fourteen shillings Currante money with Interest thereon after the rate of six Pr. Centum Pr. Annum from the said tenth day of May untill the said sum shall be paid with Costs and a Lawyers Fee.

Scot vs Ware   In the Action of Trespass on the Case between Edward Scot Plt. and Peter Ware Defendt. the Deft. appears and confesses a Judgment to the Plt for two pounds ten shillings Currant money whereupon it is considered by the Court that the Plt. do recover against the Deft. the said sum together with the Costs of this Suit and a Lawyers Fee.

Grand Jury vs Judith Ballew   On the Presentment of the Grand Jury against Judith for having one Bastard child the following Jury are sworn John McBrid, Mathew Cox, Samuell Allin, John Prier, Benjamin Bradshaw, Luke Wiles, Francis Martin, Thomas Edwards, Jacob Micheaux, George Stoveall, Edward Hatcher, John Baylor, who after some time return with their Verdict which is ordered to be recorded and is as followeth "Wee find the Defendant guilty John Mcbrid Foreman." whereupon it is considered by the Court that the Defendt. do pay unto the Church wardens of St. James's Parish the sum of five hundred pounds of tobacco with Cask with Costs and a Lawyers Fee.

Ford vs Williams   The Action of Trover and Conversion between Peter Foord Plt. and Edward Williams Defendt. is continued.

Digges vs Payne   The Action of Trespass on the Case between Dudley Digges Plt.

[40]   September Court 1730
and Josiah Payne Defendt. is dismist neither party appearing.

Woodson vs Napier   The Action of Trespass on the Case between William Woodson Plt. and Bouth Napier Defendt. is continued.

Ward vs Dean   The Action of Debt between Seth Ward Plt. and Richard Dean Deft. is continued.

Ford vs Pruit   The Action of Trespass on the Case between James Ford Plt. and Thomas Pruit Defendt. is continued.

Wood vs Burton   In the Action of Debt between Henry Wood Plt. and Nowell Burton Defendt. the Deft. appears and confesses a Judgment to the Plt. for five pounds one shilling and six pence Currant money whereupon it is considered by the Court that the Plt. do recover against the Deft. the said sum with Costs.

Turpin vs Hook ext   In the Action on the Case between Mathew Turpin Assignee of John Welsh Plt. and James Hook & John Peter Bilboe Defendts. time is granted the Plt. to mend his declaration.

Scot vs Daniell   In the Action of Detinue between Edward Scot Plt. and James Daniell Defendt. the Sherif having made return on the Alias Capias that the Deft. is not to be found and he failing to appear on the Plts. motion a Pluries Capias is awarded against the Deft. returnable to the next Court.

Mayo &c. vs Nunnary   The Action of Debt between William Mayo & Daniell Stoner Church wardens of St. James Parish Plts. and Judith Nunnary Defendt. is dismist the Plts. not prosecuting the same.

Scot vs Pruit   The Action of Trespass on the Case between Edward Scot Admr. &c. of John Stephens deced Plt. and Thomas Pruit Deft. is continued.

Lad & Powell vs Thompson   On the Petition of Amos Lad & Roger Powell against Samuell Thompson & Mary his wife the Sherif having returned the said

[41]   September Court 1730
Samuell Summoned and he failing to appear a Capias is awarded against him returnable to the next Court.

Taylor vs Lowe   The Action of Trespass on the Case between John Taylor Plt. and Thomas Lowe & Amey his wife Defts. is continued.

Surveyors of the roads   The Surveyors of the roads formerly appointed are continued.

Hatcher vs Fleming   The Action of Trespass on the Case between Edward Hatcher Plt. and John Fleming Administrator &c. of Paul Pennington deced Defendt. is dismist the Plt. not prosecuting the same.

Martin vs Fleming   The Action of Trespass on the Case between John Martin Plt. and John Fleming Administrator &c. of Paul Pennington deceased Defendt. is continued.

Hatcher vs Fleming   Edward Hatcher exhibits an Account of the funeral Expences of Paul Pennington deceased which being regulated by the Court amount to one pound ten shillings and six pence Currant money and it is ordered that John Fleming Administrator &c. of the said Paul deceased do pay unto the said Edward out of the said deceadents Estate the said sum, no costs to be taxed.

Lad vs Cannon   In the Action on the Case between Amos Lad Plt. and William Cannon Defendt. the Parties Submit themselves to the Court for tryall whereupon the witnesses being heard the Court are of Opinion the Deft. is guilty and assess the damages at twenty two shillings and six pence Currant money whereupon it is considered that the Plt. do recover against the Deft. the said Sum with Costs and a Lawyers Fee.

Hall vs Lad   On the motion of Richard Hall a Witness for Amos Lad vs William Cannon it is Ordered that the said Amos do pay him for five days attendance one hundred and fifty pounds of tobacco with Costs.

[42]   September Court 1730

Powell & Hoggat's Recognizance for Ballew's child   Roger Powell and Anthony Hoggat come into Court and acknowledges themselves indebted to our Sovereign Lord the King in the Sum of fifty pounds Currant money to be levied on the Goods & Chattles of the said Roger Powell and Anthony Hoggat on Condition nevertheless that if a Bastard child born of the body of Judith Ballew and named William shall not become chargeable to St. James's Parish then the said Recognizance to be void.

Taylor to be listed   On the motion of John Taylor himself and his Negro Sue are ordered to be added to the List of titheables.

Agee vs Sutleith   The Action of Trespass on the Case between Mathew Agee Plt. and Abraham Sutleith Defendt. is continued.

Bingley vs Boccar   The Action of Debt between Joseph Bingley Plt. and Peter Boccar Defendt. is dismist neither party appearing.

Rocket vs Dickins   In the Action of Trespass on the Case between Baldwin Rocket Plt. and Thomas Dickins Deft. an imparlance is granted the Deft.

Mayo vs Wilson   The Action of Trespass on the Case between William Mayo Plt. and Richard Wilson Deft. is dismist neither party appearing.

Mayo vs Martin   In the Action of Trespass on the Case between William

Mayo Plt. and John Martin Deft. the Deft. pleads [he] oweth nothing and for tryall thereof puts himself upon the [Country] and the Plt. likewise.

Hatcher &c. vs Symes   In the Action of Trespass on the [Case between] Henry Hatcher Assignee of Samuell Hatcher Plt. [and] Richard Symes Defendt. the Sherif having made return that [the Plt.] is not to be found and he failing to appear an Alias [Capias is aw]arded against him returnable to the next Court.

Wood vs Hoggat   In the Action of Debt between Henry Wood Plt. and Anthony Hoggat Defendt. the Deft. failing to appear on the Plts. motion Judgment is granted him against the Deft. and Tarlton Fleming

[43]   September Court 1730
Gent. Sherif for what damages shall be recovered in this Suit to be discharged nevertheless if the Deft. shall appear at the next Court.

Smith vs Kent   The Action of Trespass on the Case between George Smith Plt. and William Kent Deft. is dismist neither party appearing.

Scot vs Swift   The Action of Trespass between Edward Scot Plt. and William Swift Defendt. is dismist neither party appearing.

[Scot] vs Napier   The Action of Trespass on the Case between Edward Scot Plt. and Robert Napier Deft. is dismist neither party appearing.

[Dick]ins vs [Po]well   The Action of Trespass on the Case between Thomas Dickins Plt. and Richard Powell Deft. is dismist neither party appearing.

Cannon vs Bugg   The Attachment obtained by William Cannon against the Estate of William Bugg is continued.

Phelps vs Bugg   The Attachment obtained by John Phelps against the Estate of William Bugg is dismist the said John not appearing.

Richards vs May   In the Action of Detinue between John Richards Plt. and William May Defendt. the Plt. having failed to file his declaration on the [Defts.] motion he is nonsuited and it is thereupon considered by [the Court] that the Deft. go hence without day and that he recov[er against] the Plt. five shillings Currant money according to the [Act of Ass]embly in that Case made and provided together with his [Costs by] him in this behalf expended and a Lawyers Fee.

Digges vs Woodson   In the Ac[tion of Tr]espass on the Case between Dudley Digges Plt. and Jos[eph Woodson] Deft. an imparlance is granted the Deft.

Digges vs Woodson   The Action of Trespass on the Case between Dudley Digges Plt. and Sanburn Woodson Defendt. is dismist the Plt. not prosecuting the same.

[44]   September Court 1730
Digges vs Bruise   The Action of Trespass on the Case between Dudley [Di]gges Plt. and Peter Bruise Deft. is dismist the Plt. not prosecuting the same.

Digges vs Lansdon   In the Action of Trespass on the Case between Dudley D[igges Plt.] and William Lansdon Defendt. the Deft. pleads he oweth [nothing and] for tryall thereof puts himself upon the Country and the Plt. [likewise.]

Digges vs Pratt   The Action of Trespass on the Case between Dudley Digge[s Plt. and] Mary Pratt Adminx. &c. of Roger Pratt deceased is continued.

Wiles vs Hughes   In the Action of Trespass on the Case between Luke Wile[s Plt. and] Stephen Hughes Defendt. the declaration not being found sin[ce last] Court on the Defts. motion the Plt. is nonsuited and it is th[erefore] considered by the Court that the Deft. go hence without day [and that] he recover against the Plt. five shillings Currant money [according to] the Act of Assembly in that Case made and provided together [with] his Costs by him in this behalf expended and a Lawyers Fee.

Bryan vs Chandler   In the Action of Trespass on the Case between William Bryan Plt. and Joell Chandler Defendt. an imparlance is granted the Defendant.

Bryan vs Chandler   In the Action of Trespass on the Case between William Bryan Plt and Joell Chandler Defendt. an imparlance is granted the Defendant.

Cabbell vs Utley   In the Action of Trespass on the Case between William Cabbell Plt. and John Utley Defendt. for four hundred and sixty pounds of tobacco the Sherif having returned the Deft. not to be found and he failing to appear on the Plts. motion an Attachment is granted him against the Defts. Estate returnable to the next Court.

Dickins vs Utley   In the Action of Trespass on the Case between Thomas Dickins Plt. and John Utley Defendt. for five pounds five shillings Currant money the Sherif having returned the Deft. not to be found and he failing to appear on the Plts. motion an Attachment is granted him against the Defendants Estate returnable to the next Court.

[45]   September Court 1730
Prosser vs Scot   The Action of Trespass on the Case between Thomas Prosser Plt. and Edward Scot Deft. is dismist neither party appearing.

[Ward vs Rocket]   In the Action of Trespass on the Case between Seth Ward Plt. and Baldwin Rocket Defendt. the Plt. having failed to file his declaration on the Defts. motion he is nonsuited and it is thereupon considered by the Court that the Deft. go hence without day and that he recover against the Plt. five shillings Currant money according to the Act of Assembly in that Case made and provided together with his Costs by him in this behalf expended and a Lawyers Fee.

[Lad vs Skelton]   The Action of Trespass on the Case between Amos Lad Plt. and James Skelton Deft. is dismist neither party appearing.

[Macon vs Hughes]   In the Action of Trespass on the Case between William Macon Plt. and Stephen Hughes Defendt. the Deft. failing to appear on the Plts. motion Judgment is granted him against the Deft. and Tarlton Fleming Gent. Sherif for what damages shall be recovered in this Suit to be discharged nevertheless if the Deft. shall appear at the next Court.

Mallet vs Pruit   In the Action of Trespass between Stephen Mallet Plt. and Thomas Pruit Defendt. an imparlance is granted the Deft.

Levins vs Farrar   In the Action of Trespass on the Case between Richard Levins Plt. and William Farrar Defendt. a Special imparlance is granted the Defendant.

Then the Court adjourned to the third Tuesday in next Month.

****

[46] County Levy Court 1730
At a Court held for the County of Goochland the seventeenth day of September Annoq. Domi. 1730 for laying the County levy. Present. John Fleming, William Mayo, Allin Howard, George Payne, William Cabbell, Gent. Justices.

Goochland County Dr.	tobacco	cask
To Henry Wood Clerk for Extraordinary Services	1000	80
To Do. for attending a Court for the tryall of John Huson	200	
To Do. for attending a Court for the tryall of Cuffey a Negro of Anthony Benning's	200	
To [Tarlton] Fleming Sheriff for Extraordinary Services	1000	80
To [torn] Raley for one Wolfs head Certified by George Payne	200	
To R[torn] Parker for three Do. Certified by James Holman	600	
To Ral[ph Hud]speath for one do. Certified by William Mayo	200	
To William Tabor for three Do. Certified by William Cabbell	600	
To John [Phelps] for one Do. Certified by William Cabbell	200	
To [Thos. H]all for one Do. Certified by George Payne	200	
To [Wm.] Atkinson for one Do. Certified by Allin Howard	200	
To M[artin D]unkin for one Do. Certified by George Payne	200	
To William Halliday for four Do. Certified by William Cabbell	800	
To Joseph [Hoop]er for three Do. Certified by William Cabbell	600	
To William [Can]non for two Do. Certified by William Cabbell	400	
To Thomas [B]allew for one Do. Certified by William Cabbell	200	
To Thomas Pate for one Do. Certified by William Cabbell	200	
To William Cabbell for two Do. Certified by Allin Howard	400	
To Henry Wood for Secretarys Fees due in 1728	160	
To Henry Wood for Do. due in 1729	316	
To Charles Raley for one Wolfs head Certified by John Woodson	200	
To Charles Raley for Do. Certified by Tarlton Fleming	800	
	8076	160

	tobacco	cask.
[47] County Levy Court 1730		
Brought forward	8876	160
[To Mart]in King for two Wolfs heads Certified by William Cabbell	400	
[To Mart]in King for one Do. Certified by John Woodson	200	
[To Joell] Chandler for three Do. Certified by William Mayo	600	
[To Adam] Buttery for one Do. Certified by John Woodson	200	
[To Step]hen Hughes Admr. &c. of Sarah Atkinson deced. for keeping Ferry from October the first till May Court after the rate of eight hundred pounds of tobo. Pr. Annum	499	
[To Step]hen Hughes for keeping ferry from May Court till this [torn] after the rate of fifteen hundred pounds of tobo. pr. annum	625	
[To D]aniell Stoner late Sheriff for Summoning a Court to try [Jo]hn Huson	200	
[To Do.] for going to Williamsburgh for Commission to try Cuffey	300	
[To Do.] for Summoning the Court	200	
[To Do.] for Summoning six witness & returning the Writts	[1]20	
[To Do.] for lock and Smiths work	[4]16	
[To Do.] for Insolvents and Persons twice listed	[285]	
[To Do.] for ten days imprisonment of Cuffey	[100]	
[To Do.] for Hasp and Staple for the Prison	[20]	
[To Wi]lliam Atkinson for five Wolves heads Certified by Allin Howard	[1000]	
[To] Thomas Edwards for one Do. Certified by Allin Howard	[200]	
[To] William Atkinson for one Do. Certified by Allin Howard	[200]	
[To] Thomas Prosser for seventeen months Salary as Attorny	[1418]	112
[To] Joseph Woodson for three years rent	[2100]	168
[To] James Skelton towards building the Court house	[10000]	800
[To] Tarlton Fleming Sherif for conveniency of 10800 pounds of tobacco at 15 Pr. Cent.	1620	
[To E]dward Williams for one Wolfs head Certified by Wm. Cabbell	200	

[To] John Fleming Gent to enable him to pay Francis
    James and John Harris this Countys proportion of
    tobacco for building the Bridge over Tuckahoe Creek 6000
[To] Daniell Stoner late Sherif for an Iron Barr   30
                                                    35809 1240
                                Cask   1240
                            Salary   3704
                                              40753
            due to the County   56
                                            40809

[48]   County Levy Court 1739
                    Do.   [Cr.]
By 1259 titheables at 32 Pr. poll   [40288]
By Capt. Daniell Stoner for last years ballance   [521]

Ordered that 15 Pr. Cent be allowed the Sheriff for [Conveniency] of the tobacco levied for the Court house and Bridge.

Ordered that Tarlton Fleming Gent. Sherif do [torn] titheable person in this County the Sum of thirty [two pounds of] tobacco Pr poll and that in case of refusal or no[npayment there]of he levy the same by distress, and that [torn] of the severall sums of tobacco to the resp[ective Creditors] [torn] the same is levied. The said Tarlton Fleming ent[torn] George Payne and William Cabbell become [h]is Se[curities.]

Alford to be listed   On the motion of William Alford he is ordered to be added to the list of titheables.

****

At a Court held for Goochland County the third Tuesday in November being the seventeenth [day] of the Month Annoq. Domi. [1730.] Present. John Fleming, [torn], George Payne, James Holman, Gent. Justices.

Proclamation published   A Proclamation by the Honble. William Gooch Esqr. his Majesties Lieut. [Governour an]d Commander in chief of this Dominion is [published] for preventing the unlawfull Meetings and Combinations of Negros and other Slaves.

[49]   November Court 1730
A Proclamation by the Honble William Gooch Esqr. his Majesty's Lieut.

Governour and Commander in chief of this Dominion is published Proroguing the General Assembly.

[torn]   On the Petition of Mr. Thomas Prosser he is permitted to [torn] as a Lawyer at this barr.

[torn]   Anne David presents an Inventory and Appraisment of [the] Estate of Peter David deceased which is admitted to record.

[torn]   On Mr. William Parks's letter to the Court it is ordered th[at] there be levied for him eight hundred pounds of tobacco [with cask an]d conveniency at the next levey for which the said Parks [furnish] [torn] twelve Copys of the laws of the last Session of [the] Assembly for the use of the Justices.

[torn]   In the Action of Trespass on the Case between Henry [Wood] Plt. and William New Defendt. Joseph Thompson entred himself Special Bail for the Defendant who appears [and] confesses a Judgment to the Plt. for two pounds thirteen [shillings] and eight pence Currant money and seven hundred and seventy nine pounds of tobacco whereupon it is considered [by] the Court that the Plt. do recover against the Deft. the said sums of money and tobacco with costs. by consent of the Plt. Execution is to cease for twelve months.

Thomas vs Gee   The Action on the Case between Rowland Thomas Plt. and Gil[bert G]ee Defendt. is continued at the Plts. cost.

Present. John Woodson Gent.

Read vs Downie   In the Action on the Case between Clem Read Plt. and Robert Downie Defendt. the Parties submit themselves to the Court for tryal by [torn] Plt. the Deft. is to be admitted to his oath whereupon [torn] having settled the accounts between them and heard the Defts. oath it is considered that

[50]   November Court 1730
that the Plaintiff do recover against the Defendt. one pound nineteen shillings and two pence Currant money with the costs of this Suit and a Lawyers Fee.

Bumpuss vs Moreman   The Action of Trespass on the Case between Samuell Bumpuss Plt. and Andrew Moreman Defendt. is continued at the Defts. cost.

Pride's deed to Watkins   John Pride acknowledges a deed with the Livery of Seizin endorsed from himself to Edward Watkins to be his Act and deed and it is thereupon admitted to record.

Johnson vs Pruit   In the Action of Trespass on the Case between Charles Johnson & Elizabeth his wife Plts. and Andrew Pruit Defendt. [torn] he is not guilty and for tryal thereof puts himself [upon the Country] and the Plt. likewise.

Ward vs Farrar   The Action of Debt between Seth Ward Plt. and John [Sutton Farrar Deft.] is continued at the Defendants cost.

Levins vs Farrar   In the Action on the Case between Richard Levins [and John] Sutton Farrar Defendt. the Plt. files a new declaration [torn] imparlance is granted the Defendant.

Pruit vs Boccar   In the Action on the Case between Hugh Pruit Plt. [torn] Boccar Defendt. the Plt. files a new declaration and [torn] continued.

Sallee vs Bowie   In the Action of Trespass on the case between Isaac [Sallee] of Thomas Jevodon Plt. and John Bowie Defendt. [torn] to plead on the Plts. motion the conditional Judgment [torn]ed against the Deft. is confirmed for so much damage [torn] found upon executing a writ of Inquiry at the [torn] which the Sherif is ordered to give the Deft. notice [torn] with a copy of this order.

Webber vs White   In the Action of Trespass on the Case between Phillip [Webber]

[51]   November Court 1730
[Edward] White Defendt. the Sherif having made return on the [Plur]ies Capias that the Deft. is not to be found and he failing to appear the Plts. motion a Pluries Capias de novo is awarded against the Deft. returnable to the next Court.

Absent. James Holman Gent.

Williams's Administration   James Holman Gent. comes into Court and makes oath that Edward Williams deceased died without any will so far as he knows or believes and on his motion and giving Security for his just and faithfull Administration of the said deceadents Estate Certificate is granted him for obtaining letters of Administration in due form Thomas

Dickins Security.

Ordered that William Womack, John Williams, Stephen Cox, George Thompson, or any three of them being first sworn by some Justice of the Peace do Appraise the Estate of Edward Williams deceased and that James Holman the Administrator do return an Inventory thereof to the next Court.

   Present. James Holman Gent.

[Jackson vs Southerland] In the Action of Trespass on the Case between John Jackson Assee. of Edward Birch Plt. and George Southerland Defendt. time is granted the Plt. to mend his declaration.

[edge torn] Stephen Hughes undertakes to keep a Ferry at the Plantation where the widow Atkinson lately dwelt and to set over on all Court days all persons who live in the County and the Sherif and his Officers at all times. In Consideration of which service it is the Opinion of the Court that there be levied for the said Stephen annually sixteen hundred pounds of tobacco with Cask and conveniency, and that the said Stephen be excused from listing one titheable.

[Digges vs Napier] The Action on the Case between Dudley Digges Plt. and Bouth Napier Defendt. is continued.

[52] November Court 1730
Happer vs Woodson In the Action on the Case between William Happer Plt. and Joseph Woodson Defendt. the Deft. appears and confesses a Judgment to the Plt. for two pounds twelve shillings and six pence Currant money whereupon it is considered by the Court that the Plt. do recover against the Plt. the said sum together with the costs of this suit and a Lawyers Fee.

Happer &c. vs Woodson In the Action on the Case between William [Happer Assignee of] William Arrington Plt. and Joseph Woodson [Defendt.] [torn] appears and confesses a Judgment to the [torn] thirteen shillings and six pence Currant money [torn] it is considered by the Court that the Plt. [torn] against the Deft. the said sum together with the costs [torn] and a Lawyers Fee.

Happer vs Harper In the Action on the Case between William [Happer P]lt. and Henry Harper Defendt. the Deft. [pleads] not guilty and for tryal thereof puts himself upon the Country and the Plt. likewise.

Clopton vs Marchbanks   In the Action of Debt between Joyce Clopton Executrix William Acrill & John Syme Executors &c. of William Clopton deceased Plts. and George Marchbanks Deft. the Parties submit themselves to the Court for tryal whereupon it is considered that the Plts. take noting by their Writ aforesaid that the Deft. go hence without day and that he recover against the Plts. his Costs by him in this behalf expended.

Chamberlayne vs Marchbanks   On the motion of William Chamberlayne of New Kent County a Witness for George Marchbanks ads Joyce Clopton &c. it is ordered that the said George do pay him for one days attendance and for coming and returning sixty miles once two hundred and forty pounds of tobacco with costs.

Guerrants Administration   Peter Guerrant comes into Court and makes oath that Daniell Guerrant deceased died without any will so far as he knows

[53]   November Court 1730
or believes and on his motion and giving Security for his just and faithfull administration of the said deceadents Estate Certificate is granted him for obtaining Letters of Administration in due form   Frances Relict of the said D[anie]l deceased having relinquished her right thereto. [It is] Ordered that Edward Scot, Thomas Dickins, Stephen [Chas]tain, John Chastain, or any three of them being first [sworn] by some Justice of the Peace do Appraise the Estate [of D]aniel Guerrant deceased and that Peter Guerrant the [Adm]inistrator do return an Inventory thereof to the next Court. Anthony [torn] & John Peter Bilboe Securities.

Stid[um vs Bingley]   [In the] Action of Debt between Benjamin Stidum Plt. and [Jose]ph Bingley & William Lansdon Defts. time is granted [the] Plt. to answer the Defts. bill of Injunction.

Moseby vs Taylor   The Action of Debt between Richard Moseby Plt. and Jo[hn Taylor] Deft. is continued at the Defts. cost.

Digges vs Hughes   The Action of Trespass on the Case between Dudley Digges Plt. and Stephen Hughes Defendt. is continued at the Plts. cost.

Digges vs Mullin   In the Action on the Case between Dudley Digges Plt. and Patrick Mullin Defendt. the Deft. failing to appear on the Plts. motion the conditional Judgment formerly granted against the Deft. and Tarlton Fleming Gent. Sherif is confirmed for so much damages as shall be found upon executing a writ of Inquiry at the next Court of which the Sherif is ordered to give the Deft. notice by serving him with a copy of this order.

Digges vs Taylor   The Action of Trespass on the Case between Dudley Digges Plt. and James Taylor Deft. is continued at the Plts. cost.

Digges vs Burks   The Action of Trespass on the Case between Dudley Digges Plt. and Richard Burks Deft. is dismist the Plt. not prosecuting the same.

[54]   November Court 1730
Wood vs Woodson   The Action on the Case between Henry Wood [Plt. and] Joseph Woodson Deft. is dismist the Plt. not prosecuting the same.

Thomas vs May   In the Action of Trespass on the Case between William Thomas Plt. and William May Defendt. the Deft. pleads he oweth nothing and for tryal thereof puts himself upon the Country and the Plt. likewise.

Locket vs James   In the Action of Trespass between Thomas Locket Plt. and Francis James Defendt. the Deft. appears but failing to plead on the Plts. motion Judgment by nihil dicit is granted him against the Deft. for what damages shall be recovered in this Suit to be discharged nevertheless if the Deft. shall plead at the next Court.

Parish vs Watkins   In the Action of Trespass on the Case between John Parish Junr. Plt. and Joseph Watkins Deft. the Deft. pleads he oweth nothing to which Plea the Plt. demurrs and the Deft. joyns in demurrer.

Elliot vs Walker   The Action of Trespass on the Case between James Elliot Executor &c. of John Chiles deced Plt. and Thomas Walker Deft. is dismist the Plt. not prosecuting the same.

Winston vs Nolun   In the Action of Debt between Isaac Winston Plt. and Agnes Nolun Administratrix &c. of Thomas Nolun deced Defendt. the Deft. appears but failing to plead on the Plts. motion Judgment by nihil dicit is granted him against the Deft. for what damages shall be recovered in this suit to be discharged nevertheless if the Deft. shall plead at the next Court.

Hambleton vs Nolun   In the Action of Debt between James Hambleton Plt. and Agnes Nolun Administratrix &c. of Thomas Nolun deced

Defendt. the Deft. appears but failing to plead on the Plts. motion Judgment by nihil dicit is granted him against the Deft. for what damages shall be recovered in this suit to be discharged nevertheless if the Deft. shall plead at the next Court.

[55]　November Court 1730
　　　Present Allin Howard Gent.

Pasl[ay vs Saunders]　In the Action of Trespass on the Case between William Paslay Plt. and Thomas Saunders Defendt. the following Jury are Sworn Robert Hughes, John Prier, William New, James Daniell, Nowell Burton, Benjamin Bradshaw, John Bostick, George Southerland, Amos Lad, Nicholas Cox, William Lansdon, Samuell Allin, who after some time bring in their Verdict which on the Plts. motion is admitted to record and is as followeth "Goochland ss Wee of the Jury find for the Plt. four pounds ten shillings and eight pence Currt. money Robert Hughes Foreman." whereupon it is considered by the Court that the Plt. do recover against the Deft. the said sum of four pounds ten shillings and eight pence Currt. money by the Jurors aforesaid in their said Verdict assessed together with the costs of this suit and a Lawyers Fee.

Webb's Ordinary Lycense　On the motion of John Webb Lycense is granted him to keep an Ordinary at his Plantation in this County Stephen Hughes entring himself Security.

Macon vs Wharton　The Action on the Case between John Macon Plt. and Thomas Wharton Deft. is continued at the Plts. cost.

Waddill vs Edwards　The Action on the Case between William Waddill Junr. Plt. and Thomas Edwards Defendt. is continued.

Pruit vs Johnson　The Action on the Case between Andrew Pruit Plt. and Charles Johnson Defendt. is continued.

Marchbanks vs Croom　The Action on the Case between George Marchbanks Plt. and Daniell Croom Defendt. is continued.

Salmon vs Edwards　In the Action on the Case between Thomas Salmon Plt. and Thomas Edwards Defendt. the Deft. pleads he oweth nothing

[56]　November Court 1730
and for tryal puts himself upon the C[ount]ry and the Plt. likewise.

Boston vs Cox   The Action on the Case between Hugh Boston Plt. and Nicholas Cox Deft. is dismist the Plt. not prosecuting the same.

Pigg vs Allin   The Action on the Case between John Pigg Junr. Plt. and Samuell Allin Defendt. is continued.

Ware vs Saunders   The Action of Trespass on the Case between Susanna Ware Plt. and William Saunders Deft. is continued at the Plts. cost.

Flournoy vs Martin   In the Action of Trespass on the Case between John James Flournoy Plt. and Francis Martin Defendt. the Deft. appears but failing to plead on the Plts. motion Judgment by nihil dicit is granted him against the Deft. for what damages shall be recovered in this suit to be discharged nevertheless if the Deft. shall plead at the next Court.

Flournoy vs Martin   In the Action of Debt between John James Flournoy and Elizabeth his wife Executrix &c. of Orlando Jones deced Plts. and Francis Martin Defendt. the Deft. appears but failing to plead on the Plts. motion Judgment by nihil dicit is granted them against the Deft. for what damages shall be recovered in this suit to be discharged nevertheless if the Deft. shall plead at the next Court.

Thompson vs Edwards   In the Action of Trespass on the Case between Samuell Thompson & Mary his wife Plts. and Thomas Edwards Defendt. the Plt. files a new declaration and on the Defts. motion an Imparlance is granted him.

Justices recommended   The Court considering that there are not a Sufficient number of Justices in the Commission of Peace, and that thereby the business of the Court is sometimes delayed, Isham Randolph, James Skelton, George Rayne, and

[57]   November Court 1730
Anthony Hoggatt are therefore recommended to the Honble. William Gooch Esqr. his Majesty's Lieut. Governour as persons proper to be added to that Commission.

Bradly vs Saunders   In the Action of Trespass on the Case between Joseph Bradley Plt. and John Saunders Defendt. the Deft. appears but failing to plead on the Plts. motion Judgment by nihil dicit is granted him against the Deft. for what damages shall be recovered in this suit to be discharged nevertheless if the Deft. shall plead at the next Court.

Napier vs Ashlin   In the Action on the Case between Bouth Napier Plt. and Joseph Ashlin Deft. the Plt. files a new declaration and on the Defts. motion an imparlance is granted him.

Mayo &c. vs Dawson   The Action of Debt between William Mayo and Daniel Stoner Gent. Church wardens of St. James's Parish Plts. and Elizabeth Dawson Defendt. is dismist the Plts. not prosecuting the same.

Prosser vs Napier   In the Action of Trespass on the Case between Thomas Prosser Plt. and Bouth Napier Defendt. the Deft. pleads he oweth nothing and for tryall thereof puts himself upon the Country and the Plt. likewise.

Rocket vs Burton   In the Action of Trespass on the Case between Baldwin Rocket Plt. and Nowell Burton Defendt. Thomas Dickins appears on behalf of the Deft. and confesses a Judgment to the Plt. for three pounds seven shillings and five pence three farthings Currant money whereupon it is considered by the court that the Plt. do recover against the Deft. the said sum together with the costs of this Suit and a Lawyers Fee.

Ford vs Williams   The Action of Trover & Conversion between Peter Ford Plt. and Edward Williams Deft. is dismist the Deft. being dead.

Woodson vs Napier   In the Action of Trespass on the Case between William Woodson Plt. and Bouth Napier Defendt. the Deft. appears but failing

[58]   November Court 1730

to plead on the Plts. motion Judgment by nihil dicit is granted him against the Deft. for what damages shall be recovered in this suit to be discharged nevertheless if the Deft. still plead at the next Court.

Ward vs Dean   The Action of Debt between Seth Ward Plt. and Richard Dean Defendt. is continued.

Ford vs Pruit   In the Action of Trespass on the Case between James Ford [Plt.] and Thomas Pruit Defendt. the Deft. appears but failing to pl[ead on] the Plts. motion Judgment by nihil dicit is granted him a[gainst] the Deft. for what damages shall be recovered in this suit to [be] discharged nevertheless if the Deft. shall plead at the next Court.

Turpin &c. vs Hook &c   In the Action on the Case between Mathew

Turpin Assignee of John Welsh Plt. and James Hook & John Peter Bilboe Defendts. an imparlance is granted the Defendants.

Scot vs Daniel   In the Action of Detinue between Edward Scot Plt. and James Daniel Defendt. the Deft. pleads non detinet and for tryal thereof puts himself upon the Country and the Plt. likewise.

Scot &c. vs Pruit   The Action of Trespass on the Case between Edward Scot Administrator of John Stephens Plt. and Thomas Pruit Deft. is continued.

Bellamy's Inventory   Samuel Thompson and Mary his wife Administratrix with the will annex'd of John Bellamy deceased present an Inventory of the Estate of the said John Bellamy deced which is admitted to record.

Lad & Powel vs Thompson   On the Petition of Amos Lad and Roger Powel against Samuel Thompson and Mary his wife Administratrix &c. of John Bellamy deceased Allin Howard and George Payne Gent. are appointed to settle the Account Dr. and Cr. of the Estate of John Bellamy deceased and to report their proceedings therein for the next Court.

Taylor vs Lowe   The Action of Trespass on the Case between John Taylor Plt. and Thomas Lowe & Amey his wife Defts. is continued.

[59]   November Court 1730
Martin vs Fleming &c   The Action of Trespass on the Case between John Martin Plt. and John Fleming Administrator &c. of Paul Pennington deceased Defendt. is continued.

Agee vs Sutleith   The Action of Trespass on the Case between Mathew Agee Plt. and Abraham Sutleith Defendt. is dismist. the Plt. not prosecuting the same.

[Rock]et vs [Dic]kins   In the Action of Trespass on the Case between Baldwin Rocket Plt. and Thomas Dickins Defendt. the Deft. appears but failing to plead on the Plts. motion Judgment by nihil dicit is granted him against the Deft. for what damages shall be recovered in this suit to be discharged nevertheless if the Deft. shall plead at the next Court.

Then the Court adjourned to the third Tuesday in next Month.

****

At a Court held for Goochland County the third Tuesday in December being the fifteenth day of the Month Annoq. Domi. 1730.
Present. John Fleming, William Mayo, John Woodson, Allin Howard, William Cabbell, Gent. Justices.

Parsons's deed to Woodson   Joseph Parsons acknowledges a deed with the Livery of Seizin endorsed from himself to Josiah Woodson to be his Act and deed and it is thereupon admitted to record.

[60]   December Court 1730
Holman's deed to Crouch   James Holman acknowledges a deed with the Livery of Seizin endorsed from himself to Richard Crouch to be his Act and deed and it is thereupon admitted to record.

Absent. John Woodson Gent.

Woodson's deed to Lightfoot   John Woodson acknowledges a deed with the Livery of Seizin endorsed from himself to Phillip Lightfoot to be his Act and deed and it is thereupon admitted to record, Josiah and Stephen Woodson also acknowledge the receit endorsed on the said deed to be their Act and deed and it is thereupon admitted to record.

Woodson's deed to Lightfoot   Josiah and Stephen Woodson acknowledge a deed with the Livery of Seizin endorsed from themselves to Phillip Lightfoot to be their Act and deed and it is thereupon admitted to record they also acknowledge receit endorsed on the said deed to be their Act and deed and it is thereupon admitted to record.

Present. John Woodson & James Holman Gent.

Prison to be built   Edward Scot undertakes to build a Prison near the Court house of the County at his own cost & charge of the following [d]imentions and after the manner hereafter expressed. the Prison to be [twenty] four foot long twelve foot wide in the clear the timbers in the sides ends floor and ceiling to be framed close to each other and to be eight inches thick, the lower floor to be laid with inch planks a partition to be made with a door in it and a lock thereto, two inside Chimneys, one outside door to be well secured with a good lock bar and other iron-work, the roof sides and ends to be covered with clap boards sap'd, the upper floor to be laid with clap boards, for which Prison the Court agree to pay the said Scot at the laying the next County levey ten thousand pounds of

tobacco with Cask and Conveniency.
Mr. Thomas Prosser promises to give a lock on the outside

[61]   December Court 1730
outside door and another for the Partition door of the said Prison.

Stoner vs Hughes   On the motion of Daniel Stoner Gent. ordered that Isaac Hughes and Martha his wife Executrix of the last will and testament of George Cox deceased be Summoned to appear at the next Court to give other Security for the Estate of the said George deceased or to deliver the same to the said Daniel who was Security for the said Martha's Probate of the said Will.

Davis's Inventory   John Quantin presents an Inventory and Appraisement of the Estate of William Davis deceased which is ordered to be recorded.

[Scot vs Utley]   The Action on the Case between Edward Scot Plt. and John Utley Deft. is dismist the Plt. not prosecuting the same.

Absent William Mayo Gent.

Mayo vs Martain   In the Action of Trespass on the Case between William Mayo Plt. and John.Martain Defendt. the Deft. appears and confesses a Judgment for the Plt. for nine pounds fifteen shillings and seven pence farthing Currant money whereupon it is considered by the Court that the Plt. do recover against the Deft. the said sum together with the costs of this Suit and a Lawyers Fee.

Present William Mayo Gent.

Hatcher vs Syms   In the Action of Trespass on the Case between Henry Hatcher Assignee of Samuell Hatcher Plt. and Richard Syms Defendt. the Sherif having made return on the Alias Capias that the Deft. is not to be found and he failing to appear on the Plts. motion a Pluries Capias is awarded against the Deft. returnable to the next Court.

Wood vs Hoggat   The Action of Debt between Henry Wood Plt. and Anthony Hoggat Defendt is continued.

[62]   December Court 1730
Cannon vs Bugg   The Attachment obtained by William Cannon against the Estate of William Bugg is continued.

Digges vs Woodson   The Action of Trespass on the Case between Dudley Digges Plt. and Joseph Woodson Deft. is continued at the Defts. cost.

Digges vs Lansdon   In the Action of Trespass on the Case between Dudley Digges Plt. and William Lansdon Defendt. the Parties submit themselves to the Court for tryal whereupon their Accounts Allegations and Witnesses being heard it is considered that the Plt. do recover against the Deft. the costs of this Suit and a Lawyers Fee.

Thompson vs Digges   On the motion of James Thompson a Witness for Dudley Digges vs William Lansdon it is ordered that the said Dudley do pay him for one days attendance thirty pounds of tobacco with Costs.

Bryan vs Chandler   In the Action of Trespass on the Case between William Bryan Plt. and Joel Chandler Defendt. the Deft. appears [but failing] to plead on the Plts. motion Judgment by nihil dicit is [granted] him against the Deft. for what damages shall be recovered in this Suit to be discharged nevertheless if the Deft. shall [plead] at the next Court.

Bryan vs Chandler   In the Action of Trespass on the Case between William [Bryan] Plt. and Joel Chandler Defendt. the Deft. appears but [failing] to plead on the Plts. motion Judgment by nihil dicit [is gr]anted him against the Deft. for what damages shall be recovered in this Suit to be discharged nevertheless if the Deft. sh[all] plead at the next Court.

Absent William Cabbell Gent.

Cabbell vs Utley   In the Action of Trespass on the Case between William Cabbell Plt. and John Utley Defendt. for four hundred and

[63]   December Court 1730
sixty pounds of tobacco the Sherif having made return on the Attachment granted in September Court that he cannot find any goods of the Defts. whereon he may serve the same on the Plts. motion the Deft. failing to appear an Attachment do novo is granted against the Defts. Estate returnable to the next Court.

Present William Cabbell Gent.

Dickins vs Utley   In the Action of Trespass on the Case between Thomas Dickins Plt. and John Utley Defendt. for five pounds five shillings Currt. money the Sherif having made return on the Attachment granted in September Court that he cannot find any goods of the Defts. whereon he may serve the same on the Plts. motion the Deft. failing to appear an Attachment de novo is granted against the Defts. Estate returnable to the next Court.

Macon vs Hughes   In the Action of Trespass on the Case between William Macon Plt. and Stephen Hughes Defendt. the Deft. appears but failing to plead on the Plts. motion Judgment by nihil dicit is granted him against the Deft. for what damages shall be recovered in this Suit to be discharged nevertheless if the Deft. shall plead at the next Court.

[Mallet vs Pruit]   In the Action of Trespass between Stephen Mallet Plt. and Thomas Pruit Defendt. the Deft. appears but failing to plead on the Plts. motion Judgment by nihil dicit is granted him against the Deft. for what damages shall be recovered in this Suit to be discharged nevertheless if the Deft. shall plead at the next Court.

Levins vs Farrar   In the Action of Trespass on the Case between Richard Levins Plt. and William Farrar Defendt. is dismist the Plt. not prosecuting the same.

[64]   December Court 1730
Chastain &c. vs Woodson   In the Action of Trespass on the Case between John Chastain & Peter Chastain Exrs. &c. of Peter Chastain deceased Plts. and Joseph Woodson Defendt. an imparlance is granted the Defendant.

Winfrey vs Woodson   In the Action on the Case between Jacob Winfrey Plt. and William Woodson Deft. an imparlance is granted the Defendant.

Cox vs Harris   The Action of Trespass on the Case between John Cox Plt. and David Harris Defendt. is dismist the Plt. not prosecuting the same.

Absent. William Cabbell Gent.

Woodson &c. vs Cabbell   In the Action of Debt between Josiah Woodson & Stephen Woodson Exrs. &c. of Jacob Woodson deceased Plts. and William Cabbell Defendt. the Sherif having made return that the Deft. is not to be found and he failing to appear on the motion of the Plts. an Alias Capias is awarded against the Deft. returnable to the next Court.

Present William Cabbell Gent.

Gates vs Saunders   In the Action of Trover between William Gates [Plt. and] Robert Saunders Deft. an imparlance is granted the [Deft.]

Hix &c. vs Tabor & Stovall   In the Action of Debt between Marmaduke Hix [Assignee] of William Mayo Plt. and John Tabor & Bartholom[ew] Stovall Defendts. the Sherif having returned the Defts. not to be found and he failing to appear on the Plts. mo[tion an] Alias Capias is awarded against him returnable to the [next] Court and the Deft. Stovall failing to appear on the [torn] Judgment is granted him against the said Deft. and [torn] Stovall his Common Bail for what damages shall be [recovered] in the Suit to be discharged nevertheless if the said [Deft.] shall appear at the next Court.

Absent John Fleming Gent.

Randolph &c. vs Mcbrid   In the Action of Trespass on the Case between Will[iam Randolph,]

[65]   December Court 1730
Randolph, John Randolph, Richard Randolph & John Fleming Executors &c. of Thomas Randolph deceased Plts. and John Mcbrid Defendt. the Deft. failing to appear on the motion of the Plts. Judgment is granted them against the Deft. and Dudley Digges Tarlton Fleming James Christian, James Nolun, John Martin Junr, John Webb, Francis Martin & Ashford Hughes his Common Bail for what damages shall be recovered in this Suit to be discharged nevertheless if the Deft. shall appear at the next Court.

Randolph &c. vs Dickinson   In the Action of Trespass on the Case between William Randolph, John Randolph, Richard Randolph, & John Fleming Exec'rs. &c. of Thomas Randolph deceased Plts. and John Dickinson Defendt. the Deft. failing to appear & the Sherif having returned Francis Martin his bail the Court are of opinion that the said bail is not sufficient and thereupon on the motion of the Plts. Judgment is granted them against the Deft. and Tarlton Fleming Gent. Sherif for what damages shall be recovered in this Suit to be discharged never the less if the Deft. shall appear at the next Court.

Randolph &c. vs Martin   In the Action of Trespass on the Case between William Randolph, John Randolph Richard Randolph & John Fleming Exec'rs. &c. of Thomas Randolph deceased Plts. and Francis

Martin Defendt. the Deft. appears and is ruled to Special Bail but failing therein and being in Custody of the Sherif on the motion of the Plts. Conditional Judgment is granted them for what damages shall be recovered in this Suit to be discharged nevertheless if the Deft. shall give Special Bail at the next Court.

Chastain &c. vs Martin   In the Action of Trespass on the Case between John Chastain & Peter Chastain Executors &c. of Peter Chastain dec'd Plts. and Francis Martin Defendt. the Defendant pleads he oweth nothing and the Suit is thereupon

[66]   December Court 1730 continued.

Then the Court adjourned to the third Tuesday in next Month.

****

At a Court held for Goochland County the third Tuesday in February being the sixteenth day of the Month Annoq. Domi. 1730 [1731].

Justices Sworn   A Commission from the Honourable William Gooch Esqr. his Majestys Lieutenant Governour and Commander in Chief of this Dominion to John Fleming William Mayo John Wood[son Daniell Stoner Tarlton Fleming Allin Howard Edward Scot [George Payne] William Cabbell James Holman Isham Randolph [James] Skelton, George Raine and Anthony Hoggatt Gent[lemen Justices] of the Peace for this County is read as also the D[idi]mus Administring the Oaths then James Holman and William Cabbell Gentlemen Administer the Oaths appointed by Act of Parliament to be taken instead of the Oaths of Allegiance and Supremacy the [torn] appointed to be taken by an Act of Parliament made in the first year of the Reign of his late Majesty King George the first intituled an Act for the further Security of his Majesty's person and Government and of the Succession of the Crown of Great Britain in [torn] heirs of the last Princess Sophia being Protestants and for [establishing] the hopes of the pretended Prince of Wales and his open a[torn] abettors unto William Mayo and Daniell Stoner Gentlemen [torn] also subscribe the Test take the Oath of a Justice of the Peace [torn] of a Justice in Chancery and then Administer the said Oath[s] [torn] Allin Howard William Cabbell and James Holman Gentlemen [torn] also Subscribe the Test.

Hoggatt takes Oaths   William Mayo and Daniell Stoner Gentlemen Adminis[ter the] Oaths appointed by Act of Parliament to be taken inst[ead of] the Oaths of Allegiance [and Sup]remacy the Oath appointed to be taken by an Act of [Parliament] [torn] the first year [torn] Reign of his late Majesty George the first intituled [torn]

[67]   February Court 1730 [1731]
Act for the further Security of his Majestys person and Government and of the Succession to the Crown of Great Britain in the heirs of the late Princess Sophia being Protestants and for extinguishing the hopes of the pretended Prince of Wales and his open and secret Abettors to Anthony Hoggat Gentleman who subscribes the Test.

   Present. Daniell Stoner Allin Howard William Cabbell
   and James Holman Gentlemen

Forcees Administration granted   Anne Forcee comes into Court and makes Oath that Francis Forcee deceasd died without any Will so far as she knows or believes and on her motion and giving Security for her just and faithfull Administration of the said Decedents Estate Probate is granted her for obtaining Letters of Administration [in due] form Anthony Rapene and William Sallee Securities.
  Ordered that Edward Scot Stephen Chastain John Paine and John Harris or any three of them being first sworn by some Justice of the Peace do appraise the Estate of Francis Forcee deceas'd and that Anne Forcee the Administratrix do return an Inventory thereof to the next Court.

Sallee's [torn] granted   William Sallee comes into Court and makes Oath that Isaac Sallee deceased died without any Will as far as he knows or believes and on his motion and giving security for his just and faithfull Administration of the said Decedents Estate Certificate is granted him for obtaining Letters of Administration in due form Anthony Rapene and John James Dupee Securities.
  Ordered that Francis James Edward Scot David Lesseur and Thomas Dickins or any three of them being first Sworn by some Justice of the Peace do appraise the Estate of Isaac Sallee deceasd and that William Sallee the Administrator do return an Inventory thereof to the next Court.

   [Absent. William] Mayo Gentleman

[68]   February Court 1730 [1731]
Jones Creek bridge to be built   Edward Scot undertakes to build a good

strong and Substantial bridge over Jones's Creek fit for Carts to pass and to keep the same in repair for the Space of Seven years after the same is finished and at the expiration of the said Term to leave the said bridge in good and sufficient repair for which it is considered by the Court that there be levy'd for the said Edward Scot and in his name at the laying on of the next County levy four thousand pounds of tobacco with Cask and Conveniency Provided the said bridge be then finished And that the said Edward Scot then or at any Court before enter into Bond with good and Sufficient Security to comply with the agreement aforesaid on his part made.

Beverdam Creek bridge to be built   Edward Scot undertakes to build a good Strong and Substantial bridge over Beverdam Creek fit for Carts to pass and to keep the same in repair for the Space of Seven years after the same is finished and after the expiration of the said Term to leave the said bridge in good and Sufficient repair for which it is considered by the Court that there be levyd for the said Edward Scot [and in his name at the] laying on of the next County levy five thou[sand pounds of tobacco] with Cask and Conveniency Provided the said [bridge be then] finished And that the said Edward Scot then or at any [Court before] enter into bond with good and Sufficient Security to [comply with] the agreement aforesaid on his part made.

Surveyor of the road   Edward Scot is appointed Surveyor of all the roads below [torn] in this County and of the road passing through the Man[torn]

Bingleys Deed to Robinson   Joseph Bingley acknowledges a Deed with the livery [of Seizin] endorsed from himself to James Robinson to be his Act and Deed and it is thereupon admitted to record, then S[torn] [wife] of the said Joseph (she being first privately examined) [relinquishes] her right of Dower in the land by the said Deed conve[yed which] is also admitted to record.

Atkinson chooses a Guardian   Robert Atkinson is permitted to choose Stephen Hug[hes as his] Guardian who accepts the Charge and enters into Bond [torn] Ashford and Isaac Hughes his Securities.

[69]   February Court 1730
Surveyor of road   Ordered that the severall Male labouring titheables in the Precincts whereof James Nowlin and David Walker are appointed Surveyors do jointly assist in repairing the bridge over Beverdam Creek on the Middle road.

Raine vs Martin   The Action of trespass on the Case between George Raine Plt. and Francis Martin Defendant is continued.

Armistrong vs Southerland   The Action of trespass on the Case between Armistrong Plt. and George Southerland Defendant is continu'd.

Prosser vs Mcbrid   The Action of debt between Thomas Prosser Plaintiff and John Mcbrid Defendant is continu'd.

Raine vs Dickinson   The Action of trespass on the Case between George Raine Plaintiff and John Dickinson Defendant is continu'd.

[Woodson vs Taylor]   [In the] Action of trespass on the Case between Joseph Woodson [Plaint]iff and John Taylor Defendant is continued.

[King vs Christian]   The Action of trespass between Martin King Plaintiff and James Christian Defendant is dismist neither party appearing.

[Scot vs King]   The Action of trespass between Edward Scot Plt. and Martin King Defendant is dismist neither party appearing.

[Woodson vs Hughes]   The Action of trespass on the Case between Joseph Woodson Plaintiff and Stephen Hughes Defendant is continued.

[Fleming vs Bates]   In the Action of Debt between Tarlton Fleming Plaintiff and Isaac Bates Defendant for one thousand pounds of tobacco due for the Defendants not listing himself as a titheable in St. James's Parish the Defendant appears and confesses a Judgment to the Plt whereupon it is considered by the Court that the Plaintiff do recover against the Defendant one thousand pounds of Tobacco with Costs.

[70]   February Court 1730 [1731]
Merriwether vs Martin   The Action of Debt between William Merriwether Plaintiff and Francis Martin Defendant is continued.

Prosser vs Martin   The Action of trespass on the Case between Thomas Prosser Plt and Francis Martin Defendant is continued.

Quantin vs Taylor   The Action of Trespass on the Case between John Quantin Plaintiff and James Taylor Defendant is continued.

The Action of debt between Charles Johnson Plaintiff and John Surls Defendant is dismist neither party appearing.

Dickins vs Dept   The Action of debt between Thomas Dickins Plaintiff and Peter Dept Defendant is continued.

The action of Trespass on the Case between William Thomas Plaintiff and Walker Coley Defendant is dismist neither party appearing.

Thomas vs Gee   The Action on the Case between Rowland Thomas Plantiff and Gilbert Gee Defendant is continued.

Bumpuss vs Moreman   The Action of trespass on the Case between Samuell Bumpuss Assignee of Robert Bumpuss Plaintiff and Andrew Moreman Defendant is continued at the Defts. Costs

Johnson vs Pruit   The Action of trespass on the Case between Charles Johnson and his Wife Plaintiffs and Andrew Pruit Defendant is continued.

   Absent Allin Howard Gentleman

Howard vs Woodson   In the Action of Debt between Allen Howard Plaintiff and Joseph Woodson Defendant the Defendant failing to appear and the Sheriff having returned no Bail on the Plaintiffs motion Judgment is granted him against the Defendant and Tarlton Fleming Gentleman Sheriff for what damages shall br recovered in this Suit to be discharg'd nevertheless if the Defendant shall appear at next Court.

[71] February Court 1730 [1731]
   Present Allin Howard Gentleman

Ward vs Farrar   The action of debt between Seth Ward Plaintiff and John Farrar Defendant is continued.

Lewins vs Farrar   The Action on the Case between Richard Levins Plaintiff and John Sutton Farrar Defendant is dismist neither party appearing.

Pruit vs Boccar   The Action on the Case between Hugh Pruit Plaintiff and Peter Boccar Defendant is continued.

Sallee vs Bowie   The Action of trespass on the Case between Isaac Sallee Assignee of Thomas Jevodan Plaintiff and John Bowie Defendant is dismist the Plaintiff being dead.

Webber vs White   The Action of trespass on the Case between Philip Webber Assignee of James Elliot Plaintiff and Edward White Defendant is continued.

Jackson vs Southerland   The Action of trespass on the Case between John Jackson Assignee of Edward Birch Plaintiff and George Southerland Defendant is continued.

Digges vs Napier   The Action on the Case between Dudley Digges Plaintiff and Bouth Napier Defendant is continued.

Happer vs Harper   The Action on the Case between William Happer Plaintiff and Henry Harper Defendant is continued.

Stidum vs Bingley &c   The Action of debt between Benjamin Stidum Plaintiff and Joseph Bingley and William Lansdon Defendants is Continued.

Moseby vs Taylor   The Action of debt between Richard Moseby Plaintiff and John Taylor Defendant is continued.

[72]   February Court 1730 [1731]

Digges vs Hughes   The Action of Trespass on the Case between Dudley Digges Plaintiff and Stephen Hughes Defendant is Continued.

Digges vs Mullin   The Action on the Case between Dudley Digges Plaintiff and Patrick Mullin Defendant is continued.

Digges vs Taylor   The Action of trespass on the Case between Dudley Digges Plaintiff and James Taylor Defendant is continued.

Thomas vs May   The Action of trespass on the case between William Thomas Plaintiff and William May Defendant is continued.

Lockit vs James   The Action of trespass on the Case between Thomas Lockit Plt. and Francis James Defendant is continued.

Parish vs Watkins.   The Action of trespass on the Case between John Parish junr. Plaintiff and Joseph Watkins Defendant is Continued.

Winston vs Nolun   The Action of Debt between Isaac Winston Plaintiff and Agnes Nolun Administratrix &c of Thomas Nolun deceased is continued.

Hambleton vs Nolun   The Action of debt between James Hambleton Plaintiff and Agnes Nolun Administratrix &c of Thomas Nolun deceas'd Defendant is continued.

Macon vs Wharton   The Action of the Case between John Macon Plaintiff and Thomas Wharton Defendant is continued.

Waddill vs Edwards   The Action on the Case between William Waddell junr. Plaintiff and Thomas Edwards Defendant is continued.

Pruit vs Johnson   In the Action on the Case between Andrew Pruit Plaintiff and Charles Johnson Defendant the Plt takes Issue on the Defendants Plea of nil debet the tryall whereof is referred to the next Court.

Marchbanks vs Croom   The Action on the Case between George Marchbanks Plt and Daniel Croom Defendant is continued.

[73]   February Court 1730 [1731]
Salmon vs Edwards   The Action on the Case between Thomas Salmon Plaintiff and Thomas Edwards Defendant is continued.

Pigg vs Allen   The Action on the Case between John Pigg Junr. Plaintiff and Samuell Allen Defendant is continued.

Ware vs Saunders   The Action of trespass on the Case between Susanna Ware Plt and William Saunders Deft. is continued at the Defendants Cost.

Flournoy vs Martin   The Action of trespass on the Case between John James Flournoy Plaintiff and Francis Martin Defendant is continued.

Flournoy vs Martin   The Action of Debt between John James Flournoy and Elizabeth his Wife Executrix &c of Orland[o] Jones deceased Plaintiffs and Francis Martin Defendant is continued.

Thompson vs Edwards   The Action of trespass on the Case between Samuell Thompson and Mary his Wife Plts and Thomas Edwards Defendt. is continued.

Bradley vs Saunders   The Action of trespass on the Case between Joseph Bradley Plaintiff and John Saunders Defendant is continued.

Napier vs Ashlin   The Action on the Case between Bouth Napier

Plaintiff and Joseph Ashlin Defendant is continued at Plts Costs.

Prosser vs Napier   The Action of trespass on the Case between Thomas Prosser Plt and Bouth Napier Defendant is continued.

Woodson vs Napier   The Action of trespass on the Case between William Woodson Plaintiff and Bouth Napier Defendant is continued.

Ward vs Dean   The Action of debt between Seth Ward Plaintiff and Richard Dean Defendant is continued.

Ford vs Pruit   The Action of trespass on the Case between James Ford Plaintiff and Thomas Pruit Defendt. is continued.

[74]   February Court 1730 [1731]
Turpin vs Hook & Bilboe   The Action of the Case between Mathew Turpin Assignee of John Welsh Plaintif and John Peter Bilboe and James Hooke Defts continued.

Scot vs Daniell   The Action of Detinue between Edward Scot and James Daniell Defendant is continued at the Plts Costs.

Scot & vs Pruit   The Action of trespass on the Case between Edward Scot Administrator &c of John Stephens deceas'd Plaintiff and Thomas Pruit Defendant is continued.

Taylor vs Lowe & Ux   The Action of trespass on the Case between John Taylor Plaintiff and Thomas Lowe and Amey his Wife Defendants is Continued.

Lad & Powell vs Thompson   The Petition of Amos Lad and Roger Powell against Samuell Thompson and Mary his Wife is continued.

Martain vs Fleming   The Action of trespass on the Case between John Martain Plt and John Fleming Admr. &c of Paul Pennington Deceas'd Defendant is continued.

Rocket vs Dickins   The Action of trespass on the Case between Baldwin Rockett Plt and Thomas Dickins Defendant is continued.

The Action of trespass on the Case between Robert Downing Plt and Robert Allen Defendant is dismist neither party appearing.

The Action of trespass on the Case between Robert Downing Plt and John Cunningham Defendant is dismist neither party appearing.

Wood vs White   In the Action on the Case between Henry Wood Plaintiff and Edward White Defendant the Defendant failing to appear on the Plaintiffs motion Judgment is granted him against the Defendant and John Lad his Common Bail for what damages shall be recovered in this Suit to be discharged nevertheless if the Defendant appears at the next Court.

The Action of trespass on the Case between Andrew Moreman

[75]   February Court 1730 [1731]
Moreman Plaintiff and Valentine Amos Defendant is dismist the Defendant being dead.

The Action of trespass on the Case between John Woodson Plaintiff and Andrew Moreman Defendant is dismist neither party appearing.

David vs Quantin   The Action on the Case between Anne David Executrix &c of Peter David deceased Plaintiff and John Quantin Defendant is continued.

Hopkins vs Woodson   The Action of trespass on the Case between William Hopkins Plaintiff and Benjamin Woodson Defendant is continued.

Dickins vs Dupuy. The Action of trespass on the Case between Thomas Dickins Plt and Francis Dupuy Defendant is continued.

Burgess vs Woodson   The Action of trespass on the Case between John Burgess Plt and John Woodson Defendant is continued.

Winfrey vs Williams   The Action of trespass on the Case between Jacob Winfrey Plt and John Williams Defendant is continued.

Hatcher vs Syms   The Action of trespass on the Case between Henry Hatcher Assignee of Samuell Hatcher Plaintiff and Richard Syms Defendant is continued.

Wood vs Hoggat   The Action of debt between Henry Wood Plt and Anthony Hoggat Defendant is continued.

Cannon vs Bugg   The Attachment obtained by William Cannon Plaintiff and William Bugg Defendant is dismist the said Cannon not appearing.

Digges vs Woodson   The Action of trespass on the Case between Dudley Digges Plt and Joseph Woodson is continued.

[76]   February Court 1730 [1731]
Bryant vs Chandler   The action of trespass on the Case between William Bryant Plaintiff and Joell Chandler Defendant is continued.

Briant vs Chandler   The Action of trespass on the Case between William Bryant Plaintiff and Joell Chandler Defendant is continued.

Dickins vs Utley   The Action of trespass on the Case between Thomas Dickins Plaintiff and John Utley Defendant is continued.

Macon vs Hughes   The Action of trespass on the Case between John Macon Plaintiff and Stephen Hughes Defendant is continued.

Mallet vs Pruit   The Action of Trespass between Stephen Mallet Plaintiff and Thomas Pruit Defendant is continued.

Chastains Exec'rs vs Woodson   The Action of trespass on the Ca[se between Joh]n and Peter Chastain Executors &c of Peter Chastain [Plt. and] Joseph Woodson Defendt. is continued.

Winfrey vs Woodson   The Action on the Case between Jacob [Winfrey] Plaintiff and William Woodson Defendant is continued.

Gates vs Saunders   The Action of Trover between William Gates Plaintiff and Robert Saunders Defendant continued.

Hix vs Tabor &c   In the Action of Debt between Marmaduke Hix Assignee of William Mayo Plaintiff and John Tabor and Bartholomew Stoveall Defendants the Defendants plead they owe nothing.

Randolphs Exec'rs vs Mcbrid   The Action of trespass on the Case between William Randolph Richard Randolph John Randolph and John Fleming Executors &c of Thomas Randolph deceas'd Plaintiffs and John Mcbrid Defendant is continued at the Plaintiffs Cost.

Randolphs Exec'rs vs Dickinson   The Action of trespass on the Case between William Randolph Richard Randolph John Randolph & John

Fleming Executors &c of

[77] February Court 1730 [1731]
&c of Thomas Randolph deceas'd Plaintiffs and John Dickinson Defendant is continued.

Randolphs Exrs. vs Martin   The Action of trespass on the Case between William Randolph Richard Randolph John Randolph and John Fleming Executors &c of Thomas Randolph deceased Plts and Francis Martin Defendant is continued at the Plaintiffs Cost.

Chastains Exec'rs. vs Martin   The Action of trespass on the Case between John and Peter Chastain Exec'rs &c of Peter Chastain deceased Plaintiffs and Francis Martin Defendant is continued at Plaintifs Cost.

Dickins vs Richards   The Action of trespass on the Case between Thomas Dickins Plt and John Richards Defendant is Continued.

The Ac[tion of] [torn] between Ashford Hughes Plaintiff and Barth[olomew Cox] Defendant is Dismist the Defendant being dead.

Scot vs Stone   In the A[ction of] trespass on the Case between Edward Scot Plaintiff and [Thomas] Stone Defendant the Defendant pleads he oweth nothing [and for] tryall thereof puts himself upon the Country and the Plaintiff likewise.

Prosser vs May   The Action of Trespass on the Case between Thomas Prosser Plaintiff and William May Defendant is continued.

Davis vs Quin. The Action of Debt between George Davis Plaintiff and John Quin Defendant is Continued.

The Action of trespass on the Case between John Martin Plaintiff and Peter Boccar Defendant is dismist neither party appearing.

The Action of trespass on the Case between Thomas Stone Plt and Jacob Winfrey Defendant is dismist neither party appearing

[78] February Court 1730 [1731]
Dixon vs Napier The Action of debt between Thomas Dixon Plaintiff and Bouth Napier Defendant is continued.

Thompson vs Farrar   The Action of debt between James Thompson

Plaintiff and William Farrar Defendant is continued.

The Action of Debt between William Mills Plaintiff and Robert Wade Defendant is dismissted neither party appearing.

Ligon vs Mingo   The Action of trespass on the Case between Mathew Ligon Plaintiff and Benjamin Mingo Defendant is continued.

Stone vs Fearman   In the Action of debt between Thomas Stone Plaintiff and Phillip Fearman Defendant the Plaintiff having failed to file his declaration on the Defendants Motion he is non Suited and it is thereupon considered by the Court that the Defendant go hence without day and that he recover against the Plaintiff five shillings Currt. money together with his Costs by him in this behalf expended and Lawyers Fee.

Taylor vs Quin   The Action of trespass on the Case between James Taylor Plaintiff and John Quin Defendant is continued.

Taylor vs Quin   The Action of Debt between James Taylor Plaintiff and John Quin Defendant is continued.

The Action of trespass on the Case between Robert Hughes Plaintiff and Peter Calvit Defendant is dismist neither party appearing.

The Action of trespass on the Case between Samuell Thompson Plaintiff and William Halliday Defendant is dismist neither party appearing.

King vs Medlock   The Action of trespass on the Case between Martin King Plaintiff and William Medlock Defendant is continued.

[79]   February Court 1730 [1731]
Saunders vs Quin   The Action of debt between John Saunders Assignee of David Harris Plaintiff and John Quin Defendant is continued.

Surveyor of road   Ordered that the titheables of William Chamberlaine under the care of William May, Charles Spurlock and John Richardson and their tytheables do Assist John Mcbird in Clearing the road of which he is appointed Surveyor.

Surveyor of road   On the Motion of Henry Wood who was formerly appointed Surveyor of the road from Tuckahoe Creek Mill into the river road towards the Church and Ferry, It is Ordered that he do clear the said Road such way as he shall judge most convenient so as the same do not prejudice any Persons Plantation by passing through it.

Absent Allin Howard Gentleman

Sheriffs recommended   Pursuant to an Act of Assembly of this Colony entituled an Act Subscribing the Methods of appointing Sheriffs &c. Tarlton Fleming   Allen Howard and George Payne Gent. are recommended to the Honourable William Gooch Esqr his Majestys Lieutenant Governour of whom one may be appointed to execute the Office of Sheriff for the ensuing year.

Then the Court adjourned to the third Tuesday in next Month

****

At a Court held for Goochland County the third Tuesday in March being the sixteenth day of the Month Annoq. Domini [1730] [1731].

Justices Sworn   Daniell Stoner and Allen Howard Gentlemen
Administer

[80]   March Court 1730 [1731]
the Oaths appointed by Act of Parliament to be taken instead of the Oaths of Allegiance and Supremacy the Oath appointed to be taken by an Act of Parliament made in the first year of the Reign of his late Majesty King George the first entituled an Act for the further Security of his Majestys person and Government and of the Succession to the Crown of Great Brittain in the heirs of the late Princess Sophia being Protestants and for extinguishing the hopes of the pretended Prince of Wales and his open and secret Abettors unto John Woodson and George Payne Gentlemen who Subscribe the Test and take the Oath of a Justice of the Peace and a Justice in Chancery.

Present. John Woodson Daniell Stoner Allen Howard
George Payne Gentlemen Justices

Ballews deed to Walton   Thomas Ballew and Leonard Ballew acknowledge a Deed with the livery of Seizin endorsed from themselves to William Walton to be their Act and deed and it is thereupon admitted to Record then Susanna Wife of the said Leonard Ballew (she being first privately examined) relinquish'd her right of Dower in the Land by the said deed convey'd which is also admitted to record.

Amos's Adm'on granted   Francis Amos comes into Court and makes Oath that Valentine Amos deceased died without making any Will so farr as he knows or beleives and on his Motion and giving security for his just and faithfull administration of the said Decedents Estate Certificate is granted him for obtaining Letters of Administration in due form Stephen Hughes and Daniell Wilmoore entring themselves securities for the Same.

Ordered that Robert Wade, Samuell Burk, Jonas Lawson and James Nevills or any three of them being first Sworn by some Justice of the peace do appraise the estate of Valentine Amos deceas'd and that Francis Amos the Administrator do present an Inventory thereof to the next Court.

Burgamys Will proved   The last Will and Testament of John Burgamy deceas'd is presented.

[81]   March Court 1730 [1731]
presented in Court by Elizabeth Burgamy and the same being prove by the Oaths of Richard Parker and Mich. Parker Witnesses thereto it is admitted to record and on the Motion of the said Elizabeth (she having refused to take upon her the execution thereof or to claim anything thereby) and her performing what is usuall in Such Cases Certificate is granted her for obtaining Letters of Administration with the Will annexed in due form John Owen and Joel Chandler entring themselves securities for the same.

Ordered that Richard Parker   George Stoveall   Luke Wiles and William Mosely or any three of them being first Sworn by some Justices of the Peace do appraise the estate of John Burgamy deceas'd and that Elizabeth Burgamy his Administratrix do present an Inventory thereof to the next Court.

Farrars Admin'on granted   Richard Levins comes into Court and makes Oath that John Sutton Farrar deceased died without making any Will so farr as he knows or beleives and on his Motion and giving Security for his just and faithfull Administration of the said decedents Estate Certificate is granted him for obtaining Letters of Administration in due form Richard Moseby and Nowell Burton Securities.

Ordered that Robert Burton   Robert Adams   Thomas Wadloe and Samuell Allen or any three of them being first sworn by some Justice of the Peace do appraise the Estate of John Sutton Farrar deceas'd and that Richard Levins the Administrator do present an Inventory thereof to the next Court.

The Action of Trespass on the Case between Samuell Allen Plaintiff and

James Holman Defendant is dismist neither party appearing.

Cabbell vs Utley   In the Action of trespass on the Case between William Cabbell Plaintiff and John Utley Defendant for four hundred and sixty pounds of tobacco the Sheriff having made return on the Attachment granted at December Court that he cannot find any goods of the Defendants whereupon he may serve the same on the

[82]   March Court 1730 [1731]
Plaintiffs motion the Defendant failing to appear an Attachment de novo is granted against the Defendants Estate returnable to the next Court.

Woodson vs Cabbell   In the Action of debt between Josiah and Stephen Woodson Executors &c of Robert Woodson deceas'd Plaintiffs and William Cabbell Defendant the Plaintiffs file a new declaration.

The Action of trespass between James Holman Plaintiff and Anthony Charon Defendant is dismist neither party appearing.

Raine vs Martin   In the Action of trespass on the Case between George Paine Plaintiff and Francis Martin Defendant the Defendant failing to appear on the Plaintiffs Motion Judgment is granted him against the Defendt. and Dudley Digges who is returned his Common Bail for so much Damages as shall be recovered in this Suit to be discharged nevertheless if the Defendant shall appear at the next Court.

Armistrong vs Southerland   In the Action of trespass on the Case between Robert Armistrong Plaintiff and George Southerland Defendant the Defendant appears and confesses a Judgment for forty shillings Current money whereupon it is considered by the Court that the Plaintiff do recover against the Defendant forty shillings Current Money with the Costs of this Suit and a Lawyers Fee.

Raine vs Dickinson   In the Action of trespass on the Case between George Raine Plaintiff and John Dickinson defendant the Defendant failing to appear on the Plaintiffs motion Judgment is granted him for what damages shall be recovered in this Suit against the defendant and Tarlton Fleming Gentleman Sheriff to be discharged nevertheless if the Defendant appears at the next Court.

Woodson vs Taylor   The Action of trespass on the Case between Joseph Woodson Plaintiff and John Taylor Defendant is dismist the Plt not prosecuting the same.

[83]   March Court 1730 [1731]
Woodson vs Hughes   In the Action of trespass on the Case between Joseph Woodson Plaintiff and Stephen Hughes Defendant the Defendant pleads he oweth nothing and for tryall thereon puts himself upon the Country and the Plaintiff likewise.

Prosser vs Mcbrid   In the Action of Debt between Thomas Prosser Plaintiff and John Mcbrid Defendant the Defendant confesses Judgment for fourteen hundred pounds of sweet scented tobacco and Cask convenient to Pamunkey River and four pounds seven shillings and ninepence Current money whereupon it is considered by the Court that the Plaintiff do recover against the Defendant the said tobacco and money with the Costs of this Suit and a Lawyers Fee.

Merriwether vs Martin   In the Action of debt between William Merriwether Plaintiff and Francis Martin Defendant the Defendant failing to appear on the Plaintiffs Motion Judgment is granted him against the Defendant and Tarlton Fleming Gentleman Sheriff for what damages shall be recovered in this Suit to be discharges nevertheless if the Defendant shall appear at the next Court.

Prosser vs Martin   In the Action of trespass on the Case between Thomas Prosser Plaintiff and Francis Martin Defendant the Defendant failing to appear on the Plaintiffs Motion Judgment is granted him against the Defendant and Tarlton Fleming Gentleman Sheriff for what damages shall be recovered in this Suit to be discharged nevertheless if the Defendant shall appear at the next Court.

Quantin vs Taylor   In the Action of trespass on the Case between John Quantin Plaintiff and James Taylor Defendant the Defendant failing to appear on the Plaintiffs Motion Judgment is granted him against the Defendant and Peter Chastain his Common Bail for what damages shall be recovered in this Suit to be discharged nevertheless if the Defendant shall appear at the next Court.

[84]   March Court 1730 [1731]
Dickins vs Dept   The Action of debt between Thomas Dickins Plaintiff and Peter Dept Defendant is dismist the Plaintiff not prosecuting the same.

Thomas vs Gee   In the Action on the case between Rowland Thomas Plaintiff and Gilbert Gee Defendant the parties waive the Demurrer and thereupon the following Jury are Sworn William Womack Robert Wade

Joseph Watkins James Nevills Thomas Turpin John Price William Lansdon George Southerland Joseph Hooper Henry Harper Henry Webb Nathaniell Bassett who after some time bring in their Verdict which on the Plaintiffs Motion is ordered to be recorded by the Court and is as followeth. "Wee find for the Plaintiff thirty one Shillings and three pence William Womack foreman" whereupon it is considered by the Court that the Plaintiff do recover against the Defendant thirty one Shillings and threepence by the Jurors aforesaid in their said Verdict Assess'd together with the Costs of this Suit and a Lawyers Fee.

Wooldridge vs Thomas   John Wooldridge of Henrico County having attended twelve days as a Wittness for Rowland Thomas vs Gilbert Gee, it is Ordered that the said Rowland do pay him for the same and for coming and returning twenty Miles eleven times thirteen hundred and eighty pounds of tobacco with Costs. Ordered that only eight days attendance and seven times coming and returning be taxed in the bill of Costs.

Bumpuss vs Moreman   The Action of trespass on the Case between Samuell Bumpuss Assignee of Robert Bumpuss Plaintiff and Andrew Moreman Defendant is dismist the Plaintiff not prosecuting the same.

Ward vs Farrar   The Action of debt between Seth Ward Plaintiff and John Farrar Defendant is continued at the Plaintiffs Cost.

Pruit vs Boccar   In the Action on the Case between Hugh Pruit Plaintiff and Peter Boccar Defendant an Imparlance is granted the Defendant.

Webber vs White   In the Action of trespass on the Case between Phillip Webber Assignee of

[85]   March Court 1730 [1731]
of James Elliot Plaintiff and Edward White Defendant the Defendant failing to appear on the Plaintiffs Motion Judgment is granted him against the Defendant and John Lad who is returned his Common Bail for what damages shall be recovered in this Suit to be discharged nevertheless if the Defendant shall appear at the next Court.

Jackson vs Southerland   In the Action of trespass on the Case between John Jackson Assignee of Edward Birch Plaintiff and George Southerland Defendant the Plaintiff failing to prosecute his Suit on the Defendants Motion his is nonsuited and it is thereupon considered by the Court that the Defendant do recover against the Plaintiff five Shillings Current

Money with his Costs by him in this behalf expended and a Lawyers Fee.

Digges vs Napier   In the Action on the Case between Dudley Digges Plaintiff and Bouth Napier Defendant Thomas Dickins Attorney for the Defendant confesses a Judgment to the Plaintiff for one pound Seventeen Shillings and ten pence half penny Current money where upon it is considered by the Court that the Plaintiff do recover against the Defendant the said sum with Costs of the Suit and a Lawyers Fee.

Stidum vs Bingley & Lansdon   In the Action of debt between Benjamin Stidum Plaintiff and Joseph Bingley and William Lansdon Defendants The Defendant in Chancery who is Plaintiff at Common Law Demurrs generally to the Complainants Bill of Injunction.

Moseby vs Taylor   The Action of debt between Richard Moseby Plaintiff and John Taylor Defendant is continued.

Digges vs Hughes   In the Action of trespass on the Case between Dudley Digges Plaintiff and Stephen Hughes Defendant the Defendant appears but failing to plead judgment by nihil dicit is granted the Plaintiff against the Defendant for what damages shall be recovered in this Suit to be discharged nevertheless if the Defendant shall plead at the next Court.

[86]   March Court 1730 [1731]
Digges vs Mullin   In the Action on the Case between Dudley Digges Plaintiff and Patrick Mullen Defendant Thomas Dickins on behalf of the Defendant confesses Judgment to the Plaintiff for four pounds five Shillings and ten pence Current money whereupon it is considered by the Court that the Plaintiff do recover against the Defendant the said Sum with the Costs of this Suit and Lawyers Fee.

Digges vs Taylor   In the Action of trespass on the Case between Dudley Digges Plaintiff and James Taylor Defendant the Defendant pleads he oweth nothing and for tryall puts himself upon the Country and the Plaintiff likewise.

Thomas vs May   In the Action of trespass on the Case between William Thomas Plaintiff and William May Defendant the Plaintiff failing to prosecute his Suite on the Defendants motion he is nonsuited and it is thereupon considered by the Court that the Defendant do recover against the Plaintiff five Shillings Current money with his Costs by him in this behalf expended and a Lawyers Fee.

Locket vs James   The Action of trespass between Thomas Locket Plaintiff and Francis James Defendant is continued.

Parish vs Watkins   In the Action of trespass on the Case between John Parish junr. Plaintiff and Joseph Watkins Defendant by consent of the parties the Demurrer is waived and Judgment is to be entred against the Plaintiff for ten Shillings Current money (he failing to prosecute his Suit) and it is thereupon considered by the Court that the Defendant do recover against the Plaintiff ten shillings Current money with the Costs by him in this behalf expended wherein no Fee is to be taxed.

Raine vs McCartny   George Raine brings into Court Patrick McCartny his Servant Who having absented himself from his said Masters Service twenty five days and the expences in taking him up two severel times and the damage sustained by his selling his Cloaths being computed at nine hundred and fifty pounds of tobacco it is considered by the Court that the said Patrick do serve his

[87]   March Court 1730 [1731]
said Master Sixty four weeks and one day after his time by Custom or Indenture is expired and also for the Costs accrewing hereon according to Law.

Justice Sworn   John Woodson and Daniell Stoner Gentleman Administer the Oaths appointed by Act of Parliament to be taken instead of the Oaths of Allegiance and Supremacy the Oath appointed to be taken by an Act of Parliament made in the first year of the Reign of his late Majesty King George the first entituled an Act for the further Security of his Majesty's person and Government and of the Succession to the Crown of Great Brittain in the heirs of the late Princess Sophia being protestants and for extinguishing the hopes of the pretended Prince of Wales and his open and Secret Abettors unto George Raine Gentleman who Subscribes the Test and takes the Oath of a Justice of the Peace and of a Justice in Chancery.

Present. George Raine Gentleman

Ware vs Saunders   In the Action of trespass on the Case between Susanna Ware Plaintiff and William Saunders Defendant the following Jury are Sworn William Womack William Lansdon Joseph Watkins George Southerland Thomas Turpin Joseph Hooper John Price Henry Harper Henry Webb Robert Wade James Nevills Nathaniell Bassett but not being agreed on their Verdict at the Rising of the Court it is Ordered that they be kept together by the Sheriff untill they are agreed that they deliver their Verdict to Sheriff and that they appear to morrow and present it to the Court.

Absent. Daniel Stoner Gent.

Stoner vs Hughes   On the Petition of Daniell Stoner vs Isaac Hughes and Martha his Wife Executrix &c of George Cox deceas'd praying that the said Daniell may be discharged from his being Security for the said Martha Stephen Hughes and Ashford Hughes offer themselves to be bound with the said Isaac according to the Condicon of

[88]   March Court 1730 [1731]
the former Bond and being approved by the Court the Peticon is continued that a Bond may be prepared to be signed at the next Court.

Stoner vs Utley   In the Action of trespass on the Case between Daniell Stoner Plaintiff and John Utley Defendant the Sherif having made return that the Defendant is not to be found and he failing to appear on the Plaintiffs motion an Alias Capias is awarded against the Defendt. returnable to the next Court.

Constable Sworn   Thomas Wharton is Sworn Constable from Great Lickinghole Creek upwards.

Hughes vs Cox   On the Motion of Ashford Hughes Ordered that John and Frederick Cox be Summoned to appear at the next Court to prove the last Will of Bartholomew Cox deceas'd or to refuse the same.

Then the Court adjourned till to morrow morning ten of the Clock.

****

At a Court continued and held for Goochland County the seventeenth day of March 1730 [1731]. Present. Daniell Stoner Allen Howard George Paine William Cabbell George Raine Gent. Justices.

Manacanton road   On the Motion of Edward Scot for leave to alter the road which passes through the Manacanton low grounds it is Ordered that Glaude [Claude] Gore an[d] Gideon Chambon be Summoned to appear at the next Court to make their objections thereto.

Grand Jury to be Summoned   Pursuant to the direccons of an Act of

Assembly of this Colony intitul'd an Act concerning Jurys it is Ordered that the Sheriff Summon twenty four Freeholders of this County to appear at May Court of whom a Grand Jury may be impanelled to serve for this County.

[89]   March Court 1730 [1731]
Ware vs Saunders   The Jury Sworn yesterday in the Action of trespass on the Case between Susanna Ware Plt and William Saunders Deft. now appear and present their Verdict which on the Plts motion is admitted to record and is as followeth "Wee find for the Plt five pounds Current money and twelve hundred pounds of tobacco in Cask William Womack Foreman." the Deft. files reasons to Arrest the judgment the Arguments whereon are referred to be heard at the next Court.

Wilkinson vs Ware   On the Motion of David Wilkinson of New Kent County a Wittness for Susanna Ware vs William Saunders it is Ordered that the said Susanna do pay him for Seven days Attendance and for coming and returning fifty Miles Six times thirteen hundred and twenty pounds of tobacco with Costs. Ordered that only Six days Attendance and five times coming and returning be taxed in the Bill of Costs the Suit being continued at Novembr Court at the Plts Cost.

Dod vs Ware   On the Motion of John Dod of New Kent County a Wittness for Susanna Ware vs William Saunders it is Ordered that the said Susanna do pay him for five days Attendance and for coming and returning fifty miles four times nine hundred pounds of tobacco with Costs Ordered that only four days Attendance and three times coming and returning be taxed in the Bill of Costs the Suit being continued at November Court at the Plts Costs.

Boulton vs Ware   On the motion of Charles Boulton of New Kent County a Wittness for Susanna Ware vs William Saunders it is Ordered that the said Susanna do pay him for seven days Attendance and for coming and returning fifty two miles six times thirteen hundred and fifty six pounds of tobacco with Costs. Ordered that only Six days Attendance and five times coming and returning be taxed in the Bill of Costs the Suit being continued at November Court at the Plts Cost.

Wilkinson vs Saunders   On the motion of Francis Wilkinson of New Kent County a Witness

[90]   March Court 1730 [1731]
for William Saunders ads Susanna Ware it is Ordered that the said William

do pay him for ten days Attendance and for coming and returning fifty five miles eight times nineteen hundred and twenty pounds of tobacco with Costs Memorandum that this Wittness attended one day in August two days in September before the day of tryall and one day in February when the Suit was continued at the Defendants Costs.

Moor vs Saunders   On the motion of James Moor of New Kent County a Witness for William Saunders ads Susanna Ware it is Ordered that the said William do pay him for nine days Attendance and for coming and returning fifty miles seven times fifteen hundred and ninety pounds of tobacco with Costs Memorandum that this Wittness attended one day in August and two days in September before the day of tryall.

Present William Mayo Gent.

Clopton vs Saunders   On the motion of Joyce Clopton of New Kent County a Witness for William Saunders ads Susanna Ware it is Ordered that the said William do pay her for Seven days Attendance and for coming and returning fifty miles five times eleven hundred and seventy pounds of tobacco with Costs. Memorandum that this Witness attended one day in August and two days in September before the day of tryall.

Johnson vs Pruit   The Action of trespass on the Case between Charles Johnson and Elizabeth his Wife Plts and Andrew Pruit Deft. is continued and it is Ordered that the Issue joined thereon be try'd at the next Court.

Happer vs Harper   In the Action on the Case between William Happer Plt and Henry Harper Deft. the Deft. confesses himself indebted unto the Plt in the Sum of thirty Shillings Currt. money whereupon it is considered by the Court that the Plt do recover against the Defendt. the said sum with the Costs of this Suit and a Lawyers Fee.

[91]   March Court 1730 [1731]
Winston vs Nolun   In the Action of debt between Isaac Winston Plt and Agnes Nolun Admrx &tc. of Thomas Nolun deceased Deft. the Deft pleads plene administravit and for tryall thereof puts herself upon the Country and the Plt likewise.

Hambleton vs Nolun   In the Action of debt between James Hambleton Plt and Agnes Nolun Admrx &c. of Thomas Nolun deceas'd Deft. the Deft. failing to appear the Conditionall Judgment formerly granted in this Suit against the Deft. is on the Plts motion confirmed for so much damages as shall be found upon executing a Writt of inquiry of Damages at the next Court of the Execution whereof the Sheriff is hereby Ordered to give the Deft. notice by serving her with a Copy of this Order.

Macon vs Wharton   In the Action on the Case between John Macon Plt and Thomas Wharton Deft. the Plt in Common Law being the Respondent in Chancery and having failed to file his Answer on the mocon [motion] of the Deft. at Common Law who is the complainant in Chancery it is Ordered the Respondent do pay unto the complainant five Shillings Currt. money for want of answer and the Suit is continued.

Absent Allen Howard Gent

Howard vs Woodson   In the Action of debt between Allen Howard Plt and Joseph Woodson Deft. the Deft confesses the judgment for three pounds ten shillings Current money whereupon it is considered by the Court that the Plt do recover against the Deft. the said sum with the Costs of this Suit and a Lawyers Fee.

Present Allen Howard Gent

Scot vs Daniell   In the Action of debt between Edward Scott Plt and James Daniell Deft. the following Jury are Sworn Robert Hughes Joseph Bingley Thomas Wadloe Ashford Hughes Bartholomew Stoveall Richard Moseby John Laine David Pattison John Christian William Woodson William Lansdon John Prier the Wittnesses being heard by consent of the parties a Juror is withdrawn and the Suit is continued.

[92]   March Court 1730 [1731]
Rates of Liquors   Pursuant to the directions of an Act of Assembly of this Colony the [Rates] of Liquors &c. are Setled as follow. Rum at ten Shillings Pr. Gallon. Madera Wine at two Shillings Pr. Quart. English Strong beer at twen[ty] pence Pr. Quart. American Strong beer at Sixpence Pr. Quart. Rum Punch made of Loaf Sugar with one third Rum at one shilling Pr. Quart. Rum Punch made of brown Sugar with one third Rum at eightpence Pr. Quart. Cyder at four pence Pr. Quart. one Diet at eightpence. one Diet for a Servant at fourpence. Stableage and Fodder or Pasturage for one horse for twenty four hours Sixpence. Indian Corn or Oats at threepence Pr. Gallon. lodging one night in a Clean bed at six pence.

Waddill vs Edwards   The Action on the Case between William Waddill Junr. Plt and Thomas Edwards is continued.

Pruit vs Johnson   The Action on the Case between Andrew Pruit Plt and Charles Johnson Deft is Continued.

Marchbanks vs Croom   The Action on the Case between George Marchbanks Plt and Daniell Croom Deft is dismist the Plt not prosecuting the same.

Flournoy vs Martin   In the Action of trespass on the Case between John James Flournoy and Elizabeth his wife Exec'rs of Orlando Jones deceas'd Plts and Francis Martin Deft. times is granted the Plt. to mend his declaration.

Flournoy vs Martin   In the Action of debt between John James Flournoy and Elizabeth his Wife Exec'rs of Orlando Jones deceasd Plts and Francis Martin Deft. time is granted the Plts to mend their declaration.

Thompson vs Edwards   In the Action of trespass on the Case between Samuell Thompson and Mary his Wife Plts and Thomas Edwards Deft. the Deft. pleads he oweth nothing and for tyrall puts himself upon the Country and the Plts likewise.

Bradley vs Saunders   In the Action of trespass on the Case between Joseph Bradley Plt and John Saunders Deft. the Deft failing to appear on the Plts motion the Conditionall Judgment formerly granted in this Suit is confirmed for

[93]   March Court 1730 [1731]
for so much damages as shall be found upon executing a Writt of inquiry of damages at the next Court of the Execution whereof the Sheriff is hereby Ordered to give the Deft. notice by serving them with a Copy of this Order.

Napier vs Ashlin   In the Action of trespass on the Case between Bouth Napier Plt and Joseph Ashlin Deft. the Deft. appears but failing to plead on the Plts motion Judgment by nihil dicit is granted him against the Deft. for what damages shall be recovered in the Suite to be discharged nevertheless if the Deft. shall plead at the next Court.

Prosser vs Napier   In the Action of trespass on the Case between Thomas Prosser Plt and Bouth Napier Deft. the parties submitt themselves to the Court for tryall whereupon the Plts Oath being considered it is Ordered that the Deft. do pay unto the Plt twenty six

Shillings Current money with Costs and a Fee.

Woodson vs Napier   In the Action of trespass on the Case between William Woodson Plt and Bouth Napier Deft. the Deft. pleads non assumpsit and for tryall puts himself upon the Country and the Plt likewise.

Ford vs Pruit   In the Action of trespass on the Case between James Ford Plt and Thomas Pruit Deft. the Deft. pleads not guilty and for tryall puts himself upon the Country and the Plt likewise.

Turpin vs Hook and Bilboe   In the Action on the Case between Mathew Turpin Assignee of John Welsh Plt and James Hook and John Peter Bilboe Defts the Defts appear but failing to plead on the Plts motion Judgment is granted by nihil dicit against the Defts. for what damages shall be recovered in this Suit to be discharged nevertheless if the Defts shall plead at the next Court.

Scot vs Pruit   The Action of trespass on the Case between Edward Scot Admin'or &c. of John Stephens deceased Plt. and Thomas Pruit Deft. is continued.

Taylor vs Lowe & Uxor   In the Action of trespass on the Case between John Taylor Plt and

[94]   March Court 1730 [1731]
Thomas Lowe and Amy his Wife Defts Daniell Stoner Gent is appointed to examine State and Setle the severall matters in dispute between them and his Report is to be made the Judgment of the Court.

Lad & Powel vs Thompson   The Petition of Amos Lad and Roger Powell against Samuell Thompson and Mary his Wife is continued.

Martain vs Fleming   In the Action of trespass on the Case between John Martain Plt and John Fleming Admr etc of Paul Pennington deceas'd Deft. the Deft. failing to appear on the Plts motion Judgment is granted him against the Deft. and Tarlton Fleming Sheriff for what damages shall be recovered in this Suit to be discharged nevertheless if the Deft. shall appear at the next Court.

Rockett vs Dickins   The Action of trespass on the Case between Baldwin Rockett Plt and Thomas Dickins Deft is dismist the Plt being dead.

Wood vs White   In the Action of Case between Henry Wood Plt and Edward White Deft. the Deft. failing to appear on the Plts motion the Conditional Judgment formerly granted in this Suit against the Deft. and John Lad his Common Bail is confirmed for so much damages as shall be found upon executing a Writt of inquiry of Damages of the next Court of the Execucon whereof the Sheriff is hereby ordered to give the Deft. and John Lad notice by serving them with a Copy of this Order.

David vs Quantin   In the Action on the Case between Anne David Exec'x &c of Peter David deceased Plt and John Quantin Administrator etc. of William Davis deceasd Deft. the Deft. failing to appear on the Plts motion Judgment is granted her against the Deft. and Tarlton Fleming Sheriff for what damages shall be recovered in this Suit to be discharged nevertheless if the Deft shall appear at the next Court.

Hopkins vs Woodson   In the Action of trespass on the Case between William Hopkins Plt and Benjamin Woodson Deft. an Imparlance is granted the Deft.

[95]   March Court 1730 [1731]
Dickins vs Dupuy   The Action of trespass on the Case between Thomas Dickins Plt and Francis Dupuy Deft. is dismist neither party appearing.

Burgess vs Woodson   In the Action of trespass on the Case between John Burgess Plt and John Woodson Deft. an Imparlance is granted the Deft.

Winfrey vs Williams   In the Action of trespass on the Case between Jacob Winfrey Plt. and John Williams Deft. the Sheriff having made return that the Deft is not to be found and he failing to appear on the Plts motion an Alias Capias is Awarded against the Deft returnable to the next Court.

Hatcher vs Syms   In the Action of trespass on the Case between Henry Hatcher Assignee of Samuell Hatcher Plt and Richard Syms Deft the Sheriff having made return on the Pluries Capias that the Deft. is not to be found and he failing to appear on the Plts motion an Pluries Capias de novo is awarded against the Deft returnable to the next Court.

Wood vs Hoggatt   The Action of Debt between Henry Wood Plt and Anthony Hoggatt Deft. is continued.

Digges vs Woodson   In the Action of trespass on the Case between

Dudley Digges Plt and Joseph Woodson Deft. the Deft. appears but failing to plead on the Plts motion Judgment by nihil dicit is granted him against the Deft. for what damages shall be recovered in this Suit to be discharged nevertheless if the Deft. shall plead at the next Court.

Bryant vs Chandler   The Action of trespass on the Case between William Bryant Plt and Joell Chandler Deft. is continued.

Bryant vs Chandler   The Action of trespass on the Case between William Bryant Plt and Joell Chandler Deft is continued.

Dickins vs Utley   In the Action of trespass on the Case between Thomas Dickins Plt & John Utley Deft. the Sheriff having made Return on the Attachment granted at December Court that he cannot find any

[96]   March Court 1730 [1731]
goods of the Defts. whereon he may serve the same on the Plts mocon [motion] the Deft. failing to appear an Attachment de novo is granted him against the Defts Estate returnable to the next Court.

Macon vs Hughes   In the Action of trespass on the Case between William Macon Plt and Stephen Hughes Deft. times is granted the Plt to mend his Declaration.

Mallet vs Pruit   The Action of trespass between Stephen Mallett Plt and Thomas Pruitt Deft. is continued.

Chastains Exec'rs vs Woodson   In the Action of trespass on the Case between John Chastain and Peter Chastain Exec'rs &c. of Peter Chastain deceasd Plts and Joseph Woodson Defendt. the Deft. failing to plead on the Plts motion Judgment by nihil dicit is granted them against the Deft. for what damages shall be recovered in this Suit to be discharged nevertheless if the Deft. shall plead at the next Court.

Winfrey vs Woodson   In the Action on the Case between Jacob Winfrey Plt and William Woodson Deft. the Deft. failing to plead on the Plts motion Judgment by nihil dicit is granted him against the Deft for what damages shall be recovered in this Suit to be discharged nevertheless if the Deft. shall plead at the next Court.

Gates vs Saunders   In the Action of trover between William Gates Plt and Robert Saunders Deft. the Deft pleads he is not guilty and the Suit is thereupon continued.

Hix vs Tabor & Stoveall In the Action of debt between Marmaduke Hix Assignee of William Mayo Plt and John Tabor and Bartholomew Stoveall Defts the Plt takes issue on the Defts Plea of Nil debet the tryall whereof is referred.

Randolphs Exer's. vs Mcbrid In the Action of trespass on the Case between William Randolph Richard Randolph John Randolph and John Fleming Exer's &c of Thomas Randolph deceasd Plts and John Mcbrid Deft the Deft. failing to appear on the motion of the Plts

[97] March Court 1730 [1731]
the Conditionall Judgment formerly granted against the Deft. and Dudley Digges Tarlton Fleming James Christian James Nolun John Martin junr John Webb Francis Martin and Ashford Hughes his Common Bail is confirmed for so much damages as shall be found upon executing a Writt of inquiry of damages at the next Court of the Execucon whereof the Sheriff is hereby Order'd to give the Deft. and his said Bail notice by serving them with a Copy of this Order.

Randolphs Ex'rs vs Dickinson In the Action of trespass on the Case between William Randolph Richard Randolph John Randolph and John Fleming Executors &c. of Thomas Randolph deceased Plts and John Dickinson Deft the deft. failing to appear on the motion of the Plts the Conditionall Judgment formerly granted against the Deft and Tarlton Fleming Gent Sheriff is confirmed for so much damages as shall be found upon Executing a Writ of enquiry of damages at the next Court of the Execucon whereof the Sheriff is hereby ordered to give the Deft. notice by serving him with a Copy of this Order.

Randolphs Ex'rs vs Martin In the Actin of trespass on the Case between William Randolph Richard Randolph John Randolph and John Fleming Exec'rs &c. of Thomas Randolph deceasd Plts and Francis Martin Deft. the Deft. is in Custody of the Sheriff and Thomas Prosser appears as his Attorney and pleads that the Deft. oweth Nothing and for tryall thereof puts himself upon the Country and the Plts likewise.

Then the Court adjourned till to morrow morning ten of the Clock

****

At a Court continued and held for Goochland County the eighteenth day of March Anno Domini 1730 [1731]. Present. Daniell Stoner Allen Howard George Payne William Cabbell George Raine

Gent. Justices.

[98]   March Court 1730 [1731]
Chastains Exec'rs vs Martin   In the Action of trespass on the Case between John Chastain and Peter Chastain Exec'rs &c of Peter Chastain deceas'd Plts and Francis Martin Deft. the Deft. pleads he oweth nothing and for tryall puts himself upon the Country and the Plts likewise.

Salmon vs Edwards   In the Action on the Case between Thomas Salmon Plt and Thomas Edwards Deft. the Plt. failing to prosecute his Suite on the Defts motion he is nonsuited and it is thereupon considered by the Court that the Deft. do recover against the Plt five shillings Current Money with his Costs by him in this behalf expended and a Lawyeres Fee.

Pigg vs Allin   In the Action on the Case beteen John Pigg Junr. Plt. and Samuel Allen Deft. the Plt. failing to prosecute his Suit on the Defts motion he is nonsuited and it is thereupon considered by the Court that the Deft. do recover against the Plt five Shillings Current Money with his Costs by him in this behalf expended and a Lawyers Fee.

Ward vs Dean   In the Action of debt between Seth Ward Plt. and Richard Dean Deft. the following Jury are Sworn Robert Hughes Joseph Bingley Thomas Wadloe Bartholomew Stovall Richard Moseby John Laine David Pattison John Christian William Lansdon John Prier Thomas Edwards George Southerland the Evidence produced by the Plt. is a Copy of a Judgment of Henrico Court to which the Deft. Demurrs and the Plt joins in Demurrer the Jury are thereupon discharged and the Arguments on the Demurrer are referred to be heard at the next Court.

Dickins vs Richard   In the Action of trespass on the Case between Thomas Dickins Plt. and John Richards Deft. the Deft. failing to appear on the Plts motion Judgment is granted him against the Deft. and Tarlton Fleming Gent Sheriff for what damages shall be recovered in this Suit to be discharged nevertheless if the Deft. shall appear at the next Court.

Prosser vs May   In the Action of trespass on the Case between Thomas Prosser Plt. and William May Deft. the Deft. failing to appear on the Plts motion Judgment is granted him against the Deft. and

[99]   March Court 1730 [1731]
Tarlton Fleming Gent Sheriff for what damages shall be recovered in this Suit to be discharged nevertheless if the Deft. shall appear at the next

Court.

Dixon vs Napier   In the Action of debt between Thomas Dixon Plt and Bouth Napier Deft. the Deft. failing to appear on the Plts motion Judgment is granted him against the Deft. and Tarlton Fleming Gent Sheriff for what damages shall be recovered in this Suit to be discharged nevertheless if the Deft. shall appear at the next Court.

Dickins vs Sutleith   In the Action of trespass on the Case between Thomas Dickins Plt and Abraham Sutleith Deft. the Deft. failing to appear on the Plts motion judgment is granted him against the Deft. and Tarlton Fleming Gent Sheriff for what damages shall be recovered in this Suit to be discharged nevertheless if the Deft. shall appear at the next Court.

Rapene vs Marchbanks   In the Action of debt between Anthony Rapene Plt and George Marchbanks Deft. the Deft. failing to appear on the Plts motion Judgment is granted him against the Deft. and James Robertson his Common Bail for what damages shall be recovered in this Suit to be discharged nevertheless if the Deft. shall appear at the next Court.

Davis vs Quin   The Action of Debt between George Davis Plt and John Quin Deft. is continued at the Defts Cost.

Scot vs Stone   In the Action of trespass on the Case between Edward Scot Plt and Thomas Stone Deft. the following Jury are Sworn Robert Hughes Joseph Bingley Thomas Wadloe Bartholomew Stoveall Richard Moseby John Laine David Pattison John Christian William Lansdon John Prier Thomas Edwards George Southerland who after some time bring in their Verdict which on the Defts motion is Orderd to be recorded and is as followeth We find for the Deft. Richard Moseby Foreman. Whereupon it is considered by the Court that the Plt take nothing by his Writt aforesaid that the Deft. go hence without day and that he recover against the Plt his Costs by him in this behalf expended and a Lawyers Fee.

[100]   March Court 1730 [1731]
Thompson vs Farrar   The Action of Debt between James Thompson Plt and William Farrar Deft. is dismist the Plt not prosecuting the same.

Ligon vs Mingo   The Action of trespass on the Case between Mathew Ligon Plt and Benjamin Mingo Deft. is dismist the Plt not prosecuting the same.

Taylor vs Quin   The Action of trespass on the Case between James Taylor Plt and John Quin Deft. is continued.

Taylor vs Quin   The Action of debt between John Taylor Plt and John Quin Deft is continued.

King vs Medlock   The Action of trespass on the Case between Martin King Plt and William Medlock Deft. is dismist the Plt not prosecuting the same.

Saunders vs Quin   In the Action of debt between John Saunders Assignee of David Harris Plt and John Quin Deft. the Sheriff having made return that the Deft. is not to be found and he failing to appear on the Plts motion an Alias Capias is awarded against the Deft. returnable to the next Court.

Holman vs Cox   In the Action of trespass on the Case between James Holman Assignee of John Prier Plt. and Francis Cox Deft. the Sheriff having made return that the Deft. is not to be found and he failing to appear on the Plts motion An Alias Capias is awarded against the Deft. returnable to the next Court.

Dickins vs Quin   In the Action of debt between Thomas Dickins Plt and John Quin Deft. the Sheriff having made return that the Deft. is not to be found and he failing to appear on the Plts motion An Alias Capias is awarded against the Deft. returnable to the next Court.

Prosser vs Quin   In the Action of trespass on the Case between Thomas Prosser Plt and John Quin Deft. the Sheriff having made return that the Deft is not to be found and he failing to appear on the Plts motion an Alias Capias is awarded against the Deft. returnable to the next Court.

[101]   March Court 1730 [1731]
Cabbell vs Woodson   In the Action of trespass on the Case between Wm. Cabbell Administrator &c of Joel Carr deceas'd Plt and Josiah and Stephen Woodson Ex'rs &c. of Robert Woodson deceasd Defts the Sheriff having made return that the Defts are not to be found and they failing to appear on the Plts motion an Alias Capias is awarded against the Defts. returnable to the next Court.

Cabbell vs Williams   In the Action of trespass on the Case between William Cabbell Plt. and John Williams Deft. the Sheriff having made return that the Deft. is no Inhabitant and he failing to appear on the Plts motion an Alias Capias is awarded against the Deft. returnable to the next Court.

Quantin vs Dickins   In the Action of trespass on the Case between John Quantin Administrator &c. of William Davis deceasd Plt and Thomas Dickins Deft. the Deft. pleads he oweth nothing and for tryall thereof puts himself upon the Country and the Plt likewise.

Moony vs Pruit   In the Action of trespass on the Case between John Moony Assignee of William Birks Plt and Thomas Pruit Deft. the Plt having failed to file his declaration on the Defts motion he is nonsuited and it is thereupon considered by the Court that the Deft do recover against the Plt five shillings Current money together with his Costs by him in this behalf expended and a Lawyers Fee.

Dickins vs Quantin   In the Action of trespass on the Case between Thomas Dickins Plt and John Quantin Deft Edward Scot enters himself speciall Bail for the Deft. and pleads he oweth nothing and for tryall thereof puts himself upon the Country and the Plt likewise.

The Action of trespass on the Case between John Tuly Plt and Robert Napier Deft. is dismist the Plt not prosecuting the same.

Cabbell vs Downie   The Attachment obtained by William Cabbell against the Estate of Robert Downie is continued returnable to the next Court.

[102]   March Court 1730 [1731]
Easly vs Bingley   In the Action of trespass on the Case between William Easly Plt. and Joseph Bingley Deft. an Imparlance is granted the Deft.

Then the Court adjourned to the third tuesday in next Month

****

At a Court held for Goochland County the third Tuesday in May being the eighteenth day of the Month annoq. Domi 1731. Present. William Mayo, Allen Howard, William Cabbell and James Holman Gent. Justices.

Proclamation Published   A Proclamation proroguing the Generall Assembly is published.

Kents deed to Sampson   William Kent acknowledges a Deed with the Livery of Seizin endorsed from himself to Stephen Sampson to be his Act and deed and it is thereupon admitted to record.

Chastains deed to Forcee   Stephen Chastain acknowledges a deed with Livery of Seizin endorsed from himself to Stephen Forcee to be his Act and deed and it is thereupon admitted to record.

Forcee's deed to Chastain   Stephen Forcee acknowledges a deed with the Livery of Seizin endorsed from himself to Stephen Chastain to be his Act and deed and is thereupon admitted to record.

Boccard's deed to Harriss   Peter Boccard acknowledges a deed with the Livery of Seizin endorsed from himself to John Harris to be his Act and deed and it is thereupon admitted to record.

Buirits deed to Ford   Peter Buirit acknowledges a deed with the Livery of Seizin endorsed from himself to James Ford to be his Act and deed and it is thereupon Admitted to record.

[103]   May Court 1731
Perault's deed to Harris   Daniel Perault acknowledges a deed with the livery of Seizin endorsed from himself to John Harriss to be his Act and Deed and it is thereupon admitted to record then Mary Wife of the said Daniel (she being first privately examined) relinquished her right of Dower in the land by the said deed conveyd which is also admitted to record.

Harriss's deed to Perault   John Harriss acknowledges a deed with the Livery of Seizin endorsed from himself to Daniel Perault to be his Act and deed and it is thereupon admitted to record, then Ursula Wife of the said John (she being first privately examin'd) relinquishes her right of Dower in the land by the said Deed conveyd which is also admitted to record.

Justice Sworn   William Mayo and Allen Howard Gent. administer the Oath of a Justice of the Peace and of a Justice in Chancery unto Anthony Hoggat Gent.

   Present. Anthony Hoggat Gent.
   Absent. James Holman Gent.

Holmans deed to Kent   James Holman acknowledges a deed withthe

Livery of Seizin endorsed from himself to William Kent to be his act and deed and it is thereupon admitted to record.

Present. James Holman Gent.

Guerrants deed to Dickins   Peter Guerrant acknowledges a deed with the Livery of Seizin endorsed from himself to Thomas Dickins to be his Act and Deed and it is thereupon admitted to record.

Stoveall & Walker deed to Davis   Bartholomew Stoveall and Thomas Walker acknowledge a deed with the Livery of Seizin endorsed from themselves to George Davis to be their Act and deed and it is thereupon admitted to record then Mary Wife of the said Bartholomew (she being first privately examind) relinquishes her right of Dower in the Land by the said Deed convey'd which is also admitted to record.

[104]   May Court 1731
Martain vs Thomas   On the Motion of John Martain of Henrico County a Witness for Rowland Thomas against Gilbert Gee it is Ordered that the said Rowland do pay him for twelve days attendance and for coming and returning twenty Miles ten times thirteen hundred and twenty pounds of tobacco with Costs.

Walker Sworn under Sheriff   Thomas Walker takes the Oaths appointed by Act of Parliament to be taken instead of the Oaths of Allegiance and Supremacy the Oath to be taken by an Act of Parliament made in the first year of the Reign of his late Majesty King George the first intituld an Act for the further security of his Majesty's person and Government and of the Succession of the Crown of Great Brittain in the heirs of the late Princess Sophia being [protestants] and for extinguishing the hopes of the pretended Prince of Wales an[d his open] and secret Abettors and subscribes the Test and then takes the Oath of under Sheriff and is admitted to the execution of that Office.

Churchill Levy free   On the petition of Richard Churchill he is exempt from paying his [county] Levey.

Brook Levey free   On the petion of George Brook he is exempt from paying his [county] Levey.

Slate Levey free   On the Petition of John Slate he is exempt from paying his County Levee this year.

Present. George Payne Gent.

Oglesby's Adm'on   Susanna Oglesby comes into Court and makes Oath that Richard [Oglesb]y deceas'd died without making any Will so farr as she knows or [beleives] and on her motion and giving security for her just and faithfull administration of the said Decedents Estate Certificate is granted her for obtaining [Lett]ers of Administration in due form John Fleming and Edward Scot Securities.

Ordered that John [Lain]e Thomas Baily Thomas Chin and John Prier [or] any three of them being first sworn by some Justice of the Peace to appraise the estate of Richard Oglesby [torn] Susanna the Administrix do return an Inventory [torn]

[105]   May Court 1731
Jevodans Adm'on   Judith Jevodan comes into Court and makes Oath that Thomas Jevodan died without making any Will so far as she knows or beleives and on her motion and giving Security for her just and faithfull Administration of the said Decedents Estate Certificate is granted her for obtaining Letters of Administration in due form, John Martain and Thomas Dickins Securities. Ordered that John Levillain, John Chastain, James Sublet, and John Bernart or any three of them being first sworn by some Justice of the peace do appraise the Estate of Thomas Jevodan deceas'd and that Judith the Administratrix do return an Inventory thereof to the next Court.

[List o]f titheables [to be] taken   George Payne Gent. is appointed to take the list of titheables on the North side of James River below the lower branch of Beverdam. Allen Howard Gent. on the same side upwards including the fork of the River, Daniell Stoner Gent. on the South side of James River in St. James's Parish and Anthony Hoggat Gent. in King William Parish.

Su[rveyo]r of road   Thomas Turpin is appointed Surveyor of the Road from the Fork of the Road between Jones's Creek and Fine Creek so far as to extend over the long branch and it is ordered that all the titheables adjacent to the said Road so far up the same as to include the titheables of William Easly and James Cock do assist in Clearing it.

Surveyor [of road]   [torn] Basset is appointed Surveyor of the Road from the long branch [torn] between Jones's Creek and fine Creek upwards as far as

[106] May Court 1731
cross the Fork of Fine Creek including the upper Creek with a Slash on the upper Side.

Surveyor of road Anthony Hughes is appointed Surveyor of the road from the Slash on the upper side of the upper branch of Fine Creek to the Chappell and it is ordered that the titheables of Joel Chandler William Chandler Bartholomew Stovall and William Davis and all others within that neighbourhood do Assist in clearing the said road.

Absent. James Holman Gent.

L'grands Adm'n Katherine L'Grand Comes into Court and relinquishing her right to the Administration of John L'Grands Estate John Fleming as Executor of the last will and testament of Thomas Randolph deceas'd makes Oath that John L'Grand deceased died without making any Will so far as he knows or beleives and on his motion and giving security for his just and faithfull administration of the said decedents estate Certificate is granted him for obtaining Letters of Administration in due form James Holman Security. Ordered that William Sallee, Thomas Dickins, Edward Scot, and John Chastain or any three of them being first Sworn by some Justice of the peace do appraise the estate of John L'Grand deceas'd and that John Fleming the Administrator do return an Inventory thereof to the next Court.

Present James Holman Gent.

Surveyor of road John Franklin is appointed Surveyor of the road from Fine Creek to Solomons Creek and it is Ordered that the titheables of Daniel Stoner, Daniel Johnson, John Cox, Frederick Cox, Joseph John, Isaac Hughes, Nicholas Wilkinson and all others within that neighbourhood do assist in clearing the said road.

Grand Jury Sworn Pursuant to directions of an Act of Assembly of this Colony intitul'd an Act concerning Juries the following persons are Sworn as a Grand Jury Edward [Scot [F]oreman, John Farrar, Francis James, Nicholas Cox, Joseph Scot, William Woodson, Nowell Burton, Joel Chandler, Robert Burton, Samuell Allin, Thomas Wadloe, Stephen Chastain

[107] May Court 1731
James Robinson, Thomas Baily, Leonard Ballew, William Womack, John Williams, James Nevil, Robert Wade, Thomas Turpin, Joseph Bingley,

who after some time being in their presentments which are Ordered to be recorded and are as follow.

Presentments by the Grand Jury against James Taylor and William Lansdon for fighting. Thomas Dickins for prophaning the Sabbath. John Quantain Evidence. George and William Davis for an assault on the body of Thomas Wadloe. William Stephens for incest he having marryed or pretends to have marry'd his Brothers Daughter. The Churchwardens of St. James Parish for not finding the Copys of the Laws appointed by Act of Assembly to be read in Churches in March and October annually. The Churchwardens of King William for the same. Jacob Micheaux for retailing Strong drink contrary to Law. John Richardson for the same. Tarlton Fleming and Joseph Dabbs for being drunk. William Lansdon Evidence. John L'Villain for the same. John Quantain for the same. Henry Wood for Swearing profainly. Joseph Dabbs Witness. Thomas Dickins for the same. Capt. William Cabbell the same. Thomas Dickins for Learning his Negro boy to profain the Lords prayer. The Exers. of Col. Thomas Randolph for not keeping a passable way over Dover Mill. The Surveyor of the Road from Deep Creek to Solomon's Creek for not keeping the said road in repair. Thomas Murril for being drunk and profane swearing. John Scruggs for Swearing. Tarlton Fleming for Swearing one Oath. Judeth Bellow [Ballew] for a Bastard Child. John Burk for Swearing. William Vail for Swearing. John Mooney the same. Edward Scot Foreman. Richard Parker for beating Thomas Wadloe. Edward Scot.

Ordered that Subpœna's be issued against the severall persons presented for their appearing at the next Court to answer the presentments.

Stoveall put into Stocks   Bartholomew Stoveall behaving himself rudely in the Court it is ordered that he be put into the Stocks there to remain for the space of one hour and that he pa[y Costs.]

[108]   May Court 1731
Johnson's deed to Sorrel   Charles Johnson acknowledges a deed with the Livery of Seizin endorsed from himself to John Sorrel to be his Act and deed and it is thereupon admitted to Record then Elizabeth Wife of the said Charles (she being first privately examined) relinquishes her right of Dower in the Land by the said Deed conveyd which is also admitted to record.

Dickins to clear a road   On the Motion of Thomas Dickins leave is granted him to clear a road from his dwelling house to the Main road provided the same does not pass through any person's clear ground.

Bumpuss vs Bumpuss   On the motion of John Bumpuss of Hanover County a Witness for Samuell Bumpuss vs Andrew Moreman it is ordered that the said Samuell do pay him for Eleven days attendance and for coming and returning fifty miles nine times two thousand one hundred and ten pounds of tobacco with Costs.

Surveyor of road   Jacob Micheaux is appointed Surveyor of the road from the Fork of the Ferry road upwards unto the main [road] and it is Ordered that the titheables of John Wood, Samuell Spencer, [torn] Croom, Anthony Morgan and Paul Micheaux and of such other persons as inhabit within that Neighbourhood do assist in clearing the same.

Absent. William Cabbell Gent.

Cabbell vs Utley   In the Action of trespass on the Case between William Cabbell Plt. and John Utley Deft. the Deft. failing to appear on the Plts motion the Attachment issued against his estate is discontinued and an Als Caps. is awarded against him returnable to the next Court.

Woodson vs Cabbell   In the Action of debt between Josiah and Stephen Woodson Executors of Robert Woodson deceased Plts and William Cabbell Deft. on the Defts motion an imparlance is granted him.

Present. William Cabbell Gent.
Absent. George Raine Gent

[109]   May Court 1731
Raine vs Martin   In the Action of trespass on the Case between George Raine Plt. and Francis Martin Deft. the Deft. failing to appear on the Plts motion the Conditionall Judgment formerly granted him in this Suit against the Deft. and Dudley Digges is confirmed for so much damages as shall be found upon executing a Writ of enquiry at the next Court of which the Sheriff is hereby Ordered to give the said Deft. and Dudley Digges notice by serving them with a Copy of this Order.

Raine vs Dickinson   In the Action of trespass on the Case between George Raine Plt. and John Dickinson Deft. the Deft. failing to appear on the Plts motion the Conditionall Judgment formerly granted him in this Suit against the Deft. and Tarlton Fleming Gent. Sheriff is confirmed for so much damages as shall be found upon executing a Writ of Enquiry at the next Court of which the Sheriff is hereby Ordered to give the said

Deft. notice by Serving him with a Copy of this Order.

Present. George Raine Gent

Merrewether vs Martin   In the Action of Debt between William Merrewether Plt. and Francis Martin Deft. the Deft. failing to appear on the Plts motion the Conditionall Judgment formerly granted him in this Suit against the Deft. and Tarlton Fleming Gent. Sheriff is confirmed for so much damages as shall be found upon Executing a Writ of enquiry at the next Court of which the Sheriff is hereby Ordered to give the said Deft. notice by Serving him with a Copy of this Order.

Prosser vs Martin   In the Action of trespass on the Case between Thomas Prosser Plt. and Francis Martin Defendt. the Deft. confesses Judgment for eighteen pounds Seventeen Shillings and three pence three farthings Currt. money whereupon it is considered by the Court that the Plt. do recover against the Deft. the said Sum with the Costs of this Suit and a Lawyers Fee.

[110]   May Court 1731
Quantin vs Taylor   In the Action of trespass on the Case between John Quantin Plt. and James Taylor Deft. the Deft. failing to appear on the Plts. motion the Conditionall Judgment formerly granted him in this Suit against the Deft. and Peter Chastain is confirmed for so much damages as shall be found upon executing a Writt of Enquiry at the next Court of which the Sheriff is hereby Ordered to give the said Deft. and Peter Chastain notice by Serving them with a Copy of this Order.

Ward vs Farrar   In the Action of Debt between Seth Ward Plt. and John Farrar Deft. the Plt. files a New declaration and an imparlance is granted the Deft.

Pruit vs Boccar   The Action on the Case between Hugh Pruit Plt. and Peter Boccar Deft. is Dismist the Plt. not prosecuting the same.

Webber vs White   In the Action of trespass on the Case between Philip Webber Assignee of James Elliott Plt. and Edward White Deft. the Deft. failing to appear on the Plts motion the Conditionall Judgment formerly granted him in this Suit against the Deft. and John Lad is confirmed for so much Damages as shall be found upon Executing a Writ of Enquiry at the next Court of Which the Sheriff is hereby ordered to give the said Deft. and John Ladd notice by Serving them with a Copy of this Order.

Stidum vs Bingley &c The Action of Debt between Benjamin Stidum Plt. and Joseph Bingley and William Lansdon Defts. is dismist the Plt. not prosecuting the same.

Moseby vs Taylor The Action of debt between Richard Moseby Plt and John Taylor Deft is continued at the Defts Cost.

Locket vs James In the Action of trespass between Thomas Locket Plt. and Francis James Deft. the Deft. files a plea and time is granted the Plt. to reply.

Absent. Daniell Stoner Gent.

[111]   May Court 1731
Stoner vs Utley In the action of trespass on the Case between Daniell Stoner Plt and John Utley Deft. the Sheriff having made return on the Als Caps. that the Deft. is not to be found and he failing to appear on the Plts motion a Plurs. Caps. is awarded against him returnable to the next Court.

Ware vs Saunders In the Action of trespass on the Case between Susanna Ware Plt. and William Saunders Deft. the Arguments on the reasons filed in arrest of Judgment being heard, it is the opinion of the Court that they are not good and Sufficient in Law to barr the Plt from having his [sic] Judgment and it is thereupon considered by the Court that the Plt do recover against the Deft. five pound Currt. money and twelve hundred pounds of tobacco in Cask by the Jurors aforesaid in their said verdict assess'd with Costs and an Attorneys Fee. from which Judgment the Deft. appeals to the Sixth day of the next General Court.

Stoner vs Hughes Daniel Stoner is discharged from being Security for the Probate of George Cox's Will and Isaac Hughes Stephen Hughes and Ashford Hughes enter into Bond for the same, and it is ordered that Isaac Hughes pay Costs.

Macon vs Wharton In the Action on the Case between John Macon Plt. and Thomas Wharton Deft the Plt. at Common Law being the Respondent in Chancery and having failed to file his answer on the Motion of the Deft at Common Law who is the Complainant in Chancery it is Ordered the Respondent do pay unto the Complainant ten shillings Current money for want of an Answer and the Suit is continued.

Waddill vs Edwards The action of Case between William Waddill junr. Plt. and Thomas Edwards Deft is continued.

Mcbrid Committed to Gaol &c   John Mcbrid having misbehaved himself towards the Court it is Ordered that the Sheriff take him into his Custody and him safely keep till he enter into bond in the Sum of five pounds Sterling conditioned for his good behaviour for a year and that he pay Costs.

Flournoy vs Martin   In the Action of trespass on the Case between John James Flournoy Plt. and Francis Martin deft. time is granted the Plt to mend his declaration.

[112]   May Court 1731
Flournoy vs Martin   In the Action of debt between John James Flournoy and Elizabeth his Wife Executrix &c of Orlando Jones deceased Plts. and Francis Martin Deft. time is granted the Plts to mend their declaration.

Napier vs Ashlin   In the Action of Case between Bouth Napier Plt. and Joseph Ashlin Deft. the Deft. confesses Judgment for three hundred pounds of tobacco whereupon it is considered by the Court that the Plt. do recover against the Deft. the said Tobacco with Costs and a Lawyers Fee.

Turpin vs Hooke &c   In the action on the Case between Mathew Turpin Assignee of John Welsh Plt. and James Hook and John Peter Bilboe Defts the Plt. failing to prosecute his Suit on the Defendants motion he is nonsuited and it is thereupon considered by the Court that the Defts do recover against the Plt five shillings Current money with Costs and an Attorneys Fee.

Scot vs Pruit   In the Action of trespass on the Case between Edward Scot Administrator &c. of John Stephens deceas'd Plt. and Thomas Pruit Deft. the Plt. files a new declaration and an imparlance is granted the Deft.

Taylor vs Lowe & Uxor   The Action of trespass on the Case between John Taylor Plt. and Thomas Lowe and Amy his Wife Defts is continued

Lad & Powell vs Thompson   On the petition of Amos Lad and Roger Powell against Samuell Thompson and Mary his Wife Exec. &c. of John Bellamy deceased the said Samuell failing to appear on the motion of the petitioners (who are Securities for the probate of the last will of the said John Bellamy deceased) it is ordered that they take into their possession the Estate of the said John Bellamy deceas'd to indemnify them from their being Securities as aforesaid and that the said Samuell pay Costs unto the Petitioners.

Martain vs Fleming The Action of trespass on the Case between John Martain Plt. and John Fleming Deft. Administrator &c. of Paul Pennington deceased Deft is continued.

David vs Quantin In the Action of Case beween Anne David Executrix of the last Will

[113] May Court 1731
Will and Testament of Peter David Plt. and John Quantin Administrat'r of the goods and Chattles of William Davis deceas'd Deft. the Deft failing to appear on the Plts motion the Conditionall Judgment formerly granted her in this Suit agt. the Deft. & Tarlton Fleming Gent. Sheriff is confirmed for so much damages as shall be found upon executing a Writ of enquiry at the next Court of which the Sheriff is hereby Ordered to give the said Deft. notice by serving him with a Copy of this Order.

Hopkins vs Woodson In the Action of trespass on the Case between William Hopkins Plt. and Benjamin Woodson Deft. the Deft. failing to plead on the Plts motion Judgment by nihil dicit is granted him against the Deft. for what damages shall be recovered in this Suit to be discharged nevertheless if the Deft. shall plead at the next Court.

Burgess vs Woodson In the Action of trespass on the Case between John Burgess Plt. and John Woodson Deft. the Deft. failing to plead on the Plts motion Judgment by nihil dicit is granted him against the Deft. for what damages shall be recovered in this Suit to be discharged nevertheless if the Deft. shall plead at next Court.

Winfrey vs Williams In the Action of trespass on the Case between Jacob Winfrey Plt. and John Williams Deft. the Sheriff haveing made return on the Als Caps. that the Deft. is no inhabitant within his Bailiwick and he failing to appear on the Plts motion a plurs. Caps. is awarded against the Deft. returnable to the next Court.

Hatcher vs Sims In the Action of trespass on the Case between Henry Hatcher Assignee of Samuell Hatcher Plt. and Richard Sims Deft. the Sheriff having returned on the Plurs. Caps. that he had not time to execute it on the Plts motion Plur. Caps. de novo is awarded against him returnable to the next Court.

Wood vs Hoggat   The Action of debt between Henry Wood Plt. and Anthony Hoggat Deft. is dismist the Plt. not prosecuting the same.

Digges vs Woodson   In the Action of trespass on the Case between Dudley Digges Plt.

[114]   May Court 1731
and Joseph Woodson Deft the Deft. pleads he oweth nothing and for tryall puts himself upon the Country and the Plt. likewise.

Bryant vs Chandler   In the Action of trespass on the Case between William Bryant Plt and Joell Chandler Deft. the Deft. pleads he oweth nothing and time is granted the Plt. to reply.

Bryant vs Chandler   In the Action of trespass between William Bryant Plt. and Joell Chandler Deft. the Deft. pleads he oweth nothing and time is granted the Plt. to reply.

Dickins vs Utley   In the Action of trespass on the Case between Thomas Dickins Plt. and John Utley Deft. the Deft. failing to appear on the Plts motion the Attachment issued against his Estate is discontinued and an Alias Caps. is awarded against him returnable to the next Court.

Macon vs Hughes   In the Action of trespass on the Case between William Macon Plt. and Stephen Hughes Deft. the Deft. failing to appear on the Plts motion the Conditionall Judgment formerly granted him in this Suit against the Deft. and Tarlton Fleming Gent. Sheriff is confirmed for so much damages as shall be found upon Executing a Writ of Enquiry at the next Court of which the Sheriff is hereby Ordered to give the said Deft. notice by serving him with a Copy of this Order.

Mallet vs Pruit   In the action of trespass between Stephen Mallet Plt. and Thomas Pruit Deft. the Deft. pleads he is not guilty and for tryall puts himself upon the Countrey and the Plt. likewise.

Mcbrids recognizance   John Mcbrid comes into Court and acknowledges himself indebted unto our Soverign Lord King George in the Sum of five pounds Sterling to be levyd upon his goods and Chattles on Condition that he be of good behaviour towards all his Majestys Subjects for a year and a day, and it is thereupon Ordered that he be discharged from the Custody of the Sheriff and that he pay Costs.

[115] May Court 1731

Scot &c. vs Ridgell &c   Edward Scot and Thomas Prosser inform the Court that Richard Ridgell, Joshua Stephens and John Field neglect to take such care of their Children as by law they ought and it is thereupon Ordered that they be summoned to appear at the next Court to answer in the premisses.

Then the Court adjourned 'till to morrow morning ten a Clock

****

At a Court continued and held for Goochland County the nineteenth day of May 1731. Present. William Mayo, George Raine, William Cabbell and Anthony Hoggat Gent. Justices.

Johnson vs Pruit   In the Action of trespass on the Case between Charles Johnson and Elizabeth his Wife Plts. and Andrew Pruit Deft. the following Jury are Sworn. Bouth Napier, John Maxey, John Paine, John Radford, Abraham Micheaux, Ashford Hughes, Sanburn Woodson, William Maxey, John Ladd, John Saunders, John Prier, William Lansdon, who after some time bring in their Verdict which on the motion of the Plts is ordered to be recorded and is as followeth "Wee find for the Plt. forty shillings Currt. money, Bouth Napier." The Deft files reasons in Arrest of Judgment the arguing whereof is referred.

Collins vs Johnson   On the motion of Catherine Collins a Witness for Charles Johnson and Elizabeth his Wife against Andrew Pruit it is Ordered that the said Charles do pay her for four days Attendance 120 lbs. of tobacco with Costs.

Perry vs Johnson   On the motion of Mary Perry a Witness for Charles Johnson and Elizabeth his Wife against Andrew Pruit it is Ordered that the said Charles do pay her for four days Attendance one hundred and twenty pounds of tobacco with Costs.

Napier vs Johnson   On the motion of Robert Napier Junr. a Witness for Charles Johnson and

[116] May Court 1731

Elizabeth his Wife against Andrew Pruit it is ordered that the said Charles do pay him for four days attendance one hundred and twenty pounds of tobacco with Costs.

Perry vs Johnson   On the motion of Hannah Perry a Witness for Charles Johnson and Elizabeth his Wife against Andrew Pruit it is Ordered that the said Charles do pay her for five days attendance one hundred and fifty pounds of tobacco with Costs.

Pruit vs Pruit   On the motion of Richard Pruit of Henrico a Witness for Andrew Pruit ads Charles Johnson and Elizabeth his Wife it is Ordered that the said Andrew do pay him for Seven days attendance and for Coming and returning twenty five Miles five times seven hundred and ninety five pounds of tobacco with Costs.

Pruit vs Pruit   On the motion of Thomas Pruit a Witness for Andrew Pruit ads Charles Johnson and Elizabeth his Wife it is Ordered that the said Andrew do pay him for seven days attendance two hundred and ten pounds of tob'o. with Costs.

Chastain vs Woodson   In the Action of trespass on the Case between John and Peter Chastain Exrs. &c. of Peter Chastain deceased Plts. and Joseph Woodson Deft. the parties submitt themselves to the Court for tryall and the Plts Oaths being heard it is considered that he do recover against the Deft two pounds fifteen shillings and threepence Current money with Costs and a Lawyers Fee.

Hughes Inventory   Robert Hughes presents part of the Inventory of the Estate of Sarah Hughes deceased which is Ordered to be recorded.

Winfrey vs Woodson   The Action on the Case between Jacob Winfrey Plt and William Woodson Deft is dismist the Plt. not prosecuting the same.

Gates vs Saunders   In the Action of Trover between William Gates Plt. and Robert Saunders Deft. the Plt. files a New Declaration and an Imparlance is granted the Deft.

[117]   May Court 1731
Hix vs Stoveall   The Action of debt between Marmaduke Hix Assignee of William Mayo Plt. and John Tabor and Bartholomew Stoveall Defts is continued.

Randolph vs Mcbrid   The Action of trespass on the Case between William Randolph, Richard Randolph, John Randolph and John Fleming Executors &c. of Thomas Randolph deceased Plts and John Mcbrid Deft. is continued.

Randolph vs Dickinson   The Action of trespass on the Case between William Randolph Richard Randolph, John Randolph and John Fleming Executors &c of Thomas Randolph deceased Plts and John Dickinson Deft. is continued.

Randolph vs Martin   The Action of trespass on the Case between William Randolph, Richard Randolph, John Randolph and John Fleming Executors &c of Thomas Randolph deceased Plts and Francis Martin Deft. is continued.

Surveyor of road   Joseph Woodson is appointed Surveyor of the Road from the Courthouse to the Ferry Landing and it is Ordered that John Webb, John McBrid and David Walker, who are Surveyors of the roads adjacent and the titheables in their Severall precincts do assist in clearing the said road and that each Surveyor warn his own Gang to appear according to the appointment of Joseph Woodson aforesaid.

Ward vs Dean   In the Action of debt between Seth Ward Plt. and Richard Dean Deft. the Deft. by consent of the Plt waives the Demurrer hereto fore entered and it is Ordered that the Issue be tryed at the next Court.

Chastain vs Martain   In the Action of trespass on the Case between John and Peter Chastain Executors &c. of Peter Chastain deceased Plts and Francis Martin Deft. the Plt. files a new declaration and an Imparlance is granted the Deft.

Dickins vs Richards   In the Action of trespass on the Case between Thomas Dickins Plt. and John Richards Deft. the Deft. pleads nil debet and for tryall Submitts himself to the Court and the Plt. likewise whereupon the

[118]   May Court 1731
accounts being heard between them it is Considered by the Court that the Plt. do recover against the Deft. five pounds and Seven pence Currt money with Costs.

Prosser vs May   In the Action of trespass on the Case between Thomas Prosser Plt and William May Deft. the Deft. failing to appear on the Plts motion the Conditionall Judgment formerly granted him in this Suit against the Deft and Tarlton Fleming Gent Sheriff is Confirmed for so much damages as shall be found upon executing a Writ of enquiry at next Court of which the Sheriff is hereby ordered to give the said Deft. Notice by serving him with a Copy of this Order.

Davis vs Quin   In the Action of debt between George Davis Plt and John Quin Deft. the Deft. failing to appear and the Sheriff having failed to return Bail on the Plts motion Judgment is granted him for what Damages shall be recovered in this Suit against the Deft. and Tarlton Fleming Sheriff to be discharged nevertheless if the Deft. shall appear at the next Court.

Hughes vs Woodson   In the Action of trespass on the Case between Robert Hughes Plt. and John Woodson Deft. the Deft. failing to appear and the Sheriff having failed to return Bail on the Plts motion Judgment is granted him for what damages shall be recovered in this Suit against the Deft. and Tarlton Fleming Sheriff to be discharged nevertheless if the Deft. shall appear at next Court.

Hughes vs Cox   In the Action of trespass on the Case between Robert Hughes Plt and John Cox Deft. the Deft. failing to appear and the Sheriff having failed to return Bail on the Plts motion Judgment is granted him for what damages shall be recovered in this Suit against the Deft. and Tarlton Fleming Sheriff to be discharged nevertheless if the Deft. shall appear at next Court.

Hughes vs Johnson   In the Action of trespass on the Case between Robert Hughes Plt. and Daniell Johnson Deft. the Deft. failing to appear and the Sheriff having

[119]   May Court 1731
failed to return Bail in the Plts. motion Judgment is granted him for what Damages shall be recovered in this Suit against the Deft. and Tarlton Fleming Sheriff to be discharged nevertheless if the Deft. shall appear at the next Court.

Dixon vs Napier   The Action of Debt between Thomas Dixon Plt and Bouth Napier Deft. is continued.

Taylor vs Quin   The Action of trespass on the Case between James Taylor Plt. and John Quin Deft. is continued.

Taylor vs Quin   The Action of debt between James Taylor Plt. and John Quin Deft. is continued.

Saunders vs Quin   In the Action of debt between John Saunders

Assignee of David Harriss Plt. and John Quin Deft. the Sheriff having return'd on the Als Caps that the Deft is not to be found and he failing to appear on the Plts. motion a Plur Caps. is awarded him returnable to the next Court.

Dickins vs Quin   In the Action of debt between Thomas Dickins Plt. and John Quin Deft. the Sheriff having returned on the Als. Caps. that the Deft. is not to be found and he failing to appear on the Plts motion a Plurs Caps. is awarded against him returnable to the next Court.

Prosser vs Quin   In the Action of trespass on the Case between Thomas Prosser Plt. and John Quin Deft. the Sheriff having returned on the Als. Caps. that the Deft. is not to be found and he failing to appear on the Plts motion a Plur. Caps. is awarded against him returnable to the next Court.

Quantin vs Dickins   The Action of trespass on the Case between John Quantin Administrator &c of William Davis deceased Plt. and Thomas Dickins Deft. is continued.

Dickins vs Sutleith   In the Action of trespass on the Case between Thomas Dickins Plt. and Abraham Sutleith Deft. Joseph Woodson enters himself Special Bail for the Deft. who confesses Judgment for fourteen hundred pounds of

[120]   May Court 1731
tobacco whereupon it is Considered by the Court that the Deft. do recover against the Deft. the said Sum with Costs and a Lawyers Fee.

Dickins vs Quantin   In the Action of trespass on the Case between Thomas Dickins Plt. and John Quantin Deft. the parties submitt themselves to the Court for tryall whereupon their Accounts and allegations being heard it is considered that the Plt. do recover against the Deft. three pounds Sixteen shillings and ninepence Current money with Costs and a Lawyers Fee.

Rapene vs Marchbanks   In the Action of Debt between Anthony Rapene Churchwarden of King William Parish Plt. and George Marchbanks Deft. the Deft. appears but failing to plead on the Plts. motion Judgment by nihil dicit is granted him against the Deft. for what damages shall be recovered in this Suit to be discharged nevertheless if the Deft. shall plead at the next Court.

Cox's Will to be proved On the Motion of Ashford Hughes it is Ordered that the Executors of the last Will and Testament of Bartholomew Cox deceased do appear at the next Court and prove the same and that on their failing so to do Administration with the Will annex'd be granted to such persons to whom the right thereof both appertain.

Pruit vs Johnson In the Action on the Case between Andrew Pruit Plt. and Charles Johnson Deft. the follow Jury are Sworn, Bouth Napier, John Maxey, John Paine, John Redford, Abraham Micheaux, Ashford Hughes, Sanburn Woodson, William Maxey, John Ladd, John Saunders, John Prier, William Lansdon, who after some time bring in their Verdict which on the Plts. motion is admitted to record and is as followeth "Wee find for the Plt. one pound eighteen Shillings and four pence Current Cash Bouth Napier." Whereupon it is Considered by the Court that the Plt. do recover against the Deft. one pound eighteen Shillings and fourpence Current money by the Jurors aforesaid in their said Verdict assessd with Costs and an Attorneys Fee.

Scot vs Johnson On the Motion of Edward Scot a Witness for Charles Johnson ads Andrew Pruit it is ordered that the said Charles do pay him for five days Attendance one hundred and fifty pounds of tobacco with Costs.

[121] May Court 1731
Collins vs Johnson On the Motion of Matthew Collins a Witness for Charles Johnson ads Andrew Pruit it is Ordered that the said Charles do pay him for nine days attendance two hundred and seventy pounds of tobacco with Costs.

Bingley vs Johnson On the Motion of Joseph Bingley a Witness for Charles Johnson ads Andrew Pruit it is ordered that the said Charles do pay him for five days attendance one hundred and fifty pounds of tobacco with Costs.

Pruit vs Pruit On the Motion of Thomas Pruit a Witness for Andrew Pruit vs Charles Johnson it is Ordered that the said Andrew do pay him for nine days Attendance two hundred and seventy pounds of tobacco with Costs.

Pruit vs Pruit On the Motion of Richard Pruit of Henrico a Witness for Andrew Pruit vs Charles Johnson it is Ordered that the said Andrew do pay him for five days attendance and for coming and returning twenty five miles twice four hundred and fifty pounds of tobacco with Costs.

Scot vs Daniell   In the Action of Detinue between Edward Scot Plt. and James Daniell Deft. the following Jury are Sworn Bouth Napier, John Maxey, John Paine, John Redford, Abraham Micheaux, Ashford Hughes, Sanburn Woodson, William Maxey, John Ladd, John Saunders, John Prier, William Lansdon, who after some time bring in their Verdict, the Deft. moves the Verdict may be set aside being found contrary to Evidence and that a new tryall be ordered which being considered by the Court it is the opinion that the Jury have found Contrary to Evidence, and it is thereupon Ordered that the Verdict be rejected, that there be a new tryall at the next Court and that the Deft. pay unto the Plt. the Costs of the Suit which have hitherto accrewd.

Wadloe vs Scot   On the motion of Thomas Wadloe a Witness for Edward Scot vs James Daniell it is Ordered that the said Edward do pay him for Six days Attendance one hundred and eighty pounds of tobacco with Costs.

Scot vs Scot   On the motion of Samuell Scot a Witness for Edward Scot vs James

[122]   May Court 1731
Daniell it is Ordered that the said Edward do pay him for Seven days Attendance two hundred and ten pounds of tobacco with Costs.

Bassett vs Scot   On the motion of Thomas Bassett of Henrico a Witness for Edward Scot vs James Daniell it is Ordered that the said Edward do pay him for eight days attendance and for coming and returning forty five miles six times twelve hundred and ninety pounds of tobacco with Costs.

Holman vs Cox   The Action of trespass on the Case between James Holman Plt. and Francis Cox Deft. is dismist the Plt not prosecuting the Same.

Davids estate to be apprais'd   Ordered that Edward Scot and James Sublet being first Sworn by some Justice of the peace do appraise the Estate of Peter David deceased in the room of the other persons formerly appointed.

Easly vs Bingley   The Action of trespass on the Case between William Easly Plt. and James Taylor Deft. is dismist and Edward Scot consents to pay the Costs of the Suit.

Mims vs Levins   In the Action of trespass on the Case between David Mims Plt. and Richard Levins Administrator &c. of John Sutton Farrar deceased Deft. an Imparlance is granted the Deft.

Digges vs Levins   In the Action of trespass on the Case between Dudley Digges Plt. and Richard Levins Administrator &c. of John Sutton Farrar deceased Deft. a Special Imparlance is granted the Deft.

Wright vs Boccard   In the Action of trespass between Elizabeth Wright Plt. and Peter Boccard & Jacob Winfrey Defts. the Plt having failed to file a declaration on the Defts motion she is nonsuited and it is thereupon Ordered that she do pay unto the Defts five Shillings Current Money with Costs and an Attorneys Fee.

The Action of trespass between Elizabeth Wright Deft. and John Creasy Deft is dismist the Plt not prosecuting the Same.

[123]   May Court 1731
The Action of trespass between Edward Scot Plt. and Thomas Stone Deft. is dismist the Plt not prosecuting the same

The Action of trespass on the Case between John Bellamy Plt. and Samuell Thompson Deft. is dismist the Plt. not prosecuting the same.

The Action of trespass on the Case between William Randolph Richard Randolph John Randolph and John Fleming Executors &c of Thomas Randolph deceased Plts and Peter Dept Deft. is dismist the Plts. not prosecuting the Same.

Digges vs Fleming   In the Action of trespass on the Case between Dudley Digges Plt and Tarlton Fleming Deft. a Special imparlance is granted the Deft.

Digges vs Prier   In the Action of trespass on the Case between Dudley Digges Plt. and John Prier Deft. a Special imparlance is granted the Deft.

The Action of trespass on the Case between Thomas Dickins Plt. and Samuell Scot and Elizabeth his Wife Defts is dismist the Plt not prosecuting the same.

Tanner vs Lansdon   In the Action of trespass on the Case between

Joseph Tanner Plt. and William Lansdon Deft. the Plt. having failed to file his declaration on the Defts. motion he is Nonsuited and it is thereupon considered by the Court that the Deft. do recover against the Deft. five Shillings Currt. money with Costs and a Lawyers Fee.

The Action of trespass on the Case between David Lesseur Plt. and John Luckadoe Deft. is dismist neither party appearing.

[124]   May Court 1731

Ladd vs White   On the Attachment obtained by John Ladd against the Estate of Edward White the Sheriff hath made the following return "Aprill 27th. 1731 - Executed in the hands of John Tuly, Constant Perkins, William Walker and Anne Hooker Pr. Jos. Thompson Sub Sher." And it is thereupon Ordered that they be Sumoned to appear at the next Court to declare what is in their hands belonging to the said Edward White.

Manacanton road   Claude Gory and Gideon Chambon appear and their Objections against altering the Manacanton road being considered it is Ordered that the road passing along the River Side in the Manacanton be kept open untill the new Church be built in King William Parish and that then the said road be Stop'd and a new one cleared from the ferry landing to the back road on the hills to pass between the Land of Gideon Chambon and Claude Gory of Which Edward Scot is appointed Surveyor.

Then the Court adjourned to the third tuesday in next month

****

At a Court held for Goochland County the third Tuesday in June being the fifteenth day of the Month Anno Dm 1731. Present. William Mayo, Daniell Stoner, James Holman, Anthony Hoggat, George Payne Gent. Justices.

Randolph &c vs Martin   In the Action of trespass on the Case between William Randolph, Richard Randolph, John Randolph & John Fleming Executors &c of Thomas Randolph deceased Plts. & Francis Martin Deft. George Payne, James Holman, Anthony Hoggat & Henry Wood are appointed to examine State & Setle the Severall matters in dispute between then & their report is to be made the Judgment of the Court.

Fleming &c vs Mcbrid   John Fleming one of the Executors &c of Thomas Randolph deceasd Exhibits an Account against John Mcbrid &

makes Oath that he found the same so stated in his Testators books which is Ordered to be certified thereon.

[125]   June Court 1731
Fleming &c vs Dickinson   John Fleming one of the Executors &c of Thomas Randolph deceas'd exhibits an Account against John Dickinson & makes Oath that he found the same so Stated in his Testators books which is Ordered to be Certifyd thereon.

Bollings Adm'on   Mary Bolling Relict of James Bolling deceas'd relinquishing her right of Administration Stephen Hughes comes into Court & (being a Quaker) makes his Affirmation that James Bolling deceas'd died without making any Will so farr as he knows or beleives and on his motion and giving Security for his just and faithfull administration of the said Deceadents Estate Certificate is granted him for obtaining Letters of Administration in due form Ashford Hughes Security. Ordered that James Cunningham Mathew Cox James Nevils & Samuell Burk or any three of them being first Sworn by some Justice of the Peace do appraise the estate of James Bolling deceas'd & that Stephen Hughes the Administrator do return an Inventory thereof to the next Court.

Utleys deed to Hoggat   Thomas Cookson John Utley Junr. & Robert Willis prove a Deed from John Utley to Anthony Hoggat to be the Act and deed of the said John Utley and it is thereupon admitted to record.

Adams Negro boy judged   Toby a Negro boy belonging to Robert Adams is judged to be twelve years Old.

   Absent William Mayo Gent.

Mayos deed to Randolph   William Mayo acknowledged a deed with the livery of Seizin endors'd from himself to William Randolph to be his Act & deed & it is thereupon Admitted to record.

   Present. Wm. Mayo Gent.

Robinsons deed to Dickins   James Robinson & Susanna his Wife (she being first privately examined) acknowledge a Deed with the Livery of Seizin endorsed from themselves to Thomas Dickins to be their Act & Deed & it is thereupon Admitted to record.

[126]   June Court 1731
Arringtons Adm'on   Jane Arrington comes into Court & (being a

Quaker) makes her Affirmation that Samuell Arrington deceased died without making any Will so far as she knows or beleives and on her motion and giving Security for her just & faithfull Administration of the said Deceadents Estate, Certificate is granted her for obtaining Letters of Administration in due form   George Stoveall & Henry Atkinson Securities.

Ordered that Nicholas Cox William Spears John Spears Marmaduke Hix or any three of them being first Sworn by some Justice of the peace do appraise the estate of Samuell Arrington deceased and that Jane Arrington the Administratrix do return an Inventory thereof to the next Court.

Sallee deed to Sallee   William Sallee & Elizabeth his Wife (she being first privately examined) acknowledge a deed with the Livery of Seizin endorsed from themselves to Peter Sallee to be their Act & deed & it is thereupon admitted to record, William Sallee also acknowledges a receipt endorsed on the said deed to be his Act & deed which is also admitted to record.

Adams vs Randolphs Exec'rs to be Sumon'd   On the Petition of Robert Adams for leave to build a Mill on Dover Mill Creek, Ordered that the Executors of Thomas Randolph deceased be Sumon'd to object against the same of they can.

Burgamys Inventory   Elizabeth Burgamy presents an Inventory of the Estate of John Burgamy deceased which is admitted to record.

    Absent Anthony Hoggat Gent.

Allen fined   Samuell Allen appears on his recognizance & being accused by Anthony Hoggat for a Misbehaviour & breach of the Peace the Witnesses being heard it is Ordered that he be fined to our Sovereign Lord King George twenty four Shillings Sterling & that he enter into bond with good & Sufficient Security for his good behaviour for a Year & a day.

    Present Anthony Hoggat, George Raine Gent.

Capper levy free   On the Petition of George Capper he is exempt from payment of County Levys.

[127]   June Court 1731
Kelly Levy free   On the Petition of Giles Kelly he is exempt from

paying his County levy this year.

Le'Grands Orphans bound   Jane Magdalene L'Grand & Judeth L'Grand Orphans of John L'grand are ordered to be bound by the Churchwardens of St. James's Parish to Peter L'Grand.

Surveyor of road   Stephen Cox is appointed Surveyor of the road from the Ferry unto the main road & leave is granted him to turn the said road. Benjamin Alsup, Thomas Lawhan, John Lewis, Stephen Woodson, Josiah Woodson & their titheables are to clear the said road & also a bridle way from the Ferry to the Church.

Surveyor of road   Daniell Hix is appointed Surveyor of the road from Buck branch to the County bridge the titheables of Thomas Randolph deceased are Ordered to clear the Same.

Surveyor of road   William Womack is appointed Surveyor of the road from Buck branch to the Mill & the titheables adjacent thereto are to assist in clearing the Same.

Present. Wm. Cabbell Gent.

Surveyor of road   George Raine is appointed Surveyor of the road from Jenitoe Creek on the back road into Hoggats road the titheables under George Payne Henry Wood & Anthony Hoggat are to assist in clearing the said road.

Constable appointed   Robert Cawthon is appointed Constable & Anthony Hoggat Gent. is to Swear him.

Adams's deed to Owen   Robert Adams acknowledges a deed with the Livery of Seisin endorsed from himself to William Owen to be his Act & deed & it is thereupon admitted to Record.

Woodson vs Hughes   The Action of Trespass on the Case between Joseph Woodson Plt. and Stephen Hughes Deft. is continued.

[128]   June Court 1731
Digges vs Hughes   In the Action of trespass on the Case between Dudley Digges Plt. and Stephen Hughes Deft. the parties Submit themselves to the Court for tryall, the parties their Accounts & Witnesses being heard it is considered that the Plt do recover against the Deft. two pounds eight Shillings & fourpence farthing Currt. money with Costs &

a Lawyers Fee.

Thompson vs Digges   On the motion of James Thompson of Gloucester a Witness for Dudley Digges vs Stephen Hughes it is Ordered that the said Dudley do pay him for one days Attendance & for coming & returning Ninety miles once three hundred and thirty pounds of tobacco & for ferriages three Shillings & ninepence with Costs.

Winston vs Nolun &c   In the Action of debt between Isaac Winston Plt. and Agnes Nolun &c. Admx. &c of Thomas Nolun deceas'd Deft. the Deft. confesses Judgment for one pound ten shillings & ten pence Current money when she shall have Assets whereupon it is Considered by the Court that the Plt. do recover against the Deft. out of the said Deceadents Estate when there shall be Assets Sufficient in her hands the said Sum with the Costs of this Suit.

Absent Daniell Stoner Gent.

Bollings Negro Levy free   John Bolling on his petition is exempt from paying County Levys for Strong Jack a Negro belonging to him.

Present. Daniell Stoner Gent.

Hambleton vs Nolun &c   In the Action of debt between James Hambleton & Agnes Nolun Admx. &c of Thomas Nolun deceased Deft. the Deft. confesses Judgment for two pounds eleven shillings & four pence Currt. money when Assets whereupon it is considered by the Court that the Plt. do recover against the Deft. out of the said deceadents estate in her hands when she shall have Assets Sufficient the said Sum with Costs.

Thompson & Uxor vs Edwards   In the Action of Trespass on the Case between Samuell Thompson & Mary his Wife Plts. & Thomas Edwards Deft. the Plts. failing to prosecute their Suit on the Defts. motion they are nonsuited and it is thereupon considered by the Court that the Deft. do recover against the Plts. five Shillings Currt. money with Costs and a Lawyers Fee.

[129]   June Court 1731
Bradley vs Saunders   The Action of trespass on the Case between Joseph Bradley Plt. and John Saunders Deft. is continued at the Plts Costs.

Woodson vs Napier   The Action of Trespass on the Case between William Woodson Plt. and Bouth Napier Deft. is dismist the Plt. not prosecuting the same.

Ford vs Pruit   In the Action of Trespass on the Case between James Ford Plt. and Thomas Pruit Deft. the following Jury are sworn, Bouth Napier, William Epperson, John Prier, Ashford Hughes, George Southerland, Joseph Bingley, Francis James, John Ladd, William Womack, James Taylor, John Laine, William Lansdon who after some time being in their Verdict which on the Plts motion is Ordered to be recorded and is as followeth "We find for the Plt. one Shilling Sterling Money Bouth Napier Foreman." Whereupon it is considered by the Court that the Plt. do recover against the Deft. one Shillings Sterling Damages by the Jurors aforesaid in their said Verdict assessed & one shillings Costs.

Cox's Administ'n   The last will & testament of Bartholomew Cox deceased is presented in Court & being proved by the Oaths of Agnes Nolun & Rebecca Wood two of the Witnesses thereto it is admitted to record & the Executors refusing to take upon them the Execution thereof & relinquishing their right therein, John Bolling Gent. comes into Court and makes Oath according to Law and thereupon Certificate is granted him for obtaining Letters of Administration with the Will annext in due form William Mayo entring himself Security for the same.

Ordered that Robert Hughes, John Saunders, Samuell Spencer & Jacob Micheaux or any three of them being first sworn by some Justice of the Peace do appraise the Estate of Bartholomew Cox deceased and that John Bolling his Administrator do present and Inventory thereof to the next Court.

Wood vs White   In the Action on the Case between Henry Wood Plt. & Edward White Deft. the following Jury are Sworn, Bouth Napier, William Epperson, John Prier, Ashford Hughes, George Southerland, Joseph Bingley, Francis James, Thomas Turpin, William Womack, James Taylor, John Laine, William Lansdon who after some time bring in their Verdict which on the Plts. motion is Ordered to be recorded and is as followeth "Wee find for the Plt. one pound fifteen

[130]   June Court 1731

Shillings and three pence Currt. money Bouth Napier Foreman" whereupon it is considered by the Court that the Plt. do recover against the Deft. & John Lad his Common Bail one pound fifteen shillings & three pence Currt. money by the Jurors aforesaid in their said Verdict ass'd with Costs.

Present. Allen Howard Gent.

Ward's Servant Order'd to Serve Richard Ward brings into Court Thomas Duggins his Servant who having absented himself from his Masters Service seven Weeks it is Ordered that he do Serve his said Master for the same and for the Costs of this Order according to Law after his time by Indenture Custom or former Order of Court is expired.

Wilson to be Sumond Richard Wilson is Ordered to be Sumoned to appear at the next Court to answer his Misbehaviour in neglected to obey a Warrant granted by William Mayo Gent. & Thomas Duggins & Nicholas Roads as Witness.

Allens recognizance Samuell Allen and James Holman come into Court & Acknowledge themselves indebted unto our Soverign Lord King George in the Sum of fifty pounds Sterling to be levyd upon their Goods & Chattles on Condition that the said Samuell Allen be of good behaviour towards all his Majestys Subjects for a Year & a day and it is thereupon Ordered that he be dis[charged] from the Custody of the Sheriff & that he pay Costs.

Ford vs Pruit On the motion of Henry Wood it is the Opinion of the Court that in the Action between James Ford Plt. & Thomas Pruit Deft. no Execution ought to be issued for the Deft. against the Plt. for the Defts Costs.

Bingley vs Pruit On the motion of Joseph Bingley a Witness for Thomas Pruit ads James Ford it is Ordered that the said Thomas do pay him for three days Attendance ninety pounds of tobacco with Costs.

Chapman vs Pruit On the motion of John Chapman a Witness for Thomas Pruit ads James Ford it is Ordered that the said Thomas do pay him for three days Attendance ninety pounds of Tobacco with Costs.

On the motion of Anthony Calvit a Witness for Thomas Pruit ads James Ford

[131] June Court 1731
Ford it is Ordered that the said Thomas do pay him for three days Attendance ninety pounds of tobacco with Costs.

Scot vs Pruit On the motion of James Scot a Witness for Thomas Pruit ads James Ford it is Ordered that the said Thomas do pay him for three days Attendance ninety pounds of tobacco with Costs.

Boccar vs Pruit   On the motion of Peter Boccar a Witness for Thomas Pruit ads James Ford it is Ordered that the said Thomas do pay him for three days Attendance ninety pounds of tobacco with Costs.

Agee vs Pruit   On the motion of Anthony Agee a Witness for Thomas Pruit ads James Ford it is Ordered that the said Thomas do pay him for three days attendance ninety pounds of tobacco with Costs.

Agee vs Ford   On the motion of Mathew Agee a Witness James Ford vs Thomas Pruit it is Ordered that the said James do pay him for three days Attendance ninety pounds of tobacco with Costs.

Robertson vs Ford   On the motion of James Robertson a Witness for James Ford vs Thomas Pruit it is Ordered that the said James do pay him for three days Attendance ninety pounds of tobacco with Costs.

Forcee vs Ford   On the motion of Mary Forcee a Witness for James Ford vs Thomas Pruit it is Ordered that the said James do pay him for three days attendance ninety pounds of tobacco with Costs.

Digges vs Woodson   In the Action of trespass on the Case between Dugley Digges Plt. and Joseph Woodson Deft. the parties submitt themselves to the Court for tryall whereupon they & their witnesses being heard & their Accounts regulated it is considered that the Plt. do recover against the Deft. three pounds two Shillings & sixpence Currt. money with Costs & a Lawyers Fee.

Thompson vs Digges   On the Motion of James Thompson of York County a Witness for Dudley Digges vs Joseph Woodson it is Ordered that the said Dudley do pay him for one days attendance & for coming & returning one hundred and ten miles once three hundred & ninety pounds of tobacco & two shillings

[132]   June Court 1731
for Ferriages with Costs.

Hughes vs Edwards   On the motion of Ashford Hughes a Witness for Thomas Edwards ads Samuell Thompson & Mary his Wife it is Ordered that the said Thomas Edwards do pay him for nine days attendance two hundred & seventy pounds of tobacco with Costs.

Bradshaw vs Edwards   On the motion of Benjamin Bradshaw a Witness for Thomas Edwards ads Samuell Thompson & Mary his Wife it is Ordered that the said Thomas Edwards do pay him for thirteen days Attendance three hundred & ninety pounds of tobacco with Costs.

Skelton takes Oaths   William Mayo and Alllen Howard Gent. administer of the Oaths appointed by Act of Parliament to be taken instead of the Oaths of Allegiance & Supremacy the Oath appointed to be taken by an Act of Parliament made in the first year of the Reign of his late Majesty King George the first intituled an Act for the further Security of his Majestys person & Government & of the Succession to the Crown of Great Britain in the heirs of the late Princess Sophia being protestants & for extinguishing the hopes of the Pretended Prince of Wales and his open & Secret Abettors to James Skelton Gent who Subscribes the Test and takes the Oath of a Justice of the Peace & of a Justice in Chancery.

Then the Court adjourned till to morrow Morning ten of the Clock.

****

At a Court continued & held for Goochland County the Sixteenth day of June 1731. Present. William Mayo, Allin Howard, Anthony Hoggat, James Skelton Gent. Justices.

Cabbell vs Downie   On the Attachment obtained by William Cabbell Plt. against the Estate of Robert Downie Deft. the persons on whom the Sheriff return'd the Attachm't Served are Ordered to be Summoned to appear at the next Court and the Attachment is continued.

Cabbell &c vs Woodson   In the Action of trespass on the Case between William Cabell Administrator of

[133]   June Court 1731
Joell Carr deceas'd Plt. & Josiah & Stephen Woodson Executors &c. of Jacob Woodson deceased defts. an Imparlance is granted the Defts.

Cabbell vs Williams   In the Action of trespass on the Case between William Cabbell Plt. & John Williams Deft. the Sheriff having made return on the Als Capias that the Deft. is not an Inhabitant in his Bailiwick & he failing to appear on the Plts motion a Plurs. Caps. is awarded against the Deft. returnable to the next Court.

Raine vs Levins &c   In the Action of trespass on the Case between

George Raine Plt & Richard Levins Administrator &c of John Sutton Farrar deceased Deft. an Imparlance is granted the Deft.

Cabbell vs Utley   In the Action of trespass on the Case between William Cabbell Plt. & John Utley Deft. the Sheriff having made return on the Als Caps. that the Deft. is not to be found and he failing to appear on the Plts. motion a Plurs. Caps. is awarded against the Deft. returnable to the next Court.

Woodson vs Cabbell   In the Action of Debt between Josiah & Stephen Woodson Exec'rs &c of Jacob Woodson deceased Plts & William Cabbell Deft. the Deft. failing to appear on the Plts. motion Judgment by nihil dicit is granted them against the Deft. for what damages shall be recovered in this Suit to be discharged nevertheless if the Deft. shall plead at the next Court.

Ward vs Farrar   In the Action of Debt between Seth Ward Plt. & John Sutton Farrar Deft. the Deft. failing to plead on the Plts motion Judgment by nihil dicit is granted him against the Deft. for what damages shall be recovered, in this Suit to be discharged nevertheless if the Deft. shall plead at the next Court.

Merrewether vs Martin   In the Action of Debt between William Merrewether Plt. & Francis Martin Deft. the following Jury are Sworn, Joell Chandler, James Robertson, William Walker, Constant Perkins, John Saunders, Bartholomew Stoveall, John Laine, James Taylor, Isaac Hughes, William Epperson, Charles Johnson, John Prier who after Some time bring in their Verdict which on the Plts motion is Ordered to be recorded and is as followeth "Wee the Jury find for the Plt. twelve hundred and forty pounds of Sweet scented tobacco Cask & Conveniency John Saunders Foreman." Whereupon it is Considered

[134]   June Court 1731
by the Court that the Plt. do recover against the Deft. and Tarlton Fleming Sheriff twelve hundred & forty pounds of Sweet scented tobacco Cask & Conveniency by the Jurors aforesaid in their said Verdict assessed with Costs and an Attorneys Fee.

Present. William Cabbell Gent.

Raine vs Martin   The Action of Trespass on the Case between George Raine Plt. & Francis Martin Deft. is continued.

Raine vs Dickinson   The Action of trespass on the Case between George Raine Plt. & John Dickinson Deft. is Continued.

Present. George Raine Gent.

Webber vs White   In the Action of Trespass on the Case between Philip Webber Assignee of James Elliot Plt. & Edward White Deft. the following Jury are Sworn, Joell Chandler, James Robertson, William Walker, Constant Perkins, John Saunders, Bartholomew Stoveall, John Laine, James Taylor, Isaac Hughes, William Epperson, Charles Johnson, John Prier who after some time bring in their Verdict which on the Plts motion is Ordered to be recorded & is as followeth "Wee the Jury find for the Plt. six hundred pounds of tobacco, John Saunders Foreman." Whereupon it is considered by the Court that the Plt. do recover against the deft. and John Lad his Common Bail six hundred pounds of tobacco by the Jurors aforesaid in their said Verdict assess'd with Costs and an Attorneys Fee.

Mallet vs Pruit   In the Action of trespass between Stephen Mallet Plt. and Thomas Pruit Deft. the following Jury are Sworn, Joell Chandler, James Robertson, William Walker, Constant Perkins, John Saunders, Bartholomew Stoveall, John Laine, James Taylor, Isaac Hughes, William Epperson, Charles Johnson, John Prier who after Some time bring in their Verdict which on the Defts motion is Ordered to be recorded & is as following "Wee find for the Deft. John Saunders Foreman." Whereupon it is considered by the Court that the Plt. take nothing by his Writ aforesaid that the Deft. go hence without day and that he recover against the Plt. his Costs by him in this behalf expended & a Lawyers Fee.

Grand Jury vs Dickins   Thomas Dickins presented by the Grand jury for profaining the Sabbath pleads not guilty & Submitts tryall to the Court & upon hearing is acquitted.

[135]   June Court 1731
Grand Jury vs Davis   George Davis presented by the Grand Jury for assaulting Thomas Wadloe pleads not guilty, issue is taken thereon.

Grand Jury vs Stephens   The presentment of the Grand Jury against William Stephens is dismist the said Stephens not being an Inhabitant.

Grand Jury vs Churchward's. of St. Jam's. Parish   The Churchwardens of St. James's Parish presented for not finding the Laws to be read in Churches upon bearin [being] heard are acquited.

Grand Jury vs Church Wardens of K'g Wm Parish   The Churchwardens of King William Parish presented for not finding the Laws to be read in Churches not appearing Ordered that a Capias do issue against them returnable to the next Court.

Grand Jury vs Micheaux   Jacob Micheaux present for retailing Liquors without Licence pleads not guilty issue is taken thereon & tryall referred.

Grand Jury vs Richardson   John Richardson presented for retailing Liquors without Lycence pleads not guilty issue is taken thereon & tryall referred.

Grand Jury vs Fleming & Dabbs   Tarlton Fleming & Joseph Dabbs presented for being drunk upon being heard are acquitted.

Grand Jury vs L'villian   John L'villain presented for being drunk and not appearing, it is Ordered that a Capias do issue against him returnable to the next Court.

Gd. Jry. vs Quantin   John Quantin presented for being drunk pleads not guilty & issue is joined.

Gd. Jry. vs Dickins   Thomas Dickins presented for Learning his Negro boy to profane the Lords prayer pleads not guilty & issue is joined.

Gd. Jy. vs Randolphs Ex'rs   The Executors of Thomas Randolph presented for not keeping a passable way over Dover Mill & not appearing a Capias is awarded against them returnable to the next Court.

Gd. Jy. vs Murrell   Thomas Murrell presented for being drunk & profane swearing & not appearing a Caps. is awarded against him returnable to the next Court.

[136]   June Court 1731
Gd. Jy. vs Scruggs   John Scruggs presented for Swearing confesses Judgment for fifty pounds of tobacco and is ordered to pay the same unto the Churchwardens of St. James's Parish with Costs.

Gd. Jy. vs Ballew   Judith Ballew presented for having a Bastard Child Thomas Walker confesses Judgment for five hundred pounds of tobacco & is ordered to pay the same to the Church Wardens of St. James's Parish.

Gd. Jy. vs Birk   John Birk presented for Swearing failing to appear a

Caps. is awarded against him returnable to the next Court.

Gd. Jy. vs Vail   William Vail presented for Swearing confesses Judgment for fifty pounds of tobacco John Radford Security, & it is Ordered that the said William & John do pay the same to the Church Wardens of St. James's Parish with Costs.

Gd. Jy. vs Mooney   John Mooney presented for Swearing, James Taylor confesses Judgment for fifty pounds of tobacco & it is Ordered that the said John do pay the same to the Churchwardens of St. James parish with Costs.

Gd. Jy. vs Parker   Richard Parker presented for beating Thomas Wadloe pleads not guilty & issue is joined thereon.

Pruit fined   Thomas Pruit is Ordered to pay fifty pounds of tobacco to the Church wardens of St. James's Parish for Swearing & also to pay Costs.

Absent. William Mayo Gent.

Hix vs Tabor & Stovall   In the Action of Debt between Marmaduke Hix Assignee of William Mayo Plt. & John Tabor & Bartholomew Stoveall Defts. the following Jury are Sworn, Joell Chandler, James Robertson, William Walker, John Saunders, John Laine, James Taylor, Isaac Hughes, William Epperson, Charles Johnson, John Prier, John Radford, John Taylor who after Some time bring in their Verdict which on the Defts motion is Ordered to be recorded and is as followeth "Wee find for the Defts   John Saunders Foreman. whereupon it is considered by the Court that the Plt. take nothing by his Writ aforesaid that the Defts go hence without day and that they recover against the Deft. their Costs by them in this behalf expended and a Lawyers Fee.

[137]   June Court 1731

Scruggs vs Tabor & Stoveall   On the motion of John Scruggs a Witness for John Tabor and Bartholomew Stoveall ads Marmaduke Hix it is Ordered that the said John Tabor & Bartholomew Stoveall do pay him for two days Attendance sixty pounds of tobacco with Costs.

Davis vs Tabor & Stoveall   On the motion of George Davis a Witness for Jno. Tabor & Bartho. Stoveall ads Marmad. Hix it is Ordered that the said John Tabor & Bartho. Stovall do pay him for two days Attendance sixty pounds of tobacco with Costs.

Walton vs Tabor & Stoveall   On the motion of Thomas Walton a Witness for Jno. Tabor & Bartho. Stoveall ads Marmad. Hix it is Ordered that the said John Tabor & Bartho. Stovall do pay him for two days Attendance sixty pounds of tobacco with Costs.

Present. William Mayo Gent.

Vail vs Pruit   On the motion of William Vail a Witness for Thomas Pruit ads Stephen Mallet it is Ordered that the said Thomas Pruit do pay him for four days Attendance one hundred & twenty pounds of tobacco with Costs.

Boccar vs Pruit   On the motion of Peter Boccar a Witness for Thomas Pruit ads Stephen Mallet it is ordered that the said Thomas Pruit do pay him for four days Attendance one hundred & twenty pounds of tobacco with Costs.

Gutridge vs Pruit   On the motion of Mark Gutridge a Witness for Thomas Pruit ads Stephen Mallet it is Ordered that the said Thomas Pruit do pay him for four days attendance one hundred & twenty pounds of tobacco with Costs.

Moseby vs Taylor   The Action of Debt between Richard Moseby Plt. & John Taylor Deft. is continued at the Defts Costs.

Locket vs James   In the Action of trespass between Thomas Locket Plt. & Francis

[138]   June Court 1731
James Deft. the Plt. files his replication & the Suit is continued.

Stoner vs Utley   In the Action of trespass on the Case between Daniell Stoner Plt. & John Utley Deft. the Sheriff having returned on the Alias Capias that the Deft. is not to be found & he failing to appear on the Plts motion a Plurs. Caps. is awarded against him returnable to the next Court.

Macon vs Wharton   In the Action on the Case between John Macon Plt. & Thomas Wharton Deft. the Plt. at Common Law being the Respondent in Chancery & having failed to file his Answer on the motion of the Defendt. at Common Law who is the Complainant in Chancery it is Ordered that the Respondent do pay unto the Complainant twenty Shillings Currt. money for want of an answer & the Suit is continued.

Waddil Junr. vs Edwards   The Action on the Case between William Waddil junr. Plt. & Thomas Edwards Deft. is continued.

Flournoy vs Martin   In the Action of Trespass on the Case between John James Flournoy Plt. & Francis Martin Deft. the Plt. files a New Declaration & an Imparlance is granted the Deft.

Flournoy &c vs Martin   In the Action of Debt between John James Flournoy & Elizabeth his Wife Executrix &c of Orlando Jones Deceased Plts & Francis Martin Def't the Plts file a New Declaration & an Imparlance is granted the Deft.

Scot vs Pruit   In the Action of trespass on the Case between Edward Scot Plt. & Thomas Pruit Deft. the Deft. pleads not guilty & for tryall puts himself upon the Country & the Plt. likewise.

Taylor vs Lowe & Uxor   The Action of Trespass on the Case between John Taylor Deft. & Thos. Lowe & Amy his Wife Defts is continued.

Martin vs Fleming &c   In the Action of trespass on the Case between John Martin Plt. & John Fleming Adminr. &c of Paul Pennington deceased Deft. the Deft. failing to appear on the Plts motion the Conditionall Judgment formerly granted him in this Suit agt the Deft. & Tarlton Fleming Sheriff is confirmed for so much damages as shall be found upon Executing a Writ of Enquiry

[139]   June Court 1731
enquiry at the next Court of which the Sheriff is hereby Ordered to give the Deft. notice by Serving him with a Copy of this Order.

Hopkins vs Woodson   In the Action of trespass on the Case between William Hopkins Plt. & Benjn. Woodson the Deft. failing to appear on the Plts motion the Conditionall Judgment formerly granted him in this Suit against the Deft. is confirmed for so much damages as shall be found upon Executing a Writ if enquiry at the next Court of which the Sheriff is hereby ordered to give the Deft. notice by Serving him with a Copy of this Order.

Winfrey vs Williams   In the Action of trespass on the Case between Jacob Winfrey Plt. & John Williams Deft. the Sheriff having made return on the Plurs. Caps. that the Deft. is not an Inhabitant in this Bailiwick & he failing to appear on the Plts. motion a Plurs. Caps. de novo is awarded against him returnable to the next Court.

Hatcher vs Syms   In the Action of trespass on the Case between Henry Hatcher Assignee of Samuell Hatcher Plt. & Richard Syms Deft. the Sheriff having made return on the Plurs. Caps. that the Writ came too late to his hands to be executing & the Deft. failing to appear on the Plts motion a Plurs. Caps. do novo is awarded against him returnable to the next Court.

Bryant vs Chandler   In the Action of Trespass on the Case between William Bryant Plt. & Joell Chandler Deft. the Deft. pleads he oweth nothing & for tryall thereof puts himself upon the Country & the Plt. likewise.

Bryant vs Chandler   In the Action of trespass on the Case between William Bryant Plt. & Joell Chandler Deft. the Deft. pleads he oweth nothing & for tryall thereof puts himself upon the Country & the Plt. likewise.

Dickins vs Utley   In the Action of trespass on the Case between Thomas Dickins Plt & John Utley Deft. the Sheriff having made return on the Als Caps that the Deft is not to be found & he failing to appear on the Plts motion a Plurs. Caps. is awarded against him returnable to the next Court.

Macon vs Hughes. In the Action of trespass on the Case between William Macon Plt. & Stephen Hughes Deft. the Plt. files a New declaration and the Deft. confesses

[140]   June Court 1731
Judgment for five pounds Sixteen shillings & five pence Currt. money whereupon it is considered by the Court that the Plt. do recover against the Deft. the said Sum with Costs & a Lawyers Fee.

Gates vs Saunders   In the Action of Trover between William Gates Plt. & Robert Saunders Deft. the Deft. pleads not guilty & for tryall thereof puts himself on the Country & the Plt. likewise.

Randolph &c. vs Macbrid   In the Act of Trespass between William Randolph, Richard Randolph, John Randolph & John Fleming Execrs. &c of Tho[mas] Randolph deceased Plts & John Mcbrid Deft. is continued a[t the Defts.] Cost.

Randolph &c vs Dickinson   The Action of trespass on the Case between William Randolph, Richard Randolph, John Randolph & John

Fleming Execrs. &c of Thom[as Randolph] deceasd Plts & John Dickinson Deft. is continued.

Ward vs Dean   In the Action of debt between Seth Ward Plt. & Richard De[an Deft.] Thomas Dickins appears on behalf of the Deft. & confesses Judgment to the Plt. for two hundred & twelve pounds of tobacco, Whereupon it is considered by the Court that the Plt. do recover against the Deft. the said Sum of tobacco with Costs & a Lawyers Fee.

Chastain vs Martin   In the Action of trespass on the Case between John & Peter Chastain Executors &c of Peter Chastain deceased Plt. & [Fra]ncis Martin Deft. the Deft. pleads he oweth nothing & for tryall thereof puts himself upon the Country & the Plt. likewise.

Davis vs Quinn   In the Action of Debt between George Davis Plt. & John Quin Deft. the Deft. failing to appear on the Plts motion [the] Conditionall Judgment formerly granted him in this Suit against the Deft. & Tarlton Fleming Gent. Sheriff is confirmed for so much damage as shall be found upon executing a Writ of enquiry at the next Court of which the Sheriff is hereby Ordered to give the Deft. notice by Serving him with a Copy of this Order.

Dixon vs Napier   In the Action of Debt between Thomas Dixon Plt. & Bouth

[141]   June Court 1731
Napier Deft. the Deft. failing to appear on the Plts motion the Conditionall Judgment formerly Granted him in this Suit against the Deft. & Tarlton Fleming Gent. Sheriff is confirmed for two pounds Sixteen Shillings & seven pence half penny Currt. money & it is thereupon considered by the Court that the Plt. do recover against Tarlton Fleming Gent. Sheriff the said Sum with Costs & a Lawyers Fee.

Fleming vs [Napier]   Whereas Thomas Dixon hath this day obtained a Judgment against Tarlton Fleming Gent. Sheriff for two pounds Sixteen Shillings & seven pence half penny Currt. money with Costs by reason of the non appearance of Bouth Napier to answer the Suit of the said Thomas Dixon therefore on the motion of the said Tarlton Fleming it is Ordered that an Attachment do issue against the Estate of the said Bouth Napier returnable to the next Court.

[Johnson vs] Pruit   In the Action of Trespass on the Case between Charles Johnson & Elizabeth his Wife Plts & Andrew Pruit Deft. at last

Court the Deft. filed reasons to stay Judgment on the Verdict then found the Arguments whereon being now heard it is the opinion of the Court that the said reasons are not sufficient in Law to Stay Judgmt on the Verdict aforesaid and it is thereupon considered that the Plts do recover against the Deft. forty Shillings Currt. money by the Jurors in their said Verdict assess'd with Costs & an Attorneys Fee.

Scot vs Daniell   The [Action] of Detinue between Edward Scot Plt. & James Daniell Deft [is continued.]

Burgess vs Woodson   In the [Acti]on of Trespass on the Case between John Burgess Plt. & John [Wood]son Deft. the Deft. failing to appear on the Plts motion the Conditionall Judgment formerly granted him in this Suit against the [Deft.] is confirmed for so much damages as shall be found upon exe[cuti]ng a Writ of Enquiry at [next] Court of which the Sherif is hereby Ordered to give [the Deft. no]tice by Serving him with a Copy of this Order.

Prosser vs May   The Action of trespass on the Case between Thomas Prosser Plt.

[142]   June Court 1731
& William May Deft. is continued John Prier entring himself Speciall Bail.

Taylor vs Quin   In the Action of trespass on the Case between James Taylor Plt. & John Quin Deft. the Plt. files a new declaration & the Deft. failing to appear on the Plts motion Judgment is granted him against the Deft. & William Cabbell who returned his Common Bail for what Da[mages are to] be recovered in this Suit to be discharged neverthe[less if the Deft.] shall appear at the next Court.

Taylor vs Quin   In the Action of Debt between James Taylor Plt. & John Quin Deft. the Deft. failing to appear on the Plts motion Judgment is granted against the Deft. & William Cabbell who is returned for [torn] bail for what damages shall be recovered in this Suit to be discharged nevertheless if the Deft. shall appear at the next Court.

Saunders vs Quin   The Action of debt between John Saunders Plt. & John Quin Deft is dismist the Plt not prosecuting the same.

David &c vs Quantin &c   In the Action on the Case between Anne David Executrix &c of Peter David deceased Plt. & John Quantin Admr &c of William Davis deceased Deft. the parties Submitt themselves to

[torn] tryall whereupon the Plts. oath being heard it is considered by the [Court that] the Plt. do recover against the Deft. out of the said Deceadents [torn] hands two pounds eight shillings & a penny Currt. money [torn]

Quantin vs Dickins   In the Action of Trespass on the Case [between] John Quantin Admr &c of William Davis deceased Plt. & Thomas [Dickins] Deft. the following Jury are Sworn   Joel Chandler, James Robert[son, John] Walker, John Saunders, John Laine, James Taylor, Isaac Hug[hes, William] Epperson, Charles Johnson, William Moor, David Mims, John [torn] after some time bring in their Verdict which on the Plts motion [is order]ed to be recorded and is as followeth "Wee find for the Plt. two [pounds] eight Shillings & two pence Currt. money John Saunders Foreman." Whereupon it is considered by the Court that the Plt. do recover against the Deft. two pounds Eight shillings & two pence Currt. money by the Jurors aforesaid in their Said Verdict assessed with the Costs of this Suit & a Lawyers Fee.

[143]   June Court 1731
Processioning of Land Ordered   Pursuant to the directions of an Act of Assembly it is Ordered that the Vestrys of King William & St. James's parishes do divide their respective Parishes in so many precincts as to them shall seem most convenient for processioning every particular person's land in their Severall respective parishes and that they do appoint the particular times between the last day of September and the last day of March next ensuing when such processioning shall be made in every precinct & that they do appoint at least two Intelligent honest Freeholders of every precinct to see such processioning performed & take & return to the Vestry an Account of every persons land they shall procession & of the persons present at the Same & of what lands in their precincts they shall fail to procession & of the particular reasons of such failure.

[Rapene vs Marchbanks]   In the Action of Debt between Anthony Rapene Plt. & George Marchbanks Deft. time is granted the Plt. to mend his Declaration.

[Dickins vs] Quin   In the Action of debt between Thomas Dickins Plt. & John Quin Deft. for forty pounds Currt. money, on the Plts motion the Plurs Caps formerly granted him in this Suit against the Deft. being returned & the Deft. not taken thereon An Attachment is awarded against the Defts estate returnable to the next Court.

Prosser vs Quin   The Action of Trespass on the Case between Thomas

Prosser Plt. & Jno. Quin [Deft. is con]tinued.

Mims vs Levins &c   In the [Action of Tresp]ass on the Case between David Mims Plt. & Richard Levins [Deft. Administrator] &c of John Sutton Farrar deceased Deft. the Deft. appears [but failing] to plead on the Plts motion Judgment by nihil dicit is granted him against [the Deft.] for what Damages shall be recovered in this Suit to be [discharged] nevertheless if the Deft. shall plead at the next Court.

Digges vs Fleming   In the [Action of tre]spass on the Case between Dudley Digges Plt. & Tarlton Fle[ming Deft. time] is granted the Plt. to mend his Declaration.

Digges vs Prier   I[n the] Action of trespass on the Case between Dudley Digges Plt. & John Prier Deft. the Deft. pleads he oweth nothing & for tryall thereof puts himself upon the Country & the Plt. likewise.

Digges vs Levins &c   In the Action of trespass on the Case between Dudley Digges Plt. &

[144]   June Court 1731
Richard Levins Admr. &c. of John Sutton Farrar deceased Deft. the Deft. appears but failing to plead on the Plts motion Judgment by nihil dicit is granted him against the Deft. for what damages shall be recovered in this Suit to be discharged nevertheless if the Deft. shall plead at the next Court.

Dickins vs Scot   In the Action of trespass on the Case between Thomas Dickins Plt. & Edward Scot Deft. the Deft. appears but failing to plead on the Plts motion Judgment by nihil dicit is granted him against the Deft. for what damages shall be recovered in this Suit to be discharged nevertheless if the Deft. shall plead at the next Court.

Hughes vs Woodson   In the Action of trespass on the Case between Robert Hughes Plt. & John Woodson Deft. the Deft. failing to appear on the Plts motion the Conditionall Judgment formerly granted him in this Suit against the Deft. & Tarlton Fleming Gent Sheriff is confirmed for so much damages as shall be found upon Executing a Writ of Enquiry at the next Court of which the Sheriff is hereby Ordered to give the Deft. notice by Serving him with a Copy of this Order.

Hughes vs Cox   The Action of trespass on the Case between Robert Hughes Plt. & John Cox Deft. is dismist the Plt. not prosecuting the same

Hughes vs Johnson   The Action of Trespass on the Case between Robert Hughes Plt. & Daniell Johnson Deft. is dismist the Plt. not prosecuting the same.

Lad vs White   On the Attachment obtained by John Ladd against the Estate of Edward White Constant Perkins appears and makes Oath that he is indebted to the said Edward one hundred & sixty pounds of tobacco and William Walker makes Oath that he is indebted seventy eight pounds of tobacco & the Attach[ment] is continued.

Scot vs Ridgell &c   Richard Ridgell, Joshua Stephens & John Field failing to appear on the Summons issued against them it is Ordered that a Capias do issue against them returnable to the next Court.

[145]   June Court 1731
Anderson vs Allin   In the Action of Debt between John Anderson Plt. & Samuell Allen Deft. the Deft. failing to appear on the Plts motion Judgment is granted him against the Deft. & Tarlton Fleming Gent. Sher. for what damages shall be recovered in this Suit to be discharged nevertheless if the Deft. shall appear at the next Court.

Anderson vs Burton   In the Action of Debt between John Anderson Plt. & Nowell Burton Deft. the Sheriff having returned on the Capias that the Deft. is not to be found and he failing to appear on the Plts motion an Als Caps. is awarded against the Deft. returnable to the next Court.

Anderson vs Quin   In the A[ction] of Debt between John Anderson Plt. & John Quin Deft. the Sheriff having returned on the Capias that the Deft is not to be found & he failing to appear on the Plts motion an Alias Capias is awarded against the Deft. returnable to the next Court.

Gurrent vs Payne   In the Action of trespass on the Case between Peter Guerrant Administrator &c of Daniell Guerrant deceased Plt. & John Payne Deft. the Deft. failing to appear on the Plts motion Judgment is granted him against the Deft. & Tarlton Fleming Gent. Sheriff for what damages shall be recovered in this Suit to be discharged nevertheless if the Deft. shall appear at the next Court.

The Action of Trespass on the Case between Robert Hughes Plt and John Creasy Deft. is dismist the Plt not prosecuting the same.

The Action of Debt between Francis James Plt. & Anthony Rapene Churchwarden of King William Parish Plt. is dismist the Plt. not prosecuting the same.

Rayne vs Payne   In the Action of Trespass on the Case between George Raine Plt. vs George Payne Junr Deft. the Sheriff having returned on the Capias that the Deft. is not to be found & he failing to appear on the Plts. motion an Alias Capias is awarded against the Deft.

[146]   June Court 1731
returnable to the next Court.

Raine vs Amos   In the Action of trespass on the Case between George Raine Plt. & Francis Amos Deft. the Deft. failing to appear on the Plts motion Judgment is granted him against the Deft. & John Creasy his Common Bail for what damages shall be recovered in this Suit to be discharged nevertheless if the Deft. shall appear at the next Court.

Digges vs Thaxton   In the Action of trespass on the Case between Dudley Digges Plt. & Abell Thaxton Deft. the Sheriff having returned on the Capias that the Deft. is not to be found & he failing to appear on the Plts motion an Als Capias is awarded against the Deft. returnable to the next Court.

Digges vs Pate   In the Action of Trespass on the Case between Dudley Digges Plt. & Thomas Pate Deft. the Sheriff having returned on the Capias that the Deft. is not to be found & he failing to appear on the Plts. motion an Alias Capias is awarded against the Deft. returnable to the next Court.

Radford vs Bostick   In the Action of trespass on the Case between John Radford Plt. & Jno. Bostick Deft. the Deft. confesses Judgment for two pounds eighteen shillings & twopence Current money whereupon it is considered by the Court that the Plt. do recover against the Deft. the said Sum with Costs & a Lawyers Fee.

Radford vs Armes   In the Action of trespass on the Case between John Radford Plt. & Jno. Armes Deft. the Deft. confesses Judgment for thirty nine shillings Current money whereupon it is considered by the Court that the Plt do recover against the Deft. the said Sum with Costs & a Lawyers Fee.

The Action of Trespass on the Case between Thomas Prosser Plt & Thomas Dickins Deft. is dismist the Plt. not prosecuting the same.

Digges vs Napier Junior   In the Action of trespass on the Case between Dudley Digges Plt and Robt. Napier Junr. Deft. the Deft. failing to appear on the Plts motion Judgment is granted him against the Deft. & Bouth Napier his

[147]   June Court 1731
his Common Bail for what damages shall be recovered in this Suit to be discharged nevertheless if the Deft. shall appear at the next Court.

Cawthon vs Levins &c   In the Action of trespass on the Case between Robert Cawthon Plt & Richard Levins Administrator &c of John Sutton Farrar deceasd Deft. an Imparlance is granted the Deft.

Cawthon & Uxr vs Levins &c   In the Action of trespass on the Case between Robert Cawthon & Mary his Wife Plt. & Richard Levins Administrator &c of John Sutton Farrar deceased Deft. an Imparlance is granted the Deft.

Scot &c vs Dickins   In the Action of trespass on the Case between Edward Scot Admr. &c. of John Stephens decea'd Plt. & Thomas Dickins Deft. an Imparlance is granted the Deft.

Taylor vs Dickins   In the Action of Trespass on the Case between John Taylor Plt. & Thomas Dickins Deft. an Imparlance is granted the Deft.

Chemeno vs Hughes   In the Action of Trespass on the Case between John Chemeno Plt & Isaac Hughes Deft. the Sheriff having returned on the Capias that the Deft Writ came too late to his hands to be executed on the Plts motion an Alias Capias is awarded against the Deft. returnable to the next Court.

Stoner vs Davis   In the Action of trespass on the Case between Daniell Stoner Plt. & William Davis Deft. the Sheriff having returned on the Capias that the Deft. is not to be found & he failing to appear on the Plts motion an Alias Capias is awarded against the Deft returnable to the next Court.

Stoner vs Davis   In the Action of trespass on the Case between Daniell Stoner Plt. & George Davis Deft. the Deft. pleads he oweth nothing & for tryall thereof puts himself upon the Country & the Plt likewise Joell Chandler enters himself Speciall Bail.

The Action of trespass on the Case between John Coleman Plt. & John

Prier Deft. is dismist the Plt. not prosecuting the same.

[148]   June Court 1731
Raine vs Ripley & Mullen   In the Action of trespass between George Raine Plt. & John Ripley & Patrick Mullen Defts. the Sheriff having returnd on the Capias that the Deft. Ripley is not to be found and he failing to appear on the Plts. motion an Alias Capias is awarded against the said Deft returnable to the next Court & the Action is dismist against the other Deft. Mullen the Plt. not prosecuting the same.

Chandler vs Napier   In the Action of trespass on the Case between Joell Chandler Plt. & Robt. Napier Junr Deft. the Deft. failing to appear on the Plts motion Judgment is granted him against the Deft. & Bouth Napier his Common bail for what Damages shall be recovered in this Suit to be discharged nevertheless if the Deft. shall appear at the next Court.

The Action of trespass on the [Case] between William Jennings Plt. & Thomas Adams Deft. is dismist the Plt. not prosecuting the same.

Dabbs vs Atkinson   The Action of debt between Joseph Dabbs Plt. & Henry Atkinson Deft. is continued.

Scot vs Epperson   In the Action of trespass on the Case between Edward Scot Plt. & William Epperson Deft. the Deft. failing to appear on the Plts. motion Judgment is granted him against the Deft. & Anthony Rapene his Common Bail for what Damages shall be recovered in this Suit to be discharged nevertheless if the Deft. shall appear at the next Court.

Scot vs Moseley   On the Scire Facias obtained by Edward Scot against William Moseley the Sheriff having made return that the Writ came too late to his hands to be executed on the Plts motion it is Ordered that an Alias Scire Facias do issue against the Deft. returnable to the next Court.

Dickins vs Harris   In the Action of trespass on the Case between Thomas Dickins Plt. & John Harris Deft. the Sheriff having return'd on the Capias that the Writ came to his hands too late to be executed on the Plts motion an Alias Capias is awarded against the Deft. returnable to the next Court.

The Action of trespass on the Case between Thomas Dickins Plt. & Joseph

[149] June Court 1731
Bingley Deft. is dismist the Plt. not prosecuting the same

Allin vs Woodson   On the Attachment obtained by Samuell Allen Plt against the Estate of John Woodson Junr. Deft. the Sheriff hath made the following return "June the 12th. day 1731. Executed one Wm. Womack. Thos. Walker Sub. Sheriff" and it is Ordered that the said William Womack be Sumoned to appear at the next Court to declare what is in his hands belonging to the said John Woodson Junr.

Woodson vs Woodson   On the Attachment obtained by Joseph Woodson against the Estate of John Woodson Junr. the Sheriff hath made the following return "Executed in the hands of William Womack one of the Executors of Robert Woodson deceased Pr. Jos. Dabbs Sub Sher June 12th 1731." and it is Ordered that the said William Womack be Sumoned to appear at the next Court to declare what is in his hands belonging to the said John Woodson Junr.

Christian vs Pleasants   In the Action of Trespass on the Case between James Christian Plt & Thomas Pleasants Deft. the Sheriff having returned on the Capias that the Deft. is not an Inhabitant in his Bailiwick on the Plts motion an Alias Capias is awarded against the Deft. returnable to the next Court.

Quantin vs Taylor   In the Action of trespass on the Case between John Quantin Plt. & James Taylor Deft. the Deft. confesses Judgment to the Plt. for three pounds four Shillings and Sixpence Current money whereupon it is considered by the Court that the Plt. do recover against the Deft. the said Sum with Costs & a Lawyers Fee.

David vs Quantin   On the motion of Anne David a Witness for John Quantin vs Thomas Dickins it is Ordered that the said John do pay her for four days Attendance one hundred & twenty pounds of tobacco with Costs.

Burgew vs Quantin   On the motion of Govert Burgew a Witness for John Quantin vs Thomas Dickins it is Ordered that the said John do pay him for four days Attendance one hundred & twenty pounds of tobacco with Costs.

[150] June Court 1731
Orphans Court appointed   Ordered that an Orphans Court be held on the eighteenth day of August next and that the Clerk do issue Subpenas

for the Guardians to appear thereat.

Then the Court adjourned to the third Tuesday in next Month.

****

At a Court held for Goochland County the third Tuesday in July being the twentieth day of the Month Annoq Domi. 1731. Present. William Mayo, Daniell Stoner, George Paine, Anthony Hoggat, Gent. Justices.

Chastains deed to Forcee   Stephen Chastain acknowledges a deed from himself to Mary Forcee to be his Act and deed and it is thereupon admitted to record.

Present William Cabbell Gent.

Forcee's Inventory   Anne Epperson presents an Inventory of the Estate of Francis Forcee deceased which is ordered to be recorded.

Bollings Inventory   Stephen Hughes presents an Inventory of the Estate of James Bolling deceased which is ordered to be recorded.

Cannon vs Scot   In the Action of Debt between William Cannon Plt. and Edward Scot Administrator &c. of John Stephens deced Deft. an Imparlance is granted the Defendant.

Cannon vs Strange   In the Action of Trespass on the Case between William Cannon Plt. and Alexander Strange Deft. the Sheriff having made return that the Deft. is not to be found and he failing to appear on the Plts. motion an Alias Capias is awarded against the Defendt. returnable to the next Court.

[151]   July Court 1731
Evans vs Easly   In the Action of Debt between Richard Evans Plt. and William Easly Deft. the Deft. appears and confesses a Judgment to the Plt. for three pounds thirteen shillings and nine pence Currt. money whereupon it is considered by the Court that the Plt. do recover against the Deft. the said sum together with the costs of this Suit and a Lawyers Fee.

Absent George Payne Gent.

Stevenson vs Payne   In the Action of Trespass and the Case between John Stevenson Plt. and George Payne Deft. an Imparlance is granted the Deft.

Present George Payne Gent.

Legrands Inventory   John Fleming presents an Inventory of the Estate of John Legrand which is ordered to be recorded.

Stevenson vs Payne   In the Action of Trespass between John Stevenson Plt. and Robert Payne Deft. the Deft. pleads he oweth nothing.

Justice Sworn   William Mayo and Daniel Stoner Gent. administer the Oaths appointed by And of Parliament to be taken instead of the Oaths of Allegiance and Supremacy, the Oath appointed to be taken by an Act of Parliament made in the first year of the reign of his late Majesty King George the First entituled an Act for the further Security of his Majesty's Persons and Government and of the Succession to the Crown of Great Brittain in the Heirs of the late Princess Sophia being Protestants and for extinguishing the hopes of the pretended Prince of Wales and his open and secret abettors unto John Fleming Gent. who subscribes the Test and takes the Oath of a Justice of the Peace and of a Justice in Chancery.

Randolph's Execrs. vs Martin   The Action of Trespass on the Case between William Randolph, Richard Randolph, John Randolph, & John Fleming Exrs. &c. of Thomas Randoph deced. Plts. and Francis Martin Deft. is continued.

[152]   July Court 1731
Present [John Fleming] Gent.

Woodson vs Hughes   In the Action of Trespass on the Case between Joseph Woodson Plt. and Stephen Hughes Deft. it is ordered that Daniel Stoner, George Payne, William Cabbell & Anthony Hoggatt, Gent. or any three of them do examine state and settle the several matters in dispute between them and report their proceedings therein to the next Court.

Bradley vs Saunders   In the Action of Trespass on the Case between Joseph Bradley Plt. and John Saunders Deft. the Execution of the Writ of Inquiry is waived, the Deft. pleads he is not guilty and for tryal thereof puts himself upon the Country and the Plt. likewise whereupon the following Jury are sworn John Mcbrid, John Prior, John Robinson, James Taylor, John Paine, Thomas Christian, Samuel Coleman, John Maddox,

William Epperson, Samuel Allen, Joseph Woodson Junr., Joel Chandler, who after some time bring in their Verdict which on the Plts. motion is ordered to be recorded and is as followeth "Wee find for the Plt. one pound ten shillings Currt. money John Mcbrid Foreman." Whereupon it is considered by the Court that the Plt. do recover against the Deft. the said sum of one pound ten shillings Currt. money by the Jurors aforesaid in their said Verdict assessed together with the Costs of this Suit and a Lawyers Fee.

Scrugs vs Bradley   On the motion of John Scrugs a witness for Joseph Bradley vs John Saunders it is ordered that the said Joseph do pay him for five days attendance one hundred and fifty pounds of tobacco with Costs.

Toney vs Bradley   On the motion of Charles Toney a witness for Joseph Bradley vs John Saunders it is ordered that the said Joseph do pay him for five days attendance one hundred and fifty pounds of tobacco with Costs.

Locket vs James   In the Action of Trespass between Thomas Locket Plt. and Francis James Deft. the following Jury are sworn John Mcbrid, John Prior, John Robinson, James Taylor, John Paine, Thomas Christian, Samuel Coleman, John Maddox, William Epperson, Samuel Allen, Joseph Woodson Junr., Joel Chandler

[153]   July Court 1731
Cha[ndler who] after sometime bring in their Verdict which on the Defts. motion is ordered to be recorded and is as followeth "Wee find for the Defendt. John Mcbrid Foreman." Whereupon it is considered by the Court that the Deft. go hence without day and that he recover against the Plt. his Costs by him in this behalf expended and a Lawyers Fee.

Bates vs Locket   On the motion of Fleming Bates a witness for Thomas Locket vs Francis James it is ordered that the said Thomas do pay him for four days attendance one hundred and twenty pounds of tobacco with Costs.

Robinson vs Locket   On the motion of John Robinson a Witness for Thomas Locket vs Francis James it is ordered that the said Thomas do pay him for three days attendance ninety pounds of tobacco with Costs.

Woodson's deed to Lightfoot   Mary wife of Josiah Woodson and Elizabeth wife of Stephen Woodson (they being first privately examined) relinquish their right of Dower in land conveyed by the said Josiah and

Stephen to Phillip Lightfoot at December Court last.

    Absent William Cabbell Gent.
    Present John Woodson Gent.

Cabbell vs Downie   On the Attachment obtained by William Cabbell against the Estate of Robert Downie the Plt. makes oath to his account, and on his motion Judgment is granted him against the Deft. for 171 lbs. of tobacco & four pounds thirteen shillings and eight pence Currt. money with the costs of this Suit and a Lawyers Fee.

The Attachment obtained by William Cabbell against the Estate of Robert Downie having been served on Daniel Britt the said Daniel appears and being sworn declares that he is indebted unto the said Robert Downie four hundred pounds of tobacco or four hundred pounds of live pork and three half bushels of Corn to be paid the last day of January next

[154]   July Court 1731
and it is thereupon ordered that he pay the same unto William Cabbell and the Attachment is continued.

Cabbell vs Woodson &c   In the Action of Trespass on the Case between William Cabbell Administrator of Joel Carr deced. Plt. & Josiah Woodson & Stephen Woodson Execrs. &c. of Jacob Woodson deced. Defts. the Defts. appear but failing to plead on the Plts. motion Judgment by nihil dicit is granted him against the Defts. for what damages shall be recovered in this suit to be discharged nevertheless if the Defts. shall plead at the next Court.

Cabbell vs Williams   The Action of Trespass on the Case between William Cabbell Plt. and John Williams Deft. is dismist the Plt. not prosecuting the same.

    Present William Cabbell Gent.

Nevils deed to Hooper   James Nevil acknowledges a deed with the Livery of Seisin endorsed from himself to Joseph Hooper to be his Act and deed and it is thereupon admitted to record.

Hooper's deed to Nevil   Joseph Hooper acknowledges a deed with the Livery of Seisin endorsed from himself to James Nevil to be his act and deed and it is thereupon admitted to record.

    Present George Rayne Gent.

Christian's deed to Coleman   Thomas Christian acknowledges a deed to Samuel Coleman to be his Act and deed and it is thereupon admitted to record, then Rebecca wife of the said Thomas (she being first privately examined) relinquishes her right of Dower in the land of the said deed conveyed which is also admitted to record.

   Absent George Raine Gent.

Raine vs Levins &c   In the Action of Trespass on the Case between George Raine Plt. and Richard Levins Admr. &c. of John Sutton Farrar deced. Deft.

[155]   July Court 1731
time is granted the Plt. to mend his declaration and the Suit is continued.

   Present George Raine Gent.
   Absent William Cabbell Gent.

Cabbell vs Utley   In the Action of Trespass on the Case between William Cabbell Plt. and John Utley Deft. for four hundred and sixty pounds of tobacco the Sherif having made return on the Pluries Capias that the Deft. is not to be found and he failing to appear on the Plts. motion it is ordered that an Attachment do issue against the Defts. estate returnable to the next Court.

Woodson &ca. vs Cabbell &c   In the Action of Debt between Josiah Woodson & Stephen Woodson Execrs. &c. of Jacob Woodson Plts. & William Cabbell Admr. &c. of Joel Carr deced. Deft. the Deft. pleads he oweth nothing and for tryal thereof puts himself upon the Country & the Plts. likewise.

   Present William Cabbell Gent.

Ward vs Farrar   The Action of Debt between Seth Ward Plt. and John Farrar Deft. is continued.
  Ordered that the Deft. pay the cost of this continuance.

   Present Allin Howard Gent.

Moseby vs Taylor   In the Action of Debt between Richard Moseby Plt. and John Taylor Deft. the Arguments on the reasons in Arrest of Judgment being heard it is the Opinion of the Court that they are not good in Law to bar the Plt. from having his Judgment and it is thereupon considered that the Deft. be imprisoned one Kalender month without Bail a Mainprise and that the Plt. do recover against the Defts. his Costs and an Attornys Fee.

[156]   July Court 1731
Hix to Taylor   On the motion of Marmaduke Hix a witness for John Taylor ads. Richard Moseby it is ordered that the said John do pay him for seven days attendance two hundred & ten pounds of tobacco with costs.

Licking hole Creek Bridge to be kept up   On the motion of Isham Randolph Gent. the bridge by him built over Licking hole Creek is agreed to become a County charge from this time.

Absent Daniel Stoner Gent.

Stoner vs Utley   In the Action of Trespass on the Case between Daniel Stoner Plt. and John Utley Deft. the Sherif having made return on the Pluries Capias that the Deft. is not to be found and he failing to appear on the Plts. motion a Pluries Capias de novo is awarded against the Deft. returnable to the next Court.

Present Daniel Stoner Gent.

Macon vs Wharton   In the Action on the Case between John Macon Plt. and Thomas Wharton Deft. the Plt. files his answer upon oath to the Defts. bill of Injunction in Chancery and the parties being heard upon Bill & Answer & the witnesses examined it is decreed that the Verdict formerly obtained by the Plt. in this Suit be set aside and that the Deft. recover against the Plt. his Costs by him in this behalf expended and a Lawyers Fee.

Martin vs Wharton   On the motion of Joseph Martin of New Kent a witness for Thomas Wharton ads John Macon it is ordered that the said Thomas do pay him for seven days attendance and for coming and returning thirty five miles six times one thousand & fifty pounds of tobacco with Costs.

Martin vs Wharton   On the motion of John Martin of New Kent a witness for Thomas Wharton ads John Macon it is ordered that the said Thomas do pay him for thirteen days attendance and for coming and returning forty two miles eleven times two thousand one hundred & sixty six pounds of tobo. with Costs.

[157]   July Court 1731
Willis vs Wharton   On the motion of William Willis a witness for Thomas Wharton ads John Macon it is ordered that the said Thomas do pay him for two days attendance sixty pounds of tobacco with costs.

Dickins vs Bolling &c   In the Action of Trespass on the Case between Thomas Dickins Plt. and John Bolling Admr. &c. with the will annex'd of Bartholomew Cox deced Deft. an imparlance is granted the Deft.

The Action of Debt between Ashford Hughes Plt. and John Bolling Admr. &c. with the will annex'd of Bartholomew Cox deced Deft. is dismist the Plt. not prosecuting the same.

Waddill vs Edwards   The Action on the Case between William Waddill Junr. Plt. and Thomas Edwards Deft. is continued.

Flournoy vs Martin   In the Action of Trespass on the Case between John James Flournoy Plt. & Francis Martin Deft. the Deft. appears but failing to plead on the Plts. motion Judgment by nihil dicit is granted him against the Deft. for what damages shall be recovered in this Suit to be discharged nevertheless if the Deft. shall plead at the next Court.

Flournoy &c. vs Martin   In the Action of Debt between John James Flournoy and Elizabeth his wife Executrix &c. of Orlando Jones deced. Plts. and Francis Martin Deft. the Deft. appears but failing to plead on the Plts. motion Judgment by nihil dicit is granted him against the Deft. for what damages shall be recovered in this Suit to be discharged nevertheless if the Deft. shall plead at the next Court.

Taylor vs Lowe &c   The Action of Trespass on the Case between John Taylor Plt. and Thomas Lowe & Amey his wife Defts. is continued.

Then the Court adjourned till to Morrow morning then of the Clock.

****

[158]   July Court 1731
At a Court continued and held for Goochland County the twenty first day of July Annoq Domi. 1731. Present. Allen Howard, George Payne, William Cabbell, George Rayne, Anthony Hoggat, Gent. Justices.

Stevenson vs Johnson   In the action of Trespass between John Stephenson Plt. and Charles Johnson Deft. the Deft. pleads he oweth nothing and the Suit is continued.

Allegre vs Capoon   In the action of Trespass on the Case between Giles Allegre Plt. & Jacob Capoon Deft. the Deft. failing to appear on the Plts. motion Judgment is granted him against the Deft. and James Sublet his common bail for what damages Shall be recovered in this Suit to be discharged nevertheless if the Deft. shall appear at the next Court.

The Action of Trespass on the Case between John Chastain and Peter Chastain Exrs. &c. of Peter Chastain deced Plts. & Elizabeth Atkinson Deft. is dismist the Plts. not prosecuting the Same.

Barret vs Epperson   In the Action of Trespass on the Case between James Barret Plt. & William Epperson Deft. the Sheriff having made return that the Deft. is not to be found & he failing to appear on the Plts. motion Judgment is granted him against the Deft. and Tarlton Fleming Gent. Sher. for So much dam[a]ges as Shall be recovered in this Suit to be discharged nevertheless if the Deft. Shall appear at the Next Court.

May vs Woodson   In the action of Trespass on the Case between William May Plt. and John Woodson Deft. an imparlance is granted the Deft.

[159]   July Court 1731
The action of trespass on the Case between Dudley Digges Plt. and Gofert Burger Deft. is dismist neither party appearing.

Saunders vs Martin   In the action of Trespass on the Case between John Saunders Plt. and Frances Martin Deft. on the Defts. motion a Special imparlance is granted him.

The action of Debt between Thomas Dickins Plt. and George Southerland Deft. is dismist neither party appearing.

Dickins vs Burton   In the action of Trespass on the Case between Thomas Dickins Plt. and Nowel Burton Deft. the Deft. pleads he oweth nothing and for tryall thereof puts himself upon the Country and the Plt. likewise.

The action of Debt between Robt. Hughes Plt. and Evan Hopkins Deft. is dismist the Plt. not prosecuting the Same.

Dickins vs Burger   In the action of Trespass between Thomas Dickins

Plt. and Govert Burger Deft. the Deft. failing to appear on the Plts. motion Judgment is granted him against the Deft. and Dudley Digges his Common Bail for what damages Shall be recovered in this Suit to be discharged nevertheless if the Deft. Shall Appear at the next Court.

The action of Trespass between Charles Allin Plt. and Charles Anderson Deft. is dismist the Plt. not prosecuting the Same.

The action of Debt between Charles Johnson Plt. and Nathan Pumphrey Deft. is dismist the Plts. not prosecuting the Same.

Haskins vs Saunders   In the action of Debt between Creed Haskins Plt. and John Saunders Deft. an imparlance is granted the Deft.

The action of Debt between Daniel Stoner Plt. and Peter Guerrant Deft. is dismist neither party Appearing.

[160]   July Court 1731
Crouch vs Cholmley   In the action of Trespass between Richard Crouch Plt. and William Cholmley Deft. the Sheriff having made return that the Deft. is not to be found and he failing to appear on the Plts. motion an Alias Capias is Awarded against the Deft. returnable to the next Court.

Lansdon vs Benning   The action of partition between William Lansdon and Hester his wife Plts. and Anthony Benning and Elizabeth his wife Defts. is continued.

    Absent George Raine Gent.

Raine vs Martin   In the action of Trespass on the Case between George Raine Plt. and Francis Martin Deft. by consent of parties the Execution of the writ of inquiry is waived and the Deft. acknowledges himself indebted unto the Plt. in the Sum of Six pounds Seven Shillings and Eleven pence Currt. money whereupon on the Plts. motion the Conditional Judgment formerly granted him in the Suit against the Deft. and Dudley Digges his Common Bail is Confirmed and it is considered by the Court that the Plt. do recover against the Deft. and Dudley Digges aforesaid the Said Sum with the Cost of this Suit and a Lawyers Fee.

Raine vs Dickinson   In the action of Trespass on the Case between George Raine Plt. and John Dickinson Deft. the following Jury are Sworn John Mackbride, Nicholas Cox, John Lad, Thomas Wadloe, Robert Adams, John Laine, John Richardson, Robert Napier Junr., James

Robinson, Joel Chandler, Joseph Woodson, and John Chastain who after Some time bring in their Verdict which on the Plts. motion is admitted to record, and is as followeth "Wee find for the Plt. twelve hundred pounds of Tobacco Sweet Scented, John Mcbride Foreman." whereupon it is considered by the Court that the Plt. do recover against the Deft. and Tarlton Fleming Gent. Sheriff the Said Tobacco with the Cost of this Suit and a Lawyers Fee.

   Present George Raine Gent.

Scot vs Pruit The Action of Trespass on the Case between Edward Scot Plt. and Thomas Pruit Deft. is Continued. Ordered that the plt. pay the Cost of this Continuance.

[161] July Court 1731
Winfrey vs Williams The action of Trespass on the Case between Jacob Winfrey Plt. and John Williams Deft. is dismist the Plt. not prosecuting the Same.

Hatcher vs Syms The action of Trespass on the Case between Henry Hatcher Assignee of Samuel Hatcher Plt. and Richard Sym[s] Deft. is dismist the Plt. not prosecuting the Same.

Hopkins vs Woodson The action of Trespass on the Case between William Hopkins Plt. and Benjamin Woodson Deft. is continued. Ordered that the Deft. do pay the Cost of this continuance.

Bryan vs Chandler In the action of Trespass on the Case between William Bryan Plt. and Joel Chandler Deft. on the Plts. Motion leave is granted him to mend his Declaration.

Bryan vs Chandler In the action of Trespass on the Case between William Bryan Plt. and Joel Chandler Deft. on the Plts. Motion leave is granted him to mend his Declaration.

Dickins vs Utley In the action of Trespass on the Case between Thomas Dickins Plt. and John Utley Deft. for five pounds five Shillings Currt. money the Sheriff having made return on the plurias Capias that the Deft. is not to be found and he failing to Appear on the Plts. motion it is Ordered that an Attachment do issue against the Defts. Estate returnable to the next Court.

Gates vs Saunders The action of Trover between William Gates Plt.

and Robert Saunders Deft. is continued. Ordered that the Plt. do pay the Cost of this Continuance.

Fleming vs Napier   On the attachment obtained by Tarlton Fleming Sheriff against the Estate of Bouth Napier for two pounds Sixteen Shillings and Seven pence half penny Currt. money and one hundred and sixty one pounds of Tobacco and fifteen Shillings Currt. money or one hundred and fifty pounds of tobacco by reason of the non Appearance of the Said Bouth Napier to Answer the Suit of Thomas Dixon the

[162]   July Court 1731
Sheriff having made return that he can find no goods or Chattells whereon to Serve the Said Attachment on the motion of the Said Tarlton Fleming it is Ordered that an Attachment de novo do issue against the Estate of the Said Bouth Napier returnable to the next Court.

  Absent William Cabbell Gent.

Taylor vs Quin   In the action of Debt between James Taylor Plt. and John Quin Deft. the Deft. failing to Appear on the Plts. Motion the conditional Judgment formerly granted him in this Suit against the Deft. and William Cabbell his common Bail is confirmed for So much Damages as Shall be found upon executing a writ of inquiry at the next Court of which the Sheriff is hereby Ordered to give the Said Deft. and William Cabbell notice by Serving then with a Copy of this Order.

Taylor vs Quin   in The action of Trespass on the Case between James Taylor Plt. and John Quin Deft. the Deft. failing to appear on the Plts. motion the conditional Judgment formerly granted him in this Suit against the Deft. and William Cabbell his Common Bail is Confirmed for So much damage as Shall be found upon Executing a Writ of inquiry at the next Court of which the Sheriff is hereby ordered to give the Said Deft. and William Cabbell notice by Serving them with a Copy of this Order.

  Present William Cabbell Gent.

Repene vs Marchbanks   The action of Debt between Anthony Rapene Plt. and George Marchbanks Deft. is continued. Ordered that the Plt. do pay the Cost of this Continuance.

Dickins vs Quin   The action of Debt between Thomas Dickins plt. and John Quin Deft. is dismist the plt. not prosecuting the Same.

Prosser vs Quin   In the action of Trespass on the Case between Thomas Prosser plt. and John Quin Deft. for twenty pounds Currt. money the Sheriff having made return on the plurias Capias that the Deft. is not to be found and he failing to appear on the Plts. motion it is ordered that an Attachment do issue against the Defts. Estate returnable to the next Court.

[163]   July Court 1731
Mims vs Levins   In the Action of Trespass on the Case between David Mims Plt. and Richard Levins Administrator &c. of John Sutton Farrar deceased Defendt. time is granted the Plt. to mend his declaration.

Digges vs Fleming   In the Action of Trespass on the Case between Dudley Digges Plt. and Tarlton Fleming Defendt. an imparlance is granted the Defendt.

    Present Daniel Stoner Gent.

Digges vs Prier   The Action of Trespass on the Case between Dudley Digges Plt. and John Prier Deft. is continued   Ordered that the Plt. pay the Cost of this Continuance.

Digges vs Levins   The Action of Trespass on the Case between Dudley Digges Plt. and Richard Levins Administrator &c. of John Sutton Farrar deceased Defendt. is Continued. Ordered that the Deft. do pay the Cost of this Continuance.

Dickins vs Scot   In the Action of Trespass on the Case between Thomas Dickins Plt. and Edward Scot Defendt. the Deft. pleads he oweth nothing and for tryal thereof puts himself upon the Country and the Plt. likewise.

Lad vs White   On the Attachment brought by John Lad Against the Estate of Edward White the Said John makes oath to his Account and Judgment is granted him against the Said Edward for One thousand three hundred and forty eight pounds of Tobacco and One pound fifteen Shillings and three pence Currt. money with Costs and a Lawyers Fee.
    Ordered that Constant Purkins do pay unto the Said John Lad one hundred and sixty pounds of Tobacco which he is indebted unto the Said Edward towards discharging this judgment.

[164]   July Court 1731
    Ordered that William Walker do pay unto the Said John Lad seventy

eight pounds of tobacco which he is indebted unto the Said Edward towards discharging this Judgment.

Anderson vs Allin   In the Action of Debt between John Anderson Plt. and Samuel Allin Defendt. the Deft. failing to Appear on the Plts. Motion the Conditional Judgment formerly granted him in this Suit Against the Deft. and Tarlton Fleming Gent. Sherif is Conformed for So much damages as Shall be found upon Executing a Writ of inquiry at the next Court of which the Sherif is hereby Ordered to give the Deft. notice by Serving him with a Copy of this Order.

Anderson vs Burton   In the Action of Debt between John Anderson Plt. and Nowel Burton Deft. the Defendt. failing to appear and the Alias Capias being returned Executed on the Plts. Motion Judgment is granted him against the Deft. and Tarlton Fleming Gent. Sherif for what damages shall be recovered in this Suit to be discharged nevertheless if the Deft. Shall Appear at the next Court.

Anderson vs Quin   The Action of Debt between John Anderson Plt. and John Quin Deft. is Dismist the Plt. not prosecuting the Same.

Guerrant vs Paine   The Conditional Judgment formerly granted in the Action of Trespass on the Case between Peter Guerrant Administrator &c. of Daniel Guerrant Deceased Plt. and John Paine Defendt. is Continued.

Absent George Raine Gent.

Raine vs Payne   The Action of Trespass on the Case between George Raine Plt. and George Payne Junr. Deft. is dismist the Plt. not prosecuting the Same.

Raine vs Amos   In the Action of Trespass on the Case between George Raine Plt. and Francis Amos Deft. the Deft. failing to appear on the Plts. Motion the Conditional Judgment formerly granted him

[165]   July Court 1731
in this Suit against the Deft. and John Cresy is confirmed for So much damages as Shall be found upon executing a Writ of inquiry at the next Court of which the Sheriff is Ordered to give the Deft. and the Said John Creasy Notice by Serving them with a Copy of this Order.

Present George Raine Gent.

Digges vs Thaxton   In the Action of Trespass on the Case between Dudley Digges Plt. and Abell Thaxton Defendt. the Sherif having made return on the Alies Capias that the Defendt. is not to be found and he failing to Appear on the Plts. Motion it is Ordered that a Pluries Capias do issue against the Deft. returnable to the next Court.

Digges vs Pate   In the Action of Trespass on the Case between Dudley Digges Plt. and Thomas Pate Deft. the Sherif having made return on the Alies Capias that the Deft. is not to be found and he failing to Appear on the Plts. Motion it is Ordered that a pluries Capias do issue against the Deft. returnable to the next Court.

Digges vs Napier   In the action of Trespass on the Case between Dudley Digges Plt. and Robert Napier Junr. Deft. the Defendt. Appears but failing to plead on the Plts. Motion Judgment by nihil dicit is granted him for what damages shall be recovered in this Suit to be discharged nevertheless if the Deft. shall plead at the next Court.

Cawthon vs Levins   In the Action of Trespass on the Case between Robert Cawthon Plt. and Richard Levins Administrator &c. of John Sutton Farrar deceased Deft. the deft. appears but failing to plead on the plts. Motion Judgment by nihil dicit is granted him for what damages Shall be recovered in this Suit to be discharged nevertheless if the Deft. Shall plead at the next Court.

[166]   July Court 1731
Cawthon vs Levins   In the Action of Trespass on the Case between Robert Cawthon and Mary his Wife Plts. and Richard Levins Administrators &c. of John Sutton Farrar deceased Deft. the deft. Appears but failing to plead on the Plts. Motion Judgment by nihil dicit is granted them for what damages shall be recovered in this Suit to be discharged nevertheless if the deft. Shall plead at the next Court.

Scot vs Dickins   In the Action of Trespass on the Case between Edward Scot Administr. &c. of John Stephens deceased Plt. and Thomas Dickins Defendt. Judgment by nihil dicit is granted him for what damages shall be recovered in this Suit to be discharged nevertheless if the Deft. shall plead at the next Court.

Taylor vs Dickins   In the Action of Trespass on the Case between John Taylor Plt. and Thomas Dickins Deft. the Deft. Appears but failing to plead on the Plts. Motion Judgment by nihil dicit is granted him for what damages Shall be recovered in this Suit to be discharged nevertheless if the Deft. Shall plead at the next Court.

Chemino vs Hughes   In the Action of Trespass on the Case between John Chemino Plt. and Isaac Hughes Deft. the Sherif having made return on the Alies Capias that the Deft. is not to be found & he failing to appear on the Plts. Motion it is Ordered that a pluries Capias do issue against the Defendt. returnable to the next Court.

   Absent Daniel Stoner Gent.
   Present John Fleming Gent.

Stoner vs Davis   In the Action of Trespass on the Case between Daniel Stoner Plt. and William Davis Deft. for ten pounds Currt. money the Sherif having made return on the Alies Capias that the Deft. is not to be found and he failing to Appear on the Plts. Motion it is Order'd that an Attachment do issue against the Defendts. Estate returnable to the next Court.

[167]   July Court 1731
Stoner vs Davis   The Action of Trespass on the Case between Daniel Stoner Plt. and George Davis Deft. is dismist the Plt. not prosecuting the Same.

   Present Daniel Stoner Gent.
   Absent George Raine Gent.

Raine vs Ripley   In the Action of Trespass between George Raine Plt. and John Ripley Deft. the Sherif having made Return on the Alies Capias the Deft. is not to be found and he failing to appear on the Plts. Motion it is Ordered that a pluries Capias do issue against the Deft. returnable to the next Court.

   Present George Raine Gent.

Chandler vs Napier   In the Action of Trespass on the Case between Joell Chandler Plt. and Robert Napier Junr. Deft. the Deft. appears but failing to plead on the Plts. Motion Judgment by nihil dicit is granted him against the Deft. for So much damages as Shall be recovered in this Suit to be discharged nevertheless if the Deft. shall plead at the next Court.

Dabbs vs Atkinson   The action of Debt between Joseph Dabbs Plt. and Henry Atkinson Deft. is dismist the Plt. not prosecuting the Same.

Scot vs Epperson   In the action of Trespass on the Case between Edward Scot Plt. & William Epperson Deft. the Deft. failing to Appear on the Plts. Motion the Conditional Judgment formerly granted him in this Suit against the Deft. and Anthony Rapene his Common Bail is Confirmed for Much damages as Shall be found upon Executing a Writ of Inquiry at the next Court of which the Sherif is hereby Ordered to give the Said Deft. & Anthony Rapene notice by Serving them with a Copy of this Order.

Absent John Fleming Gent.

[168]   July Court 1731
Randolph vs Mcbrid   In the Action of Trespass on the Case between Richard Randolph, William Randolph, John Randolph and John Fleming Executors &c. of Thomas Randolph deceased Plts. and John Mcbrid Deft. the parties Submit the tryal of the Writ of Inquiry to the Court whereupon the Accounts being regulated and the Defts. oath heard it is considered by the Court that the Plts. Executors as aforesaid do recover against the Deft. and Dudley Digges, Tarlton Fleming, James Christian, James Nolun, John Martin Junr., John Webb, Francis Martin, and Ashford Hughes his Bail ten pounds four Shillings and three pence Currt. money with the Costs of this Suit and a Lawyers Fee.

Randolph vs Dickinson   In the Action of Trespass on the Case between William Randolph, Richard Randolph, John Randolph, and John Fleming Executors &c. of Thomas Randolph deceased Plts. and John Dickinson Deft. the following Jury are Swore to enquire of the damages. John Mcbrid, Nicholas Cox, John Lad, Thomas Wadloe, Robert Adams, John Laine, John Richardson, Robert Napier Junr., James Robertson, Joell Chandler, Joseph Woodson, John Chastain, Who after Some time bring in their Verdict which on the Plts. Motion is Ordered to be recorded & is as followeth "Wee find for the Plts. One pound four Shillings and three pence half penny Currt. money John Mcbrid Foreman." Whereupon it is Considered by the Court that the Plts. do recover against the Deft. & Tarlton Fleming Gent. Sherif the Said Sum with the Costs of this Suit and a Lawyers Fee.

Martin vs Fleming   The Action of Trespass on the Case between John Martin Plt. and John Fleming Administrator &c. of Paul Pennington deceased Deft. is dismist the Plt. not prosecuting the Same.

Present John Fleming Gent.

Chastain vs Martin   The Action of Trespass on the Case between John Chastain and Peter Chastain Administrators &c. of Peter Chastain deceased Plts. and Francis Martin Deft. is Continued. Ordered that the Deft. pay the Cost of this Continuance.

[169]   July Court 1731
Davis vs Quin   In the Action of Debt between George Davis Plt. and John Quin Deft. the following Jury are Sworn to enquire of the damages. John Mcbrid, Nicholas Cox, John Lad, Thomas Wadloe, Robert Adams, John Laine, John Richardson, Robert Napier Junr., James Robertson, Joell Chandler, Joseph Woodson, John Chastain, who after Some time bring in their Verdict which on the Plts. Motion is Admitted to record and is as followeth. "Wee find for the Plt. forty Shillings Currt. Money John Mcbrid Foreman." whereupon it is Considered by the Court that the Plt. do recover against the Deft. & Tarlton Fleming Gent. Sheriff the Said Sum with the Costs of this Suit & a Lawyers Fee.

Scot vs Moseley   On the Scire facias brought by Edward Scot Against William Moseley to renew a Judgment of this Court Obtained the twenty first day of October One thousand Seven Hundred and twenty Nine for two pounds Nineteen Shillings and one penny Currt. Money & eight seven pounds of tobacco & fifteen Shillings Currt. Money or one hundred and fifty pounds of tobacco being the Costs of Suit the Alies Scire Facias being returned Executed and the Deft. not Appearing on the Motion of the said Edward the Said Judgment is renewed and the Deft. is Ordered to pay the Costs of this Suit no Attorny's Fee to be taxed.

Dickins vs Harris   The Action of trespass on the Case between Thomas Dickins Plt. and John Harris Deft. is dismist the Plt. not prosecuting the Same.

Allin vs Woodson   On the Attachment obtained by Samuel Allin Against the Estate of John Woodson Junr. William Womack being returned Summoned and failing to Appear on the Motion of the Said Samuel Ordered that a Capias do issue Against the Said William Womack returnable to the next Court.

Woodson vs Woodson   The Attachment Obtained by Joseph Woodson Junr. Against the Estate of John Woodson Junr. is dismist no prosecution.

Christian vs Pleasants   The action of Trespass on the Case between James Christian Plt. and Thomas Pleasants Deft. is dismist the Plt. not prosecuting the Same.

[170] July Court 1731
Absent John Fleming Gent.

Adams vs Randophs Exrs   The Petition of Robert Adams for leave to build a mill is dismist at the motion of John Fleming one of the Executors &c. of Thomas Randolph deceased for the uncertainty of the said petition.

Present John Fleming Gent.

Scot vs Daniel   The Action of detinue between Edward Scot Plt. and James Daniel Deft. is Continued; Ordered that the Plt. pay the Cost of this Continuance.

Wilson to be Summoned   The Summons issued last Court Against Richard Wilson being returned not Executed and the Said Wilson failing to Appear to Answer his misbehaviour in neglecting to obey a precept directed to him by William Mayo Gent. Ordered that a new Sumons do issue against him & Thomas Duggins & Nicholas Roads as Witnesses.

Grand Jury vs George Davis   On the Presentment of the Grand Jury Against George Davis for beating Thomas Wadloe the Said George Appears and confesses himself guilty and it is Ordered that he be fined to Our Lord the King five Shillings Sterling & that he pay Costs.

Davis's Recognizance   George Davis Comes into Court and Acknowledges himself indebted unto Our Lord the King in the Sum of ten pounds Sterling to be levied on his goods and Chattles on Condition that if the Said George keep the peace towards all his Majesty's Subjects for a year & a day and also appear at the next Court to be held for this County after the Said Year & a day are Expired then this recognizance to be Void.

Grand Jury vs Wm. Davis   Ordered that a Sumons do issue against William Davis for his Appearance at the next Court to answer the presentment of the Grand Jury.

[171] July Court 1731
Cone's Acct. of Estate &c   Daniel Stoner Gent. is appointed to Examine the Account Debter and Credit of the Estate of John Cone deceased and to Make report thereof to the next Court.

Burges vs Woodson   The Action of Trespass on the Case between John

Burgess Plt. and John Woodson Deft. is dismist the Plt. not prosecuting the same.

Absent John Fleming Gent.

Adams vs Randolph's Exrs   On the Petition of Robert Adams praying leave to build a mill on Dover mill Creek the same is referred for the Exrs. of Thomas Randolph deced. to be heard against the same.

Present John Fleming Gent
Absent Allin Howard Gent.

Prosser vs May   In the Action of Trespass on the Case between Thomas Prosser Plt. and William May Deft. the Plt. waives the execution of the Writ of inquiry the Deft. pleads he oweth nothing and for tryal submits himself to the Court and the Plt. likewise whereupon the Accounts being regulated and the Plts. oath heard it is considered by the Court that the Plt. do recover against the Deft. forty shillings Currt. money with Costs.

Hughes vs Woodson   In the Action of Trespass on the Case between Robert Hughes Plt. and John Woodson Deft. the Plt. waives the Execution of the Writ of inquiry the Deft. pleads he oweth nothing and for tryal submits himself to the Court and the Plt. likewise whereupon the parties being heard and their Accounts regulated it is considered by the Court that the Plt. do recover against the Deft. two pounds five shillings Currt. money with Costs and an Attorneys Fee.

[172]   July Court 1731
The Deft. offers a Surveyors Fee of five hundred and sixty pounds of tobacco in discount which Fee the Court are of Opinion the Plt. chargeable with but that it ought not to be allowed in discount of the Plts. debt which is Money.

Esham vs Hughes   On the Motion of George Esham a witness for Robert Hughes vs John Woodson it is ordered that the said Robert do pay him for two days attendance sixty pounds of tobacco with Costs.

Powell vs Hughes   On the motion of Richard Powel a witness for Robert Hughes ads John Woodson it is ordered that the said Robert do pay him for two days attendance sixty pounds of tobacco with Costs.

Grand Jury vs Micheaux   On the Presentment of the Grand Jury vs Jacob Micheaux for retailing Liquors without License the following Jury are sworn John Mcbrid, John Laine, David Mims, John Prier, John Biby, Charles Anderson, John Scrugs, Hugh Morris, John Lad, Joseph Woodson, Sanburn Woodson, Joseph Woodson Junr. who after some time bring in their Verdict in these words "Wee find the Deft. not guilty John Mcbrid Foreman." whereupon the said Presentment is dismist.

Grand Jury vs Richardson   On the Presentment of the Grand Jury vs John Richardson for retailing Liquors without License the following Jury are sworn John Mcbrid, John Laine, Davis Mims, John Prier, John Biby, Charles Anderson, John Scrugs, Hugh Morris, John Lad, Joseph Woodson, Sanburn Woodson, Joseph Woodson Junr., who after sometime bring in their Verdict in these words "Wee find the Deft. not guilty John Mcbrid Foreman." whereupon the Presentment is dismist.

Grand Jury vs Parker   On the Presentment of the Grand Jury against Richard Parker for beating Thomas Wadloe the following Jury are sworn John Mcbrid, John Laine, Davis Mims, John Prier, John Biby, Charles Anderson, John Scrugs, Hugh Morris, John Lad, Joseph Woodson, Sanburn Woodson, Joseph Woodson Junr. who

[173]   July Court 1731
who after some time bring in their Verdict in these words "Wee find Richard Parker guilty of beating Thomas Wadloe. John Mcbrid Foreman." whereupon it is ordered that the said Richard be fined to our Lord the King ten shillings Sterling and that he pay Costs.

The said Richard Parker not appearing ordered that a Capias do issue against him returnable to the next Court for the fine and his appearance then to give Security for keeping the Peace.

Webb vs Parker   On the Motion of John Webb a witness for the King against Richard Parker it is ordered that the said Richard do pay him for one days attendance thirty pounds of tobacco with Costs.

Amos vs Parker   On the Motion of Francis Amos a Witness for the King against Richard Parker it is ordered that the said Richard do pay him for one days attendance thirty pounds of tobacco with Costs.

Wadloe vs Parker   On the Motion of Thomas Wadloe a witness for the King against Richard Parker it is ordered that the said Richard do pay him for one days attendance thirty pounds of tobacco with Costs.

Grand Jury vs Quantin   On the Presentment of the Grand Jury against John Quantin for being Drunk Edward Scot appears for the said John and confesses the Presentment to be true and it is ordered that the said John do pay unto the Church wardens of King William Parish fifty pounds of tobacco with Costs.

Grand Jury vs Dickins   On the Presentment of the Grand Jury against Thomas Dickins for learning his Negro boy to profane the Lords Prayer the tryall being submitted to the Court the Presentment is dismist.

[174]   July Court 1731
Grand Jury vs Church Wardens of Kg. Wm. parish   On the Presentment of the Grand Jury against the Church wardens of King William Parish for not finding the laws appointed to be read in Churches the tryall being submitted to the Court the Presentment is dismist.

Grand Jury vs L'Villain   On the Presentment of the Grand Jury against John L'Villain for being Drunk Thomas Dickins appears for the said John and confesses the Presentment to be true whereupon it is ordered that the said John do pay unto the Church wardens of King William Parish five shillings Currt. money with Costs.

Absent John Fleming Gent.

Grand Jury vs Randolph's Exrs   On the Presentment of the Grand Jury against the Exrs. of Thomas Randolph deced for not keeping a passable way over Dover mill Dam the tryall being submitted to the Court the Presentment is dismist.

Present John Fleming Gent.

Grand Jury vs Murrell   On the Presentment of the Grand Jury against Thomas Murrell the Deft. pleads he is not guilty issue is taken thereon and the tryall referred to the next Court.

Grand Jury vs Burk   On the Presentment of the Grand Jury against John Burk for swearing it is ordered that the said John do pay unto the Church wardens of St. James Parish five shillings Currt. money or 50 lbs. of tobacco with Costs.

Scott &c. vs Ridgell &c   The information of Edward Scot and Thomas Prosser against Richard Ridgell, Joshua Stephens, and John Field is dismist.

Absent. John Fleming Gent.

Jevodan vs Fleming   In the Action of Trespass on the Case between Judith Jevodan

[175]   July Court 1731
Jevodan Admx. &c. of Thomas Jevodan deced Plt. and John Fleming Admr. &c. of John Legrand deced Deft. an Imparlance is granted the Deft.

Carnar vs Fleming &c   In the Action of Trespass on the Case between Susanna Carnar Plt. and John Fleming Admr. of John Legrand deced Deft. an Imparlance is granted the Deft.

Present John Fleming Gent.

Then the Court adjourned to the third Tuesday in next Month.

****

At a Court held for Goochland County the third Tuesday in August being the seventeenth day of the Month Annoq Domi. 1731. Present. John Fleming, William Mayo, Daniell Stoner, George Payne, George Raine, Gent. Justices.

Surveyor of road   James Spears is appointed Surveyor of the road from the widow Blackburns to the County line.

Informacon vs Locket &c   William Lansdon Constable informs the Court that Thomas Locket Junr, William Mosely, and John Tabor, have tended Seconds this year on their several plantation, and it is ordered that the Kings Deputy Attorny do prosecute them for the same.

Absent John Fleming, George Raine, Gent.

[176]   July Court 1731
Present William Cabbell Gent.

Sherifs sworn   Tarlton Fleming Gent. produces a Commission from the Honble William Gooch Esqr. his Majesty's Lieut. Governour & Commander in chief of this Dominion to be Sherif of this County which being read the said Tarlton Fleming together with John Fleming and George Raine, Gent. enter into bond according to Law and acknowledging the same to be their Act and deed it is ordered to be recorded then Tarlton Fleming, Joseph Dabbs and Thomas Walker take the Oaths appointed to be taken by Act of Parliament instead of the Oaths of Allegiance and Supremacy the Oath appointed to be taken by an Act of Parliament made in the first year of the reign of his late Majesty King George the First Entituled an Act for the further Security of his Majestys Person and Government and the Succession of the Crown in the Heirs of the late Princess Sophia being Protestants and for extinguishing the hopes of the pretended Prince of Wales and his open and secret abettors and Subscribe the Test. Tarlton Fleming also takes the Oath of a Sherif and Joseph Dabbs and Thomas Walker take the Oath of an Under sherif.

Present John Fleming, George Raine, Gent.

Souillee's deed to Rapene   Nicholas Souillee acknowledges a deed with the Livery of Seisin endorsed from himself to Anthony Rapene to be his Act and deed and it is thereupon admitted to record.

Rapene's deed to Souillee   Anthony Rapene & Margaret his wife (she being first privately examined) acknowledge a deed with the Livery of Seisin endorsed from themselves to Nicholas Souillee to be their Act and deed and it is thereupon admitted to record.

Williams's Inventory   James Holman presents an Inventory of the Estate of Edward Williams deced. which is ordered to be recorded.

Parsons deed to Burton   Joseph Parsons acknowledges a deed with the Livery of Seisin endorsed from himself to Nowel Burton to be his Act and deed

[177]   August Court 1731
and it is thereupon admitted to record then Sarah wife of the said Joseph (She being first privately examined) relinquishes her right of Dower in the land by this deed conveyed which is also admitted to record.

Parsons deed to Woodson   Sarah wife of Joseph Parsons (she being first privately examined) relinquishes her right of Dower in land formerly conveyed by her husband to Josiah Woodson which is ordered to be recorded.

James deed to Lansdon   Mary wife of Francis James (she being first privately examined) relinquishes her right of Dower in land formerly conveyed by her husband to William Lansdon which is ordered to be recorded.

Guerrant's Inventory   Peter Guerrant presents an Inventory of the Estate of Daniel Guerrant deced which is ordered to be recorded.

Sallee's Inventory   William Sallee presents an Inventory of the Estate of Isaac Sallee deced which is ordered to be recorded.

Owens deed to Cocke   John Owen acknowledges a deed with the Livery of Seisin endorsed from himself to James Cocke to be his Act and deed and it is thereupon admitted to record then Sarah wife of the said John (she being first privately examined) relinquishes her right of Dower in the land by this deed conveyed which is also admitted to record.

Prison received   Daniel Stoner, William Cabbell, & Tarlton Fleming, Gent. are appointed to view the Prison who report that it is built according to the Agreement made with Edward Scot and it is thereupon received by the Court.

Sherif's Protest   Tarlton Fleming Gent. Sherif protests against the Justices for not building a sufficient Prison without alled[g]ing any particular reason for such his protest.

[178]   August Court 1731
Cannon vs Scot   The Action of Debt between William Cannon Plt. and Edward Scot Admr. &c. of John Stephens deced. is dismist the Plt. not prosecuting the same.

Absent George Payne Gent.

Stevenson vs Payne   In the Action of Trespass on the Case between John Stevenson Plt. and George Payne Deft. the Deft. pleads he oweth nothing and the Suit is continued.

Present George Payne Gent.

Cannon vs Strange   In the Action of Trespass on the Case between William Cannon Plt. and Alexander Strange Deft. the Deft. appears and making no objection or discount against his bond it is ordered that he do pay unto the Plt. thirty five shillings Currt. money with Interest after the rate of Six Pr. Centum Pr. Annum from the 13th. day of March 1724 [1725] till the date of this Judgment with Costs and an Attorneys Fee.

Stevenson vs Payne   In the Action of Trespass between John Stevenson Plt. and Robert Payne Deft. the Plt. files a new declaration and an imparlance granted the Deft.

Randolph vs Martin   The Action of Trespass on the Case between William Randolph, Richard Randolph, John Randolph, & John Fleming, Exrs. &c. of Thomas Randolph deced Plts. and Francis Martin Deft. is continued.

Woodson vs Hughes   In the Action of Trespass on the Case between Joseph Woodson Plt. and Stephen Hughes Deft. the Auditors present their report which is ordered to be recorded in these words "Pursuant to an order of Goochland County Court we have examined stated & settled the Acco'ts. between Joseph Woodson Plt. & Stephen Hughes Defendant and find that there is justly due unto Stephen Hughes two pounds eighteen shills. and one penny farthing & seven hundred and ten pounds of tobacco Certified this fourteenth day of Augst. 1731. Pr. us Daniel Stoner, Geo. Payne, Antho. Hoggatt." whereupon

[179]   August Court 1731
whereupon it is considered by the Court that the Plt. take nothing by his writ aforesaid that the Deft. go hence without day and that he recover against the Plt. his Costs by him in this behalf expended.

       Absent. George Raine Gent.

Raine vs Levins &c   In the Action of Trespass on the Case between George Raine Plt. and Richard Levins Admr. &c. of John Sutton Farrar deced. Deft. an imparlance is granted the Deft.

Murrells deed to Lewis   Thomas Murrell acknowledges a deed with the Livery of Seisin endorsed from himself to Joseph Lewis to be his Act and deed and it is thereupon admitted to record then Elizabeth wife of the said Thomas (she being first privately examined) relinquishes her right of Dower in the land by this deed conveyed which is also admitted to record.

       Present Allin Howard Gent.

Orphan to be bound   Ordered that Tom the Son of Dole a Mulatto be bound by the Church wardens of St. James's Parish unto James Cocke according to Law.

Ward vs Farrar   In the Action of Debt between Seth Ward Plt. and John Farrar Deft. the Deft. files a Demurrer and time is granted the Plt. to reply.

Dickins vs Bolling   In the Action of Trespass on the Case between Thomas Dickins Plt. and John Bolling Admr. &c. of Bartholomew Cox Deced. Deft. the Deft. failing to plead on the Plts. motion Judgment by nihil dicit is granted him against the Deft. for what damages shall be recovered in this Suit to be discharged nevertheless if the Deft. shall plead at the next Court.

[180]   August Court 1731
Waddill vs Edwards   The Action on the Case between William Waddill Junr. Plt. and Thomas Edwards Deft. is continued.

Flournoy vs Martin   In the Action of Trespass on the Case between John James Flournoy Plt. and Francis Martin Deft. on the Defts. motion leave is granted him to plead several matters and thereupon he files pleas & time is granted the Plt. to reply.

Flournoy vs Martin   In the Action of Debt between John James Flournoy & Elizabeth his wife Exec'x. of Orlando Jones deced Plts. and Francis Martin Deft. Deft. on the Defts. motion leave is granted him to plead several matters whereupon he files pleas and time is granted the Plts. to reply.

Taylor vs Lowe   The Action of Trespass on the Case between John Taylor Plt. and Thomas Lowe & Amey his wife Defts. is continued.

Stevenson vs Johnson   In the Action of Trespass between John Stevenson Plt. and Charles Johnson Deft. the Plt. files a new declaration and an imparlance is granted the Deft.

Allegre vs Capoon   The Action of Trespass on the Case between Giles Allegre Plt. & Jacob Capoon Deft. is dismist neither party appearing.

Barret vs Epperson   The Action of Trespass on the Case between James Barret Plt. & William Epperson Deft. is dismist the Plt. not prosecuting the same.

May vs Woodson   In the Action of Trespass on the Case between William May Plt. & John Woodson Deft. time is granted the Plt. to mend his declaration.

Saunders vs Martin   In the Action of Trespass on the Case between John Saunders Plt. and Francis Martin Deft. the Deft. failing to plead on the Plts. motion Judgment by nihil dicit is granted him against the Deft.

for what damages shall be recovered in this Suit to be discharged nevertheless if the Deft. shall plead at the next Court.

[181]   August Court 1731
         Absent William Mayo, William Cabbell, Gent.

Cabbell vs Downie   The Attachment obtained by William Cabbell against the Estate of Robert Downie is continued and a Subpena is ordered to issue against John Cunningham in whose hands the Attachment is served.

Cabbell vs Woodsons   In the Action of Trespass on the Case between William Cabbell Admr. &c. of Joell Carr deced Plt. and Josiah and Stephen Woodson Exrs. &c. of Jacob Woodson deced Defts. the Defts. plead they owe nothing and for tryal put themselves upon the Country and the Plt. likewise.

Cabbell vs Utley   In the Action of Trespass on the Case between William Cabbell Plt. and John Utley Deft. the Sherif having returned the Attachment served in the hands of Anthony Hoggatt it is ordered that a Summons do issue against the said Anthony returnable to the next Court.

Woodson vs Cabbell   In the Action of Debt between Josiah & Stephen Woodson Exrs. &c. of Jacob Woodson deced. Plts. and William Cabbell Deft. is continued. Ordered that the Plts. pay the cost of this continuance.

         Present William Cabbell Gent.
         Absent Daniel Stoner Gent.

Stoner vs Utley   In the Action of Trespass on the Case between Daniel Stoner Plt. and John Utley Deft. for twelve pounds five shillings nine pence Currt. money due by bond the Sherif having made return on the Pluries Capias that the Deft. is not to be found and he failing to appear on the Plts. motion an Attachment is granted him against the Defts. Estate returnable to the next Court.

[182]   August Court 1731
         Present William Mayo, Daniel Stoner Gent.

Dickins vs Burton   In the Action of Trespass on the Case between Thomas Dickins Plt. and Nowel Burton Deft. the Deft. appears and confesses a Judgment for eight pounds four shillings & six pence half penny Currt. money whereupon it is ordered that he do pay the same unto the Plt. with Costs and an Attorneys Fee.

Dickins vs Burger   In the Action of Trespass on the Case between Thomas Dickins Plt. and Govert Burger Deft. the Deft. failing to appear on the Plts. motion the Conditional Judgment formerly granted in this suit against the Deft. and Dudley Digges his Common Bail is confirmed for so much damages as shall be found upon executing a Writ of inquiry at the next Court of which the Sherif is ordered to give the Deft. and the said Dudley Digges notice by serving them with a Copy of this order.

Haskins vs Saunders   In the Action of Debt between Creed Haskins Plt. and John Saunders Deft. the Plt. files a new declaration and on the motion of the Deft. an imparlance is granted him.

Crouch vs Cholmly   In the Action of Trespass between Richard Crouch Plt. and William Cholmly Deft. the Sherif having made return on the Alias Capias that the Deft. is not to be found and he failing to appear on the Plts. motion a Pluries Capias is awarded him against the Deft. returnable to the next Court.

Lansdon vs Benning   In the Action of Partition between William Lansdon and Hester his wife Plts. and Anthony Benning & Elizabeth his wife Defts. the said Anthony & Elizabeth his wife who is within Age come & defend the force & injury when &c. and the said Anthony saith nothing in barr of the Action aforesaid of the said Plts. by which the same Plts. remain against the said Anthony Benning & Elizabeth his wife thereof undefended therefore it is considered of that the Partition between the said Plts. and the aforesaid Defts. of the lands and tenements in the declaration mentioned with the appurtenances may be made and it is ordered that a

[183]   August Court 1731
a Writ de partitione facienda do issue returnable to the next Court.

Scot vs Pruit   The Action of Trespass on the Case between Edward Scot Admr. & John Stephens deced Plt. and Thomas Pruit Deft. is continued. Ordered that the Plt. pay the Cost of this continuance.

Hopkins vs Woodson   On the Action of Trespass on the Case between William Hopkins Plt. and Benjamin Woodson Deft. time is granted the Plt. to mend his declaration and the suit is continued. Ordered that the Plt. pay the Cost of this continuance.

Bryant vs Chandler   In the Action of Trespass on the Case between William Bryant Plt. and Joel Chandler Deft. the Plt. files a new declaration and an imparlance is granted the Deft.

Bryant vs Chandler   The Action of Trespass on the Case between William Bryant Plt. and Joel Chandler Deft. is dismist the Plt. not prosecuting the same.

Dickins vs Utley   In the Action of Trespass on the Case between Thomas Dickins Plt. and John Utley Deft. the Sherif having returned the Attachment served in the hands of Anthony Hoggat it is ordered that a Summons do issue against the said Anthony returnable to the next Court.

Gates vs Saunders   The Action of Trover between William Gates Plt. & Robert Saunders Deft. is continued. Ordered that the Deft. pay the Cost of this continuance.

Fleming vs Napier   On the Attachment obtained by Tarlton Fleming Sher. against the Estate of Bouth Napier for two pounds sixteen shillings and seven pence half penny Currt. money & one hundred & sixty pounds one pounds of tobacco and fifteen shillings Currt. money or one hundred and fifty pounds of tobacco by reason of the non appearance of the said Bouth Napier to answer the Suit of Thomas Dixon the Coroner having made return that

[184]   August Court 1731
that he can find no Goods or Chattels whereon to serve the said Attachment on the motion of the said Tarlton Fleming it is ordered that an Attachment de novo do issue against the Estate of the said Bouth Napier returnable to the next Court.

Absent William Cabbell, William Mayo, Gent.

Taylor vs Quin   In the Action of Debt between James Taylor Plt. and John Quin Deft. the following Jury are Sworn Joseph Bingley, John Merriman, William Cannon, David Mims, John Prior, Samuel Allen, Peter Jefferson, John Maddox, William Lansdon, Francis James, James Daniel Junr., John Paine, who after sometime bring in their Verdict in these words "Wee find for the Defendt. Joseph Bingley Foreman." whereupon it is considered by the Court that the Plt. take noting by his Writ aforesaid that the Deft. go hence without day and that he recover against the Plt. his Costs by him in this behalf expended and a Lawyers Fee.

Present William Cabbell, James Skelton, Gent.

Taylor vs Quin   The Action of Trespass on the Case between James Taylor Plt. and John Quin Deft. is continued. Ordered that the Plt. pay the Cost of this continuance.

Repene vs Marchbanks   In the Action of Debt between Anthony Rapene Church warden of King William Parish Plt. and George Marchbanks Defendt. the Plt. files a new declaration and an imparlance is granted the Deft.

Mims vs Levins &c   In the Action of Trespass on the Case between David Mims Plt. and Richard Levins Admr. &c. of John Sutton Farrar deced Deft. the Deft. failing to plead on the Plts. motion Judgment by nihil dicit is granted him against the Deft. for what damages shall be recovered in this suit to be discharged nevertheless if the Deft. shall plead at the next Court.

[185]   August Court 1731
Digges vs Fleming   The Action of Trespass on the Case between Dudley Digges Plt. and Tarlton Fleming Deft. is continued. Ordered that the Plt. pay the Cost of this continuance.

Digges vs Prier   The Action of Trespass on the Case between Dudley Digges Plt. and John Prier Deft. is continued. Ordered that the Plt. pay the Cost of this continuance.

Digges vs Levins   The Action of Trespass on the Case between Dudley Digges Plt. and Richard Levins Admr. &c. of John Sutton Farrar deced. Deft. is continued. Ordered that the Plt. pay the Cost of this continuance.

Dickins vs Scot   In the Action of Trespass on the Case between Thomas Dickins Plt. and Edward Scot Deft. Henry Wood is appointed to Examine state settle the several Accts. in dispute between them and his report is to be made the Judgment of this Court.

Anderson vs Allen   In the Action of Debt between John Anderson Plt. and Samuel Allen Deft. is continued. Ordered that the Plt. pay the Cost of this continuance.

Chastain vs Martin   In the Action of Trespass on the Case between John & Peter Chastain Exrs. &c. of Peter Chastain Plts. & Francis Martin Deft. the following Jury are sworn Joseph Bingley, John Merriman,

William Cannon, David Mims, John Prier, Samuel Allin, Peter Jefferson, John Maddox, William Lansdon, Francis James, James Daniel Junr., John Paine, the Plts. produce their Acct. the sum of which not being cognizable by the Court on the Defts. motion the Plts. are nonsuited and it is thereupon ordered that they do pay unto the Defts. five shillings Currt. money with Costs.

    Present William Mayo Gent.

Grand Jury vs Murrell   On the Presentment of the Grand Jury against Thomas Murrell for being drunk & profane swearing the following Jury are sworn John Merriman, William Cannon, Davis Mims, John Prier, Peter Jefferson, John Mattox, William Lansdon, James Daniel Junr, John Paine, Stephen Woodson, William Kent, Benjamin Bradshaw, who after some time bring in their

[186]   August Court 1731
their Verdict in these words "Wee find Thomas Murrell guilty." whereupon it is considered by the Court that the said Thomas do pay unto the Church wardens of St. James's Parish ten shillings Currt. money or one hundred pounds of tobacco with costs.

Anderson vs Burton   In the Action of Debt between John Anderson Plt. and Nowell Burton Deft. time is granted the Plt. to mend his declaration.

Rapene vs Napier &c   On the Petition of Anthony Rapene Church warden of King William Parish, Robert Napier Junr. and James Taylor come into Court and consent to enter into bond with condition to save harmless the said Parish from the charge of Agnes and Judith two Children belonging to Anne Farmar.

Fleming vs Parsons   In the Action of Trespass on the Case between Tarlton Fleming Plt. Joseph Parsons Deft. the Deft. confesses himself indebted three hundred & eighteen pounds of tobacco whereupon it is ordered that he do pay the same unto the Plt. with Costs and an Attorneys Fee.

Guerrant vs Paine   In the Action of Trespass on the Case between Peter Guerrant Plt. & John Paine Deft. Thomas Dickins & Thomas Walker are appointed to Examine state and settle the several matters in dispute between [them] and their report is to be made the Judgment of this Court.

Raine vs Amos   The Action of Trespass on the Case between George Raine Plt. and Francis Amos Deft. is continued.

Prosser vs Quin   In the Action of Trespass on the Case between Thomas Prosser Plt. & John Quin Deft. for twenty pounds Currt. money the Sherif having made return on the Attachment issued last Court that he can find no goods of the Defts. whereon to serve the same on the Plts. motion it is ordered that an Attachment de novo do issue against the Defts. Estate returnable to the next Court.

Digges vs Thaxton   The Action of Trespass on the Case between Dudley Digges Plt. and Abell Thaxton Deft. is continued.

[187]   August Court 1731
Digges vs Napier   The Action of Trespass on the Case between Dudley Digges Plt. and Robert Napier Junr. Deft. is continued. Ordered that the Plt. pay the Cost of this continuance.

Digges vs Pate   The Action of Trespass on the Case between Dudley Digges Plt. and Thomas Pate Deft. is dismist the Plt. not prosecuting the same.

Cawthorn vs Levins   The Action of Trespass on the Case between Robert Cawthorn Plt. and Richard Levins Admr. &c. of John Sutton Farrar deced. Deft. is continued. Ordered that the Deft. pay the Cost of this continuance.

Cawthorn vs Levins   The Action of Trespass on the Case between Robert Cawthorn & Mary his wife Plts. & Richard Levins Admr. &c. of John Sutton Farrar deced. Deft. is continued. Ordered that the Deft. pay the Cost of this continuance.

Scot vs Dickins   In the Action of Trespass on the Case between Edward Scot Admr. &c. of John Stephens Plt. & Thomas Dickins Deft. the Deft. pleads he oweth nothing & for tryal thereof puts himself upon the Country & the Plt. likewise.

Taylor vs Dickins   In the Action of Trespass on the Case between John Taylor Plt. and Thomas Dickins Deft. the Deft. pleads he oweth nothing & for tryal thereof puts himself upon the Country and the Plt. likewise.

Chemino vs Hughes   In the Action of Trespass on the Case between John Chemino Plt. & Isaac Hughes Deft. the Deft. appears & confesses a Judgment to the Plt. for thirty shillings Currt. money whereupon it is considered by the Court that the Plt. do recover against the Deft. the said sum together with the Costs of this Suit and a Lawyers Fee.

Stoner vs Davis   In the Action of Trespass on the Case between Daniel Stoner Plt. and William Davis Deft. for ten pounds Currt. money the Sherif having made return on the Attachment issued last Court that he can find no goods of the Defts. whereon to serve the same on the Plts. motion it is ordered that an Attachment de novo do issue against the Defts. Estate returnable to the next Court.

Raine vs Ripley   In the Action of Trespass between George Raine Plt. and John Ripley

[188]   August Court 1731
Ripley Deft. the Sherif having made return on the Pluries Capias that the Deft. is not to be found and he failing to appear on the Plts. motion a Pluries Capias de novo is awarded him against the Deft. returnable to the next Court.

Chandler vs Napier   In the Action of Trespass on the Case between Joel Chandler Plt. and Robert Napier Junr. Deft. on the Defts. motion leave is granted him to plead several matters whereupon he files pleas & time is granted the Plt. to reply.

Scot vs Epperson   The Action of Trespass on the Case between Edward Scot Plt. and William Epperson Deft. is continued.

Allin vs Woodson   The Attachment obtained by Samuel Allin against the Estate of John Woodson Junr. is dismist the Plt. not prosecuting the same.

Wilson to be Summoned   Richard Wilson is ordered to be Summoned to appear at the next Court to answer his misbehaviour in neglecting to obey a Warrant granted by William Mayo Gent. & Thomas Duggins & Nicholas Roads as Witnesses.

Scot vs Daniel. The Action of Detinue between Edward Scot Plt. and James Daniel Deft. is continued.

Grand Jury vs Davis   On the Presentment of the Grand Jury against William Davis for an Assault on the body of Thomas Wadloe the Deft. pleads he is not guilty and issue is joined thereupon.

Grand Jury vs Parker   Richard Parker acknowledges himself indebted unto our Lord the King in the Sum of twenty five pounds Sterling, Edward Scot twelve pounds ten shillings Sterling, William Womack twelve pounds ten shillings Sterling to be levied on their Goods & Chattles on condition that if the said Richard Parker keep the peace towards all his Majestys Subjects for a year & a day and also appear at the next Court to be held for this County after the year & a day are expired then this recognizance is to be void.

Jevodan vs Fleming   The Action of Trespass on the Case between Judith Jevodan Admx. &c. of Thomas Jevodan deced. Plt. & John Fleming Admr. &c. of John Legrand deced Deft. is dismist the Plt. not prosecuting the same.

[189]   August Court 1731
Carnar vs Fleming   The Action of Trespass on the Case between Susanna Carnar Plt. and John Fleming Admr. &c. of John Legrand deced Deft. is dismist the Plt. not prosecuting the same

  Absent John Fleming Gent.

Adams vs Randolph's Exrs   On the Petition of Robt. Adams praying leave to build a mill on a branch of Dover mill Creek the Court are of opinion the building of the said mill will be prejudicial to a mill already built below on the same run belonging to the Estate of Thomas Randolph deced but now out of repair nevertheless leave is granted the petitioner to build a mill according to the prayer of his petition if the other mill below do not grind within the space of four months.

  Present John Fleming Gent.

Surveyors   The Surveyors of the roads are continued.

Alves vs Joplin   In the Action of Debt between George Alves Plt. and Thomas Joplin Deft. the Sherif having made return that the Deft. is not to be found and he failing to appear on the Plts. motion an Alias Capias is awarded him against the Deft. returnable to the next Court.

  Absent John Fleming Gent.

Sallee vs Fleming   In the Action of Trespass on the Case between William Sallee Plt. and John Fleming Admr. &c. of John Legrand deced. Deft. the Plt. having failed to file his declaration on the Defts. motion he is nonsuited and it is thereupon considered by the Court that the Deft. go hence without day and that he recover against the Plt. five shillings Currt. money according to the Act of Assembly in that case made and provided together with his Costs by him in this behalf expended.

Present John Fleming Gent.

[190] August Court 1731

Quantin vs Dickins   In the Action of Detinue between John Quantin Plt. and Thomas Dickins time is granted the Plt. to mend his declaration.

Goodall vs Chemino   In the Action of Trespass on the Case between James Goodall Plt. & John Chemino Deft. time is granted the Plt. to mend his declaration.

Woodson vs Hughes   In the Action of Debt between John Woodson Plt. & Robert Hughes Deft. time is granted the Plt. to mend his declaration.

Woodson vs Hughes   In the Action on the Case between Joseph Woodson Plt. and Stephen Hughes Deft. the Deft. pleads he oweth nothing .

Absent John Fleming Gent.

Benning vs Fleming   The Action of Trespass on the Case between Anthony Benning Plt. and John Fleming Admr. &c. of John Legrand deced. Deft. is dismist the Plt. not prosecuting the same.

Burnar vs Fleming   The Action of Trespass on the Case between David Burnar Plt. and John Fleming Admr. &c. of John Legrand deced Deft. is dismist the Plt. not prosecuting the same.

Present John Fleming Gent.

Stevenson vs Payne   The Action of Trespass on the Case between John Stevenson Plt. & George Paine Junr. Deft. is dismist the Plt. not prosecuting the same.

Landson vs Mooney   In the Action of Trespass between William Lansdon Plt. & John Mooney Deft. is dismist the Plt. not prosecuting the same.

Woodson vs Woodson   On the Attachment obtained by Joseph Woodson Junr. against the Estate of John Woodson Junr. a new declaration is filed and the Attachment is dismist on the motion of the Plts. Attorney.

Then the Court adjourned to the third Tuesday in next month.

****

[191]   September Court 1731
At a Court held for Goochland County the third Tuesday in September being the twenty first day of the Month Annoq Domi. 1731. Present. John Woodson, Daniel Stoner, Allin Howard, Anthony Hoggatt, Gent. Justices.

Stevenson vs Payne   In the Action of Trespass on the Case between John Stevenson Plt. & George Payne Deft. the Plt. files a new declaration & an imparlance is granted the Deft.

Stevenson vs Payne   In the Action of Trespass between John Stevenson Plt. & Robert Payne Deft. the Deft. appears but failing to plead on the Plts. motion Judgment by nihil dicit is granted him against the Deft. for what damages shall be recovered in this Suit to be discharged nevertheless if the Deft. shall plead at the next Court.

Present. George Payne, William Cabbell, Gent.

Randolph vs Martin   In the Action of Trespass on the Case between William Randolph, Richard Randolph, John Randolph, & John Fleming Exrs. &c. of Thomas Randolph deced. Plts. & Francis Martin Deft. the Suit is continued for the Auditors report. The Deft. moves that the Issue may be tryed by a Jury and the order for an Audit set aside which motion is denied by the Court.

Farrars Acct. of Estate   George Payne & George Raine Gent. are appointed to examine the Account Dr. & Cr. of the Estate of John Sutton Farrar deced.

Raines vs Levins &c   In the Action of Trespass on the Case between George Raine Plt. and Richard Levins Admr. &c. of John Sutton Farrar deced. Deft. the Deft. pleads he hath fully Administred and for tryal thereof puts himself upon the Country and the Plt. likewise.

Christians deed to Harris   Thomas Christian acknowledges a deed with the Livery of Seisin endorsed from himself to Mathew Harris & Lee Harris to be his Act & deed and it is thereupon admitted to record then Rebacca wife of

[191a]   September Court 1731
of the said Thomas (she being first privately examined) relinquishes her right of Dower in the land by the said deed conveyed which is also admitted to record.

Ward vs Farrar   In the Action of Debt between Seth Ward Plt. and John Farrar Deft. the Plt. joyns in Demurrer the arguing whereof is referred.

Dickins vs Bolling &c   In the Action of Trespass on the Case between Thomas Dickins Plt. and John Bolling Admr. &c. of Bartholomew Cox Deft. the Deft. failing to plead on the Plts. motion the conditional Judgment formerly granted in this Suit is confirmed for so much damages as shall be found upon executing a Writ of inquiry at the next Court of which the Sherif is ordered to give the Deft. notice by serving him with a Copy of this order.

Informacon vs Logan &c   Thomas Wharton Constable informs the Court that Henry Harper, and Alexander Logan have tended Seconds this year on their several Plantations and it is ordered that the Kings Deputy Attorney do prosecute them for the same.

Waddill vs Edwards   The Action on the Case between William Waddill Junr. Plt. and Thomas Edwards Deft. is continued.

Flournoy vs Martin   In the Action of Trespass on the Case between John James Flournoy Plt. and Francis Martin Deft. the Plt. takes issue on the Defts. pleas & the Suit is continued.

Flournoy vs Martin   In the Action of Debt between John James Flournoy & Elizabeth his wife Ex'x. &c. of Orlando Jones deced. Plts. & Francis Martin Deft. the Plt. takes issue on the Defts. pleas and the Suit is continued.

Taylor vs Lowe   The Action of Trespass on the Case between John Taylor Plt. & Thomas Lowe & Amey his wife Defts. is continued.

Stevenson vs Johnson   In the Action of Trespass between John Stevenson Plt. & Charles Johnson Deft. the Deft. pleads he is not guilty and for tryal thereof puts himself upon the Country and the Plt. likewise.

May vs Woodson   In the Action of Trespass on the Case between William May Plt. & John Woodson the Plt. files a new declaration & an imparlance is granted the Deft.

[192]   September Court 1731
Saunders vs Martin   In the Action of Trespass on the Case between John Saunders Plt. & Francis Martin Plt. the Deft. pleads he oweth nothing & for tryal thereof puts himself upon the Country and the Plt. likewise.

  Absent William Cabbell Gent.

Cabbell vs Downie   The Attachment obtained by William Cabbell against the Estate of Robert Downie is continued.

Cabbell vs Woodson   In the Action of Trespass on the Case between William Cabbell Admr. &c. of Joell Carr deced. Plt. & Josiah & Stephen Woodson Exrs. &c. of Jacob Woodson deced Defts. the parties submit themselves unto the Court for tryal whereupon the Accts. between them and the Defts. oath being considered it is ordered that the Defts. do pay unto the Plt. Admr. as aforesaid out of the said deceadents Estate in their hands three shillings Currt. money with Costs.

  Present William Mayo Gent.

Rule of Court   On the motion of Thomas Prosser it is entered as a Rule that a Fee be taxed where any person is taxed at the Kings Suit.

Cox's & Hughes land to be viewed   On the Petition of Nicholas Cox & Stephen Hughes ordered that John Saunders, George Stoveall, & Joell Chandler, being sworn in Court do value the improvements on their land on Muddy Creek being two thousand six hundred sixty six acres and make their report to the next Court.

  Present George Raine, William Cabbell, Gent.

Poe whipped   Robert Poe & Elizabeth his wife appear on his Recognizance & the said Elizabeth being accused with stealing a grubbing hoe from Mark Lively upon hearing the witnesses & the Prisoner it is the opinion of the Court that she is guilty and thereupon ordered that she do receive at the Common whipping post five lashes on her bare back and that her husband pay Costs & a Lawyers Fee.

[193]   September Court 1731
Lee to be bound   Ordered that Marmaduke Hix deliver unto the Church wardens of St. James's Parish James Lee an Orphan to be bound by them according to law.

Absent William Cabbell, Anthony Hoggatt, Gent.

Cabbell vs Utley   In the Action of Trespass on the Case between William Cabbell Plt. and John Utley Deft. the Plt. makes Oath to his debt & on the motion Judgment is granted him against the Deft. for four hundred & sixty pounds of tobacco with the costs of this Suit and a Lawyers Fee.
   The Attachment obtained by William Cabbell against the Estate of John Utley having been served on Anthony Hoggatt & he failing to appear on the Summons on the Plts. motion it is ordered that a Capias do issue against the said Anthony returnable to the next Court.

Woodon vs Cabbell   In the Action of Debt between Josiah & Stephen Woodson Exrs. &c. of Jacob Woodson deced. Plts and William Cabbell Deft. the following Jury are sworn Bouth Napier, Nicholas Cox, David Pattison, John Harris, Nathaniel Basset, John Paine, Joel Chandler, John Prier, Henry Harper, Robert Hughes, Benjamin Bradshaw, William Walton, who after some time bring in their Verdict in these words "Wee find for the Plt. three hundred pounds of tobacco. Bouth Napier Foreman." whereupon it is considered by the Court that the Plts. Exrs. as aforesaid do recover against the Deft. the said sum with the Costs and an Attorneys Fee.

Wadloe vs Woodsons   On the motion of Thomas Wadloe a witness for Josiah & Stephen Woodson Exrs. &c. of Jacob Woodson deced vs William Cabbell it is ordered that the said Josiah & Stephen do pay him for two days attendance sixty pounds of tobacco with Costs.

Stokes vs Woodsons   On the motion of Young Stokes a witness for Josiah & Stephen Woodson vs William Cabbell it is ordered that the said Josiah & Stephen do pay him for one days attendance thirty pounds of tobacco with Costs.

Powell vs Cabbell   On the motion of Roger Powell a witness for William Cabbell ads Josiah & Stephen Woodson it is ordered that the said William do pay him for one days attendance thirty pounds of tobacco with Cost.

[194] September Court 1731
Absent Daniel Stoner Gent.

Stoner vs Utley   In the Action of Trespass on the Case between Daniel Stoner Plt. and John Utley Deft. the Sherif having returned the Summons issued against Anthony Hoggatt Executed and he failing to appear on the Plts. motion it is ordered that a Capias do issue against the said Anthony returnable to the next Court.

Arrington's Inventory   Jane Arrington presents an Inventory on the Estate of Samuel Arrington deced. which is ordered to be recorded.

Dawson's deed to Logan   Thomas Dawson acknowledges a deed with the Livery of Seisin endorsed from himself to Alexander Logan to be his Act & deed and it is thereupon admitted to record then Mary wife of the said Thomas (she being first privately examined) relinquishes her right of Dower in the land by this deed conveyed which is also admitted to record.

Willis vs Holman Admr. &c   On the Petition of Robert Willis praying to be allowed the funeral charges of Edward Williams the Court having regulated his Acct. there of it is ordered that James Holman Admr. &c. of the said Edward deced. do pay unto the Petitioner out of the said deceadents Estate two pounds six shillings and three half pence with costs.

County levey to be laid   Ordered that the County levey be laid the day after the next November Court.

The King vs Wilson   Richard Wilson appears to answer a complaint made against him for refusing or neglecting to Execute a Warrant directed to him by William Mayo Gent. and upon examination thereof the Court are of opinion he is guilty of a contempt and it is thereupon ordered that he do sit in the Stocks two hours and give bond with Security in the sum of ten pounds Sterl. for his good behaviour for a year and a day and that he pay costs and an Attorneys Fee.

[195] September Court 1731
Wilson's Recognizance   Richard Wilson acknowledges himself indebted unto our Lord the King in the sum of five pounds Sterling, William Gates fifty shillings Sterling, James Gates fifty shillings Sterling to be levied on their goods & chattles on condition that if the said Richard Wilson keep

the Peace towards all his Majesty's Subjects for a year & a day and also appear at the next Court to be held for this County after the year and a day are expired then this recognizance to be void.

Prosser apps. on his bond &c   Thomas Prosser appears pursuant to his Bond to Our Lord the King for his good behaviour and Proclamation being made no person objects any thing against him whereupon he is discharged from the Penalty of the said bond.

Surveyor of the road   Ordered that Thomas Dickins's titheables at Long Acre be added to James Spears Surveyor of the road.

Prison bound to be laid out   Stephen Hughes is appointed to lay out the Prison bounds and to make report thereof to the next Court.

Then the Court adjourned till to morrow ten of the Clock.

[End of Order Book 2]

Appendices

APPENDIX A

COUNTY OFFICIALS

The lists below include the men who served Goochland County during the time period of this volume, May 21, 1728 through September 21, 1731.

GENTLEMEN JUSTICES

William Cabbell
John Fleming
Tarlton Fleming
Anthony Hoggat
James Holman
Allin Howard
William Mayo

George Paine (Payne)
George Raine
William Mayo
Edward Scot
James Skelton
Daniel Stone
John Woodson

CLERK OF THE COURT

Henry Wood

SHERIFFS, UNDER SHERIFFS, SUB SHERIFFS

Joseph Bingley
John Bowie
Joseph Dabbs
Tarlton Fleming

Daniel Stoner
Joseph Thompson
Thomas Walker

APPENDIX B

GLOSSARY and ABBREVIATIONS

&c	etcetera; and so forth
acct	account
ads	against, versus
assee	assignee; a person who has been assigned another person's rights or property (Harris, 25)
capias (capius)	an order to seize or take. Plurius capias is the third order in a case. The first order in a case is a capias, the second is an alias capias, the third is a plurius capias. (Drake, 34)
cask	casks which contained tobacco
C^r	credit
curr^t money	current money
deced	deceased
Deft.; Defts.	defendant; defendants; defendant's
demurrer	a delay or stay; a document filed by the defendant asking the court not to accept the plaintiff's declaration even if true as sufficient evidence to support a judgment in behalf of the plaintiff (Harris, 74)
de novo	a new plurius capius order (Webster, 339)
de partitione facienda	"de repartitione facienda," the name of a writ which lies by one tenant in common against the other, to cause him to aid in repairing the common property (Law-dictionary.org)
detinet	a common law action alleging that the defendant is withholding money or items owed
detinue	an action to recover or obtain compensation for personal property that has been illegally detained. (Harris, 76; Drake, 68)
D°.	ditto, repeated item
dower	the portion of her husband's estate to which the widow is entitled by law, usually one-third of real estate
D^r.	debtor; debt; one who owes
D.S. tree	District Survey tree, used by county governments as a boundary point (Paul Drake)
Exr; Exrs; Exx	executor; executors; executrix

GLOSSARY and ABBREVIATIONS

gaol	early word for jail; sometimes misspelled as goal in these court orders
Gent.	gentleman; gentlemen; a person of affluence or high station (Drake, 103)
go without day	go without his day in court; the case is dismissed with prejudice, meaning that the suit cannot be brought again unless the facts are changed for some reason other than the plaintiff's own activity for that purpose. (Drake, personal response)
honble	honorable
imparlance	an extension or granting of time for a party to a lawsuit to further plead their cause. (Drake)
instant	during the same month
lease & release	a method of buying land to avoid paying English court fees, in which the land was leased for a period until all rights were finally purchased through a release (Harris, 134)
levy	a tax; in this record, the tax imposed on the county taxables (titheables) in pounds of tobacco
livery of seizin	the common law ceremony when possession of property was delivered to the buyer (Drake)
nihil dicit	a legal claim sustained against someone who failed to plead or answer a complaint, or after doing so, abandoned his defense. (Drake, 149)
nil debet	a pleading; a general issue in debt, a simple contract. (Law-Dictionary.org)
non damnificatus	pleading: a plea to an action of debt by which the defendant asserts that the plaintiff has received no indemnity, by which the defendant asserts that the plaintiff has received no damage; in other words that he is not damnified. (Law-Dicitionary.org)
non est factum	factum is a deed; a man's own act and deed. When a man denies by his plea that he made a deed on which he is sued, he pleads non est factum. (Law-Dictionary.org)
non sum informatus	pleading: I am not informed. (Law-Dictionary)
nonsuit	dismissal of a law suit at the order of a court (Drake, 150)

GLOSSARY and ABBREVIATIONS

ordinary	a tavern and place for eating and drinking where the rates were usually set by the county court (Drake, 155)
p; pr	per as in per annum
Petr. Petrs.	petitioner; petitioner's; petitioners
Plt; Plts	plaintiff; plaintiffs; plantiff's; plaintiffs'
relict	widow or widower
rundlet	a small cask measuring 18 gallons of liquid or 15 gallons in English measurement. (Harris, 193)
scire facias	a writ in which the person is required to show why a matter of record should not be enforced (Harris, 196)
severalty	property held by one person only and not jointly or in common. (Harris, 200)
ss	scilicet; namely, that is to say; appears as "ss" after the name of a county (Drake)
tobo	tobacco
trover	an action to recover the value of goods wrongfully converted by another person to his own use (Webster, 1266); gaining possession of goods by finding or other means such as smuggling, poaching, salvage (Harris, 221)
uxor; et ux	the spouse of the person named. (Drake, 85, 221; Harris, 224)
vizt	videlicet; that is to say; namely

BIBLIOGRAPHY

Blomquist, Ann K. *Goochland County Virginia Court Order Book 3 1731-1735.* Westminster, MD: Heritage Books, 2006.

Blomquist, Ann K. *Goochland County Virginia Court Order Book 5 1741-1745.* Westminster, MD: Heritage Books, 2007.

Cocke, Charles Francis. *Parish Lines, Diocese of Southern Virginia.* Richmond VA: Virginia State Library, 1981.

Cocke, Charles Francis. *Parish Lines, Diocese of Virginia.* Richmond VA: Virginia State Library, 1967.

Doran, Michael. *Atlas of County Boundary Changes in Virginia 1634-1895.* San Bernardino, CA: Borgo Press, 1989.

Drake, Paul. *What Did They Mean By That? A Dictionary of Historical Terms for Genealogists.* Bowie, MD: Heritage Books, 1994.

Grundset, Eric. *Historical Boundary Atlas of Central Virginia.* Fairfax, VA: Grundset, 1999.

Harris, Maurine and Glen. *Concise Genealogical Dictionary.* Salt Lake City, UT: Ancestry, 1989.

Hopkins, William L. *St. James Northam Parish Vestry Book 1744-1850 Goochland County, Virginia.* Richmond, 1987.

Hudgins, Dennis R. *Goochland County, Virginia Order Books I and II 1728-1731.* Goochland, 1997.

Lurvey, A. Jean. *Goochland County, Virginia Tithe Lists 1735-1747.* Springfield MO, 1985.

Lurvey, A. Jean. *Goochland County, Virginia Tithe Lists 1748-1749.* Springfield MO, 1979.

Sweeny, Mrs. William M. "Goochland County Tithables 1747, 1751," *The Virginia Genealogist,* Vol 6, No. 1, January 1962.

TLC Genealogy. *Goochland County, Virginia Court Order Books 1728-1735, An Every-Name Index.* Miami Beach, 1992.

INDEX

Variant spellings should be checked.
Names may appear more than once on a page.

Acrill, William 229, 245, 267, 286
Adams, Ebenezer 7, 10, 74, 167, 198
Adams, Mourning 36
Adams, Robert 31, 36, 41, 114, 119, 120, 169, 179, 180, 181, 233, 310, 349, 350, 351, 381, 388, 389, 390, 391, 406
Adams, Thomas 371
Adding justices 74
Adkins, Henry 131
Adultery 32
Agee, see Ogee
Agee, Anne 5
Agee, Anthony 355
Agee, Mathew 5, 195, 209, 224, 237, 244, 257, 276, 291, 355
Akin, James 270
Alexander, John 38, 50, 56, 58, 71, 91, 104, 112, 115, 134
Alford, William 282
Allegre, Giles 73, 195, 210, 217, 229, 238, 380, 398
Allen, see Allin
Allin, Charles 241, 381
Allin, David 217
Allin, Robert 304
Allin, Robert Jr 56
Allin, Samuel 39, 42, 58, 59, 61, 63, 72, 73, 77, 92, 96, 97, 99, 100, 108, 114, 117, 133, 136, 156, 158, 159, 164, 169, 174, 176, 182, 183, 184, 190, 191, 204, 205, 212, 220, 236, 242, 252, 254, 262, 269, 272, 274, 288, 289, 303, 310, 325, 332,

Allin, Samuel (con't) 350, 354, 368, 372, 375, 385, 389, 401, 402, 403, 405
Alsup, Benjamin 100, 351
Alsup, William 236
Alter road 316, 348
Alves, see Alvis
Alvis, George 5, 9, 14, 22, 27, 32, 36, 37, 48, 49, 58, 60, 75, 82, 113, 122, 139, 151, 167, 175, 185, 196, 200, 201, 223, 237, 406
Amos, Francis 310, 369, 385, 392, 404
Amos, John 101, 225
Amos, Valentine 305, 310
Anderson, Charles 381, 392
Anderson, John 368, 385, 402, 403
Anderson, Mary 102, 11
Appomattox ridge 8, 58
Applebury, Thomas 126
Armes, John 369
Armistrong, see Armstrong
Armistrong 300
Armstrong, Robert 194, 227, 311
Arrington, Jane 139, 349, 412
Arrington, Samuel 139, 226, 242, 350, 412
Arrington, William 228, 244, 247, 267, 285
Ashlin, Joseph 16, 28, 29, 37, 49, 50, 60, 72, 92, 93, 143, 158, 175, 196, 211, 253, 264, 272, 290, 304, 320, 337
Askew 131

Assault 196, 202, 203, 333, 358, 405
Atkins, Sarah 146
Atkinson, Elizabeth 18, 264, 380
Atkinson, Henry 18, 41, 53, 81, 99, 101, 110, 111, 120, 121, 137, 146, 197, 211, 264, 350, 371, 387
Atkinson, Robert 299
Atkinson, Sarah iv, 7, 68, 70, 74, 87, 89, 107, 108, 117, 124, 140, 143, 146, 154, 169, 172, 176, 189, 190, 207, 208, 217, 219, 221, 223, 232, 235, 257, 262, 263, 264, 281
Atkinson, Thomas 124, 140, 154, 176, 178, 190, 208, 232, 262
Atkinson, Widow 285
Atkinson, William 280, 281
Atkinson's ferry ii, 7, 74, 87, 220, 281, 285
Attorney imprisoned 258

Back Road 8, 74, 86, 131, 351
Bailey, see Baily
Baily, Henry 30, 124, 141, 154, 193
Baily, Thomas 182, 183, 184, 331, 332
Baise, see Baize
Baize, Edward 44, 55, 66, 88, 106, 113, 125, 139, 146, 149, 192, 216, 218, 231
Baize, Peter 9, 32, 116, 118, 119, 120, 122, 144, 180
Baize, Sarah 180
Baker, Francis 41, 53, 63, 80, 81, 82
Baldridge, Thomas 69, 91, 92
Baldwin, Henry 80, 81, 98
Ballew, Giles 72

Ballew, Judith 161, 175, 192, 211, 225, 246, 274, 333, 359
Ballew, Leonard 8, 9, 32, 36, 88, 104, 107, 108, 109, 182, 309, 332
Ballew, Susannah 309
Ballew, Thomas 9, 102, 143, 280, 309
Ballew, William 276
Ballow, see Ballew
Barnes, William 11, 43, 55, 64, 65, 79, 97, 234
Barnit, see Burnet
Barnit, John 76, 78, 80, 81, 168
Barret, James 143, 218, 222, 224, 226, 241, 242, 258, 380, 398
Barret, Sarah 226, 241
Barrett, see Barret
Barringer, Joseph 199
Barrow 78
Basket 77
Bass, Edward 73, 93. 116
Basset, see Bassett
Bassett 331
Bassett, Nathaniel 8, 20, 21, 24, 47, 49, 58, 64, 104, 107, 108, 110, 147, 313, 315, 411
Bassett, Thomas 346
Bastard child 45, 161, 274, 333, 359
Bates, Fleming 181, 375
Bates, Isaac 300
Battery 59, 184
Baylor, John 274
Beating 196, 203, 333, 360, 390, 392
Beaver Dam, see Beverdam
Becket, John 33
Bedstead 77
Beer 13, 319
Behavior 135, 189, 196, 202, 203, 234, 259, 263, 337, 339,

Behavior (con't) 350, 354, 390, 405, 412, 413
Bellamy, John 97, 114, 138, 155, 291, 310, 337, 347
Bellamy, Judith 114
Bellamy, Mary 97, 114, 125
Benning, Anthony 31, 32, 52, 68, 85, 89, 107, 117, 146, 169, 177, 219, 257, 260, 280, 381, 400, 407
Benning, Elizabeth 85, 381, 400
Benning, William 36
Bernart, John 331
Beverdam 253, 272, 331
Beverdam Bridge 8, 161, 191, 197, 198, 299
Beverdam Creek 8, 86, 197, 223, 299
Beverdam Road 191
Beverly, Peter 2
Bibe, Elizabeth 138, 179, 180, 268
Bibe, Thomas 3, 179
Biby, John 392
Bilboe, John Peter 256, 275, 286, 291, 304, 321, 337
Bingley, John 4
Bingley, Joseph 16, 19, 29, 39, 41, 43, 44, 48, 50, 51, 55, 61, 62, 64, 65, 66, 69, 76, 79, 81, 84, 85, 92, 96, 97, 98, 109, 110, 118, 120, 137, 142, 152, 153, 159, 160, 162, 171, 180, 187, 188, 190, 193, 197, 204, 206, 215, 218, 228, 229, 230, 231, 234, 240, 245, 251, 252, 258, 266, 268, 276, 286, 299, 302, 314, 319, 325, 326, 328, 332, 336, 345, 353, 354, 372, 401, 402
Bingley, Judith 19, 160
Bingley, Mathew 65, 124, 127, 140

Bingley, S (wife) 299
Birch, Edward 167, 227, 243, 266, 285, 302, 313
Bird Creek 8
Bird River 198
Birk, Birks, see Burk
Birks, John 86, 194, 209, 359
Birks, Katherine 86
Birks, William 328
Blackburn, Widow 394
Blankets 78
Boccar 284
Boccar, Peter 44, 193, 194, 213, 226, 242, 266, 276, 301, 307, 313, 329, 335, 347, 355, 361
Boccard, Boccor, see Boccar
Boccard, Stephen 44
Bolling, James 68, 349, 373
Bolling, John 12, 13, 29, 42, 54, 63, 72, 192, 352, 353, 379, 398, 409
Bolling, Major 8
Bolling, Mary 349
Bolling's Mill 44, 74, 131, 197
Bondurant, John Peter v, 149, 163, 171, 215, 248
Bostick, John 39, 47, 76, 198, 288, 369
Boston, Hugh 157, 165, 174, 190, 205, 220, 236, 252, 271, 289
Bottom, William 24, 25, 34, 35, 49, 52, 113, 149
Boulton, Charles 317
Bound out 5, 145, 215, 250, 351, 397, 411
Bowen, Griffith 136, 161, 162, 206, 211, 214, 263
Bowey, see Bowie
Bowie, John 84, 85, 113, 158, 214, 226, 242, 266, 284, 301
Bradford, Ambrose 81
Bradley, Joseph 7, 11, 14, 20,

Bradley, Joseph (con't) 25, 26, 133, 248, 253, 272, 289, 303, 320, 352, 374, 375
Bradshaw, Ann 46
Bradshaw, Benjamin 45, 46, 144, 269, 274, 288, 356, 403, 411
Bread tray 77
Breaking and entering 178
Bridges, see each
  Beverdam, County, Jones Creek, Lickinghole Creek, Muddy Creek, Tuckahoe Creek
Bridle way 351
Brigs, Charles 112
Britt, Daniel 376
Brook, George 330
Brooks, Jacob 17, 19, 20, 21, 29, 103, 114, 123, 139, 153
Brown, John 7, 11
Bruise, Peter 5, 278
Bryan, see Bryant
Bryan, Thomas 12, 19, 23, 34, 40, 51, 62, 78
Bryan, William 61, 257, 278, 294, 382
Bryant, see Bryan
Bryant, James 194
Bryant, William 306, 323, 339, 363, 401
Buck Branch 351
Bugg, William 277, 293, 306
Buirit, Peter 329
Bullington, John 72, 87, 102, 111, 121, 138, 153
Bumpuss, John 334
Bumpuss, Robert 124, 237, 301, 313
Bumpuss, Samuel 124, 140, 151, 186, 200, 221, 237, 265, 283, 301, 313, 334
Burgamy, Elizabeth 310, 350

Burgamy, John 12, 350
Burger, Gofert/Govert 372, 380, 381, 400
Burgess 29
Burgess, Daniel 70, 73, 91
Burgess, John 124, 149, 305, 322, 338, 365, 391
Burk, see Birk, Birks, Burks
Burk, Catherine 14
Burk, Theodorick 149, 182, 199, 218
Burks, John 14, 56, 161, 175, 393
Burks, Richard 247, 268, 287
Burks, Samuel 13, 149, 232, 233, 247, 260, 310, 349
Burnar, David 407
Burnet, see Barnit
Burnet, John 176
Burton, John 273
Burton, Nowell 9, 11, 12, 22, 29, 31, 32, 39, 40, 46, 47, 51, 57, 62, 66, 69, 70, 72, 76, 88, 91, 92, 94, 96, 99, 101, 104, 107, 108, 109, 112, 114, 115, 117, 119, 121, 128, 131, 134, 138, 143, 146, 153, 158, 164, 169, 173, 176, 179, 180, 181, 184, 190, 191, 193, 197, 199, 212, 218, 219, 223, 228, 231, 232, 233, 235, 242, 243, 249, 250, 254, 256, 269, 272, 274, 288, 290, 310, 332, 368, 380, 385, 395, 399, 403
Burton, Robert 29, 31, 38, 41, 47, 49, 50, 60, 76, 88, 96, 104, 107, 109, 110, 118, 119, 120, 134, 136, 147, 211, 249, 254, 256, 310, 332
Butler, Samuel 58, 136
Buttery, Adam 12, 28, 37, 49

Cabbell 328
Cabbell, Elizabeth 114
Cabbell, William 6, 9, 28, 29, 32, 37, 49, 56, 58, 59, 60, 61, 62, 71, 72, 74, 79, 80, 81, 83, 84, 85, 92, 93, 94, 99, 103, 105, 106, 108, 110, 113, 115, 117, 120, 121, 124, 126, 129, 131, 133, 134, 136, 137, 140, 143, 145, 148, 150, 153, 157, 158, 160, 163, 168, 169, 172, 177, 179, 183, 184, 188, 189, 190, 192, 198, 202, 204, 207, 210, 213, 220, 223, 230, 234, 250, 252, 258, 262, 269, 278, 280, 281, 282, 292, 294, 295, 296, 297, 298, 311, 316, 324, 327, 333, 334, 340, 351, 356, 357, 365, 373, 374, 376, 377, 379, 383, 394, 396, 399, 401, 402, 408, 410, 411
Cable, Edward 178
Calvet, see Calvit
Calvit, Anthony 354
Calvit, Peter 44, 55, 66, 88, 231, 308
Calvit, William 145, 215
Canady, Michael 39, 40, 41, 51, 56, 57, 66, 67, 94, 115, 134
Cannon, Charles 38
Cannon, John 158, 164, 173, 189
Cannon, William 29, 68, 70, 73, 89, 91, 92, 107, 116, 123, 132, 137, 140, 154, 156, 163, 174, 182, 194, 205, 206, 208, 210, 212, 219, 222, 223, 224, 228, 232, 233, 237, 242, 257, 273, 276, 277, 280, 293, 306, 373, 396, 401, 403
Capoon, Elizabeth 103
Capoon, Jacob 57, 73, 91, 103, 113, 115, 131, 221, 380, 398

Capper, George 350
Cardwell, Thomas 130
Carnar, Susannah 6, 7, 10, 11, 12, 14, 20, 41, 53, 86, 101, 111, 121, 137, 146, 194, 197, 394, 406
Carol, Elizabeth 70, 91
Carol, Roger 70, 91
Carr, Joel 169, 234, 327, 356, 376, 377, 399, 410
Carrington, George 134
Carter, John 1
Carter, Mary 161
Carter, Robert 77, 78, 101, 102, 156, 161, 172, 173, 190, 193, 197, 200, 201
Carts 299
Cary, Henry 169
Cawthon, Mary 370, 386, 404
Cawthon, Robert 351, 370, 386, 404
Cawthorn, see Cawthon
Chamberlaine, Samuel 40
Chamberlaine, William 25, 35, 43, 55, 64, 74, 82, 100, 111, 112, 145, 167, 214, 216, 217, 243, 286, 308
Chamberlayne, see Chamberlaine
Chambers, John 57
Chambon, Gideon 86, 316, 348
Champaigne, Peter 5, 9, 14, 22, 31, 34
Chandler, Joel 3, 25, 29, 58, 59, 61, 71, 91, 93, 96, 99, 104, 115, 128, 131, 132, 134, 147, 156, 159, 202, 262, 264, 265, 266, 278, 281, 294, 306, 323, 332, 339, 357, 358, 360, 363, 366, 370, 371, 375, 382, 387, 388, 389, 401, 405, 410, 411
Chandler, William 332
Chapel 332
Chapman, John 354

Charon, see Sherrone
Charon, Anthony 311
Chastain, John 31, 39, 72, 163, 171, 260, 286, 295, 297, 306, 307, 323, 325, 331, 332, 341, 342, 364, 380, 382, 388, 389, 402
Chastain, Peter 39, 52, 163, 171, 253, 295, 297, 306, 307, 312, 323, 325, 335, 341, 342, 364, 380, 389, 402
Chastain, Stephen 7, 8, 31, 32, 39, 44, 81, 95, 103, 110, 133, 180, 215, 216, 286, 298, 329, 332, 373
Chemeno, see Chemino
Chemino, John 370, 387, 404, 407
Chest 77
Children neglected 340
Chiles, Henry 179, 180, 262
Chiles, John 248, 270, 287
Chin, Thomas 331
Chisels 20
Chiswell, Charles 24, 34, 47, 48, 60, 74, 95
Cholmley, see Chumley
Cholmley, William 381, 400
Christian, James 145, 161, 231, 296, 300, 324, 372, 388, 389
Christian, John 43, 54, 64, 79, 97, 109, 110, 119, 134, 135, 136, 319, 325, 326
Christian, Rebecca 377, 409
Christian, Robert 231
Christian, Thomas 32, 36, 89, 118, 119, 128, 131, 132, 144, 145, 147, 156, 159, 161, 169, 200, 201, 204, 223, 228, 374, 375, 377, 409
Christian, Thomas Jr 161, 169, 201, 204
Chumley, see Cholmley

Chumley, William 254
Church 308, 333, 348, 351, 358, 359, 393
Church wardens 5, 145, 175, 215, 250, 253, 256, 272, 274, 275, 290, 333, 344, 351, 358, 359, 360, 368, 393, 397, 402, 403, 411
Churchill, Richard 330
Clark, Christopher 68, 71, 89, 107, 116, 132, 181
Clark, John 73, 93, 104, 116
Clarkson, David 58, 136, 229
Clarkson, James 229
Clayton, Arthur 219
Clear road 263, 308, 332, 333, 351
Clerk 280
Clerk, see Clark
Clopton, Joyce 229, 245, 267, 286, 318
Clopton, William 50, 229, 267, 286
Clopton, William Jr 38, 58
Coal pit 8
Cocke, James 9, 127, 331, 396, 397
Cocke, Richard 131, 193
Coleman, John 370
Coleman, Samuel 101, 102, 111, 121, 179, 374, 375, 377
Coley, Walker 301
Collins, Catherine 340
Collins, Mathew 123, 136, 162, 170, 187, 201, 220, 236, 251, 271, 345
Committed to gaol 337
Commodities, see each
    beer, corn, fodder, sugar, tobacco, wine
Cone, John 68, 89, 104, 116, 131, 148, 195, 215, 216, 390
Cone, Mary 215, 216, 234

Conner, Thomas 73
Constable 4, 13, 65, 93, 127, 143, 316, 351, 394, 409
Cooker, Samuel 249
Cookson, Thomas 349
Copy of the laws 283, 333
Corn 13, 58, 77, 132, 148, 163, 319, 376
Coroner 148, 168, 204, 401
County attorney 281
County bridge 351
County levy 261
County line 4, 8, 19, 30, 86, 133, 144, 394
Court day 7
Court house i, 4, 7, 44, 45, 74, 87, 131, 172, 220, 257, 261, 281, 282, 292, 342
Coutain, John 163
Cox 15
Cox, Bartholomew 56, 124, 140, 151, 186, 201, 202, 247, 269, 307, 316, 345, 353, 379, 398, 409
Cox, Francis 346
Cox, Fredorick iv, 7, 11, 14, 20, 25, 26, 79, 80, 107, 108, 110, 124, 128, 131, 132, 140, 145, 154, 155, 163, 181, 192, 200, 201, 206, 208, 210, 212, 215, 218, 233, 235, 265, 316, 332
Cox, George 2, 3, 7, 293, 316, 336
Cox, John 8, 83, 99, 202, 215, 295, 316, 332, 343, 367
Cox, Martha 2, 3, 7
Cox, Mathew 8, 70, 79, 80, 83, 169, 172, 179, 180, 181, 190, 192, 193, 197, 204, 208, 215, 232, 233, 269, 274, 349
Cox, Nicholas 21, 105, 125, 157, 165, 174, 179, 180, 181, 190, 205, 218, 220, 222, 232,

Cox, Nicholas (con't) 233, 236, 240, 241, 252, 258, 271, 288, 289, 350, 381, 388, 389, 410, 411
Cox, Stephen 32, 58, 59, 61, 245, 261, 285, 351
Cragwarr, William 123, 129, 130
Creasy, Creesey, Cressy, see Creesey
Creesey, John 30, 264, 347, 368, 369, 385
Creesey, William 5, 30, 215, 264
Croom 334
Croom, Daniel 3, 7, 13, 125, 141, 154, 186, 195, 200, 220, 236, 251, 271, 288, 303
Crouch, Richard 292, 381, 400
Crump, Stephen 16, 39, 46, 47, 61, 76
Cunningham, James 349
Cunningham, John 305, 399
Curd, Edward 42, 54, 63, 78, 131, 214

Dabbs, Joseph 213, 333, 359, 371, 372, 387, 394, 395
Dale, Christopher 71, 90, 115, 131, 181, 198, 218, 225
Dandrige, John 106, 107
Dandy, William 57
Daniel, James 256, 275, 288, 291, 304, 319, 346, 365, 390, 405
Daniel, James Jr 401, 403
Darracote, John 219
David, Anne 260, 283, 305, 322, 338, 365, 372
David, Peter iv, 47, 57, 114, 143, 163, 260, 261, 283, 305, 322, 338, 346
Davis, George 135, 149, 176, 182, 191, 203, 208, 307, 326,

Davis, George (con't) 330, 343, 358, 360, 364, 370, 387, 389
Davis, John 43, 54, 64, 83
Davis, William 56, 101, 111, 135, 196, 197, 203, 261, 293, 322, 328, 332, 333, 338, 344, 365, 366, 370, 387, 390, 405
Dawson, Elizabeth 253, 272, 290
Dawson, John 144
Dawson, Mary 412
Dawson, Thomas 26, 412
Dean, Richard 57, 67, 69, 70, 72, 91, 93, 96, 99, 103, 104, 112, 115, 116, 118, 119, 120, 121, 123, 124, 129, 130, 131, 140, 142, 152, 154, 169, 172, 179, 180, 181, 182, 187, 192, 199, 200, 201, 203, 204, 217, 218, 233, 235, 240, 253, 255, 265, 274, 290, 304, 325, 342, 364
Deceased persons
  Amos, Valentine
  Arrington, Samuel
  Atkinson, Sarah
  Baize, Edward
  Ballew, Giles
  Bass, Edward
  Bellamy, John
  Bibe, Thomas
  Boccard, Stephen
  Bolling, James
  Canady, Michael
  Carol, Roger
  Carr, Joel
  Chastain, Peter
  Chiles, John
  Clopton, William
  Cone, John
  Cox, George
  Cox, Bartholomew
  Dale, Christopher

Deceased persons
  David, Peter
  Davis, William
  Downie, Robert
  Farrar, John Sutton
  Forcee, Francis
  Green, Paul
  Griffith, John
  Guerrant, Daniel
  Howl, William
  Hughes, Sarah
  Jevodan, Thomas
  Jones, Orlando
  King, Julius
  Lafeat, Tobias
  Laforce, Rene
  Legrand, John
  Meaux, John
  New, Edmund
  Nolun, Thomas
  Oglesby, Richard
  Pennington, Paul
  Pratt, Roger
  Runals, William
  Sallee, Isaac
  Scot, John Jr
  Stephens, John
  Taylor, James
  White, Edward
  Williams, Edward
  Woodson, Benjamin
  Woodson, Jacob
  Woodson, Robert
  Wright, John
Deep Creek 8, 241, 333
Defendant imprisoned 378
Dendy, William 67, 87
Dennet, John 176
Denton, Thomas 99, 225
Dep, see Dept
Dept, Peter 17, 44, 301, 312, 347
Dickason, John 42

Dickins, Thomas 33, 34, 40, 52, 53, 72, 74, 77, 81, 82, 92, 95, 97, 98, 99, 108, 110, 117, 120, 123, 128, 133, 136, 137, 139, 142, 145, 147, 153, 158, 161, 162, 164, 165, 167, 169, 175, 181, 183, 185, 187, 191, 195, 196, 206, 211, 219, 225, 237, 246, 248, 256, 262, 268, 271, 276, 277, 279, 285, 286, 290, 291, 294, 298, 301, 304, 305, 306, 307, 312, 314, 321, 322, 323, 325, 326, 327, 328, 330, 331, 332, 333, 342, 344, 347, 349, 358, 359, 363, 366, 367, 369, 370, 371, 372, 379, 380, 382, 383, 384, 386, 389, 393, 398, 399, 400, 401, 402, 403, 404, 407, 409, 413

Dickinson, Frances 109

Dickinson, John 11, 16, 28, 53, 63, 77, 78, 79, 83, 102, 296, 300, 307, 311, 324, 334, 342, 349, 358, 364, 381, 388

Diet 13, 319

Digges, Dudley 9, 86, 101, 102, 173, 227, 228, 229, 238, 244, 245, 246, 247, 249, 255, 267, 268, 278, 285, 286, 287, 294, 296, 302, 311, 314, 323, 324, 334, 339, 347, 351, 355, 367, 369, 370, 380, 381, 384, 386, 388, 400, 402, 404

Digges, Edward 274

Digges, William 306

Dillon, James Theophilus v, 228, 238, 248

Ditoway/Dittoway, Barbary 81, 94, 110, 171

Dixon, Thomas 307, 326, 343, 364, 401

Dockery, James 216

Dod, John 317

Doran, John 68, 89, 108, 117, 136

Dover Mill 257, 333, 359

Dover Mill Creek 350, 391, 406

Dover Mill Dam 393

Downie, Robert 112, 121, 138, 150, 185, 199, 219, 235, 265, 283, 328, 356, 376, 399, 410

Downing, Robert 72, 304, 305

Drunkenness 333, 359, 392, 393, 403

Duggins, Thomas 354, 390, 405

Dumas, Jeremiah 86

Dumas, Unity 86

Duncan, see Dunkin

Dunkin, Martin 32, 198, 280

Dupee, John James 298

Dupuy, Bartholomew 3

Dupuy, Francis 305, 322

Ear mark 273

Easly, Robert 134

Easly, Sarah 130

Easly, Warham 69, 88, 91, 92, 130, 263

Easly, William 163, 171, 328, 331, 346, 373

East, William 34, 43, 50

Eastham, George 72, 73, 92

Edwards, Thomas 9, 12, 40, 41, 48, 53, 58, 59, 61, 62, 75, 76, 78, 79, 80, 83, 88, 98, 110, 119, 126, 137, 141, 144, 145, 147, 150, 155, 182, 183, 184, 186, 199, 200, 218, 220, 235, 236, 240, 245, 250, 251, 253, 264, 269, 271, 272, 274, 281, 288, 289, 303, 319, 320, 325, 326, 336, 352, 355, 356, 362, 379, 398, 409

Elk ford 198

Elk lick 198

Ellidge, Francis 32

Elliot, James 248, 270, 287, 302, 313, 335, 358
Epes, Francis 161
Epperson, Anne 373
Epperson, Francis 225
Epperson, William 353, 357, 358, 360, 366, 371, 375, 380, 388, 398, 405
Esham, George 391
Evans, Richard 373
Evans, Tabitha 12
Exempt from clearing road 21
Exempt from levy 3, 27, 87, 215, 221, 222, 235, 236, 330, 350, 352

Farcee, see Forcee
Farguson, John 40
Farmar, Agnes 403
Farmar, Judith 403
Farmer, Anne 403
Farrall, Daniel 53
Farrar, Catherine 21
Farrar, John 168, 226, 242, 265, 301, 313, 332, 335, 377, 397, 409
Farrar, John Sutton v, 66, 227, 242, 266, 284, 301, 310, 347, 357, 367, 384, 370, 377, 386, 397, 402, 404, 408
Farrar, Joseph 172, 180, 181, 190, 193, 197, 201, 232, 233
Farrar, Thomas 21
Farrar, William 113, 122, 251, 252, 254, 279, 295, 308, 326
Fauqua, Joseph 33
Fauquinou, Daniel iv, 47, 57, 113, 123, 139, 147, 158, 185
Fauquinou, Mary 183
Fearman, Phillip 308
Felps, see Phelps
Felps, John 143, 156, 159
Fenton, Thomas 176, 191, 205,

Fenton, Thomas (con't) 221, 236
Ferriage 74, 173, 270, 352, 355
Ferry 7, 27, 45, 58, 65, 74, 87, 143, 144, 173, 220, 281, 285, 308, 351
Ferry landing 342
Ferry rates 74
Ferry road 334
Field 15
Field, John 11, 340, 368, 393
Fighting 333
Fine Creek 8, 58, 65, 133, 241, 331, 332
Fleming, John 1, 4, 8, 13, 20, 27, 31, 38, 41, 45, 51, 69, 72, 74, 84, 85, 93, 100, 101, 111, 120, 137, 143, 146, 177, 178, 179, 184, 188, 201, 204, 244, 245, 258, 262, 269, 270, 275, 276, 280, 282, 291, 292, 296, 297, 304, 306, 307, 321, 324, 331, 332, 338, 341, 342, 347, 348, 349, 362, 363, 364, 374, 387, 388, 390, 391, 393, 394, 395, 397, 406, 407, 408
Fleming, Tarlton ii, 1, 2, 4, 7, 8, 13, 20, 21, 27, 29, 30, 31, 38, 45, 46, 58, 61, 65, 73, 74, 76, 82, 83, 84, 85, 86, 93, 100, 101, 103, 134, 143, 144, 145, 148, 155, 160, 167, 168, 171, 177, 179, 183, 188, 192, 202, 204, 211, 213, 217, 234, 238, 247, 268, 269, 277, 279, 280, 281, 282, 286, 296, 297, 300, 301, 311, 312, 321, 322, 324, 325, 326, 333, 334, 335, 338, 339, 342, 343, 347, 357, 359, 362, 364, 367, 368, 380, 383, 384, 385, 388, 389, 394, 395, 396, 401, 402, 403
Flournoy, Elizabeth 253, 272,

Flournoy, Elizabeth (con't) 289, 303, 320, 337, 362, 379, 398, 409
Flournoy, John James v, 253, 272, 289, 303, 320, 337, 362, 379, 398, 409
Fodder 13, 319
Forcee, Anne 298
Forcee, Francis 79, 113, 298, 373
Forcee, Mary 355, 373
Forcee, Stephen 329
Ford, Anne 85
Ford, James 230, 256, 274, 290, 304, 321, 329, 353, 354, 355
Ford, John 8, 58, 66, 85
Ford, Judith 66
Ford, Peter 31, 32, 36, 44, 55, 56, 65, 66, 87, 180, 255, 274, 290
Fox, Joseph 179
Franklin, John 17, 25, 36, 56, 101, 172, 219, 332
Frazer/Frazur, Allin 40, 51, 94, 115, 134
Freedom dues 163
Freedom granted 57
Funeral charges 412

Gallemore, William 41, 53, 63, 68, 78, 89, 97, 104, 107, 116, 129
Gaol (jail) 189, 196, 202, 217, 229, 259
Gates, James 412
Gates, William 102, 241, 296, 306, 323, 341, 363, 382, 401, 412
Gathwrite, Ephraim 137
Gathwrite, Michael 33, 69
Gee, Gilbert 42, 48, 63, 81, 82, 98, 110, 120, 137, 150, 184, 199, 218, 235, 265, 283,

Gee, Gilbert (con't) 301, 312, 313, 330
Gevedon, Gevodan, see Jevodan
Gill, John 25, 35, 49, 61, 64
Gill, Joseph 245
Gloucester County 352
Goddard, William 222
Golsby, Thomas 58, 136
Golsby, Thomas Jr 260
Good, Joseph 80
Goodall, James 407
Gore/Gory, Claude 316, 348
Grand jury 67, 159, 160, 161, 175, 192, 210, 211, 225, 245, 268, 332, 333, 358, 359, 392, 393, 403, 405
Great Licking Hole Creek 198, 316
Green, Frances iii, 45, 46, 143, 144
Green, Paul 25, 27, 35, 44, 48, 55, 56, 60, 75, 95, 109, 118, 147, 182
Gregory, Samuel 214
Griffith, John 184
Griffith, Mary 17, 20, 52
Grundy, Joseph 112, 121
Guardian 59, 114, 125, 181, 234, 299, 373
Guerrant, Daniel 286, 3868, 385, 396
Guerrant, Daniel Jr 3, 12, 19, 32, 39
Guerrant, Frances 286
Guerrant, Peter 286, 330, 368, 381, 385, 396, 403
Guin, see Gunn
Gunn, John 27, 32, 36, 71, 90, 98, 110, 115, 120, 131, 137, 150, 161, 169, 181, 184, 188, 198, 216, 218,
Gutridge, Mark 361

Hall, Richard 276
Halliday, see Holliday
Halliday, William 280, 308
Hambleton, James 248, 270, 287, 303, 318, 352
Hamilton, Francis 38
Hancocke, Samuel 59, 83
Hand saw 20
Handcocke, see Hancocke
Hanover County 86, 96, 99, 100, 101, 127, 166, 188, 201, 210, 212, 219, 246
Happer, William 227, 228, 244, 267, 285, 302, 318
Harbour, Thomas 194
Hardcastle, William ii, 234
Harding, Mary 118
Harding, Thomas 118
Hardwick, Robert 195
Harper, Henry 20, 21, 24, 27, 44, 47, 49, 55, 161, 169, 172, 228, 244, 258, 262, 264, 265, 266, 267, 285, 302, 313, 315, 318, 409, 411
Harris, David 83, 295, 308, 327, 344
Harris, Edward 155
Harris, Elizabeth 155
Harris, John 32, 44, 47, 49, 51, 55, 65, 87, 88, 104, 107, 108, 110, 131, 132, 181, 182, 183, 184, 251, 252, 282, 298, 329, 371, 389, 411
Harris, Lee 409
Harris, Mathew 409
Harris, Peter 27
Harris, Ursula 329
Harrison, Benjamin 149, 173, 182
Haskins, Creed 381, 400
Hatcher, Edward 21, 269, 274, 275
Hatcher, Henry 277, 293, 305,

Hatcher, Henry (con't) 322, 338, 363, 382
Hatcher, Samuel 277, 293, 305, 322, 338, 363, 382
Hathaway, David 128
Haws, Henry 42, 53
Henrico County 4, 193, 211, 263, 270, 313, 330, 341, 345, 346
Henrico Court 325
Henson, Benjamin 157, 164, 174, 189, 210, 212, 221, 242, 243, 246
Hinson, John 73, 92
Hix, Agnes 232
Hix, Daniel 86, 245, 260, 351
Hix, Joan 260
Hix, Marmaduke 26, 29, 30, 70, 91, 103, 232, 241, 296, 306, 324, 341, 350, 360, 361, 378, 411
Hodges, John 13
Hodges, Robert 12, 13, 16
Hodges, Susan 14
Hodges, William 12
Hoggat, Anthony 6, 10, 14, 19, 21, 24, 28, 32, 34, 36, 37, 39, 47, 49, 50, 61, 67, 75, 76, 78, 80, 86, 88, 89, 93, 95, 104, 106, 107, 108, 109, 110, 118, 119, 127, 134, 136, 147, 156, 165, 167, 166, 194, 206, 207, 209, 222, 223, 224, 240, 248, 252, 262, 271, 276, 277, 289, 297, 293, 305, 322, 329, 331, 339, 340, 348, 349, 350, 351, 356, 373, 374, 379, 397, 399, 401, 408, 411, 412
Hoggat, Eleanor 206, 207
Hoggat, Phillip 12, 15, 102, 111
Hoggat Road 351
Hoggatt, see Hoggat
Holland, Judith 179, 180

Holland, Michael 33, 38, 39, 40, 41, 48, 50, 51, 52, 61, 62, 70, 71, 73, 76, 80, 90, 96, 109, 118, 123, 142, 152, 179, 186, 187, 203, 222, 223, 260, 262
Holliday, see Halliday
Holliday, William 143
Holman, James 30, 70, 74, 81, 84, 85, 86, 98, 102, 104, 105, 116, 132, 133, 143, 146, 155, 160, 163, 168, 171, 177, 179, 198, 213, 223, 230, 231, 260, 262, 280, 282, 284, 285, 292, 297, 298, 311, 327, 328, 329, 330, 332, 346, 348, 354, 395, 412
Holman, Sarah 85
Hook, James 18, 23, 33, 46, 52, 124, 140, 172, 219, 256, 275, 291, 304, 321, 337
Hooker, Anne 348
Hooper, Joseph 143, 280, 313, 315, 376
Hopkins, Evan 159, 163, 173, 189, 192, 207, 208, 209, 221, 237, 262, 266, 380
Hopkins, William 305, 322, 338, 362, 382, 400
Horse 13, 21, 74, 92, 99, 144, 173, 234, 319
Horseley, Robert 47
Howard, Allin/Allen 1, 2, 4, 7, 8, 13, 20, 27, 29, 30, 31, 38, 44, 45, 46, 57, 58, 65, 69, 74, 83, 84, 85, 86, 100, 103, 107, 115, 126, 127, 133, 143, 144, 145, 159, 160, 167, 168, 172, 177, 178, 179, 188, 198, 204, 205, 211, 213, 214, 223, 230, 234, 243, 250, 258, 261, 262, 263, 269, 271, 280, 281, 288, 291, 292, 297, 298, 301, 309, 316, 319, 324, 328, 329, 331,

Howard, Allin (con't) 354, 356, 377, 379, 391, 391, 397, 408
Howard, James 14, 86
Howl, Mary 51, 215
Howl, Susannah 215
Howl, William 51, 52, 69, 81, 94, 95, 101, 110, 111, 120, 137, 146, 184, 239
Huckaby, John 69, 90
Hudson, John 6
Hudspeath/Hudspith, Ralph 33, 280
Huetson, John 167, 175, 196, 223, 237
Hughes, Anthony 332
Hughes, Ashford 30, 32, 36, 41, 47, 49, 53, 56, 58, 59, 61, 63, 75, 78, 82, 83, 88, 93, 96, 97, 99, 109, 118, 119, 120, 128, 129, 130, 131, 134, 179, 180, 215, 218, 228, 234, 296, 299, 307, 316, 319, 324, 336, 340, 345, 346, 349, 353, 355, 379, 388
Hughes, Elizabeth 105, 115
Hughes, Isaac 293, 299, 316, 332, 336, 357, 358, 360, 366, 370, 387, 404
Hughes, Martha 293, 316
Hughes, R[obt] 129
Hughes, Robert 3, 20, 21, 24, 32, 36, 42, 51, 53, 58, 59, 61, 68, 70, 88, 89, 91, 93, 104, 116, 129, 130, 131, 148, 181, 207, 215, 217, 235, 251, 252, 266, 288, 308, 319, 325, 326, 341, 343, 353, 367, 368, 380, 391, 407, 411
Hughes, Sarah 215, 235, 341
Hughes, Stephen iii, iv, 5, 11, 16, 39, 42, 45, 47, 53, 61, 63, 71, 72, 73, 76, 77, 79, 82, 83, 85, 87, 92, 93, 99, 100, 101,

Hughes, Stephen (con't) 104, 105, 116, 124, 125, 126, 132, 136, 140, 141, 150, 154, 161, 166, 167, 169, 174, 176, 178, 189, 190, 196, 205, 207, 208, 215, 217, 220, 229, 232, 234, 235, 246, 250, 258, 259, 262, 263, 264, 268, 278, 279, 281, 285, 286, 288, 295, 299, 300, 302, 306, 310, 312, 314, 316, 323, 336, 339, 349, 351, 352, 363, 373, 374, 397, 407, 410, 413
Hulmes, Charles 142
Hulsey, Charles 161
Hulsey, Susannah 161
Huson, John iv, 103, 112, 121, 124, 135, 140, 155, 163, 180, 182, 280, 281

Illegitimate child 32
Incest 333
Innis, John ii, 126, 162, 170, 188, 189, 206, 207, 232, 251, 252
Inquest 144

Jackson, John 16, 23, 33, 227, 243, 266, 285, 302, 313
Jackson, Joseph 114, 141, 152, 186, 203, 222, 232, 233, 237, 258, 263, 266, 267, 268
Jail, see Gaol
James, Francis 51, 145, 147, 248, 270, 282, 287, 298, 302, 315, 332, 336, 353, 361, 368, 375, 395, 401, 403
James, Mary 395
James River 8, 27, 45, 86, 173, 178, 223, 331
Jefferson, Peter 169, 204, 258, 262, 264, 401, 403

Jeffs, John 68, 70, 79, 81, 90, 94, 103, 104, 115, 123, 128, 148, 182, 194, 199, 218, 219
Jenitoe Creek 351
Jennings, William 371
Jevodan, Judith 331, 394, 406
Jevodan, Thomas 39, 72, 75, 76, 78, 79, 80, 223, 226, 242, 266, 284, 301, 331, 394, 406
John, Joseph 332
Johnson, Charles 36, 42, 56, 56, 70, 90, 113, 122, 139, 151, 185, 200, 212, 219, 224, 235, 247, 251, 265, 271, 284, 288, 300, 301, 303, 318, 320, 333, 340, 341, 345, 357, 358, 360, 364, 366, 379, 381, 398, 409
Johnson, Daniel 124, 140, 154, 332, 343, 368
Johnson, Elizabeth 212, 224, 265, 284, 318, 333, 340, 341, 364
Johnson, Widow 27
Johnson, William 176, 191, 205, 221, 236
Jones Creek 298, 299, 331
Jones, Esther/Hester 65, 66, 86, 157, 164, 174
Jones, Orlando 272, 289, 303, 320, 337, 379, 398, 409
Jones, Rees 113
Jones, Rice 122, 181
Joplin, Thomas 106, 136, 406
Jordan, Elizabeth 59, 181
Jouany, Esther 31
Jury confined 173

Karnar, see Carner
Kelly, Giles 350
Kelly, John 235
Kennon, William 21
Kenny, William 112, 121
Kent, William 17, 32, 56, 143,

Kent, William (con't) 157, 163, 277, 329, 330, 403
Kerby, John 40
Kilpatrick, Alexander 130
King, Julius 68, 90, 108, 117, 136
King, Martin 41, 43, 53, 54, 63, 64, 80, 82, 107, 108, 109, 198, 258, 281, 300, 308, 327
King William Parish 4, 5, 86, 223, 331, 333, 344, 348, 359, 366, 368, 393, 402, 403
Knife 78
Knight, William 27, 214

Lad, Amos 47, 49, 114, 123, 138, 140, 154, 155, 161, 169, 177, 192, 194, 205, 216, 224, 237, 245, 250, 251, 252, 255, 257, 258, 262, 264, 265, 266, 267, 269, 275, 276, 279, 288, 291, 304, 321, 337
Lad, Constantine 101
Lad, John 305, 313, 322, 335, 340, 345, 346, 348, 353, 358, 368, 381, 384, 388, 389, 392
Ladd, see Lad
Lafait, Tobias 31, 66, 157, 164, 174
Lafeat, Lafeit, see Lafait
Laforce, Rene 1, 21, 84
Laine, John 20, 21, 24, 27, 43, 44, 54, 56, 64, 75, 76, 78, 79, 80, 83, 93, 96, 97, 99, 110, 119, 134, 135, 136, 143, 156, 159, 172, 182, 183, 184, 198, 200, 201, 204, 206, 208, 210, 212, 228, 242, 262, 264, 265, 266, 267, 319, 325, 326, 331, 353, 357, 358, 360, 366, 381, 388, 389, 392
Laine, William 144
Lankford, John 149

Lankford, West 149, 169, 195
Lansdon, Esther/Hester 85, 147, 381, 400
Lansdon, William 32, 43, 44, 50, 58, 59, 61, 65, 74, 75, 76, 78, 79, 80, 83, 85, 88, 93, 96, 99, 112, 114, 118, 119, 123, 127, 128, 131, 132, 139, 142, 145, 147, 152, 153, 156, 172, 179, 180, 181, 187, 190, 193, 195, 196, 197, 200, 201, 206, 208, 210, 212, 218, 222, 223, 228, 229, 230, 233, 237, 245, 262, 264, 265, 266, 268, 278, 286, 288, 294, 302, 313, 314, 315, 319, 325, 326, 333, 336, 340, 345, 346, 348, 353, 381, 394, 395, 400, 401, 403, 407
Lashes to the back 126, 178, 234, 410
Lavillain, Levillain, see L'Villain
Lawhan, Thomas 351
Lawson, David 144
Lawson, John 12, 28, 37, 49
Lawson, Jonas 227, 244, 267, 310
Lax, William 41, 53, 56, 61, 63, 78, 81, 97, 99, 109, 110, 120, 125, 141, 172
Leather 21, 126
Lee, James 411
Legrand, see L'Grand
Leister, see Lester
Leister, Henry 224, 237, 257
Leister, Jeremiah 224, 237, 257
Lesseur, David 29, 52, 68, 89, 107, 117, 143, 146, 169, 172, 261, 298, 348
Lester, see Leister
Lester, Henry 195, 209, 237, 238
Lester, Jeremiah 195, 209, 237
Letalone Creek 21, 88, 159

Levins, Richard 113, 122, 227, 242, 266, 279, 284, 295, 301, 310, 347, 357, 367, 370, 377, 384, 386, 397, 402, 404, 408
Lewis, John 125, 189, 202, 351
Lewis, Joseph 147, 156, 159, 397
Lewis, Mary 127
Lewis, William 28, 37, 127, 128, 211
L'Grand, Jane Magdalene v, 351
L'Grand, John 30, 260, 261, 332, 351, 394, 406, 407
L'Grand, Judith 351
L'Grand, Katherine 332
L'Grand, Peter 351
License 93, 391, 392
Licking Hole Creek 139
Licking Hole Creek Bridge 378
Lightfoot, Phillip 292, 376
Ligon, Mathew 113, 122, 161, 308, 326
Linen 178
Liquor rates 13, 319, 359, 391, 392
List of titheables 4
Little Licking Hole Creek 191
Littlepage, Frances 39, 46
Lively, Mark 247, 410
Lock 281, 292, 293
Locket, Thomas 113, 122, 181, 248, 249, 258, 269, 270, 273, 287, 302, 315, 336, 361, 375
Locket, Thomas Jr 270
Lodging 13, 319
Logan, Alexander 41, 48, 62, 80, 193, 209, 233, 253, 409, 412
Long acre 413
Long branch 331
Lowe, Amey 26, 68, 90, 108, 117, 133, 149, 192, 209, 221, 236, 257, 275, 291, 304, 321,

Lowe, Amey (con't) 337, 362, 379, 398, 409
Lowe, Thomas 68, 90, 108, 117, 133, 142, 149, 155, 183, 192, 201, 209, 221, 222, 236, 257, 275, 291, 304, 321, 337, 362, 379, 398, 409
Luckadoe, John 348
L'Villain, John 9, 31, 39, 162, 170, 187, 201, 222, 237, 257, 331, 333, 359, 393
Lyles, David 9, 87, 115, 257

Macbrid, Macbride, see Mcbrid
MacDaniel, Henry 41, 56
Macon, John 16, 23, 33, 46, 59, 74, 82, 94, 99, 100, 105, 108, 110, 116, 117, 120, 132, 134, 136, 137, 149, 150, 161, 162, 169, 183, 196, 199, 218, 235, 250, 271, 288, 303, 306, 319, 336, 361, 378, 379
Macon, William 279, 295, 323, 339, 363
Maddox, John 374, 375, 401, 403
Main Road 65, 173, 263, 334, 351
Mallet, Stephen 30, 160, 230, 279, 295, 306, 323, 339, 358, 361
Man, John 26
Manacantown 348
Manaconton road 316
Manakin Creek 133
Manakin Town 21, 58, 88, 159
Manakin Town ferry 45
Marchbanks, George 18, 25, 35, 43, 55, 64, 68, 82, 90, 100, 104, 107, 108, 109, 111, 117, 125, 132, 136, 141, 147, 154, 167, 186, 200, 220, 229, 236, 245, 251, 267, 271, 286, 288,

Marchbanks, George (con't) 303, 320, 326, 344, 366, 383, 402
Marshall, Alexander 27, 59, 83
Martain, John 293, 304, 321, 330, 331, 338
Martin, Francis 71, 80, 98, 110, 120, 137, 150, 159, 163, 173, 179, 184, 188, 189, 190, 193, 197, 208, 222, 223, 228, 252, 269, 272, 274, 289, 296, 297, 300, 303, 307, 311, 312, 320, 324, 325, 334, 335, 337, 342, 348, 357, 362, 364, 374, 379, 380, 381, 388, 389, 397, 398, 402, 408, 409, 410
Martin, James 61
Martin, John 7, 28, 37, 49, 61, 68, 75, 90, 98, 103, 110, 115, 120, 123, 126, 128, 140, 148, 151, 182, 185, 186, 199, 218, 275, 277, 291, 307, 362, 378, 388
Martin, John Jr 80, 81, 137, 142, 149, 153, 192, 212, 213, 296, 324, 388
Martin, Joseph 378
Martin, Thomas 178
Matlock, William 73, 92
Mattox, John 403
Maxey, Edward 51, 149
Maxey, John 11, 87, 124, 140, 340, 345, 346
Maxey, Nathaniel 28, 38, 40, 50, 52, 59, 62, 65, 80
Maxey, William 340, 345, 346
May, Anne 214
May, William 6, 10, 11, 14, 15, 19, 23, 72, 92, 107, 113, 117, 131, 141, 152, 156, 160, 161, 165, 186, 195, 203, 209, 213, 214, 222, 224, 237, 240, 248, 264, 267, 268, 270, 277, 287,

May, William (con't) 302, 307, 308, 314, 325, 342, 365, 380, 391, 398, 410
Mayo, George 135
Mayo, Joseph 134, 159
Mayo, Sarah 135
Mayo, William 1, 2, 4, 7, 8, 13, 30, 46, 57, 58, 65, 70, 74, 84, 85, 86, 90, 94, 96, 103, 115, 119, 126, 127, 143, 144, 145, 155, 160, 166, 168, 172, 173, 177, 178, 180, 188, 198, 204, 213, 214, 215, 223, 230, 245, 250, 253, 256, 258, 262, 269, 272, 275, 276, 277, 280, 281, 290, 292, 293, 296, 297, 298, 306, 318, 324, 328, 329, 340, 341, 348, 349, 353, 354, 356, 360, 361, 373, 374, 390, 394, 399, 401, 403, 405, 410, 412
Mcbrid, John 4, 8, 19, 20, 21, 24, 29, 31, 32, 47, 49, 83, 93, 96, 99, 118, 119, 134, 136, 143, 144, 147, 156, 159, 161, 162, 169, 170, 172, 179, 180, 181, 188, 189, 190, 193, 196, 197, 200, 201, 206, 207, 208, 211, 216, 219, 222, 223, 228, 232, 233, 251, 252, 269, 274, 296, 300, 306, 308, 312, 324, 337, 339, 341, 342, 348, 363, 374, 375, 381, 382, 388, 389, 392
Mcbride, see Mcbrid
McCartney, Patrick 315
McCulloch, John 103, 114, 123, 139, 153
McDaniel, Henry 19, 20, 21
McDermore, Michael 273
McKenny, Daniel 149, 182
McLoughland, James 201
Meaux, John 34
Medlock, William 308, 327

Meriwether, David 34
Meriwether, William 25, 67, 300, 312, 335, 357
Merriman, John 218, 219, 222, 223, 228, 231, 401, 402, 403
Michaux, see Micheaux
Micheaux, Abraham 30, 144, 340, 345, 346
Micheaux, Elizabeth 3
Micheaux, Jacob 3, 7, 9, 27, 29, 65, 83, 93, 96, 99, 101, 111, 139, 156, 157, 163, 165, 172, 174, 175, 179, 180, 181, 182, 183, 184, 189, 190, 193, 197, 204, 205, 215, 269, 274, 333, 334, 353, 359, 391
Micheaux, John 3, 7, 25, 32, 36, 42, 70, 90
Micheaux, Judith 7
Micheaux, Paul 334
Micheaux, Sarah 3
Michell, Archelaus 199
Michell, Thomas 199
Middle Road 299
Mill 8, 44, 45, 58, 74, 86, 131, 136, 197, 257, 308, 333, 350, 351, 359, 390, 391, 393, 406
Mills, William 308
Mims, David 18, 347, 366, 367, 384, 392, 401, 402, 403
Mims, Lionel 27, 36, 253
Mingo, Benjamin 308, 326
Misbehavior in court 337
Monford, Stephen 3
Mooney, John 333, 360, 407, 328
Moor, Edward 11, 15, 22, 32, 46, 59, 179
Moor, Job 106, 107
Moor, John 113, 131, 318
Moor, Thomas 3, 6, 9, 18, 71, 77, 82
Moor, William 44, 47, 49, 55,

Moor, William (con't) 66, 88, 106, 116, 131, 242, 366
Moore, see Moor
Moreman 13
Moreman, Andrew 124, 130, 132, 140, 151, 161, 186, 198, 200, 204, 211, 237, 265, 283, 301, 305, 313, 334
Moreman, Susannah 14, 130
Morgan, Anthony 31, 182, 334
Morgan, Edward 52, 69
Morris, Hugh 43, 54, 64, 79, 88, 89, 100, 138, 141, 155, 186, 200, 206, 210, 212, 213, 220, 225, 251, 252, 392
Morris, John 6, 10, 14, 162, 170, 187, 201, 208, 213, 220, 224, 236, 240, 246, 252, 271
Morris, Mary 88, 141, 155, 186, 200, 220
Morris, Sarah 43, 64, 79, 88, 89, 100, 138
Morris, William 112, 121
Moseby, Richard 66, 112, 122, 138, 150, 185, 200, 206, 208, 209, 210, 212, 218, 219, 221, 245, 268, 286, 302, 310, 314, 319, 325, 326, 336, 361, 377, 378
Moseley, Arthur 59, 83
Moseley, William 155, 310, 371, 389
Moss, Elizabeth 232
Moss, James 58, 107, 136
Moss, Thomas 67, 88, 116, 132, 148, 183, 184
Moss, William 183, 232
Muddy Creek 8, 241, 410
Mulatto, Dole 397
Mulatto, Hannah 250
Mulatto, Tom 397
Mullen, see Mullin
Mullin, Mary 67

Mullin, Patrick 194, 211, 246, 268, 286, 302, 314, 371
Murder of child 45
Murrell, Elizabeth 45, 397
Murrell, Thomas 27, 45, 58, 59, 61, 75, 76, 78, 80, 86, 113, 128, 144, 156, 169, 175, 206, 208, 210, 211, 212, 216, 225, 231, 232, 233, 237, 333, 359, 393, 397
Musket 58, 132, 163

Napier, Bouth 18, 19, 23, 24, 25, 28, 33, 34, 35, 37, 39, 46, 47, 48, 49, 58, 59, 60, 74, 75, 94, 95, 106, 107, 109, 117, 118, 130, 134, 136, 142, 147, 152, 162, 170, 172, 182, 187, 188, 190, 193, 197, 199, 203, 204, 206, 207, 208, 210, 212, 218, 222, 223, 227, 244, 253, 254, 255, 267, 272, 274, 285, 290, 302, 303, 304, 307, 314, 320, 321, 326, 337, 340, 343, 345, 346, 353, 364, 383, 401, 411
Napier, Bouth Jr 247
Napier, Mary 193
Napier, Robert 16, 28, 39, 199, 277, 328
Napier, Robert Jr 69, 73, 93, 104, 116, 124, 131, 140, 151, 181, 186, 189, 201, 202, 217, 233, 269, 340, 370, 371, 381, 386, 387, 388, 389, 403, 404, 405
Napier, Sarah 130
Nash, Samuel 73, 92
Neglect of children 340
Negro, see mulatto
Negro 27, 359
Negro, Betty 133
Negro, Cain 86
Negro, Charles 9
Negro, Cuffey iii, 177, 178, 280, 281
Negro, Fanny 86
Negro, Guy 231
Negro, Hannah 9, 133
Negro, Jack 7, 145
Negro, Jenny 7
Negro, Jupiter 133
Negro, Kate iii, 145, 177
Negro, Nero 9
Negro, Robin 9
Negro, Rochester 262
Negro, Roger 126
Negro, Strong Jack 352
Negro, Sue 276
Negro, Toby 9, 349
Negro, Tom 231
Nevil, Nevill, Nevills, see Neville
Neville, James 29, 173, 240, 310, 313, 315, 332, 349, 376
New, Edmund 8, 43, 54, 64, 79, 88, 89, 138, 141, 155, 186, 200
New Kent County 169, 183, 243, 286, 317, 378
New, Mary 8, 11, 19
New, William 8, 11, 19, 43, 44, 54, 55, 63, 66, 79, 88, 89, 100, 141, 142, 153, 155, 176, 186, 187, 191, 200, 205, 206, 213, 220, 221, 225, 234, 265, 283, 288
Nolun, see Nowlin
Nolun, Agnes 181, 213, 222, 225, 240, 241, 248, 249, 270, 287, 302, 303, 318, 352, 353
Nolun, James 296, 324, 388
Nolun, Thomas 16, 28, 29, 37, 38, 49, 50, 60, 61, 72, 75, 76, 92, 95, 99, 108, 109, 112, 117, 118, 121, 134, 136, 138,

Nolun, Thomas (con't) 150, 153, 181, 183, 185, 213, 222, 225, 240, 248, 270, 287, 302, 303, 318, 352
Nowlin, see Nolun
Nowlin, James 8, 20, 21, 24, 32, 57, 161, 169, 184, 189, 216, 299
Nunnary, Judith 256, 275

Oats 319
Ogee, see Agee
Ogee, Anne 127
Ogee, Mathew 127
Oglesby, Richard 9, 93, 96, 99, 104, 107, 108, 110, 136, 206, 208, 210, 212, 232, 233, 242, 251, 252, 331
Oglesby, Susannah 331
Ordinary 13, 93, 126, 262, 288
Orphans 5, 145, 215, 250, 351, 397, 411
Orphans court 372
Owen, John 396
Owen, Sarah 396
Owen, William 198, 351

Pail 77
Paine, see Payne
Paine, George 8, 9, 20, 21, 24, 31, 41, 74, 75, 76, 84, 85, 93, 94, 103, 105, 115, 119, 125, 126, 131, 134, 136, 143, 144, 145, 155, 166, 177, 179, 191, 198, 204, 205, 211, 212, 311, 316, 373
Paine, George Jr 99, 188, 407
Paine, John 12, 18, 69, 87, 90, 93, 96, 99, 180, 298, 340, 345, 346, 374, 385, 401, 403, 411
Paine, Josiah 29
Paine, Josias 143

Pamunkey River 312
Parentan, Isaac 160, 204, 218
Parents, Isaac 76
Parish, John 105, 106, 188
Parish, John Jr 248, 270, 287, 302, 315
Parker 280
Parker, Michael 310
Parker, Richard 21, 88, 159, 256, 310, 333, 360, 392, 406
Parks, William 283
Parsons, Joseph 13, 16, 69, 91, 92, 292, 395, 403
Parsons, Sarah 395
Paslay/Pasley, William 248, 271, 288
Pate, Benjamin 101
Pate, Thomas 280, 369, 386, 404
Patrick's Ford 8
Pattison, David 41, 53, 54, 63, 64, 73, 75, 76, 78, 79, 80, 83, 88, 104, 105, 107, 128, 131, 132, 144, 172, 199, 319, 325, 326, 411
Pattison, David Jr 43, 82, 108, 109, 189, 196, 197, 199, 202, 203, 212
Pattison, Thomas 189, 199, 202
Pavement, Thomas 17, 29, 102, 111, 121, 179
Payne, see Paine
Payne, George 32, 106, 129, 148, 160, 167, 176, 213, 218, 223, 234, 250, 258, 269, 271, 280, 282, 291, 297, 309, 324, 331, 348, 351, 373, 374, 376, 379, 394, 396, 397, 408
Payne, George Jr 234, 385, 369
Payne, John 223, 228, 229, 368
Payne, Josiah 255, 274
Payne, Robert 374, 396, 408
Pennington, Paul 124, 141, 154,

Pennington, Paul (con't)   193, 245, 270, 275, 276, 291, 304, 321, 338, 362, 388
Perault, see Perro
Perault, Daniel   329
Perault, Mary   329
Perkins, Abraham   131
Perkins, Constant   32, 86, 161, 200, 201, 216, 242, 348, 357, 358, 368, 384
Perkins, Constantine   27
Perkins, Richard   144
Perrin, George   123, 136
Perro, see Perault
Perro, Daniel   160
Perry, Hannah   341
Perry, Mary   340
Phelps, John   67, 157, 163, 170, 175, 182, 183, 187, 206, 232, 242, 251, 277, 280
Phenix, Abraham   127, 166
Pigg, John Jr   156, 164, 174, 190, 205, 220, 236, 252, 272, 289, 303, 325
Pillory   44, 144
Pleasants, John   48, 51, 69, 81, 94, 95, 101, 110, 111, 120, 137, 146, 184, 239
Pleasants, Thomas   372, 389
Poe, Elizabeth   ii, 410
Poe, Robert   410
Poisoning   177
Poveall, John   179
Powell, Richard   42, 47, 71, 77, 91, 109, 115, 262, 277
Powell, Robert   37, 391
Powell, Roger   26, 28, 60, 114, 129, 138, 155, 177, 257, 275, 276, 291, 304, 321, 337, 411
Pratt, Mary   180, 215, 238, 239
Pratt, May   229, 278
Pratt, Roger   43, 44, 55, 56, 65, 66, 87, 160, 180, 215, 229,

Pratt, Roger (con't)   238, 239, 278
Prewit, see Pruit
Price, John   313, 315
Pride, John   10, 211, 225, 246, 268, 284
Prier, Edward   165
Prier, John   32, 36, 79, 80, 83, 128, 131, 132, 156, 159, 161, 169, 172, 179, 180, 181, 190, 193, 197, 198, 200, 201, 206, 208, 210, 212, 218, 222, 223, 228, 233, 237, 245, 262, 264, 265, 266, 267, 274, 288, 319, 325, 326, 327, 331, 340, 345, 346, 347, 353, 357, 358, 360, 367, 371, 374, 375, 384, 392, 401, 402, 403, 411
Prier, Rebecca   158, 165
Prier, Samuel   158
Prince George County   257, 273
Prior, see Prier
Prison   i, 4, 7, 135, 217, 229, 230, 281, 292, 293, 396, 413
Pritchet, James   144, 157, 158, 162, 163, 173, 174, 196, 210, 24, 265
Pritchett, John   102
Profane language   333
Profaning the Lord's prayer   393
Profaning the Sabbath   358
Prophet, Silvester   199
Prosser, Elizabeth   57, 67, 87
Prosser, Thomas   iii, 5, 13, 35, 43, 57, 59, 61, 66, 74, 84, 86, 87, 94, 95, 96, 97, 98, 135, 136, 145, 146, 157, 159, 161, 162, 165, 169, 179, 183, 184, 189, 196, 197, 210, 237, 254, 257, 258, 259, 263, 272, 279, 281, 283, 290, 293, 300, 304, 307, 312, 320, 324, 325, 327, 335, 340, 342, 344, 365, 367,

Prosser, Thomas (con't) 369, 384, 391, 393, 404, 410, 413
Pruit, Andrew 6, 42, 58, 79, 98, 113, 122, 136, 139, 151, 185, 200, 212, 219, 224, 235, 251, 271, 284, 288, 301, 303, 318, 320, 340, 341, 345, 364
Pruit, Hugh 65, 194, 226, 242, 266, 284, 301, 313, 335
Pruit, Richard 341, 345
Pruit, Thomas 5, 9, 11, 14, 22, 28, 31, 34, 38, 40, 43, 50, 52, 55, 56, 59, 62, 65, 79, 80, 97, 256, 274, 275, 279, 290, 291, 295, 304, 306, 321, 323, 328, 337, 339, 345, 353, 354, 355, 358, 360, 361, 362, 382, 400
Pryer, see Prier
Public claims 178
Pumfree, Margaret 168
Pumfree, Sylvanus 168
Pumfree, Sylvanus Jr 168
Pumphrey, Nathan 381
Purkins, see Perkins

Quaker 31, 51, 77, 111, 178, 349, 350
Quantain, see Quantin
Quantin, John 213, 225, 261, 293, 300, 305, 312, 322, 328, 333, 335, 344, 359, 365, 366, 372, 392, 407
Quin, John 6, 7, 8, 10, 11, 12, 14, 15, 16, 18, 20, 22, 23, 25, 27, 29, 32, 33, 38, 40, 43, 46, 50, 51, 54, 55, 56, 61, 62, 64, 70, 71, 72, 76, 78, 80, 82, 83, 90, 91, 92, 94, 98, 100, 102, 107, 108, 112, 117, 121, 124, 133, 136, 138, 140, 145, 146, 150, 151, 153, 154, 155, 157, 160, 164, 165, 168, 173, 174, 181, 183, 185, 186, 191, 195,

Quin, John (con't) 197, 200, 213, 216, 217, 220, 224, 227, 235, 240, 244, 251, 271, 307, 308, 326, 327, 343, 344, 364, 365, 366, 367, 368, 383, 384, 385, 389, 401, 402, 404
Quin, Susannah 16

Radford, John 87, 340, 360, 369
Raine, see Rayne
Raine, George 297, 300, 311, 315, 324, 334, 335, 340, 350, 351, 357, 358, 369, 371, 377, 381, 382, 385, 387, 394, 395, 397, 404, 405, 408, 410
Raley 280
Raley, Charles 29, 43, 54, 64, 82, 100, 101, 102, 111, 280
Raley, James 73
Randolph, Isham 133, 263, 289, 297, 378
Randolph, John 296, 306, 307, 324, 341, 342, 347, 348, 363, 374, 388, 397, 408
Randolph, Richard 9, 18, 21, 29, 159, 296, 306, 307, 324, 341, 342, 347, 348, 374, 388, 397, 408
Randolph, Thomas 1, 2, 4, 13, 15, 18, 20, 27, 29, 30, 31, 34, 38, 39, 41, 45, 46, 48, 52, 56, 57, 59, 66, 67, 69, 71, 72, 74, 77, 80, 82, 84, 85, 86, 93, 98, 100, 102, 103, 106, 107, 108, 111, 117, 119, 121, 125, 126, 128, 130, 133, 135, 138, 141, 149, 153, 166, 245, 269, 296, 306, 307, 324, 332, 333, 341, 342, 347, 348, 349, 350, 351, 359, 363, 364, 374, 388, 390, 391, 393, 397, 406, 408
Randolph, William 296, 306, 307, 324, 341, 342, 347, 348,

Randolph, William (con't) 349,
    363, 374, 388, 397, 408
Rapene, Anthony 6, 10, 11, 12,
    31, 39, 44, 51, 61, 76, 81, 96,
    98, 109, 110, 118, 120, 137,
    153, 159, 160, 162, 170, 177,
    180, 188, 190, 192, 193, 204,
    212, 213, 218, 229, 234, 238,
    245, 252, 258, 267, 298, 326,
    344, 366, 368, 371, 383, 388,
    395, 402, 403
Rapene, Margaret 395
Rapine, see Rapene
Rayne, see Raine
Rayne, George 289, 379
Raynold, Henry 143
Read, Clement 112, 121, 138,
    150, 185, 199, 219, 235, 265,
    283
Record book 143
Redford, John 195, 345, 346
Reed, Thomas 128
Release from gaol 263
Revis, Edward 226
Reynolds, see Raynold, Runals
Reynolds, Henry 69, 144, 198
Richard, see Richards
Richards, John 7, 10, 19, 23, 40,
    52, 277, 307, 325, 342
Richardson, John 308, 333, 359,
    381, 388, 389, 392
Ridgell, Richard 340, 368, 393
Right, see Wright
Right, John 17, 198
Ripley, John 371, 387, 405
River Road 8, 13, 136, 173,
    241, 308
Roads, Nicholas 354, 390, 405
Roberts, John 229
Roberts, Maurice 230
Robertson, James 326, 355,
    357, 358, 360, 366, 388, 389
Robertson, John 25

Robinson, Isaac 133
Robinson, James 299, 332, 349,
    382
Robinson, John 96, 127, 225,
    374, 375
Robinson, Susannah 349
Robinson, Wife 299
Rocket, Baldwin 6, 10, 67, 69,
    71, 91, 194, 209, 225, 233,
    254, 272, 276, 279, 290, 291,
    304, 321
Rogers, Robert 16, 18, 56
Rug 78
Rule for court time 103
Rule of court 410
Rum 13, 319
Rum punch 13
Runals, see Reynolds
Runals, Mary 234
Runals, William 234
Runals, William [jr] 234
Russell, John 273

Saddle 21
Sadler, William 235
Sallee, Abraham 39, 72
Sallee, Elizabeth 350
Sallee, Isaac 30, 72, 226, 242,
    261, 266, 284, 298, 301, 396
Sallee, Peter 350
Sallee, William 30, 32, 36, 39,
    43, 54, 64, 70, 75, 76, 78, 79,
    80, 83, 91, 298, 332, 350,
    396, 406
Salmon, Thomas 12, 15, 23, 33,
    126, 141, 154, 155, 186, 200,
    220, 236, 251, 271, 288, 303,
    325
Sampson, Stephen 27, 329
Sanders, see Saunders
Saunders, John 3, 8, 17, 24, 25,
    26, 36, 45, 57, 67, 88, 115,
    128, 212, 216, 217, 229, 243,

Saunders, John (con't) 244, 253, 267, 272, 289, 303, 308, 320, 327, 340, 343, 345, 346, 352, 353, 357, 358, 360, 365, 366, 374, 375, 380, 381, 398, 400, 410
Saunders, John Jr 26
Saunders, Joseph 248
Saunders, Robert 145, 296, 306, 323, 341, 363, 383, 401
Saunders, Thomas 34, 39, 40, 51, 53, 62, 67, 69, 76, 78, 96, 97, 109, 115, 118, 131, 157, 164, 174, 181, 189, 198, 201, 206, 208, 210, 221, 242, 243, 246, 248, 255, 271, 288
Saunders, William 20, 21, 24, 125, 176, 191, 208, 221, 236, 252, 272, 289, 303, 315, 317, 318, 336
Scot, Anne 105
Scot, Edward ii, 1, 9, 19, 21, 23, 25, 27, 28, 34, 35, 37, 44, 48, 49, 52, 55, 56, 60, 66, 75, 79, 84, 85, 95, 97, 105, 109, 118, 123, 126, 133, 142, 147, 155, 157, 162, 164, 174, 177, 182, 194, 196, 209, 210, 214, 224, 226, 227, 230, 231, 233, 241, 243, 244, 247, 249, 253, 254, 255, 256, 258, 261, 263, 265, 267, 273, 274, 275, 277, 279, 286, 291, 292, 293, 297, 298, 299, 300, 304, 307, 316, 319, 321, 326, 328, 331, 332, 333, 337, 340, 345, 346, 347, 362, 365, 367, 370, 371, 373, 382, 384, 386, 388, 389, 390, 392, 393, 396, 400, 402, 404, 405, 406
Scot, Elizabeth 347
Scot, James 354
Scot, John Jr 105, 240

Scot, Joseph 52, 256, 261, 332
Scot, Samuel 240, 346, 347
Scott, see Scot
Scott, Walter 18
Scoyles, William 163, 171
Scrugs, see Scruggs
Scruggs, John 26, 30, 72, 102, 128, 176, 191, 208, 333, 359, 360, 375, 392
Secretary of the colony 1
Selling strong drink 333
Serjeant, Mary 188
Servant 315, 354
Servant absent 315
Servant freed 57
Sharrone, see Charon
Sharrone, Anthony 114
Shelton, John 67, 87
Sheriff 2, 29, 83, 90, 119, 122, 131, 134, 143, 146, 163, 165, 175, 176, 191, 192, 194, 195, 197, 208, 209, 211, 280, 281, 301, 309, 311, 312, 321, 322, 324, 325, 326, 334, 335, 338, 342, 343, 357, 362, 364, 367, 368, 382, 383, 389
Sheriff's protest 396
Shooting a horse 234
Simon, Benjamin 17
Sims, George 246
Sims, Mathew 162, 187, 206
Sims, Richard 338
Skeeman, see Skeyman
Skelton, James i, 261, 279, 281, 297, 356, 402
Skelton, John 57
Skeyman, George 32, 149, 182, 199, 218
Slate, John 330
Smith, George 222, 277
Smith, James 114, 193
Smith, John 5, 18, 215
Snugs, William 5

Solomon's Creek 8, 65, 332, 333
Sorrell, John 5, 9, 14, 22, 32, 36, 113, 122, 125, 126, 136, 139, 151, 168, 185, 200, 201, 333
Souille/Souillie, Nicholas 44, 180, 258, 395
Southerland, George 194, 227, 232, 233, 237, 240, 243, 245, 258, 262, 264, 265, 266, 267, 285, 288, 300, 302, 311, 313, 315, 325, 326, 353, 380
Spears, James 20, 21, 24, 47, 49, 270, 394, 413
Spears, John 350
Spears, Robert 25, 35, 49, 61, 64, 269
Spears, William 350
Spencer, Peter 71, 91, 108, 117, 133
Spencer, Samuel 41, 53, 63, 78, 97, 104, 116, 129, 334, 353
Spradley, Andrew 30, 67, 143
Spurlock, Charles 308
St. James Parish 4, 85, 86, 145, 175, 215, 223, 250, 253, 256, 272, 274, 275, 276, 290, 300, 331, 333, 351, 358, 359, 360, 366, 393, 397, 403, 411
Stableage 13, 319
Statutes 65
Stealing 126, 167, 410
Stealing leather 126
Stephens, John 256, 275, 291, 304, 321, 337, 370, 373, 386, 396, 400, 404
Stephens, Joseph 393
Stephens, Joshua 73, 340, 368
Stephens, Mary 32
Stephens, William 333, 358
Stephenson, John 379
Stevenson, John 374, 396, 398, 407, 408, 409

Stewart, John 179
Stidum, Benjamin 43, 55, 64, 79, 97, 142, 152, 187, 195, 187, 195, 206, 210, 217, 228, 229, 230, 238, 245, 268, 302, 314, 336
Stocks 44, 333, 412
Stokes, Young 411
Stone, John 103
Stone, Thomas 198, 307, 308, 326, 347
Stoner, Daniel 1, 2, 3, 8, 29, 30, 40, 42, 44, 48, 62, 63, 68, 71, 73, 74, 76, 77, 79, 81, 82, 83, 84, 89, 90, 91, 94, 95, 101, 102, 104, 111, 113, 118, 122, 131, 134, 137, 138, 139, 142, 143, 145, 146, 157, 158, 163, 165, 175, 176, 191, 192, 194, 195, 197, 208, 209, 215, 226, 227, 228, 229, 233, 241, 244, 253, 256, 272, 281, 282, 290, 293, 297, 298, 309, 315, 316, 321, 324, 331, 332, 336, 348, 352, 361, 370, 373, 374, 378, 381, 384, 387, 390, 394, 396, 397, 399, 405, 408, 412
Stoner, Mary 8
Stony Creek 8
Store 18, 46, 174, 179
Stovall, Bartholomew 3, 4, 20, 21, 26, 93, 134, 136, 149, 168, 182, 183, 184, 262, 264, 265, 266, 267, 296, 306, 319, 324, 325, 326, 330, 332, 333, 341, 357, 358, 360, 361
Stovall, Elizabeth 216
Stovall, George 8, 17, 24, 26, 143, 182, 183, 184, 216, 226, 241, 262, 263, 264, 269, 274, 310, 350, 410
Stovall, Mary 330
Stovall, Thomas 128

Stoveall, see Stovall
Strange, Alexander 16, 373, 396
Stubblefield, John 11, 15, 22, 24, 25, 32, 34, 46, 47, 59
Sublet, James 331, 346
Sublet, Peter Lewis 73, 91, 115, 131
Subsheriff, see sheriff
Sugar 13, 319
Suille, see Souille
Surls, John 300
Surveyor 4, 19, 21, 22, 27, 44, 45, 58, 65, 74, 86, 88, 127, 131, 133, 136, 144, 159, 161, 169, 173, 191, 198, 241, 275, 299, 308, 331, 332, 333, 334, 342, 348, 351, 391, 394, 406, 413
Sutleith, Abraham 56, 195, 209, 224, 237, 257, 276, 291, 326, 344
Sutlet, Suleth, Sutlief, see Sutleith
Swearing 161, 175, 333, 359, 360, 393, 403
Swett, Robert 102, 112
Swift, William 157, 158, 164, 173, 174, 189, 196, 210, 211, 234, 250, 271, 277
Syme, John 6, 10, 14, 21, 229, 245, 267, 286
Syms, Mathew 170, 232, 251
Syms, Richard 277, 293, 305, 322, 363, 382

Table 77
Tabor, John 6, 9, 296, 306, 324, 341, 360, 361
Tabor, William 280
Tanner, Joseph 348
Tapley, John 42, 54, 63
Taylor, Avis 17, 24
Taylor, Elizabeth 28, 37, 50

Taylor, James 17, 18, 20, 21, 25, 28, 32, 33, 34, 35, 37, 49, 50, 52, 67, 88, 89, 102, 107, 108, 112, 114, 116, 117, 118, 119, 120, 123, 124, 128, 131, 132, 139, 140, 146, 147, 148, 151, 153, 156, 159, 161, 171, 172, 179, 180, 181, 183, 186, 189, 192, 196, 197, 200, 204, 206, 207, 208, 209, 210, 212, 219, 220, 221, 223, 233, 235, 237, 245, 247, 251, 256, 261, 265, 266, 267, 268, 271, 287, 300, 302, 308, 312, 314, 327, 333, 335, 343, 346, 353, 357, 358, 360, 365, 366, 372, 374, 375, 383, 401, 402, 403
Taylor, John 11, 15, 17, 22, 24, 25, 26, 36, 45, 57, 67, 68, 88, 90, 102, 108, 111, 112, 114, 115, 117, 122, 128, 133, 138, 142, 149, 150, 155, 159, 162, 172, 173, 182, 183, 184, 185, 192, 195, 200, 201, 209, 221, 222, 236, 245, 252, 257, 258, 264, 267, 268, 275, 276, 286, 291, 300, 302, 304, 311, 314, 321, 327, 336, 337, 360, 361, 362, 370, 377, 378, 379, 386, 398, 404, 409
Taylor, Sarah 68
Taylor, William 171
Temple, Joseph 112, 121, 138, 153, 184, 199, 218, 219, 235, 250
Thaxton, Abell 369, 386, 404
Thomas, Edward 118
Thomas, Joseph 8
Thomas, Michael 79, 94, 104
Thomas, Phillip 126, 159
Thomas, Rowland 42, 48, 63, 81, 82, 98, 110, 120, 137, 150, 184, 199, 218, 235, 265,

Thomas, Rowland (con't) 283, 301, 312, 313, 330
Thomas, William 248, 270, 287, 301, 302, 314
Thomason, Arnold 40
Thomason, John 216
Thompson, George 58, 136, 260, 285
Thompson, James 294, 307, 326, 352, 355
Thompson, Joseph 231, 283, 348
Thompson, Mary 138, 155, 177, 253, 272, 275, 289, 291, 303, 304, 320, 321, 337, 352, 355, 356
Thompson, Samuel 138, 155, 161, 176, 177, 191, 192, 194, 209, 212, 233, 247, 253, 257, 272, 275, 289, 291, 303, 304, 308, 320, 321, 337, 347, 352, 355, 356
Thornton, John 12, 15, 23, 33
Tindall, Thomas 9, 156
Titheables 86, 223
Tobacco seconds 394, 409
Toney, Charles 375
Town proposed 178
Townes, see Towns
Towns, William 28, 37, 49, 61, 67, 75, 88, 95, 106, 109, 118, 119, 127, 156, 165, 166, 167
Treasurers run 8
Tryce, James 113, 122
Tub 77
Tuckahoe Bridge 22, 159, 161
Tuckahoe Creek 8, 19, 45, 86, 136, 282
Tuckahoe Creek Mill 308
Tuckahoe Mill 58
Tuly, John 85, 100, 133, 328, 348
Tuly, Sarah 85

Turner, Hannah 175, 192, 210, 225, 246, 268
Turner, James 25, 42, 47, 71, 91, 109, 115, 156, 165, 174, 189, 205
Turner, Joanna 45
Turpin, Mathew 256, 304, 321, 337
Turpin, Thomas 8, 204, 232, 233, 237, 238, 240, 245, 251, 252, 258, 275, 291, 313, 315, 331, 332, 353
Tyre, James 40, 51, 62, 78, 96

Undersheriff, see sheriff
Upper Creek 332
Utley, John 16, 18, 19, 23, 27, 33, 36, 38, 40, 46, 48, 51, 60, 62, 74, 75, 78, 82, 94, 96, 106, 107, 112, 113, 117, 118, 119, 120, 121, 122, 138, 141, 147, 182, 194, 199, 209, 218, 233, 263, 278, 279, 293, 294, 306, 311, 316, 323, 334, 336, 357, 361, 363, 377, 378, 382, 399, 401, 411, 412
Utley, John Jr 349
Utley, Thomas 339

Vail, William 333, 360, 361
Vanderhood, Henry 6, 9, 10, 14, 22, 32, 69, 90, 103, 175
Vanderhoode, see Vanderhood
Vaughan/Vaughn, George 43, 54, 64, 79, 99, 100, 101
Vigne, Adam 3
Virginia laws 143

Waddill, William 53, 62, 80, 98, 110, 119, 336
Waddill, William Jr 40, 137, 150, 183, 199, 218, 235, 250, 271, 288, 303, 319, 362, 379,

Waddill, William Jr (con't) 398, 409
Wade, Robert 81, 99, 101, 111, 120, 130, 137, 153, 184, 198, 223, 308, 310, 312, 315, 332
Waders, see Wotars
Waders, William 29, 37, 38
Wadley, Thomas 31
Wadloe, Thomas 58, 59, 61, 87, 88, 136, 147, 159, 161, 169, 200, 201, 204, 232, 233, 237, 242, 251, 310, 319, 325, 326, 332, 333, 346, 358, 360, 381, 388, 389, 390, 392, 405, 411
Walker, David 74, 131, 181, 190, 193, 197, 200, 201, 233, 299, 342
Walker, John 6, 9, 206, 252, 366
Walker, Thomas 2, 6, 77, 84, 85, 181, 215, 248, 253, 267, 268, 270, 287, 330, 359, 372, 394, 395, 403
Walker, William 42, 54, 63, 78, 182, 183, 184, 200, 201, 204, 214, 249, 348, 357, 358, 360, 368, 384
Walton, Thomas 361
Walton, Thomas Jr 12
Walton, William 309, 411
Ward, Richard 11, 12, 15, 20, 354
Ward, Seth 142, 152, 187, 203, 204, 226, 242, 255, 265, 274, 279, 284, 290, 301, 304, 313, 325, 335, 342, 357, 364, 377, 397, 409
Ware, Peter 42, 47, 49, 67, 70, 74, 75, 76, 78, 79, 80, 88, 93, 94, 99, 104, 106, 107, 108, 109, 120, 125, 134, 136, 147, 156, 178, 227, 254, 255, 258, 262, 264, 265, 266, 267, 273, 274

Ware, Susannah 17, 40, 53, 62, 78, 97, 115, 131, 176, 181, 191, 198, 201, 208, 221, 236, 252, 272, 289, 303, 315, 317, 318, 336
Warwick 178
Waters, see Wotars, Waders
Waters, William 28
Watkins, Edward 284
Watkins, Joseph 106, 136, 139, 147, 237, 240, 245, 248, 251, 252, 262, 264, 265, 266, 267, 270, 287, 302, 313, 315
Watkins, Martha 32
Watkins, Thomas 10, 11, 15, 20, 22, 32, 40, 51, 62, 77, 94, 113, 115, 123, 134
Watkins, William 11, 15, 20, 22, 32, 40, 51, 62, 77, 94, 113, 115, 123, 134
Webb, Agnes 66
Webb, Henry 30, 66, 109, 139, 190, 193, 197, 219, 222, 232, 233, 237, 313, 315
Webb, John 8, 9, 47, 49, 58, 59, 61, 75, 76, 78, 79, 80, 83, 93, 96, 99, 100, 128, 131, 132, 161, 179, 180, 215, 288, 296, 324, 342, 388, 392
Webb, William 256
Webber, Phillip 41, 42, 53, 54, 63, 78, 80, 81, 82, 106, 116, 130, 132, 226, 242, 266, 284, 302, 313, 335, 358
Webster, Elizabeth 124
Weldy, William 138
Welsh, John 256, 275, 291, 304, 321, 337
Westbrook, Frances 73, 93, 116
Westbrook, James 73, 93, 104, 116, 188
Wetherford, William 210, 246
Wharton, Thomas 16, 23, 33,

Wharton, Thomas (con't) 39, 46, 59, 73, 74, 94, 108, 117, 134, 150, 155, 175, 183, 191, 199, 218, 235, 250, 271, 288, 303, 316, 319, 336, 361, 378, 379, 409
Whipping ii, 44, 126, 178, 234, 410
White, Edward 158, 165, 180, 226, 242, 266, 284, 302, 305, 313, 322, 335, 348, 353, 358, 368, 384, 385
White, Samuel 42, 54, 63, 78, 106, 116, 132
Whiteman, Thomas 20
Wiers, John 41, 43, 48, 50, 56, 62, 66, 227, 243
Wild Boar Swamp 198
Wilds, see Wiles
Wiles, Francis 208
Wiles, John 232
Wiles, Luke 11, 124, 125, 140, 141, 143, 154, 176, 190, 232, 258, 259, 262, 263, 264, 265, 266, 267, 269, 274, 278, 310
Wilkinson, David 317
Wilkinson, Francis 317
Wilkinson, John 144
Wilkinson, Nicholas 181, 332
Williams, Edward 12, 15, 41, 42, 48, 67, 70, 82, 88, 93, 94, 99, 106, 120, 125, 143, 226, 241, 251, 252, 255, 265, 274, 281, 284, 290, 395, 412
Williams, John ii, 43, 54, 64, 79, 83, 99, 100, 101, 144, 218, 222, 223, 228, 231, 240, 245, 247, 285, 305, 322, 327, 332, 338, 356, 362, 376, 382
Williams, Welcome 12
Williamsburg 45, 46, 144, 281
Willis Creek 8, 173
Willis, Robert 27, 144, 349, 412

Willis, William 379
Wilmore, Daniel 310
Wilson, Richard 17, 276, 354, 390, 405, 412
Winfree, see Winfrey
Winfrey, Jacob 7, 28, 37, 49, 61, 69, 75, 83, 92, 231, 247, 295, 305, 306, 307, 322, 323, 341, 347, 362, 382
Winfrey, James 338
Winston, Isaac 248, 270, 287, 302, 318, 352
Womack, William 8, 9, 20, 21, 22, 24, 104, 106, 107, 108, 109, 110, 158, 163, 164, 173, 226, 241, 245, 285, 312, 313, 315, 317, 332, 351, 353, 372, 389, 406
Wood, Edward 169
Wood, Henry v, 1, 2, 3, 19, 26, 29, 31, 38, 45, 46, 51, 57, 58, 59, 65, 73, 74, 83, 93, 103, 112, 115, 122, 126, 136, 138, 143, 162, 175, 176, 178, 179, 180, 187, 191, 205, 206, 212, 221, 223, 227, 229, 234, 239, 247, 256, 265, 269, 274, 277, 280, 283, 287, 293, 305, 308, 322, 333, 339, 348, 351, 353, 354, 402
Wood, John 334
Wood, Rebecca 353
Woodall, John 181
Woodson, Benjamin 29, 32, 36, 37, 38, 50, 58, 60, 71, 76, 96, 109, 118, 134, 136, 142, 147, 152, 161, 186, 193, 211, 227, 233, 234, 255, 256, 305, 322, 338, 362, 382, 400
Woodson, Elizabeth 375
Woodson, Jacob 42, 63, 77, 97, 114, 295, 356, 357, 376, 377, 399, 410, 411

Woodson, John 1, 2, 4, 8, 15, 20, 21, 24, 27, 29, 30, 31, 38, 39, 41, 45, 46, 47, 51, 52, 56, 57, 58, 59, 61, 65, 76, 84, 85, 93, 100, 102, 103, 111, 113, 122, 123, 124, 125, 126, 127, 133, 139, 140, 143, 144, 145, 146, 151, 156, 157, 159, 161, 162, 167, 168, 172, 177, 178, 181, 185, 192, 200, 211, 218, 226, 242, 250, 280, 281, 283, 292, 297, 305, 309, 315, 322, 338, 343, 365, 367, 376, 380, 391, 398, 407, 408, 410

Woodson, John Jr 372, 389, 405, 408

Woodson, Joseph 11, 13, 16, 25, 34, 42, 47, 49, 123, 125, 126, 131, 140, 144, 151, 157, 163, 165, 170, 174, 175, 185, 186, 187, 189, 190, 201, 205, 222, 227, 228, 231, 237, 244, 247, 257, 267, 269, 278, 281, 285, 287, 294, 295, 300, 301, 306, 311, 312, 319, 323, 339, 341, 342, 344, 351, 355, 372, 374, 382, 388, 392, 397, 407

Woodson, Joseph Jr 375, 389, 392, 408

Woodson, Josiah 42, 53, 54, 63, 77, 97, 114, 292, 295, 311, 327, 334, 351, 356, 357, 375, 376, 377, 395, 399, 410, 411

Woodson, Mary 375

Woodson, Robert 34, 41, 81, 98, 105, 106, 107, 116, 132, 159, 163, 171, 226, 241, 311, 327, 372

Woodson, Robert Jr 52

Woodson, Samuel 127

Woodson, Sanburn 242, 278, 340, 345, 346, 392

Woodson, Sarah 69, 91, 106,

Woodson, Sarah (con't) 107, 125

Woodson, Stephen 32, 42, 53, 54, 63, 69, 71, 77, 91, 114, 134, 136, 159, 179, 180, 181, 233, 240, 251, 252, 258, 292, 295, 311, 327, 334, 351, 356, 357, 375, 376, 377, 399, 403, 410, 411

Woodson, Tarlton 195, 209, 224, 237, 257

Woodson, William 29, 32, 38, 50, 58, 59, 60, 61, 75, 76, 78, 80, 81, 83, 88, 93, 96, 98, 104, 105, 108, 109, 110, 114, 116, 118, 119, 120, 128, 131, 132, 147, 148, 156, 160, 162, 163, 164, 170, 171, 174, 183, 184, 188, 190, 205, 207, 210, 211, 212, 218, 220, 222, 223, 228, 232, 233, 236, 237, 242, 255, 274, 290, 295, 304, 306, 319, 321, 323, 341, 353

Woodson's Mill Creek 22

Wooldridge, John 313

Wooldridge, Thomas 230

Worley, John 69, 90, 103, 249, 269, 270, 273

Wotars, William 13, 49, 50, 60, 71, 75, 93, 96, 99, 108, 109, 118, 133, 149, 158, 165, 175, 192, 194, 197, 208, 209, 232, 233

Wright, Elizabeth 217, 231, 250, 347

Wright, John 217, 231

York County 355

www.ingramcontent.com/pod-product-compliance
Lightning Source LLC
Chambersburg PA
CBHW071222230426
43668CB00011B/1266